Jewish Philosophy
and the Crisis of Modernity

SUNY Series in the Jewish Writings of Leo Strauss
Kenneth Hart Green, editor

Jewish Philosophy
and the Crisis of Modernity

Essays and Lectures
in Modern Jewish Thought

BY LEO STRAUSS

EDITED WITH AN
INTRODUCTION BY

Kenneth Hart Green

State University of New York Press

Published by
State University of New York Press, Albany

© 1997 State University of New York

All rights reserved

Printed in the United States of America

For information, address State University of New York
Press, State University Plaza, Albany, N.Y., 12246

Production by Diane Ganeles
Marketing by Nancy Farrell

Library of Congress Cataloging-in-Publication Data

Strauss, Leo.
    Jewish philosophy and the crisis of modernity : essays and
  lectures in modern Jewish thought / by Leo Strauss ; edited with an
  introduction by Kenneth Hart Green.
        p.   cm. — (SUNY series in the Jewish writings of Leo Strauss)
    Includes index.
    ISBN 0-7914-2773-0 (ch. : alk. paper). — ISBN 0-7914-2774-9 (pbk.
  : alk. paper)
    1. Philosophy, Jewish—History. 2. Philosophy, Modern—History.
  3. Judaism and philosophy. 4. Judaism—20th century. I. Green,
  Kenneth Hart, 1953–   . II. Title. III. Series: SUNY series in the
  Jewish writings of Strauss.
  B5800.S77 1997
  181'.06—dc20   95-8058
                                                                      CIP

10 9 8 7 6 5 4 3 2 1

To my parents,
Patrick and Freda Hart Green

"Ask your father, he will inform you,
your elders, they will tell you."

(Deut. 32:7)

Contents

Acknowledgments   ix

Editor's Preface   xi

Editor's Introduction: Leo Strauss as a Modern Jewish Thinker   1

Part I: Essays in Modern Jewish Thought

1. Progress or Return? (1952)   87
2. Preface to *Spinoza's Critique of Religion* (1965)   137

Part II: Studies of Modern Jewish Thinkers

3. How to Study Spinoza's *Theologico-Political Treatise* (1948)   181
4. Preface to Isaac Husik, *Philosophical Essays* (1952)   235
5. Introductory Essay to Hermann Cohen,
   Religion of Reason out of the Sources of Judaism (1972)   267

Part III: Lectures on Contemporary Jewish Issues

6. Freud on Moses and Monotheism (1958)   285
7. Why We Remain Jews (1962)   311

Part IV: Studies on the Hebrew Bible

8. On the Interpretation of Genesis (1957)   359
9. Jerusalem and Athens (1967)   377

Part V: Comments on Jewish History

10. What Is Political Philosophy? [The First Paragraph] (1954)   409
11. Review of J. L. Talmon, *The Nature of Jewish History* (1957)   411
12. Letter to the Editor: The State of Israel (1957)   413

Part VI: *Miscellaneous Writings on Jews and Judaism*

13. Introduction to *Persecution and the Art of Writing* (1952)   417
14. Perspectives on the Good Society (1963)   431

Part VII: *Autobiographical Reflections*

15. An Unspoken Prologue (1959)   449
16. Preface to *Hobbes Politische Wissenschaft* (1965)   453
17. A Giving of Accounts (1970)   457

Appendix 1: Plan of a Book Tentatively Entitled
          Philosophy and the Law: Historical Essays (1946)   467
Appendix 2: Restatement on Xenophon's *Hiero*
          [The Last Paragraph] (1950)   471
Appendix 3: Memorial Remarks for Jason Aronson (1961)   475

Sources   477

Bibliography   479

Index   489

Acknowledgments

The editor gratefully acknowledges permission to reprint the writings of Leo Strauss from the following sources:

"Progress or Return? The Contemporary Crisis in Western Civilization" is reprinted by permission of the Johns Hopkins University Press from *Modern Judaism* 1 (1981): 17–45. It appears in the present book as sections I and II of "Progress or Return?"

"The Mutual Influence of Theology and Philosophy" is reprinted by permission of *The Independent Journal of Philosophy* 3 (1979): 111–18. It appears in the present book as section III of "Progress or Return?"

"Preface to the English Translation of *Spinoza's Critique of Religion*" from *Spinoza's Critique of Religion* by Leo Strauss, translated by Elsa M. Sinclair. Copyright © 1965 by Schocken Books, Inc. Reprinted by permission of Schocken Books, published by Pantheon Books, a division of Random House, Inc.

"How to Study Spinoza's *Theologico-Political Treatise*" is reprinted by permission of the American Academy for Jewish Research from *Proceedings of the American Academy for Jewish Research* 17 (1948): 69–131.

"Preface to Isaac Husik, *Philosophical Essays: Ancient, Medieval, and Modern*" is reprinted by permission of Basil Blackwell, Inc., from *Philosophical Essays: Ancient, Medieval, and Modern* by Isaac Husik, edited by Milton Nahm and Leo Strauss. Copyright © 1952 Basil Blackwell.

"Introductory Essay" by Leo Strauss is reprinted from *Religion of Reason out of the Sources of Judaism* by Hermann Cohen. Copyright © 1972 by Frederick Ungar Publishing Co., Inc. Reprinted by permission of the publisher.

"Freud on Moses and Monotheism" is published with the permission of Joseph Cropsey and the Estate of Leo Strauss.

"Why We Remain Jews" is published with the permission of Joseph Cropsey and the Estate of Leo Strauss.

"On the Interpretation of Genesis" is reprinted by permission of *L'Homme: revue française d'anthropologie* 21 (1981): 5–36.

"Jerusalem and Athens" is reprinted by permission of The City College, The City University of New York from *Jerusalem and Athens: Some Preliminary Reflections*, The City College Papers, Number 6. The First Frank Cohen Public Lecture in Judaic Affairs. New York: The City College, 1967.

The first paragraph of "What Is Political Philosophy?" is reprinted by permission of The Free Press, a division of Macmillan, Inc., from *What Is Political Philosophy? and Other Studies* by Leo Strauss. Copyright © 1959 The Free Press.

"Review of J.L. Talmon, *The Nature of Jewish History*" is reprinted by permission of Joseph Cropsey and the Estate of Leo Strauss from *The Journal of Modern History* 29 (1957): 306, which is published by the University of Chicago Press.

"Letter to the Editor: The State of Israel" is reprinted by permission of *National Review*, Inc., 150 East 35th Street, New York, New York, 10016.

"Introduction to *Persecution and the Art of Writing*" is reprinted by permission of the University of Chicago Press from *Persecution and the Art of Writing* by Leo Strauss. Copyright © 1988 by The University of Chicago Press.

"Perspectives on the Good Society" is reprinted by permission of The Divinity School, The University of Chicago from *Criterion* 2, no. 3 (Summer 1963): 2–9.

"An Unspoken Prologue to a Public Lecture at St. John's College" is reprinted by permission of *Interpretation: A Journal of Political Philosophy* 7, no. 3 (1978): 1–3.

"Preface to *Hobbes Politische Wissenschaft*" is reprinted by permission of both *Interpretation: A Journal of Political Philosophy* 8, no. 1 (1979–80): 1–3, and the translator, Professor Donald J. Maletz.

"A Giving of Accounts" is reprinted by permission of *The St. John's Review* from *The College* 22, no. 1 (April 1970): 1–5.

"Plan of a Book Tentatively Entitled *Philosophy and the Law: Historical Essays*," the last paragraph of "Restatement on Xenophon's *Hiero*," and "Memorial Remarks for Jason Aronson," are published with the permission of Joseph Cropsey and the Estate of Leo Strauss.

The editor gratefully acknowledges the Connaught Fund of the University of Toronto for a generous fellowship and aid to publication grant, which was a great help in the editing and production of the present work.

And the editor also gratefully acknowledges the Jewish Studies Program at the University of Toronto, and its director, David Novak, for a further grant that assisted in the publication of this book.

Editor's Preface

The following is a collection of essays and lectures written by Leo Strauss in the field of modern Jewish thought, which have been gathered together for the first time. It is meant to offer the reader an introduction to the enormous range of Strauss's Jewish interests. In doing so, I have been guided by two intentions: first, to present the best of Strauss's shorter writings in modern Jewish thought; and second, to present a comprehensive view of how Strauss expressed himself as a modern Jewish thinker.

Strauss wrote the pieces in this volume during a period of approximately thirty years, with one essay published in the last year of his life (on Hermann Cohen's *Religion of Reason*). Since Strauss did not himself place these pieces together in this form or order, the editor alone assumes full responsibility for their selection and arrangement. The decisions as to the contents were made by the editor with the permission of, and in consultation with, the executor of Strauss's literary estate, Professor Joseph Cropsey, to whom my sincere thanks are due. In considering how to make the decisions about the arrangement of the essays and lectures, I have been instructed by Strauss's own words and example in his edition of Isaac Husik's philosophical essays: they have been arranged primarily in the logical order suggested by the contents, and only secondarily "by the dates of publication."[1]

It should be noted, however, that I have included only those works of Strauss that were produced in the years following 1945. The reason for excluding all but the later writings is simply that this is merely one of five volumes to appear in a State University of New York Press series, "The Jewish Writings of Leo Strauss" (series editor, K. H. Green). The series will consist of the following volumes: the early German Jewish writings, 1921–32; a new translation of *Philosophy and Law* (1995); Strauss's writings on Moses Mendelssohn; Strauss's writings on Moses Maimonides; and the present work.

Most of this volume consists of essays that were previously published by Strauss during his life, such as his compelling Preface to *Spinoza's Critique of Religion,* and his groundbreaking study of Spinoza's *Theologico-Political Treatise,* with its implications for modern Judaism.

Some of the lectures in this volume were never finalized by Strauss in written form. Two spoken lectures, one published here for the first time, have been placed together in a single section for this reason. "Freud on Moses and Monotheism" is previously unpublished, and "Why We Remain Jews" was first published only in 1994. They were both originally delivered as talks, and though now appearing in print, they are still just that: transcriptions of "essentially oral material, much of which was developed spontaneously, and none of which was prepared with publication in mind."[2] Previously, photocopies of typescripts of both the original lecture transcriptions were passed separately from hand to hand—although the transcriptions were neither produced nor approved by Strauss himself. However, they do perhaps convey something of his charm, humor, and power as a teacher.

Also reprinted in the present volume are Strauss's two sustained studies of the Hebrew Bible: "On the Interpretation of Genesis" and "Jerusalem and Athens." Both are justifiably famous to those familiar with them, though they are scarcely known well enough, and rarely put in the context of modern Jewish thought.[3] Strauss proceeds on the basis of a new approach to the reading of the Hebrew Bible, which he regards as neither traditional nor modern but what he calls "postcritical." It is beyond doubt that this new approach has not yet received as full or adequate an articulation as it deserves.[4]

I might also mention that among these essays and lectures is a piece that is untypical of Strauss for its more passionate, but not less reasonable, argument: a letter to the editor, the only one he ever wrote of which I am aware. This letter was sent to the *National Review* in 1957 in order to defend the state of Israel against unjust attacks regularly launched against it by several authors on so-called conservative grounds.[5]

Finally, Appendix 1 reproduces a previously unpublished proposal Strauss sketched in 1946 for a book of essays in Jewish philosophy which he wanted to publish, and which he entitled *Philosophy and the Law.* It is not clear to me whether he ever submitted it to a publisher. The book he did publish, which used some of the same contents, was *Persecution and the Art of Writing* (1952), but it appeared in quite a different form from the book sketched in the proposal. The proposal does reflect concisely Strauss's mature view of the state of Jewish philosophy, and contains his suggestion for the direction in which it should move.

Appendix 2 publishes for the first time the last paragraph of Strauss's "Restatement on Xenophon's *Hiero*" in its original English version. It is what might be called his metaphysical confession of faith. Appendix 3 presents Strauss's "Memorial Remarks for Jason Aronson," the only place in his writings in which he speaks as a comforter to his fellow Jews.

It is hoped that this book will help to establish for some, and will enhance for others, the stature of Leo Strauss as a modern Jewish thinker. Put together in the present form, which renders accessible the full range of Strauss's mature writings on modern Judaism, it should bring to light the power, depth, and originality of his Jewish thought. Indeed, I would suggest that this book represents one of the most impressive achievements of Jewish philosophy in the twentieth century, and will yet bear fruit in the twenty-first century. This is a book that should be of interest to all who search for the truth, whether expressed in the spirit of philosophy or in the spirit of religion. Perhaps these essays and lectures will also perform the modern Maimonidean function to which Strauss dedicated himself in the introductory remarks to one of his lectures not reprinted in the present book: to "help the Jewish students . . . towards facing the perplexities of the modern Jew with somewhat greater clarity."[6] Or, to use the terms of Maimonides himself: to liberate such students, and those like them, from the "heartache and great perplexity" into which they may have sunk due to the conflicts between modern philosophy and Judaism, and to illuminate some of the forgotten stores of wisdom in the Jewish tradition.[7] If this collection[8] succeeds in helping to guide the reader in that direction, Strauss's legacy will have been served well.

Notes

1. "Preface to Isaac Husik, *Philosophical Essays*," infra, 264.

2. I quote from the editorial "warning" on the title page of the original typed transcription of "Why We Remain Jews," although it was not written by Strauss himself but by the transcribers, Werner Dannhauser and James Lane. Essentially the same thing can be said about "Freud on Moses and Monotheism."

3. But see "Strauss, Soloveitchik, and the Genesis Narrative: Conceptions of the Ideal Jew as Derived from Philosophical and Theological Readings of the Bible," by Jonathan Cohen, which appeared in the *Journal of Jewish Thought and Philosophy* 5, no. 1 (1995): 99–143. See also note 4, infra.

4. I am aware of only three students of the Hebrew Bible who have in recent years been attempting to apply Strauss's new approach: Hillel Fradkin, Leon Kass, and Robert Sacks. As far as I know, nothing has yet been written that discusses critically or even acknowledges this new approach. For Strauss's articulation of his manner of reading the Hebrew Bible, see infra, "On the Interpretation of Genesis," 359–62, 367–70, and "Jerusalem and Athens," 379–82, as well as "Progress or Return?," 117–20. See Robert Sacks: *A Commentary on the Book of Genesis* (Lewiston, N.Y.: Edwin Mellen Press, 1991); and also his forthcoming *A Commentary on the Book of Job*. And see Leon Kass: "Evolution and the Bible: Genesis 1 Revisited," *Commentary* 86, no. 5 (November 1988): 29–39; "A Woman for All Seasons," *Commentary* 92, no. 3 (September 1991): 30–35; "Man and Woman: An Old Story," *First Things* no. 17 (November 1991): 14–26; "Regarding Daughters and Sisters," *Commentary* 93, no. 4 (April 1992): 29–38; "Seeing the Nakedness of His Father," *Commentary* 93, no. 6 (June 1992): 41–47; "Why the Dietary Laws?," *Commentary* 97, no. 6 (June 1994): 42–48; "Educating Father Abraham: The Meaning of Wife," *First Things* no. 47 (November 1994): 16–26; "Educating Father Abraham: The Meaning of Fatherhood," *First Things* no. 48 (December 1994): 32–43; "A Genealogy of Justice," *Commentary* 102, no. 1 (July 1996): 44–51; and his recent book, *The Hungry Soul* (New York: Free Press, 1994). And see Hillel Fradkin: "God's Politics—Lessons from The Beginning," *This World* no. 4 (Winter 1983): 86–104; and "Poet Kings: A Biblical Perspective on Heroes," in *Political Philosophy and the Human Soul*, eds. Michael Palmer and Thomas L. Pangle, 55–66 (Lanham, Maryland: Rowman and Littlefield, 1995). Strauss's manner of reading, uniquely enabling him to see the Hebrew Bible in a fresh light, has been noted and duly appreciated in a passing remark of the distinguished literary critic Harold Bloom: see his Foreword to Yosef H. Yerushalmi, *Zakhor: Jewish History and Jewish Memory* (New York: Schocken, 1989): xiii. He fittingly calls Strauss a "political philosopher and Hebraic sage." See also his Introduction to Martin Buber, *On the Bible: Eighteen Studies* (New York: Schocken, 1982): xxvi–xxvii; and *Ruin the Sacred Truths* (Cambridge: Harvard University Press, 1989), 171: "Evasiveness is purposive; it writes between the lines, to borrow a fine trope from Leo Strauss." As for Strauss's own characterization of his new approach to the Hebrew Bible, he offered the following somewhat elusive view in a letter of 8 April 1964 to Seth Benardete, as a response to a remark of Benardete's about the great modern biblical scholar Umberto Cassuto. In this remark, Benardete apparently likened Strauss's approach to that of Cassuto, and Strauss responded as follows:

> I have heard frequently of Cassuto. He is very highly thought of, especially by the more thoughtful or conservative Jews, but I have never read any of his works. What you tell me about my agreement with him regarding Genesis 1 was good to hear. I believe the difference is this, that Cassuto does not look at the text as much from the outside as I do. This has both its advantages and disadvantages, as I do not have to explain to you.

What Strauss means by saying that he tries as much as possible to "look at the text . . . from the outside" is not immediately evident, but perhaps the following passage from "Jerusalem and Athens" (infra, 382), helps to make this notion somewhat clearer: "We shall start from the uppermost layer [of the Bible]— from what is first for us, even though it may not be the first simply. We shall start, that is, where both the traditional and the historical study of the Bible necessarily start. In thus proceeding we avoid the compulsion to make an advance decision in favor of Athens against Jerusalem." By attempting not to make "an advance decision in favor of Athens against Jerusalem," Strauss wants not to decide *against* traditional biblical faith (i.e., "against Jerusalem"), and hence *for* Greek philosophy, as modern biblical criticism would seem to presuppose or to require. However, he also does not decide simply *for* Jerusalem, which is why he claims still to "look at the text . . . from the outside." In other words, Strauss tries in a certain measure to stand beyond both antagonists. Whether he has been able to maintain such a stance—indeed, whether he has been able to avoid a decision from the beginning—is something which needs to be reflected on deeply, for as "Progress or Return?" makes clear, Strauss himself does not seem to believe in a third position which is not *either* philosophy *or* theology. (See 116–17, infra.) However, the one thing which Strauss allows himself and seems to believe in from the beginning to the end of his studies, and which is not either philosophy or theology, is *history*. And yet history, as Strauss views it, is not something higher than the two fundamental alternatives, but rather is something which helps to comprehend, and hence to choose between, the two fundamental alternatives. Thus, Strauss's "postcritical" approach to the Bible represents a new beginning in study of the biblical text, which is sympathetic to the Bible in the very fact of his viewing "the text . . . from the outside." He searches for an intellectually defensible position which permits him to remain free of traditional premises either debilitated or refuted by biblical criticism, yet which also permits him to exploratively presuppose the "cognitive value" of the Bible precisely as an exact historical interpreter, a presupposition dogmatically disallowed by biblical criticism.

5. Some enlightening commentary on Strauss's letter is provided by Werner Dannhauser in his contribution to "The Achievement of Leo Strauss," by Walter Berns, Herbert J. Storing, Harry V. Jaffa, and Werner Dannhauser, which appeared in *National Review* 25 (1973): 1347–57.

6. This was the first sentence of Strauss's lecture posthumously published with the title "An Introduction to Heideggerian Existentialism," a sentence which does not appear in that published version. See *The Rebirth of Classical Political Rationalism: Essays and Lectures*, by Leo Strauss, and edited by Thomas L. Pangle (Chicago: University of Chicago Press, 1989), 27–46. The full sentence reads as follows: "This series of lectures—a reminder of the perplexities of modern man—should help the Jewish students in particular towards facing the perplexities of the modern Jew with somewhat greater clarity." We should note, as Alan Udoff put it, "the deeply suggestive Maimonidean resonances with which the essay began." See "On Leo Strauss: An Introductory Account," in *Leo Strauss's Thought: Toward a Critical Engagement*, edited by Alan Udoff (Boulder,

Colo.: Lynne Rienner, 1991), p. 25, note 39. See also Udoff's review of *The Rebirth of Classical Political Rationalism* in the *Review of Metaphysics* 63, no. 3 (March 1990): 648–50, and especially p. 649. However, the lecture has since been republished in a complete form by David Bolotin, Christopher Bruell, and Thomas L. Pangle, which contains the previously missing first sentence, and which is presented with its original, simpler title: "Existentialism." See *Interpretation* 22, no. 3 (Spring 1995): 303–20.

7. Strauss himself first wrote something like this about another Jewish thinker whom he revered: "Cohen was a faithful warner and comforter to many Jews. At the very least he showed them most effectively how Jews can live with dignity as Jews in a non-Jewish, even hostile, world while participating in that world. . . . It is a blessing for us that Hermann Cohen lived and wrote." (See his "Introductory Essay to Hermann Cohen, *Religion of Reason*," infra, 281–82.) Something similar has already been written twice about Strauss. First, see Emil L. Fackenheim, "Leo Strauss and Modern Judaism," in *Claremont Review of Books* 4, no. 4 (Winter 1985): 23. Fackenheim, however, substitutes "lived and taught" for "lived and wrote" as the source of Strauss's "blessing." (See also Editor's Introduction, note 1, infra.) Second, see Alan Udoff, "On Leo Strauss: An Introductory Account," in *Leo Strauss's Thought*, 22. See also Martin D. Yaffe, "Leo Strauss as Judaic Thinker: Some First Notions," in *Religious Studies Review* 17, no. 1 (January 1991): 33–41. For a sadly misconceived caricature of Strauss's attitude toward, and familiarity with, the sources of Judaism and of Jewish philosophy, see the vehement polemic "written from an absolute Torah point of view" (p. 1), i.e., in what might be called an "ultraorthodox" spirit, by Chaim Zimmerman, *Torah and Existence: Insiders and Outsiders of Torah*, 206–9 (Brooklyn: Judaica Press, 1986).

8. I would like to make a comment on the title of the present book, *Jewish Philosophy and the Crisis of Modernity*. It is, of course, entirely the responsibility of the editor. The first half of the title may surprise some, while the second half of the title probably will not. As is well known, Strauss used most hesitantly the term "Jewish philosophy"; while he did use it on occasion, he did so apparently only because it is generally accepted and commonly employed in the English-speaking world. See, e.g., "Preface to Isaac Husik, *Philosophical Essays*," infra, 247–56. In light of these passages, one must qualify somewhat Warren Zev Harvey's unconditional rule: "Strauss refused to speak of 'Jewish philosophy'"; however, Harvey was right to suggest that the term seemed to Strauss "self-contradictory." See "The Return of Maimonideanism," *Jewish Social Studies* 42 (1980): 249–68, and esp. p. 254. Similarly, the statement by Laurence Berns would need to be accepted if and only if it is read most carefully: "Leo Strauss was a Jew, a Jewish scholar, and, if I know anything about the meaning of the word, he was a philosopher; but he insisted that strictly speaking there is no such thing as Jewish philosophy." See "Leo Strauss: 1899–1973," *The Independent Journal of Philosophy* 2 (1978): 1–3, esp. p. 2. If Berns's statement is essentially correct, as I believe it is, then the choice of the title is based on the need to speak loosely—

but acquiescing in this need is justified for a specific reason which I will explain shortly. Why did Strauss make such a point about the term "Jewish philosophy"? This is because he held the view that Judaism and philosophy are not readily compatible things; indeed, they may be—in the decisive respect—fundamentally divergent, irreconcilable, or even contradictory things. See "Introduction to *Persecution and the Art of Writing*," infra, 426–28; as well as *Persecution and the Art of Writing*, pp. 43, 104–5, and "How To Begin To Study *The Guide of the Perplexed*," p. xiv. See also by the present writer: "Religion, Philosophy, and Morality: How Leo Strauss Read Judah Halevi's Kuzari," in *Journal of the American Academy of Religion* 61, no. 2 (Summer 1993): 225–73, and esp. pp. 231–32, 234–35, 248–49, 267–68. In my judgment, however, no available alternate term seems to cover adequately the significant difference, generally accepted and commonly employed, between "Jewish philosophy" and "Jewish thought." This represents a significant difference in the following sense: on the one hand, "Jewish philosophy" is thinking informed by Western philosophy as well as by the sources of Judaism which articulates an encounter between Western philosophy and the sources of Judaism; on the other hand, "Jewish thought" is thinking which reflects on and expresses the beliefs of Judaism in their native form and content, or which meditates on Jewish history as much as possible from its own theological-moral grounds alone. The latter term may include the former, but generally speaking the former term excludes the latter. Did Strauss believe in the very possibility of Jewish philosophy? See Michael L. Morgan, "Leo Strauss and the Possibility of Jewish Philosophy," in *Dilemmas in Modern Jewish Thought* (Bloomington, Ind.: Indiana University Press, 1992), 55–67. See now also his essay, "Teaching Leo Strauss as a Jewish and General Philosopher," in *Jewish Philosophy and the Academy*, eds. Emil L. Fackenheim and Raphael Jospe, 174–88 (London: Associated University Presses, 1996). For the term "crisis of modernity," which Strauss used free of qualification, see "Progress or Return?," infra, 104.

Editor's Introduction:
Leo Strauss as a Modern Jewish Thinker

I am sure many people who never met Strauss in person simply were gripped by a book of his, and it did change their lives. . . . It was a great blessing for the future of Jewish philosophy that Leo Strauss lived and taught.

Emil Fackenheim[1]

I suppose one could say that I saw in you what I had in vain searched for in rabbis but which I knew to be their vocation—science and piety, learning of a synoptic variety about the things of this world.

Allan Bloom[2]

. . . a professor [cannot] give meanings to his students. What [he] may give, however, is an example, the existential example of personal commitment to the search for truth.

Viktor Frankl[3]

The Importance of Leo Strauss

It has long been established that Leo Strauss (1899–1973) is one of the leading political thinkers of the twentieth century. In recent years, however, another side of Leo Strauss has been discovered that may be of equal, if not greater, significance: his contribution as a Jewish scholar, and as a major Jewish thinker in his own right.

This book brings together the most noteworthy essays and lectures by Leo Strauss in the field of modern Jewish thought, composed between 1945 and 1973.[4] The present work should help to establish beyond doubt that Strauss deserves to be counted in the select company of the few truly original Jewish philosophic thinkers of the twentieth century.

I would venture to guess that however high a standing he may deserve, Leo Strauss is scarcely known as a Jewish thinker and scholar, except to those who specialize in the field of medieval Jewish philosophy.[5] Even those who are acquainted with Strauss's groundbreaking historical research on medieval Jewish philosophic thought will likely not be familiar with Strauss's views on modern Judaism, since he scrupulously avoided expressing these views in his purely scholarly works. This might lead one to the conclusion that Strauss was solely a man of academic interests who never responded to the issues of contemporary Jewish thought and life, and hence who was a thoroughly detached scholar who exercised little or no influence on the thinking of his contemporaries. To draw such a conclusion from Strauss's undoubted seriousness as a historical scholar, however, would be to make a grave error. The most prominent of his students in Jewish philosophic thought, Emil L. Fackenheim, acknowledges

> it was Leo Strauss . . . whose example has convinced me, more than that of any other Jewish thinker alive in my own lifetime, of the possibility, and therefore the necessity, of a Jewish philosophy for our age.[6]

The astonishing fact that Fackenheim, himself one of the most important Jewish thinkers of the post-1945 era, states that he was inspired by the example of Leo Strauss *"more than [by] that of any other Jewish thinker alive in [his] own lifetime,"* should by itself cause one to see Strauss in a new and different light. And Fackenheim was not the only one to acknowledge his debt to Leo Strauss. Other Jewish scholars and thinkers have also paid tribute to Strauss—figures such as Gershom Scholem, Shlomo Pines, Alexander Altmann, Steven Schwarzschild, and Marvin Fox. Moreover, if one begins to search through Strauss's writings, one starts to uncover a surprisingly diverse array of essays and lectures on modern Jewish topics, ranging from a penetrating study of the origins of modern Judaism in the philosophic thought of Baruch Spinoza to a cogent critique of Sigmund Freud's analysis of biblical religion.

These essays and lectures of Leo Strauss, written during a period of approximately thirty years, reveal themselves as the products of a mind intensely engaged with the issues affecting Jews and Judaism in the modern age. Strauss emerges from these writings as one who somehow expertly manages to unite a diversity of commitments: an unfaltering devotion to philosophy and its eternal questions, a deep reverence for the Jewish religious tradition, and a vital grasp of the exigencies of the Jewish political situation. In addition to this largeness of vision, Strauss's works also reveal a critical incisiveness of mind that leads one to consider whether Strauss has not set an intellectual standard by which future Jewish thought will be measured.

Leo Strauss as Jewish Thinker: His Life and Work

This discovery of Leo Strauss as an important modern Jewish thinker surely leads one to ask: Who was this man who seemed content to remain in the shadows of contemporary Jewish discourse, but whose thinking has already quietly exercised a considerable influence on the direction of contemporary Jewish philosophic thought?[7] Let us begin by looking at the life and work of Leo Strauss from the perspective of his experience as a Jew and his involvement in Judaism.

Leo Strauss was born 20 September 1899 in Kirchhain, Hesse, Germany. He was raised in an orthodox Jewish home, and received a basic if not deep instruction in the sources of the Jewish religious tradition. Strauss's sense of a living Judaism was in a certain measure also gleaned from *where* he was raised: Jewish life in towns like Kirchhain, Hesse, was much closer to traditional Jewish society in the towns and villages of eastern Europe than it was to the modernized Jewish life of such cities as Berlin or Frankfurt. The impression made on Strauss by the orthodox Jewish piety of his parents is referred to obliquely in two remarks.[8] First, the Jewish laws "were rather strictly observed" in his family home, although "very little Jewish knowledge" was communicated to him.[9] Second, an attitude of Jewish solidarity was transmitted to him in the care shown by his parents for persecuted Jewish refugees fleeing to Germany from the 1905 pogroms of czarist Russia.[10]

The first great transformative experience of Strauss's youth occurred in his seventeenth year when, as he put it, he was "converted" to "political Zionism, pure and simple," calling himself a follower of Vladimir Jabotinsky.[11] As a result, for several years he immersed himself in the activities of the German Zionist youth movement, and wrote several compelling essays pertaining to its controversies. Drifting away from his parents' orthodoxy, Strauss began to define himself as one of "those [modern Jews] who cannot be orthodox," but who must remain loyal to Judaism.[12] Political Zionism, at this point in his life, seemed to serve that very purpose. It would subsequently be supplemented with another devotion—to Jewish learning.

Following World War I, Strauss spent the next seven years (1918–25) studying philosophy, history, mathematics, and the natural sciences at various German universities: Marburg, Frankfurt, Berlin, Hamburg, Freiburg, and Giessen. He completed his doctoral dissertation at the University of Hamburg in 1921, supervised by Ernst Cassirer, on the topic: "The Problem of Knowledge in F. H. Jacobi's Philosophical Teaching."[13] Strauss made contact with Franz Rosenzweig, who deeply impressed him and who recruited Strauss to teach for two years at the Free Jewish House of Learning in Frankfurt (1923–25). He was then brought to the attention of Julius Guttmann by his study of "Cohen's Analysis of Spinoza's Bible Science," which had been published by Martin Buber in the periodical that he edited, *Der Jude* (1924).

Strauss was subsequently appointed to the Academy for the Science of Judaism in Berlin as a research fellow in Jewish philosophy, a position he held from 1925 to 1932.[14] While working there Strauss published his first important book in Jewish thought, *Spinoza's Critique of Religion* (1930), which he dedicated "to the memory of Franz Rosenzweig." He also completed the editing of volumes 2 and 3 (part 1) of the *Jubilee Edition of the Complete Works of Moses Mendelssohn* (1931 and 1932), which contain his introductions to some of Mendelssohn's metaphysical and theological writings.

Strauss was able to leave Germany in 1932 just prior to Hitler's accession to power, having been awarded a Rockefeller Grant with the help of recommendations from Ernst Cassirer, Julius Guttmann, and Carl Schmitt.[15] While an itinerant scholar in France and England from 1932 to 1938, he researched the medieval Jewish philosophy of Moses Maimonides and Levi Gersonides, as well as the political philosophy of Thomas Hobbes. Schocken Press published the second of Strauss's important Jewish books, *Philosophy and Law: Contributions to the Understanding of Maimonides and His Predecessors* (1935), during the last years it was able to operate in Nazi Germany. It was in this period that Strauss also worked on volume 3 (part 2) of *Moses Mendelssohn's Complete Works*, dealing with the eighteenth-century Mendelssohn-Jacobi controversy regarding the legacy of G. E. Lessing. This volume appeared in print only posthumously (1974), since the publication project had been halted by the rise of Nazism in Germany.

During those same years Strauss married Miriam Bernson Petri. He and his wife raised two children, a son, Thomas, and a daughter, Jenny Ann.[16] Other than his wife, son, and daughter, all the members of Strauss's family were killed by, or perished due to their flight from, Hitler Germany.[17]

In 1938 Strauss secured both a permanent home in the United States as a naturalized citizen, and his first true academic position as a lecturer in philosophy at the New School for Social Research in New York. During the next eleven years (1938–49) he rose to the rank of full professor. He was also appointed a fellow of the prestigious American Academy for Jewish Research. He subsequently served as an active member of the executive committee of the Leo Baeck Institute in New York.[18] Strauss lectured in the field of Jewish philosophy at the Jewish Theological Seminary on several occasions during those years.[19]

In 1949 Strauss was persuaded by Robert Maynard Hutchins to relocate to the University of Chicago, where he taught in the Department of Political Science for the next nineteen years (1949–68). During those years Strauss became renowned for his excellence as a teacher and his influence as a thinker. In 1960 he was named Robert Maynard Hutchins Distinguished Service Professor. It was also in this period of his life that he published *Persecution and the Art of Writing* (1952). He also wrote the introductory essay, "How to Begin to Study *The Guide of the Perplexed*," to the English translation by Shlomo Pines of Maimonides' *Guide* (1963). And he delivered the first "Frank Cohen Public Lecture in Judaic Affairs" at the City College of New York, which was published as *Jerusalem and Athens: Some Preliminary Reflections* (1967).

Still a vital and committed Jewish scholar and thinker, Strauss delivered occasional lectures on the Hebrew Bible and taught seminars on Maimonides' *Guide* to students at the University of Chicago. He also spoke on numerous occasions at its Hillel House regarding topics of contemporary Jewish concern.[20]

Strauss spent a year in Israel, teaching at the Hebrew University of Jerusalem (1954–55), while also delivering there its esteemed Judah L. Magnes Lectures. Strauss retained his youthful convictions about political Zionism as a moral force in modern Jewish history, and remained devoted to the state of Israel during his entire life.[21] Twice Strauss was considered for teaching positions at the Hebrew University: first, in Jewish philosophy (during 1934–35), with the sponsorship of his friend Gershom Scholem (which was not finally offered to him but to Julius Guttmann); second, in social philosophy (during 1949–50), with the sponsorship of Martin Buber and Scholem, which he declined to accept.

It should be noted that in 1954 en route to his year of teaching in Israel, Strauss paid a very brief visit of several days to Germany, his only return trip subsequent to his choice to leave in 1932. This trip was made for the purpose of visiting his father's grave in Kirchhain. In 1965 Strauss was awarded an honorary doctorate in political philosophy by the University of Hamburg, from which he had received his original doctorate.[22] He was also awarded an honorary doctorate in 1966 by the Hebrew Union College in Cincinnati, which recognized him for his important contribution to Jewish thought.

When Strauss retired from the University of Chicago in 1968, he taught briefly at Claremont College in Berkeley, California, and then in 1969 removed to St. John's College in Annapolis, Maryland. St. John's named him its first Scott Buchanan Scholar in Residence. During these last years of his life, he contributed the "Introductory Essay" to the English translation of Hermann Cohen's *Religion of Reason out of the Sources of Judaism* (1972).

Leo Strauss died 18 October 1973. He was buried in the cemetery of the Kneseth Israel synagogue of Annapolis. At his funeral Psalm 114 was read in his memory, which was chosen because it was known to have been a favorite of his.[23] Memorial meetings were held in his honor in several locations, with friends, colleagues, and students gathering together to speak of aspects of his legacy: at the University of Chicago, Harvard University, the University of Toronto, Claremont College, St. John's College, and the Hebrew University of Jerusalem. He leaves as a legacy a set of powerful writings in Jewish thought which continue to challenge, and a unique position as a Jewish thinker which remains unrefuted, as well as an array of remarkable students who carry on his philosophic thought and teaching to the present day.[24]

Jewish Philosophy and the Crisis of Modernity

What characterizes Strauss's basic position as a Jewish thinker? He began his career as a Jewish philosophic thinker by initiating a critique of contemporary philosophy and its subsequent influence on modern Jewish thought. In this critique, Strauss judged contemporary philosophy to be morally and intellectually bankrupt due to its surrender to radical historicism. As a result, Strauss began to reconsider the wisdom, and explicate afresh the texts, of the medieval and ancient philosophers.

This culminated in Strauss's focus on Maimonides, whom he viewed as an exemplary Jewish philosophic thinker, able to achieve a perfect balance between philosophy, morality, politics, and religion. Strauss saw the enduring basis of Maimonides' position as grounded in his adherence to the idea of the eternal truth, in whose light a defense of both revelation and reason is made possible. Indeed, Strauss's own Jewish thought may be characterized as a "return to Maimonides." He made a modern effort to revive Maimonideanism as a corrective to the contemporary dilemmas and defects of modern Jewish thought. In doing so, Strauss also recovered the notion of philosophic "esotericism," or of "writing between the lines." He brought to light the forgotten reasons why thinkers like Maimonides considered it imperative to express what they truly thought in a concealed and diversionary manner. Indeed, he eventually turned to Maimonides, in a seemingly paradoxical formulation, as the deeper thinker about and wiser guide to the perplexities of the modern Jew.[25]

What was the point of departure for Strauss's efforts in Jewish thought? Strauss's perspective on the essential condition of contemporary Jewish philosophic thought can only be understood properly by beginning with his conviction that this is an era of grave crisis for modern Judaism, which he called the "theological-political crisis." This crisis was in great measure brought to light by the historical events of the twentieth century, such as communism in Russia and Nazism in Germany, which administered a traumatic shock to modern Jewish thought, since they called into question the ideas of human rationality and liberalism.[26] This made problematic the related belief of the Enlightenment that in the progress of history not only was the triumph of liberalism guaranteed, but also the Jews and Judaism would flourish in freedom through its triumph.[27] The erosion of these beliefs, on which the political hopes of modern Jews rested, suggested that the ground on which modern Judaism had been built was about to collapse.[28]

But the apparent overturning of liberal politics was not the only cause of the contemporary crisis for modern Jews. The decline of rational philosophy posed a threat of perhaps even greater profundity to the viability of modern Judaism. The "theological-political crisis" first manifested itself to Strauss in his youth by the observation that most Jewish philosophic responses to the challenges of modernity were in a state of critical disintegration. For Strauss, this applied to *all* the leading theological positions representing modern Jewish thought from Spinoza to Buber.

Especially by 1933 Strauss recognized that the leading positions in modern Jewish thought were faced with a fundamental dilemma: they could no longer adequately defend their spiritual integrity. This spiritual integrity had been based on previously authoritative philosophic positions (e.g., Spinoza, Locke, Rousseau, Kant, Hegel), which were no longer persuasive or had lost their value to most modern thinkers. In other words, modern Jewish thinkers had only been able to establish their own well-fortified positions because they were authentic Jewish responses to serious philosophic challenges. Once the seriousness of the challenges were removed, how crucial were the responses?[29]

In Strauss's view, the modern rationalist philosophy to which most Jewish thinkers adhered was faced with a gradual devastation due to the wave of thought that was conquering every sphere of traditional moral authority and vital philosophical life.[30] Specifically, the thought of Nietzsche and especially Heidegger, whose thought Strauss calls "radical historicism," was responsible for bringing about the triumph of such notions as: the priority of will to reason in man; the radical doubts about a fixed human nature; history as true but not rational; atheism and the fundamental abyss; man as creator of his own meanings and values; eternal truth as a defunct, if not a pious, fraud; the challenge of nihilism; the will to power, resoluteness, and authenticity.

In Strauss's estimation, this thought in both its subtle and crude forms has exercised an enormous, if not the decisive, influence on philosophic, religious, moral, and political thought in the last hundred years. Indeed, this has been the major cause of the theological-political crisis in Western civilization and in modern Judaism, the proportions of which are difficult to measure because it is still unfolding. Thus, modern Jewish thought (along with modern rationalist philosophy) was challenged by the same need to justify and account for itself according to the categories of the "new thinking" enunciated by those two thinkers, and certainly could not hope to return to the "naive" state it assumed prior to their appearance.

Ironically, Strauss accepted much of the critique of the modern philosophic positions made by the new thinking, because he believed that this thought did accurately highlight the serious flaws contained in the modern rationalist tradition of philosophy, which has been dominant since the Enlightenment. But unlike Nietzsche and Heidegger, Strauss was not attracted to the types of irrationalism which they preached. He sought a philosophy based on reason—i.e., on rational enquiry and rational principles—though not of the sort presented in the dominant forms of modern reason, if only because it proved susceptible to such a devastating critique.

He then asked whether there might still be found a rational philosophy of a different sort, one that would still be able to claim confidently to teach *the* truth. This is what led him to reconsider and ultimately "return" to the position of the medieval Jewish rational theologian Maimonides. It was this same concern that also led him to reflect on the ancient philosophic thought of Plato and Aristotle. In the tradition of their philosophy, Maimonides' own thought was itself grounded. In other words, Strauss began to search in premodern sources of philosophic thought in order to help guide modern Judaism toward an adequate resolution of its contemporary crisis.

Spinoza (Baruch and Benedict)

What specifically did Strauss regard as the most serious flaws of modern reason, and how did this manifest itself to him in the leading positions of modern Judaism? Strauss began with the beginning: he started with Spinoza. Indeed, in Strauss's view, modern Judaism can be defined as "a synthesis between rabbinical Judaism and Spinoza."[31] Not daunted by Spinoza's reputation as a modern saint, a canonization promoted by Moses Mendelssohn and confirmed by German romanticism, Strauss quickly advanced to the heart of Spinoza's originality: his critique of religious orthodoxy, both Jewish and Christian.

Strauss focused on Spinoza's relatively obscure *Theologico-Political Treatise* rather than on his well-known *Ethics* as the proper introduction to his philosophy. This was unconventional but highly fortuitous since, as Strauss observed, in the former work Spinoza had to give reasons and arguments for his critique of orthodoxy, while in the latter work most of these reasons and arguments are simply taken for granted. He became aware that in Spinoza, because of his famous boldness, one may readily detect the fundamentally "antitheological" premises of modern philosophy. Hence one may also see the most dubious grounds of those premises, in a clearer light than in any of his predecessors or even successors. As such, Strauss reached the following conclusion: Spinoza wrote his *Treatise* essentially in order to refute religious orthodoxy insofar as it is based on the Bible. As Strauss discovered, this explains why Spinoza needed to invent biblical criticism—in order to subvert, if not to refute, belief in the orthodox religious teachings.

As Strauss conceived it, Spinoza was neither revolutionary nor saint, but rather the heir of the modern revolt against the premodern Western tradition both philosophic and religious, a revolt known as the Enlightenment. He applied to Judaism the critique of religion initiated by Machiavelli, and executed by Bodin, Bacon, Descartes, and Hobbes. Spinoza attacked (as well as mocked) not only the orthodox religious teachings embraced by the multitude of simple Jewish believers, but also the chief medieval philosophic defense and reform of Judaism, which was elaborated by Maimonides.

What Strauss was not deceived by was Spinoza's artful rhetoric. To most unsuspecting readers of his *Treatise*, he appears in the guise of a modern religious reformer attempting to correct what he viewed as erroneous methods of reading the Bible. As Spinoza presents himself, he is a man who still believes in the Bible as the genuine word of God, however far removed he may be from a fanatical orthodoxy. But as Strauss discovered, this is certainly not Spinoza's genuine belief. Strauss was able to trace Spinoza's philosophic thought to its true source in the *Treatise* only by avoiding such rhetorical traps set by Spinoza for the unwary reader. Hence Strauss listens very carefully to Spinoza's seemingly random denials of the cognitive value of every crucial biblical teaching, and his apparently incidental expressions of fundamental doubt about every important religious belief.[32]

Strauss also rejects the notion that Spinoza was some sort of martyr for the cause of the eternal truth, because, as Strauss discerned, Spinoza never entertained the possibility that the Bible might contain something of this highest truth. Since this possibility was never even taken seriously by Spinoza, it was doubtful to Strauss if he is the model, as he has been mythically presented by modern philosophy, of the genuinely open-minded thinker who sacrifices himself for the truth which he discovered and maintained with the greatest difficulty. Indeed, Spinoza advocates modern philosophy from the start, which means he presupposes both the notion of truth developed in modern science by his predecessors Bacon, Descartes, and Hobbes, as well as "his belief in the final character of his [own] philosophy as *the* clear and distinct and, therefore, *the* true account of the whole."[33] If Spinoza can show the biblical teachings to be self-contradictory, immature, confused, and hence absurd, then the logical conclusion to be drawn from this absurdity is that the Bible offers nothing to the genuine searcher for the truth. For Spinoza, truth by definition, as it were, cannot be given by God, and thus the entire notion of divine revelation is *impossible* pure and simple.

The doubt that animated Strauss is whether Spinoza has ever been able to truly show this. If Spinoza can only demonstrate that there are contradictions and other such difficulties in the text and the teachings of the Bible, this is still certainly compatible with belief in the truth of the biblical God:

> But what is Spinoza actually proving? In fact, nothing more than that it is not *humanly* possible that Moses wrote the Pentateuch . . . This is not denied by the opponents. . . . [This is because,] on the assumption that Scripture is revealed, it is more apposite to assume an unfathomable mystery, rather than corruption of the text, as the reason for obscurity.[34]

In Strauss's view, Spinoza could only meet his claim to "refute" the Bible if the biblical God has already been proven to be false, if the mysterious God—the one omnipotent and transcendent God whose will is unfathomable—is somehow an "absurd" notion. But does Spinoza prove this?

According to Strauss's assessment, Spinoza's critique of religion is rooted in a single genuinely cogent argument, an argument which pertains to all revealed religion.[35] Strauss recognized that in order to dispose of both the Bible as the basis for all revealed religion, and its claim to teach the suprarational truth, Spinoza must disprove or refute philosophically the notion of revelation per se. But Strauss argues that revelation can only occur in a certain kind of universe: one in which the human mind can naturally achieve perfect knowledge only to a certain degree, and in which God, Who is all-powerful and Who "acts with unfathomable freedom,"[36] can satisfy man's yearning for such perfect knowledge insofar as He chooses to let man know. As Strauss discerned, the unequalled cogency of Spinoza's critique of the notion of revelation (especially as this was philosophically defended by Maimonides) lies in his awareness that the possibility of such revelation can only be refuted if the universe and the human mind are so constructed as to disallow it unconditionally. Strauss considers Spinoza's entire position, his attempt at unfolding the completed philosophic system, as an uncompromising attempt to do just that: to think it through as far as possible and, as a result, to construct the universe and the human mind so as to prevent the possibility of any revelation from ever occurring in them.

Although Spinoza already attempts to achieve this goal in the *Theologico-Political Treatise*, Strauss proves by paying careful and critical attention to Spinoza's actual arguments that he is not in fact able to construct the universe and the human mind in this fashion. As Strauss observes, this claim about the superiority of the completed system of Spinoza does not even succeed in retrospective terms against the medieval Maimonides. Maimonides was perhaps Spinoza's toughest-minded philosophical opponent. Spinoza attacks his hermeneutical method, his Aristotelianism and "scholastic" attitude to science, his view of man and of Jewish society and faith, his prophetology and attitude toward miracles. However, inasmuch as these attacks do not fall into logical fallacies or meet with other rational limitations, they all still assume the refutation of revelation as a human or natural possibility. If, as directed by Strauss, we finally turn to the *Ethics* in anticipation of discovering the truly systematic refutation, our hopes will be disappointed: this completed system, rather than being a refutation of revelation, presupposes its falsity from the very first page of the *Ethics*. Thus Spinoza never refutes it *in* the system, since its falsity is presupposed *by* the system.

But why is it necessary for Spinoza to simply presuppose such falsity? What premise is so difficult to refute or even to face directly? To Strauss, the difficulty lies in the following concept: God as unfathomable will. If God is unfathomable will because He is omnipotent, Who reveals Himself as He wills, revelation is possible. It could be refuted only if man could attain the clear and distinct knowledge of the whole, the knowledge which Spinoza strives to contain in the *Ethics*, the knowledge which in principle makes all causes explicable and hence renders all things intelligible. In a completely comprehensible universe, the mysterious God would be a superfluous hypothesis. Since, according to Strauss, Spinoza never adequately demonstrates his view,[37] the system presented in the *Ethics*, "the clear and distinct account of everything . . . remains fundamentally hypothetical. As a consequence, its cognitive status is not different from that of the orthodox account." For this reason, Spinoza cannot refute, or even "legitimately deny," the *possibility* of the theological view presented in the Bible—i.e., there is then no justification whatever for his not considering the revealing God and revelation per se as possibly the truth.[38]

Not only in matters of theological argument, but also in purely "personal" terms, Strauss was certainly not impressed with the attitude or behavior of Spinoza as a Jew in the *Treatise*. Insofar as Spinoza might be styled the hidden "lawgiver" of modern Judaism, Strauss asked whether his consistently hostile attitude to traditional Judaism reflects an essential flaw in modern Judaism itself, which learned so much from him. Can it be relegated to a mere idiosyncracy of Spinoza's character, a regrettably skewed emphasis resulting from his unhappy personal experience with the Amsterdam Jewish community? Or rather, does this hostile attitude not detract from the honorableness of the intention of mounting "true" criticisms of traditional Judaism, as a result of which any possibly honest conclusion about their truth has been seriously compromised?

Strauss had undoubtedly been taught by Hermann Cohen not to be deceived by the aura surrounding Spinoza as a modern saint so as to miss the "antitheological ire" that moved his criticisms of Judaism. This aura had been acquired in some measure by the ban pronounced against him by the Amsterdam rabbis, not to mention by his support for Dutch liberal republicanism, and perhaps also by his family's persecuted Marrano origins. The mystique of Spinoza's life combined to issue in an even greater aura entirely unrelated to a sober assessment of his philosophic thought and its Jewish implications. Strauss acknowledged that this aura was somehow allowed to vindicate Spinoza's words and actions as a plainly unjust accuser against Judaism, since his supposedly "pure" intentions are used to serve as an exoneration.

At the same time, Strauss detected that Spinoza's disloyalty as a Jew may not just be evidence of moral depravity, but may also be derived from a much bigger political exigency he was involved in meeting—the need to destroy the "medieval" order. Strauss knew that Spinoza followed with full conviction the modern project first suggested by Machiavelli, to build a wall of separation between the political and the religious realms. This modern project aimed to subordinate the religious realm in order to ensure the supremacy and autonomy of the political realm, which would be commanded by statesmen liberated from religion and devoted to glory, guided by benevolent scientists free to pursue unhampered knowledge, and supported by an enlightened people disenchanted of supernatural religion, busy with commerce, and moved by patriotism.[39]

Although some of these beliefs were clearly antithetical, in whole or in part, to traditional Judaism, they supported a greater aim with which Jews certainly could, and mostly did, sympathize. Jews were distinctly unfriendly to the survival of the medieval Christian order, which the Enlightenment aimed to destroy. For them its meaning was clear, as Strauss put it so well: "The action most characteristic of the Middle Ages is the Crusades; it may be said to have culminated not accidentally in the murder of whole Jewish communities."[40] If only for this reason, Strauss recognized that it is difficult for modern nonorthodox Jews to stand in a critical relation to Spinoza, as "the first philosopher who was both a democrat and a liberal," and hence as the thinker who is responsible for some of the greatest blessings of modernity in his commanding argument for liberal democracy, as the only modern regime which has been more or less consistently friendly to the Jews.[41] It is only in this regime that they have been allotted an honorable settlement, though one not always free of contradictions, i.e., as individual human beings with natural rights.

Strauss thus uncovers the Machiavellian political considerations which permitted Spinoza to tactically attack things Jewish if it helped him strategically win his battle to separate Christian religious faith and European political life.[42] Spinoza's Machiavellian moral calculus may be stated as follows: he needed to make a direct attack on the Jews both in order to make surreptitiously a greater attack on the Christians, and in order to protect his own safety as a lone attacker against a powerful and oppressive order. As Strauss further perceived, Spinoza could make an argument against Christianity acceptable to Christians via an argument against Judaism and the Jewish Bible, because his attack was put in the disguised form of an attack on the Jews who were despised by his Christian readers, and hence they would be receptive to it. Spinoza could meanwhile vindicate himself by claiming to liberate the Jews both from their own oppressive religion, and from the oppressive medieval Christian order. Eventually, once the war has been victorious, i.e., the common enemy has been demolished and liberal democracy has been established, the Jews will be grateful to him.[43]

This led to Strauss's mature conclusion that Spinoza was not entirely a bad Jew, despite his amoral Machiavellian tactics and strategy. Strauss thus moved to a greater appreciation for Spinoza's contribution to modern Judaism. Strauss's earlier view of Spinoza as entirely unconcerned with the Jews and Judaism seems to have been qualified decisively, for in his later essays Strauss recognized in Spinoza's suggestions for reforming the Jews, so as to make possible their accommodation to his projected liberal democracy, a vital and even deep remaining "sympathy with his people." Although he may have been definitely set against Judaism, he was not set against the Jews, especially once they have been freed by him from any ultimate ties to what he regarded as their "effeminating" traditional religion.[44] Strauss refers directly to perhaps the most important "solution to the Jewish problem," which Spinoza first suggested, namely, "liberal assimilationism," which enables the Jews as secular individual citizens to fit in with a liberal democracy so as to derive the decent benefits and protections of their "natural rights."

In fact, Strauss credits Spinoza not only with the idea of liberal assimilationism, but also with the quite different possibility of a "solution to the Jewish problem" on the basis of a restored Jewish political autonomy in their ancestral homeland. Although it is Strauss's view that this option sketched by Spinoza is atheistic in its origins and impulses, and derives from liberalism while pointing correctly to the limits of liberalism,[45] it nevertheless restores to the Jews a fighting spirit, teaches them to resist by arms the evils which befall them, and forces them to control their own political destiny. Spinoza, witness to the Shabbetai Zevi messianic episode, which illustrated to him how theology led the Jews astray, made this "Zionist" suggestion as a logical deduction from his liberalism. He envisioned that once the Jews have been liberated from the "debilitating" aspects of their religion, this will enable them to choose either individual or collective freedom in the modern age. Although both of these political suggestions are in full conformity with what Strauss calls "Spinoza's egoistic morality," a morality which in his analysis is not compatible with Judaism, they do prove to Strauss that Spinoza was not unmoved by the political plight and suffering of the Jews.[46]

In the subtle and dialectical approach of Leo Strauss, Spinoza is presented as a highly complex, original, and yet questionable figure. He was a keen student of Machiavelli and his "disciples," Bacon, Descartes, and Hobbes, and was animated by the "antitheological ire" of the modern project. Yet he advocated its aim to dismantle the medieval Christian order so as to establish the humane liberal democracy devised originally in his philosophy. He was a philosophic system builder, and a defender of the open-minded pursuit of modern science and philosophy in complete freedom. Yet he was also a closed-minded antagonist of revelation, especially in its claim to knowledge, and he even attempted to "refute" it by a brilliant but unavailing argument. He was a hostile critic of orthodox Judaism, an unjust attacker of the basis of its faith, and the consequent author of biblical criticism. Yet he was also the originator of the powerful modern Jewish ideas of political Zionism and liberal Jewish religion.

For Strauss, this leads to the unassailable conclusion that modern Judaism simply cannot be separated from the dubious figure of Spinoza, in whom such troublesome contradictions coincide. In Strauss's search for the causes of the contemporary crisis of modern Judaism and for a way toward its possible resolution, he tried to comprehend Spinoza in his full complexity: as a bold and original modern philosopher in his own right, as a Jewish thinker compared against the standard of Maimonides, and as the benefactor of modern Judaism in the light of whose legacy his modern Jewish heirs were viewed and measured. By this means Strauss hoped to attain a solid ground beyond the present predicament, a ground that somehow encompasses both the true importance, and the problematic nature, of Spinoza.

Moses Mendelssohn

If Strauss viewed Spinoza as a sort of mastermind of modern Judaism in directing it by remote suggestion to its diverse forms, he recognized Moses Mendelssohn as the actual and direct father of modern Judaism. Strauss acknowledged Mendelssohn as undoubtedly the first modern Jewish philosophical thinker who was not only a knowledgeable Jew, as Spinoza admittedly was too, but also a relatively loyal and devoted Jew, unlike Spinoza. But for Strauss, it was of much greater import to decide whether Mendelssohn had been a deep enough thinker to vindicate intellectually the perhaps extravagant claims he made for the ready and uncomplicated synthesis of traditional Judaism with modern philosophy and the modern order.[47]

In fact, Strauss was led to conclude that, although Mendelssohn's "synthesis" seemingly depended on the acceptance of the two blended elements, Jewish orthodoxy and Enlightenment, as somehow equally compelling in terms of essential truth, the equal treatment of the two truth claims never did occur. As this implies, Mendelssohn renounced even token resistance to modern philosophy and science as futile by accepting the claim of this philosophy and science to stand beyond rational critique. And so he capitulated from the start by denying the very idea of truths unique to Judaism. In Strauss's view, Mendelssohn set the direction of modern Jewish life and thought since he attuned Jewish thought to the commanding ideas of modern religious liberalism, and thus formulated it in an entirely "apologetic" vein. Mendelssohn as well as his immediate Jewish followers were apologetic thinkers because they assumed what Strauss regarded as a not adequately critical attitude, either as Jews or as philosophers, toward the radical Enlightenment, especially as it was defined by such thinkers as Bacon, Hobbes, Spinoza, and Rousseau, and as they accepted it in the palatable versions of Locke, Leibniz, and Lessing.

Mendelssohn's position was essentially subservient to the Enlightenment, because he held to the Jewish element of the synthesis only inasmuch as it could be made conformable with modern philosophy in its popular teaching. As he construed it, this meant the one natural religion and morality teaching required by the modern liberal political order. The attempts by Mendelssohn and his Jewish followers at a supposed synthesis never served as a basis for developing a reciprocal critique of modern philosophy and science. Such a dialectical method of Jewish theological critique in response to the challenges of philosophy might still have been learned, as Strauss emphasized, from the different sort of effort in which Maimonides had been engaged in a similar, even though medieval, situation.

Strauss discerned that Mendelssohn's basic strategy was to argue that Judaism need not conflict with the entire Enlightenment teaching, because this is just what Judaism itself teaches and what has always been taught by it. Strauss recognized, however, that in the synthesis produced by Mendelssohn, Judaism was forced on almost every point to conform, to one degree or another, with modern reason. But in Strauss's estimation, notwithstanding this rather one-sided synthesis, the encounter between Judaism and modern reason could have been made to serve a useful purpose. That is to say, if by this encounter Judaism had been helped to learn how to defend itself against the charges brought by modern philosophy, and hence if it was forced to think through what it itself believed *in contrast with* modern reason prior to committing itself to a synthesis, perhaps the process started by Mendelssohn could have been rendered legitimate.

However, as Strauss contends, this was never done by Mendelssohn or by his followers. Indeed, they never asked whether the need of Judaism to conform with modern reason was fully rational and hence necessary, because it was never asked if modern reason was in itself fully rational and hence necessary. Further, they never raised the question of whether the conclusions of modern science and philosophy were as solid, as irrefutable, or as comprehensive as they claimed to be. And finally, the problem never seems to have been addressed whether modern reason could ever be a fair and impartial judge of Judaism—that is, whether it possesses even the rational credibility and sufficiency to set itself up as an authoritative judge of Judaism.

It was, as a consequence, doubtful to Strauss whether Judaism and modern reason could ever be synthesized in the way proposed by Mendelssohn, if only because of the specific hostility of modern reason to Judaism as a revealed religion, and the essential hostility of Judaism to any unqualified and complete "system" of rationalism. Thus, Strauss discovered that Mendelssohn was forced by modern reason to sacrifice almost everything unique to Jewish teaching. Mendelssohn was constrained, based mostly on the charges against Judaism brought by the philosophy of Spinoza, to "prove" that Judaism neither believed in miracles, revelation, the chosenness of the Jews, nor offered special salvation for those who obey the commandments of the Torah, because these beliefs were dismissed as "irrational dogmas." Besides everything else, it seems he did not ever ask whether it was possible for Judaism to do this and still survive as an autonomous and self-sustaining religious tradition.

In comparison with the apologetics and compromises of Mendelssohn, Strauss discerned in the sheer stubborn resistance of Jewish orthodoxy to the radical Enlightenment an expression of a greater intellectual honesty than Mendelssohn's version of synthesis. This, Strauss concluded, was the source for the apologetic religious liberalism that dominates in modern Judaism, which in his view amounted to a virtual "unconditional surrender" to modern philosophy.

Hermann Cohen

During Strauss's youth, the most powerful spokesman for the vitality of modern Jewish philosophic thought was Hermann Cohen. Strauss encountered a Jewish thinker who had been a major figure in German academic philosophy, and who also claimed audaciously to apply his neo-Kantian philosophic teaching to Judaism so as to enable it to resolve its fundamental modern dilemmas. As Strauss interpreted modern Judaism, and as he experienced its vicissitudes in his own life,

Hermann Cohen emerged as perhaps the most appealing and yet some-how also the least persuasive modern figure.[48] Essentially, Cohen was appealing to Strauss as "a passionate philosopher and a Jew passion-ately devoted to Judaism."[49] In point of fact, Cohen exercised a forma-tive influence on Strauss's intellectual development: in his youth, Strauss was persuaded by Cohen's Marburg neo-Kantianism, and he affirmatively viewed Cohen as one who was able to blend happily a strict devotion to philosophy with a passionate commitment to Judaism.

Strauss was also impressed with how much Cohen had been determined to wrestle with the conflict between Judaism and philoso-phy, produced by their fundamental differences, in the hope of yielding a decisive resolution to their conflict.[50] Cohen remained for Strauss until the very end the image of the proud and self-respecting modern Jew who engages in philosophic activity; he served as a kind of exemplar, standing for the virtues which he hoped to imitate in the sphere of mod-ern Jewish thought.[51]

Yet Cohen was also not persuasive to Strauss precisely because of his vaunted modern synthesis, constructed on the basis of his neo-Kantian system of philosophy, with Judaism (represented by its classical and medieval texts) playing a leading role. Strauss concluded even in his youth that insofar as Cohen's "idealizing" method of interpreting Jewish texts presupposed the truth of the neo-Kantian philosophic sys-tem, it could not do simple philosophic justice to the religious thought of the sources of Judaism.[52] This is because, as Strauss started to believe, the neo-Kantian philosophic system of Cohen was itself deeply flawed, especially in its supplementing of Kant with the Hegelian premise of a necessary dialectical progress in history. Thus, it was Strauss's view that Cohen's philosophic teaching about man and history aroused exag-gerated hopes about the modern liberal order, because it was not grounded in a sober assessment of the true achievements of modern man in politics and in science.

Alert to the growing philosophic critique of Cohen (in the form of Husserl and phenomenology), Strauss calls himself, already in 1922, "a doubting and dubious adherent of the Marburg school of neo-Kantianism."[53] From a purely Jewish perspective, it also seemed evi-dent to Strauss that none of his fundamental doubt about Cohen's philo-sophico-historical synthesis of modernity as it was applied to modern Judaism could be dispelled by Cohen's resort to the ancient Jewish sources in order to secure and bolster the ground beneath his philo-sophical teaching. Thus, Strauss was critical of Cohen for approaching the ancient Jewish sources by his peculiar style of "idealization" in order to make his historical arguments. This method of interpretation assumed that Cohen could uncover in the classical Jewish texts their "highest possibility." However, as Strauss perceived, this amounted to the explication of the texts so that neo-Kantian wisdom, only fully made available in the present, was the single true "highest possibility" of those ancient sources.

Insofar as Cohen claimed to make a historical argument, he does not do justice to the historical truth about those texts; insofar as he claimed to make a philosophical argument, he did not provide modern Jews with any autonomous Jewish standard by which to criticize the defective present and its thought. By doing so, to Strauss, Cohen made this ancient tradition and its classical texts of an even greater irrelevance than that to which they had been consigned by modern Judaism hitherto.

Of course, what also seemed so faulty to Strauss, in common-sense terms, was Cohen's firm belief in modern Germany as the chief ground of hope for modern Jews. For him that hopeful teaching did not express a view of modernity which corresponded to his own experience of actual political reality as a Jew in post–World War I Germany, which scarcely seemed on the verge of the triumph of liberalism and the rejection of anti-Semitism. As Strauss observed, how could Cohen be right if the most powerful voices at work in modern Germany, which seemed to him determinative of the immediate historical reality, had not actually been inspired by Kant or even by Hegel, but by Nietzsche and especially by Heidegger?[54]

Consequently Strauss began to drift away from Cohen both due to gnawing doubts about his neo-Kantian philosophic system, and to massive political forces not discussed or predicted by Cohen by which Strauss was threatened, and with which he, unlike Cohen, had to deal. Perhaps because of these doubts about Cohen provoked by historical events, and perhaps also in anticipation of not yet fully articulated philosophical doubts, Strauss was not able to discover in Cohen the resources to deal with his immediate perplexities. As a solution to the Jewish political problem, Strauss had been moved to embrace political Zionism at the youthful age of seventeen. He continued to accept the force of its essential argument, although one might think that this would have been put in doubt by Cohen's strictures. Responding to deeper spiritual needs, he also grew attracted to Rosenzweig's return to a revised orthodox theology, although certainly it too was not in basic accord with the spirit of Cohen. Rosenzweig stressed the individual's experience of revelation in an encounter with God, a notion contradicting Cohen's emphasis on the primacy of autonomy in man, which excluded any such encounter.[55]

Disregarding for the moment the precarious Jewish political situation of Strauss's youth, to which he was so alert in his thinking, and which forced a Zionist political direction and neo-orthodox theological orientation on it, let us investigate in somewhat greater detail what Cohen's grand modern philosophical synthesis entailed, and try to explain why it would not provide enough philosophical or theological sustenance for Strauss as a young Jewish thinker. In Cohen's synthesis, it was argued that the modern West was constituted by the bringing together of the Hebrew prophetic idea of ethical monotheism with the Platonic idea of philosophy as science. This was so especially as the two have been raised to modern systematic perfection by the critical philosophy of Kant, in which the essential ideas of both are taken into account and given their highest possible rational articulation, culminating in the moral idea and messianic task of humanity.

Strauss was in a definite sense impressed with the bold uniqueness of Cohen's enterprise. As a philosophic thinker who was also a Jewish thinker, Cohen tried to defend the integrity of the Jewish tradition—with all "necessary" qualifications, such as the divestment of its mysticism—as compatible with the modern requirement, defined by neo-Kantianism, that religion not detract from the absolute moral autonomy and pure rational creativity of man. Thus, Cohen showed in his synthesis how Jewish thought was sufficient to the task of responding with a true seriousness to the enormous challenges of Kantian ethics and epistemology, while seemingly not surrendering or reducing the Jewish religious view of man and the world.

Strauss, however, could not help but observe that in this synthesis classical Jewish theology was ultimately required to surrender or reduce its own religious view, especially in regard to its claim to genuine knowledge of things, and in its expression of moral principles. This is because Kantian (or neo-Kantian) philosophy conceived of religion in terms of postulated belief rather than as a source of knowledge, and also viewed morality as in its very nature defined as a consequence of human autonomy, and not as a revealed (i.e., heteronomous) set of fundamental principles. Hence, Cohen allowed the Jewish religious view to stand only inasmuch as it was transferable from a claim of knowledge to a claim of belief, and only insofar as it could be interpreted as consistent with human autonomy of reason and freedom of will, as such notions were conceived in Cohen's neo-Kantian epistemology and moral philosophy.

Moreover, Strauss saw that Cohen needed the sources of Judaism clearly to ratify his modern synthesis, and hence in this light he reworked them as needed to suit his preordained end. But Cohen did not perceive that the elements of this synthesis, as well as this synthesis itself, were entirely creatures of his own construction. For him it was apparently a simple historical fact that purely rational ethics had been manifested originally, though unconsciously, by the Hebrew prophets. This historical fact he believed to be confirmed by his study of the ancient sources of Judaism.

In Strauss's view, Cohen could achieve such full evidence often only by reading those Jewish sources with the utmost selectiveness, and hence by seeing them in a distorting light. As Cohen chose to interpret the sources of Judaism, the "highest possibility" of the ancient Jewish religious view was its promise of Kantian (or neo-Kantian) ethics, in the sense that this modern philosophy supposedly represents its first completely rational articulation. In Cohen's reading, the ancient Jewish religious view could be reconstructed as a postulated belief necessary to support and fulfill a correctly rational morality. It was this that had been developed unsystematically by ancient Jewish religious thinkers.[56] Though not neo-Kantian philosophers, they acted on "primitive" or unconscious impulses yielded in a historical dialectic: they carried through and expressed imaginatively the logical consequences, or the moral implications, of the rational idea of the one God as creator, which they discovered in their own native tradition.

Strauss also discerned that Cohen's synthesis was a defense of modernity, in the face of the massive critique of the modern project that emerged in Nietzsche. On the positive side of the scale, it seemed to Strauss to have been rooted in a rare modern seriousness about both reason and revelation. This had somehow been revived by Cohen in recognizing a deep need of the modern sensibility that had been made visible in the critique of modernity. Strauss was certainly impressed with Cohen's historical justification of Jewish sources on the very highest philosophic plane, which in his system were praised for their once decisive contribution to modern Western civilization. However, on the negative side of the scale, Strauss noticed that while for Cohen this idea of ethical monotheism had originally been contributed to Western civilization by the Jews, it puts a high value on the Jewish tradition in an *ultimately* philosophic translation and as *primarily* a historical artifact. Even if Jews must persist as the teachers of "the pure monotheism," Judaism is reduced to an idea.[57] Even if a historical future is preserved for the Jews, as adherents of "the pure monotheism" in their relation to the fulfillment of the messianic task to build one humanity in the *idea* of the future, it is no longer as a vital and self-creative people.

And, as should also be mentioned, both of the two original elements of the final modern synthesis, Platonism and Judaism, do not possess in themselves the same vitality or dynamic which the synthesis itself possesses as it unfolds. By the unadmitted Hegelian logic of Cohen's historical synthesis, they have been perforce "sublated" by it. It is not evident from Cohen's argument, then, whether once the truth of the ethical monotheistic idea has been done justice in modern Kantian or neo-Kantian philosophy, there is any further *essential* need for the Jewish religion, or anything genuinely new for the Jews to do, but proclaim the old teaching while working for the victory of European liberalism in the form of democratic socialism.

Moreover, as mentioned previously, Strauss also grew to doubt the neo-Kantian philosophic system as this had been devised by Cohen, both because of the influence of Husserl's phenomenological critique of Cohen's idea of modern scientific reason, and because of the exposure to neo-orthodox theology in the 1920s, offered by Franz Rosenzweig and Karl Barth. This put in doubt the adequacy of Cohen's historically progressive notion of revelation. Strauss was never able to restore his faith in Cohen's system because of these criticisms, which suggested it was not able to meet the type of challenge issued by radical historicism to its view of modern scientific reason—a view that indeed verged on, if it did not merge with, positivism, and hence is itself only a step away from historicism.[58]

In one respect only, then, was there a role of fundamental importance for Cohen to play in Strauss's mature Jewish thought: Strauss revered Cohen ultimately neither for the supposedly final modern synthesis of his philosophic system, nor for the acknowledged philosophic depth evident in his thought, but for the general attempt at such a synthesis, however misguided and unfulfilled Cohen's specific effort. He showed not just the possibility of a modern Jewish philosophy, which resembled and even imitated its medieval ancestor, but also an unavoidable modern Jewish need. Cohen was the model for Strauss himself of the modern Jewish philosopher: an undoubtedly original philosophic thinker, who is immersed in the Western tradition of philosophy and science. And yet Cohen still remains devoted to Judaism in the highest sense, trying by an exacting scholarly consideration, on the ground of intellectual honesty and consistency, to reconcile his two commitments.

Consequently, Strauss defends Cohen against the charges laid against him by Isaac Husik, a leading historian of medieval Jewish philosophy. Husik thought that the integrity of Cohen as a modern Jewish philosopher was diminished, if not nullified, by the dubiousness of Cohen's scholarly efforts in the history of Jewish thought.[59] In this context, Strauss carries through a true "vindication" of Hermann Cohen against Husik's sharp criticisms.[60] In doing so, Strauss was compelled to also defend the very idea of a modern Jewish philosophy, since it was Husik's view that there could not be such a thing. This is because, as Husik believed, Jewish philosophy means, and can only mean, *medieval* Jewish philosophy. In his view, this entity called "Jewish philosophy" only made sense in terms of the fixed coordinates which once made it possible, things now known to be noble medieval delusions which have been irrevocably dispelled: belief in the literal truth of the Torah as a once only historical revelation, and belief in a comprehensive, rigorous, and completed (Aristotelian) science. But as Strauss counters here quite simply, the lack in modern Jewish philosophy of the identical fixed coordinates which perhaps once "historically" defined medieval Jewish philosophy *cannot* be the last word, since these fixed coordinates do not define, in the most basic sense, what Judaism is or what philosophy is.

This leads Strauss to the trenchant observation that "the fundamental problem," which aroused the need for Jewish philosophy during the medieval period and beyond, remains the same. If this is so, then ultimately Husik's and Cohen's approaches coalesce. They both recognize that this still "fundamental problem" is most evident in the vital need to wrestle with and to reconcile "the relation of the spirit of science and of the spirit of the Bible."[61]

However, in spite of Strauss's admiration for Cohen as a model of the modern Jewish philosophic thinker, and for his revival of Jewish philosophy pursued with exemplary passion, Strauss was not able to revive his interest in Cohen's actual philosophic thought. Cohen remained beholden to the very modern philosophy to which Strauss was searching for a rational alternative.[62] Strauss graciously relegated the intellectual faults and moral vices of Cohen's thought to the effects and limits of his historical experience. Such awareness of subsequent events did not permit Strauss to even consider trying to revive Cohen's thought.[63] Thus, Strauss rests his case against the adequacy of Cohen's thought on its pre–World War I character:

> The worst things that he experienced were the Dreyfus scandal and the pogroms instigated by czarist Russia: he did not experience communist Russia and Hitler Germany.[64]

For Strauss these historical experiences make the "naive" belief in historical progress and in the rationality of the historical process impossible. As a result, Strauss was convinced that we must reconsider and rethink as radically as possible all our modern premises which have brought us to this pass—indeed, he insisted on it already by 1935.

However, that conviction did not lead him either to call for an embrace of irrationalism in its "ultramodern" forms, or to argue for a supposedly simple "rejection" of reason in favor of revelation, as this is known in the modern Jewish tradition. But it did arouse in him the notion of a reassessment of the theological value and rational truth possibly still contained in a premodern Jewish philosophic tradition of rational theology, whose wisdom may not have been entirely surpassed by modern Jewish thinkers like Cohen.

In other words, a reconsideration or rethinking of the modern tradition of philosophy and theology, however radical, never entailed for Strauss a simple rejection of modern reason, which he did not regard as a sober option worth entertaining. Thus, Strauss did resemble Cohen in one highly important regard: he was like him in maintaining an adherence to modern liberal democracy, not to mention to modern science and to biblical criticism, i.e., for all practical purposes, to the unavoidable legacy of Spinoza judiciously appropriated.[65] And Strauss also stood with Cohen, although put in his own terms, on the need for modern Jewish thinkers to wrestle with the deepest conflicts between reason and revelation, which have not been resolved by modern man, in light of the pressing moral concerns, powerful historical experiences, and most serious intellectual difficulties and impasses of modern man.

At the same time, in contradistinction to Cohen, Strauss was growing attracted to the form of premodern rational thought which he discovered in Maimonides. The move toward it required a much greater radical turn of thought and critical reassessment of the modern than was available to him in Cohen's system. Responding to the extreme terms and unprecedented light in which modernity was placed by Nietzsche and Heidegger, Strauss would come to doubt in theory the entire modern project which Cohen could not think beyond, and did not see any reason to think beyond. Strauss goes to the point of connecting the origins of modernity with Machiavelli, and hence he views it as rooted in what would be regarded in traditional terms as an amoral philosophic thought, contrary to Cohen's Kantian idealization of the primacy of a traditional moral impulse in the move to modernity and Enlightenment.

The shock of recognition of this ambiguous origin and impulse in which the idea of the modern arose is for Strauss a sobering realization that seemed to help him account for the repeated collapse in our century of liberal morality, politics, and religion as bulwarks against tyranny, as well as against subtler forms of evil. In addition, Strauss was fully aware that the challenge presented by Nietzsche to the ideas of traditional morality, of reason in human nature, and of the rationality of history was greater than Cohen imagined. Cohen was virtually a full-fledged Hegelian in his faith in the march of modern progress toward rationality and morality.[66]

It was Cohen's views on Judaism, however, that were ultimately unsatisfactory to Strauss. In particular, Strauss assessed the position of Cohen on divine revelation as defective.[67] He concluded that the unique elements in the Jewish teaching on revelation are not adequately comprehended by Cohen's notion of the greater "originalness" of Judaism as a cultural or historical source (such as is brought to light by his difficulties with "God as a reality").[68] Strauss also did not believe Cohen's position did justice to revelation's claim to universal truth, especially insofar as this truth may contradict modern ideas, such as human rational and moral autonomy. Although Cohen's system admits that in the divine revelation of Judaism there is displayed a primitive form of Kantian moral reasoning and human autonomy, revelation still remains on the most basic level a relic or artifact of the past, however impressive. It is not a vital teaching of the present, or even a teaching which may be needed to instruct the present. In Strauss's judgment, if this is all there is to the truth of Judaism as a divinely revealed teaching, as a magnificent anticipation of modern (neo-Kantian) ideas, then Cohen does not provide a fully compelling reason why we must preserve and give priority to the *unchanged* sources and traditions of Judaism, which had been the essence of the debate between Spinoza and Jewish orthodoxy.

This leads Strauss to stress that Cohen does not believe in "revealed truths or revealed laws in the precise or traditional sense of the terms." Strauss would perhaps admit that Cohen provides us with a motive for maintaining a liberal Jewish religion, as a perfectly acceptable and even in some respects superior version of the religion of reason.[69] But then over and above everything else, Strauss seems to doubt whether this rationale is likely to provide a motive for devotion to the sources of Judaism, if they are no longer a teaching of revealed truths separate from, and claiming superiority to, the truths of reason.

Franz Rosenzweig

Strauss considered Franz Rosenzweig to be responsible for undoubtedly the most important change in the previous direction of modern Jewish theology.[70] In Strauss's view, Rosenzweig contributed the most powerful idea which may be attributed to what Strauss calls the movement of return in modern Judaism. This is his idea that divine revelation is a present possibility and thus is something which can be "genuinely known," rather than just received opinion, and hence something which should be "merely believed."[71] Strauss was especially impressed with Rosenzweig's interpretation of revelation as not just a historic fact from the past, but also as something which can be experienced in every historic situation, through a type of communication or encounter in the human soul, from divine subject to human subject.

However, the other ways in which the Rosenzweig's "new thinking" transformed modern Jewish theology were treated by Strauss more or less critically.[72] One of the primary reasons Strauss was not persuaded by Rosenzweig stemmed from the fact that Strauss viewed this "new thinking" as originating in the problematic ideas of Kierkegaard and Nietzsche. As this further suggested to Strauss, the new thinking was grounded in the fundamental belief of these thinkers that a fatal blow had been struck against reason itself with the collapse of the Hegelian synthesis in philosophy. Hence, reason was abandoned for the sake of "anxiety," "commitment," "authenticity," and "probity." In Strauss's reading, Rosenzweig began his analysis of the individual human being not with his relations to his fellow man, to society, to science, or even to God, but like Heidegger with his "being toward death," or with mortal fear. This move is based on the assumption that reason as unfolded by Hegel and the entire preceding Western philosophic tradition was sterile, if not actually destructive, of what is most human in man. Although reason had once been advanced as the great hope of modern man, what has actually been wrought by it, according to this view, is mediocrity, conformity, isolation, hopelessness, and even nihilism. Thus, in its critical and scientific function, according to the critique made by the new thinking, modern reason has been consumed by its own children.

While Strauss was not willing to dispense with the idea of reason (even if he was sharply critical of reason in its *modern* forms), he did follow Rosenzweig in his simple rejection of the sufficiency of Hegelian dialectical reason. It issued in the idea of a necessary "progress" in human history. Strauss reached the conclusion that this notion of progress is simply unbelievable for us in the twentieth century, if only because of a single assumption which is essential to it, but which he discerned to be manifestly flawed: progress should enable us to attain a certain "fixed level of being" that, once we attain it, is permanently established. This is a level beneath which we cannot fall.[73] However, the barbarity of our contemporary history proves otherwise:

> This contention [of progress], however, is empirically refuted by the incredible barbarization which we have been so unfortunate as to witness in our century. We can say that the idea of progress, in the full and emphatic sense of the term, is based on wholly unwarranted hopes.[74]

It was Rosenzweig's apparent abandonment of faith in reason, and his move toward a sort of irrationalism, with which Strauss was most dissatisfied, and for which he faulted Rosenzweig.[75] In stark contrast to him, Strauss expounds Judaism undoubtedly in the spirit of both Maimonides and Hermann Cohen, viewing it as a faith which claims only to possess "suprarational," and not "irrational," truths. Hence, the truths which Judaism teaches, according to Strauss's thought, do not contradict reason, but only pass beyond what unaided reason can apprehend by its own efforts and abilities alone.[76] This means that Judaism travels as far as possible with reason, in order to apprehend its true powers and their possible limits, prior to reaching any decision about those sources which might claim to surpass it in terms of knowledge. He uses as his proof text a favorite Torah verse (Deut. 4:6), which he often cites in order to emphasize the rational character of the Jewish tradition: "Jewish orthodoxy based its claim to superiority to other religions from the beginning on its superior rationality."[77]

Thus, in Strauss's final judgment, Rosenzweig pursued the assumptions of the new thinking to their furthest reaches, and indeed, beyond even Heidegger.[78] However, Strauss was dissatisfied with Rosenzweig's version of the new thinking for three reasons. First, its chief assumption may not have been as self-evident as Rosenzweig's version of the new thinking claims. That is, the collapse of the Hegelian synthesis might not only issue in the rehabilitation of orthodoxy, but might also result in the resuscitation of the original challenges of the Enlightenment, not to mention premodern philosophy. Second, Strauss believed that the original grounds of this assumption may not have been as deeply grasped by Rosenzweig as they were by Heidegger. He seemed to comprehend with greater accuracy and precision what is contained in both the Enlightenment and in the premodern Western tradition of philosophy, and what would be required if one is to judge properly whether they have been truly surpassed or refuted. Third, Strauss also questioned whether Rosenzweig exemplified his own thought as consistently as might have been done. In other words, is it the new thinking which justifies the merely qualified return to orthodoxy, or do the qualifications rest on another basis, i.e., on the Enlightenment in its critique of religion? But this is a position that is supposed to have been surpassed or discredited, according to Rosenzweig himself.

In light of these concerns, it is possible to see why Strauss put such weight on his criticism of Rosenzweig's thought for its derivative modern notions about the premodern Western philosophic tradition: the old thinking can scarcely be regarded as completely defeated if the refutation of it is still somehow rooted in the old thinking, and if one does not make evident in one's arguments such detailed and thorough knowledge of the old thinking as would be required for its refutation in adequate terms.

Together with this, however, Strauss recognized that Rosenzweig was a thinker of greater profundity than Heidegger regarding the Bible, biblical religion, and divine revelation. Indeed, as Strauss would seem to maintain, the atheistic new thinking of Heidegger insofar as it rests on biblically derived categories—such as anguish, conscience, guilt, and anxiety—remains rooted in the biblical view of man and human life, i.e., in the "biblical morality" which, as Strauss learned from Nietzsche, requires the biblical God. As a result, Rosenzweig appears to have been able to grasp better than Heidegger the deepest impulse presupposed by the new thinking: it would seem, according to Strauss, that this thought is moved by a sort of defense of biblical revelation. Hence it constitutes a type of vindication (witting in Rosenzweig, and unwitting in Heidegger) of the biblical God against his modern philosophic deniers.[79]

Consequently, it is no wonder that Strauss approved of the conclusion Rosenzweig drew from the new thinking in its critique of modern reason—the return to orthodoxy. Strauss seemed to view this as a consistent and honest deduction derived from the rest of his arguments. Strauss, however, regarded as untenable what he viewed as Rosenzweig's unwillingness to follow through with what is clearly implied in the logic of his own thought. That is, this "new thinking" constitutes fundamentally a revived defense of orthodox theological notions. If there is a need for an unqualified return to Jewish orthodoxy pure and simple, then certainly this is something which is philosophically defensible. But Strauss could not ignore that Rosenzweig attempted no such defense. Thus, Strauss saw Rosenzweig's return to orthodoxy as a merely *qualified* return, characterized by doubts and reservations about several key orthodox Jewish beliefs, developed in actuality in light of the old thinking of Mendelssohn, which is itself ultimately rooted in the philosophy of Spinoza.

As Strauss lucidly discerned, Rosenzweig never adequately accounts for and justifies the new thinking's radical dependency on a critique launched by the old thinking (as its insights, to be sure, had been transformed by the modern Enlightenment) against the very religious tradition he wished to defend.

Theodor Herzl and Political Zionism

Prior to turning to Strauss's Maimonideanism, I must complete my review of the reconsideration Strauss made of modern Jewish thought in an era of "theological-political crisis." I have been led to emphasize the theological concerns of Strauss, and I have been brought by them to a conundrum about Strauss's own position. Is it true for Strauss that perhaps ultimately this crisis of Jews and Judaism is entirely brought about by political causes? Strauss's great respect for the political in the mature stages of the development of his thought might tempt one to proceed in such a direction. But his "Platonic" leanings, and his constantly linking the political with the theological, should cause one to hesitate in the face of such a temptation to read Strauss as a thoroughly "modern" Jewish philosophic thinker.

Notwithstanding such cautions, no doubt politics, and especially Jewish politics, stood close to the very epicenter of Strauss's concerns. Besides liberal democracy, the leading Jewish political option which remained compelling to Strauss in both moral and historical terms was Zionism. Thus it is crucial to explore his complex view of it, both because of the formative influence which it exercised on his Jewish thought, and in order to fully comprehend his subsequent attraction to Maimonides for the roundedness and unity of his Jewish political and theological vision.

Although "converted," as he put it, to political Zionism at seventeen, Strauss continued to deepen his commitment to Zionism by not exempting it from his critical philosophical reflection. It is interesting that this critical reflection did not diminish his admiration for the father of political Zionism, Theodor Herzl. To be sure, Strauss was aware that Herzlian "political Zionism is problematic for obvious reasons."[80] Among other things, Zionism could not provide *the* solution to the Jewish problem, since it could not reconcile its explicit secularism with its implicit theology, as will be discussed shortly. However, it could achieve what its father Herzl chiefly aimed for: "the restoration of [Jewish] honor through the acquisition of statehood and therefore of a country," i.e., as a matter of principle, if we disregard merely Jewish preferences, any state in any country will do. Nevertheless, it is also instructive that this "problematic" aim of political Zionism certainly did not nullify for Strauss Herzl's cogent political analysis of the modern Jewish situation. In his view this analysis has only been confirmed, rather than refuted, by subsequent history.[81]

Strauss perceived that the growth of Zionism, and "the truth [it] proclaimed," was inextricably tied to what he called "the limitations of liberalism." By this he meant the following: although those countries that have been guided by the idea of liberal democracy have mostly been friendly to the Jews, at least in principle, they have not in moments of crisis always been true to their own principles. Liberal democracy makes a promise to the Jews that, if they "assimilate" (and this term implies that conversion is not required), their natural rights as individual citizens, as human beings irrespective of religious affiliation, will be protected. This means that they will be legally equal and socially accepted, they will be free to participate in all aspects of society and only limited by their abilities, and, they will be awarded honors for their accomplishments as worthy individual citizens. And yet liberal democracy has frequently been shown to manifest grave limits in its ability to deliver on this comprehensive promise.

The cause of liberalism in Europe advanced on the strength of a truth supplied by reason concerning the natural equality of all human beings. But "as a demand of reason it had no effect on the feelings of non-Jews." Certainly Strauss's turn to Zionism did not amount to a simple rejection of modern Western liberal democracy. Strauss never ceased to regard it as still the best modern political option available to Jews, even in Israel. Rather, his fidelity to Zionism was rooted in a sober historical and philosophical assessment of the weakness of Western liberal democracy since, combined with Jewish "assimilationism," it has not been able to offer, and cannot offer, *the* decisive "solution to the Jewish problem" of diaspora Jews. This is sufficient to impair its moral authority as the highest hope of modern Jews. In this respect, Strauss's attitude to Zionism is defined by an awareness of what must be learned from modern Jewish history: that it provides the best demonstration, a living proof, of the necessary and hence permanent limits of liberalism.[82]

As will be recalled, Strauss traced modern Zionism to a suggestion made in passing by Spinoza, who first consistently deduced it from his liberalism as merely a logical implication. Strauss was most interested in the core of this modern idea, a core that he regarded as best expressed in purely political Zionism, since it was originally as an entirely secular, indeed atheistic, political movement that this idea was propounded. It arose from thoroughly secular modern Jews, like Leon Pinsker and Theodor Herzl. They made an incisive analysis of the hard and cold facts of the Jewish situation in modern liberal Europe. They perceived what these facts implied about the futility of Jewish hopes for assimilation and true acceptance in modern Europe: not only was it far-fetched to rest hope for the Jewish masses on the liberalization of Russia, but also they focused on the peculiarly exasperating failures of liberalism in Europe in its repeated betrayal of the Jews (and not just in principle), not to mention the aspect of its principles that made it impossible to act in defense of the Jews.

The aspect of its principles to which this refers is the liberal assertion of the rights and freedoms of the private sphere to dwell in legally protected safety, in which religion was confined, as opposed to the rights and duties of the public order, and it was this that entailed the legal defense of anti-Semitism if it remained in the private sphere. In this protected sphere it could flourish unimpeded so long as it did not (for a while) impinge on the public order. Spinoza's redesigned political order, his liberal democracy otherwise humane and decent toward Jews if only formally, was susceptible to use by secular fanatics, even "scientific" ones not tied to religion, who aimed to breed a culture of hatred and evil bound to destroy the very order that permitted it to be produced. This was a possibility that, as Strauss discerned, was not fully anticipated by the fathers of modern liberalism like Spinoza. They relied too much on the "historical" or political identification of evil and fanaticism with traditional revealed religion, rather than on a "natural" or philosophical analysis of the human soul entirely detached from any relation to specific religions.

As Jewish political thinkers like Pinsker and Herzl acknowledged, liberal "assimilationism" in its diverse kinds and degrees was not working. The attempt to apply for acceptance with the promise to change oneself in order to receive it has been humiliating and demoralizing for modern European Jewry. As Strauss emphasized, however, their conclusion was not to abandon liberalism, but to devise a better scheme which will guarantee its success. Since so-called anti-Semitism—or as Strauss prefers to call it, "hatred of Jews"[83]—will not disappear as long as there are Jews, so they must return en masse to their ancestral homeland. They must rebuild not their ancient kingdom and third temple, but a modern state as a model of liberalism, with all that this entails. This amounts to the political "normalization" or rehabilitation of the Jews as modern human beings in the modern world as a remedy for Jewish vulnerability. If the Jews want to reach the goal of liberalism, then they can achieve it with much greater efficacy by affirming rather than denying that they are Jews. To provide a decisive solution to the Jewish problem, it is imperative to pursue an honestly and purely political program.

As Herzl presented it in political arguments and by his historical figure, which both deeply impressed the youthful Strauss, Jews must no longer ask for their freedom and honor individually, but they must assert it and achieve it on their own by a fight for their freedom and honor collectively. Herzl reasoned that this can be accomplished by a massive transfer of population, as a voluntary movement, in order to aid in the establishment of their own state (liberal, modern, and secular) on their own land, whether or not it is their own ancestral homeland which they are able to secure.

Thus, according to Strauss, purely political Zionism cannot ultimately be characterized adequately as a completely "liberal" movement if what is meant by liberalism is some sort of universalizing tendency that denies the importance of national traditions, and desires to bring about an unqualified homogeneity between all peoples and indeed all individual human beings. While political Zionism accepted the essential truths of earlier liberalism, it obviously arose in the wake of the later liberal discovery of nationalism. Its main thrust was not to enable the Jews to "assimilate" to the diverse European cultures, but rather to save them from the ravages wrought by such assimilation, and to defend their right to their own national particularity as a point of honor. It preferred to view this as an attempt to "modernize" the Jews, which is not the same as assimilation, in that it is a process they control, and it preserves their own unity as a national culture in a process of modernization not different from the European states.[84] It is in this sense that Zionism is of much greater significance as what Strauss would prefer to call a "conservative" movement. As Strauss puts it:

> The moral spine of the Jews was in danger of being broken by the so-called emancipation, which in many cases had alienated them from their heritage, and yet not given them anything more than merely formal equality; it had brought about a condition which has been called "external freedom and inner servitude"; political Zionism was the attempt to restore that inner freedom, that simple dignity, of which only people who remember their heritage and are loyal to their fate are capable. . . . I can never forget what it achieved as a moral force in an era of complete dissolution. It helped to stem the tide of "progressive" leveling of venerable, ancestral differences; it fulfilled a conservative function.[85]

In spite of this greatness, Strauss continued to believe that "political Zionism is problematic for obvious reasons." Why precisely is it "problematic," and what are those "obvious reasons"? Strauss articulates his main criticisms of political Zionism in the following terms.

First, it is "problematic" in terms of messianism. In Strauss's view, Zionism and its fulfillment in the state of Israel does not end the *galut*, "exile," in the theological sense, but is only an important political and religious modification of the exile. Although Zionism teaches the Jews to control their own political destiny by a return to their ancestral homeland and restores to them a fighting spirit, it neither claims to bring the messianic era, nor does it aspire messianically to bridge the gap between unredeemed man and the redeeming God.[86] However, precisely by setting itself very limited aims, and proclaiming them as such—it merely wants to help the Jews to achieve a political liberation—it neither dispels nor resolves the deeper religious impulses that lead to messianism. As Strauss perceived, however, the fulfillment of the political Zionist program in the modern state of Israel only highlights these unresolved religious impulses. This is especially so, insofar as it both arouses and denies the messianic hopes that it needed to draw on for the efficacy of its appeal to the Jews.

Second, Zionism is "problematic," according to Strauss, in terms of its relation to liberalism. Zionism aims not only to terminate Jewish homelessness by purely human means, but it also does so entirely in the spirit of modern liberalism. This presupposes a dramatic break with traditional Jewish thought vis-à-vis the limits of human action. This also, in Strauss's view, uncovers a fundamental contradiction in the heart of Zionism: on the one hand, Zionist thought honestly recognizes the futility of the original hopes of modern liberalism to assimilate the Jews into European culture; on the other hand, it also relies on the premises of modern liberalism in order to "solve" the "Jewish problem" by human means alone, i.e., as a merely human problem susceptible of a simple human solution. As Strauss perceived, Zionism was inspired by liberalism while simultaneously exposing liberalism's own limitations. Moreover, the *essential* limits of modern liberalism may have been revealed by its defective ability to "help" the Jews.

This led Strauss to raise a philosophic question about the universal implications of the "Jewish problem." Is it not a problem that eludes or transcends even the best human efforts and, according to Strauss, does this not illuminate what an "absolute, infinite problem" looks like? In any case, although Strauss acknowledged that "it is particularly difficult for a nonorthodox Jew to adopt a critical posture toward liberalism," he nevertheless believed that this contradiction in Zionism highlights the greater critical need for modern Jewish philosophic thought to ascertain the limits of liberalism in a clearer and deeper manner than has been the case hitherto.

Third, Strauss also regarded Zionism as "problematic" in terms of its concept of honor. Unlike all previous modern Jewish movements, Zionism is unapologetically motivated by the conscious pursuit of worldly honor, a pursuit defined by modern men who generally do not respect traditional religious categories and authorities. It is in this specific sense that Strauss designates Zionism as "atheistic." Breaking with "traditional Jewish hopes," Zionism was convinced that it had discovered the psychological key to the modern Jewish dilemma: the political dependency or vulnerability of the Jews, which had resulted in a loss of honor. It also believed it could restore Jewish honor "through the acquisition of statehood." Strauss perceived that in order to be concerned with the acquisition of humanly measured honor (not to mention putting one's faith in the termination of the exile by purely human means), with the end in view of establishing a secular liberal state, one had to have already lost some faith in divine promises, divine election, and special providence. Yet Strauss also believed that however much the achievement of Zionism has been limited by its preoccupation with worldly honor (a preoccupation that might be regarded as a weakening of traditional Jewish disregard for the bad "opinion" of the Gentiles toward the Jews), this has been vindicated by the freedom and strengthening of Jews and Judaism issued in by the existence of the state of Israel. Indeed, Strauss views this as an essential gain, beyond any detriment associated with the concern with honor. As he succinctly puts it, the establishment of the state of Israel has "cleansed" Jewish honor, and so has "procured a blessing for all Jews . . . whether they admit it or not."

However, on this point too Strauss believed we should be aware that the accomplishments of Zionism, however great, are not free from contradiction. Political Zionism was guided by concerns which represent a break with traditional Judaism. Yet in the modern state of Israel, a state created by political Zionism, traditional Judaism has been enabled to flourish in an unparalleled fashion. Consequently, if "traditional Jewish hopes" have been paradoxically assisted by the pursuit of human honor as Zionism strives to attain, Strauss suggests we must continue to ponder whether the Jewish faith can be fully reconciled religiously to this high rank assigned to the pursuit of "worldly" honor, as the sustenance of a Jewish state in political freedom would seem to require.

Finally, it was Strauss's contention that Zionism is also "problematic" in terms of its relation to secular culture. As has already been mentioned, purely political Zionism defined itself in great measure in purely secular terms, and it denied any fundamental connection with the previous Jewish religious tradition. In order to "normalize" the Jews through a modern state, political Zionism also needed to modernize them in order to remake them as fit citizens. This meant that it was forced by its desire for a modern state to consider also the domestic realm in which this state would operate, i.e., a modern national culture. Precisely for the sake of the very efficacy political Zionism held in view—to establish a Jewish state with a modern national culture—even political Zionism needed to "make its peace" with Jewish tradition and to recognize the need for a spiritual "return," at least in the sense of articulating its relation to past Jewish culture in order to make profitable use of it.[87] As Strauss thus perceived, no matter how secularized one's political Zionism was, if one wanted a "Jewish state" and not just a "state of Jews," one needed not just a universal Western culture, but also a particular Jewish culture—and hence the almost unavoidable rise of cultural Zionism, with which political Zionism would need to ally itself. Indeed, with his clear-eyed "Platonic" vision, Strauss saw that this secular project for creating a modern Jewish national culture as a support and even as a guide for the Zionist political project would never be able to sever itself fully from the traditional Judaism against which it had rebelled, yet to which it could not help but be tied. In other words, as Strauss saw, Zionism could not afford to forget that its origins lie in the very Jewish history it planned to daringly redirect. But since the prior "culture" it needed to rely on consisted of sources which could never be rendered fully secular, this led Strauss to also perceive that cultural Zionism, once it reflects on itself, "turns into religious Zionism." And religious Zionism, once it reflects on itself, must admit it is primarily "Jewish faith and only secondarily Zionism." In point of fact, Strauss seems to doubt whether the secular marriage of political and cultural Zionism in modern Israel, however impressive its achievements, is enough to sustain the Jews in their spiritual life for the duration, beyond the immediate and admittedly urgent political needs of the present era.

This brought Strauss to suggest the paradoxical conclusion that since even secular political Zionism is rooted in Judaism, so the state of Israel should fortify or nourish its traditional theological roots in the sources of Judaism if it is to remain healthy politically, and if it is to continue to flourish culturally.

While Strauss fully respected the adherence to secular political Zionism for its "highly honorable" approach to the modern "Jewish problem," he also believed it was not a "sufficient" one to meet the full needs of the present.[88] Although the state of Israel procured what Strauss called both the "blessing" and the "cleansing" for all Jews, it does not resolve the most fundamental dilemmas. Indeed it sets in motion a host of subsidiary dilemmas peculiar to it. Strauss seemed convinced that the possible alliance of the political approach of Zionism with the theological trends in modern Judaism already discussed also cannot yield an integrated approach, insofar as this would be able to do away with the difficulties which each of these approaches manifests in its own terms.

The search for such a fully integrated approach and unified view, one which addressed Strauss's modern Jewish theological *and* political concerns, and yet also addressed his philosophical and moral questions about "radical historicism" and its problematic relation to contemporary rational philosophy, is what drove Strauss on. This is, I believe, what led him to Maimonides. Maimonides alone seemed to offer Strauss an impressive awareness of most, if not all, of the concerns that preoccupied him from his youth, which at least pointed in the direction of their possible integrated spiritual resolution.[89]

Strauss's Maimonideanism

Leo Strauss in point of fact grounded his own unique position as a modern Jewish thinker in the medieval Jewish thought of Maimonides. In doing so, Strauss showed it is possible to cross the great divide between modern and premodern philosophic thought in order to reappropriate the essential truth of the premodern thinkers. In particular, Strauss believed that Maimonides' theological and political approach is possessed of an enduring and universal validity. It is actually as relevant for us in our modern dilemmas as it was for the medieval Jewish community for whom it was written.

What is Strauss's "Maimonideanism," and why does he claim so much for it? First, if we recall Strauss's criticism of Spinoza, perhaps the main point in contention for Strauss was that modern philosophy (following Spinoza's lead) never proved its own highest speculative premises to be true, but just acted as if they were, and so proceeded on this faulty basis to attack revealed religion. But if, as Strauss counters, these premises are not true, as rationally knowable or demonstrable, the entire refutation, defeat, and dismissal of revelation as "irrational" is not sound. Modern philosophy has thus been misled by its own *hubris*, i.e., by a mere assertion of knowledge of things, which is not in its power. Thus, according to Strauss, if modern reason does not seem to actually possess such knowledge, it also does not know what is good pure and simple for man. To prove his case, Strauss allows modern (especially twentieth-century) history to be brought to light as evidence against the faulty assumptions of modern reason.

There is, then, according to Strauss, a need to recover the original meaning of what philosophy is, and of what reason is. Paradoxically, this should also lead us to recover an original awareness of what revelation is as well; reason and revelation are true natural rivals, whose opposition cannot be done away with, despite the pretensions of modern reason. In Strauss's perception, this dispute is not only the source of the modern view of morality (although the modern view claims to reject both premodern sources as well as their dispute), but it remains the only sound basis from which the Western philosophic thinker is able to truly derive his knowledge of what is good for man. Does reason deserve to be victorious—that is, can it demonstrate that divine revelation is implausible, not to mention refutable? If it cannot do this, should all wisdom from the past—e.g., the "medieval" or orthodox legacy of Jewish thought—have been rejected as benighted?

Following careful study of the medieval Jewish texts, Strauss reached the conclusion that the medieval thinkers, such as Maimonides, were actually wiser about the very things on which the moderns claimed proud and decisive superiority, such as on the fundamental relations between philosophy, religion, and politics. In his monumental work *Philosophy and Law*, Strauss oriented his "return to Maimonides" toward this very point: he stressed that what distinguishes Maimonides' position as a Jewish thinker is his defense of divine law. Belief is not the key notion for revealed religion, as the moderns maintained it was, since such a notion artificially detaches belief from law or commandment, which is in actuality primary. In other words, revelation counted for Maimonides as a philosopher insofar as it appears in the form of a divinely revealed law, which (as Strauss's research on Spinoza showed) has never been refuted by reason.

Strauss discerned that law received such a high estimation for Maimonides in great measure because he was a Jewish philosophic thinker in the tradition of Plato. In this tradition, originally cultivated by some of the great Islamic philosophers who preceded Maimonides, it was recognized that the freedom of philosophy, as this means absolutely free reflection on God, man, and the world, is not the natural beginning point of its own activity. It is not self-evident why such free philosophizing should be permitted to arise in the context of a revealed religion, grasped as revealed not in the modern sense of religion as belief, but as a polity-forming comprehensive divine law which defines what actions are commanded by God as lawgiver. It is law that constitutes and defines the religious community. But, as Strauss further perceived, philosophy poses a potential threat to the religious community, since one might reach conclusions other than those prescribed by the divine law. As an activity which arises in the polity guided by divine law, free philosophic thought (as a form of action in theological-political life) rightly needs to be considered by the law, which is the highest authority of the religious community. Hence, such free reflection needs to be justified in terms of the law, and limited according to the law.

Strauss also comprehended that for Maimonides, as for Plato and Aristotle, man is naturally a political animal. Because of this view, Maimonides was in a philosophic sense fully able to justify the great authority of law in Judaism. Law is the natural expression of civilized political life, and is the proper instrument for the fulfillment of the imperatives of human nature. What distinguishes divine law, according to Maimonides, is its concern with the full perfection of human nature, i.e., in terms of both body and soul. But the divine law's teaching, which bears on the perfection of the human soul, is presented in a form which is not always clear, and hence this teaching (or the text on which it is based) is in need of interpretation. In Maimonides' view, the needful explication of the text of the divine law is the basis for the free reflection which is permitted—nay, commanded—to the philosophic believer, in order to know rationally the true meaning of this revealed teaching, so long as he does not use his rational freedom to subvert or circumvent the law.

If Maimonides was so much concerned with philosophic pursuits, as Strauss seems to have been convinced, why was it so important *philosophically* to him to defend the Jewish law, and to make himself a legal authority? As a loyal citizen of the Jewish polity, Maimonides obviously believed it to be essential to remain devoted to its imperatives in the highest sense. By contrast with Maimonides, Spinoza did not regard himself as bound by such considerations; indeed, he made it a point of honor to stand free of such considerations. This is because Spinoza believed that a better (if humanly devised) law could be constructed by modern reason. Around this point their fundamental argument revolves, with regard to what best constitutes a good and truly binding law. Maimonides was persuaded that only a prophet, as stringently defined by him, could bring a "perfect" and hence divine law.

Further, Maimonides acknowledged that it was this law which made possible his activity as a Jewish philosopher. He must remain attached and obedient to the polity which created him, as Socrates argued in the *Crito*, lest philosophy itself be discredited by the liberties which the philosopher allows himself with the commitments he makes, and with the debts he owes. Spinoza in contrast believed in the philosopher who can lead a life remote from the crowd. As a cosmopolitan citizen of the world, the philosopher or scientist possesses a political freedom from any undue attachment to specific polities which serve the ignorant multitude. But Maimonides denied that such a world posited by Spinoza existed in any essential sense other than in the mind or imagination of the philosopher or the scientist, who does not lead his life detached from his body, and whose soul does not produce or educate itself.

The political wisdom of Maimonides,[90] which Strauss was very much influenced by, did not, however, exhaust his interest in Maimonides. Strauss was further impressed with how this political acuity allowed Maimonides to unfold a rational defense of the Jewish tradition as laws and ritual life in a highly elaborate, even "scientific," fashion which did not aim to diminish the importance of those laws. Maimonides ordered the laws so as to bring to light their purpose with regard to enlightenment, and so as to reflect the proper order of the soul. According to him, the laws are able to educate human beings by acting as imaginative or poetic expressions of rational truths. The theological and moral teaching of the divine law is not compromised by its complex and dialectical political aims, but rather it is connected with and dependent on them. In order to enhance the rationality of human beings in society, it is imperative to ensure decent relations between human beings, and to convey true notions about God. But according to Strauss's reading of Maimonides, this would not have been possible on any other basis than by a prophet, who is the most perfect man—a philosopher-lawgiver. Strauss perceived that by taking seriously the key political role played by the prophet, i.e., in the bringing of a good and binding law, and by combining it with a defense of the Jewish philosophic life as an attempted imitation of the prophet, Maimonides was even able to give a plausible philosophic account of the seemingly "obsolete" laws of the ancient temple sacrifices in purely anthropological and historical terms. Maimonides was able to achieve this while not detracting from the sense of permanent obligation to obey the laws, since these laws (and others like them) are the fundamental support of Jewish political life, and fidelity to them is required of every loyal citizen.

Further, Maimonides safeguarded the duty to obey the law by his teaching the philosophizing Jews who learned from him to respect the perennial wisdom about human nature and human need that is contained in even the most "ritualistic" laws: that is, he taught that the law is divine because it is guided by one highest aim—to serve the cause of knowing the truth. This "explanation" of the laws is not, as with Spinoza, moved by the intention of philosophical refutation or historical debunking, but to provide a theological understanding and political overview whose aim is to deepen the reasons for "philosophical" obedience.[91]

But Strauss recognized that this rationalistic justification for Judaism was not sufficient for a defense of Judaism in its uniqueness even according to the Jewish thought of Maimonides himself. On the matter of the highest truth taught by Judaism, to what is Maimonides ultimately loyal: to revelation or to reason? Does Maimonides' interpretation of Judaism acknowledge nothing beyond what unaided reason can achieve on its own, hence claiming only to accord with rational philosophical truth?[92] Or, does Maimonides acknowledge that Judaism, even if this religion is called "the most rational," still teaches a supra-rational theological truth which surpasses what unaided reason can achieve on its own, and which needs some faith, commitment, or act of will in order to "know" its highest truth?

According to Strauss, Maimonides did not accede to that simple either/or alternative, since he did not believe the fundamental choice is between radical human rational autonomy versus irrational or blind religious commitment. Most illustrative is Maimonides' view on the matter of creation versus eternity. He regarded this much debated matter as of decisive religious importance, and yet he did not resolve it dogmatically. He argues for the "relative" rationality of the belief in the creation of the world on the ground that this teaching is not of any greater irrationality than the eternity of the world, if the Aristotelian philosophic arguments for eternity are critically scrutinized and honestly assessed for their true rationality.

Proceeding from this argument for the belief in creation, Strauss perceived that all of the theological issues treated in Maimonides' *Guide* may be reduced to a fundamental issue at stake, which separates between philosophy and Judaism: the philosophic belief in the autonomous, all-comprehensive, and self-encompassing principle of "nature" ruled by divine mind and knowable by the human mind versus the theological belief in unqualified divine omnipotence mitigated by an absolutely moral will which has been revealed to man in history by the supreme prophet. In the first place, it seems that Maimonides himself adhered with full awareness, and with much greater consistency than is usually the case, to the Jewish doctrine of an absolute divine omnipotence which is yet morally and naturally self-limiting in opposition to philosophy which relies on "nature."

At the same time, Maimonides did not surrender or compromise his commitment to rationality, and even to "the supremacy of reason," on any point.[93] As this implies, he did not accept any "irrational" religious dogmas. He accepted only such religious dogmas as could be made at least cognitively consistent with rationally knowable, i.e., demonstrated, truth. He achieved this feat of balance between divine omnipotence and "nature" by maintaining that human intellect, which knows as much as man can know about "nature," is the chief expression of the divine image in man.

Thus, over and above everything else, as Strauss seems to have been persuaded, Maimonides' fruitful adherence to the notion of divine omnipotence (as passing beyond but not denying "nature") was based on the belief that only on this religious ground is a "genuine" moral code made possible, i.e., a moral code which is both rationally true and absolutely binding.[94] Morality is revealed, however, not by some spectacular miracle (as divine omnipotence might suggest), but through the prophet as the most perfect man, i.e., whose supreme excellence of the moral and the rational-intellectual in one human being makes him most suitable to receive the truth of these moral and speculative commandments in what he calls a divine "overflow." What apparently guides divine law, and what accounts for its appeal to all human beings, is the depth of comprehension by the prophet of the full range of needs, high and low, of the human soul, and of how best to satisfy and harmonize those needs. The prophet as philosopher-lawgiver conveys this harmonizing wisdom in the form of a law, which, for those who want to learn, is a wisdom and prudence about how a measured accommodation of the law to those needs helps to produce well-ordered souls in a well-ordered society—the supreme aim of a divine law.[95]

Indeed, what defines the highest type of prophet is he who is able to enshrine virtue, piety, and wisdom in a law. This law alone is divine because it perfectly balances those various and sundry conflicting human needs, while never forgetting the requirements of morality and truth. If political and theological history may serve as a roundabout proof for its moral and religious excellence, the law of Moses has been the inspiration for two great "imitators," as Maimonides would put it, by whose teaching Western civilization has been guided for several millennia. Apparently to Maimonides this is no accident, but a function of the superior spirituality that emanates from the original model, the Torah of Moses.

At the same time, however, Strauss suggested surreptitiously that perhaps Maimonides himself did not fully embrace this vision of perfection in prophecy; that is, perhaps he did not remain completely satisfied with traditional religion as a comprehensive or self-contained mode of thought. Strauss perceived that Maimonides subtly leaves room for doubt in the very heart of his own theology, and he reserves a lawful place for doubt for a very specific reason. This is because Maimonides, like every philosopher, was aware of the problematic character and even questionability of every final resolution, and hence even of his own seemingly "perfect" one, to the perplexities of the Torah.

Indeed, according to Strauss's mature reading of Maimonides, the crucial element of fundamental or radical doubt, essential to the philosophic experience, led Strauss to perceive a hidden dimension in the writings of Maimonides: his use of esotericism, so that his true philosophic defense of medieval Judaism could be comprehended only by the Jewish spiritual elite. Only members of such an elite would be able to handle philosophic doubt in their resolute encounter with the tough questions of theology, and in their subtle uncoverings of the problems of the law.

How did Strauss comprehend the theological logic which animated Maimonides' use of such esotericism? He maintained that this logic could only be grasped if seen in the light of Maimonides' philosophic view of the perfection of the prophet. The true prophet, according to Maimonides, possesses the unique or superhuman ability to communicate on two levels simultaneously, the imaginative and the intellectual. These levels are expressions of separate teachings dialectically or pedagogically intertwined. While the Torah is a ladder of ascent to the truth with numerous rungs, still in the decisive respect it remains a three-tiered system, as represents human nature: it trains all people to religious piety and moral goodness; it prepares the life of the better and most decent human being, and it does so through leading a noble life dedicated to fulfilling God's law and educating to the highest belief possible about Him; and it guides the philosopher (or better: the potential prophet), since the Torah makes allowance for the search for wisdom, with a promise to culminate in knowledge of *the* truth. The Torah, it would seem, tries especially to harmonize the two higher human types of the three: the moral-religious man and the philosophic man. But this suggests that the life of search for wisdom and the life of elevated or moral piety are not in harmony but in conflict; between the two higher types, a higher discord emerges.[96] According to Strauss, this fundamental conflict was taken most seriously by Maimonides, who believed it needed to be resolved, and it was that need which gave rise to Maimonidean esotericism.

Maimonidean esotericism, as Strauss rediscovered it, was a method employed to both conceal and reveal the conflict between the two most basic and permanent classes of human beings, the philosophic few and the nonphilosophic many, in the life of Judaism. Study of the religious texts is used as a common ground for these opposed types to be able to encounter one another on a high plane, and especially as a common ground on which the few can learn vital truths about the many. To be sure, such a "textual encounter" could potentially lead to a clash, in that the Jewish philosophical student could be brought to attack the religious texts as philosophically "primitive," and to unthinkingly reject them as sources of knowledge or wisdom. But in the subtle method of Maimonides, this textual encounter emerges as the basis for harmony, in that by studying these texts the Jewish philosophical student learns fundamental lessons about religion, prophecy, and wisdom, and perceives vital truths about how precarious the life of thought is in any society, but especially in a religious society based on revelation.

Thus, in order to avoid this clash, and to ensure that the Jewish philosophical student is taught a prudent and wise respect for the religion, and especially revealed texts, which had been perplexing to him, Maimonides needed to conceal with numerous artful literary devices his most radical arguments and conclusions. They might be a threat both to the piety of the simple faithful and, in a preliminary stage, to the proper moral and cognitive development of the Jewish philosophical student. However, this concern for the proper order in the uncovering of truth is balanced in creative tension, as Strauss recognized, with a contrary aim in the pedagogic regimen of Maimonides: it is also true that to recognize these same radical truths, even to learn how to think them through for themselves, is essential to the very production of the elite of Jewish philosophical students, which he aimed to educate and hence to create. Indeed, this learning is not in any sense intended to diminish respect for a religious society based on revelation, but just the opposite is true. Thus, it is meant to raise respect for its unique excellence, because as has already been observed, divine revelation by the one omnipotent God is for Maimonides the only ground on which a "genuine" morality can be conceived and established.

Strauss made his name in Jewish scholarly circles by his careful study and detailed reiteration of the subtle method used by Maimonides in writing the *Guide* as peculiarly as he did. But a mere scholarly discovery, however prodigious, was scarcely Strauss's main contribution to modern Jewish thought. Rather, it is the examination of Maimonides' thought concealed beneath the discovery which reveals Strauss's deeper insight. This can be discerned in Strauss's analysis of why Maimonides entertained such a passion for the life of the mind in his approach to Judaism. In Strauss's reading, Maimonides regarded the production of the highest intellectual excellence or virtue in an elite class of Jewish philosophical students as the most difficult task, one fraught with risks. But he also regarded no other task as so imperative for the well-being and future survival of the Jewish people. Maimonides saw that from the days of the patriarchs and prophets, the distinguishing mark of the Jews, what has been the key to their ability to discern and receive the highest religious truths, has been their devotion to the life of the mind, to pursuit of knowledge in the philosophic and scientific sense, and to human perfection in the form of comprehensive wisdom about God.

It was this notion of the history of Judaism that guided Maimonides in his efforts as a great teacher, a notion which Strauss found highly appealing. He sought to stress it in his reading of the philosophic argument concealed beneath esotericism. Although the elite of Jewish philosophical students receive the same moral education as everyone else, and are held to the same if not higher moral standards, their intellectual excellence is the guarantee of the health of their souls and of the soul of the people: the moral excellence of man is a prerequisite of his intellectual perfection. Once such perfection is achieved, it overflows to an even higher moral excellence informed by intellectual truth. Strauss, with his concern for defending both political morality and the moral integrity of philosophy, was further drawn to the depth of wisdom he uncovered in Maimonides. For Maimonides it would seem, as for Socrates, proper knowledge is true virtue.

In this light, Strauss learned from Maimonides that religion is essential to any healthy political society, and certainly for the moral life of human beings. Over and above this, Maimonides convinced Strauss that Jewish religion, based on the Hebrew Bible, is most essential to ground a "genuine" morality for almost every human being, and to aid some to apprehend the highest truths. As Strauss would seem to concede, it is possible some rare philosopher may reach the same moral truths on the basis of his own rational speculation. But this possibility is certainly no guarantee that he will reach them or be guided by them in his life. Most if not all philosophers are also still in need of the morality and religion taught by the Hebrew Bible. Moreover, Strauss was convinced that philosophy not only cannot dispute the imperative character and usefulness of biblical religion, or the fundamentally formative role that is played by this religion in the ennoblement of human beings toward their highest moral and spiritual stature, but also (and indeed of much greater importance) has not been able to disprove or refute the truth claims of revealed or monotheistic religion.

Together with this, however, Strauss did not forget the previously mentioned truth about philosophy: it must be free to doubt. Indeed, the philosopher must, in his search for knowledge, doubt some of the most fundamental beliefs and dearly held opinions of the moral and religious tradition. But most people cannot live with such excruciating doubts about the universe and the meaning and value of life, which are most interesting and essential to the life of the philosopher, whatever decent or defective final conclusions he may reach. As a result, Strauss followed Maimonides in defending the view that such speculations must be confined to an elite who need this activity of doubt, and they must be hidden as much as possible from society, i.e., preferably confined to thought or communicated only to trustworthy friends. If they publish their speculations, they must communicate them esoterically; they must "write between the lines," in order to mask their doubts about the generally accepted or traditional truths. This means that even they must be guided by a higher authority, and in the case of Judaism, by the law brought by Moses, the highest prophet, whose law harmonizes the conflict of the human types in society. To Strauss, this Maimonidean wisdom permits philosophy to flourish in freedom while the moral life of society is preserved and shielded from the doubts that the philosophers must ever bring to bear against it.

Conclusion

Although Strauss did not go so far as to regard Maimonides' teaching as a prescription to solve all modern Jewish theological or political problems, his deep reflection on Maimonides did lead him to maintain that this teaching is a vital source of wisdom which modern Judaism needs in order to help it resolve its contemporary crisis. If Strauss himself was not as traditionally pious as it is suggested a "true" Maimonidean would likely be, this was perhaps because for him the Maimonidean inspiration resided in the general approach and not in the specific details of Maimonides' medieval philosophical theology. Strauss scarcely was asking the Jews to return to their premodern status, nor did he define complete obedience to the law as the *only* authentic form of modern Judaism.

Thus, while Strauss was one of the first to speak about a "movement of return" in modern Judaism, with which he identified himself, he meant this in the broadest possible sense. Strauss in fact applied that phrase "movement of return" to those modern Jews who had begun to doubt the virtually "religious" faith in liberalism and its promise of an actualizable "universal human society." They had consequently also begun to wonder whether a greater loyalty to, and genuine respect for, the particular Jewish tradition is not somehow the wiser position to assume.

Yet simultaneously Strauss counted himself among "those who cannot be orthodox."[97] This was perhaps because he regarded himself as compelled to accept not only the conclusions but "even the premises of biblical criticism,"[98] and also because he was both a youthful adherent and a mature supporter of political Zionism, as well as a friend of liberal democracy. Whatever the reasons, Strauss never made himself an advocate of the precise and systematic details of Maimonides' theology and legal code—or of any other "orthodox" theology and legal code, whether in medieval or modern form. In other words, whatever one concludes about Strauss's "return" to Maimonides, he remained emphatically a modern Jew, committed to learning from the past while not attempting to revive it.

This apparent acceptance of the condition of the modern Jew, however, did not lead Strauss to believe that things could continue as previously constituted. Strauss argued that Jewish thought needs to rethink the entire range of modern positions to discover what has been rendered obsolete, and what can endure. In consequence of this need, and together with careful study of Maimonides' writings, Strauss was undoubtedly persuaded that it would be better for future Jewish theology to adapt or embrace some of the most essential arguments (and even structures) of Maimonides' teaching as a model for Jewish life and thought.

In Strauss's view, Maimonides' theology is superior in its theoretical reasoning and practical wisdom on fundamental points as compared with almost every modern Jewish thinker, even though such wisdom and reasoning is usually dismissed as distressingly "medieval." Strauss pointed to such fundamental theological points as: the belief in creation, and the powerful arguments which can be made for it; the need for the law, and its rational-moral character; the prophets as searchers for knowledge and bearers of truth; the proper relations of the theological sphere to the political sphere; and his metaphysical-moral notion of human perfection.

Strauss also deemed it desirable to learn from the basic approach of Maimonides as a Jewish philosophic thinker, something he believed is reflected in the literary character of his books. As a philosophizing Jew, Strauss admired Maimonides for his unconditional devotion as a Jew to the life of thought. This is exemplified in his courageous, clearsighted, and consistent thinking through of the logic of the positions he defended. As Strauss further suggests, this entails that Maimonides exposes (even if this is not on the surface, but only "written between the lines") the price one must pay for reaching certain philosophic positions, inasmuch as they render other positions "impossible" if one is to retain one's intellectual honesty. Though subtly communicated, he never hid *the* truth either from himself or from his best readers. The seriousness and rigor of thought that Maimonides displays in his analysis of Jewish philosophical problems is a model to Strauss for teaching one how to think.

Indeed, this same type of unflinchingly radical investigation of theological issues, which Strauss saw exemplified in Maimonides, he also acknowledged and praised in the medieval Jewish mystics who followed Maimonides. Perhaps paradoxically, they seem to have been instructed by Maimonides himself in the proper method of theological thought:

> Gershom Scholem . . . shows to what amazing lengths some of our mystics went by thinking through these beliefs; and then they came

out with views to which many of the objections, which many of us would have to such traditional beliefs, would no longer be tenable. That would be the kind of thing which I would regard as satisfactory. But, I believe, by simply replacing God by the creative genius of the Jewish people, one gives away, one deprives oneself—even if one does not believe—of a source of *human* understanding.[99]

As for those contemporary Jews who are driven to despair of reason, or to despise it, because of the "catastrophes and horrors" that have occurred in the modern West during the present century, Strauss would caution against too quickly saying "farewell to reason," even if it is said in the name of revelation.[100] Neither intellectual honesty nor love of truth impels one to a simple rejection of all things modern and Western, such as science and philosophy, liberal democracy, or even modern individualism, because of the evident deficiencies that have been displayed by them. Certainly one is entitled, based on sound Jewish and even Maimonidean principles, to respond with revulsion to contemporary moral relativism and philosophic nihilism. But the question stands, whether Judaism is not at its origin closer to genuine philosophic rationalism than it is to any fideistic orthodoxy, whether religious or secular. Such views as are currently fashionable, which stand against reason in the name of Judaism, are answered by Strauss in no uncertain terms:

> The victory of orthodoxy through the self-destruction of rational philosophy was not an unmitigated blessing, for it was a victory, not of Jewish orthodoxy, but of any orthodoxy, and Jewish orthodoxy based its claim to superiority to other religions from the beginning on its superior rationality (Deut. 4:6).[101]

In this light, Strauss regarded the modern West to be still a better hope than any available alternative, especially since the things rejected as modern and Western by those antirationalist defenders of revelation are not plainly antithetical to Judaism. In this sense, Strauss seems to suggest that the modern West did not arise from sources entirely extraneous to Judaism. Its impulses (however transformed) were actually produced by aspects of ancient and medieval Jewish thought—although Strauss made no definitive statement on the relation of Judaism to modernity. Yet in Strauss's eminently sober view, Jews cannot act as if the threats to Judaism that they see around them will cease to be true challenges by closing their eyes to them. In this regard, Maimonides should also be looked to as the model of the Jewish philosophic thinker, determined to face the most formidable intellectual challenges to

Judaism. Perhaps this is because Strauss perceived that Maimonides maintained a supreme confidence in the fundamental cognitive integrity of Judaism, which he combined with a belief that it possesses a tough core of truth able to withstand or survive any attack.

In the face of the retreat from both reason and revelation in the contemporary era, Strauss points to the wisdom of Maimonides to serve as a guide for meeting the true challenges of Western philosophic thought, while simultaneously showing how to defend honestly what is most essential in Judaism. As an important task for contemporary Jewish thought, this would require thinking through with greater critical awareness the relations between Judaism and Western civilization, especially Western philosophy, in light of our modern historical experience and modern intellectual legacy. We must still face the difficult questions put to Judaism by premodern Western philosophy, which are perennial—indeed, just as perennial as is Judaism's basic questioning of it. And we must also rethink the historical doubts raised by modern Western philosophy about the entire premodern tradition, i.e., about the original texts and revelations of Judaism, in order to know which doubts are still valid or true.

As has been shown, Strauss came to maintain that the search for wisdom in the midst of our contemporary crisis seems to require us to return to the original sources of our wisdom. Over and above everything else, this meant in Strauss's mind that we need especially to turn to the Hebrew Bible, the most fundamental Jewish source, in order to consider whether this book contains a unity of forgotten knowledge that had provided us with our first light, and with an unrefuted truth that we can still recover.

Just as Maimonides focused on the Hebrew Bible in order to meet the medieval philosophic challenge and the crisis it provoked, Strauss believed that modern Jews should return to studying the Hebrew Bible as one book with one teaching about God, man, and the world. As this suggests, Strauss thought that we are in need of its essential teaching— blurred by tradition and obscured by modern critique—which we must try to grasp afresh. This is because, to Strauss, it is only in the original sources of our wisdom that true wisdom may reside and can best be rediscovered.

Notes

1. "Leo Strauss and Modern Judaism," *Claremont Review of Books* 4, no. 4 (Winter 1985): 21, 23. In his quoted passage, Fackenheim paraphrases the

famous remark that Strauss made about Hermann Cohen (see the last line of "Introductory Essay to Hermann Cohen, *Religion of Reason*," infra, 282), but with at least one crucial difference: he calls the life and work of Strauss "a great blessing" rather than just "a blessing." For the other important difference, Fackenheim speaks about the "blessing" of both Cohen and Strauss for their having "lived and taught," rather than "lived and wrote," as Strauss originally said about Cohen. Either Fackenheim quoted erroneously from memory, or perhaps he made this "error" deliberately (if put together with his remark about Strauss's books) in order to emphasize that the "great blessing" of Strauss as a thinker is only fully evident in his comprehensive power *both* as a teacher *and* as a writer, i.e., in the charm, wisdom, learning, profundity, and piety which students encountered in Strauss during his teaching, and which inspired them to imitate him; and in the artfulness, power, and depth of thought which readers encounter in him as a writer, and which exemplifies a classical style. In a recent comment, Fackenheim attributed an even greater significance to Strauss's thought: "Perhaps a time will come when Heidegger will be remembered mainly because, without him, Leo Strauss would not have been who he was and became." This means, as he suggests, that Strauss's thought will assume the leading position not only in the Jewish thought of the future, but also in philosophy of the future. See "Reply to My Critics: A Testament of Thought," *Fackenheim: German Philosophy and Jewish Thought*, edited by Louis I. Greenspan and Graeme Nicholson (Toronto: University of Toronto Press, 1992), 298. See also note 6, infra.

2. Letter to Leo Strauss, 22 April 1964. Bloom also made the following bold suggestion about the true stature of Strauss in contemporary philosophy: ". . . I believe our generation may well be judged by the next generation according to how we judged Leo Strauss." See "Leo Strauss," *Political Theory* 2, no. 4 (November 1974): 372–92, especially p. 392; idem, *Giants and Dwarfs* (New York: Simon and Schuster, 1990), 235–55, especially p. 255.

3. *The Unconscious God* (New York: Simon and Schuster, 1975), 120–21.

4. What was undoubtedly one of the single most important essays of Strauss in the field of modern Jewish thought, written prior to the period covered by the present volume (i.e., between 1923 and 1945), is his "Einleitung" to *Philosophie und Gesetz* (Berlin: Schocken, 1935). A new and reliable English translation by Eve Adler of *Philosophy and Law* has recently been published (1995) in the same SUNY series ("The Jewish Writings of Leo Strauss") in which the present volume appears. Strauss's "Introduction" to that book should be read in this new translation, and may be fruitfully compared with the essays in the present volume. Also, a volume in this same SUNY series (forthcoming shortly) will publish in English translation Strauss's impressive youthful German Jewish essays (i.e., which appeared between 1923 and 1932), translated, edited, and introduced by Michael Zank. That volume will place together and make known for the first time to the English-speaking world the formative stage in the development of Strauss's Jewish thought. Mention should also be made of the two

remaining volumes in the same series, one of which will present Strauss's writings on Moses Mendelssohn (edited by Martin D. Yaffe) and the other, his writings on Moses Maimonides (edited by the present writer).

5. For a sample of Strauss's powerful contributions as a Jewish scholar, the reader is especially directed to essay 3 in the present volume, i.e., the essay on Benedict (né Baruch) Spinoza and his *Theologico-Political Treatise*. These contributions to Jewish scholarly research also indicate Strauss's novel and unconventional approach to Jewish thought, and his scholarly and philosophic insistence on both careful reading and historical exactness. As for Strauss's seeming desire to avoid the entrapments of modern fame, Harvey C. Mansfield, Jr., finds the enlightening power of Strauss's philosophic thought not at all diminished by his relative obscurity, since Strauss "counseled against seeking the limelight" both for himself and for his students. And hence he "is not obscure in the usual way, by having done nothing remarkable." See "Democracy and the Great Books," *New Republic* 4 April 1988, 33–37.

6. Emil L. Fackenheim, *To Mend the World* (New York: Schocken, 1982), x. In spite of statements by Jewish thinkers such as Fackenheim (and see also supra, note 1), nevertheless it has not been enough to prevent a philosopher and student of Strauss of the high caliber and brilliance of Stanley Rosen from writing of Strauss's mere "exoteric flirtation with Hebraic tradition." See *Hermeneutics as Politics* (New York: Oxford University Press, 1987), 17, as well as pp. 15–17, 87–140. He even makes an unambiguous statement about Strauss's clear-cut choice between philosophy and Judaism, Athens and Jerusalem: "No competent student of Leo Strauss was ever in doubt as to his teacher's choice." Rosen implies a seemingly simple choice for Greek philosophy (ibid., 112). Rosen's wholly unambiguous claim about Strauss's often deliberately ambiguous self-depictions, and usually unambiguous asseverations of deep and serious loyalty to the Jewish tradition in the highest sense, is subsequently qualified significantly by Rosen. These qualifications amount to a partial retraction of the two just quoted statements in a significant sense: "At the same time, it does not follow that there was not for Strauss a real problem in choosing between Jerusalem and Athens. Neither does it follow that Strauss was an unmitigated 'ancient' or resident of Athens." This means either, as Allan Bloom suggests, the choice was difficult because of an idiosyncrasy of his personality, due to the accident of his Jewish origins, or it means that this approach of both Bloom and Rosen is not adequate in dealing with the character and depth of Strauss's Jewish attachment, and its affect on his thought. This tendency to override Strauss's declared statements about his own lifelong attachment to Judaism, and to dismiss them as either intentionally "exoteric" or as idiosyncratic and hence unessential products of his own personal life experience, is perhaps crystalized in the publication of Strauss's "An Introduction to Heideggerian Existentialism" lacking its, as it were, "parochial" Jewish first sentence: but see also Editor's Preface, note 6, supra. Harry V. Jaffa, although not concerned with Strauss as a Jewish thinker per se, has expressed quite a different view of the relation between

Judaism and philosophy, or Jerusalem and Athens, or reason and revelation, in his debates with Thomas L. Pangle on the character of Strauss's thought. Jaffa's argument, as I should like to restate it in my own terms, maintains that this theme of Jerusalem and Athens in Strauss's thought has been completely misinterpreted by the "Straussians," among whom he used to count himself. Strauss never made such a simple choice between Judaism and philosophy because he knew *precisely as a philosopher* that he could not, in good philosophical conscience, make this simple choice for one side alone. In other words, Strauss meant seriously (and *not* merely as an obvious ploy or as an "exoteric teaching") his argument that philosophy has never been able to "refute" the biblical God or the biblical revelation. If this is the case, then philosophy is not an activity which rests on a truly solid ground, on "evident and necessary knowledge" (see "Progress or Return?" and "Preface to *Spinoza's Critique of Religion*," infra): there is no basis for assuming the "false" character of biblical revelation if philosophy does not truly know the whole, i.e., if it does not know *the* one complete truth, which knowledge would provide what is needed for a genuine refutation—and certainly not if philosophy is "mere" quest for wisdom. In other words, as this would also seem to imply, if philosophy is defined as a "self-evident" (Socratic) search for knowledge based on ignorance that man "naturally" wants to alleviate, it would also be a most serious error for philosophy to claim to know that revelation is false. As a result of this, he further believes that the entire "Straussian" reading, at least as it emerges in Pangle's presentation of Strauss as Jaffa's arguments highlight it, is in error about Strauss's true position as a thinker. See his "The Primacy of the Good: Leo Strauss Remembered," *Modern Age* 26 (1982): 266–69; "The Legacy of Leo Strauss," *Claremont Review of Books* 3, no. 3 (Fall 1984): 14–21; "'The Legacy of Leo Strauss' Defended," *Claremont Review of Books* 4, no. 1 (Spring 1985): 20–24; "Crisis of the Strauss Divided: The Legacy Reconsidered," *Social Research* 54 (1987): 579–603; "Dear Professor Drury," *Political Theory* 15, no. 3 (August 1987): 316–25. It might still be preferable to commence with Alexander Altmann's characterization: he wrote about Strauss's "noble piety" and "profound reverence for the Jewish tradition." See his "Leo Strauss: 1899–1973," *Proceedings of the American Academy for Jewish Research* 41–42 (1975): xxxiii–xxxvi. This suggests something of greater substance than *either* at best an "exoteric flirtation with Hebraic tradition" which constructs a Strauss who decided unambiguously against Jerusalem although he retained a pious connection with it for some undefined reason (Rosen), *or* at worst a homogenization of "biblical thought and the thought of the Greek poets" in order to make Strauss contrast them on par with the higher wisdom of philosophy (Pangle).

7. The relative obscurity of Leo Strauss as a Jewish thinker may be beginning to change. See the recent book by the present writer, *Jew and Philosopher: The Return to Maimonides in the Jewish Thought of Leo Strauss* (Albany: State University of New York Press, 1993), with its bibliography of the growing number of works on Strauss's Jewish thought. Also the "Jewish Writings of Leo Strauss" are appearing in a series of five volumes, edited by the present writer, published by

the State University of New York Press. A recent conference on "Jerusalem and Athens Revisited: Leo Strauss and Judaism" was held at the University of Virginia on 10–11 October 1993. French translations of some of the most important Jewish works of Leo Strauss have been published. See *Maïmonide*, edited and translated by Rémi Brague (Paris: Presses Universitaires de France, 1988), and *Le Testament de Spinoza*, edited and translated by Gérard Almaleh, Albert Baraquin, and Mireille Depadt-Ejchenbaum (Paris: Les Editions du Cerf, 1991). For Strauss's Jewish thought as starting to exercise an influence through the production of progeny, see David R. Lachterman, "Torah and Logos," *Graduate Faculty Philosophy Journal* 17, nos. 1–2 (1994): 3–27. Perhaps also noteworthy is the recognition represented by the separate entry on his contribution to Jewish philosophic thought in the just-published *Routledge History of Jewish Philosophy*, edited by Daniel Frank and Oliver Leaman (London: Routledge, 1997). As for the relative obscurity of Leo Strauss as a philosophic thinker, see also *Leo Strauss's Thought: A Critical Engagement*, edited by Alan Udoff (Boulder, Colo.: Lynne Rienner, 1991), for essays on several aspects of Strauss's Jewish thought. A special issue dedicated to his philosophic thought is in *Revue de Métaphysique et de Morale* 94, no. 3 (July–September 1989). Essential reading is the essay by Allan Bloom, "Leo Strauss: September 20, 1899–October 18, 1973," in *Giants and Dwarfs* (New York: Simon and Schuster, 1990), 235–55. As for his political thought, for which he is perhaps best known, as well as essays on his Jewish and philosophic thought, see also the special issues dedicated to him in the following journals: *Review of Politics* 53, no. 1 (Winter 1991), and *The Vital Nexus* 1, no. 1 (May 1990). And one must not forget to mention Allan Bloom, *The Closing of the American Mind* (New York: Simon and Schuster, 1987), for the controversy which it aroused, and the essays and books which flowed from it, since some of these put Strauss's name and thought in the center of the debate. For comparisons and contrasts, see: *Carl Schmitt and Leo Strauss: The Hidden Dialogue*, by Heinrich Meier (Chicago: University of Chicago Press, 1995); *Leo Strauss and Nietzsche*, by Laurence Lampert (Chicago: University of Chicago Press, 1996); *Hannah Arendt and Leo Strauss*, eds. Peter Graf Kielmansegg, Horst Mewes, and Elisabeth Glaser-Schmidt (New York: Cambridge University Press, 1995). Also perhaps noteworthy, however rarefied the achievement for most people, is Stanley Rosen's election to the presidency of the Metaphysical Society of America (1991–92), which represents the rise to academic prominence and the recognition of a thinker trained in, though occasionally critical of, and yet still derived from, Strauss's school of thought. See also the recently issued *Faith and Political Philosophy*, edited by Peter Emberley and Barry Cooper (University Park, Pa.: Pennsylvania State University Press, 1993), which contains the philosophic letters between Strauss and Eric Voegelin, and philosophic essays by both, on the nexus between religion and politics; it also is graced with cogent "commentaries" on the correspondence by eight prominent thinkers of diverse stripes, from the Christian theologian Thomas J. J. Altizer to the Heideggerian hermeneuticist Hans-Georg Gadamer. And see *On Tyranny* (revised and augmented edition), edited by Victor Gourevitch and Michael S. Roth (New York: Free Press, 1991), for the philosophic letters between Strauss and Alexandre Kojève, and their interpretive exchange concerning Xenophon. And further, see the sixteen essays in *Leo Strauss: Political*

Philosopher and Jewish Thinker, edited by Kenneth L. Deutsch and Walter Nicgorski (Lanham, Md.: Rowman and Littlefield, 1994). See also Hans-Georg Gadamer, "Interview on Leo Strauss," in *Interpretation* 12 (1984): 1–13. Also recently published is a detailed and subtle explication by Susan Orr of the text of "Jerusalem and Athens" and other works by Strauss, one that presents a complete interpretation of Strauss's views on this debated issue. See her *Jerusalem and Athens: Reason and Revelation in the Works of Leo Strauss* (Lanham, Md.: Rowman and Littlefield, 1995). Another important, recently published work is *Leo Strauss and Judaism: Jerusalem and Athens Revisited,* edited by David Novak (Lanham, Md.: Rowman and Littlefield, 1996). And Heinrich Meier is editing the complete writings of Strauss, rendered in the German language. Thus, if the recent expressions of interest in Strauss, especially of the last ten years, are any indication of the shape of things to come, the growing rumblings might threaten to turn into a virtual avalanche in the next ten years. Indeed, the relative quiet and obscurity during most of Strauss's life (and the twenty years following his death) may go into a reversal and emerge as a veritable posthumous celebration—but such a course of events might at least help serve to correct an undeserved neglect.

8. Strauss seems to prefer not to discuss his earlier experiences in his parents' home, and their formative influence on him and hence on his later thought. Indeed, he refuses to dwell on the details about the facts of his life because he does not regard them as finally *determinative.* Thus he says:

> Those thoughts [concerning matters of public concern], it is true, are connected with our lives, and I for one will have to say something about my life. But this is of interest even to me only as a starting point of considerations, of studies, which I hope are intelligible to those who do not know my starting point.

"A Giving of Accounts," infra, 459. But he is certainly aware that one's own experience may influence one's approach to the issues, and he mentions this in "Why We Remain Jews," infra, 313:

> Now this and many other experiences, which it would be absolutely boring and improper to rehearse, are the bases of my lecture.

9. Thus, it was even a matter to be decided by religious law whether Strauss could raise pet rabbits. See Ralph Lerner, "Leo Strauss: 1899–1973," *American Jewish Year Book* 76 (1976): 91–97, esp. p. 91. See also George Anastaplo, "On Leo Strauss: A Yahrzeit Remembrance," *University of Chicago Magazine* 67 (Winter 1974): 30–38, esp. p. 37.

10. "Why We Remain Jews," infra, 312–13. If it was, as Strauss recalls, at about the age of five or six, he was probably faced with the consequences of the repeated government-sponsored attacks of czarist Russia on the Jews, which were launched again in 1905, and the Jewish flight from Russia in which it issued. See Salo W. Baron, *The Russian Jew Under Tsars and Soviets* (New York: Schocken, 1987), 56–62; Louis Greenberg, *The Jews in Russia* (New York:

Schocken, 1976), vol. 2, 50–54, 76–82. Toward the very end of his life, in his last Jewish writing which introduced Hermann Cohen's *Religion of Reason out of the Sources of Judaism*, Strauss makes a passing remark about Cohen's pious "fidelity" to Judaism and Jews, which could readily also be applied to him: "He does not speak of the moral obligation not to desert one's people especially when they are in need—and when are Jews not in need?—because for him this went without saying." See "Introductory Essay to Hermann Cohen, *Religion of Reason*," infra, 281. For the atmosphere of 1905 in Russia, and how it represented a precipitous deterioration in the already oppressed condition of Russian Jewry, see also the novel by Sholem Aleichem, *In the Storm* (*In shturm*), translated by Aliza Shevrin (New York: New American Library, 1985). Strauss certainly showed fidelity toward his father: not only did he dedicate *Philosophie und Gesetz* (1935) "to the memory of Meyer Strauss," but on his single return trip to Germany (1954), he visited his father's grave. See also the comments by Edward C. Banfield, "Leo Strauss," in *Remembering the University of Chicago*, edited by Edward Shils (Chicago: University of Chicago Press, 1991), 490–591, esp. pp. 493, 497. See also the sentence quoted supra in note 8, at the end.

11. "Why We Remain Jews," infra, 319; "A Giving of Accounts," infra, 460. Hans-Georg Gadamer, in his "Interview on Leo Strauss," expresses an interesting opinion in passing: one's adult identity is fully formed between the ages of 14 and 18. See also the comments of William James on the importance of youthful or teenage conversion in *The Varieties of Religious Experience* (New York: Library of America, 1990), lecture 9, 185–87; but see also in lecture 1, 17–23, his pointed cautions against any reductionism that an emphasis on this youthful factor might seem to imply. Certainly these were key years in Strauss's life, to mention only the highlights: departure from his parents' orthodoxy, encounter with German humanism, conversion to Zionism, the army and World War I. We not only do not know who "converted" Strauss to Zionism, but also we do not know what experiences, interests, ideas, or passions might have been decisive so as to predispose him toward such a "conversion." He does refer in "Why We Remain Jews" to his youthful friends who became important figures in the state of Israel, but he mentions no one by name. In referring to them, he offers perhaps a much greater clue as to what might have been decisive in cooling (rather than warming) his youthful Zionist ardor:

> In this student group [a political Zionist youth organization], when I talked to my friends—some of whom are now very high officials in Israel—I made this observation. They were truly passionate Zionists, and worked very much, and were filled with enthusiasm. But, after all, you cannot always make speeches, and have political discussions, or do other administrative work: you also have to have, so to say, a life of your own. I was struck by the fact that the substance of the intellectual life of some of these estimable young men—to the extent that it was not merely academic, and therefore of no particular interest outside of academic halls—consisted of their concern with people like Balzac.

("Why We Remain Jews," infra, 319.) This suggests that during his period of most active involvement with Zionist student politics, he, like his friend Gershom Scholem, eventually experienced a disillusionment with the effect of such politics on the souls of his Jewish contemporaries. As for Strauss's friendship with Gershom Scholem and their common activism in the German Zionist youth movement, Scholem mentions that at a crucial moment he turned to Walter Benjamin and Strauss to help distribute in this circle a polemic against Oskar Goldberg, the leader of a "Jewish sect" of "metaphysical magicians": see his *Walter Benjamin: The Story of a Friendship*, translated by Harry Zohn (New York: Schocken, 1981), 98. See also *From Berlin to Jerusalem: Memories of My Youth*, translated by Harry Zohn (New York: Schocken, 1980), 146–49.

12. "Jerusalem and Athens," infra, 380. It might be said by some in disparagement that, through his frequently articulated defense of Jewish orthodoxy, he merely alludes obliquely or even unconsciously to the affirmative qualities of his parents' traditional Jewish piety. As this would seem to mean, his defense of orthodoxy is not fully serious, but may be reduced to a product of his own peculiar biography, and hence may be dismissed as at best an exoteric teaching, or at worst an idiosyncratic atavism. In my view, the argument that his defense of modern or enlightened orthodoxy (combined with political Zionism), and his philosophic position on Judaism, can somehow be reduced to properly fulfilled filial piety as well as ethnic solidarity, is not sustainable. Anastaplo approaches rather too close to this tendency in the skewed emphasis ("above all") of the following remark:

> Mr. Strauss showed them [i.e., "sophisticated young Jews"], as well as their Gentile fellow-travelers, that there was indeed much in Jewish faith and tradition to be respected and salvaged. There was, perhaps above all for him, an obligation of every Jew (mindful of family feeling, honor, gratitude) to stand firm with his people around the world and through the ages. (See Plato, *Apology* 34d.)

In "Freud on Moses and Monotheism," he speaks about some modern Jews who believe that what is best in them is due to their Judaism. This most certainly applies to Strauss himself, and suggests a deeper relation to his Judaism than mere filial piety or ethnic solidarity and loyalty. See "Freud on Moses and Monotheism," infra, 286–88. In an early letter to Walter Benjamin of 29 March 1935, Gershom Scholem characterized Strauss's *Philosophy and Law*, not as an effort at a rehabilitation of Maimonides in philosophic, religious, and theological-political terms, but rather as follows:

> Any day now, Schocken will bring out a book by Leo Strauss (I devoted great energy to obtaining an appointment for Strauss in Jerusalem), marking the occasion of the Maimonides anniversary. The book begins with an unfeigned and copiously argued (if completely ludicrous) affirmation of atheism as the most important Jewish watchword. Such admirable boldness for a book that will be read by every-

body as having been written by a candidate for Jerusalem! It even out-
does the first 40 pages of your postdoctoral dissertation! I admire this
ethical stance and regret the—obviously conscious and deliberately
provoked—suicide of such a capable mind. As is to be expected here,
only three people at the very most will make use of the freedom to
vote for an appointment of an atheist to a teaching position that serves
to endorse the philosophy of religion. (*The Correspondence of Walter
Benjamin and Gershom Scholem, 1932–1940*, edited by Gershom Scholem,
and translated by Gary Smith and Andre Lefevere [New York:
Schocken, 1989], 156–57)

Benjamin's response to Scholem (in a letter of 20 May 1935) is also worth noting:
"I am also very interested in Leo Strauss's book. What you tell me about him fits
in with the pleasant image of him that I have always made for myself" (p. 160).
See also Scholem's further comments about these letters between himself and
Benjamin with regard to Strauss in *Walter Benjamin: The Story of a Friendship*, trans-
lated by Harry Zohn (New York: Schocken, 1981), 201. See also his brief mention
of Strauss in *From Berlin to Jerusalem: Memories of My Youth*, translated by Harry
Zohn (New York: Schocken, 1980), 149. To return to Scholem, his opinion of Jewish
philosophy and Jewish philosophers was never very high: see esp. "General
Characteristics of Jewish Mysticism," *Major Trends in Jewish Mysticism* (New York:
Schocken, 1961), 11, 22–39; and Strauss's reply in "How to Begin to Study
Medieval Philosophy," *Rebirth of Classical Political Rationalism* (Chicago: University
of Chicago Press, 1989), 212–16. As for Scholem's strange use of the term "atheist"
to characterize Strauss's position as a Jewish thinker—although, as a careful reading would prove, "atheism" had been clearly and distinctly rejected by Strauss in
the very book to which Scholem refers (see *Philosophie und Gesetz*, 9–10, 22–28;
Philosophy and Law, translated by Eve Adler [Albany: State University of New
York Press, 1995], 21–22, 32–38; see also *On Tyranny* [rev.], 185–86)—one might
recall what Scholem writes in a later essay, "Reflections on Jewish Theology"
(1974). Scholem presents as "the experience of modern man" the loss of orthodox
belief in God combined with a passionate interest in authentic religious faith.
Thus, it is authentic "modern man" per se whom he characterizes as "the pious
atheist," i.e., as the "one for whom nothing has remained of God but the void . . .
to be sure, the void of God." See *On Jews and Judaism in Crisis* (New York:
Schocken, 1976), 283. Thus, I would regard as mostly untenable Scholem's characterization of Strauss's position as "atheist," even if he means by it some sort of
praiseworthy "pious atheism," and even if he refers to this position as an "ethical
stance" that he can "admire." For a quite different approach to Strauss as, at the
very least, a "cognitive theist," see my *Jew and Philosopher: The Return to
Maimonides in the Jewish Thought of Leo Strauss* (Albany: State University of New
York Press, 1993), 10–11, 25–27, 166 note 119, and 167 note 127. And for a persuasive account of Strauss's paramount importance in contemporary Jewish thought,
see Martin D. Yaffe, "Leo Strauss as Judaic Thinker: Some First Notions," *Religious
Studies Review* 17, no. 1 (January 1991): 33–41. For Strauss and Scholem, see Steven
B. Smith, "Gershom Scholem and Leo Strauss," *Modern Judaism* 13 (1993): 209–29.

13. In "A Giving of Accounts," infra, 460, Strauss refers to his thesis as "a disgraceful performance." To be fairer to him than he was to himself, Strauss was only twenty-two on its completion. A doctoral dissertation in a German university of those days meant something quite different from what it meant, or means, in an American context. See Max Weber, "Science as a Vocation," *From Max Weber: Essays in Sociology*, edited, translated, and introduced by H. H. Gerth and C. Wright Mills (New York: Oxford University Press, 1946), 129–56, and esp. pp. 129–34.

14. See Hillel Fradkin, "Leo Strauss," *Interpreters of Judaism in the Late Twentieth Century*, edited by Steven T. Katz (Washington, D.C.: B'nai B'rith, 1993), 343–67, esp. p. 343.

15. See Ralph Lerner, "Leo Strauss: 1899–1973," *American Jewish Year Book* 76 (1976): 91–97, esp. pp. 91–92.

16. See Fradkin, "Leo Strauss," p. 344.

17. Letters from their families in the 1930s (which contains letters about the fate of some family members) are preserved in the Leo Strauss Archive, University of Chicago Library (boxes 4 and 5). I refer especially to the deaths of his sister Bettina and his brother-in-law Paul Kraus in the phrase "perished due to their flight from Hitler Germany." They would not have been in Egypt if they did not need to accept any means of escape from Nazi Germany. For some of the details surrounding the fate of his brother-in-law, in an unpublished letter to Alexander Altmann of 2 December 1969, Strauss reported that he had received new and reliable proof from L'Institut Française of Cairo that Paul Kraus had not committed suicide, as had been originally reported, but had in fact been assassinated as a supposed Zionist spy. This assassination had been engineered by fanatical Arabs, but Strauss was still not certain how they had actually committed the crime and how they had made this appear as a suicide. With respect to his sister Bettina, I do not know of the circumstances in which she perished.

18. See Alexander Altmann, "Leo Strauss: 1899–1973," *Proceedings of the American Academy for Jewish Research* 41–42 (1975): xxxiii–xxxvi, esp. p. xxxiv.

19. He mentions Louis Finkelstein as a friend in "Why We Remain Jews," Question and Answer Section, infra, 335. Also, in a letter Strauss wrote concerning the attempt with which he was involved to help establish a chair in Jewish studies at the University of Chicago, he again refers to a consultation with Finkelstein, as a result of which they were in accord on what should be expected of the projected chair holder, both in terms of educational training and character. (See Leo Strauss Archive, box 1, folder 1. For a detailed description of the contents of the archive, see the "Guide to the Leo Strauss Papers," by Hildegard Korth, 28 pp.) With respect to Strauss's research position in the Columbia University department of history in 1937–38, it should be noted that Salo Wittmayer Baron, the great Jewish historian and the first man to occupy a

chair in Jewish history in North America, was a member of the department during this period (from 1930), although I do not know what role Baron played, if any, in Strauss's appointment. They were both members of the American Academy for Jewish Research, and it was in the book which Baron edited on Maimonides that Strauss published his first great monograph on Maimonides' esotericism, "The Literary Character of the *Guide of the Perplexed*." None of this necessarily means any special connection between them. It would seem it was also during this period that Strauss made contact with other scholars of Jewish philosophy with whom he was to maintain friendly relations in spite of great differences between them, Isaac Husik and Harry Austryn Wolfson. They were undoubtedly already familiar with him from his books and articles on Cohen, Spinoza, and Maimonides. As for his lectures at the Jewish Theological Seminary, I repeat a story told by Marvin Fox to Harry Jaffa about one of those "events": "Strauss had given one of his virtuoso performances at the Seminary. As the audience was leaving, one of its number, a famous talmudic scholar, was overheard to exclaim: 'Such a terrible loss! Such genius! What a great talmudist he would have made, had he not wasted his life on philosophy!'"

20. Also consider the words of Werner Dannhauser, one of Strauss's students at the University of Chicago. His commitment to Judaism was deepened by his contact with Strauss as a teacher:

> I simply wish to record that he astounded me by the care with which he studied books by Jews like Maimonides, thus showing me that one could not afford to treat the whole tradition of Jewish learning as relics in one's mind. In this unobtrusive way he caused me to revise—to broaden and deepen—my whole understanding of Judaism. He helped me to become not indeed a good Jew but a better one than I had been. Since I know that this experience is in no way peculiar to me, I dare say that in his role of teacher, Leo Strauss was a most loyal Jew.

Werner Dannhauser, "Leo Strauss as Jew and Citizen," *Interpretation* 17, no. 3 (Spring 1991): 433–47, esp. p. 446. Similar comments have been made by Ralph Lerner, "Leo Strauss: 1899–1973," *American Jewish Year Book* 76 (1976): 91–97, and esp. p. 97, and Milton Himmelfarb, "On Leo Strauss," *Commentary* 58, no. 8 (August 1974): 60–66, and esp. p. 64. Related comments have often been made by both friend and foe on the "Jewish" quality of Strauss's single-minded and "religious" devotion to learning. See, e.g., Löwith's remark in the "Correspondence Between Karl Löwith and Leo Strauss," *The Independent Journal of Philosophy* 5/6 (1988): 177–92, esp. pp. 180–81. Similarly, some perceive a Jewish relic in Strauss's manner of reading texts, which pays the most careful attention to the significance of every minute detail in great philosophic writers, i.e., as a style of talmudic or even kabbalistic thinking. To these critical observers, Strauss attributes a virtually revealed quality to the texts of great writers, which in their view is not appropriate for reading human, all too human, authors. Thus, see the critical comment by Hans-Georg Gadamer on

Strauss's misapplied "talmudism," in his "Interview on Leo Strauss," *Interpretation* 12 (1984): 1–13; and Alexander Altmann's critical remark about what he regards as Strauss's strange tendency toward "kabbalism":

> [Strauss] even ventures to read symbolical significance into the numbers designating the sequence of chapters (pp. xxx and xviii). Here he obviously enters into a realm of pure speculation, and few will follow in a credulous mood this kind of "kabbalistic" exegesis. It seems far remote from Maimonides' way of thinking. (Review of *The Guide of the Perplexed*, in *Journal of Religion* 44 [1964]: 260–61)

But see for an affirmative assessment of such attributes, e.g., Ralph Lerner, "Leo Strauss," p. 91, and George Anastaplo, "On Leo Strauss," p. 37. I quoted the words of Allan Bloom at the beginning of this essay with regard to his finding in Strauss what he had been seeking in rabbis. I would like to add to it the sentence that follows immediately in the same letter for what it may say about the attraction of Strauss to some of his Jewish students: "I suppose the fact that I was somehow a Jew and respected the rabbinic idea provided the crucial precondition."

21. The 1954–55 Magnes Lectures were published as "What Is Political Philosophy?," and were reprinted in Leo Strauss, *What Is Political Philosophy?* (New York: Free Press, 1959), 9–55. For Strauss's convictions about Zionism most distilled, see especially "The State of Israel," infra, and the Editor's Introduction, section 8, supra.

22. During his stay he apparently also delivered some sort of a lecture on Socrates at the University of Heidelberg, sponsored by Hans-Georg Gadamer. See Gadamer, "Interview," p. 2, for his mention of the lecture, and Korth, "Guide," p. 4, for the doctorate.

23. It was selected by family and friends as a fitting special reading to put it in the funeral service because it was apparently one of Strauss's favorite psalms. See "Jerusalem and Athens," infra, 381. I would like to note (because it may have been significant to Strauss) that this psalm is one of the Hallel prayers. The unit of six Psalms, 113–118, "full Hallel," is recited in synagogues only on certain Jewish holy days—the three pilgrimage festivals of the liberation from Egypt, Chanukah, and (in the state of Israel) on Independence Day. Hallel signalizes the importance of the events commemorated as specially testifying to God's miraculous power to save the people Israel, with its tacit promise of future redemption. With respect to Psalm 114 on its own, Strauss writes "one is tempted to ascribe to the Bible what one may call the poetic concept of miracles." However, as he hastens to add, this ascription disregards an essential differentiation: "the concept of poetry—as distinguished from that of song—is foreign to the Bible" (ibid.). For Strauss and prayer, see: George Anastaplo, "On Leo Strauss," p. 38; and James V. Schall, "Leo Strauss on Prayer," *Crisis* 3 (July 1984): 46–47.

24. See Lerner, "Leo Strauss," p. 93.

25. See my *Jew and Philosopher: The Return to Maimonides in the Jewish Thought of Leo Strauss* (Albany: State University of New York Press, 1993), which deals elaborately (chapters 3 through 6) with the stages in the development of Strauss's thought, especially as they relate to his views on Maimonides. Arnaldo Momigliano refers to Strauss's "beloved Maimonides," to whom he "returned repeatedly." See "Hermeneutics and Classical Political Philosophy in Leo Strauss," in his *Essays on Ancient and Modern Judaism* (Chicago: University of Chicago Press, 1994), 179.

26. As a young man, Strauss was apparently alerted to the feeble condition of modern liberalism: by the shortsighted attitude of the Western democracies toward Germany in the years following World War I; by the consequent fate of the liberal Weimar Republic in Germany; and by the comatose reaction of the Western democracies to the rise of Hitler Germany, which prepared World War II. As for the decrepit state of rational philosophy, he seems to have been alerted to it by the pallid aestheticism of Ernst Cassirer as the best defense made by the party of reason against Martin Heidegger, in their famous encounter at the Davos conference of 1929. The "radical historicism" of Heidegger, in his concentrated reflection on the entire Western tradition of rational philosophy in order to "deconstruct" it and rediscover Being, was possessed of a much greater vigor than its opponent, and was energized by an almost warlike spiritual devotion to its cause: to discredit and delegitimize Western rationalism which according to Heidegger is life-destroying, and hence the chief cause of the truly unjust modern world. See "An Introduction to Heideggerian Existentialism," *The Rebirth of Classical Political Rationalism* (Chicago: University of Chicago Press, 1989), 28. Strauss also was alerted by a growing awareness that in this era (Strauss, writing in 1959, seems to refer to the era since 1918), none of the four great recent philosophers (Bergson, Whitehead, Husserl, and Heidegger) defends the important tradition of Western political philosophy, as did even Hermann Cohen. See "What Is Political Philosophy?," *What Is Political Philosophy?* (New York: Free Press, 1959), 27; and also "Preface to *Spinoza's Critique of Religion*," infra, 147–53, 171–73. I discuss Strauss's view of the importance of Heidegger for contemporary philosophy in my book *Jew and Philosopher*. In the Preface I refer to the

> one prior decisive conviction that Strauss adhered to unchanged in spite of other significant variations in his thought. This was his conviction about the moral and intellectual bankruptcy of contemporary philosophy, a bankruptcy that he regarded as issuing in a grave "theological-political crisis" both for modern Judaism and for modern Western civilization. Strauss suggested that the most serious and deepest reason for this bankruptcy may be attributed to philosophy's surrender to "radical historicism" (i.e., Heidegger). He believed it led to the self-destruction of reason and the misguiding of religion, and was based finally on the abandonment or "forgetfulness" of truth. (p. xii)

27. Strauss, as a critic of historicism, did not view the events of the twentieth century in a historicist scheme as necessitated by the dialectics of history, but rather he regarded the victories of Lenin and Hitler as intelligible by a purely political explanation:

> The victory of national socialism became necessary in Germany for the same reason that the victory of communism had become necessary in Russia: the man who had by far the strongest will or single-mindedness, the greatest ruthlessness, daring, and power over his following, and the best judgment about the strength of the various forces in the immediately relevant political field was the leader of the revolution. ("Preface to *Spinoza's Critique of Religion*," infra, 138.) See also Hiram Caton, "Explaining the Nazis: Leo Strauss Today," *Quadrant* (October 1986): 61–65.

28. To Strauss, even in the case of Hermann Cohen's philosophic thought, it is deeply limited by its pre–World War I character:

> The worst things that he experienced were the Dreyfus scandal and the pogroms instigated by czarist Russia: he did not experience communist Russia and Hitler Germany. (See "Jerusalem and Athens," infra, 399.)

29. Because of those recent historical events, in Strauss's judgment the leading positions of modern Jewish thought no longer speak to the deepest and most immediate spiritual needs of contemporary Jews. As a result, what continues to impose itself unwanted and willy-nilly on most Jews is a sense of unresolved predicament, a sense justified by the unprecedented and radical challenges to everything held dear by modern Judaism. This sense of an unresolved predicament is constantly reawakened in the political sphere by the perennial challenges to liberalism, and is with even greater vehemence reawakened in the theological sphere by the perennial challenges to reason. The comprehensiveness of the Jewish dilemma, inasmuch as it embraces doubts about both the adequacy of the deepest intellectual responses of modern Jewish thought as well as about the solidity of ordinary life in a liberal democracy as based on modern Jewish historical experience, is one reason why Strauss chooses to call the present situation a "theological-political crisis." Strauss claimed that his own thought was always rooted in actual historical experience as the primary consideration. For modern Judaism, this means especially the "catastrophes and horrors of a magnitude hitherto unknown," which dominate our recent history. (See "Jerusalem and Athens," infra, 399.) He himself was immersed in and affected by this history, and he was ever attentive to its implications. But he also believed that to comprehend these implications with regard to the causes of modern historical events, we are required to search for ultimate causes in those previously mentioned intellectual responses to our deepest concerns. This is perhaps mainly because, to Strauss, from the start and until the present, the modern liberal order (on which modern Judaism was

grounded) made a claim to its own necessity that was based on its correlation with the necessity of the modern order of reason. Indeed, the specifically modern intention was to correlate modern philosophical-scientific reason with the modern liberal political order as much as was possible. As a result, even though he fully recognized that historical events possess a life of their own, he also saw that fundamental confusions and errors in modern philosophy and theology are also reflected in modern political life to an even greater extent than in any previous political life. Hence fundamental confusions and errors of thought are potentially of a much greater destructiveness in our political life. In the thought of Strauss, this lends to our pressing philosophical, theological, and political dilemmas perhaps a greater power and gravity than that which they receive from most contemporary Jewish thinkers. And this also helps to explain a seeming paradox in Strauss's approach to modern Judaism: he claimed to preserve both an awareness of the "theological" dimension in Jewish thought and a properly political approach to historical events by proceeding through what he calls political philosophy, which for him meant philosophy whose primary but not ultimate orientation is to the human realm. In his view, once we have been fully apprised of the political nature of historical events in their specificity, we need to look away from those political events, in order to make even political sense of those events, to the light shed by a higher source on those events—modern philosophic thought and its dilemmas. See his remarks on the priority to be accorded to the "high" and the "low" in "Preface to *Spinoza's Critique of Religion*," infra, 138. Eventually, he wondered whether it might not be "unwise to say farewell to reason" (173). Consequently, he regarded himself, as also those who are persuaded by him, as compelled to ask and to investigate thoroughly whether rational "enlightenment is necessarily modern Enlightenment" (*Philosophie und Gesetz*, 28; *Philosophy and Law*, 38), or to consider if modern "Enlightenment deserves its name or whether its true name is Obfuscation." See *Thoughts on Machiavelli* (Glencoe, Ill.: Free Press, 1958), 173. On the vital contemporary Jewish *theological* need for political philosophy, in light of the idea of covenant, see David Novak, "Jewish Theology," in *Modern Judaism* 10 (1990): 311–23, and esp. p. 322, which points specifically to Strauss as needed by future Jewish religious thought.

30. Although I speak only of rational philosophy, I believe that for Strauss (as also for Franz Rosenzweig: see *The Star of Redemption*, part I, book 1), whatever "irrationalism" preceded Nietzsche in modern philosophy, it was still tied to and dependent on modern rational philosophy (i.e., as the Romantics were to Spinoza and Rousseau, as Kierkegaard was to Kant and Hegel, etc.), but this cannot be said of those who followed Nietzsche. For Strauss's notion of the three "waves" in the history of modern philosophy, each launched respectively by Machiavelli (in the sixteenth century), Rousseau (in the eighteenth century), and Nietzsche (in the nineteenth century)—a scheme also reflected in his mature approach to the history of modern Jewish philosophy—see "The Three Waves of Modernity," in *An Introduction to Political Philosophy* (Detroit: Wayne State University Press, 1989), 81–98. According to Strauss, we dwell in the midst of the

onslaught of the third wave, launched by Nietzsche and carried on by his "student" Heidegger. Our situation perhaps cannot be changed fundamentally, but with a full and proper awareness of our situation we can choose to mount a philosophical "resistance" by thinking through our opposition to the Nietzsche-Heidegger school of thought and its vast number of contemporary *epigonoi*. For Strauss, who did not want to commit the error of leading a fanatical resistance to fanaticism, this also meant that we accept calmly and with confidence that the importance of such philosophical "resistance" will likely be appreciated only once this wave has been allowed to run its course. In this sense, it may be said that Strauss like his friend Gershom Scholem were the first two modern Jewish thinkers who fully absorbed the teaching of Nietzsche via Heidegger (which still dominates modern philosophy in the derivative forms of Benjamin, Kojève, Gadamer, Foucault, Rorty, Derrida, radical feminism), yet who were not conquered by it. Prior to Strauss and Scholem, Berdyczewski—who did receive the first impact of Nietzsche on Jewish thought—still thought of him in terms of the "heroic," not in terms of nihilism. Following Strauss and Scholem, both Levinas and Fackenheim are engaged in an honest wrestling with Heidegger, though it amounts to the thinking through of a post-Holocaust rejection of his thought, and with him of his mentor Nietzsche, a rejection begun in the 1930s by Scholem and Strauss. For Strauss's own youth, he wrote to his friend Karl Löwith in a letter of 23 June 1935:

> I can only say that Nietzsche so dominated and bewitched me between my 22nd and 30th years, that I literally believed everything that I understood of him—and that is, as I see clearly from your work, only a part of his teaching. . . . [On the other hand,] I think that you do not take seriously enough those intentions of Nietzsche which point beyond Nietzsche's teaching. . . . For it is not sufficient simply to stop where Nietzsche is no longer right; rather one must ask whether or not Nietzsche himself became untrue to his intention to repeat antiquity, and did so as a result of his confinement within modern presuppositions or in polemics against these. [*The Independent Journal of Philosophy* 5/6 (1988): 183–84]

31. See "Preface to *Spinoza's Critique of Religion*," infra, 168–69. See also infra, 154–70, passim, for his remarks on Spinoza in the debate between the leading advocates of the "movement of return," i.e., between Cohen and Rosenzweig, concerning the status and importance of Spinoza in grounding modern Judaism.

32. See "How to Study Spinoza's *Theologico-Political Treatise*," infra, 212, for Strauss's view of Spinoza's procedure, which is summarized in the following statement: "To exaggerate for purposes of clarification, we may say that each chapter of the *Treatise* serves the function of refuting one particular orthodox dogma while leaving untouched all other orthodox dogmas."

33. See "How to Study Spinoza's *Theologico-Political Treatise*," infra, 190.

34. *Spinoza's Critique of Religion* (New York: Schocken, 1965), 143, 157. Strauss applies the same insight to the attack on Maimonides' exegesis: "In principle, no critique of Scripture can touch Maimonides' position, since such critique is capable of no more than establishing what is *humanly* possible or impossible, whereas his opponent assumes the divine origin of Scripture." (p. 157)

35. Ibid., 159–60.

36. Ibid., 155.

37. If there are still true "Spinozists" in philosophy, who are persuaded of the complete adequacy of the *Ethics* as the final philosophic system, in which all its truths about God, man, and the world are fully and properly demonstrated by its geometrical method, then to them Strauss's entire argument and ultimate conclusions will appear to be specious logic. Strauss briefly summarizes his own doubts about Spinoza's *Ethics* as follows:

> But is Spinoza's account of the whole clear and distinct? Those of you who have ever tried their hands, for example, at his analysis of the emotions, would not be so certain of that. But more than that, even if it is clear and distinct, is it necessarily true? Is its clarity and distinctness not due to the fact that Spinoza abstracts from those elements of the whole which are not clear and distinct and which can never be rendered clear and distinct?

See "Progress or Return?," infra, 130–31. As to the failure of Spinoza to refute orthodoxy, Strauss remarks: "Spinoza and his like owed such success as they had in their fight against orthodoxy to laughter and mockery." Thus Strauss was also "tempted to say": "mockery does not succeed the refutation of the orthodox tenets but is itself the refutation." ("Preface to *Spinoza's Critique of Religion*," infra, 170. See also the "Einleitung" to *Philosophie und Gesetz*, 18–19; and the "Introduction" to *Philosophy and Law*, 29–30.)

38. See "Preface to *Spinoza's Critique of Religion*," infra, 170–71; *Spinoza's Critique of Religion*, 144–46, 204–14, 42.

39. This also meant that the Machiavellian modern project wanted to ensure the control and diminution of the religious realm, which will be allowed by the political realm to play only a pedagogical role, and solely in the sphere of liberal moral training. In other words, religion will be banished from the spheres both of the claim to know the truth, and of ambition for political power. This is because it is the view of Spinoza and the Enlightenment that religion, if it is not otherwise kept to the function of teaching a liberal morality, is one of the chief causes, if not *the* chief cause by itself alone, of evil, wickedness, and suffering in human life. This controlling aim of the modern project, to subordinate if not also to refute the truth claims made by biblical religion, and hence to prevent it from exercising any political influence on statesmen or on the people, resulted even-

tually in the full articulation by Spinoza of the beliefs in liberalism, progress, science, natural morality and religion, the secular state, and popular enlightenment, as both the necessary and the sufficient beliefs of modern man.

40. See "Preface to *Spinoza's Critique of Religion,*" infra, 139.

41. See "Preface to *Spinoza's Critique of Religion,*" infra, 137–44.

42. This amoral aspect of Spinoza, his Machiavellian logic of evil permitted (i.e., in the form of telling lies about the Jews) if it is calculated to achieve good (i.e., in the justified destruction of the medieval order), was entirely missed by Cohen—although it is not true that Strauss speaks better of Spinoza in moral terms than Cohen spoke. "Our case against Spinoza is in some respects even stronger than Cohen thought." See "Preface to *Spinoza's Critique of Religion,*" infra, 159. In spite of his powerful rhetoric, Cohen's misgivings about Spinoza were weaker than Strauss's precisely because Cohen's dependence on Spinoza was greater, if only in his lacking (by resistance or denial) the awareness of his dependence on Spinoza, perhaps because of its humiliating character. Cohen's modern Judaism required Spinoza's "sacrileges" in order to establish a clean break with premodern or orthodox Judaism. As Strauss summarizes his argument against Cohen's critique of Spinoza: "Cohen commits the typical mistake of the conservative." By this Strauss means, he forgets that the continuity of the tradition which he reveres and defends was originally established by radical discontinuity, and even revolution, against a prior tradition. (See ibid., 169.) And in the spirit of Rosenzweig, Strauss also does not refrain from criticizing Cohen for his lack of a proper appreciation of Spinoza for originating the modern Jewish tradition which Cohen himself cherished and in which his Jewish philosophy was ultimately rooted. Already in his youth Strauss formulated the correct or "radical" question which Cohen should have been trying to answer: "Which Jewish motives are alive in Spinoza's Bible science?" See "Cohens Analyse der Bibel-Wissenschaft Spinozas," 314. (See the translation by Michael Zank, as "Cohen's Analysis of Spinoza's Scientific Study of the Bible," forthcoming in his edition of *Leo Strauss's Early Jewish Writings,* "The Jewish Writings of Leo Strauss," SUNY Press.) Strauss subsequently summarized his own final appreciation of Spinoza's "Jewish motives" in the following words:

> However bad a Jew he may have been in all other respects, he thought of the liberation of the Jews in the only way in which he could think of it, given his philosophy. ("Preface to *Spinoza's Critique of Religion,*" infra, 161).

43. For those familiar with Jewish history in the twentieth century, this way of expressing Spinoza's amoral (or immoral) logic is deliberately intended to echo a most shameful "liberal" Machiavellian argument made during World War II. Allied Western leaders (i.e., Roosevelt and Churchill) argued, for their own primarily disreputable reasons, that they could do nothing special to help the millions of Jews being murdered by the Nazi Germans, because it would

distract from the main war effort, and hence would delay the final victory. But, they added, the Jews would be helped ultimately by the defeat of Hitler Germany, toward which they were called to redouble their effort and contribution. It was apparently illegitimate for the Jews to ask for any sort of special help, even though the Jews alone had been isolated by the Nazi plan for systematic murder, a plan for systematic murder (it has now been definitively established) known to the Allied command. Certainly the Jews were finally alerted by this to what Strauss calls the "limitations of liberalism," as represented by the mass "conversion" of world Jewry to support for political Zionism in the years following 1945. However, the evidence still suggests that it has been most difficult for Western Jews to absorb in a complete manner what might be called the full historical "lesson" of the Holocaust with respect to liberalism. On another level, for those who would here demur at the notion that this is a "lesson" which can be learned from the Holocaust, at least it is possible for Jewish thought to learn from Strauss how to philosophically absorb "the limitations of liberalism," however one may relate them to the course of modern Jewish history. For Strauss's brief statement of those "limitations," together with a defense of liberalism, see infra, "Preface to *Spinoza's Critique of Religion*," 143–44. As Strauss viewed modern liberalism, it "cannot provide a solution to the Jewish problem," or it can only provide an "uneasy" one, but even so it is still the best one available. As the basis of liberal democracy, it makes for the most decent political life in modern circumstances. It was evident to Strauss from these and other forceful arguments he made against the alternatives that liberalism is the modern order whose decency is least corruptible and most defensible not only for the Jews, but also for modern man as such. For Strauss, this obviously means it is best in the state of Israel as well. For brief accounts of the previously mentioned historical (and hypocritical) argument made by the Allied command to Jewish leaders, see, e.g., Walter Lacqueur, *The Terrible Secret* (New York: Penguin, 1982), 95, 162, 202–4; David S. Wyman, *The Abandonment of the Jews* (New York: Pantheon Books, 1984), 337–40. As for whether what we called "liberal religious reform" is liable to the same critique, it is difficult to say. If we mean simply forms of modern Judaism of a nonorthodox but distinctively religious character, Strauss does not seem to have been inclined to reject them, insofar as the changes they make are not to the fundamental religious beliefs and moral principles of Judaism. Whether this absolute limit on changes to the fundamentals can still be maintained about contemporary forms of nonorthodox religious Judaism is perhaps not as self-evident as it was during Strauss's life (1899–1973). But it would seem to have been Strauss's view that some such absolute limitation, however defined, must be obeyed by any modern religious movement, if it is to remain authentically Jewish. Otherwise, Judaism is defined relative to the current modern ideas, which means it is not able to resist those ideas if they break with fundamental Jewish notions of piety and decency. See the comment by Emil Fackenheim on the importance of "moral constancy" in modern Judaism in his Preface, xiii–xvii, to *Where Judaism Differs*, by Abba Hillel Silver (New York: Collier, 1989). The type of concerns which are distinctive to Strauss were clearly and eloquently restated by Hillel Halkin in a recent book review, even though Halkin writes apparently not on Straussian grounds, and even though I believe Strauss would not limit Halkin's point to the followers of Mordecai Kaplan, or even to American Jews, but would apply it to modern Judaism per se:

> . . . [they] fail to make the distinction between Jewishness, the socio-logical and cultural condition of the modern Jew that Kaplan was really talking about, and Judaism, a more than 3,000-year-old religion that is profoundly in conflict with "the context of twentieth-century thought" and that can only retain its integrity in opposition to that context. No confusion in American Jewish life today is more wide-spread or intellectually debilitating. (*Jerusalem Report* vol. 4, no. 9 [9 September 1993]: 46–47)

44. See "Preface to *Spinoza's Critique of Religion*," infra, 142. For Spinoza's view of the Jews and Judaism, see his *Theologico-Political Treatise*, and for these points, especially chapter 3, toward the end. Spinoza regarded the Mosaic law as binding only so long as the Jews possessed their own state and their own land, and hence he viewed himself as no longer obligated to obey it; for him it was, in any case, primarily a political, not a religious, law. By way of contrast, he also believed that the Jews could reconstitute their state, "so ultimately changeable are human affairs," and this suggests they might need the Mosaic law again. Is it only the rabbinic law of the exile which "emasculates," precisely because it does not inculcate virtues (civic and martial) which would constantly drive them to attempt to reconquer their land, and rebuild their state? Strauss seems to have been convinced that this argument of Spinoza's was not merely an imi-tation of Machiavelli's attitude to Christianity, and yet it is also difficult not to reduce it to specious logic on its own. As Strauss would seem to hold in contrast to the "judgment" of Spinoza, the Jews deserve praise for what Lessing called their "heroic obedience," i.e., for their astonishingly courageous fidelity to their tradition, in spite of periodic persecutions and constant contempt on the one hand, and temptations to convert in order to escape such contempt and perse-cutions on the other hand. See "Why We Remain Jews," infra, 322–23. If Spinoza is referring to their lack of training in the rigors of command, based on their supposed unwillingness to reflect on the virtues required for political freedom, Strauss was fond of the passage in Maimonides' *Letter on Astrology*, which he often cited, in which an account is offered of why the Jews lost their ancient state:

> In the same vein Maimonides declares that the ruin of the Jewish king-dom was caused by the "sins of the fathers," namely, by their idolatry; but idolatry worked its effect in a perfectly natural manner: it led to astrology and thus induced the Jewish people to devote themselves to astrology instead of to the practice of the arts of war and the conquest of countries. (*On Tyranny* [rev.], 183–84; idem, *What Is Political Philosophy?*, 102–3)

See the same pages—as well as *Thoughts on Machiavelli*, 176–80—for Strauss's prior discussion of Machiavelli's remark on "the 'unarmed heaven' and 'the effeminacy of the world,' which, according to him, are due to Christianity." See also "Notes on Maimonides' *Letter on Astrology*," in *Studies in Platonic Political Philosophy* (Chicago: University of Chicago Press, 1983), 207; and "On Abravanel's Philosophical Tendency and Political Teaching," *Isaac Abravanel*, edited by J. B. Trend and H. Loewe (Cambridge: Cambridge University Press, 1937), 106–7.

45. See, e.g., "Preface to *Spinoza's Critique of Religion*," infra, 141–44, in which Strauss explains in somewhat greater detail this idea that we have been compelled to indicate in a rather cryptic phrase.

46. Ibid., 161, 166, 168. The recent book by Yirmiyahu Yovel, *Spinoza and Other Heretics* (Princeton: Princeton University Press, 1989), might seem to offer an elaborate restatement of Strauss's thesis in much greater detail. However, Yovel breaks philosophically with Strauss in terms of presenting what Martin D. Yaffe called a mostly "deep-psychological" approach to Spinoza. Thus, Yovel resorts to a historical (and hence virtually reductionist) explanation of Spinoza based on his Marrano origins, as these Marrano origins are supposed to represent an autonomous "Jewish" tradition which exercised the decisive influence on him, rather than attempting a philosophical interpretation of Spinoza as a thinker who knew what he was doing at least as well, if not better, than we do, irrespective of our supposedly "superior" historical perspective on the Marranos. See Martin D. Yaffe, "Two Recent Treatments of Spinoza's *Theologico-Political Treatise* (1670): A Review Essay," *Modern Judaism* 13 (1993): 309–15.

47. See the recent book by Allan Arkush, *Mendelssohn and the Enlightenment* (Albany: State University of New York Press, 1994), which discusses these issues in greater depth.

48. In his youth, Strauss writes, "Cohen was the center of attraction for philosophically minded Jews who were devoted to Judaism; he was the master whom they revered." See "Introductory Essay to Hermann Cohen, *Religion of Reason*," infra, 267. In most personal terms, Cohen exercised a spiritual influence upon Strauss, as upon his non-Jewish friend Kurt Riezler, "by the fire and power of his soul." See also *What Is Political Philosophy?*, 242. But by 1922 Strauss was what he calls "a doubting and dubious adherent of the Marburg school of neo-Kantianism." Husserl seems to have been responsible for turning him away from Cohen and toward "phenomenology," while Heidegger turned him away from Husserl. Cohen asserted the reality only of constructed ideals in the human mind, rejecting the basis of science as grounded in any actual sense perception. Even the prescientific world and man as they are eventually known by science are a product of the creative human rational mind, which not only cannot know the intelligible things in themselves, but also must create ideas of what things are like based originally on merely phenomenal impressions, which are not, however, even the sensible things in themselves. Cohen regarded any

alternative view as a compromise of the Kantian notion of purity in reason as based on reason as not only legislator but also as generator of the scientific laws as they are operative in nature, with no possible reference to claims about how things actually are. Husserl began by rejecting Cohen's premise as self-contradictory: How is science possible if it is not based on a prescientific actual awareness of what the sensible things are like? The things of sense perception must be what is primarily and actually known. These must also appear as actual sense perceptions in a sort of reasonable order, which science merely improves on. Otherwise, how do we know we do not merely imagine what the things are like, which science deals with? Reliable prediction may be a sound test for our grasp of natural things, but what does one do especially with things in and of man? Phenomenology provides us with a better sense, as precise description, of what those prescientific phenomenal impressions are like (even if also not of the things in themselves), and what the prescientific order they represent is like, which enables us to attain a surer basis for scientific understanding or explanation. Heidegger, for Strauss, "radicalized Husserl's critique of the school of Marburg and turned it against Husserl: what is primary is not the object of sense perception but the things which we handle and with which we are concerned, *pragmata*. What [Strauss] could not stomach was his moral teaching." See "A Giving of Accounts," infra, 461, as well as "Philosophy as Rigorous Science and Political Philosophy," *Studies in Platonic Political Philosophy*, 31. The ultimate conflict between Heidegger's radical modern historicism, on the one hand, and Strauss's restored classical naturalism or rationalism, on the other hand, may be said to have been prepared by Husserl also in his critique of Cohen. What Strauss seems to mean by tracing the conflict to Husserl is something like the following. Husserl recognized with profundity the fact that "the scientific understanding of the world," which for Cohen is simply primary, is actually "derivative" from "our natural understanding of the world," and this is "prescientific." Hence, in order to understand this "prescientific" or "natural" ground, which is the true basis for all "scientific understanding," we must first understand how we arrive at the idea of "nature" as something that can and should be scientifically understood, and especially also what the human conditions are which lead to such a breakthrough to "science." For Strauss, Husserl raised the right question in asking whether the dubious, specifically modern "separation of the ideas of wisdom (i.e., the approach to man) and of rigorous science (i.e., the approach to nature)" is tenable. Hence, Husserl also correctly asked about the proper relation between "the two kinds of philosophy," the human and the natural, and about whether one is necessarily prior to the other. Husserl's answer, however, Strauss rejects. Husserl asserts that this separation cannot be surpassed and properly ordered. He thus maintains there is no comprehensive or universal "natural" approach to man (i.e., the "idea of philosophy") which is presupposed by what is merely considered at present to be the prior eternal "idea of science" with regard to nature. It is then, according to Husserl, only in the arbitrary sphere of *Weltanschauungen*—i.e., in particular and historically relative acts of faith by one man or some men or by a human society about how best to construe the world—that this relation must be

who by far surpassed in spiritual power all other German professors of philosophy of his generation." See "Preface to *Spinoza's Critique of Religion*," infra, 154. See also *What Is Political Philosophy?*, 242. But Strauss also calls himself, even in 1922, "a doubting and dubious adherent of the Marburg school of neo-Kantianism." See "Philosophy as Rigorous Science and Political Philosophy," *Studies in Platonic Political Philosophy*, 31; and "A Giving of Accounts," infra, 460.

51. See one of Strauss's last works, "Introductory Essay to Hermann Cohen, *Religion of Reason*," infra, 281–82, in which he still praises Cohen as:

> a faithful warner and comforter to many Jews. At the very least he showed them most effectively how Jews can live with dignity as Jews in a non-Jewish, even hostile, world while participating in that world. . . . It is a blessing for us that Hermann Cohen lived and wrote.

According to Alexander Altmann, Strauss was closely bound to Cohen from beginning to end. Cohen started him thinking about Spinoza and the Enlightenment, about the Platonic character of Maimonides' thought, and about the dilemmas of modern Judaism. By Strauss's consenting to write the introductory essay to the translation of Cohen's *Religion of Reason*, as Altmann puts it, "the circle of his life's course was complete." Thus, Altmann noted what he regarded as perhaps the most significant pattern in the course of Strauss's Jewish writings—the unbroken connection with Hermann Cohen:

> Cohen's critique of Spinoza had challenged him at the beginning of his career to reexamine the latter's attack on orthodox religion, and in *Philosophie and Gesetz* he had quoted Cohen's utterance about Maimonides being more of a Platonist than an Aristotelian, thereby claiming Cohen's support for his political interpretation of Maimonides' *Guide*. Introducing the *Religion of Reason* and, more so, its author to English readers was more than an act of piety. It meant that the circle of his life's course was complete. ("Leo Strauss: 1899–1973," *Proceedings of the American Academy for Jewish Research* 41–42 (1973–74): xxxiii–xxxvi, and esp. p. xxxvi)

The last book of his essays, which Strauss arranged to publish "in their present order" prior to his death (Joseph Cropsey), also finished with his introductory essay to Cohen's *Religion of Reason*. Alan Udoff quotes a letter Strauss wrote in 1931 in which, speaking of himself, he declares "as emphatically as possible": "I am in no way a Cohenian." Notwithstanding this unambiguous declaration, he proceeds to follow this with a revealing statement:

> Cohen is much too original and deep a thinker that the doubtfulness of his teaching can release us thereby from listening, in any event, to that which he says.

See Udoff's entire essay for several suggestive remarks about Strauss's complex but positive relation to Cohen's thought: "On Leo Strauss: An Introductory

Account," *Leo Strauss's Thought: Toward a Critical Engagement*, 1–29 (Boulder, Colo.: Lynne Rienner, 1991), and esp. 22–23, note 3. By way of contrast, Thomas L. Pangle, in his "Introduction" to *Studies in Platonic Political Philosophy*, reads the relation of Strauss to Cohen in quite a different, and mostly negative, light:

> . . . there is a discernible kinship between the hopes of modern philos-
> ophy and the hopes for the Messiah. In the hands of the penetrating
> and truly noble Kantian Jew Hermann Cohen, that kinship became
> the leitmotif of a new, supposedly superior or "historically progres-
> sive" grand synthesis of Jerusalem and Athens. Strauss closes his last
> work by returning again to Cohen and demonstrating, with the great-
> est respect but with relentless clarity, what a delusion was thus con-
> structed by the man who had been in a sense the hero of Strauss's
> youth. (p. 26)

Pangle seems to attribute to Strauss's thought the notion that this "messianic" component of modern philosophy reaches its apotheosis in Cohen. It is my view that Strauss attributed a seriously "messianic" religious component or residual faith to modern philosophy in its very beginnings, irrespective of whether these were Machiavellian or Hobbesian. For Strauss, this is what differentiates modern philosophers from premodern: the belief that they can transform, and even perfect, the nature of man and the world. To return to Cohen again, he is present in the entire course of Strauss's Jewish writings, beginning with his first major work, the article "Cohen's Analysis of Spinoza's Bible Science" (1924), and ending with his last major work, the Introductory Essay in the English translation of Hermann Cohen's *Religion of Reason out of the Sources of Judaism* (1972). Perhaps I should also observe the curious fact that Strauss only consented to write introductory essays to two English translations, in spite of the number of great works he commented on and which his students translated. The two books are both great works of Jewish philosophy: Maimonides' *Guide* and Hermann Cohen's *Religion of Reason*. Through this fact does Strauss mean to say something to us about the type of works, besides his own, with which he wanted his name to be permanently associated? Thus, in spite of Strauss's youthful break with Cohen, it is by no means remote to suggest that Cohen continued to exercise a decided influence on Strauss's reading of Maimonides in his construction of a *primarily* political, nonmetaphysical Maimonides, whose theoretical bent was ultimately turned to establishing "the primacy of practical reason," albeit of a nonmoral type. This is, of course, the reading fully developed by Shlomo Pines in the revision of his views expressed in his essay, "The Limits of Knowledge According to Al-Farabi, Ibn Bajja, and Maimonides," *Studies in Medieval Jewish History and Literature*, edited by Isadore Twersky (Cambridge: Harvard University Press, 1979), 82–109. (This represents a dramatically changed point of view from the quite differently interpreted Maimonides in his Translator's Introduction to *The Guide of the Perplexed*.) It is, however, my judgment that this revised reading by Pines of Maimonides is not to be identified with Strauss's own deeper reading of Maimonides or with

Strauss's own views. For a critique of Pines's revised "practical" reading of Maimonides, see R. Zev Friedman, "Maimonides and Kant on Metaphysics and Piety," *Review of Metaphysics* 45, no. 4 (June 1992): 773–801. But see *Philosophie und Gesetz*, 120–22, and *Philosophy and Law*, 131–33, for what I believe most concisely articulates Strauss's position on that issue.

52. Strauss acknowledged the debt he owed to the "resurrection" of theology in the 1920s by Barth and Rosenzweig. See "Preface to *Hobbes Politische Wissenschaft*," infra, 453–54, and "A Giving of Accounts," infra, 460. With regard to the *contents* of what they taught him, he mentions Barth's liberating biblical hermeneutic as he enunciated it in the "Preface" to his *Commentary on Paul's Letter to the Romans*. There Barth emphasizes that the truth expounded by Scripture can only be of interest to us if it is just as vital and relevant for us here and now as it was then and there. This amounts to a declaration of independence from the historical approach to Scripture, which can only be exculpated from the charge of participating in historicist triumphalism and reductionism by duly subordinating itself to the eternal truth taught by Scripture. Cohen was guilty of precisely such complicity with moderate historicism, albeit of a rationalist variety, since in his efforts he understands the past better than it understood itself, rather than as it understood itself. Strauss maintained that this rationalism still represents a surrender to historicism. Either it does not need the past to validate itself, since it stands on its claim to be the absolute moment of rational insight in history, which transcends history and predefines all understanding of the past, making the study of history redundant and superfluous. Or it does need the past, but then there is a distorting light cast on all of its understanding of the past by its filtering and discarding all "extraneous" facts which do not confirm the absolute moment as the absolute teaching, and hence which cannot achieve true historical understanding. This belief in the eternal truth, as Barth so well brings to theological light, requires that history remain subordinate to such truth, whether one conceives of its nature in theological or philosophical terms. See also "Cohens Analyse der Bibel-Wissenschaft Spinozas," in *Der Jude* 8 (1924): 295–314, and esp. pp. 312–14.

53. See "A Giving of Accounts," infra, 460, and "Philosophy as Rigorous Science and Political Philosophy," *Studies in Platonic Political Philosophy*, 31. Strauss first encountered Cohen's system as it was taught in the philosophy faculty at the University of Marburg, where it had been established as a school by Cohen himself. But when Strauss arrived "the school was in a state of disintegration," since "Cohen belonged definitely to the pre–World War I world."

54. For Strauss's purely political analysis:

The Weimar Republic was weak. It had a single moment of strength, if not of greatness: its strong reaction to the murder of the Jewish Minister of Foreign Affairs, Walther Rathenau, in 1922. On the whole it presented the sorry spectacle of justice without a sword or of justice unable to use the sword. The election of Field Marshal von

Hindenburg to the presidency of the German Reich in 1925 showed everyone who had eyes to see that the Weimar Republic had only a short time to live: the old Germany was stronger—stronger in will—than the new Germany. ("Preface to *Spinoza's Critique of Religion*," infra, 137)

Strauss speaks of Max Weber as one of a handful of Germans who were friendly toward the Jews ("Why We Remain Jews," 335–36), but he is also fond of referring to Weber's essay, "Science as a Vocation" (1918), which deeply impressed him in his youth. It was in this essay that Weber, precisely as a friend, addressed Jewish students who aspired to an academic career in Germany with the harsh advice: you are like one who is about to enter hell, and as Dante put it, "Abandon hope!" (*lasciate ogni speranza*). See "Science as a Vocation," *From Max Weber: Essays in Sociology*, translated, edited, and introduced by H. H. Gerth and C. Wright Mills (New York: Oxford University Press, 1946), 129–56, and esp. p. 134.

55. See "Progress or Return?," infra, 103–4; "Why We Remain Jews," infra, 344; "Preface to *Spinoza's Critique of Religion*," infra, 154; "Jerusalem and Athens," infra, 398–99.

56. See "Preface to *Spinoza's Critique of Religion*," infra, 165–66, for "idealizing" versus historical interpretation, i.e., seeing "a teaching in light of its highest possibility" (even if such was unknown to its originator) or "as meant by its originator." See also "Preface to Isaac Husik, *Philosophical Essays*," infra, 251–56.

57. See "Introductory Essay to Hermann Cohen, *Religion of Reason*," infra, 267–69.

58. See "Social Science and Humanism," 8–12, "Relativism," 21–24, and "An Introduction to Heideggerian Existentialism," 32, all in *The Rebirth of Classical Political Rationalism*. See also Hilail Gildin, "Introduction" to *An Introduction to Political Philosophy*, pp. xiii–xviii. Also consider *Natural Right and History* (Chicago: University of Chicago Press, 1971), 9–79. See also Steven Schwarzschild, "Authority and Reason Contra Gadamer," in *Studies in Jewish Philosophy*, edited by Norbert M. Samuelson (Lanham, Md.: University Press of America, 1987), 161–90, esp. pp. 168–69, in which he tries to defend Cohen against the "historicality of reason" made fundamental by Heidegger and Gadamer. It seems to me that this attempted defense illustrates about as well as could have been done Strauss's point about the positivist as well as Cohenian slide toward historicism: the purely regulative function of reason, which is filled by the content of the current historical state of scientific knowledge, is saved from the positivism of infinite pursuit, regulated only by "method," by the moral addition of the infinite "messianic task" of reason. Hence, it is only a step away from the positivist surrender to historicism, once doubts about the moral and cognitive value of science enter the purview of the thinker. Schwarzschild seems willing to jettison the guard wall which protected Kant

from such a slide toward positivism, because he seems to doubt the truth of what is "frequently alleged" about Kant's "metaphysical commitment to Euclidean geometry and Newtonian science"; but for Cohen and Marburg neo-Kantianism, he puts beyond "legitimate dispute" the fact that this school accepts the "historical character of the cognitive (and other) categories."

59. See "Preface to Isaac Husik, *Philosophical Essays*," infra, 251–52. In beginning a critique of Julius Guttmann (the other leading historian of medieval Jewish philosophy), Strauss wisely laid down the following dictum: "There is no inquiry into the history of philosophy that is not at the same time a *philosophic* inquiry." In this light, one sees why it was that Strauss was especially critical of the tacit *philosophic* premise of Husik as a historian of Jewish philosophy: he was concerned to isolate those chief difficulties which beset Husik's philosophic position as it was directly applied to and reflected by his historical research in Jewish philosophy. Strauss reduces these difficulties of Husik to three problems: "the problems of objectivity, of historical evolution, and of the idea of a Jewish philosophy."

60. Ibid., infra, 255–56.

61. Ibid., infra, 255. Consider also:

This Jewish heritage, [Husik] felt, is as essential for civilization as the Greek spirit of science and philosophy. From this conclusion, he was naturally led to demand that the Jewish heritage—"the passion for justice" or "the fear of the Lord"—[must] be brought into some working relation with philosophy and science, or, more precisely, with modern philosophy and science. He was led, in other words, to subscribe to the demand for a modern philosophy of Judaism. . . . This whole strand in Husik's thought is in full agreement with the principles of Hermann Cohen. It is therefore hard to see how Husik could with consistency have avoided agreeing with the principle of Cohen's approach to Jewish medieval philosophy.

Strauss elaborates on his critique, beginning with the following quoted words of Husik himself:

"All will not be well in Judaism until the position of the Bible as a Jewish authority is dealt with in an adequate manner by Jewish scholars who are competent to do it . . . the scholar who is going to undertake it . . . must be a philosopher and thinker of eminent abilities. And he must have a love of his people and sympathy with its aspirations." That is to say, what is needed is a modern Jewish philosopher. . . . For the fundamental problem for the modern Jewish philosopher—the relation of the spirit of science and of the spirit of the Bible—was also the fundamental problem for the medieval Jewish philosopher. The modern Jewish philosopher will naturally try to learn as much as possible for his own task from his illustrious predecessors. Since he has achieved greater clarity at least about certain aspects of the fundamental issue than the medieval thinkers had, he will not be exclusively concerned with what the medieval thinkers explicitly or actually intended in elaborating their doctrines. He will be much more concerned with what these doctrines mean in the light of the fundamental issue, regardless of whether the medieval thinkers were aware of that meaning or not. (Ibid., infra, 255–56)

62. For Strauss's critical remarks on Cohen's faulty political morality, see "Preface to *Spinoza's Critique of Religion*," infra, 162–63. As he summarizes Cohen's neglect of "the law of reason or the natural law": "Revolutions are political but not legal acts. . . . They do not necessarily occur without the killing of human beings; Cohen, the sworn enemy of capital punishment, reflects only on the death of 'the revolutionary martyrs' who voluntarily sacrifice their lives, but not on the death of their victims."

63. Strauss does not seem to have been convinced that Cohen's philosophic thought was *entirely* a product of philosophic pursuits as they emerged in modern Germany prior to 1914. This would make it of a most dubious philosophic usefulness to subsequent Jewish thought. He did recognize that its importance for modern Judaism per se must be admitted; however, this is still limited by a fundamentally defective historical vision.

64. See "Jerusalem and Athens," infra, 399. Strauss, from his youth, was unable to conceal from himself as a Jew his doubts about Germany, which did not move him to loyalty, knowing as well as he did how powerfully anti-Semitism ran wild in the hidden and not so hidden regions of post-1918 Germany, expressing itself most plainly in its growing legitimacy among the intellectuals and the professors.

65. See "Preface to *Spinoza's Critique of Religion*," infra, 154, 170–71.

66. Strauss shows most succinctly in his critique of Cohen his awareness of the need for the greater radicalism in theory than Cohen could muster, paradoxically combined with a greater conservatism in practice than Cohen could affirm, and the need to be able to distinguish between the two in thinking: "Is the conservatism which is generally speaking the wise maxim of practice also the sacred law of theory?" See "Preface to *Spinoza's Critique of Religion*," infra, 166.

67. See esp. "Introductory Essay to Hermann Cohen, *Religion of Reason*," infra, 267–72.

68. *Philosophie und Gesetz*, 33, 38–39; *Philosophy and Law*, 44–45, 49–51.

69. See "Introductory Essay to Hermann Cohen, *Religion of Reason*," infra, 267–69.

70. According to Strauss, Franz Rosenzweig "is thought to be the greatest Jewish thinker" produced by German Jewry, a judgment which by his wording he seems to raise doubts about. See "Preface to *Spinoza's Critique of Religion*," infra, 147.

71. "Preface to *Spinoza's Critique of Religion*," infra, 146.

72. "Preface to *Spinoza's Critique of Religion*," infra, 151–54, for Rosenzweig as compared with Maimonides by Strauss. Those aspects of Rosenzweig's thought which are treated in Strauss's critique embrace: its supposedly "empirical," but actually dogmatic, point of departure in "Israel" rather than in "Torah," yet for Strauss and the old thinking, what is actually "primary or authoritative" for Jewish *experience* is "Torah," while "Israel" is merely "the primary condition of [its] possibility"; its revitalized method of biblical interpretation, which however he regards as enmeshed in historicism; its accepting the need for a "principle of selection" in regard to the "traditional beliefs and rules," which refers itself to "a force" possessed by each Jewish person, which he observes is only possible in "the conditions of modern 'individualism'"; its determined stance against "orthodox austerity or sternness" concerning the Law, which in Strauss's view may however be shallower than the orthodox view as regards "the power of evil in man"; and its often doubting attitude toward miracles, which he believes does not sufficiently reckon with God's omnipotence. See also Michael L. Morgan, "The Curse of Historicity: The Role of History in Leo Strauss's Jewish Thought," *Journal of Religion* 61 (1981): 345–63; idem, *Dilemmas in Modern Jewish Thought* (Bloomington: Indiana University Press, 1992), 40–54.

73. The crisis of contemporary Western man derives from the liberal promise to offer through modern reason, liberal democracy, science, and technology the final solution to all fundamental human problems. If things were not yet perfect (whether in 1789, 1848, 1917, 1939, or the present), then it was believed "progress" would guarantee that this would eventually be brought about. But Strauss carefully analyzed what the notion of "progress" implies, and how it stands in the present. Thus, as Strauss succinctly indicates, in the very "progress" of modern reason and universal homogeneous civilization, its faith in itself as a force of absolute good for man gradually fails and eventually collapses due to both irrationalist philosophical developments and the events of history revealing the dubious benevolence in the modern human self-assertion against nature. Strauss speaks of "the self-destruction of rational philosophy" in our day. Modern rationalism, as Jews adapted the Jewish tradition to it, not only leaves Judaism more exposed to attack by its opponents for its suprarational claims, but also leaves it appearing less inspired than medieval or premodern philosophy ever did in its happy adaptation to such philosophy. See *Philosophie und Gesetz*, 21–22; *Philosophy and Law*, 31–33; "Preface to *Spinoza's Critique of Religion*," infra, 143–54, 172.

74. See "Progress or Return?," infra, 100.

75. Indeed, according to Strauss, even in the collapse of modern rationalism through "the victory of orthodoxy" or irrationalist philosophy, its virtual antipode, Judaism is not actually helped, as Rosenzweig especially would have us believe. See *Philosophie und Gesetz*, p. 9 note 1; *Philosophy and Law*, p. 135 note

1: "'Irrationalism' is but a variety [*Spielart*] of modern rationalism, which is itself already 'irrational' enough." For Strauss's comments about Mendelssohn's modern Jewish "rationalist" theology in relation to the history of modern philosophy, see *Moses Mendelssohn, Gesammelte Schriften: Jubiläumsausgabe*, volume 3, part 2, pp. lx–lxx, cxvi–cx. See also the Translator's Introduction, *Philosophy and Law*, translated by Eve Adler (Albany: State University of New York Press, 1995), 1–4.

76. It might be asked, is not to "pass beyond" reason also to contradict it? Does reason itself ever distinguish between "suprarational" and "irrational" truths? As it might seem, either a proposition is defensible in terms of reason or it is not, in which case it is not "suprarational" but "irrational." Such might seem to be the Platonic or classical rationalist critique of the possible truth contained in religious propositions as derived from the *Euthryphro*. In response to this, I would argue that Strauss was deeply impressed by Maimonides' pivotal discussion in the *Guide* of the creation versus the eternity of the universe. First, the Hebrew biblical (or monotheistic) challenge to philosophy is fundamentally and radically different from the challenge of Greek (or any pagan) piety— if only because in its articulate and defensible metaphysical claims, philosophy meets a true rival. Second, in matters of physics and metaphysics, rather than morals (which the *Euthyphro* focuses its attention on), the philosophers cannot demonstrate which is *the* true rational and which is *the* irrational position. This lends greater "rational" credence and plausibility to the religious (or so-called irrational) position. For some passing remarks by Strauss on the *Euthyphro* and monotheism, see "On the *Euthyphron*," in *The Rebirth of Classical Political Rationalism*, 202, 206. Also see "Progress or Return?," infra, 127–28.

77. See "Preface to *Spinoza's Critique of Religion*," infra, 172, along with *Spinoza's Critique of Religion*, 170–71, 169; *Philosophie und Gesetz*, 54–55; *Philosophy and Law*, 65–67; "How to Begin to Study *The Guide of the Perplexed*," in Moses Maimonides, *The Guide of the Perplexed*, translated by Shlomo Pines (Chicago: University of Chicago Press, 1963), p. xxii; "Jerusalem and Athens," infra, 382, 396; see also the *Guide* itself, 2.11 and 3.31. Maimonides also favored this verse, and his two uses of it in the *Guide* (just cited) suggest that it resonates the same as it did for Strauss: once to defend the compatibility of the Torah with the pure sciences, physics and astronomy, and once to defend the rationality and usefulness of the laws in the Torah.

78. On the relation between Rosenzweig's and Heidegger's thought, see the still definitive essay by Karl Löwith, an essay which Strauss himself recommends: "M. Heidegger and F. Rosenzweig: A Postscript to *Being and Time*," in *Nature, History, and Existentialism*, edited by Arnold Levison (Evanston, Ill.: Northwestern University Press, 1966), 51–78; idem, "M. Heidegger and F. Rosenzweig, or Temporality and Eternity," *Philosophy and Phenomenological Research* 3 (1943): 53–77.

79. See "Preface to *Spinoza's Critique of Religion*," infra, 146–51, 172–73. As Strauss concludes: "Considerations of this kind seemed to decide the issue in

favor of Rosenzweig's understanding of the new thinking, or in favor of the unqualified return to biblical revelation." Strauss makes the further point about Heidegger that "in this most important respect he is much more Christian than Nietzsche"; he also speaks about "the Christianity without God which . . . limits Heidegger's perspective." *What Is Political Philosophy?*, 252.

80. See "Letter to the Editor: The State of Israel," infra, 414, in which Strauss speaks of a simple moral truth about Zionism:

> . . . the founder of Zionism, Herzl, was fundamentally a conserva- tive man, guided in his Zionism by conservative considerations. . . . I can never forget what it achieved as a moral force in an era of complete dissolution. It helped to stem the tide of "progressive" leveling of venerable, ancestral differences; it fulfilled a conserva- tive function.

He also says Zionism, through the establishment of the state of Israel, "pro- cured a blessing for all Jews everywhere regardless of whether they admit it or not." See "Preface to *Spinoza's Critique of Religion*," infra, 142. Yet as Strauss views the matter, secular political Zionism in spite of its being "an act or a progress of Jewish assimilation" also acts unwittingly to preserve Judaism as a separate religious tradition precisely by its simple "reassertion of the differ- ence between Jews and non-Jews." (See "Why We Remain Jews," infra, 326.) It is enlightening in this context to contrast the attitude of Strauss toward Zionism and the state of Israel with that of his Jewish friends Alexandre Kojève and Isaiah Berlin. In terms of their attitudes toward what it means to be a philoso- pher, Strauss was much closer to Kojève; in terms of their attitudes toward what it means to be a Jew, Strauss was much closer to Berlin. Kojève was an atheist Hegelian attached to a vision of the "universal and homogeneous state" as *the* absolute "end of history"; perhaps as a logical consequence, he was what one might call a thoroughly "assimilated" Western Jew. Berlin defines himself as a "pluralist" liberal; yet notwithstanding that, he has been able to remain a firmly convinced Zionist. Berlin recalls that he once discussed the future of the Jews with Kojève; in this discussion, Strauss would undoubtedly have been in an unqualified sympathy with the argument of Berlin. The following repro- duces this discussion as it is recalled by Berlin. Kojève: "The Jews have the most interesting history of any people. Yet now they want to be what? Albania? How can they?" Berlin: "For the Jews to be like Albania constitutes progress. Some 600,000 Jews in Rumania were trapped like sheep to be slaughtered by the Nazis and their local allies. A good many escaped. But 600,000 Jews in Palestine did not leave because Rommel was at their door. That is the difference. They considered Palestine to be their own country, and if they had to die, they would die not like trapped animals, but for their own country." See *Conversations with Isaiah Berlin*, ed. Ramin Jahanbegloo (London: Orion, 1993), p. 86; see also pp. 19–22, 81–88, 99–106, 119–24. Yet Berlin also criticized Strauss's argument for a rationally-grounded adherence to "eternal truths" and "absolute values." In Berlin's view, this argument actually requires that Strauss make the wildly improbable claim to possess the "magical" faculty of a "metaphysical eye." See ibid., 31–33, 108–9. Strauss made a critical assessment of Berlin's book, *Two Concepts of Liberty* (1958). Strauss regarded the book not as a solution, but rather as a manifestation, of the problem of modern freedom and its standard contemporary defense, or as "a characteristic document of the crisis of liberalism." This crisis of liberalism "is due to the fact that [it] has abandoned its absolutist basis and is trying to become entirely relativistic." In Strauss's view, the fatal flaw in Berlin's argument arises in essence from his already compromised aim, which is to establish "an impossible middle ground between relativism and absolutism." See "Relativism," in *Relativism and the Study of Man*, eds. Helmut Schoeck and J. W. Wiggins (Princeton: Van Nostrand, 1961), 135–57.

81. However "problematic" Strauss knew this political analysis to be, he acknowledged that Herzl was perhaps the first affirmative Jewish thinker ever to take the "low" seriously, and to give it its full due with all possible clarity, rather than viewing it in what Herzl regarded as the distorting light of the "high." But as Strauss knew, Herzl himself did not disregard or deny the actuality and compelling power of the "high" in political action, especially if limited to the noble. For Strauss's own mature (though brief) statement on the proper relations between the "high" and the "low," see "Preface to *Spinoza's Critique of Religion*," infra, 138. See also *Natural Right and History* (Chicago: University of Chicago Press, 1971), 128–29.

82. Strauss's clearest statement on the limits of liberal democracy, which political option still offers the Jews their best hope, but must be supplemented by Zionism, is in "Preface to *Spinoza's Critique of Religion*," infra, 142–44. His view is perhaps best summarized in the following statement:

> Finite, relative problems can be solved; infinite, absolute problems cannot be solved. In other words, human beings will never create a society which is free from contradictions. From every point of view it looks as if the Jewish people were the chosen people, at least in the sense that the Jewish problem is the most manifest symbol of the human problem insofar as it is a social or political problem.

83. "Our worst enemies are called (since I do not know how many years) 'anti-Semites,' a word which I shall never use, and which I regard as almost obscene. I think that if we are sensible we abolish it from our usage. I said in a former speech here that it was coined by some German or French pedant: I smelled them. But then I learned, a few weeks ago, that it was coined by a German pedant, a fellow called Marr. The reason he coined it was very simple. 'Anti-Semitism' means hatred of Jews. Why not call it as we Jews call it? It is *rish'us*, 'viciousness.' 'Hatred of Jews' is perfectly intelligible." See "Why We Remain Jews," infra, 320.

84. This does not mean that Strauss read Herzl too much in the light of Ahad Ha'am; he knew about Herzl's penchant for Jews speaking the German

language and for their duty to cultivate the opera. But he also acknowledged as integral to Herzl's vision the desire to establish a Jewish national culture, however defective may have been his final vision of it.

85. See "Letter to the Editor: The State of Israel," infra, 414. The phrase "external freedom and inner servitude" is borrowed from the title of a famous essay by Aḥad Ha'am. It is discussed in somewhat greater detail by Strauss, "Why We Remain Jews," infra, 341.

86. As Strauss notes, modern Zionism assumes no traditional Jewish messianic posture: it neither "waits" for the messiah, nor does it hope by force to restore the Davidic kingdom in order to rebuild the third temple.

87. "Preface to Spinoza's Critique of Religion," infra, 142–43.

88. Philosophie und Gesetz, 28; Philosophy and Law, 38.

89. The two areas in which Zionism would seem to reach a superior position to Maimonides, precisely because it is modern, would consist of the following two issues. First, is Maimonides not the advocate of the priestly city, or the rule of priests, which it had been the aim of Machiavelli to delegitimate? See Thoughts on Machiavelli, 184–85, as well as "Marsilius of Padua," in History of Political Philosophy 2d ed. (Chicago: University of Chicago Press, 1963), 252–57, which show Strauss's doubts about drawing any such conclusions about Maimonides' true views. Second, is Maimonides not guilty of fostering those attitudes which make for that supposed "effeminacy" of the Jewish religious mind, as this was mocked by Spinoza with the aim in mind of subverting such attitudes on which it was based, in which Jews are not compelled to control their own fate by force of arms and cunning, and hence to embrace a warlike spirit? But see also: The City and Man (Chicago: University of Chicago Press, 1964), 33–34; Thoughts on Machiavelli, 176–231, 82; "The Literary Character of The Guide of the Perplexed," in Persecution and the Art of Writing (Glencoe, Ill.: Free Press, 1952), p. 91 note 156; "Maimonides' Statement on Political Science," in What Is Political Philosophy?, 157–58; and "Note on Maimonides' Letter on Astrology," in Studies in Platonic Political Philosophy, 207, which again show Strauss's doubts about drawing any such conclusions about Maimonides' true views.

90. As Strauss learned, the political was just as encompassing for Maimonides as it was for modern political Zionism, but he was able to transcend its limited political vision of Jewish life toward theology and philosophy. In the spirit of modern political Zionism, Maimonides attributed the loss of the ancient Jewish kingdom to purely natural "political" causes—the Jews turned to a preoccupation with "idolatrous" astrology, and neglected to learn the arts of war and conquest, an analysis by which Strauss was most impressed—but he was able to see even these political matters in a higher light. For Maimonides, the purpose of Jewish political return led by the King Messiah, whose qualifications for such a title would be measured by his political-military

success since his failure in battle would mean he is not the Messiah, was not just to end the oppression of the Jews by the Gentiles, but to make possible a society in which the study of the Torah, and the knowledge of God, would be plentiful and accessible to most members of society, and would inform and excite its spirit. See "Note on Maimonides' *Letter on Astrology*," in *Studies in Platonic Political Philosophy*, 101–3; *On Tyranny* (rev.), 183–84.

91. Perhaps only a certain type of philosopher or a certain type of Zionist could be satisfied with such a rationalistic argument for the "political" necessity of obedience to Jewish law. Even for Maimonides, it is not enough to secure his loyalty to the Jewish tradition, which as he knew also claims to teach *the* highest truth just as much as does philosophy, and surely in opposition to it on specific points. Even if Judaism amazes by its rationality as a religion, and even if Jewish law can be shown to command adherence to nothing plainly irrational, must the philosopher not need to reject everything which Judaism still teaches in opposition to philosophy? If compared with modern Jewish thought, then, this is the point at which there is a conflict between Cohen and Rosenzweig.

92. If this is so in Maimonides' view of Judaism, then it means that he accepts the sufficiency and autonomy of human reason to potentially know everything there is which it is essential or important to know in speculative truth (i.e., matters physical and metaphysical), and to determine what things are essential or important to know, as well as able to articulate rationally and definitively what is morally imperative or what needs to be done in human life.

93. This phrase is used by Aḥad Ha'am to characterize Maimonides' position in Judaism, and I would say that for Strauss it is correct as far as it goes. But Aḥad Ha'am does not grasp the political dimension (or the "esotericism") of Maimonides' "supreme rationality" as well as does Strauss. As a result, he cannot come to a conclusion about strange aspects of the *Guide* which strike him, but do not accord with what he thinks Maimonides should think.

94. Indeed, such are the limits of reason in the production of a truly compelling and sanctioned morality that this may be the only "genuine" moral code known to man in history. The omnipotent God, who created the world from nothing with His absolutely binding will, can alone reveal to man a Ten Commandments, so as to make them the morally supreme code. The philosopher can merely advise or suggest, he cannot command, because with regard to specific actions he does not and cannot know rationally of categorical imperatives. Strauss obviously believed Maimonides achieved by a theological argument what Cohen could not achieve by pure modern critical reason. See my "Religion, Philosophy, and Morality: How Leo Strauss Read Judah Halevi's *Kuzari*," in *Journal of the American Academy of Religion* 61, no. 2 (Summer 1993): 225–73. See also "Progress or Return?," infra, 108–10.

95. See Maimonides, *Introduction to the Talmud*, chapter 8, "The Gemara," in which he asks the "parenthetical" question why the two most essential and

unchangeable types of human beings need to exist? Curiously, his answer unites two quite disparate reasons: to meet the requirements for the difficult production of the most perfect human individual; and to alleviate the burden of loneliness for even the most perfect individual.

96. To illustrate why the conflict is fundamental: Strauss refers to the ambiguity about what the Hebrew Bible teaches concerning especially creation out of nothing, as is known to everyone who studies the text honestly. Yet Maimonides apparently makes a cardinal point of precisely creation out of nothing. Perhaps his reasons for doing so were related more to an exigency arising from the cause of the defense of morality previously discussed, and less to the dictates of conveying the best or most complete textual interpretation which he usually obeyed—which, if he does so, is a rare lapse, but one to which a careful reader is pointed by Maimonides himself! Strauss makes the following statement:

> Now I do not deny that a man can believe in God without believing in creation, and particularly without believing in creation out of nothing. After all, the Bible itself does not explicitly teach creation out of nothing, as one might see. But still, Judaism contains the whole notion of man's responsibility and of a final redemption. . . . But the very notion of the certainty of final redemption is untenable without belief in a God concerned with justice—and this is such a most important issue. ("Why We Remain Jews," infra, 344–45)

97. See "Why We Remain Jews," infra, 328–29, 343–45; "Progress or Return?," infra, 87–94; "Preface to *Spinoza's Critique of Religion*," infra, 144, 154, 170; "Jerusalem and Athens," infra, 380.

98. "Jerusalem and Athens," infra, 381.

99. See "Why We Remain Jews," infra, 345. The "creative genius of the Jewish people" is a notion used by several modern Jewish thinkers, both religious and secular, from Abraham Geiger to Ahad Ha'am, to account in a modern form for aspects of traditional Jewish theology. In this passage, it seems that Strauss was concerned with its radical use as a substitute for belief in God especially by cultural Zionism. For a similar comment by his friend Scholem:

> I would venture to say that it is no great distance from such a subjective [existentialist] conception, which transplants Revelation into the human heart, to a secular-humanist conception, as is perhaps most readily apparent in Ahad Ha'am. Here some profane, more or less romantic or pragmatic categories such as the *Volksgeist* (genius of the people), assume the place of ethical-religious authority. As a former follower of Ahad Ha'am, I have no illusions regarding the weakness of humanistic foundations for religious statements, in which God can show up at best as a fiction, though perhaps as a necessary one.

("Reflections on Jewish Theology," in *On Jews and Judaism in Crisis*, 261–97, edited by Werner Dannhauser [New York: Schocken, 1976], and esp. pp. 274–75)

See also "Why We Remain Jews," infra, 343–45. As for the Jewish mystics in relation to Maimonides, Scholem acknowledges (based on the research of Strauss) that the rigorous "esotericism" of the Kabbala was borrowed or learned from Maimonides, especially as this appeared in the generations immediately subsequent to Maimonides—which seems to encompass the author of the Zohar, Moses de Leon. See Gershom Scholem, *On the Kabbala and Its Symbolism* (New York: Schocken, 1965), 50–51.

100. "Jerusalem and Athens," infra, 381–82; "Preface to *Spinoza's Critique of Religion*," infra, 173.

101. Ibid., infra, 172.

I

Essays in Modern Jewish Thought

1

Progress or Return?
The Contemporary Crisis
in Western Civilization

The title of this lecture indicates that progress has become a problem—that it could seem as if progress has led us to the brink of an abyss, and it is therefore necessary to consider alternatives to it. For example, to stop where we are, or else, if this should be impossible, to return. "Return" is the translation for the Hebrew word *teshuva*. *Teshuva* has an ordinary and an emphatic meaning. Its emphatic meaning is rendered in English by "repentance." Repentance is return, meaning the return from the wrong way to the right one. This implies that we were once on the right way before we turned to the wrong way. Originally we were on the right way; deviation or sin or imperfection is not original. Man is originally at home in his father's house. He becomes a stranger through estrangement, through sinful estrangement. Repentance, return, is homecoming.

I remind you of a few verses from the first chapter of Isaiah: "How is the faithful city become a harlot. It was full of judgment, righteousness lodged in it. But now murderers. . . . Therefore, saith the Lord . . . I will restore thy judges as at the first and thy counselors as at the beginning. Afterwards thou shalt be called the city of righteousness, the faithful city."[1] Repentance is return; redemption is restoration. A perfect beginning—the faithful city—is followed by defection, decline, sin; and this is followed by a perfect end. But the perfect end is the restoration of the perfect beginning: the faithful city at the beginning and at the end. At the beginning, men did not roam a forest left to themselves, unprotected and unguided. The beginning is the garden of Eden. Perfection results in the beginning—in the beginning of time, the oldest time. Hence perfection is sought derivatively in the old time—in the father, the father of fathers, the patriarchs. The patriarchs are the divine chariot which Ezekiel had seen in his vision.[2] The great time—the classic time—is in the past: first the period of the desert; later the period of the temple. The life of the Jew is the life of recollection. It is at the same time a life of anticipation, of hope, but the hope for redemption is restoration—*restituto in integro*. In the words of Jeremiah: "Their children shall be as aforetime."[3] Redemption consists in the return of the youngest, the most remote from the past, the most future ones, so to speak, to the pristine condition. The past is superior to the present. This thought is, then, perfectly compatible with hope for the future. But does the hope for redemption—the expectation of the Messiah—not assign a much higher place to the future than to the past, however venerable?

This is not unqualifiedly true. According to the most accepted view, the Messiah is inferior to Moses.[4] The messianic age will witness the restoration of the full practice of the Torah, part of which was discontinued owing to the destruction of the temple. Belief in the Torah was always the way in Judaism, whereas messianism frequently became dormant. For example, as I learn from Gershom Scholem, Kabbala prior to the sixteenth century concentrated upon the beginning; it was only with Isaac Luria that Kabbala began to concentrate upon the future—upon the end. Yet even here, the last age became as important as the first. It did not become more important. Furthermore (I quote Scholem), "by inclination and habit, Luria was decidedly conservative. This tendency is well expressed in persistent attempts to relate what he had to say to older authorities." For Luria, "salvation means actually nothing but restitution, reintegration of the original whole, or *tikkun*, to use the Hebrew term. . . . For Luria, the appearance of the Messiah is nothing but the consummation of the continuous process of restoration. . . . The path to the end of all things is also the path to the beginning."[5] Judaism is a concern with return; it is not a concern with progress. "Return" can easily be expressed in biblical Hebrew; "progress" cannot. Hebrew renderings of progress seem to be somehow artificial, not to say paradoxical.[6] Even if it were true that messianism bespeaks the predominance of the concern with the future, or of living toward the future, this would not affect in any way the belief in the superiority of the past to the present. The fact that the present is nearer in time to the final redemption than is the past does not mean, of course, that the present is superior in piety or wisdom to the past, especially to the classic past.

Today the word *teshuva* has acquired a still more emphatic meaning. Today, *teshuva* sometimes means, not a return which takes place within Judaism, but a return to Judaism on the part of many Jews who, or whose fathers, had broken with Judaism as a whole. That abandonment of Judaism—that break with Judaism—did not understand itself, of course, as a defection or desertion, as leaving the right way; nor did it understand itself as a return to a truth which the Jewish tradition in its turn had deserted; nor even merely a turn to something superior. It understood itself as progress. It granted to the Jewish tradition, as it were, that Judaism is old, very old, whereas it itself had no past of which it could boast. But it regarded this very fact, the antiquity of Judaism, as a proof of its own superiority and of Judaism's inadequacy. For it questioned the very premise underlying the notion of return, that premise being the perfect character of the beginning and of the olden times. It assumed that the beginning is most imperfect and that perfection can be found only in the end—so much so that the movement from the beginning toward the end is in principle a progress from radical imperfection toward perfection. From this point of view, age did not have any claim whatsoever to veneration. Antiquity rather deserved contempt, or possibly contempt mitigated by pity.

Let us try to clarify this issue somewhat more fully by contrasting the life characterized by the idea of return with the life characterized by the idea of progress. When the prophets call their people to account, they do not limit themselves to accusing them of this or that particular crime or sin. They recognize the root of all particular crimes in the fact that the people have forsaken their God. They accuse their people of rebellion. Originally, in the past, they were faithful or loyal; now they are in a state of rebellion. In the future they will return, and God will restore them to their original place. The primary, original, initial is loyalty; unfaithfulness, infidelity, is secondary. The very notion of unfaithfulness or infidelity presupposes that fidelity or loyalty is primary. The perfect character of the origin is a condition of sin—of the thought of sin. Man who understands himself in this way longs for the perfection of the origin, or of the classic past. He suffers from the present; he hopes for the future.

Progressive man, on the other hand, looks back to a most imperfect beginning. The beginning is barbarism, stupidity, rudeness, extreme scarcity. Progressive man does not feel that he has lost something of great, not to say infinite, importance; he has lost only his chains. He does not suffer from the recollection of the past. Looking back to the past, he is proud of his achievements; he is certain of the superiority of the present to the past. He is not satisfied with the present; he looks to future progress. But he does not merely hope or pray for a better future; he thinks that he can bring it about by his own effort. Seeking perfection in a future which is in no sense the beginning or the restoration of the beginning, he lives unqualifiedly toward the future. The life which understands itself as a life of loyalty or faithfulness appears to him as backward, as being under the spell of old prejudices. What the others call rebellion, he calls revolution or liberation. To the polarity faithfulness-rebellion, he opposes the polarity prejudice-freedom.

To repeat, the return to Judaism succeeds a break with Judaism which eventually, or from the beginning, understood itself as a progress beyond Judaism. That break was effected in a classic manner by a solitary man—Spinoza. Spinoza denied the truth of Judaism: Judaism, which includes, of course, the Bible, is a set of prejudices and superstitious practices of the ancient tribes. Spinoza found in this mass of heterogeneous lore some elements of truth, but he did not consider this as peculiar to Judaism. He found the same elements of truth in paganism as well. Spinoza was excommunicated by the Jewish community in Amsterdam. He ceased to regard himself as a Jew. He has sometimes been accused of having been hostile to Judaism and to Jews. I do not find that he was more opposed to Judaism than to Christianity, for example, and I do not find that he was hostile to Jews. He acquired a strange, or perhaps not so strange, neutrality in regard to the secular conflict between Judaism and Christianity. Looking at the Jews and the Jewish fate from this neutral point of view, he even made some suggestions as to the redemption of the Jews. One suggestion is almost explicit. After having asserted that the Jews have not been elected in any other sense than that in which the Canaanites too had been elected earlier, and that therefore the Jews have not been elected for eternity, he tries to show that their survival after the loss of the land can be explained in a perfectly natural manner. In this context, he makes the following remark: "If the foundations of their religion did not effeminate their minds, I would absolutely believe that they might again restore their state, under auspicious circumstances, considering the fact that human things are mutable."[7] This means that the hope for divine redemption is altogether baseless. The sufferings of the exiles are altogether meaningless. There is no guarantee whatsoever that these sufferings will ever cease. But the first condition of entertaining any reasonable hope for the end of the exile is that the Jews should get rid of the foundations of their religion, that is to say, of the spirit of Judaism. For that spirit, Spinoza thought, is adverse to warlike enterprise and to the energy of government. As far as I know, this is the earliest suggestion of a purely political solution to the Jewish problem—the substitution of a purely political solution for the miracle of redemption toward which men can contribute, if at all, only by a life of piety. It is the first inkling of unqualifiedly political Zionism. But Spinoza intimated still another solution. In his *Theologico-Political Treatise*, he sketches the outline of what he regarded as a decent society. That society, as described by him, can be characterized as a liberal democracy. Incidentally, Spinoza may be said to be the first philosopher who advocated liberal democracy. Spinoza still regarded it as necessary to underwrite liberal democracy with a public religion or a state religion. Now, it is very remarkable that that religion, that state religion, which is emphatically not a religion of reason, is neither Christian nor Jewish. It is neutral in regard to the differences between Judaism and Christianity. Furthermore, Spinoza claims to have proved, on the basis of the Bible, that the Mosaic law was binding only for the period of the Jewish commonwealth. If one considers these two facts, first, that the state religion is neutral in regard to the differences between Judaism and Christianity, and second, that the Mosaic law is no longer binding, one is entitled to say that Spinoza laid the foundation for another purely political solution of the Jewish problem. In fact, he laid the foundation for the alternative to political Zionism, the solution known as assimilationism.

In Spinoza's liberal democracy, Jews do not have to become baptized in order to acquire full citizen rights. It is sufficient if they accept the extremely latitudinarian state religion, and they may then forget about the Mosaic law. In this neutral atmosphere, the sufferings of the exiles could be expected to wither away. Spinoza has merely intimated the two classical alternatives which followed from the radical break with Judaism. The practical consequences were fully developed in the course of the nineteenth century. But when they were exposed to the test of practice, they led into certain difficulties.

On the premise of assimilationism, Jewish suffering—suffering for Judaism—becomes meaningless. That suffering is merely the residue of a benighted past, a residue which will cease in proportion as mankind makes further progress. But the results were somewhat disappointing. The decrease of the power of Christianity did not bring about the expected decrease of anti-Jewish feeling. Even where legal equality of the Jews became a fact, it contrasted all the more strongly with the social inequality which continued. In a number of countries, legal inequality and the cruder forms of social inequality gave way to subtler forms of social inequality, but the social inequality did not for this reason become less of a hardship. On the contrary, sensitivity increased with social ascent. Our ancestors had been immune to hatred and contempt because it merely proved to them the election of Israel. The uprooted assimilated Jew had nothing to oppose to hatred and contempt except his naked self. Full social equality proved to require the complete disappearance of the Jews as Jews—a proposition which is impracticable, if for no other reason, then at least for the perfectly sufficient one of simple self-respect. Why should we, who have a heroic past behind and within us, which is not second to that of any other group anywhere on earth, deny or forget that past? That past is all the more heroic, one could say, since its chief characters are not the glitter and trappings of martial glory and of cultural splendor, although it does not lack even these. Assimilation proved to require inner enslavement as the price of external freedom. Or, to put it somewhat differently, assimilationism seemed to land the Jews into the bog of philistinism, of shallow satisfaction with the most unsatisfactory present—a most inglorious end for a people which had been led out of the house of bondage into the desert with careful avoidance of the land of the Philistines. To quote the words of the Torah: "And it came to pass when Pharaoh had let the people go, that God led them not through the way of the land of the Philistines, although that was near."[8] It is always near. Once progress was indeed achieved, hatred of the Jews could no longer present itself among educated or half-educated people as hatred of the Jews. It had to disguise itself as "anti-Semitism," a term invented by some bashful German or French pedant of the nineteenth century. It is certainly a most improper term. The shock administered by the continued existence of social inequality and by the emergence of anti-Semitism, especially in Germany and France, proved to be a fair warning for what was going to happen in Germany, especially between 1933 and 1945.

Those European Jews who realized that assimilation was no solution to the Jewish problem and looked out for another purely human or political solution turned to political Zionism. But political Zionism led to difficulties of its own. The basic idea underlying purely political Zionism was not Zionist at all. It could have been satisfied by a Jewish state anywhere on earth. Political Zionism was already a concession to the Jewish tradition. Those who were seeking a solution of the Jewish problem other than the disappearance of the Jews had to accept not only the territory hallowed by Jewish tradition but its language, Hebrew, as well. They were forced to accept, furthermore, Jewish culture. "Cultural Zionism" became a very powerful rival of political Zionism. But the heritage to which cultural Zionism had recourse rebelled against being interpreted in terms of "culture" or "civilization," meaning, as an autonomous product of the genius of the Jewish people. That culture or civilization had its core in the Torah, and the Torah presents itself as given by God, not created by Israel. Thus the attempts to solve the Jewish problem by purely human means ended in failure. The knot which was not tied by man could not be untied by man. I do not believe that the American experience forces us to qualify these statements. It is very far from me to minimize the difference between a nation conceived in liberty and dedicated to the proposition that all men are created equal, and the nations of the old world, which certainly were not conceived in liberty. I share the hope in America and the faith in America, but I am compelled to add that that faith and that hope cannot be of the same character as that faith and that hope which a Jew has in regard to Judaism and which the Christian has in regard to Christianity. No one claims that the faith in America and the hope for America is based on explicit divine promises.

The attempt to "solve the Jewish problem" has failed because of the overwhelming power of the past. The experience of that power is part of what is sometimes called the discovery of history. The discovery was made in the nineteenth century. As a discovery, it consisted in the realization of something which was not realized previously: that the acceptance of the past or the return to the Jewish tradition is something radically different from a mere continuation of that tradition. It is quite true that Jewish life in the past was almost always more than a continuation of a tradition. Very great changes within that tradition have taken place in the course of the centuries. But it is also true that the change which we are witnessing today, and which all of us are participating in, is—in one way or the other—qualitatively different from all previous changes within Judaism.

Let me try to clarify that difference. Those who today return to Judaism do not assert that, say, Spinoza was altogether wrong. They accept at least the principle of that biblical criticism which was regarded as the major offense of Spinoza. Generally speaking, those who today return to Judaism admit that modern rationalism, to use this vague term, had a number of important insights which cannot be thrown overboard and which were alien to the Jewish tradition. Therefore, they modify the Jewish tradition consciously. You only have to contrast that with the procedure of Maimonides in the twelfth century, who, when introducing Aristotelian philosophy into Judaism, had to assume that he was merely recovering Israel's own lost inheritance. These present-day Jews who return to the tradition try to do in the element of reflection what traditionally was done unconsciously or naively. Their attitude is historical rather than traditional. They study the thought of the past as thought of the past and therefore as not necessarily binding on the present generation as it stands. But still, what they are doing is meant to be a return—that is to say, the acceptance of something which was equally accepted by the Jewish tradition. Thus the question arises as to the relative importance of these two elements: the new element and the unchanged element, the new element being the fact that present-day

Judaism is forced to be what has been called "postcritical." Are we wiser than our ancestors in the decisive respect or only in a subordinate respect? In the first case, we still would have to claim that we have made decisive progress. But if the insights implied in the "postcritical" character of present-day Judaism are only of a subordinate character, the movement which we are witnessing can justly claim to be a return. Now, this movement of return would not have had the effect which it has had, but for the fact that, not only among Jews but throughout the Western world more generally, progress has become a matter of doubt. The term "progress" in its full and emphatic meaning has practically disappeared from serious literature. People speak less and less of "progress" and more and more of "change." They no longer claim to know that we are moving in the right direction. Not progress, but the "belief" in progress, or the "idea" of progress as a social or historical phenomenon, is a major theme for the present-day student of society. A generation or so ago, the most famous study on this subject was entitled *The Idea of Progress.*[9] Its opposite number in present-day literature is entitled *The Belief in Progress.*[10] The substitution of belief for idea is in itself worthy of note. Now, to understand the crisis of the belief in progress, we must first clarify the content of that belief.

What is progress? Now progress, in the emphatic sense, presupposes that there is something which is simply good, or the end, as the goal of progress. Progress is change in the direction of the end. But this is only the necessary, not the sufficient, condition of the idea of progress. A sign of this is the notion of the Golden Age, which also presupposes a notion of the simply good; but that simply good, that end, is here located in the beginning. The end of man, the simply good, must be understood in a specific manner if it is to become the basis of the idea of progress. I suggest that the end of man must be understood primarily as perfection of the understanding in such a manner that the perfection of the understanding is somehow akin to the arts and crafts. It has always been controversial whether man's beginning was perfect or imperfect, but both parties to the controversy admitted that the arts and the crafts, and certainly their perfection, do not belong to man's beginning. Therefore, to decide the question of progress, disregarding the perfection or imperfection of man's beginning, depends upon how the question of the value of the arts and crafts is decided. At any rate, the idea of progress presupposes that there is the simply good life and that the beginning of life is radically imperfect. Accordingly, we find in Greek science or philosophy a full consciousness of progress: in the first place, of progress achieved, and its inevitable concomitant, looking down on the inferiority or the weakness of the ancients; and as regards future progress, Aristotle himself noted: "In the art of medicine, there is no limit to the pursuit of health, and in the other arts there is no limit to the pursuit of their several ends. For they aim at accomplishing their ends to the uttermost."[11] The possibility of infinite progress, at least in certain respects, is here stated. Yet *the* idea of progress is different from the Greek conception of progress. What is the relative importance of fulfillment, on the one hand, and of future progress, on the other? The most elaborate statements on progress seemed to occur in Lucretius and Seneca, where the possibility of infinite progress in the sciences and arts is clearly stated. Yet Lucretius was an Epicurean, and Seneca was a Stoic, which means they both presupposed that the fundamental issue has been settled already, either by Epicurus or by the Stoa. No future progress, then, in the decisive respect is envisioned. Generally speaking, it seems that in classical thought the decisive questions were thought to have been answered as far as they can be answered. The only exception of which I know is Plato, who held that the fulfillment proper, namely, full wisdom, is not possible, but only quest for wisdom, which in Greek means philosophy. He also insisted that there are no assignable limits to that quest for wisdom, and therefore it follows from Plato's notion that indefinite progress is possible in principle.

Hitherto I have spoken of intellectual progress. What about social progress? Are they parallel? The idea that they are necessarily parallel, or that intellectual progress is accompanied in principle by social progress, was known to the classics. We find there the idea that the art of legislation, which is the overarching social art, progresses like any other art. Yet Aristotle, who reports this doctrine, questions this solution, and he notes the radical difference between laws and arts or intellectual pursuits.[12] More generally stated, or more simply stated, he notes the radical difference between the requirements of social life and the requirements of intellectual life. The paramount requirement of society is stability, as distinguished from progress. If I may summarize this point, in the classical conception of progress, it is clearly admitted that infinite intellectual progress in secondary matters is theoretically possible. But we must add immediately, there is no practical possibility for that. For according to the one school, the visible universe is of finite duration; it has come into being and will perish again. And, according to the other view, which held that the visible universe is eternal, they asserted, especially Aristotle, that there are periodic cataclysms which will destroy all earlier civilization.[13] Hence, eternal recurrence of the same progressive process occurs, followed by decay and destruction.

Now what is lacking in the classical conception as compared to the modern? I see two points. First, there is lacking the notion of a guaranteed parallelism between intellectual and social progress; and secondly, there is no necessary end of the progressive process through telluric or cosmic catastrophes. As to the first point—the guaranteed parallelism between social and intellectual progress—in the classical statements about progress the emphasis is on intellectual progress rather than on social progress. The basic idea can be stated as follows: science or philosophy is the preserve of a small minority, of those who have "good natures," as they called it, or who are "gifted," as we say. Their progress, the progress of this tiny minority, does not necessarily affect society at large—far from it. It was this thought which was radically challenged in the seventeenth century, at the beginning of modern philosophy, and with the introduction of the crucial notion of the idea of method. Method brings about the leveling of the natural differences of the mind, and methods can be learned in principle by everyone. Only discovery remains the preserve of the few. But the acquisition of the results of the discovery, and especially of the discovery of methods, is open to all. And there was a very simple proof: mathematical problems which formerly could not be solved by the greatest mathematical geniuses are now solved by high-school boys; the level of intelligence—that was the conclusion—has enormously been raised; and since this is possible, there is a necessary parallelism between intellectual and social progress.

As for the second point—the guarantee of an infinite future on earth not interrupted by telluric catastrophes—we find this thought fully developed in the eighteenth century. The human race had a beginning but no end, and it began about seven thousand years ago—as you see, that man did not accept the biblical chronology.[14] Hence, since mankind is only seven thousand years old, it is still in its infancy. An infinite future is open, and look what we have achieved in this short span—compared with infinity—of seven thousand years! The decisive point is then this: there is a beginning and no end. Obviously the argument presupposes a beginning; otherwise you cannot figure out this infinite progress. The origin of this idea—a beginning but no end—could perhaps be found in Plato's dialogue *Timaeus*, if one takes that literally.[15] Yet Plato certainly admitted regular telluric catastrophes. The source, I think, has to be found in a certain interpretation of the Bible, which we find, for example, in Maimonides, where you have the beginning—the creation—and no end, and cataclysms are excluded, not by natural necessity, but by the covenant of God with Noah.[16] Yet precisely on the basis of the Bible, the beginning cannot be imperfect. Moreover, such additional important notions as the power of sin and of the need for greater redemption counter the effect of the notion of progress necessarily. Then again, in the Bible the core of the process from the beginning to the end is not progress. There is a classic past, whether we seek it at Mount Sinai or in the patriarchs or wherever else. Furthermore, and quite obviously, the core of the process as presented in the Bible is not intellectual-scientific development. The availability of infinite time for infinite progress appears, then, to be guaranteed by a document of revelation which condemns the other crucial elements of the idea of progress. Progress in the full and emphatic sense of the term is a hybrid notion.

This difficulty explains why the idea of progress underwent a radical modification in the nineteenth century. I quote one specimen:

> Truth . . . can no longer be found in a collection of fixed dogmatic propositions . . . but only in the process of knowing, . . . which process ascends from the lower to ever higher stages. . . . All those stages are only perishable phases in the endless development from the lower to the higher. . . . There is no final absolute truth and no final absolute stage of the development. . . . Nothing is imperishable except the uninterrupted process of becoming and perishing, of the endless ascent from the lower to the higher. . . . We do not have to consider here the question as to whether this view agrees with the present state of natural science, for at present natural science predicts a possible end to the existence of the earth and a certain end to the inhabitability of the earth. Natural science therefore assumes today that human history consists not only of an ascending, but also of a descending, process. However this may be, we are certainly still rather remote from the point where decline begins to set in. . . .

That statement was made by Friedrich Engels, the friend and coworker of Karl Marx.[17] Here we see infinite progress proper is abandoned, but the grave consequences of that are evaded by a wholly incomprehensible and unjustifiable "never mind." This more recent form of the belief in progress is based on the decision just to forget about the end, to forget about eternity.

The contemporary crisis of Western civilization may be said to be identical with the climactic crisis of the idea of progress in the full and emphatic sense of the term. I repeat, that idea consists of the following elements: the development of human thought as a whole is a progressive development; certainly the emergence of modern thought since the seventeenth century marks an unqualified progress beyond all earlier thought. There is a fundamental and necessary parallelism between intellectual and social progress. There are no assignable limits to intellectual and social progress. Infinite intellectual and social progress is actually possible. Once mankind has reached a certain stage of development, there exists a solid floor beneath which man can no longer sink. All these points have become questionable, I believe, to all of us. To mention only one point, perhaps the most massive one, the idea of progress was bound up with the notion of the conquest of nature, of man making himself the master and owner of nature for the purpose of relieving man's estate. The means for that goal was a new science. We all know of the enormous successes of the new science and of the technology which is based on it, and we all can witness the enormous increase of man's power. Modern man is a giant in comparison to earlier man. But we have also to note that there is no corresponding increase in wisdom and goodness. Modern man is a giant of whom we do not know whether he is better or worse than earlier man. More than that, this development of modern science culminated in the view that man is not able to distinguish in a responsible manner between good and evil—the famous "value judgment." Nothing can be said responsibly about the right use of that immense power. Modern man is a blind giant. The doubt of progress led to a crisis of Western civilization as a whole, because in the course of the nineteenth century, the old distinction between good and bad, or good and evil, had been progressively replaced by the distinction between progressive and reactionary. No simple, inflexible, eternal distinction between good and bad could give assurance to those who had learned to take their bearings only by the distinction between progressive and reactionary, as soon as these people had become doubtful of progress.

The substitution of the distinction between progressive and reactionary for the distinction between good and bad is another aspect of the discovery of history, to which I referred before. The discovery of history, to state this very simply, is identical with the substitution of the past or the future for the eternal—the substitution of the temporal for the eternal. Now, to understand this crisis of Western civilization, one cannot leave it at understanding the problematic character of the idea of progress, for the idea of progress is only a part, or an aspect, of a larger whole, of what we shall not hesitate to call modernity. What is modernity? A hard question which cannot be discussed in detail here. However, I would like to offer one or two somewhat rambling considerations. First, one might remember the decisive steps which led up to the contemporary crisis of Western civilization, and to those who are familiar with these things I must apologize for the superficiality of what is now offered in brief; but I think it is important to recall these things nevertheless. Therefore regard this as a stenogram, not as an analysis.

Western civilization has two roots: the Bible and Greek philosophy. Let us begin by looking at the first of these elements, the Bible, the biblical element. Modern rationalism rejected biblical theology and replaced it by such things as deism, pantheism, and atheism. But in this process, biblical morality was in a way preserved. Goodness was still believed to consist in something like justice, benevolence, love, or charity; and modern rationalism has generated a tendency to believe that this biblical morality is better preserved if it is divorced from biblical theology. Now this was, of course, more visible in the nineteenth century than it is today; it is no longer so visible today because one crucial event happened between 1870 and 1880: the appearance of Nietzsche. Nietzsche's criticism can be reduced to one proposition: modern man has been trying to preserve biblical morality while abandoning biblical faith. That is impossible. If the biblical faith goes, biblical morality must go too, and a radically different morality must be accepted. The word which Nietzsche used is "the will to power." Nietzsche meant it in a very subtle and noble manner, yet the crude and ignoble way in which it was later understood is not altogether independent of the radical change of orientation he suggested.

As for the other major component of Western civilization, the classical element, that is, the idea of philosophy or science, that too began to change. In the seventeenth century, a new philosophy and a new science began to emerge. They made the same claims as all earlier philosophy and science had done, but the result of this seventeenth-century revolution produced something which had never existed before—the emergence of Science with a capital S. Originally the attempt had been made to replace traditional philosophy and science by a new philosophy and a new science; but in the course of a few generations it appeared that only a part of the new philosophy and science was successful and, indeed, amazingly successful. No one could question these developments, e.g., Newton. But only a part of the new science or philosophy was successful, and then the great distinction between philosophy and science, which we are all familiar with, came into being. Science is the successful part of modern philosophy or science, and philosophy is the unsuccessful part—the rump. Science is therefore higher in dignity than philosophy. The consequence, which you know, is the depreciation of all knowledge which is not scientific in this peculiar sense. Science becomes the authority for philosophy in a way perfectly comparable to the way in which theology was the authority for philosophy in the Middle Ages. Science is *the* perfection of man's natural understanding of the world. But then, certain things took place in the nineteenth century, e.g., the discovery of non-Euclidean geometry and its use in physics, which made it clear that science cannot be described adequately as the perfection of man's natural understanding of the world, but rather as a radical modification of man's natural understanding of the world. In other words, science is based on certain fundamental hypotheses which, being hypotheses, are not absolutely necessary and which always remain hypothetical. The consequence was again drawn most clearly by Nietzsche: science is only one interpretation of the world among many. The scientific interpretation of the world has certain advantages, but that of course does not give it any ultimately superior cognitive status. The last consequence stated by some men in our age is as you know: modern science is in no way superior to Greek science, as little as modern poetry is superior to Greek poetry. In other words, even science with its enormous prestige—a prestige higher than any other power in the modern world—is also a kind of giant with feet of clay, if you consider its foundations. As a consequence of this chain of scientific development the notion of a rational morality, the heritage of Greek philosophy, has, to repeat myself, lost its standing completely; all choices are, it is argued, ultimately nonrational or irrational.

II

The immediate cause of the decline of the belief in progress can perhaps be stated as follows: the idea of progress in the modern sense implies that once man has reached a certain level, intellectual and social or moral, there exists a firm level of being below which he cannot sink. This contention, however, is empirically refuted by the incredible barbarization which we have been so unfortunate as to witness in our century. We can say that the idea of progress, in the full and emphatic sense of the term, is based on wholly unwarranted hopes. You can see this even in many critics of the idea of progress. One of the most famous critics of the idea of progress, prior to World War I, was the Frenchman, Georges Sorel, who wrote a book, *The Delusions of Progress*.[18] But strangely, Sorel declared that the decline of the Western world was impossible because of the vitality of the Western tradition. I think that we have all now become sufficiently sober to admit that, whatever may be wrong in Spengler—and there are many things wrong in Spengler—the very title, in the English translation especially, of the work *The Decline of the West* is more sober, more reasonable, than these hopes which lasted so long.[19]

This barbarization which we have witnessed and which we continue to witness is not altogether accidental. The intention of the modern development was, of course, to bring about a higher civilization, a civilization which would surpass all earlier civilizations. Yet the effect of the modern development was different. What has taken place in the modern period has been a gradual corrosion and destruction of the heritage of Western civilization. The soul of the modern development, one may say, is a peculiar "realism," the notion that moral principles and the appeal to moral principles—preaching, sermonizing—is ineffectual, and therefore that one has to seek a substitute for moral principles which would be much more efficacious than ineffectual preaching. Such substitutes were found, for example, in institutions or in economics, and perhaps the most important substitute is what was called "the historical process," meaning that the historical process is, in a way, a much more important guarantee for the actualization of the good life than what the individual could or would do through his own efforts. This change shows itself, as already noted, in the change of general language, namely, in the substitution of the distinction between progressive and reactionary for the distinction between good and bad—the implication being that we have to choose and to do what is conducive to progress, what is in agreement with the historical trends, and it is indecent or immoral to be squeamish in such adaptations. Once it became clear, however, that historical trends are absolutely ambiguous and therefore cannot serve as a standard, or, in other words, that to jump on the bandwagon or the wave of the future is not more reasonable than to resist those trends, no standard whatever was left. The facts, understood as historical processes, indeed do not teach us anything regarding values, and the consequence of the abandonment of moral principle proper was that value judgments have no objective support whatsoever. To spell this out with the necessary clarity—although one knows this from the study of the social sciences—the values of barbarism and cannibalism are as defensible as those of civilization.

I have spoken of modernity as of something definite and hence knowable. An analysis of this phenomenon is out of the question here, as goes without saying. Instead I would like briefly to enumerate those characteristic elements of modernity which are particularly striking, at least to me. But I must make one observation in order to protect myself against gross misunderstanding. A modern phenomenon is not characterized by the fact that it is located, say, between 1600 and 1952, because premodern traditions of course survived and survive. And more than that, throughout the modern period, there has been a constant movement against this modern trend, from the very beginning. One phenomenon which is very well known, perhaps unduly well known, is the quarrel between the ancients and moderns at the end of the seventeenth century, which in its most well-known form was concerned with the relatively unimportant question of whether the French drama of the seventeenth century was really comparable to the classical drama. The real quarrel between the ancients and moderns did not concern the drama, of course, but concerned modern science and philosophy. But there was a resistance to that modern science and philosophy from the very beginning: the greatest man in English letters who represented this is Swift; but then you have it again very strongly in German classicism in the second half of the eighteenth century;[20] and then indeed in the nineteenth century this movement, this countermovement, was completely pushed to the wall as a great intellectual movement. But in a way, of course, the tradition still persisted. So having made clear that by modernity I do not mean something which is simply chronological, let me now indicate what I think are the most striking elements of modernity in a purely enumerative fashion without attempting an analysis.

The first characteristic feature of modern thought as modern thought, one can say, is its anthropocentric character. Although apparently contradicted by the fact that modern science with its Copernicanism is much more radically antianthropocentric than earlier thought, a closer study shows that this is not true. When I speak of the anthropocentric character of modern thought, I contrast it with the theocentric character of biblical and medieval thought, and with the cosmocentric character of classical thought. You see this most clearly if you look at modern philosophy which, while it does not have the general authority which modern science has, is nevertheless a kind of conscience or consciousness of modern science. One has only to look at the titles of the most famous books of modern philosophy to see that philosophy is, or tends to become, analysis of the human mind. You could also see this same trait easily, but that would be too laborious, by looking at what philosophic disciplines emerged in modern times that were unknown to earlier philosophy: all are parts of the philosophy of man or of the human mind. The underlying idea, which shows itself not in all places clearly but in some places very clearly, is that all truths or all meaning, all order, all beauty, originate in the thinking subject, in human thought, in man. Some famous formulations: "We know only what we make"—Hobbes. "Understanding prescribes nature its laws"—Kant. "I have discovered a spontaneity, little known previously, of the monads of the thoughts"—Leibniz. To give you a very simple popular example, certain human pursuits which were formerly called imitative arts are now called creative arts. One must not forget that even the atheistic, materialistic thinkers of classical antiquity took it for granted that man is subject to something higher than himself, e.g., the whole cosmic order, and that man is not the origin of all meaning.

Connected with this anthropocentric character is a radical change of moral orientation, which we see with particular clarity in the fact of the emergence of the concept of rights in the precise form in which it was developed in modern social thought. Generally speaking, premodern thought put the emphasis on duty, and rights, as far as they were mentioned at all, were understood only as derivative from duties and subservient to the fulfillment of duties. In modern times, we find the tendency, again not always expressed with the greatest clarity but definitely traceable, to assign the primary place to rights and to regard the duties as secondary if, of course, very important. This is connected with another fact: in the crucial period of the seventeenth century, where the change becomes most visible, it is understood that the basic right coincides with a passion. The passions are in a way emancipated, because in the traditional notion, the passion is subordinate to the action, and the action means virtue. The change which we can observe throughout the seventeenth century in all the most famous revolutionary thinkers is that virtue itself is now understood as a passion. In other words, a notion that virtue is a controlling, refraining, regulating, ordering attitude towards passion—think of the image in Plato's *Phaedrus*, the horses and the charioteer—is given up when virtue itself is understood as a passion. This leads to another change which becomes manifest only at a somewhat later age, namely, that freedom gradually takes the place of virtue; so that in much present-day thought you find, not that freedom is the same as license (that it is not goes without saying), but that the distinction between freedom and license takes on a different meaning, a radically different meaning. The good life does not consist, as it did according to the earlier notion, in compliance with a pattern antedating the human will, but consists primarily in originating the pattern itself. The good life does not consist of both a "what" and a "how," but only of a "how." To state it somewhat differently, and again repeating that I am only enumerating, man has no nature to speak of. He makes himself what he is; man's very humanity is acquired. That is granted, I think, in many quarters; that is, what is absolutely stable are certain so-called biological characteristics and perhaps some very elementary psychological characteristics, the character of perception, etc. But all interesting things are not modeled on a pattern antedating human action, but are a product of human activity itself. Man's very humanity is acquired.

And this leads me to the third point, which became fully clear only in the nineteenth century, and which is already a kind of corrective of this radical emancipation of man from the superhuman. It became ever more clear that man's freedom is inseparable from a radical dependence. Yet this dependence was understood as itself a product of human freedom, and the name for that is history. The so-called discovery of history consists in the realization, or in the alleged realization, that man's freedom is radically limited by his earlier use of his freedom, and not by his nature or by the whole order of nature or creation. This element is, I think, increasing in importance; this is so much so that today one tends to say that the specific character of modern thought is "history," a notion which is in this form, of course, wholly alien to classical thought or to any premodern thought or to biblical thought as well, naturally. If I had the time I would try to show that precisely in this so-called historicization of modern thought the problem of modernity becomes most visible from a technical point of view, and a technical point of view has a peculiarly convincing character, at least to a certain type of person. So I leave it at that.

The crisis of modernity on which we have been reflecting leads to the suggestion that we should return. But return to what? Obviously, to Western civilization in its premodern integrity, to the principles of Western civilization. Yet there is a difficulty here, because Western civilization consists of two elements, has two roots, which are in radical disagreement with each other. We may call these elements, as I have done elsewhere, Jerusalem and Athens, or, to speak in nonmetaphorical language, the Bible and Greek philosophy. This radical disagreement today is frequently played down, and this playing down has a certain superficial justification, for the whole history of the West presents itself at first glance as an attempt to harmonize, or to synthesize, the Bible and Greek philosophy. But a closer study shows that what happened and has been happening in the West for many centuries, is not a harmonization but an attempt at harmonization. These attempts at harmonization were doomed to failure for the following reason: each of these two roots of the Western world sets forth one thing as the one thing needful, and the one thing needful proclaimed by the Bible is incompatible, as it is understood by the Bible, with the one thing needful proclaimed by Greek philosophy, as it is understood by Greek philosophy. To put it very simply and therefore somewhat crudely, the one thing needful according to Greek philosophy is the life of autonomous understanding. The one thing needful as spoken by the Bible is the life of obedient love. The harmonizations and synthesizations are possible because Greek philosophy can *use* obedient love in a subservient function, and the Bible can *use* philosophy as a handmaid; but what is so used in each case rebels against such use, and therefore the conflict is really a radical one. Yet this very disagreement presupposes some agreement. In fact, every disagreement, we may say, presupposes some agreement, because people must disagree about something and must agree as to the importance of that something. But in this case the agreement is deeper than this purely formal one.

Now, what then is the area of agreement between Greek philosophy and the Bible? Negatively we can say, and one could easily enlarge on this position, that there is a perfect agreement between the Bible and Greek philosophy in opposition to those elements of modernity which were described above. They are rejected explicitly or implicitly by both the Bible and Greek philosophy. But this agreement is, of course, only an implicit one, and we should rather look at the agreement as it appeared directly in the texts. One can say, and it is not misleading to say, that the Bible and Greek philosophy agree in regard to what we may call, and we do call in fact, morality. They agree, if I may say so, regarding the importance of morality, regarding the content of morality, and regarding its ultimate insufficiency. They differ as regards that "x" which supplements or completes morality, or, which is only another way of putting it, they disagree as regards the basis of morality.

I will give you first a brief statement, a reminder rather, of the agreement. Now, some people assert that there is a radical and unqualified opposition between biblical morality and philosophic morality. If one heard certain people speak, one would believe that the Greek philosophers did nothing but preach pederasty, whereas Moses did nothing but curb pederasty. Now these people must have limited themselves to a most perfunctory reading of a part of Plato's *Banquet* or of the beginning of the *Charmides*; but they cannot have read the only work in which Plato set forth specific prescriptions for human society, namely, Plato's *Laws*; and what Plato's *Laws* say about this subject agrees fully with what Moses says.[21] Those theologians who identified the second table of the Decalogue, as the Christians call it, with the natural law of Greek philosophy, were well-advised. It is as obvious to Aristotle as it is to Moses that murder, theft, adultery, etc., are unqualifiedly bad.[22] Greek philosophy and the Bible agree as to this, that the proper framework of morality is the patriarchal family, which is, or tends to be, monogamous, and which forms the cell of a society in which the free adult males, and especially the old ones, predominate. Whatever the Bible and philosophy may tell us about the nobility of certain women, in principle both insist upon the superiority of the male sex. The Bible traces Adam's Fall to Eve's temptation. Plato traces the fall of the best social order to the covetousness of a woman.[23] Consisting of free men, the society praised by the Bible and Greek philosophy refuses to worship any human being. I do not have to quote the Bible for I read it in a Greek author, who says: "You worship no human being as your Lord, but only the gods," and he expresses an almost biblical abhorrence of human beings who claim divine honors.[24] Bible and Greek philosophy agree in assigning the highest place among the virtues, not to courage or manliness, but to justice. And by justice both understand primarily, obedience to the law. The law that requires man's full obedience is in both cases not merely civil, penal, and constitutional law, but moral and religious law as well. It is, in biblical language, the guidance, the Torah, for the whole life of man. In the words of the Bible, "It is your life," or, "It is the tree of life for those who cling to it"; and in the words of Plato, "The law effects the blessedness of those who obey it."[25] Its comprehensiveness can be expressed, as Aristotle does it, by saying, "What the law does not command, it forbids"; and substantially that is the biblical view as well, as is shown by such commandments as "Thou shall eat and be full," and "Be fruitful and multiply."[26] Obedience to a law of this kind is more than ordinary obedience; it is humility. No wonder that the greatest prophet of the Bible as well as the most law-abiding among the Greeks are praised for their humility.[27] Law and justice, thus understood, are divine law and divine justice. The rule of law is fundamentally the rule of God, theocracy. Man's obedience and disobedience to the law is the object of divine retribution. What Plato says in the tenth book of the *Laws* about man's inability to escape from divine retribution is almost literally identical with certain verses of Amos and Psalm 139.[28] In this context, one may even mention, and without apology I think, the kinship between the monotheism of the Bible and the monotheism toward which Greek philosophy is tending, and the kinship between the first chapter of Genesis and Plato's *Timaeus*.[29] But the Bible and Greek philosophy agree not merely regarding the place which they assign to justice, the connection between justice and law, the character of law, and divine retribution. They also agree regarding the problem of justice, the difficulty created by the misery of the just and the prospering of the wicked. One cannot read Plato's description in the second book of the *Republic* of the perfectly just man who suffers what would be the just fate of the most unjust man without being reminded of Isaiah's description of him who has done no violence, neither was any deceit in his mouth, yet who was oppressed and afflicted and brought as a lamb to the slaughter.[30] And just as Plato's *Republic* ends with restoring all kinds of prosperity to the just, the book of Job ends with the restoration to the just Job of everything he had temporarily lost.[31]

Now, in the course of these extremely summary remarks, I have tacitly replaced morality by justice, understanding by "justice" obedience to the divine law. This notion, the divine law, it seems to me is the common ground between the Bible and Greek philosophy. And here I use a term which is certainly easily translatable into Greek as well as into biblical Hebrew. But I must be more precise. The common ground between the Bible and Greek philosophy is the problem of divine law. They solve that problem in a diametrically opposed manner.

Before I speak of the root of their difference, I would like to illustrate the fundamental antagonism between the Bible and philosophy by enumerating some of its consequences. I have indicated the place of justice in both Bible and Greek philosophy. We may take Aristotle's *Ethics* as the most perfect, or certainly the most accessible, presentation of philosophic ethics. Now, Aristotle's *Ethics* has two foci, not one: one is justice, the other, however, is magnanimity or noble pride. Both justice and magnanimity comprise all other virtues, as Aristotle says, but in different ways. Justice comprises all other virtues insofar as the actions flowing from them relate to other men; magnanimity, however, comprises all other virtues insofar as they enhance the man himself. Now there is a close kinship between Aristotle's justice and biblical justice, but Aristotle's magnanimity, which means a man's habitual claiming for himself great honors while he deserves these honors, is alien to the Bible. Biblical humility excludes magnanimity in the Greek sense. There is a close relation between the magnanimous man and the perfect gentleman. There occur a few, very few, gentlemen and ladies in the Bible— I hope that this remark is not understood as a criticism of the Bible. There is Saul, who disobeys a divine command and by so doing does the noble thing—he spared his brother, King Agag, and destroys only what is vile and refuse. For this he was rejected by God, and Agag was hewn to pieces by the prophet Samuel before the Lord. Instead of Saul, God elected David, who did a lot of things a gentleman would not do, who was one of the greatest sinners, but at the same time one of the greatest repenters, who ever lived. There is a gentleman, Jonathan, who was too noble to compete with his friend David for kingship in Israel. There is a lady, Michal, the wife of David, who saw David leaping and dancing before the Lord, and she despised him in her heart and ridiculed him for having shamelessly compromised his royal dignity by leaping and dancing before the riffraff, but she was punished by God with sterility. I need not dwell on the obvious connection between the biblical rejection of the concept of a "gentleman" and the biblical insistence on man's duties to the poor.[32] The Greek philosophers were very far from being vulgar worshipers of wealth—must I say so? Socrates lived in thousandfold poverty, as he himself says, and he failed to see why a horse can be good without having money, whereas a man cannot.[33] But they held that, as far as the general run of men is concerned, virtue presupposes a reasonable economic underpinning. The Bible, on the other hand, uses poor and pious or just as synonymous terms. Compared with the Bible, Greek philosophy is heartless in this as well as in other respects. Magnanimity presupposes a man's conviction of his own worth. It presupposes that man is capable of being virtuous, thanks to his own efforts. If this condition is fulfilled, consciousness of one's shortcomings or failings or sins is something which is below the good man. Again I quote Aristotle: "Sense of shame," which is such consciousness of human failing, "befits young men who cannot yet be fully virtuous, but not men of mature age who are free not to do the wrong thing in the first place."[34] Or to quote the remark made by one twentieth-century gentleman about another, "Disgrace was impossible because of his character and behavior."[35] The Greek philosophers differed as to whether man can become fully virtuous, but if some deny this possibility, as Socrates does, he merely replaces the self-satisfaction, the self-admiration of the virtuous man, by the self-satisfaction or self-admiration of him who steadily progresses in virtue.[36] He does not imply, as far as the happy few are concerned, that they should be contrite, repentant, or express a sense of guilt. Man's guilt was indeed the guiding theme of tragedy. Hence Plato rejects tragedy from his best city. (I do not say that this is the whole story; that this is only a part of the story you see from the fact that tragedy is replaced by songs praising the virtuous.) And according to Aristotle, the tragic hero is necessarily an average man, not a man of the highest order. However, it should be noted that tragedy is composed and performed for the benefit of the multitude. Its function is to arouse the passions of fear and pity while at the same time purging them.[37]

Now fear and pity are precisely the passions which are necessarily connected with the feeling of guilt. When I become guilty, when I become aware of my being guilty, I have at once the feeling of pity toward him whom I have hurt or ruined and the feeling of fear of him who avenges my crime. Humanly speaking, the unity of fear and pity combined with the phenomenon of guilt might seem to be the root of religion. God, the king or the judge, is the object of fear; and God, the father of all men, makes all men brothers, and thus hallows pity. According to Aristotle, without these feelings, which have to be purged by tragedy, the better type of man is liberated from all morbidity and thus can turn wholeheartedly to noble action. Greek philosophy has frequently been blamed for the absence from it of that ruthless examination of one's intentions which is the consequence of the biblical demand for purity of the heart. "Know thyself" means for the Greeks, know what it means to be a human being, know what is the place of man in the universe, examine your opinions and prejudices, rather than "Search your heart." This philosophic lack of depth, as it is called, can consistently be maintained only if God is assumed not to be concerned with man's goodness or if man's goodness is assumed to be entirely his own affair. The Bible and Greek philosophy agree, indeed, as regards the importance of morality or justice, and as to the insufficiency of morality, but they disagree as to what completes morality. According to the Greek philosophers, as already noted, it is understanding or contemplation. Now this necessarily tends to weaken the majesty of the moral demands, whereas humility, a sense of guilt, repentance, and faith in divine mercy, which complete morality according to the Bible, necessarily strengthen the majesty of the moral demands. A sign of this is the fact that contemplation is essentially a transsocial or asocial possibility, whereas obedience and faith are essentially related to the community of the faithful. To quote the Jewish medieval thinker, Yehuda Halevi, "The wisdom of the Greeks has most beautiful blossoms, but no fruits," with "fruits" here meaning actions.[38] That asocial perfection which is contemplation normally presupposes a political community, the city, which accordingly is considered by the philosophers as fundamentally good, and the same is true of the arts, without whose services, and even model, political life and philosophic life are not possible. According to the Bible, however, the first founder of a city was the first murderer, and his descendants were the first inventors of the arts. Not the city, not civilization, but the desert, is the place in which the biblical God reveals Himself. Not the farmer Cain, but the shepherd Abel, finds favor in the eyes of the biblical God.[39]

The force of the moral demand is weakened in Greek philosophy because in Greek philosophy this demand is not backed up by divine promises. According to Plato, for example, evil will never cease on earth, whereas according to the Bible the end of days will bring perfect redemption. Hence the philosopher lives in a state above fear and trembling as well as above hope, and the beginning of his wisdom is not, as in the Bible, the fear of God, but rather the sense of wonder; whereas biblical man lives in fear and trembling as well as in hope. This leads to a peculiar serenity in the philosopher which I would like to illustrate here by only one example which I think is not wholly accidental. The prophet Nathan seriously and ruthlessly rebukes King David for having committed one murder and one act of adultery. I contrast that with the way in which a Greek poet-philosopher playfully and elegantly tries to convince a Greek tyrant, who has committed an untold number of murders and other crimes, that he would derive greater pleasure if he would have been more reasonable.[40] Now let me leave it with these examples, which naturally are to a certain extent arbitrary, but I think not misleading. I think I can illustrate the difference also as follows by two characteristic events or accounts. Contrast the account of the *Akeida*—the binding of Isaac—in the story of Abraham. There the crucial point is that Abraham obeys an unintelligible command, the command being unintelligible because he has been promised that his name would be called through Isaac and in the descendants of Isaac, and now he is asked to slaughter that son. Yet, Abraham obeys the command unhesitatingly. The only analogy in Greek philosophy of which I can think would be the example of Socrates who is, or believes at least that he has been, commanded by Apollo to something, and yet the action consists not in unhesitating obedience, but in examining an unintelligible saying of Apollo.[41]

Now, after these illustrations, what is the difference? These principles were clarified, particularly in the medieval discussion, in the heyday of theological discussion; Maimonides especially, in *The Guide of the Perplexed*, is probably the greatest analyst of this fundamental difference. The issue as he stated it was as follows: philosophy teaches the eternity of the world, and the Bible teaches the creation out of nothing.[42] This conflict must be rightly understood, because Maimonides is primarily thinking of Aristotle, who taught the eternity of the visible universe. But if you enlarge that and apply it not only to this cosmos, to this visible universe in which we live now, but to any cosmos or chaos which might ever exist, certainly Greek philosophy teaches the eternity of cosmos or chaos; whereas the Bible teaches creation, implying creation out of nothing. The root of the matter, however, is that only the Bible teaches divine omnipotence, and the thought of divine omnipotence is absolutely incompatible with Greek philosophy in any form. And I think one can even trace that back to the very beginnings of Greek literature—though technically much beyond philosophy—to the passage in the *Odyssey*, where Hermes shows Odysseus a certain herb against Circe.[43] Now, in this context, the gods can do everything, the gods are omnipotent, one can say, but it is very interesting what this concept means in this context. Why are the gods omnipotent? Because they know the natures of all things, which means, of course, they are not omnipotent. They know the natures of things which are wholly independent of them, and through that knowledge they are capable of using all things properly. In all Greek thought, we find in one form or the other an impersonal necessity higher than any personal being; whereas in the Bible the first cause is, as people say now, a person. This is connected with the fact that the concern of God with man is absolutely, if we may say so, essential to the biblical God; whereas that concern is, to put it very mildly, a problem for every Greek philosopher. Stated somewhat differently, what is now called religious experience is underlined in the Bible and is understood by the Bible as genuine experience; whereas from the point of view of the Greek philosophers, this religious experience is a questionable interpretation—I take the example of Plato—a questionable interpretation of experiences of the soul as an all-pervasive principle.[44]

We must try, as far as it is possible, to understand this antagonism. It can well be questioned whether what I am going to say can in truth be called an attempt at understanding, and so you can take it as a kind of illustration from the point of view of, say, social science. In order to clarify this antagonism, it is proposed that we go back to the common stratum between the Bible and Greek philosophy, to the most elementary stratum, a stratum which is common, or can be assumed to be common, to all men. How can we find that? I think it is easier to start from philosophy, for the simple reason that the question which I raise here is a scientific or philosophic question. We have to move in the element of conceptual thought, as it is called, and that is of course the element of Greek philosophy. With a view to this fact, I would like to state the issue more precisely. What distinguishes the Bible from Greek philosophy is the fact that Greek philosophy is based on this premise: that there is such a thing as nature, or natures—a notion which has no equivalent in biblical thought. It should be noted that there is no Hebrew-biblical term for nature, the Hebrew word being derived very indirectly from a Greek word which is an equivalent of "nature" in Greek, *charakter*, *teva* in Hebrew. So the issue from this point of view would be this: we have to go back behind that discovery or invention of nature. We have to try to discern what we may call the prephilosophical equivalent of nature, and, by starting from that, perhaps we can arrive at a purely historical understanding of the antagonism we are analyzing. Let me add, parenthetically, another point. Philosophy is the quest for principles, meaning—and let us be quite literal—for the beginnings, for the first things. This is, of course, something common to philosophy and myth, and I would suggest for the time being that philosophy, as distinguished from myth, comes into being when the quest for the beginnings is understood in the light of the idea of nature.

Now what is the prephilosophic equivalent of nature? I think we can find the answer to this question in such notions as "custom" or "way." This answer occurred to me, very simply, as a result of reading Maimonides, who knew the true roots of which I speak very well indeed. In the beginning of his great legal work, the *Mishneh Torah*, in the first section, the "Hilkhot Yesodei ha-Torah," "Laws Regarding the Foundations of the Torah," chapter 4, paragraph 2, he speaks of the four elements. Before he introduces the term nature, he speaks first of the custom or way—the custom of fire, and the way of earth; and somewhat later he refers to the nature of water. And this insight goes, I think, to the root of the problem. The rubrics "custom" or "way" are biblical notions and are, of course, also to be found in Greek sources. Moreover, I would assume, until the contrary has been proven, that these ideas are really universal ones. People in all times and places have observed that things behave in a regular manner, that they have customs of behaving and ways of behaving. Take, for example, a biblical expression, *derekh nashim*, the way of women, menstruation, or in Greek, an expression such as *boskaematon dikei*, the custom of beasts, meaning the same as the nature of beasts. Or again, in biblical Hebrew, the word *mishpat* means the custom or the law of a thing as reflected in its regular behavior. In this context it is clear that no distinction is made between the custom of dogs and the custom of the Philistines; for example: a Philistine regularly behaves in his way and the dog regularly behaves in his way. You can also take lions and Hebrews, if you think I employ only poor examples. So things have regular behavior, customs or ways. I have also learned from a Hindu student that the Hindi term *dharma*, which is usually translated as "religion," means custom or way, and can refer to such things as the custom or way of iron, of trees, and of whatnot. And since the custom or way of human beings is, of course, the Hindu religion, it means derivatively, if most importantly, what is according to religion.

If we now assume that this idea of the "way" is really the prephilosophical equivalent of nature, we have immediately to add this very obvious observation: that there is one way, among the many ways, which is particularly important, and that is the way of the group to which one belongs: "our way." Now, our way is, of course, the right way. And why is it right? The answer: because it is old and because it is one's own, or, to use the beautiful expression of Edmund Burke, because it is "home-bred and prescriptive."[45] We can bring it altogether under the term "ancestral." Hence the original notion is that the ancestral is identical with the good. The good is necessarily ancestral, which implies, since man was always a thinking being, that the ancestors were superior. If this were not the case, in what sense would the ancestral be good? The ancestors are superior, and therefore the ancestors must be understood, if this notion is fully thought through, as gods, or sons of gods, or pupils of gods. In other words, it is necessary to consider the "right way" as the divine law, *theos nomos*. Whether this conclusion is always reached is, of course, uninteresting to us, because we admit the possibility that sometimes people do not think with sufficient penetration; but in those places where they did, they arrived at this understanding.

Unfortunately, the divine law, the *theos nomos*, to use the Greek image, leads to *two* fundamental alternatives: one is the character of Greek philosophy; the other is the character of the Bible. Now why is this problematic? The answer is all too familiar, i.e., the variety of divine laws. We find everywhere such orders claiming to be divine, and these orders are not only different from each other—that would not technically be a difficulty, because different gods could have assigned different codes to different tribes—but they contradict each other. In every code of this kind, there are some elements which claim to be universal. For example, one only has to read Herodotus to get very beautiful examples of conflicting claims: one tribe burned the dead, and the other tribe buried them. Now, the alternative burial custom was not only looked upon as a different folk-more, a different cultural pattern, but as an abomination. So we may say that different laws contradict each other, and they contradict each other especially regarding what they say about the first things, because no early code, written or unwritten, is thinkable without a preamble which explains the obligations involved and which provides an account of the first things. Given this variety and this contradictory character of the various allegedly divine codes, it becomes necessary to transcend this whole dimension, to find one's bearings independently of the ancestral, or to realize that the ancestral and the good are two fundamentally different things despite occasional coincidences between them.

There is, too, the basic question of how to find one's bearings in the cosmos. The Greek answer fundamentally is this: we have to discover the first things on the basis of inquiry, that everyone knows. We can note two implications of what inquiry means here. In the first place, inquiry implies seeing with one's own eyes as distinguished from hearsay, to observe for oneself. And secondly, the notion of inquiry presupposes the realization of the fundamental difference between human production and the production of things which are not manmade, so that no conclusion from human production to the production of non-manmade things is possible except if it is first established by demonstration that the visible universe has been made by thinking beings. This implication, I think, is decisive: it was on the basis of the principles of Greek philosophy that what later became known as demonstrations of the existence of God or gods came into being. This is absolutely necessary, and that is true not only in Aristotle, but in Plato as well, as you see, for example, from the tenth book of the *Laws*. An ascent from sense perception and reasoning on sense data, an ascent indeed guided, according to Plato and Aristotle, by certain notions, leads upwards; and everything depends on the solidity of the ascending process, on the demonstration. Because the quest for the beginning, for the first things, becomes now philosophic or scientific analysis of the cosmos, the place of the divine law, in the traditional sense of the term (where it is a code traced to a personal god), is replaced by a natural order which may even be called, as it was later to be called, a natural law—or at any rate, to use a wider term, a natural morality. So the divine law, in the real and strict sense of the term, is only the starting point, the absolutely essential starting point, for Greek philosophy, but it is abandoned in the process. And if it is accepted by Greek philosophy, it is accepted only politically, meaning, for the education of the many, and not as something which stands independently.

To understand the biblical notion in the sense of understanding to which I refer, one can say this: the Bible, biblical thought, clings to this notion that there is one particular divine law; but it contends that this particular divine law is the only one which is truly divine law. All these other codes are, in their claim to divine origin, fraudulent. They are figments of man. Since, however, one code is accepted, then no possibility of independent questioning arises and is meant to arise. Now what, then, is it that distinguishes the biblical solution from the mythical solution? I think it is this: that the author or authors of the Bible were aware of the problem of the variety of the divine laws. In other words, they realized—and I am now speaking not as a theologian but as a historian—they realized what are the absolutely necessary conditions if one particular law should be *the* divine law. How has one to conceive of the whole if one particular, and therefore contingent, law of one particular, contingent tribe is to be *the* divine law? The answer is: it must be a personal God; the first cause must be God; He must be omnipotent, not controlled and not controllable. But to be knowable means to be controllable, and therefore He must not be knowable in the strict sense of the term. Thus in the language of later thought, of already Graecified thought, God's essence is not knowable; as the Bible says, one cannot see God's face. But this is not radical enough, and the divine name given in Exodus, which literally translated means, "I shall be What I shall be," is the most radical formulation of that.[46] It is just the opposite of the Greek notion of essence, where it means the being is what it is and was and will be. But here the core, one could say, is inaccessible; it is absolutely free: God is what He shall be. It is a free God, unpredictable. Why then can man trust Him? Answer: only because of the covenant.

God has freely bound Himself, but all trust depends on the trust in God's word, in God's promise; there is no necessary and therefore intelligible relation; and, needless to say, this covenant is not a free covenant, freely entered into by originally independent partners; it is a covenant which, according to the Bible, God commanded man to perform.

To complete this extremely sketchy picture by a few points, I would like to say this. There is no doubt that the Greek philosophers of the classical period did not know the Bible, and it is, I think, generally admitted that the authors of the Bible did not know the Greek philosophers. But the extraordinary fact is that if one studies both the Greek philosophers and the Bible a little more carefully, one sees that in both sources of Western thought the alternative was, if I may say so, divine. Even in Aristotle you will find passages where he speaks of certain very crude notions in Greece which pointed fundamentally to what we know in the Bible in a more developed form, e.g., the notion that maybe it is bad to devote oneself to the philosophical rebellion against God.

By way of comparison, now consider the perfect agreement, as to the decisive biblical message, between the first account of creation and the second account of creation, the account which culminates in the story of the Fall.[47] It is the same notion which underlies the account of the first chapter of Genesis, the depreciation of heaven, and which underlies the account of the second chapter of Genesis, the prohibition against the eating of the fruit of the tree of knowledge of good and evil. This is because the knowledge of good and evil means, of course, not one special branch of knowledge, as is shown by the fact that in God's knowing of the created things, the verses always end, "And He saw that it was good." The completed thing, the complete knowledge of the completed thing, is knowledge of the good, the notion being that the desire for, and the striving for, knowledge is forbidden. Man is not meant to be a theoretical, a knowing, a contemplating being; man is meant to live in childlike obedience. Needless to say, this notion was modified in various ways in the later tradition, but it seems to me that the fundamental thought was preserved, if we disregard some marginal developments.

What then is the principle underlying the seemingly changed attitude of later times? I think we can understand this from the Bible itself. You recall that the story of the Fall is followed by the account of Cain and later on by the genealogy of Cain, where the city and the arts are assigned to this undesirable branch of mankind; and yet later on we find that there is a very different attitude toward the city and the arts: think of the holy city of Jerusalem, and of the arts which Bezalel used in adorning the temple, etc.[48] I think we find the clearest discussion of this issue later on, in the discussion of kingship, of the institution of human kingship in Israel, in the first book of Samuel, where we see what the general trend of the biblical solution is. Fundamentally, the institution of human kingship is bad—it is a kind of rebellion against God, as is the *polis* and the arts and knowledge. But then it becomes possible, by divine dispensation, that these things, which originate in human rebellion, become dedicated to the service of God and thus become holy. And I think that this is the biblical solution to the problem of human knowledge: human knowledge, if it is dedicated to the service of God, and only then, can be good; and perhaps, in that sense, it is even necessary. But without that dedication, it is a rebellion. Man was *given* understanding in order to understand God's commands. He could not be freely obedient if he did not have understanding. But at the same time this very fact allows man to emancipate the understanding from the service, from the subservient function, for which it was meant, and this emancipation is the origin of philosophy or science from the biblical point of view. And so the antagonism between them. Even if you take later versions as your model, e.g., so-called Jewish medieval philosophy, you will still find that this difficulty is very noticeable.

However this may be, it seems to me that this antagonism must be considered by us in action. That is to say: it seems to me that the core, the nerve, of Western intellectual history, Western spiritual history, one could almost say, is the conflict between the biblical and the philosophic notions of the good life. This was a conflict which showed itself primarily, of course, in arguments—arguments advanced by theologians on behalf of the biblical point of view, and by philosophers on behalf of the philosophic point of view. There are many reasons why this is important, but I would like to emphasize only one: it seems to me that this unresolved conflict is the secret of the vitality of Western civilization. The recognition of two conflicting roots of Western civilization is, at first, a very disconcerting observation. Yet this realization has also something reassuring and comforting about it. The very life of Western civilization is the life between two codes, a fundamental tension. There is, therefore, no reason inherent in the Western civilization itself, in its fundamental constitution, why it should give up life. But this comforting thought is justified only if we live that life, if we live that conflict. No one can be both a philosopher and a theologian, or, for that matter, some possibility which transcends the conflict between philosophy and theology, or pretends to be a synthesis of both. But every one of us can be and ought to be either one or the other, the philosopher open to the challenge of theology, or the theologian open to the challenge of philosophy.

III

1.

When we attempt to return to the roots of Western civilization, we observe soon that Western civilization has two roots which are in conflict with each other, the biblical and Greek philosophic, and this is to begin with a very disconcerting observation. Yet this realization has also something reassuring and comforting. The very life of Western civilization is the life between two codes, a fundamental tension. There is, therefore, no reason inherent in the Western civilization itself, in its fundamental constitution, why it should give up life. But this comforting thought is justified only if we live that life, if we live that conflict, that is. No one can be both a philosopher and a theologian, or, for that matter, a third which is beyond the conflict between philosophy and theology, or a synthesis of both. But every one of us can be and ought to be either the one or the other, the philosopher open to the challenge of theology, or the theologian open to the challenge of philosophy.

There is a fundamental conflict or disagreement between the Bible and Greek philosophy. This fundamental conflict is blurred to a certain extent by the close similarity in points. There are, for example, certain philosophies which come seemingly close to the biblical teaching—think of philosophic teachings which are monotheistic, which speak of the love of God and of man, which even admit prayer, etc. And so the difference becomes sometimes almost invisible. But we recognize the difference immediately if we make this observation. For a philosopher or philosophy there can never be an absolute sacredness of a particular or contingent event. This particular or contingent is called, since the eighteenth century, the "historical." Therefore people have come to say that revealed religion means historical religion as distinguished from natural religion, and that philosophers could have a natural religion, and furthermore, that there is an essential superiority of the historical to the natural. As a consequence of this interpretation of the particular and contingent as historical, it came to be held, and that is very frequently held today, that the Bible is in an emphatic sense historical, and that the Bible (or the biblical authors), as it were, discovered history, whereas philosophy as philosophy is essentially nonhistorical. This view is underlying much of present-day interpretation of biblical thought. What is called "existentialism" is really only a more elaborate form of this interpretation. I do not believe that this approach is very helpful for the understanding of the Bible, at least as far as its basic parts are concerned. As an explanation, I will suggest here only one consideration: that these present-day concepts, such as History with a capital *H*, are very late concepts, and very derivative, and by this very fact are not as capable of unlocking to us early thought, thought which is in no way derivative, but at the beginning of a tradition.

One can begin to describe the fundamental disagreement between the Bible and Greek philosophy, and doing that from a purely historical point of view, from the fact that we observe first a broad agreement between the Bible and Greek philosophy regarding both morality and the insufficiency of morality; the disagreement concerns that "x" which completes morality. According to Greek philosophy, that "x" is *theoria*, contemplation, and the biblical completion we may call, I think without creating any misleading understanding, piety, the need for divine mercy or redemption, obedient love. To be more precise (the term "morality" itself is one of these derivative terms which are not quite adequate for the understanding of earlier thought), we may replace the term "morality" by the term "justice," a term common to both sources; and justice means primarily obedience to law, and law in the full and comprehensive sense means divine law. Going even back behind that, we suggest as a starting point of the whole moral development of mankind, if we may say so, a primeval identification of the good with the ancestral. Out of this primeval equation, which we still understand, and of which we still make use in actual life, the notion of a divine law necessarily arose. And then, in a further step, the problem of divine law arises: the original notion of a divine law or divine code implies that there is a large variety of them. The very variety and, more specifically, the contradiction between the various divine codes makes the idea of a divine law in the simple and primary sense of the term radically problematic.

There are two diametrically opposed solutions to this problem possible, the one is the philosophic and the other is the biblical solution. The philosophic solution we may describe in the following terms: the philosophers transcend the dimension of divine codes altogether, the whole dimension of piety and of pious obedience to a pregiven code. Instead they embark on a free quest for the beginnings, for the first things, for the principles. And they assume that on the basis of the knowledge of first principles, of the first principles, of the beginnings, it will be possible to determine what is by nature good, as distinguished from what is good merely by convention. This quest for the beginnings proceeds through sense perception, reasoning, and what they called *noesis*, which is literally translated by "understanding" or "intellect," and which we can perhaps translate a little bit more cautiously by "awareness," an awareness with the mind's eye as distinguished from sensible awareness. But while this awareness has certainly its biblical equivalent, and even its mystical equivalent, this equivalent in the philosophic context is never divorced from sense perception and reasoning based on sense perception. In other words, philosophy never becomes oblivious of its kinship with the arts and crafts, with the knowledge used by the artisan, and with this humble but solid kind of knowledge.

Now turning to the biblical alternative, here the basic premise is that one particular divine code is accepted as truly divine; that one particular code of one particular tribe is *the* divine code. But the divine character of all other allegedly divine codes is simply denied, and this implies a radical rejection of mythology. This rejection of mythology is also characteristic of the primary impulse of philosophy, but the biblical rejection of mythology proceeds in the opposite direction to what philosophy does. To give some meaning to the term "mythology," which I am here forced to use, I would say that mythology is characterized by the conflict between gods and impersonal powers behind the gods. What is in Greek sometimes called *moira*, for example. Now philosophy replaces this impersonal fate, as we might say, by nature and intelligible necessity. The Bible, on the other hand, conceives of God as the cause of everything else, impersonal necessities included. The biblical solution, then, stands or falls by the belief in God's omnipotence. The notion of omnipotence requires, of course, monotheism, because if you have more than one God clearly none of them can be omnipotent. Only the biblical authors, we may say, understand what omnipotence really means, because only if God is omnipotent can one particular code be the absolute code. But an omnipotent God who is in principle perfectly knowable to man is in a way subject to man, insofar as knowledge is in a way power. Therefore a truly omnipotent God must be a mysterious God, and that is, as you know, the teaching of the Bible. Man cannot see the face of God; and especially the divine name, "I shall be That I shall be," means it is never possible in any present to know that, i.e., what God shall be. But if man has no hold whatever over the biblical God, how can there be any link between man and God? The biblical answer is the covenant, a free and mysterious action of love on the part of God; and the corresponding attitude on the part of man is trust, or faith, which is radically different from theoretical certainty. The biblical God is known in a humanly relevant sense only by His actions, by His revelations. The book, the Bible, is the account of what God has done and what He has promised. In the Bible, as we would say, men tell about God's actions and promises on the basis of their experience of God. This experience, and not reasoning based on sense perception, is the root of biblical wisdom.

This radical difference between the Bible and Greek philosophy shows itself also in the literary character of the Bible, on the one hand, and of Greek philosophic books, on the other. The works of the Greek philosophers are really books, works, works of one man, who begins at what he regards as the necessary beginning, either the beginning simply or the best beginning for leading people up to what he regards as the truth. And this one man–one book was characteristic of Greek thought from the very beginning: Homer. But the Bible is fundamentally, as is today generally held, a compilation of sources, which means the Bible continues already a tradition with a minimum of changes, and therefore what follows are the famous difficulties with which the biblical scholars are concerned. The decisive point, I think, is this: here there is no beginning made by an individual, no beginning made by man, ultimately. There is a kinship between this art of writing and the favored form of writing, favored in the Jewish tradition, namely, the commentary, always referring back to something earlier. Man does not begin.

In my analysis I presupposed that the equation of the good with the ancestral is the primeval equation. That may be so in chronological terms, but one cannot leave it at that, of course, because the question arises: why should this be so, what evidence does this equation have? That is a very long question, and I do not propose to answer it now. I would only refer to a Greek myth according to which Mnemosyne, memory, is the mother of the muses, meaning the mother of wisdom. In other words, primarily the good, the true, however you might call it, can be known only as the old because, prior to the emergence of wisdom, memory occupied the place of wisdom. Ultimately, I think, one would have to go back to a fundamental dualism in man in order to understand this conflict between the Bible and Greek philosophy, to the dualism of deed and speech, of action and thought—a dualism which necessarily poses the question as to the primacy of either—and one can say that Greek philosophy asserts the primacy of thought, of speech, whereas the Bible asserts the primacy of deed. That is, I know very well, open to misunderstandings, but permit me to leave it at this for the moment.

2.

Now we are at any rate confronted with the fact that there is a radical opposition between Bible and philosophy, and this opposition has given rise to a secular conflict from the very beginning. This conflict is characteristic of the West, the West in the wider sense of the term, including even the whole Mediterranean basin, of course. It seems to me that this conflict is the secret of the vitality of the West. I would venture to say that as long as there will be a Western civilization, there will be theologians who will suspect the philosophers, and philosophers who will be annoyed or feel annoyed by the theologians. But, as the saying goes, we have to accept our fate, and it is not the worst fate which men could imagine. We have this radical opposition: the Bible refuses to be integrated into a philosophical framework, just as philosophy refuses to be integrated into a biblical framework. As for this biblical refusal, there is the often-made remark that the god of Aristotle is not the God of Abraham, Isaac, and Jacob; and, therefore, any attempt to integrate the biblical understanding into philosophic understanding means to abandon that which is meant by the God of Abraham, Isaac, and Jacob.[49] As for philosophy, that is perhaps a little bit obscured by a number of facts, and therefore we must dwell upon it for a moment. The obscuration, I believe, is ultimately due to the fact that, in the discussions regarding the relation of theology and philosophy, philosophy is identified with the completed philosophic system: in the Middle Ages, of course, primarily with Aristotle—by which I do not mean to say that Aristotle has a system, although it is sometimes believed that he had—but certainly with Hegel in modern times. That is, of course, one very special form of philosophy: it is not the primary and necessary form of philosophy. I have to explain that.

In a medieval work, the *Kuzari*, by Yehuda Halevi, we find this statement: "Socrates says to the people, 'I do not reject your divine wisdom, I simply do not understand it. My wisdom is merely human wisdom.'"[50] Now in the mouth of Socrates, as in this apothegm, "human wisdom" means imperfect wisdom or quest for wisdom, that is to say, philosophy. Since Socrates realizes the imperfection of human wisdom, it is hard to understand why he does not go from there to divine wisdom. The reason implied in this text is this: as a philosopher, he refuses assent to anything which is not evident to him, and revelation is for him not more than an unevident, unproven possibility. Confronted with an unproven possibility, he does not reject; he merely suspends judgment. But here a great difficulty arises which one can state as follows: it is impossible to suspend judgment regarding matters of utmost urgency, regarding matters of life and death. Now the question of revelation is evidently of utmost urgency. If there is revelation, unbelief in revelation or disobedience to revelation is fatal. Suspense of judgment regarding revelation would then seem to be impossible. The philosopher who refuses to assent to revelation because it is not evident therewith rejects revelation. But this rejection is unwarranted if revelation is not disproved. Which means to say that the philosopher, when confronted with revelation, seems to be compelled to contradict the very idea of philosophy by rejecting without sufficient grounds. How can we understand that? The philosophic reply can be stated as follows: the question of utmost urgency, the question which does not permit suspense, is the question of how one should live. Now this question is settled for Socrates by the fact that he is a philosopher. As a philosopher, he knows that we are ignorant of the most important things. The ignorance, the evident fact of this ignorance, evidently proves that quest for knowledge of the most important things is the most important thing for us. Philosophy is, then, evidently the right way of life. This is, in addition, according to him, confirmed by the fact that he finds his happiness in acquiring the highest possible degree of clarity which he can acquire. He sees no necessity whatever to assent to something which is not evident to him. And if he is told that his disobedience to revelation might be fatal, he raises the question: what does fatal mean? In the extreme case, it would be eternal damnation. Now, the philosophers of the past were absolutely certain that an all-wise God would not punish with eternal damnation, or with anything else, such human beings as are seeking the truth or clarity. We must consider later on whether this reply is quite sufficient. At any rate, philosophy is meant—and that is the decisive point—not as a set of propositions, a teaching, or even a system, but as a way of life, a life animated by a peculiar passion, the philosophic desire or *eros*; it is not understood as an instrument or a department of human self-realization. Philosophy understood as an instrument or as a department is, of course, compatible with every thought of life, and therefore also with the biblical way of life. But this is no longer philosophy in the original sense of the term. This has been greatly obscured, I believe, by the Western development, because philosophy was certainly in the Christian Middle Ages deprived of its character as a way of life, and became just a very important compartment.

I must therefore try to restate why, according to the original notion of philosophy, philosophy is necessarily a way of life and not a mere discipline, if even the highest discipline. I must explain, in other words, why philosophy cannot possibly lead up to the insight that another way of life apart from the philosophic is the right one. Philosophy is quest for knowledge regarding the whole. Being essentially quest and being not able ever to become wisdom, as distinguished from philosophy, the problems are always more evident than the solutions. All solutions are questionable. Now, the right of way of life cannot be fully established except by an understanding of the nature of man, and the nature of man cannot be fully clarified except by an understanding of the nature of the whole. Therefore, the right way of life cannot be established metaphysically except by a completed metaphysics, and therefore the right way of life remains questionable. But the very uncertainty of all solutions, the very ignorance regarding the most important things, makes quest for knowledge the most important thing, and therefore makes a life devoted to it the right way of life. So philosophy in its original and full sense is, then, certainly incompatible with the biblical way of life. Philosophy and the Bible are the alternatives or the antagonists in the drama of the human soul. Each of the two antagonists claims to know or to hold the truth, the decisive truth, the truth regarding the right way of life. But there can be only one truth: hence, conflict between these claims, and necessarily conflict among thinking beings; and that means inevitably argument. Each of the two opponents has tried for millennia to refute the other. This effort is continuing in our day, and in fact it is taking on a new intensity after some decades of indifference.

3.

Now I have to say a few words about the present-day argument. The present-day argument in favor of philosophy, we can say, is practically nonexistent because of the disintegration of philosophy. I have spoken on a former occasion of the distinction between philosophy and science, as understood today—a distinction which necessarily leads to a discrediting of philosophy. The contrast between the lack of results in philosophy and the enormous success of the sciences brings this about. Science is the only intellectual pursuit which today successfully can claim to be the perfection of the human understanding. Science is neutral in regard to revelation. Philosophy has become uncertain of itself. Just one quotation, a statement of one of the most famous present-day philosophers: "Belief in revelation is true, but not true for the philosopher. Rejection of revelation is true for the philosopher, but not true for the believer."[51] Let us turn to the more promising present-day argument in favor of revelation. I shall not waste words on the most popular argument which is taken from the needs of present-day civilization, the present-day crisis, which would simply amount to this: that we need today, in order to compete with communism, revelation as a myth. Now this argument is either stupid or blasphemous. Needless to say, we find similar arguments also within Zionism, and I think this whole argument has been disposed of, in advance, a long time ago by Dostoyevsky in *The Possessed.*[52]

Now, the serious argument in favor of revelation can be stated as follows: there is no objective evidence whatever in favor of revelation, which means there is no shred of evidence in favor of revelation except, first, the experience, the personal experience, of man's encounter with

God, and secondly, the negative proof of the inadequacy of any non-believing position. Now as to the first point—there is no objective evidence in favor of revelation except the experience of one's encounter with God—a difficulty arises. Namely, what is the relation of this personal experience to the experience expressed in the Bible? It becomes necessary to distinguish between what the prophets experience, what we may call the Call of God or the Presence of God, and what they said; and this latter would have to be called, as it is today called by all nonorthodox theologians, a "human interpretation" of God's action. It is no longer God's action itself. The human interpretation cannot be authoritative. But the question arises, is not every specific meaning attached to God's Call or to God's Presence a human interpretation? For example, the encounter with God will be interpreted in radically different manners by the Jew on the one hand, and by the Christian on the other, to say nothing of the Muslim and others. Yet only one interpretation can be the true one. There is, therefore, a need for argument between the various believers in revelation, an argument which cannot help but allude somehow to objectivity. As for the second point—the negative proof of the inadequacy of any nonbelieving position—that is usually very strong insofar as it shows the inadequacy of modern progressivism, optimism, or cynicism, and to that extent I regard it as absolutely convincing.

But that is not the decisive difficulty. The decisive difficulty concerns classical philosophy, and here the discussions, as far as I know them, do not come to grips with the real difficulty. To mention only one point, it is said that classical philosophy is based on a kind of delusion which can be proved to be a delusion. Classical philosophy is said to be based on the unwarranted belief that the whole is intelligible. Now this is a very long question. Permit me here to limit myself to saying that the prototype of the philosopher in the classical sense was Socrates, who knew that he knew nothing, who therewith admitted that the whole is not intelligible, and who merely wondered whether by saying that the whole is not intelligible we do not admit to having some understanding of the whole. For of something of which we know absolutely nothing, we could of course not say anything, and that is the meaning, it seems to me, of what is so erroneously translated by the intelligible, that man as man necessarily has an awareness of the whole. Let me only conclude this point. As far as I know, the present-day arguments in favor of revelation against philosophy are based on an inadequate understanding of classical philosophy.

Now, to find our bearings, let us return to a more elementary stratum of the conflict. What is truly significant in the present-day argument will then become clearer, and we shall understand also the reasons for the withdrawal from objectivity in the argument in favor of revelation in present-day theology. The typical older view regarding revelation and reason is today accepted fully only by the Catholic church and by orthodox Jews and orthodox Protestants. I shall speak, of course, only of the Jewish version. The question is: how do we know that the Torah is from Sinai, or is the word of the living God? The traditional Jewish answer is primarily that our fathers have told us, and they knew it from their fathers, an uninterrupted chain of reliable tradition, going back to Mount Sinai. If the question is answered in this form, it becomes inevitable to wonder, is the tradition reliable? I will mention only one specimen from the earlier discussion. At the beginning of his legal code, Maimonides gives the chain of tradition from Moses down to talmudic times, and there occurs the figure of Ahijah the Shilonite, who is said to have received the Torah from King David, and who also is introduced as a contemporary of Moses, who had received the Torah from Moses.[53] Now, whatever Maimonides may have meant by the insertion of this talmudic story, from our point of view it would be an indication of the fact that this chain of the tradition, especially in its earlier parts, contains what today are called "mythical," that is to say, unhistorical elements. I shall not dwell on the very well-known discrepancies in the Bible. The question, Who wrote the Pentateuch?, was traditionally answered, as a matter of course: by Moses; this was so much so that when Spinoza questioned the Mosaic origin of the Torah it was assumed that he denied its divine origin. Who wrote the Pentateuch: Moses himself, or men who knew of the revelation only from hearsay or indirectly? The details are of no interest to us here; we have to consider the principle.

Is a historical proof of the fact of revelation possible? A historical proof of the fact of revelation would be comparable to the historical proof of the fact, say, of the assassination of Caesar by Brutus and Cassius. That is demonstrably impossible. In the case of historical facts proper, or historical facts in the ordinary sense of the term, there is always evidence by impartial observers or by witnesses belonging to both parties. For example, here, friends and enemies of Caesar. In the case of revelation, there are no impartial observers. All witnesses are adherents, and all transmitters were believers. Furthermore, there are no pseudoassassinations or pseudowars, but there are pseudorevelations and pseudoprophets. The historical proof presupposes, therefore, criteria for distinguishing between genuine and spurious revelation. We know the biblical criterion, at least the decisive one in our context: a prophet cannot be a genuine prophet if he contradicts the preceding classic revelations, the Mosaic revelation. Therefore the question is, how to establish the classic revelation?

The usual traditional answer was: "miracles." But here the difficulty arises in this form: miracles as miracles are not demonstrable. In the first place, a miracle as a miracle is a fact of which we do not know the natural causes, but our ignorance of the cause of a given phenomenon does not entitle us to say it cannot have been produced by any natural cause, but only supernaturally. Our ignorance of the power of nature—that is Spinoza's phrasing of the argument—our ignorance of the power of nature disqualifies us from ever having recourse to supernatural causation.[54] Now this argument in this form is not quite adequate for the following reason: while our knowledge of the power of nature is certainly very limited, of certain things we know, or at least men like Spinoza believed themselves to know, that they are impossible by nature. I mention only the resurrection of a dead man, to take the strongest example, which Spinoza would admit could never have taken place naturally. Therefore the argument taken from the ignorance of the power of nature is supplemented by the following argument: that it might be possible theoretically to establish in given cases that a certain phenomenon is miraculous, but it so happens that all these events regarding which this claim is made are known only as reported, and many things are reported which have never happened. More precisely, all miracles which are important, certainly to the Jew and even to the Protestant (the case of Catholicism is different), took place in a prescientific age. No miracle was performed in the presence of first-rate physicists, etc. Therefore, for these reasons, many people today say, and that was also said by certain famous theologians of the past, that miracles presuppose faith; they are not meant to establish faith. But whether this is sufficient, whether this is in accordance with the biblical view of miracles, is a question. To begin with, one could make this objection: that if you take the story of the prophet Elijah on Carmel, you see that the issue between God and Baal is decided by an objective occurrence, equally acceptable to the sense perception of believers as well as unbelievers.[55]

The second ordinary traditional argument in favor of revelation is the fulfillment of prophecies. But I need not tell you that this again is open to very great difficulties. In the first place, we have the ambiguity of prophecies. And even in the case of unambiguous prophecies—for example, the prophecy of Cyrus in the fortieth chapter of Isaiah—that is today generally taken to be a prophecy after the event, the reasoning being that such a prophecy would be a miracle if established; but it is known only as reported, and therefore the question of historical criticism of the sources comes in.[56]

Much more impressive is the other line of the argument, which proves revelation by the intrinsic quality of revelation. The revealed law is the best of all laws. Now this, however, means that the revealed law agrees with the rational standard of the best law; but if this is the case, is then the allegedly revealed law not in fact the product of reason, of human reason, the work of Moses and not of God? Yet the revealed law, while it never contradicts reason, has an excess over reason; it is suprarational, and therefore it cannot be the product of reason. That is a very famous argument, but again we have to wonder what does suprarational mean? The "supra" has to be proved, and it cannot be proved. What unassisted reason sees is only a nonrational element, an element which, while not contradicting reason, is not in itself supported by reason. From the point of view of reason, it is an indifferent possibility: possibly true, possibly false, or possibly good, possibly bad. It would cease to be indifferent if it were proved to be true or good, which means if it were true or good according to natural reason. But again, if this were the case, it would appear to be the product of reason, of human reason. Let me try to state this in more general terms. The revealed law is either fully rational—in that case, it is a product of reason—or it is not fully rational—in that case, it may as well be the product of human unreason as of divine superreason. Still more generally, revelation is either a brute fact, to which nothing in purely human experience corresponds—in that case, it is an oddity of no human importance—or it is a meaningful fact, a fact required by human experience to solve the fundamental problems of man—in that case, it may very well be the product of reason, of the human attempt to solve the problem of human life. It would then appear that it is impossible for reason, for philosophy, to assent to revelation as revelation. Moreover, the intrinsic qualities of the revealed law are not regarded as decisive by the revealed law itself. Revealed law puts the emphasis not on the universal, but on the contingent, and this leads to the difficulties which I have indicated before.

Let us turn now to the other side of the picture; these things are, of course, implied in all present-day secularism. Now all these and similar arguments prove no more than that unassisted human reason is invincibly ignorant of divine revelation. They do not prove the impossibility of revelation. Let us assume that revelation is a fact, if a fact not accessible to unassisted reason, and that it is meant to be inaccessible to unassisted reason. For if there were certain knowledge, there would be no need for faith, for trust, for true obedience, for free surrender to God. In that case, the whole refutation of the alleged rejection of the alleged objective historical proofs of revelation would be utterly irrelevant. Let me take this simple example of Elijah on Carmel: were the believers in Baal, whom Elijah or God convinced, impartial scientific observers? In a famous essay, Francis Bacon made a distinction between idolators and atheists, and said that the miracles are meant only for the conviction, not of atheists, but of idolators, meaning of people who in principle admit the possibility of divine action.[57] These men were fearing and trembling, not beyond hope or fear like philosophers. Not theology, but philosophy, begs the question. Philosophy demands that revelation should establish its claim before the tribunal of human reason, but revelation as such refuses to acknowledge that tribunal. In other words, philosophy recognizes only such experiences as can be had by all men at all times in broad daylight. But God has said or decided that He wants to dwell in mist. Philosophy is victorious as long as it limits itself to repelling the attack which theologians make on philosophy with the weapons of philosophy. But philosophy in its turn suffers a defeat as soon as it starts an offensive of its own, as soon as it tries to refute, not the necessarily inadequate proofs of revelation, but revelation itself.

4.

Now there is today, I believe, still a very common view, common to nineteenth- and twentieth-century freethinkers, that modern science and historical criticism have refuted revelation. Now, I would say that they have not even refuted the most fundamentalistic orthodoxy. Let us look at that. There is the famous example which played such a role still in the nineteenth century and, for those of us who come from conservative or orthodox backgrounds, in our own lives: the age of the earth is much greater than the biblical reports assume. But this is obviously a very defective argument. The refutation presupposes that everything happens naturally; but this is denied by the Bible. The Bible speaks of creation; creation is a miracle, *the* miracle. All the evidence supplied by geology, paleontology, etc., is valid against the Bible only on the premise that no miracle intervened. The freethinking argument is really based on poor thinking. It begs the question. Similarly, this applies to textual criticism—the inconsistencies, repetitions, and other apparent deficiencies of the biblical text: if the text is divinely inspired, all those things mean something entirely different from what they would mean if we were entitled to assume that the Bible is a merely human book. Then they are just deficiencies, but otherwise they are secrets.

Historical criticism presupposes unbelief in verbal inspiration. The attack, the famous and very effective attack, by science and historical criticism on revelation is based on the dogmatic exclusion of the possibility of miracles and of verbal inspiration. I shall limit myself to miracles, because verbal inspiration itself is one miracle. Now this attack, which underlies all the scientific and historical arguments, would be defensible if we knew that miracles are impossible. Then we would indeed be able to draw all these conclusions. But what does that mean? We would have to be in possession of either a proof of the nonexistence of an omnipotent God, Who alone could do miracles, or of a proof that miracles are incompatible with the nature of God. I see no alternative to that. Now, the first alternative—a proof of the nonexistence of an omnipotent God—would presuppose that we have perfect knowledge of the whole, so, as it were, we know all the corners, and there is no place for an omnipotent God. In other words, the presupposition is a completed system. We have the solution to all riddles. And then, I think, we may dismiss this possibility as absurd. The second alternative— namely, that miracles are incompatible with the nature of God—would presuppose human knowledge of the nature of God: in traditional language, natural theology. Indeed, the basis, the forgotten basis, of modern free thought is natural theology. When the decisive battles were waged, not in the nineteenth century but in the eighteenth and seventeenth centuries, the attempted refutation of miracles, etc., was based on an alleged knowledge of the nature of God—natural theology is the technical name for that.

Let us sketch the general character of this argument. God is the most perfect being. This is what all men mean by God, regardless of whether He exists or not. Now, the philosophers claim that they can prove the incompatibility of revelation and of any other miracle with divine perfection. That is a long story, not only in the seventeenth and eighteenth centuries but of course also in the Middle Ages. I will try to sketch this argument by going back to its human roots. Fundamentally, the philosophic argument in natural theology is based on an analogy from human perfection. God is the most perfect being. But perfection we know empirically in the form of human perfection, and human perfection is taken to be represented by the wise man, or by the highest human approximation to the wise man. For example, just as the wise man does not inflict infinite punishment on erring human beings, God, still more perfect, would do it even less. A wise man does not do silly or purposeless things; but to use the miracle of verbal inspiration, for example, in order to tell a prophet the name of a pagan king who is going to rule centuries later, would be silly. I mean, that is the argument underlying these things, or something of that kind. To this I would answer as follows: God's perfection implies that He is incomprehensible. God's ways may seem to be foolish to man; this does not mean that they are foolish. Natural theology would have to get rid, in other words, of God's incomprehensibility in order to refute revelation, and that it never did.

There was one man who tried to force the issue by denying the incomprehensibility of God's essence, and that man was Spinoza. (May I say this in passing, that I have leaned very heavily in my analysis of these things on Spinoza.) One can learn much from Spinoza, who is the most extreme, certainly of the modern critics of revelation, not necessarily in his thought but certainly in the expression of his thought. I like to quote the remark of Hobbes, you know, a notoriously bold man, who said that he had not dared to write as boldly as Spinoza.[58] Now, Spinoza says: "We have adequate knowledge of the essence of God"; and if we have that, God is clearly fully comprehensible.[59] What Spinoza called the adequate knowledge of the essence of God led to the consequence that miracles of any kind are impossible. But what about Spinoza's adequate knowledge of the essence of God? Let us consider that for one moment, because it is really not a singular and accidental case. Many of you will have seen Spinoza's *Ethics*, his exposition of that knowledge. Spinoza's *Ethics* begins, as you know, with certain definitions. Now these definitions are in themselves absolutely arbitrary, especially the famous definition of substance: substance is what is by itself and is conceived by itself. Once you admit that, everything else follows from that; there are no miracles possible then. But since the definitions are arbitrary, the conclusions are arbitrary. The basic definitions are, however, not arbitrary if we view them with regard to their function. Spinoza defines by these definitions the conditions which must be fulfilled if the whole is to be fully intelligible. But they do not prove that these conditions are in fact fulfilled—that depends on the success of Spinoza's venture. The proof lies in the success. If Spinoza is capable of giving a clear and distinct account of everything, then we are confronted with this situation. We have a clear and distinct account of the whole, and, on the other hand, we have obscure accounts of the whole, one of which would be the biblical account. And then every sane person would prefer the clear and distinct account to the obscure account. That is, I think, the real proof which Spinoza wants to give. But is Spinoza's account of the whole clear and distinct? Those of you who have ever tried their hands, for example, at his analysis of the emotions, would not be so certain of that. But more than that, even if it is clear and distinct, is it necessarily true? Is its clarity and distinctness not due to the fact that Spinoza abstracts from those elements of the whole which are not clear and distinct and which can never be rendered clear and distinct? Now fundamentally, Spinoza's procedure is that of modern science according to its original conception—to make the universe a completely clear and distinct, a completely mathematizable, unit.

Let me sum this up: the historical refutation of revelation—and I say here that this is not changed if you take revelation in the most fundamentalist meaning of the term—presupposes natural theology, because the historical refutation always presupposes the impossibility of miracles, and the impossibility of miracles is ultimately guaranteed only by the knowledge of God. Now a natural theology which fills this bill presupposes in its turn a proof that God's nature is comprehensible, and this in its turn requires completion of the true system, of the true or adequate account of the whole. Since such a true or adequate account, as distinguished from a merely clear and distinct account, of the whole, is certainly not available, thus philosophy has never refuted revelation. Nor, to come back to what I said before, has revelation, or rather theology, ever refuted philosophy. For from the point of view of philosophy, first, revelation is only a possibility; and secondly, man, in spite of what the theologians say, can live as a philosopher, that is to say, untragically. It seems to me that all these attempts (made, for example, by Pascal and by others),[60] to prove that the life of philosophy is fundamentally miserable, presuppose faith; such "proofs" are not acceptable and possible as a refutation of philosophy. Generally stated, I would say that all alleged refutations of revelation presuppose unbelief in revelation, and all alleged refutations of philosophy presuppose already faith in revelation. There seems to be no ground common to both, and therefore superior to both.

If one can say colloquially, the philosophers have never refuted revelation and the theologians have never refuted philosophy, that would sound plausible, considering the enormous difficulty of the problem from any point of view. And to that extent we may be said to have said something very trivial; but to show that it is not quite trivial, I submit to you this consideration in conclusion. And here when I use the term philosophy, I use it in the common and vague sense of the term where it includes any rational orientation in the world, including science and what have you, common sense. If this is so, philosophy must admit the possibility of revelation. Now that means that philosophy itself is possibly not the right way of life. It is not necessarily the right way of life, not evidently the right way of life, because this possibility of revelation exists. But what then does the choice of philosophy mean under these conditions? In this case, the choice of philosophy is based on faith. In other words, the quest for evident knowledge rests itself on an unevident premise. And it seems to me that this difficulty underlies all present-day philosophizing, and that it is this difficulty which is at the bottom of what in the social sciences is called the "value problem": that philosophy or science, however you might call it, is incapable of giving an evident account of its own necessity. I do not think I have to prove that showing the practical usefulness of science, natural and social science, does not, of course, prove its necessity at all. I mean I shall not speak of the great successes of the social sciences, because they are not so impressive; but as for the great successes of the natural sciences, we in the age of the hydrogen bomb have the question completely open again whether this effort is really reasonable with a view to its practical usefulness. That is, of course, not the most important reason theoretically, but one which has practically played a great role.

Notes

["Progress or Return?" is based on a series of written lectures delivered by Leo Strauss at the Hillel House, University of Chicago, on 5, 12, and 19 November 1952. The written lectures were published posthumously in two parts. The first part appeared in print as "Progress or Return? The Contemporary Crisis in Western Civilization" in *Modern Judaism* 1 (1981): 17–45. It appears in the present book as sections I and II of "Progress or Return?" The second part appeared in print as "The Mutual Influence of Theology and Philosophy" in *The Independent Journal of Philosophy* 3 (1979): 111–18. It appears in the present book as section III of "Progress or Return?" The notes below to these lectures are entirely the work of the present editor. —Ed.]

1. Isaiah 1:21, 26.

2. See Ezekiel 1 and 10. Compare with Genesis 1–2, and with 2 Kings 2:12.

3. Jeremiah 30:20.

4. In speaking about "the most accepted view" of Judaism on the Messiah, Strauss likely bases himself on the legal works of Moses Maimonides; in these, "the most accepted view" is articulated authoritatively by him as law. See, e.g., *Mishneh Torah, Book of Judges,* "Laws of Kings," chap. 11, paras. 1, 3, 4; chap. 12, paras. 1, 2, 4.

5. Strauss appears to combine several passages from Gershom Scholem, *Major Trends in Jewish Mysticism* (New York: Schocken, 1946), 256, 268, 274.

6. In this sentence Strauss refers to the "paradox" that both of the modern Hebrew terms for progress—*kidma* or *hitkadmut*—derive from the root *kdm*, to precede. The root *kdm* is most often used in forms which convey "old," "early," "former," or "prior," as with *kedem*, "ancient days." Thus in modern Hebrew "progress" cannot help but suggest or imply "return."

7. Benedict Spinoza, "On the Vocation of the Hebrews," chap. 3, toward the end, in *Theologico-Political Treatise.*

8. Exodus 13:17.

9. J. B. Bury, *The Idea of Progress* (London: Macmillan, 1920).

10. John Baillie, *The Belief in Progress* (London: Oxford University Press, 1950).

11. Aristotle, *Politics* 1257b25–28.

12. Ibid., 1268b25–1269a29.

13. Strauss speaks about a first school of Greek thought, in which he seems to think of Plato. He also speaks about a second school of Greek thought, specifically associated with Aristotle. For periodic telluric cataclysms in Plato, see *Timaeus* 22b–23c. For the eternity of the visible universe in Aristotle, see *Physics* 251b20ff., and *Metaphysics* 1071b5ff.; for periodic telluric cataclysms in Aristotle, see *Politics* 1269a5–8.

14. Abbé de Saint-Pierre, *Observations on the Continuous Progress of Universal Reason*. Cited by J. B. Bury, *The Idea of Progress* (London: Macmillan, 1920), 136. (My thanks to Ernest Fortin for the reference.) See also Bury, p. 132, for a reference to the orthodox belief in a "six thousand year" chronology of human history since the creation, a belief which was denied by the Abbé de Saint-Pierre, but which was still held by the Abbé's immediate predecessor, Emeric Cruce in his *Nouveau Cynée* (1623), who otherwise advocated similar modern "progressive" ideas about establishing a perpetual peace.

15. Plato, *Timaeus* 41a–b.

16. Moses Maimonides, *The Guide of the Perplexed*, trans. Shlomo Pines (Chicago: University of Chicago Press, 1963), 2.27–28.

17. Friedrich Engels, "Ludwig Feuerbach and the End of Classical German Philosophy," sect. 1, toward the beginning. It appears that this series of passages has been translated by Strauss himself. For the original German, see "Ludwig Feuerbach und der Ausgang der klassischen deutschen Philosophie," in *Karl Marx und Friedrich Engels: Werke*, ed. Institut für Marxismus-Leninismus beim ZK der SED, vol. 21, pp. 267–68 (Berlin: Dietz, 1962).

18. Georges Sorel, *Les illusions du progrès* (Paris: Rivières, 1908); *The Illusions of Progress*, translated by John and Charlotte Stanley (Berkeley: University of California Press, 1969).

19. Oswald Spengler, *Der Untergang des Abendlandes* (Munich: C. H. Beck, 1918); *The Decline of the West*, translated by Charles Francis Atkinson (New York: Alfred Knopf, 1926).

20. Strauss seems especially to think of Gotthold Ephraim Lessing. See Leo Strauss, "Exoteric Teaching," in *Interpretation* 14, no. 1 (January 1986): 51–59; and "Correspondence between Karl Löwith and Leo Strauss," in *The Independent Journal of Philosophy* 5/6 (1988): 177–92, and esp. p. 190: "Read Swift—who next to Lessing was the freest mind of modernity." See also in Appendix 1, infra, the very last item in Strauss's proposed table of contents.

21. Plato, *Laws* 636b–d and 836c–e; Leviticus 18:22 and 20:13. Also consider Deuteronomy 22:5, 23:18–19. A reference was also made in passing (five paragraphs prior to the present one) to the character of virtue in Plato: see *Phaedrus* 246a–247c.

22. Aristotle, *Nicomachean Ethics* 1107a9ff.; Exodus 20:13–14 and Deuteronomy 5:17–18.

23. Plato, *Republic* 549c–d; Genesis 3:1–7.

24. Perhaps Strauss was thinking of Herodotus, *The History* 7.136. (My thanks to Seth Benardete for the reference.) But consider also Xenophanes, fragment 23, and Sophocles, *Antigone* 450–60; Deuteronomy 4:16 (and Exodus 20:4–5).

25. Deuteronomy 32:47 and Proverbs 3:18; Plato, *Laws* 718b.

26. Aristotle, *Nicomachean Ethics* 1138a8; Deuteronomy 8:10 (or Leviticus 25:19) and Genesis 1:28.

27. Plato, *Apology of Socrates* 21d, 22d–e, and *Crito* 50c4–54d1; Xenophon, *Memorabilia* 1.2.62–63, 4.3.1–18; Numbers 12:3, with Micah 6:8. See also Mishna Avot 5:22, and Babylonian Talmud, Makkot 24a.

28. Compare Plato, *Laws* 905a with Amos 9:1–4 and Psalm 139:7–12.

29. Compare Plato, *Timaeus* 28–38 with Genesis 1.

30. Isaiah 53:7, 9; Plato, *Republic* 361e.

31. Plato, *Republic* 611e–621d; Job 42.

32. For the magnanimous or great-souled man as he is related to the perfect gentleman, see Aristotle, *Nicomachean Ethics* 1123a33–1125a35. For King Saul and King Agag, see 1 Samuel 15. For the sins of David against Uriah and Bathsheba, and for his repentance, see 2 Samuel 11–12. For the friendship of Jonathan and David, see 1 Samuel 18–20 and 2 Samuel 1. For Michal and David, see 2 Samuel 6:12–23. For some of the duties to the poor and the reasons for them, see: Exodus 22:20–26; Deuteronomy 15:7–11, as well as 24:14, 17–20; Isaiah 3:14–17, 9:14–16, 10:1–3, and 58:6–12; Amos 2:6–7, 5:11–12.

33. For the "thousandfold poverty" of Socrates, see Plato, *Apology of Socrates* 23b–c. For Socrates' statement on the goodness of man and horse relative to monetary value, see Xenophon, *Oeconomicus* 11.3–6. See also Leo Strauss, "Liberal Education and Responsibility," in *Liberalism Ancient and Modern* (New York: Basic Books, 1968), 13–14; *Xenophon's Socratic Discourse* (Ithaca, N.Y.: Cornell University Press, 1970), 159–66.

34. Aristotle, *Nicomachean Ethics* 1128b10–21.

35. Winston Churchill, "Arthur James Balfour," in *Great Contemporaries* (London: Thornton Butterworth, 1937), 237–57, and esp. p. 239. (My thanks to Laurence Berns for the reference.)

36. Xenophon, *Memorabilia* 4.8.6. See also Leo Strauss, *On Tyranny*, edited by Victor Gourevitch and Michael S. Roth (New York: Free Press, 1991), 197, 203–5; *Xenophon's Socrates* (Ithaca, N.Y.: Cornell University Press, 1972), 124–26.

37. Plato, *Republic* 398a1–b3, 605c2–608b2; Aristotle, *Poetics* 1453a7–11, 1449b24–28.

38. Yehuda Halevi, "For the sake of the house of our God," in *Selected Poems of Jehudah Halevi*, ed. Heinrich Brody (Philadelphia: Jewish Publication Society, 1924), p. 16, lines 53–54. See also Leo Strauss, *Persecution and the Art of Writing* (Glencoe, Ill.: Free Press, 1952), p. 109 note 39.

39. Genesis 4:2, 4, 8, 17, 20–22; Exodus 19–20.

40. Compare Xenophon, *Hiero, or, On Tyranny*, with 2 Samuel 11–12. See also Leo Strauss, *On Tyranny*.

41. Compare Genesis 22 with Plato, *Apology of Socrates* 21a–23c.

42. Maimonides, *Guide* 2.13–24. See also 2.25–31.

43. Homer, *Odyssey* 10.302.

44. Plato, *Laws*, book 10, and perhaps especially 891c–900b.

45. Edmund Burke, "Fourth Letter on a Regicide Peace" (1795), in *The Writings and Speeches of Edmund Burke*, gen. ed. Paul Langford. Vol. 9, ed. R. B. McDowell (Oxford: Clarendon Press, 1991), 83. In the following paragraph, Strauss mentions Herodotus on conflicting burial customs. See *The History* 1.98, 216; 2.85–90; 3.24, 38; 4.26, 71–73, 94, 190; 5.4–5, 8. In what is likely the crucial passage to which Strauss refers, 3.38, Herodotus mentions the saying of Pindar: "Custom is king of all."

46. Exodus 33:20, with 3:14.

47. Compare Genesis 1:1–2:4a with 2:4b–3:24.

48. For the Fall, see Genesis 3. For Cain and Abel, see Genesis 4:1–15. For Cain's genealogy, see Genesis 4:17–24. For Jerusalem, see, e.g., Isaiah 2:1–4, 66:20. For Bezalel, see Exodus 35–39. For kingship, see 1 Samuel 8, 10, 12.

49. See: Yehuda Halevi, *Kuzari* 4.12–19, as well as 1.11 and 25; Blaise Pascal, *Pensées* # 556, and *Mémorial* (1654): "God of Abraham, God of Isaac, God of Jacob, not of philosophers and scholars."

50. Halevi, *Kuzari* 4.14.

51. I have not been able to locate the author or the source of the quoted statement.

52. Fyodor Dostoyevsky, *The Possessed*, trans. Constance Garnett (New York: Modern Library, 1963). See especially the conversation of Shatov and Stavrogin in the chapter entitled "Night," pp. 250–60.

53. Maimonides, *Mishneh Torah, The Book of Knowledge*, ed. Moses Hyamson (New York: Philipp Feldheim, 1981), p. 1b, lines 17–19.

54. Spinoza, "On Miracles," chap. 6, toward the beginning, in *Theologico-Political Treatise*. In Spinoza's account of the first of four points he enumerates on miracles, he states: ". . . miracles were brought about according to the understanding of the vulgar, who are wholly ignorant of the power of nature."

55. 1 Kings 18. See also Leo Strauss, *Spinoza's Critique of Religion* (New York: Schocken, 1965), 212–14.

56. See especially Isaiah 44:28 and 45:1. See also Jeremiah 29:10–14, and compare with 2 Chronicles 36:17–23.

57. Francis Bacon, "Of Atheism," at the beginning, in *Essays of 1625*. But see also *The Advancement of Learning* 2.25.24.

58. John Aubrey, "Thomas Hobbes," in *Brief Lives*, ed. Andrew Clark (Oxford: Clarendon Press, 1898), vol. 1, p. 357. See also Leo Strauss, *Persecution and the Art of Writing* (Glencoe, Ill.: Free Press, 1952), 183; and *What Is Political Philosophy?* (New York: Free Press, 1959), 171.

59. Benedict Spinoza, *Ethics* part 2, proposition 47.

60. Pascal, *Pensées* # 72–73, 82–83, 361, 365, 374, 389, 397–99, 412, 525, 556.

2

Preface to *Spinoza's Critique of Religion*

The study on Spinoza's *Theologico-Political Treatise* to which this was a preface was written during the years 1925–28 in Germany. The author was a young Jew born and raised in Germany who found himself in the grips of the theologico-political predicament.

At that time Germany was a liberal democracy. The regime was known as the Weimar Republic. In the light of the most authoritative political document of recent Germany, Bismarck's *Thoughts and Recollections*, the option for Weimar reveals itself as an option against Bismarck. In the eyes of Bismarck, Weimar stood for leanings to the West, if not for the inner dependence of the Germans on the French and above all on the English, and a corresponding aversion to everything Russian. But Weimar was, above all, the residence of Goethe, the contemporary of the collapse of the Holy Roman Empire of the German nation, and of the victory of the French Revolution and Napoleon, whose sympathetic understanding was open to both antagonists and who identified himself in his thought with neither. By linking itself to Weimar the German liberal democracy proclaimed its moderate, nonradical character: its resolve to keep a balance between the dedication to the principles of 1789 and the dedication to the highest German tradition.

The Weimar Republic was weak. It had a single moment of strength, if not of greatness: its strong reaction to the murder of the Jewish Minister of Foreign Affairs, Walther Rathenau, in 1922. On the whole it presented the sorry spectacle of justice without a sword or of justice unable to use the sword. The election of Field Marshal von Hindenburg to the presidency of the German Reich in 1925 showed everyone who had eyes to see that the Weimar Republic had only a short time to live: the old Germany was stronger—stronger in will—than the new Germany. What was still lacking then for the destruction of the Weimar Republic was the opportune moment; that moment was to come within a few years. The weakness of the Weimar Republic made certain its speedy destruction. It did not make certain the victory of national socialism. The victory of national socialism became necessary in Germany for the same reason that the victory of communism had become necessary in Russia: the man who had by far the strongest will or single-mindedness, the greatest ruthlessness, daring, and power over his following, and the best judgment about the strength of the various forces in the immediately relevant political field was the leader of the revolution.[1]

Half-Marxists trace the weakness of the Weimar Republic to the power of monopoly capitalism and the economic crisis of 1929, but there were other liberal democracies which were and remained strong although they had to contend with the same difficulties. It is more reasonable to refer to the fact that the Weimar Republic had come into being through the defeat of Germany in World War I, although this answer merely leads to the further question as to why Germany had not succeeded in becoming a liberal democracy under more auspicious circumstances (for instance, in 1848), i.e., why liberal democracy had always been weak in Germany. It is true that the Bismarckian regime as managed by William II had become discredited already prior to World War I and still more through that war and its outcome, and correspondingly liberal democracy had become ever more attractive; but at the crucial moment the victorious liberal democracies discredited liberal democracy in the eyes of Germany by the betrayal of their principles through the Treaty of Versailles.

It is safer to try to understand the low in the light of the high than the high in the light of the low. In doing the latter one necessarily distorts the high, whereas in doing the former one does not deprive the low of the freedom to reveal itself fully as what it is. By its name the Weimar Republic refers one to the greatest epoch of German thought and letters, to the epoch extending from the last third of the eighteenth century to the first third of the nineteenth century. No one can say that classical Germany spoke clearly and distinctly in favor of liberal democracy. This is true despite the fact that classical Germany had been initiated by Rousseau. In the first place Rousseau was the first modern critic of the fundamental modern project (man's conquest of nature for the sake of the relief of man's estate) who therewith laid the foundation for the distinction, so fateful for German thought, between civilization and culture. Above all, the radicalization and deepening of Rousseau's thought by classical German philosophy culminated in Hegel's *Philosophy of Right*, the legitimation of that kind of constitutional monarchy which is based on the recognition of the rights of man, and in which government is in the hands of highly educated civil servants appointed by a hereditary king. It has been said, not without reason, that Hegel's rule over Germany came to an end only on the day that Hitler came to power. But Rousseau prepared not only the French Revolution and classical German philosophy but also that extreme reaction to the French Revolution which is German romanticism. To speak politically and crudely, "the romantic school in Germany . . . was nothing other than the resurrection of medieval poetry as it had manifested itself . . . in art and in life."[2] The longing for the Middle Ages began in Germany in the same moment in which the actual Middle Ages—the Holy Roman Empire ruled by a German—ended, in what was then thought to be the moment of Germany's deepest humiliation. In Germany, and only there, did the end of the Middle Ages coincide with the beginning of the longing for the Middle Ages. Compared with the medieval Reich, which had lasted for almost a millennium until 1806, Bismarck's Reich (to say nothing of Hegel's Prussia) revealed itself as a little Germany not only in size. All profound German longings—for those for the Middle Ages were not the only ones nor even the most profound ones—all these longings for the origins or, negatively expressed, all German dissatisfactions with modernity pointed toward a third Reich, for Germany was to be the core even of Nietzsche's Europe ruling the planet.[3]

The weakness of liberal democracy in Germany explains why the situation of the indigenous Jews was more precarious in Germany than in any other Western country. Liberal democracy had originally defined itself in theologico-political treatises as the opposite, less of the more or less enlightened despotism of the seventeenth and eighteenth centuries, than of "the kingdom of darkness," i.e., of medieval society. According to liberal democracy, the bond of society is universal human morality, whereas religion (positive religion) is a private affair; in the Middle Ages religion, i.e., Catholic Christianity, was the bond of society. The action most characteristic of the Middle Ages is the Crusades; it may be said to have culminated not accidentally in the murder of whole Jewish communities. The German Jews owed their emancipation to the French Revolution or its effects. They were given full political rights for the first time by the Weimar Republic. The Weimar Republic was succeeded by the only German regime—by the only regime that ever was anywhere—which had no other clear principle except murderous hatred of the Jews, for "Aryan" had no clear meaning other than "non-Jewish." One must keep in mind the fact that Hitler did not come from Prussia, nor even from Bismarck's Reich.

While the German Jews were politically in a more precarious situation than the Jews in any other Western country, they originated "the science of Judaism," the historical-critical study by Jews of the Jewish heritage. The emancipation of the Jews in Germany coincided with the greatest epoch of German thought and poetry, with the epoch in which Germany was the foremost country in thought and poetry. One cannot help comparing the period of German Jewry with the period of Spanish Jewry. The greatest achievements of Jews during the Spanish period were partly rendered possible by the fact that Jews became open to the influx of Greek thought, which was understood to be Greek only accidentally. During the German period, however, the Jews became open to the influx of German thought, of the thought of the particular nation in the midst of which they lived—of a thought which was understood to be German essentially: the political dependence was also spiritual dependence. This was the core of the predicament of German Jewry.

Three quotations may serve to illustrate the precarious situation of the Jews in Germany. Goethe, the greatest among the cosmopolitan Germans, a "decided non-Christian," summarizes the results of a conversation about a new society to be founded, between his Wilhelm Meister and "the gay Friedrich," without providing his summary with quotation marks, as follows:

> To this religion [the Christian religion] we hold on, but in a particular manner; we instruct our children from their youth on in the great advantages which [that religion] has brought to us; but of its author, of its course, we speak to them only at the end. Then only does the author become dear and cherished, and all reports regarding him become sacred. Drawing a conclusion which one may perhaps call pedantic, but of which one must at any rate admit that it follows from the premise, we do not tolerate any Jew among us; for how could we grant him a share in the highest culture, the origin and tradition of which he denies?[4]

Two generations later Nietzsche could say: "I have not yet met a German who was favorably disposed toward the Jews."[5] One might try to trace Nietzsche's judgment to the narrowness of his circle of acquaintances: no one would expect to find people favorably disposed toward Jews among the German Lutheran pastors among whom Nietzsche grew up, to say nothing of Jakob Burckhardt in Basel. Nietzsche has chosen his words carefully; he surely excluded himself when making the judgment quoted, as appears, in addition, from the context. But he does not say something trivial. While his circle of acquaintances was limited—perhaps unusually limited—he was of unusual perspicacity. Besides, being favorably disposed toward this or that man or woman of Jewish origin does not mean being favorably disposed toward Jews. Two generations later, in 1953, Heidegger could speak of "the inner truth and greatness of national socialism."[6]

In the course of the nineteenth century many Western men had come to conceive of many, if not all, sufferings as problems which as such were held to be soluble as a matter of course. Thus, they had come to speak also of the Jewish problem. The German-Jewish problem was never solved. It was annihilated by the annihilation of the German Jews. Prior to Hitler's rise to power most German Jews believed that their problem had been solved in principle by liberalism: the German Jews were Germans of the Jewish faith, i.e., they were no less German than the Germans of the Christian faith or of no faith. They assumed that the German state (to say nothing of German society or culture) was or ought to be neutral to the difference between Christians and Jews or between non-Jews and Jews. This assumption was not accepted by the strongest part of Germany and hence by Germany. In the words of Herzl: "Who belongs and who does not belong, is decided by the majority; it is a question of power." At any rate it could seem that in the absence of a superior recognized equally by both parties the natural judge on the Germanness of the German Jews was the non-Jewish Germans. As a consequence, a small minority of the German Jews, but a considerable minority of German-Jewish youth studying at the universities, had turned to Zionism. Zionism was almost never wholly divorced from the traditional Jewish hopes. On the other hand, Zionism never intended to bring about a restoration like the one achieved in the days of Ezra and Nehemiah: the return to the land of Israel was not thought to culminate in the building of the third temple and in the restoration of the sacrificial service.

The peculiarity of Zionism as a modern movement comes out most clearly in the strictly political Zionism as presented in the first place by Leon Pinsker in his *Autoemancipation*, and then by Theodor Herzl in *The Jews' State*. Pinsker and Herzl started from the failure of the liberal solution, but continued to see the problem to be solved as it had begun to be seen by liberalism, i.e., as a merely human problem. They radicalized this purely human understanding. The terrible fate of the Jews was in no sense to be understood any longer as connected with divine punishment for the sins of our fathers or with the providential mission of the chosen people and hence to be borne with the meek fortitude of martyrs. It was to be understood in merely human terms: as constituting a purely political problem which as such cannot be solved by appealing to the justice or generosity of other nations, to say nothing of a league of all nations. Accordingly, political Zionism was concerned primarily with nothing but the cleansing of the Jews from millennial degradation, or with the recovery of Jewish dignity, honor, or pride.

The failure of the liberal solution meant that the Jews could not regain their honor by assimilating themselves as individuals to the nations among which they lived or by becoming citizens like all other citizens of the liberal states: the liberal solution brought at best legal equality, but not social equality; as a demand of reason it had no effect on the feelings of the non-Jews. To quote Herzl again: "We are a nation—the enemy makes us a nation whether we like it or not." In the last analysis this is nothing to be deplored, for "the enemy is necessary for the highest effort of the personality." Only through securing the honor of the Jewish nation could the individual Jew's honor be secured. The true solution of the Jewish problem requires that the Jews become "like all the nations" (1 Samuel 8), that the Jewish nation assimilate itself to the nations of the world or that it establish a modern, liberal, secular (but not necessarily democratic) state. Political Zionism strictly understood was then the movement of an elite on behalf of a community, constituted by common descent and common degradation, for the restoration of their honor through the acquisition of statehood and therefore of a country—of any country: the land which the strictly political Zionism promised to the Jews was not necessarily the land of Israel.

This project implied a profound modification of the traditional Jewish hopes—a modification arrived at through a break with these hopes. For the motto of his pamphlet Pinsker chose these words of Hillel: "If I am not for myself, who will be for me? And if not now, when?" He omitted the sentence which forms the center of Hillel's statement: "And if I am only for myself, what am I?" He saw the Jewish people as a herd without a shepherd to protect and gather it; he did not long for a shepherd, but for the transformation of the herd into a nation which can take care of itself. He regarded the Jewish situation as a natural sickness which can be cured only by natural means. What the change effected by strictly political Zionism means, one sees most clearly when, returning to the origin, one ponders over this sentence of Spinoza: "If the foundations of their religion did not effeminate the minds of the Jews, I would absolutely believe that they will at some time, given the occasion (for human things are mutable), establish their state again."

Strictly political Zionism became effective only through becoming an ingredient, not to say the backbone, of Zionism at large, i.e., by making its peace with traditional Jewish thought. Through this alliance or fusion it brought about the establishment of the state of Israel and therewith that cleansing which it had primarily intended; it thus procured a blessing for all Jews everywhere regardless of whether they admit it or not.[7] It did not, however, solve the Jewish problem. It could not solve the

Jewish problem because of the narrowness of its original conception, however noble. This narrowness was pointed out most effectively by cultural Zionism: strictly political Zionism, concerned only with the present emergency and resolve, lacks historical perspective; the community of descent, of the blood, must also be a community of the mind, of the national mind; the Jewish state will be an empty shell without a Jewish culture which has its roots in the Jewish heritage. One could not have taken this step unless one had previously interpreted the Jewish heritage itself as a culture, i.e., as a product of the national mind, of the national genius.[8] Yet the foundation, the authoritative layer, of the Jewish heritage presents itself, not as a product of the human mind, but as a divine gift, as divine revelation. Did one not completely distort the meaning of the heritage to which one claimed to be loyal by interpreting it as a culture like any other high culture? Cultural Zionism believed itself to have found a safe middle ground between politics (power politics) and divine revelation, between the subcultural and the supracultural, but it lacked the sternness of the two extremes. When cultural Zionism understands itself, it turns into religious Zionism. But when religious Zionism understands itself, it is in the first place Jewish faith and only secondarily Zionism. It must regard as blasphemous the notion of a human solution to the Jewish problem. It may go so far as to regard the establishment of the state of Israel as the most important event in Jewish history since the completion of the Talmud, but it cannot regard it as the arrival of the messianic age, of the redemption of Israel and of all men. The establishment of the state of Israel is the most profound modification of the *galut* which has occurred, but it is not the end of the *galut*: in the religious sense, and perhaps not only in the religious sense, the state of Israel is a part of the *galut*. Finite, relative problems can be solved; infinite, absolute problems cannot be solved. In other words, human beings will never create a society which is free from contradictions. From every point of view it looks as if the Jewish people were the chosen people, at least in the sense that the Jewish problem is the most manifest symbol of the human problem insofar as it is a social or political problem.

To realize that the Jewish problem is insoluble means never to forget the truth proclaimed by Zionism regarding the limitations of liberalism. Liberalism stands and falls by the distinction between state and society or by the recognition of a private sphere, protected by the law but impervious to the law, with the understanding that, above all, religion as particular religion belongs to the private sphere. As certainly as the liberal state will not "discriminate" against its Jewish citizens, as certainly is it constitutionally unable and even unwilling to prevent "discrimination" against Jews on the part of individuals or groups. To recognize a private sphere in the sense indicated means to permit private "discrimination," to protect it, and thus in fact to foster it. The liberal state cannot provide a solution to the Jewish problem, for such a solution would require the legal prohibition against every kind of "discrimination," i.e., the abolition of the private sphere, the denial of the difference between state and society, the destruction of the liberal state. Such a destruction would not by any means solve the Jewish problem, as is shown in our days by the anti-Jewish policy of the U.S.S.R. It is foolish to say that that policy contradicts the principles of communism, for it contradicts the principles of communism to separate the principles of communism from the communist movement. The U.S.S.R. owes its survival to Stalin's decision not to wait for the revolution of the Western proletariat, i.e., for what others would do for the U.S.S.R., but to build up socialism in a single country where his word was the law, by the use of any means, however bestial, and these means could include, as a matter of course, means successfully used before, not to say invented, by Hitler: the large-scale murder of party members and anti-Jewish measures. This is not to deny that communism has not become what national socialism always was, the prisoner of an anti-Jewish ideology, but it makes use of anti-Jewish measures in an unprincipled manner, when and where they seem to be expedient. It is merely to confirm our contention that the uneasy "solution of the Jewish problem" offered by the liberal state is superior to the communist "solution."

There is a Jewish problem which is humanly soluble:[9] the problem of the Western Jewish individual who or whose parents severed his connection with the Jewish community in the expectation that he would thus become a normal member of a purely liberal or of a universal human society, and who is naturally perplexed when he finds no such society. The solution to his problem is return to the Jewish community, the community established by the Jewish faith and the Jewish way of life—*teshuva* (ordinarily rendered by "repentance") in the most comprehensive sense. Some of our contemporaries believe that such a return is altogether impossible because they believe that the Jewish faith has been overthrown once and for all, not by blind rebellion, but by evident refutation. While admitting that their deepest problem would be solved by that return, they assert that intellectual probity forbids them to bring the sacrifice of the intellect for the sake of satisfying even the most vital need. Yet they can hardly deny that a vital need legitimately induces a man to probe whether what seems to be an impossibility is in fact only a very great difficulty.

The founder of cultural Zionism could still deny that the Jewish people have a providential mission on the ground that Darwin had destroyed the most solid basis of teleology.[10] At the time and in the country in which the present study was written, it was granted by everyone except backward people that the Jewish faith had not been refuted by science or by history. The storms stirred up by Darwin and to a lesser degree by Wellhausen had been weathered; one could grant to science and history everything they seem to teach regarding the age of the world, the origin of man, the impossibility of miracles, the impossibility of the immortality of the soul and of the resurrection of the body, the Jahvist, the Elohist, the third Isaiah, and so on, without abandoning one iota of the substance of the Jewish faith. Some haggling regarding particular items, which issued sometimes in grudging concessions, was still going on in outlying districts, but the battle for the capital had been decided by the wholesale surrender to science and history of the whole sphere in which science and history claim to be or to become competent, and by the simultaneous depreciation of that whole sphere as religiously irrelevant. It had become religiously relevant, it was affirmed, only through a self-misunderstanding of religion, if of a self-misunderstanding which was inevitable in earlier times and which on the whole was even harmless in earlier times. That self-misunderstanding consisted in understanding revelation as a body of teachings and rules which includes such teachings and rules as could never become known to the unassisted human mind as true and binding, such as the human mind would reject as subrational were they not proved to be suprarational by the certainty that they are the word of God; men who were not earwitnesses of God's declaring these teachings and rules could have that certainty only through a reliable tradition which also vouches for the reliable transmission of the very words of God, and through miracles. The self-misunderstanding is removed when the content of revelation is seen to be rational, which does not necessarily mean that everything hitherto thought to be revealed is rational. The need for external credentials of revelation (tradition and miracles) disappears as its internal credentials come to abound. The truth of traditional Judaism is the religion of reason, or the religion of reason is secularized Judaism. But the same claim could be made for Christianity, and however close secularized Judaism and secularized Christianity might come to each other, they are not identical, and as purely rational they ought to be identical. Above all, if the truth of Judaism is the religion of reason, then what was formerly believed to be revelation by the transcendent God must now be understood as the work of the human imagination in which human reason was effective to some extent; what has now become a clear and distinct idea was originally a confused idea.[11] What, except demonstrations of the existence of God by theoretical reason or postulations of His existence by practical reason which were becoming ever more incredible, could prevent one from taking the last step, i.e., to assert that God Himself is a product of the human mind, at best "an idea of reason"?

These and similar denials or interpretations suddenly lost all their force by the simple observation that they contradict not merely inherited opinions but present experience. At first hearing one may be reminded of what Leibniz had said when overcoming Bayle's doubt regarding revelation: "Toutes ces difficultés invincibles, ces combats prétendus de la raison contre la foi s'évanouissent.

> Hi motus animorum atque haec discrimina tanta
> Pulveris exigui jactu compressa quiescunt."[12]

God's revealing Himself to man, His addressing man, is not merely known through traditions going back to the remote past and is therefore now "merely believed," but is genuinely known through present experience which every human being can have if he does not refuse himself to it. This experience is not a kind of self-experience, of the actualization of a human potentiality, of the human mind coming into its own, into what it desires or is naturally inclined to, but of something undesired, coming from the outside, going against man's grain; it is the only awareness of something absolute which cannot be relativized in any way as everything else, rational or nonrational, can; it is the experience of God as the Thou, the father and king of all men; it is the experience of an unequivocal command addressed to me here and now as distinguished from general laws or ideas which are always disputable and permitting of exceptions; only by surrendering to God's experienced call which calls for one's loving Him with all one's heart, with all one's soul, and with all one's might can one come to see the other human being as one's brother and love him as oneself. The absolute experience will not lead back to Judaism—for instance, to the details of what the Christians call the ceremonial law—if it does not recognize itself in the Bible and clarify itself through the Bible, and if it is not linked up with considerations of how traditional Judaism understands itself and with meditations about the mysterious fate of the Jewish people. The return to Judaism also requires today the overcoming of what one may call the perennial obstacle to the Jewish faith: of traditional philosophy, which is of Greek, pagan origin. For the respectable, impressive, or specious alternatives to the acceptance of revelation, to the surrender to God's will, have always presented themselves and still present themselves as based on what man knows by himself, by his reason. Reason has reached its perfection in Hegel's system; the essential limitations of Hegel's system show the essential limitations of reason and therewith the radical inadequacy of all rational objections to revelation. With the final collapse of rationalism the perennial battle between reason and revelation, between unbelief and belief, has been decided in principle, even on the plane of human thought, in favor of revelation. Reason knows only of subjects and objects, but surely the living and loving God is infinitely more than a subject and can never be an object, something at which one can look in detachment or indifference. Philosophy as hitherto known, the old thinking, so far from starting from the experience of God, abstracted from such experience or excluded it; hence, if it was theistic, it was compelled to have recourse to demonstrations of the existence of God as a thinking or a thinking and willing being. The new thinking as unqualified empiricism speaks of God, man, and the world as actually experienced, as realities irreducible to one another, whereas all traditional philosophy was reductionist. For if it did not assert that the world and man are eternal, i.e., deny the creator-God, it sought for the reality preceding world and man as it precedes world and man and as it succeeds world and man, i.e., for what cannot be experienced by man, by the whole man, but can only be inferred or thought by him. Unqualified empiricism does not recognize any such Without or Beyond as a reality, but only as unreal forms, essences, or concepts which can never be more than objects, i.e., objects of mere thought.[13]

The new thinking had been originated, above all, by Franz Rosenzweig, who is thought to be the greatest Jewish thinker whom German Jewry has brought forth. It was counteracted by another form of the new thinking, the form originated by Heidegger.[14] It was obvious that Heidegger's new thinking led far away from any charity as well as from any humanity. On the other hand, it could not be denied that he had a deeper understanding than Rosenzweig of what was implied in the insight or demand that the traditional philosophy which rested on Greek foundations must be superseded by a new thinking. He would never have said as Rosenzweig did that "we know in the most precise manner, we know it with the intuitional knowledge of experience, what God taken by Himself, what man taken by himself, what the world taken by itself 'is'." Nor did he assume, as Rosenzweig assumed, that we possess without further ado an adequate understanding of Greek philosophy, of the basic stratum of that old thinking which has to be overcome: with the questioning of traditional philosophy the traditional understanding of the tradition becomes questionable. For this reason alone he could not have said as Rosenzweig did that most Platonic dialogues are "boring."[15] This difference between Rosenzweig and Heidegger, about which much more could be said, was not unconnected with their difference regarding revelation. At that time Heidegger expressed his thought about revelation by silence or deed rather than by speech. Rosenzweig's friend Martin Buber quotes a much later utterance of Heidegger which gives one, I believe, an inkling of Heidegger's argument—especially if it is taken in conjunction with well-known utterances of Nietzsche whom Heidegger evidently follows in this matter.

"The 'prophets' of these religions [sc. Judaism and Christianity]," says Heidegger according to Buber, "do not begin by foretelling the word of the Holy. They announce immediately the God upon whom the certainty of salvation in a supernatural blessedness reckons."[16] Buber comments on this statement as follows:

> Incidentally, I have never in our time encountered on a high philo-sophical plane such a far-reaching misunderstanding of the prophets of Israel. The prophets of Israel have never announced a God upon whom their hearers' striving for security reckoned. They have always aimed to shatter all security and to proclaim in the opened abyss of the final insecurity the unwished for God who demands that His human creatures become real, they become human, and confounds all who imagine that they can take refuge in the certainty that the temple of God is in their midst.

Heidegger does not speak of the prophets' "hearers," but he clearly means that the prophets themselves were concerned with security.[17] This assertion is not refuted by the well-known facts which Buber points out—by the fact, in a word, that for the prophets there is no refuge and fortress except God: the security afforded by the temple of God is noth-ing, but the security afforded by God is everything. As Buber says sev-enteen pages earlier in the same publication, "He who loves God only as a moral ideal, can easily arrive at despairing of the guidance of a world the appearance of which contradicts, hour after hour, all princi-ples of his moral ideality."[18] Surely the Bible teaches that in spite of all appearances to the contrary the world is guided by God or, to use the traditional term, that there is particular providence, that man is pro-tected by God if he does not put his trust in flesh and blood but in God alone, that he is not completely exposed or forsaken, that he is not alone, that he has been created by a being which is, to use Buber's expression, a Thou. Buber's protest would be justified if the biblical prophets were only, as Wellhausen may seem to have hoped, prophets of insecurity, not to say of an evil end,[19] and not also predictors of the messianic future, of the ultimate victory of truth and justice, of the final salvation and security, although not necessarily of the final salvation and security of all men. In other words, the biblical experience is not simply undesired or against man's grain: grace perfects nature; it does not destroy nature. Not every man but every noble man is concerned with justice or right- eousness and therefore with any possible extrahuman, suprahuman support of justice, or with the security of justice. The insecurity of man and everything human is not an absolutely terrifying abyss if the high- est of which a man knows is absolutely secure. Plato's Athenian Stranger does not indeed experience that support, that refuge and fortress as the biblical prophets experienced it, but he does the second best: he tries to demonstrate its existence. But for Heidegger there is no security, no happy ending, no divine shepherd; hope is replaced by thinking; the longing for eternity, belief in anything eternal is under- stood as stemming from "the spirit of revenge," from the desire to escape from all passing away into something that never passes away.[20]

The controversy can easily degenerate into a race in which he wins who offers the smallest security and the greatest terror, and regard- ing which it would not be difficult to guess who would be the winner. But just as an assertion does not become true because it is shown to be comforting, it does not become true because it is shown to be terrifying. The serious question concerns man's certainty or knowledge of the divine promises or covenants. They are known through what God Himself says in the Scriptures. According to Buber, whose belief in rev- elation is admittedly "not mixed up with any 'orthodoxy'," what we read in the Bible is in all cases, even when God is said to have said something (as for example and above all in the case of the Ten Commandments), what the biblical authors say, and what the biblical authors say is never more than a human expression of God's speechless call or a human response to that call or a manmade "image," a human interpretation—an experienced human interpretation, to be sure—of what God "said." Such "images" constitute not only Judaism and Christianity but all religions. All such "images" are "distorting and yet correct, perishable like an image in a dream and yet verified in eter- nity."[21] The experience of God is surely not specifically Jewish. Besides, can one say that one experiences God as the creator of heaven and earth, i.e., that one knows from the experience taken by itself of God that He is the creator of heaven and earth, or that men who are not prophets expe- rience God as a thinking, willing, and speaking being? Is the absolute experience necessarily the experience of a Thou?[22] Every assertion about the absolute experience which says more than that what is experienced is the Presence or the Call, is not the experiencer, is not flesh and blood, is the wholly other, is death or nothingness, is an "image" or interpretation; that any one interpretation is the simply true interpretation is not known, but "merely believed." One cannot establish that any particular interpretation of the absolute experience is the most adequate interpretation on the ground that it alone agrees with all other experiences, for instance, with the experienced mystery of the Jewish fate, for the Jewish fate is a mystery only on the basis of a particular interpretation of the absolute experience, or rather the Jewish fate is the outcome of one particular interpretation of the absolute experience. The very emphasis on the absolute experience as experience compels one to demand that it be made as clear as possible what the experience by itself conveys, that it not be tampered with, that it be carefully distinguished from every interpretation of the experience, for the interpretations may be suspected of being attempts to render bearable and harmless the experienced which admittedly comes from without down upon man and is undesired, or to cover over man's radical unprotectedness, loneliness, and exposedness.[23]

Yet—Buber could well have retorted—does not precisely this objection mean that the atheistic suspicion is as much a possibility, an interpretation, and hence is as much "merely believed" as the theistic one? And is not being based on belief, which is the pride of religion, a calamity for philosophy? Can the new thinking consistently reject or (what is the same thing) pass by revelation? Through judging others, Nietzsche himself had established the criterion by which his doctrine is to be judged. In attacking the "optimistic" as well as the "pessimistic" atheism of his age, he had made clear that the denial of the biblical God demands the denial of biblical morality, however secularized, which, so far from being self-evident or rational, has no other support than the biblical God; mercy, compassion, egalitarianism, brotherly love, or altruism must give way to cruelty and its kin.[24] But Nietzsche did not leave things at "the blond beast." He proclaimed "the overman," and the overman transcends man as hitherto known at his highest. What distinguishes Nietzsche in his view from all earlier philosophers is the fact that he possesses "the historical sense,"[25] i.e., the awareness that the human soul has no unchangeable essence or limits, but is essentially historical. The most profound change which the human soul has hitherto undergone, the most important enlargement and deepening which it has hitherto experienced, is due, according to Nietzsche, to the Bible. "These Greeks have much on their conscience—falsification was their particular craft, the whole European psychology suffers from the Greek *superficialities;* and without that little bit of Judaism, etc. etc." Hence the overman is "the Roman Caesar with Christ's soul."[26] Not only was biblical morality as veracity or intellectual probity at work in the destruction of biblical theology and biblical morality; not only is it at work in the questioning of that very probity, of *"our* virtue, which alone has remained to us";[27] biblical morality will remain at work in the morality of the overman. The overman is inseparable from "the philosophy of the future." The philosophy of the future is distinguished from traditional philosophy, which pretended to be purely theoretical, by the fact that it is consciously the outcome of a will: the fundamental awareness is not purely theoretical, but theoretical and practical, inseparable from an act of the will or a decision. The fundamental awareness characteristic of the new thinking is a secularized version of the biblical faith as interpreted by Christian theology.[28] What is true of Nietzsche is no less true of the author of *Sein und Zeit.* Heidegger wishes to expel from philosophy the last relics of Christian theology like the notions of "eternal truths" and "the idealized absolute subject." But the understanding of man which he opposes to the Greek understanding of man as the rational animal is, as he emphasizes, primarily the biblical understanding of man as created in the image of God. Accordingly, he interprets human life in the light of "being towards death," "anguish," "conscience," and "guilt"; in this most important respect he is much more Christian than Nietzsche.[29] The efforts of the new thinking to escape from the evidence of the biblical understanding of man, i.e., from biblical morality, have failed. And, as we have learned from Nietzsche, biblical morality demands the biblical God.

Considerations of this kind seemed to decide the issue in favor of Rosenzweig's understanding of the new thinking, or in favor of the unqualified return to biblical revelation. In fact, Rosenzweig's return was not unqualified. The Judaism to which he returned was not identical with the Judaism of the age prior to Moses Mendelssohn. The old thinking had brought about since the days of Mendelssohn, to say nothing of the Middle Ages, some more or less important modifications of native Jewish thought. While opposing the old thinking, the new thinking was nevertheless its heir. Whereas the classic work of what is called Jewish medieval philosophy, the *Guide of the Perplexed*, is primarily not a philosophic book, but a Jewish book, Rosenzweig's *Star of Redemption* is primarily not a Jewish book, but "a system of philosophy." The new thinking is "experiencing philosophy." As such it is passionately concerned with the difference between what is experienced, or at least capable of being experienced, by the present-day believer and what is merely known by tradition; that difference was of no concern to traditional Judaism. As experiencing philosophy it starts in each case from the experienced, and not from the nonexperienced "presuppositions" of experience. For instance, we experience things "here" or "there," in given "places"; we do not experience the homogeneous infinite "space" which may be the condition of the possibility of "places." I experience a tree; in doing so, I am not necessarily aware of my "Ego" which is the condition of possibility of my experiencing anything.

Accordingly, when speaking of the Jewish experience, one must start from what is primary or authoritative for the Jewish consciousness, and not from what is the primary condition of possibility of the Jewish experience: one must start from God's Law, the Torah, and not from the Jewish nation. But in this decisive case Rosenzweig proceeds in the opposite manner; he proceeds, as he puts it, "sociologically." He notes that the Jewish dogmaticists of the Middle Ages, especially Maimonides, proceeded in the first manner: traditional Jewish dogmatics understood the Jewish nation in the light of the Torah; it was silent about the "presupposition" of the Law, viz. the Jewish nation and its chosenness. One begins to wonder whether our medieval philosophy, and the old thinking of Aristotle of which it made use, was not more "empirical," more in harmony with the "given," than an unqualified empiricism which came into being through opposition to modern constructionist philosophy as well as to modern scientific empiricism: if the Jewish nation did not originate the Torah, but is manifestly constituted by the Torah, it is necessarily preceded by the Torah, which was created prior to the world and for the sake of which the world was created. The dogma of Israel's chosenness becomes for Rosenzweig "the truly central thought of Judaism" because, as he makes clear, he approaches Judaism from the point of view of Christianity, because he looks for a Jewish analogon to the Christian doctrine of the Christ.[30] It is not necessary to emphasize that the same change would have been effected if the starting point had been mere secularist nationalism.

Rosenzweig never believed that his return to the biblical faith could be a return to the form in which that faith had expressed or understood itself in the past. What the author of a biblical saying or a biblical story or the compilers of the canon meant is one thing; how the text affects the present-day believer, and hence what the latter truly understands, i.e., appropriates and believes, is another. The former is the concern of history as history which, if it regards itself as self-sufficient, is one of the decayed forms of the old thinking; the latter, if it is practiced with full consciousness, calls for the new thinking. Since the new thinking is the right kind of thinking, it would seem that the understanding of the Bible of which it is capable is in principle superior to all other forms. At any rate, Rosenzweig agrees with religious liberalism as to the necessity of making a selection from among the traditional beliefs and rules. Yet his principle of selection differs radically from the liberal principle.

The liberals made a distinction between the essential and the unessential, i.e., they made a distinction which claimed to be objective. Rosenzweig's principle is not a principle strictly speaking, but "a force": the whole "reality of Jewish life," even those parts of it which never acquired formal authority (like "mere" stories and "mere" customs), must be approached as the "matter" out of which only a part can be transformed into "force"; only experience can tell which part will be so transformed; the selection cannot but be "wholly individual."[31] The sacred law, as it were the public temple, which was a reality thus becomes a potential, a quarry, or a storehouse out of which each individual takes the materials for building up his private shelter. The community of the holy people is henceforth guaranteed by the common descent of its members and the common origin of the materials which they transform by selecting them. This conscious and radical historicization of the Torah—the necessary consequence of the assumed primacy of the Jewish people under the conditions of modern "individualism"[32]—is in Rosenzweig's view perfectly compatible with the fact that the Jewish people is the ahistorical people.

Rosenzweig could not believe everything which his orthodox Jewish contemporaries in Germany believed. His system of philosophy supplies the reasons why he thought that in spite of their piety they were mistaken. He has discussed by themselves two points regarding which he disagreed with them and which are of utmost importance. First, he opposed to their inclination to understand the Law in terms of prohibition, denial, refusal, and rejection, rather than in terms of command, liberation, granting, and transformation, the opposite inclination. It is not immediately clear, however, whether the orthodox austerity or sternness does not rest on a deeper understanding of the power of evil in man than Rosenzweig's at first glance more attractive view, which resembles one of "the favorite topics" of Mittler in Goethe's *Elective Affinities*.[33] Second, Rosenzweig was unable simply to believe all biblical miracles. All biblical miracles were indeed susceptible of becoming credible to him. For instance, when the story of Balaam's speaking she-ass was read from the Torah, it was not a fairy tale for him, whereas on all other occasions he might doubt this miracle.[34] The orthodox Jew would reproach himself for his doubts as for failings on his part, for he would not determine what he is obliged to believe by his individual and temporary capacity or incapacity to believe; he would argue, with Maimonides' *Treatise on the Resurrection of the Dead*, that if God has created the world out of nothing and hence is omnipotent, there is no reason whatever for denying at any time any miracle vouched for by the word of God.

Considerations like those sketched in the preceding paragraphs made one wonder whether an unqualified return to Jewish orthodoxy was not both possible and necessary—was not at the same time the solution to the problem of the Jew lost in the non-Jewish modern world and the only course compatible with sheer consistency or intellectual probity. Vague difficulties remained like small faraway clouds on a beautiful summer sky. They soon took the shape of Spinoza—the greatest man of Jewish origin who had openly denied the truth of Judaism and had ceased to belong to the Jewish people without becoming a Christian. It was not the "God-intoxicated" philosopher, but the hardheaded, not to say hardhearted, pupil of Machiavelli and philologic-historical critic of the Bible. Orthodoxy could be returned to only if Spinoza was wrong in every respect.

That Spinoza was wrong in the decisive respect had been asserted about a decade earlier by the most authoritative German Jew who symbolized more than anyone else the union of Jewish faith and German culture: Hermann Cohen, the founder of the neo-Kantian school of Marburg. Cohen was a Jew of rare dedication, the faithful guide, defender, and warner of German Jewry, and at the same time, to say the least, the one who by far surpassed in spiritual power all the other German professors of philosophy of his generation. It became necessary to examine Cohen's attack on Spinoza. That attack had been occasioned by a particularly striking act of celebration of Spinoza on the part of German Jews.

There were two reasons why contemporary Jews were inclined to celebrate Spinoza. The first is Spinoza's assumed merit about mankind and only secondarily about the Jews; the second is his assumed merit about the Jewish people and only secondarily about mankind. Both reasons had induced contemporary Jews, not only informally to rescind the excommunication which the Jewish community in Amsterdam had pronounced against Spinoza, but even, as Cohen put it, to canonize him.

The great revolt against traditional thought or the emergence of modern philosophy or natural science was completed prior to Spinoza. One may go further and say that, far from being a revolutionary thinker, Spinoza is only the heir of the modern revolt and the medieval tradition as well. At first glance he might well appear to be much more medieval than Descartes, to say nothing of Bacon and Hobbes. The modern project as understood by Bacon, Descartes, and Hobbes demands that man should become the master and owner of nature, or that philosophy or science should cease to be essentially theoretical. Spinoza, however, attempts to restore the traditional conception of contemplation: one cannot think of conquering nature if nature is the same as God. Yet Spinoza restored the dignity of speculation on the basis of modern philosophy or science, of a new understanding of "nature." He thus was the first great thinker who attempted a synthesis of premodern (classical-medieval) and of modern philosophy. His speculation resembles neo-Platonism; he understands all things as proceeding from, not made or created by, a single being or origin; the One is the sole ground of the Many. Yet he no longer regards this process as a descent or decay, but as an ascent or unfolding: the end is higher than the origin. According to his last word on the subject, the highest form of knowledge, which he calls intuitive knowledge, is knowledge not of the one substance or God, but of individual things or events: God is fully God, not qua substance or even in His eternal attributes, but in His noneternal modes understood *sub specie aeternitatis*. The knowledge of God as presented in the first part of the *Ethics* is only universal or abstract; only the knowledge of individual things or rather events qua caused by God is concrete.[35]

Spinoza thus appears to originate the kind of philosophic system which views the fundamental *processus* as a progress: God in Himself is not the *ens perfectissimum*. In this most important respect he prepares German idealism. Furthermore, just as he returned to the classical conception of *theoria*, he returned in his political philosophy to classical republicanism. The title of the crowning chapter of the *Theologico-Political Treatise* is taken as literally as possible from Tacitus. But just as his theoretical philosophy is more than a restatement of classical doctrines and in fact a synthesis of classical and modern speculation, his political philosophy is more than a restatement of classical republicanism. The republic which he favors is a liberal democracy. He was the first philosopher who was both a democrat and a liberal. He was the philosopher who founded liberal democracy, a specifically modern regime. Directly and through his influence on Rousseau, who gave the decisive impulse to Kant, Spinoza became responsible for that version of modern republicanism which takes its bearings by the dignity of every man rather than by the narrowly conceived interest of every man. Spinoza's political teaching starts from a natural right of every human being as the source of all possible duties. Hence it is free from that sternness and austerity which classical political philosophy shares with ancient law—a sternness which Aristotle expressed classically by saying that what the law does not command it forbids. Hence Spinoza is free from the classical aversion to commercialism; he rejects the traditional demand for sumptuary laws. Generally speaking his polity gives the passions much greater freedom and correspondingly counts much less on the power of reason than the polity of the classics. For whereas for the classics the life of passion is a life against nature, for Spinoza everything that is, is natural. For Spinoza there are no natural ends, and hence in particular there is no end natural to man. He is therefore compelled to give a novel account of man's end (the life devoted to contemplation): man's end is not natural, but rational, the result of man's figuring it out, of man's "forming an idea of man, as of a model of human nature." He thus decisively prepares the modern notion of the "ideal" as a work of the human mind or as a human project, as distinguished from an end imposed on man by nature.

The formal reception of Spinoza took place in 1785 when F. H. Jacobi published his book *On the Doctrine of Spinoza, in Letters to Herr Moses Mendelssohn*. Jacobi made public the fact that in Lessing's view there was no philosophy but the philosophy of Spinoza. The philosophy of Kant's great successors was consciously a synthesis of Spinoza's and Kant's philosophies. Spinoza's characteristic contribution to this synthesis was a novel conception of God. He thus showed the way toward a new religion or religiousness which was to inspire a wholly new kind of society, a new kind of Church. He became the sole father of that new Church which was to be universal in fact, and not merely in claim as other churches, because its foundation was no longer any positive revelation—a Church whose rulers were not priests or pastors, but philosophers and artists and whose flock were the circles of culture and property. It was of the utmost importance to that Church that its father was not a Christian, but a Jew who had informally embraced a Christianity without dogmas and sacraments. The millennial antagonism between Judaism and Christianity was about to disappear. The new Church would transform Jews and Christians into human beings—into human beings of a certain kind: cultured human beings, human beings who, because they possessed science and art, did not need religion in addition. The new society, constituted by the aspiration common to all its members toward the True, the Good, and the Beautiful, emancipated the Jews in Germany. Spinoza became the symbol of that emancipation which was to be not only emancipation but secular redemption. In Spinoza, a thinker and a saint who was both a Jew and a Christian and hence neither, all cultured families of the earth, it was hoped, will be blessed. In a word, the non-Jewish world, having been molded to a considerable extent by Spinoza, had become receptive to Jews who were willing to assimilate themselves to it.

The celebration of Spinoza had become equally necessary on purely Jewish grounds. As we have seen, the emphasis had shifted from the Torah to the Jewish nation, and the Jewish nation could not be considered the source of the Torah if it was not understood as an organism with a soul of its own; that soul had expressed itself originally and classically in the Bible, although not in all parts of the Bible equally. From the days of the Bible, there was always the conflict between prophet and priest, between the inspired and the uninspired, between profound subterranean Judaism and official Judaism. Official Judaism was legalistic and hence rationalistic. Its rationalism had received most powerful support from the philosophic rationalism of alien origin which had found its perfect expression in the Platonic conception of God as an artificer who makes the universe by looking up to the unchangeable, lifeless ideas. In accordance with this, official Judaism asserted that God has created the world and governs it *sub ratione boni*. Precisely because he believed in the profoundly understood divinity of the Bible, Spinoza revolted against this official assertion in the name of the absolutely free or sovereign God of the Bible—of the God Who will be What He will be, Who will be gracious to whom He will be gracious and will show mercy to whom He will show mercy. Moved by the same spirit, he embraced with enthusiasm Paul's doctrine of predestination. The biblical God has created man in His image: male and female did He create them. The male and the female, form and matter, cogitation and extension, are then equally attributes of God; Spinoza rejects both Greek idealism and Christian spiritualism. The biblical God forms light and creates darkness, makes peace and creates evil; Spinoza's God is simply beyond good and evil. God's might is His right, and therefore the power of every being is as such its right; Spinoza lifts Machiavellianism to theological heights. Good and evil differ only from a merely human point of view; theologically the distinction is meaningless. The evil passions are evil only with a view to human utility; in themselves they show forth the might and the right of God no less than other things which we admire and by the contemplation of which we are delighted. In the state of nature, i.e., independently of human convention, there is nothing just and unjust, no duty and no guilt, and the state of nature does not simply vanish when civil society is established: pangs of conscience are nothing but feelings of displeasure which arise when a plan has gone wrong. Hence there are no vestiges of divine justice to be found except where just men reign. All human acts are modes of the one God Who possesses infinitely many attributes each of which is infinite and only two of which are known to us, Who is therefore a mysterious God, Whose mysterious love reveals itself in eternally and necessarily bringing forth love and hatred, nobility and baseness, saintliness and depravity, and Who is infinitely lovable not in spite of but because of His infinite power beyond good and evil.

Compared with the fantastic flights of the Spinoza enthusiasts in the two camps, of the moralists and the immoralists, Cohen's understanding of Spinoza is sobriety itself. All the more impressive is his severe indictment of Spinoza.[36] He shows first that in his *Theologico-Political Treatise* Spinoza speaks from a Christian point of view and accordingly accepts the entire Christian critique of Judaism, but goes much even beyond that Christian critique in his own critique. Spinoza accepts against his better knowledge the assertion of Jesus that Judaism commands the hatred of the enemy. He opposes spiritual and universalistic Christianity to carnal and particularistic Judaism: the core of Judaism is the Mosaic law as a particularistic, not to say tribal, law which serves no other end than the earthly or political felicity of the Jewish nation; the Torah does not teach morality, i.e., universal morality; the Mosaic religion is merely national; Moses' God is a tribal and in addition a corporeal God. By denying that the God of Israel is the God of all mankind Spinoza has blasphemed the God of Israel. He reduces Jewish religion to a doctrine of the Jewish state. For him, the Torah is of merely human origin.

Cohen shows next that the Christianity in the light of which Spinoza condemns Judaism is not historical or actual Christianity, but an idealized Christianity, and hence that while he idealizes Christianity, he denigrates Judaism. He shows then that Spinoza admits the universalistic character of the Old Testament prophecy, thus contradicting himself grossly. This contradiction clearly proves his lack of good faith.[37] Nor is this all. While taking the side of spiritual and transpolitical Christianity against carnal and political Judaism, Spinoza contradicts this whole argument by taking the side of the state not only against all churches but against all religion as well. "He put religion altogether," i.e., not merely Judaism, "outside the sphere of truth." Starting like all other sophists from the equation of right and might, he conceives of the state entirely in terms of power politics, i.e., as divorced from religion and morality, and he puts the state thus conceived above religion. This does not mean that he deifies the state. On the contrary, he is concerned above everything else with what he calls philosophy, which he assumes to be wholly inaccessible directly or indirectly to the large majority of men. He has no compunction whatever about affirming the radical and unmodifiable inequality of men without ever wondering "how can nature, how can God answer for this difference among men?" Hence his sympathy for democracy is suspect. He is compelled to erect an eternal barrier between popular education and science or philosophy, and therewith between the state and reason. There is no place in his thought for the enlightenment of the people. He has no heart for the people, no compassion. He cannot admit a messianic future of mankind when all men will be united in genuine knowledge of God. This is the reason why he is altogether blind to biblical prophecy and hence to the core of Judaism.[38]

On the basis of all these facts Cohen reached the conclusion that so far from deserving celebration, Spinoza fully deserved the excommunication. Far from rescinding the excommunication, Cohen confirmed it, acting as a judge in the highest court of appeal. The grounds of his verdict were not the same as the grounds of the lower court. He was not concerned with Spinoza's transgression of the ceremonial law and his denial of the Mosaic authorship of the Pentateuch. He condemned Spinoza because of his infidelity in the simple human sense, of his complete lack of loyalty to his own people, of his acting like an enemy of the Jews and thus giving aid and comfort to the many enemies of the Jews, of his behaving like a base traitor. Spinoza remains up to the present day the accuser par excellence of Judaism before an anti-Jewish world; the disposition of his mind and heart toward Jews and Judaism was "unnatural," he committed a "humanly incomprehensible act of treason," he was possessed by "an evil demon."[39]

Our case against Spinoza is in some respects even stronger than Cohen thought. One may doubt whether Spinoza's action is humanly incomprehensible or demoniac, but one must grant that it is amazingly unscrupulous. Cohen is justly perplexed by the fact that "the center of the whole [theologico-political] treatise" is the disparagement of Moses and the idealization of Jesus, although the purpose of the work is to secure the freedom of philosophizing. He explains this anomaly by Spinoza's belief that the suppression of philosophy goes back to the Mosaic law. Cohen does not assert that Moses championed the freedom of philosophy, but he raises the pertinent question whether Jesus championed it.[40] Why then does Spinoza treat Judaism and Christianity differently? Why does he take the side of Christianity in the conflict between Judaism and Christianity, in a conflict of no concern to him as a philosopher? Cohen believes that Spinoza had a genuine reverence for Jesus' teachings. According to Spinoza's own statements he preferred spiritual Christianity to carnal Judaism.[41] But is Spinoza a spiritualist? Cohen says that spirit or mind, if applied to God, is no less a metaphor than hand, voice, or mouth. He thus merely repeats what Spinoza himself asserts; Spinoza may be said to have denied that God has a spirit or mind. The question returns: why does Spinoza treat Christianity differently from Judaism? Cohen comes closest to the truth in saying that Spinoza's motive was fear,[42] surely a "humanly comprehensible" motive. Or, to start again from the beginning, Spinoza, attempting to achieve the liberation of philosophy in a book addressed to Christians, cannot but appeal to the Christian prejudices which include anti-Jewish prejudices; he fights Christian prejudices by appealing to Christian prejudices; appealing to the Christian prejudice against Judaism, he exhorts the Christians to free essentially spiritual Christianity from all carnal Jewish relics (e.g., the belief in the resurrection of the body). Generally speaking, he makes the Old Testament against his better knowledge the scapegoat for everything he finds objectionable in actual Christianity. In spite of all this he asserts that the prophets were as universalistic as Jesus and the apostles or, more precisely, that both Testaments teach with equal clarity everywhere the universal divine law or the universal religion of justice and charity. Why this strange reversal, this flagrant contradiction?

At this point Cohen fails to follow Spinoza's thought. The purpose of the *Treatise* is to show the way toward a liberal society which is based on the recognition of the authority of the Bible, i.e., of the Old Testament taken by itself and of the two Testaments taken together. The argument culminates in the fourteenth chapter in which he enumerates seven dogmas which are the indispensable fundamentals of faith, of biblical faith—the seven "roots," as the Jewish medieval thinkers would say. They are essential to "the catholic or universal faith," to the religion which will be the established religion in the well-ordered republic; belief in these seven dogmas is the only belief necessary and sufficient for salvation. They derive equally from the Old Testament taken by itself and from the New Testament taken by itself.[43] They do not contain anything specifically Christian nor anything specifically Jewish. They are equally acceptable to Jews and to Christians. The liberal society with a view to which Spinoza has composed the *Treatise* is then a society of which Jews and Christians can be equally members, of which Jews and Christians can be equal members. For such a society he wished to provide. The establishment of such a society required in his opinion the abrogation of the Mosaic law insofar as it is a particularistic and political law, and especially of the ceremonial laws: since Moses' religion is a political law, to adhere to his religion as he proclaimed it is incompatible with being the citizen of any other state, whereas Jesus was not a legislator, but only a teacher.[44] It is for this reason that Spinoza is so anxious to prove that Moses' law lost its obligatory power, and that the Jews ceased to be the chosen people, with the loss of the Jewish state: the Jews cannot be at the same time the members of two nations and subject to two comprehensive legal codes. Spinoza stresses the abrogation of the ceremonial law, however, not only because that abrogation is in his opinion a necessary condition of civic equality of the Jews but also as desirable for its own sake: the ceremonial law is infinitely burdensome, nay, a curse.[45]

In providing for the liberal state, Spinoza provides for a Judaism which is liberal in the extreme. The "assimilationist" "solution to the Jewish problem" which Spinoza may be said to have suggested was more important from his point of view than the "Zionist" one which he likewise suggested. The latter as he understood it could seem to require the preservation of the ceremonial law although the abandonment of the spirit which has animated it hitherto.[46] The former suggestion and the general purpose of the *Theologico-Political Treatise* are obviously connected: freedom of philosophy requires, or seems to require, a liberal state, and a liberal state is a state which is not as such either Christian or Jewish. Even Cohen sensed for a moment that Spinoza was not entirely free from sympathy with his people.[47] Spinoza may have hated Judaism; he did not hate the Jewish people. However bad a Jew he may have been in all other respects, he thought of the liberation of the Jews in the only way in which he could think of it, given his philosophy. But precisely if this is so, we must stress all the more the fact that the manner in which he sets forth his proposal—to say nothing of the proposal itself—is Machiavellian: the humanitarian end seems to justify every means; he plays a most dangerous game;[48] his procedure is as much beyond good and evil as his God.

All this does not mean, however, that Cohen's critique of Spinoza's *Theologico-Political Treatise* is altogether convincing. His political thought claims to be inspired by biblical prophecy and hence is messianic. In opposition to Spinoza, it starts from the radical difference between nature and morality, the Is and the Ought, egoism and pure will. The state is essentially moral, and morality cannot be actual except in and through the state. The difficulty presented by the fact that morality is universal and the state is always particular is overcome by the consideration that the state is part of a universal moral order, as is shown by the existence of international law and by the intrinsic possibility, which is at the same time a moral necessity, of a universal league of states. The radical difference between nature and morality does not amount to a contradiction between nature and morality: nature does not render impossible the fulfillment of the moral demands. The morally demanded infinite progress of morality, and in particular the "eternal progress" toward "eternal peace," nay, every single step of morality, requires for its "ultimate security" the infinite duration *a parte post* of the human race and hence of nature; this infinite duration or eternity is secured by the idea of God "who signifies the harmony of the knowledge of nature and of moral knowledge," who is not a person, nor living, nor existing, nor a spirit or mind, but an idea, "our" idea, i.e., our *hypothesis* in what Cohen regards as the Platonic meaning of the term. This is the Cohenian equivalent of Creation and Providence. Without "the idea of God" as Cohen understands it morality as he understands it becomes baseless. That idea is the basis of his trust in infinite progress or of his belief in history, of his "optimism," of his certainty of the ultimate victory of the good: "there is no evil."

But eternal progress also requires eternal tension between the actual state and the state as it ought to be:[49] immorality is coeval with morality. Here Cohen seems to join Spinoza, whose political thought is based on the truth, allegedly proven by experience, that there will be vices as long as there will be human beings and who takes it therefore for granted that the state is necessarily repressive or coercive. Cohen too cannot well deny that the state must use coercion, but, opposing the Kantian distinction between morality and legality, he denies that coercion is the principle of law: coercion means nothing other than law and needs therefore not to be mentioned. He is as uneasy about coercion as he is about power: the state is law, for the state is essentially rational, and coercion begins where reason ends. All this follows from the premise that morality is self-legislation and that it can be actual only in and through the state. A further consequence is that Cohen must understand punishment, not in terms of the protection of society or other considerations which may be thought to regard the criminal not as "an end in himself" and only as a means, but in terms of the self-betterment of the criminal alone.[50] Cohen obscures the fact that while the self-betterment is necessarily a free act of the criminal, his forcible seclusion for the purpose of that self-betterment, in which he may or may not engage, is not. In other words, all men are under a moral obligation to better themselves, but the specific difference of the condemned criminal is that he is put behind bars. For it goes without saying that Cohen denies the justice of capital punishment. However justly Spinoza may deserve condemnation for his Machiavelli-inspired hardheartedness, it is to be feared that Cohen has not remained innocent of the opposite extreme. Since he attacks Spinoza in the name of Judaism, it may suffice here to quote a Jewish saying: "But for the fear of the government, men would swallow each other alive."[51]

One may doubt whether Cohen's political teaching is unqualifiedly superior to Spinoza's from the moral point of view. Cohen "rejects war." On the other hand he does not reject revolution, although, as he emphasizes, Kant had "coordinated wars to revolutions." Revolutions are political but not legal acts, and hence the state is not simply law; revolutions "suspend" positive law, but are justified by natural law. They do not necessarily occur without the killing of human beings; Cohen, the sworn enemy of capital punishment, reflects only on the death of "the revolutionary martyrs" who voluntarily sacrifice their lives, but not on the death of their victims. Kant had questioned the legitimacy of revolution on the ground that its maxim does not stand the test of publicity, which in his view every honest maxim stands: the preparation of every revolution is necessarily conspiratorial or secret. To counter this argument Cohen observes that the moral basis of revolutions is the original contract which, "being only an idea, is always only an interior, hence secret presupposition." The same reasoning would lead to the further conclusion that the original contract, nay, Cohen's theology, must never be publicly mentioned, let alone be taught. It is altogether fitting that Cohen, who was no friend of the "irrational" or of "mysticism," should be driven in his defense of the revolutionary principle to become friendly to the "irrational" and to "mysticism."[52] To say nothing of other things, he would never have been driven to this surrender of reason if he had taken seriously the law of reason or the natural law which may be said to indicate the right mean between hardheartedness and softheartedness.

While admitting "the deep injustice" of Cohen's judgment on Spinoza, Rosenzweig asserts that Cohen has honestly complied in his critique of the *Theologico-Political Treatise* with the duty of scholarly objectivity.[53] This assertion must be qualified. Since Cohen accuses Spinoza of having been unfair in his treatment of the universalism of the prophets, one must consider in fairness to Spinoza whether the Jewish tradition with which Spinoza was directly confronted had preserved intact that universalism. Cohen failed to make this investigation. Once one makes it, one observes that Spinoza recognized the universalism of the prophets in some respects more clearly than some of the greatest traditional Jewish authorities. In his critique of Spinoza, Cohen is silent about the fact, which he mentions elsewhere, that prophetic universalism had become obscured in later times for easily understandable reasons.[54] Cohen is particularly indignant about Spinoza's using a remark of Maimonides in order to prove that according to Judaism non-Jews cannot be saved unless they believe in the Mosaic revelation,[55] i.e., unless, as one is tempted to say, they are Christians or Muslims. More precisely, Spinoza quotes a passage from Maimonides' *Code* in which it is said that a Gentile is pious and has a share in the world to come if he performs the seven commandments given to Noah qua commanded by God in the Torah, but that if he performs them because of a decision of reason, he does not belong to the pious Gentiles nor to the wise ones. Cohen accuses Spinoza of having used a false reading of a single passage of the *Code*—of a passage which expresses only Maimonides' private opinion and which in addition is contradicted by two other passages of the *Code*—in order to deny the universalism of postbiblical Judaism. He (or the authority to which he defers) notes that according to the most authoritative commentator on the *Code*, Joseph Caro, the qualification stated by Maimonides (viz. that piety requires recognition of the Mosaic revelation) is his private opinion, but Cohen fails to add that Caro adds that the opinion is correct. Caro would not have said this if Maimonides' opinion contradicted the consensus of Judaism.

Cohen (or his authority) also notes that, according to the most authentic text of the *Code*, the Gentile who performs the seven Noahidic commandments because of a decision of reason does not indeed belong to the pious Gentiles, but to the wise ones.[56] But Cohen does not show that Spinoza knew that reading to be the most authentic reading. The reading used by Spinoza is still the common reading, which it would not be if it were in shocking contrast to the consensus of Judaism as Cohen asserts and hence would have shocked every Jewish reader.[57] In addition, the allegedly best reading does not necessarily improve the fate of the wise Gentiles unless one proves first that the fate of the wise Gentiles is as good as that of the pious Gentiles. Cohen finally asserts that the passage in question contradicts two other passages of the *Code* which in his opinion do not demand that the pious Gentile believe in the revealed character of the Torah. It suffices to say that the two passages are silent on what precisely constitutes the piety of the Gentiles and are therefore irrelevant to the issue.[58] Cohen also refers to a different treatment of the subject in Maimonides' *Commentary on the Mishna*; but this merely leads to the further question whether that commentary, composed much earlier than the *Code*, is equal in authority to it.

But, to return to the main issue, i.e., to the question whether the ordinary reading, used by Spinoza, of the passage under consideration makes sense as a Maimonidean utterance: can Maimonides have taught, as Spinoza asserts he did, that Gentiles who perform the seven Noahidic commandments because reason decides so are not wise men? The answer is simple: Maimonides must have taught it because he denied that there are any rational commandments. Cohen might have objected to this argument on the ground that if Maimonides' denial of the rationality of any commandments or laws were his last word, he could not well have attempted to show that all or almost all commandments of the Torah have "reasons."[59] The reply is obvious: according to Maimonides all or almost all commandments of the Torah serve the purpose of eradicating idolatry, an irrational practice, and are in this sense "rational"; they are rational in the sense in which, not a healthy body, but a medicine, is "healthy."[60] One could say that Maimonides' denial of the rationality of any law is implied in the incriminated passage itself regardless of which of the two readings one prefers; for the term which Cohen renders by "reason" (*da'at*) does not necessarily mean reason in particular, but may mean thought or opinion in general:[61] it makes sense both to assert and to deny that opinion justifies the seven Noahidic commandments.

These and similar considerations do not affect the main issue, namely, the fact that Cohen may well be right in asserting that Spinoza acted ignobly in basing his denial of the universalism of traditional, postprophetic Judaism on a single Maimonidean utterance. In the words of Rosenzweig, beneath the deep injustice of Cohen's judgment lies its still much deeper justification. What Rosenzweig meant may be stated as follows. Cohen was a more profound thinker than Spinoza because unlike Spinoza he did not take for granted the philosophic detachment or freedom from the tradition of his own people; that detachment is "unnatural," not primary, but the outcome of a liberation from the primary attachment, of an alienation, a break, a betrayal; the primary is fidelity, and the sympathy and love which go with fidelity. Genuine fidelity to a tradition is not the same as literalist traditionalism and is in fact incompatible with it. It consists in preserving not simply the tradition but the continuity of the tradition. As fidelity to a living and hence changing tradition, it requires that one distinguish between the living and the dead, the flame and the ashes, the gold and the dross: the loveless Spinoza sees only the ashes, not the flame; only the letter, not the spirit. He is not excusable on the ground that Jewish thought may have declined in the centuries preceding him from its greatest height; for he "on whose extraction, whose gifts, whose learning the Jews had put the greatest hope" was under an obligation to understand contemporary Judaism, and still more Maimonides, to say nothing of Scripture itself, in the light of the highest or, if necessary, better than they understood themselves. Within a living tradition, the new is not the opposite of the old, but its deepening: one does not understand the old in its depth unless one understands it in the light of such deepening; the new does not emerge through the rejection or annihilation of the old, but through its metamorphosis or reshaping. "And it is a question whether such reshaping is not the best form of annihilation."[62] This is indeed the question: whether the loyal and loving reshaping or reinterpretation of the inherited, or the pitiless burning of the hitherto worshiped, is the best form of annihilation of the antiquated, i.e., of the untrue or bad. On the answer to this question the ultimate judgment on Spinoza as well as on Cohen will depend: is the right interpretation "idealizing" interpretation—the interpretation of a teaching in the light of its highest possibility regardless of whether or not that highest possibility was known to the originator—or is it historical interpretation proper which understands a teaching as meant by its originator? Is the conservatism which is generally speaking the wise maxim of practice also the sacred law of theory?

It would not be reasonable to demand from Cohen that he should give the benefit of idealizing interpretation to Spinoza, who had become an ingredient of the modern tradition on which Cohen's philosophy as a philosophy of culture is based. For the kind of interpretation which Spinoza calls for is not idealizing since his own doctrine is not idealistic. As was shown before, Cohen's political philosophy did not pay sufficient attention to the harsh political verities which Spinoza has stated so forcefully. Accordingly, he does not pay sufficient attention to the harsh necessity to which Spinoza bowed by writing in the manner in which he wrote. He did not understand Spinoza's style, which was indeed entirely different from his own. Cohen sometimes writes like a commentator on a commentary on an already highly technical text and hence like a man whose thought is derivative and traditional in the extreme; and yet he surprises time and again with strikingly expressed original and weighty thoughts. Be this as it may, he goes so far as to deny that in Spinoza's time the freest minds were compelled to withhold and to deny the truth; "Think only of Jean Bodin who in his *Heptaplomeres* not only directed the strongest attacks against Christianity but also celebrated Judaism most highly. It must appear strange that this writing, which was known to Leibniz and Thomasius, which was at that time widely distributed, should have remained unknown to Spinoza." He forgets here to say what he says elsewhere: "Leibniz had seen the manuscript of the *Heptaplomeres* and had advised against its being printed";[63] it was not printed before the nineteenth century. Once one takes into consideration the consequences of persecution, Spinoza's conduct in the *Theologico-Political Treatise* ceases to be that "psychological riddle" which Cohen saw in it. He wondered whether that conduct could not be traced to the fact that the Spanish Jews' feelings of anxiety caused by the terrors of the Inquisition had eventually turned into hatred for that for the sake of which they had been so cruelly persecuted. A different explanation was suggested by Nietzsche in his verses addressed to Spinoza. After having paid homage to Spinoza's *amor dei* and to his being "blissful through intelligence," he goes on to say that beneath the love of the "One in all" there was eating a secret desire for revenge: *am Judengott frass Judenhass.* Nietzsche understood Spinoza in his own image. He traced his own revolt against the Christian God to his Christian conscience. The premise of this explanation is Hegelian dialectics: every form of the mind perishes through its antithesis which it necessarily produces. Spinoza's break with the Torah is the consequence of the *sitrei Tora* in the double sense of the expression: the secrets of the Torah and the contradictions of the Torah. Spinoza was not swayed by Hegelian dialectics, but by the Aristotelian principle of contradiction.

Cohen read Spinoza on the one hand not literally enough and on the other hand much too literally; he understood him too literally because he did not read him literally enough. Hence he did not find his way among the contradictions in which the *Theologico-Political Treatise* abounds. As he exclaims on one occasion, "No reason of reasonable men can understand, let alone overcome, these difficulties." A single example must here suffice. He wonders whether Spinoza does not contradict himself by admitting that the Mosaic law is a divine law although he understands by a divine law a law which aims only at the highest good, viz. true knowledge of God and love of God, or intellectual love of God, and he denies that the Mosaic law aims at that highest good. The contradiction disappears once one considers the fact, which Cohen observes, that according to Spinoza a law may also be called divine with a view to its origin: the Mosaic law is human as regards its end, since it aims only at political felicity, but it is divine qua divinely revealed. Cohen quotes Spinoza's explanation: the Mosaic law "may be called the law of God or divine law since we believe that it is sanctioned by the prophetic light." He remarks: "But why do we believe this? This question is not answered by the anonymous author." But does not the community consisting of the anonymous author who speaks as a Christian and his Christian readers believe it as a matter of course, so that the question as to why "we believe it" does not have to arise? Spinoza had originally said that the divine law aims only at the highest good; immediately before saying that the Mosaic law can be called divine with a view to its origin as distinguished from its aim, he says according to Cohen that the divine law "consists chiefly in the highest good": hence, Cohen infers, Spinoza admits now a secondary content of the divine law without stating immediately what that secondary content is, namely, the sensual means which sensual men need. But Spinoza did not say that the divine law consists in the highest good; he says that it consists in the prescriptions regarding the means required for achieving the highest good: the divine law consists chiefly of the prescriptions regarding the proximate means and secondarily of the prescriptions regarding the remote means; since "sensual man" is incapable of intellectual love of God, his needs fall wholly outside of the divine law as here considered by Spinoza. It must be added that according to Spinoza even the divine law in the strictest sense is of human origin; every law is prescribed by human beings to themselves or to other human beings. Cohen throws some light on Spinoza's teaching regarding the divine law by making this remark on Spinoza's assertion that "the highest reward of the divine law is the law itself": "here he has literally taken over a sentence of the Mishna from the well-known *Sayings of the Fathers,* only adding the word 'highest'." Cohen underestimates the importance of Spinoza's addition: Spinoza's egoistic morality demands for the fulfillment of the commandments rewards other than the commandments or perhaps additional commandments; it does not leave room for martyrdom.[64]

Rosenzweig finds Cohen guilty of injustice to Spinoza, not because of defective objectivity, but rather because of defective "subjectivity," i.e., of "insufficient reflection about the conditions and foundations of his own person. He ought to have made his attack with a clearer consciousness of the fact that, not indeed he himself, but the times which had borne and raised him, Cohen himself, would not have been possible without Spinoza." The distinction between Cohen himself and his time, which is due to idealizing or apologetic interpretation, is immaterial here, for if Cohen's thought had nothing to do with the thought of his time, he would not have met Spinoza by reflecting about the presuppositions of "his own person." Cohen accuses Spinoza of blindness to biblical prophetism, but this phenomenon as Cohen understood it was brought to light by what he calls "the historical understanding of the Bible," and this understanding is not possible without higher criticism of the Bible, i.e., without a public effort which was originated with the necessary comprehensiveness by Spinoza. Cohen blames Spinoza for disregarding the difference between mythical and historical elements of the Bible, a distinction which, as Cohen states, was alien to our traditional exegesis; and as regards the doctrinal elements of the Bible, he blames him for not distinguishing between the less and the more mature biblical statements; he blames him for the immaturity or incompetence of his biblical criticism, not at all for his biblical criticism itself: for Cohen, biblical criticism is a matter of course.

Similarly, he states that Spinoza opposed rabbinical Judaism, especially its great concern with the ceremonial law, and that his sharp opposition had a certain salutary effect on the liberation of opinion; he notes without any disapproval that "modern Judaism" has freed itself from part of the ceremonial law; he fails to admit that modern Judaism is a synthesis between rabbinical Judaism and Spinoza. As for Spinoza's denial of the possibility of miracles, Cohen gives an extremely brief summary of the chapter which Spinoza devotes to the subject of miracles without saying a word in defense of miracles.[65] In brief, Cohen does not discuss at all the issue between Spinoza and Jewish orthodoxy, i.e., the only issue with which Spinoza could have been concerned, since there was no modern or liberal Judaism in his time. One may say that in his critique of Spinoza, Cohen commits the typical mistake of the conservative, which consists in concealing the fact that the continuous and changing tradition which he cherishes so greatly would never have come into being through conservatism, or without discontinuities, revolutions, and sacrileges committed at the beginning of the cherished tradition and at least silently repeated in its course.

This much is certain: Cohen's critique of Spinoza does not come to grips with the fact that Spinoza's critique is directed against the whole body of authoritative teachings and rules known in Spinoza's time as Judaism and still maintained in Cohen's time by Jewish orthodoxy. Cohen took it for granted that Spinoza had refuted orthodoxy as such. Owing to the collapse of "the old thinking" it became then necessary to examine the *Theologico-Political Treatise* with a view to the question of whether Spinoza had in fact refuted orthodoxy. Cohen's critique remained helpful for this purpose almost only insofar as it had destroyed the prejudice in favor of Spinoza, or the canonization of Spinoza by German or Jewish romanticism, to say nothing of the canonization by liberalism. Cohen's critique had the additional merit that it was directed chiefly against the *Theologico-Political Treatise*. The seeming neglect of the *Ethics* proved to be sound, and thus to be obligatory for the reexamination of Spinoza's critique of orthodoxy, for the following reason. The *Ethics* starts from explicit premises by the granting of which one has already implicitly granted the absurdity of orthodoxy and even of Judaism as understood by Cohen or Rosenzweig; at first glance these premises seem to be arbitrary and hence to beg the whole question. They are not evident in themselves, but they are thought to become evident through their alleged result: they and only they are held to make possible the clear and distinct account of everything; in the light of the clear and distinct account, the biblical account appears to be confused. The *Ethics* thus begs the decisive question—the question as to whether the clear and distinct account is as such true and not merely a plausible hypothesis. In the *Theologico-Political Treatise*, however, Spinoza starts from the premises which are granted to him by the believers in revelation; he attempts to refute them on the bases of Scripture, of theologoumena formulated by traditional authorities, and of what one may call common sense. For in the *Treatise* Spinoza addresses men who are still believers and whom he intends to liberate from their "prejudices" so that they can begin to philosophize; the *Treatise* is Spinoza's introduction to philosophy.

The results of this examination of Spinoza's critique may be summarized as follows. If orthodoxy claims to know that the Bible is divinely revealed, that every word of the Bible is divinely inspired, that Moses was the writer of the Pentateuch, that the miracles recorded in the Bible have happened and similar things, Spinoza has refuted orthodoxy. But the case is entirely different if orthodoxy limits itself to asserting that it believes the aforementioned things, i.e., that they cannot claim to possess the binding power peculiar to the known. For all assertions of orthodoxy rest on the irrefutable premise that the omnipotent God, Whose will is unfathomable, Whose ways are not our ways, Who has decided to dwell in the thick darkness, may exist. Given this premise, miracles and revelations in general, and hence all biblical miracles and revelations in particular, are possible. Spinoza has not succeeded in showing that this premise is contradicted by anything we know. For what we are said to know, for example, regarding the age of the solar system, has been established on the basis of the assumption that the solar system has come into being naturally; miraculously it could have come into being in the way described by the Bible. It is only naturally or humanly impossible that the "first" Isaiah should have known the name of the founder of the Persian empire; it was not impossible for the omnipotent God to reveal to him that name. The orthodox premise cannot be refuted by experience nor by recourse to the principle of contradiction. An indirect proof of this is the fact that Spinoza and his like owed such success as they had in their fight against orthodoxy to laughter and mockery. By means of mockery they attempted to laugh orthodoxy out of its position from which it could not be dislodged by any proofs supplied by Scripture or by reason. One is tempted to say that mockery does not succeed the refutation of the orthodox tenets, but is itself the refutation. The genuine refutation of orthodoxy would require the proof that the world and human life are perfectly intelligible without the assumption of a mysterious God; it would require at least the success of the philosophic system: man has to show himself theoretically and practically as the master of the world and the master of his life; the merely given world must be replaced by the world created by man theoretically and practically. Spinoza's *Ethics* attempts to be the system, but it does not succeed; the clear and distinct account of everything which it presents remains fundamentally hypothetical. As a consequence, its cognitive status is not different from that of the orthodox account. Certain it is that Spinoza cannot legitimately deny the possibility of revelation. But to grant that revelation is possible means to grant that the philosophic account and the philosophic way of life are not necessarily, not evidently, the true account and the right way of life: philosophy, the quest for evident and necessary knowledge, rests itself on an unevident decision, on an act of the will, just as faith. Hence the antagonism between Spinoza and Judaism, between unbelief and belief, is ultimately not theoretical, but moral.

For the understanding of that moral antagonism the Jewish designation of the unbeliever as Epicurean seemed to be helpful, especially since from every point of view Epicureanism may be said to be the classic form of the critique of religion and the basic stratum of the tradition of the critique of religion. Epicureanism is hedonism, and traditional Judaism always suspects that all theoretical and practical revolts against the Torah are inspired by the desire to throw off the yoke of the stern and exacting duties so that one can indulge in a life of pleasure. Epicureanism can lead only to a mercenary morality, whereas traditional Jewish morality is not mercenary: "the reward for [the fulfillment of] the commandment is the commandment." Epicureanism is so radically mercenary that it conceives of its theoretical doctrines as the means for liberating the mind from the terrors of religious fear, of the fear of death, and of natural necessity. Characteristically modern unbelief is indeed no longer Epicurean. It is no longer cautious or retiring, not to say cowardly, but bold and active. Whereas Epicureanism fights the religious "delusion" because of its terrible character, modern unbelief fights it because it is a delusion: regardless of whether religion is terrible or comforting, qua delusion it makes men oblivious of the real goods, of the enjoyment of the real goods, and thus seduces them into being cheated of the real, "this-worldly" goods by their spiritual or temporal rulers who "live" from that delusion. Liberated from the religious delusion, awakened to sober awareness of his real situation, taught by bad experiences that he is threatened by a stingy, hostile nature, man recognizes as his sole salvation and duty not so much "to cultivate his garden" as in the first place to plant a garden by making himself the master and owner of nature. But this whole enterprise requires, above all, political action, revolution, a life and death struggle: the Epicurean who wishes to live securely and retiredly must transform himself into an "idealist" who has learned to fight and to die for honor and truth. But in proportion as the systematic effort to liberate man completely from all nonhuman bonds seems to succeed, the doubt increases whether the goal is not fantastic—whether man has not become smaller and more miserable in proportion as the systematic civilization progresses.

Eventually the belief that by pushing ever farther back the "natural limits" man will advance to ever greater freedom, that he can subjugate nature and prescribe to it his laws, begins to wither away. In this stage the religious "delusion" is rejected, not because it is terrible, but because it is comforting: religion is not a tool which man has forged for dark reasons in order to torment himself, to make life unnecessarily difficult, but a way out chosen for obvious reasons in order to escape from the terror, the exposedness, and the hopelessness of life which cannot be eradicated by any progress of civilization. A new kind of fortitude which forbids itself every flight from the horror of life into comforting delusion, which accepts the eloquent descriptions of "the misery of man without God" as an additional proof of the goodness of its cause, reveals itself eventually as the ultimate and purest ground for the rebellion against revelation. This new fortitude, being the willingness to look man's forsakenness in its face, being the courage to welcome the most terrible truth, is "probity," "intellectual probity." This final atheism with a good conscience, or with a bad conscience, is distinguished from the atheism at which the past shuddered by its conscientiousness. Compared not only with Epicureanism but with the unbelief of the age of Spinoza, it reveals itself as a descendant of biblical morality. This atheism, the heir and the judge of the belief in revelation, of the secular struggle between belief and unbelief, and finally of the short-lived but by no means therefore inconsequential romantic longing for the lost belief, confronting orthodoxy in complex sophistication formed out of gratitude, rebellion, longing, and indifference, and in simple probity, is according to its claim as capable of an original understanding of the human roots of the belief in God as no earlier, no less complex-simple philosophy ever was. The last word and the ultimate justification of Spinoza's critique is the atheism from intellectual probity which overcomes orthodoxy radically by understanding it radically, i.e., without the polemical bitterness of the Enlightenment and the equivocal reverence of romanticism. Yet this claim, however eloquently raised, cannot deceive one about the fact that its basis is an act of will, of belief, and that being based on belief is fatal to any philosophy.

The victory of orthodoxy through the self-destruction of rational philosophy was not an unmitigated blessing, for it was a victory, not of Jewish orthodoxy, but of any orthodoxy, and Jewish orthodoxy based its claim to superiority to other religions from the beginning on its superior rationality (Deut. 4:6). Apart from this, the hierarchy of moralities and wills to which the final atheism referred could not but be claimed to be intrinsically true, theoretically true: "the will to power" of the strong or of the weak may be the ground of every other doctrine; it is not the ground of the doctrine of the will to power: the will to power was said to be a fact. Other observations and experiences confirmed the suspicion that it would be unwise to say farewell to reason. I began therefore to wonder whether the self-destruction of reason was not the inevitable outcome of modern rationalism as distinguished from premodern rationalism, especially Jewish-medieval rationalism and its classical (Aristotelian and Platonic) foundation. The present study was based on the premise, sanctioned by powerful prejudice, that a return to premodern philosophy is impossible. The change of orientation which found its first expression, not entirely by accident, in the article published at the end of this volume[66] compelled me to engage in a number of studies in the course of which I became ever more attentive to the manner in which heterodox thinkers of earlier ages wrote their books. As a consequence of this, I now read the *Theologico-Political Treatise* differently than I read it when I was young. I understood Spinoza too literally because I did not read him literally enough.

Notes

[The "Preface to *Spinoza's Critique of Religion*" first appeared in print in 1965, along with the English translation of Strauss's original book of 1930. A subsequent version of the "Preface" was published in 1968 in Leo Strauss, *Liberalism Ancient and Modern*, with some slight editorial changes made by Strauss. This present edition is based essentially on the earlier 1965 version, but incorporates almost all of the slight editorial changes made by Strauss in the later 1968 version, on the assumption that the 1968 version is Strauss's final statement. —Ed.]

1. Consider Leon Trotsky, *The History of the Russian Revolution*, translated by Max Eastman (Ann Arbor: University of Michigan Press, 1957), I, 329–31 and III, 154–55.

2. Heinrich Heine, "Die romantische Schule," in *Sämtliche Werke*, ed. Elster, V, 217. See the discussion of romanticism in Hegel's *Aesthetik*.

3. Consider *Jenseits von Gut und Böse*, chap. 8.

4. *Wilhelm Meisters Wanderjahre*, bk. 3, ch. 11.

5. *Jenseits von Gut und Böse*, no. 251; see *Morgenröte*, no. 205.

6. *Einführung in die Metaphysik* (Tübingen: Max Niemeyer, 1953), 152. This book consists of a course of lectures given in 1935, but as stated in the Preface: "Errors have been removed." See also the allusion on p. 36 to a recent "cleansing" of the German universities.

7. See Gerhard Scholem, "Politik der Mystik. Zu Isaac Breuer's 'Neuem Kusari'," *Jüdische Rundschau* 39, no. 57 (1934).

8. See Yehezkel Kaufmann, *The Religion of Israel*, translated and abridged by Moshe Greenberg (Chicago: University of Chicago Press, 1960), 2, 233–34.

9. Maimonides, *Mishneh Torah, Hilkhot Teshuva* 6.3.

10. Ahad Ha'am in his essay "External Freedom and Internal Servitude."

11. See Spinoza, *Tractatus theologico-politicus*, praef. (sect. 7 Bruder).

12. *Théodicée*, Discours de la Conformité de la foi avec la raison, sect. 3, and Vergil, *Georgica* IV, 86–87. The poet speaks of the battle between two rival queens for the rule of a single beehive. The philosopher seems to think of the question whether philosophy or revelation ought to be the queen.

13. See Franz Rosenzweig, *Kleinere Schriften* (Berlin: Schocken, 1937), 354–98.

14. On the relation between Rosenzweig's and Heidegger's thought, see Karl Löwith, *Gesammalte Abhandlungen* (Stuttgart: W. Kohlhammer, 1960), 68–92.

15. Rosenzweig, *Kleinere Schriften*, 380, 387.

16. *Eclipse of God* (New York: Harper, 1952), 97; see the German original, *Gottesfinsternis* (Zürich: Manesse, 1953), 87–88. I have not attempted to bring the translation somewhat closer to Heidegger's German statement which, incidentally, is not quite literally quoted by Buber. See Heidegger, *Nietzsche*, II, 320.

17. Hermann Cohen, *Ethik des reinen Willens*, 4th ed., 422: "Der Prophet hat gut reden: Himmel und Erde mögen vergehen; er denkt sie in seinem Felsen, den ihm Gott bildet, wohlgegründet."

18. *Eclipse of God*, 81; *Gottesfinsternis*, 71. I believe that the translator made a mistake in rendering "Führung einer Welt" by "conduct of the world," and I changed his translation accordingly, but I do not know whether I am right; it does not appear from the Preface that Buber has approved the translation.

19. See the reasoning with which Wellhausen justifies his athetesis of Amos 9:13–15: "Roses and lavender instead of blood and iron." *Skizzen und Vorarbeiten* (Berlin: Reimer, 1893), V, 94.

20. *Der Satz vom Grund*, 142; *Was heisst Denken?*, 32ff.

21. *Gottesfinsternis*, 143, 159–61; *Eclipse of God*, 154, 173–75. See Rosenzweig, 192, 530. See above all the thorough discussion of this theme by Gershom Scholem, *On the Kabbala and its Symbolism* (New York: Schocken, 1965), chapters 1 and 2.

22. Compare *Gottesfinsternis*, 34 with 96–97 and 117, or *Eclipse of God*, 39–40 with 106, 127.

23. Heidegger, *Sein und Zeit*, sect. 57. See C. F. Meyer's *Die Versuchung des Pescara*.

24. See *Fröhliche Wissenschaft*, no. 343.

25. *Jenseits*, nos. 45, 224; *Götzen-Dämmerung*, "Die 'Vernunft' in der Philosophie," nos. 1–2.

26. Letter to Overbeck of 23 February 1887. See *Jenseits*, no. 60; *Genealogie der Moral*, I, no. 7, III, nos. 23, 28 beginning; Nietzsche, *Werke*, ed. Schlechta, III, 422.

27. *Fröhliche Wissenschaft*, no. 344; *Jenseits*, no. 227; *Genealogie der Moral*, III, no. 27.

28. *Jenseits*, I; *Fröhliche Wissenschaft*, nos. 347, 377. Thomas Aquinas, *S. th.* 1 qu. 1. a. 4. and 2-2 qu. 1. a. 1.

29. *Sein und Zeit*, 48–49, 190 n. 1, 229–30, 249 n. 1.

30. *Kleinere Schiften*, 31–32, 111, 281–82, 374, 379, 382, 391, 392.

31. Ibid., 108–9, 114, 116–17, 119, 155–56.

32. Nietzsche, *Also sprach Zarathustra*, "Of Thousand Goals and One."

33. See also Kant, *Die Religion innerhalb der Grenzen der blossen Vernunft*, ed. Kehrbach, 43.

34. *Kleinere Schriften*, 154; *Briefe* (Berlin: Schocken, 1935), 520.

35. *Ethics* V, prop. 25 and prop. 36 schol.; see *Tr. theol-pol.* VI, sect. 23. See Goethe's letter to F. H. Jacobi of 5 May 1786.

36. "Spinoza über Staat und Religion, Judentum und Christentum," *Hermann Cohens Jüdische Schriften*, ed. Bruno Strauss (Berlin: C. A. Schwetschke, 1924), III, 290–372; "Ein ungedruckter Vortrag Hermann Cohens über Spinozas Verhältnis zum Judentum," eingeleitet von Franz Rosenzweig, *Festgabe zum zehnjährigen Bestehen der Akademie für die Wissenschaft des Judentums, 1919–1929*, 42–68. See Ernst Simon, "Zu Hermann Cohens Spinoza-Auffassung," *Monatsschrift für Geschichte und Wissenschaft des Judentums* 79 (1935): 181–94.

37. *Jüdische Schriften*, 293, 320, 325–26, 329–31, 343, 358, 360; *Festgabe*, 47–50, 57, 61–64.

38. *Jüdische Schriften*, 299, 306–9, 329, 360–62.

39. *Jüdische Schriften*, 333, 361, 363–64, 368, 371; *Festgabe*, 59.

40. *Festgabe*, 46, 47, 49–50; *Jüdische Schriften*, 344.

41. *Jüdische Schriften*, 317–21, 323, 337–38.

42. *Jüdische Schriften*, 367; *Festgabe*, 56. Compare *Tr. theol.-pol.* I, sects. 35 and 37 with the titles of *Ethics* I and II (see *Cogitata Metaphysica* II, 12) and V, 36 cor.

43. *Tr.* XII, 19, 24, 37; XIII, 23; XIV, 6, 22–29, 34–36; XX, 22, 40; *Tr. pol.* VIII, 46. See especially *Tr.* XII, 3, where Spinoza takes the side of the Pharisees against the Sadducees. The contrast of *Tr.* XIV with Hobbes' *Leviathan*, ch. 43, is most revealing.

44. *Tr.* V, 7–9.

45. Ibid., V, 13, 15, 30–31; XVII, 95–102; XIX, 13–17.

46. Cohen, *Jüdische Schriften* III, 333.

47. Ibid.

48. Cohen, *Kants Begründung der Ethik*, 2nd ed., 490, speaks of the "gewagte Spiel" of Kant in his *Die Religion innerhalb der Grenzen der blossen Vernunft*, a work according to Cohen rich in "ambiguities and inner contradictions."

49. *Ethik*, 61, 64, 94, 439–58, 468–70, 606. See *Kants Begründung der Ethik*, 2nd ed., 356–57.

50. Spinoza, *Tr. pol.* I, 2. Cohen, *Ethik*, 64, 269, 272, 285–86, 378, 384–86; *Kants Begründung der Ethik*, 394–406, 454. See, however, Hegel, *Rechtsphilosophie*, sect. 94ff.

51. *Pirkei Avot* 3:2.

52. *Kants Begründung der Ethik*, 309, 430, 431, 439, 446, 452, 511, 544–45, 554.

53. *Festgabe*, 44 (*Kleinere Schriften*, 355).

54. *Jüdische Schriften* II, 265–67. Cf. *Tr.* III, 25, 33, 34, e.g., with Rashi on Isaiah 19:25, Jeremiah 1:5, and Malachi 1:10–11, and Kimchi on Isaiah 48:17.

55. *Festgabe*, 64–67; *Jüdische Schriften* III, 345–51. See *Tr.* V, 47–48.

56. Misreading his authority or Caro, Cohen erroneously asserts that Caro declares the reading "but to the wise ones" to be the correct reading.

57. See also Manasse ben Israel, *Conciliator* (Frankfurt: 1633), Deut. q. 2. (p. 221).

58. In one of the passages (*Edut* 11.10) Maimonides says that the pious idolators have a share in the world to come; but how do we know that he does not mean by a pious idolator an idolator who has forsworn idolatry (see *Issurei Bia* 14.7) on the ground that idolatry is forbidden to all men by divine revelation? In the other passage (*Teshuva* 3.5) he merely says that the pious Gentiles have a share in the world to come; the sequel (3.6ff., see esp. 14) could seem to show that the pious Gentile is supposed to believe in the revealed character of the Torah.

59. *Jüdische Schriften* III, 240.

60. *Guide* 3.29 at the end; Aristotle, *Metaphysics* 1003a33ff.

61. See *M.T., Hilkhot Yesodei ha-Torah* 1.1.

62. Cohen, *Die Religion der Vernunft aus den Quellen des Judentums* (Frankfurt: J. Kauffmann, 1929), 205.

63. *Festgabe*, 53; *Jüdische Schriften* III, 365; see also II, 257.

64. *Jüdische Schriften*, 335–36; *Tr.* IV, 17 (see 9–16), 21.

65. *Jüdische Schriften* III, 351; *Festgabe*, 50–54.

66. "Comments on *Der Begriff des Politischen* by Carl Schmitt" (1932). See *Spinoza's Critique of Religion* (New York: Schocken, 1965), 331–51.

II

Studies of Modern Jewish Thinkers

3

How to Study Spinoza's
Theologico-Political Treatise

I

Before attempting to answer the question of how to proceed in a particular historical investigation, one must clarify the reasons why the investigation is relevant. In fact, the reasons which induce one to study a particular historical subject immediately determine the general character of the procedure. The reason why a fresh investigation of Spinoza's *Theologico-Political Treatise*[1] is in order, is obvious. The chief aim of the *Treatise* is to refute the claims which had been raised on behalf of revelation throughout the ages; and Spinoza succeeded, at least to the extent that his book has become *the* classic document of the "rationalist" or "secularist" attack on the belief in revelation. The study of the *Treatise* can be of real importance only if the issue discussed in it is still alive. A glance at the present scene is sufficient to show one that the issue which, until a short while ago, was generally believed to have been settled by Spinoza's nineteenth-century successors once and for all, and thus to be obsolete, is again approaching the center of attention. But we cannot help noticing that the most fundamental issue—the issue raised by the conflicting claims of philosophy and revelation—is discussed in our time on a decidedly lower level than was almost customary in former ages. It is with a view to these circumstances that we open the *Treatise* again. We shall therefore listen to Spinoza as attentively as we can. We shall make every effort to understand what he says exactly as he means it. For if we fail to do so, we are likely to substitute our folly for his wisdom.

To understand the words of another man, living or dead, may mean two different things which for the moment we shall call interpretation and explanation. By interpretation we mean the attempt to ascertain what the speaker said and how he actually understood what he said, regardless of whether he expressed that understanding explicitly or not. By explanation we mean the attempt to ascertain those implications of his statements of which he was unaware. Accordingly, the realization that a given statement is ironical or a lie belongs to the interpretation of the statement, whereas the realization that a given statement is based on a mistake, or is the unconscious expression of a wish, an interest, a bias, or a historical situation, belongs to its explanation. It is obvious that the interpretation has to precede the explanation. If the explanation is not based on an adequate interpretation, it will be the explanation, not of the statement to be explained, but of a figment of the imagination of the historian. It is equally obvious that, within the interpretation, the understanding of the explicit meaning of a statement has to precede the understanding of what the author knew but did not say explicitly: one cannot realize, or at any rate one cannot prove, that a statement is a lie before one has understood the statement in itself.

The demonstrably true understanding of the words or the thoughts of another man is necessarily based on an exact interpretation of his explicit statements. But exactness means different things in different cases. In some cases exact interpretation requires the careful weighing of every word used by the speaker; such careful consideration would be a most inexact procedure in the case of a casual remark of a loose thinker or talker.[2] In order to know what degree or kind of exactness is required for the understanding of a given writing, one must therefore first know the author's habits of writing. But since these habits become truly known only through the understanding of the writer's work, it would seem that at the beginning one cannot help being guided by one's preconceived notions of the author's character. The procedure would be more simple if there were a way of ascertaining an author's manner of writing prior to interpreting his works. It is a general observation that people write as they read. As a rule, careful writers are careful readers and vice versa. A careful writer wants to be read carefully. He cannot know what it means to be read carefully but by having done careful reading himself. Reading precedes writing. We read before we write. We learn to write by reading. A man learns to write well by reading well good books, by reading most carefully books which are most carefully written. We may therefore acquire some previous knowledge of an author's habits of writing by studying his habits of reading. The task is simplified if the author in question explicitly discusses the right manner of reading books in general, or of reading a particular book which he has studied with a great deal of attention. Spinoza has devoted a whole chapter of his *Treatise* to the question of how to read the Bible, which he had read and reread with very great care.[3] To ascertain how to read Spinoza, we shall do well to cast a glance at his rules for reading the Bible.

Spinoza holds the view that the method of interpreting the Bible is identical with the method of interpreting nature. The reading of the book of nature consists in inferring the definitions of natural things from the data supplied by "natural history." In the same way, the interpretation of the Bible consists in inferring the thought of the biblical authors, or the definitions of the biblical subjects qua biblical subjects, from the data supplied by "the history of the Bible." The knowledge of nature must be derived solely from data supplied by nature herself, and not at all from considerations of what is fitting, beautiful, perfect, or reasonable. In the same way the knowledge of the Bible must be derived solely from data supplied by the Bible itself, and not at all from considerations of what is reasonable. For we have no right to assume that the views of the biblical authors agree with the dictates of human reason. In other words, the understanding of the biblical teaching and the judgment on whether that teaching is reasonable or not, have to be kept strictly separate. Nor can we identify the thought of the biblical authors with its traditional interpretation unless we prove first that that interpretation goes back to oral utterances of the biblical authors. Besides, seeing that there is a variety of biblical authors, we have to understand each of them by himself; prior to investigation we have no right to assume that they all agree with each other. The Bible has to be understood exclusively by itself, or nothing can be accepted as a biblical teaching if it is not borne out clearly by the Bible itself, or the whole knowledge of the Bible must be derived exclusively from the Bible itself.[4]

"The history of the Bible," as Spinoza conceives of it, consists of three parts: a) thorough knowledge of the language of the Bible; b) collection and lucid arrangement of the statements of each biblical book regarding every significant subject; c) knowledge of the lives of all biblical authors, as well as of their characters, mental casts, and interests; knowledge of the occasion and time of the composition of each biblical book, of its addressees, of its fate, etc. These data or, more specifically, the collected and properly arranged biblical statements understood in the light of grammar, paleography, history, etc., are the basis of the interpretation proper, which consists in inferring, by legitimate reasoning, from the data mentioned, the thought of the biblical authors. Here again one has to follow the model of natural science. One has to ascertain first the most universal or most fundamental element of biblical thought, i.e., what all biblical authors explicitly and clearly present as a teaching meant for all times and addressed to all men; thereafter one has to descend to derivative or less universal themes, such as the biblical teaching about less general subjects, and the teachings peculiar to the individual biblical authors.[5]

Spinoza's formulation of his hermeneutic principle ("the whole knowledge of the Bible must be derived exclusively from the Bible itself") does not express precisely what he actually demands. In the first place, the knowledge of the language of the Bible has to be derived primarily, as he maintains, not from the Bible, but from a certain tradition.[6] Besides, as for the knowledge of the lives, etc., of the authors, and of the fate of their books, it may not be impossible to derive it partly from the Bible, but there is certainly no reason why it should be an indispensable duty to derive it exclusively from the Bible; Spinoza himself welcomed every reliable extraneous information shedding light on matters of this kind.[7] Furthermore, he does not say a word to the effect that the biblical statements regarding the various significant subjects must be arranged according to principles supplied by the Bible itself; there are reasons for believing that his own arrangement of biblical subjects would have had no biblical basis whatever, but would have corresponded to what he considered the natural order of the subjects in question.[8] Above all, the interpretation proper, as he conceives of it, consists in ascertaining the definitions of the subjects dealt with by the Bible; but these definitions are admittedly not supplied by the Bible itself; in fact, qua definitions they transcend the horizon of the Bible; thus the interpretation of the Bible consists, not in understanding the biblical authors exactly as they understood themselves but in understanding them better than they understood themselves. We may say that Spinoza's formulation of his hermeneutic principle is not more than an exaggerated and therefore inexact expression of the following view: the only meaning of any biblical passage is its literal meaning, except if reasons taken from the indubitable usage of the biblical language demand the metaphorical understanding of the passage; certainly the disagreement of the statement of a biblical author with the teaching of reason, of piety, of tradition, or even of another biblical author, does not justify one in abandoning the literal meaning. Spinoza's exaggeration is sufficiently justified by the power of the position which he challenges: he had to make himself heard amidst the clamor raised by the myriads of his opponents.

There is a certain agreement between Spinoza's hermeneutic principle ("the Bible must be understood exclusively by itself") and the principle to which we adhere ("the Bible must be understood exactly as it was understood by its authors, or by its compilers"). His demand that the interpretation of the biblical teaching and the judgment on the truth or value of that teaching be kept strictly separate, partly agrees with what we meant by distinguishing between interpretation and explanation. Yet, as we have indicated, the difference between the two

principles is fundamental. According to our principle, the first questions to be addressed to a book would be of this kind: what is its subject
matter, i.e., how is its subject matter designated, or understood, by the
author?; what is his intention in dealing with his subject?; what questions does he raise in regard to it, or with what aspect of the subject is he
exclusively, or chiefly, concerned? Only after these and similar questions have found their answer, would we even think of collecting and
arranging the statements of the author regarding various topics discussed or mentioned in his book; for only the answers to questions like
those we have indicated would enable us to tell what particular topics
referred to in his book are significant or even central. If we followed
Spinoza's rule, we would start to collect and to arrange the biblical
statements regarding all kinds of subjects without any guidance supplied by the Bible itself as to what subjects are central or significant,
and as to what arrangement agrees with the thought of the Bible.
Furthermore, if we followed Spinoza, we would next look out for the
most universal or most fundamental teaching of the Bible as a teaching
clearly presented everywhere in the Bible. But is there any necessity,
or even likelihood, that the most fundamental teaching of a book should
be constantly repeated? In other words, is there any necessity that the
most universal or most fundamental teaching of a book should be its
clearest teaching?[9] Be this as it may, we need not dwell on what we consider the deficiencies of Spinoza's biblical hermeneutics. For any objection which we could raise against that hermeneutics would be based on
the premise that the Bible is substantially intelligible, and Spinoza
denies that very premise. According to him, the Bible is essentially unintelligible, since its largest part is devoted to unintelligible matters, and it
is accidentally unintelligible since only a part of the data which could
throw light on its meaning is actually available. It is the essential unintelligibility of the Bible—the fact that it is a "hieroglyphic" book—which
is the reason why a special procedure has to be devised for its interpretation: the purpose of that procedure is to open up an indirect access
to a book which is not accessible directly, i.e., by way of its subject matter. This implies that not all books, but only hieroglyphic books require
a method of interpretation that is fundamentally the same as that
required for deciphering the book of nature. Spinoza is primarily concerned with what the Bible teaches clearly everywhere, because only
such a ubiquitous teaching could supply a clue to every hieroglyphic
passage that might occur in the Bible. It is because of its essential unintelligibility that the Bible must be understood exclusively by itself: the
largest part of the Bible is devoted to matters to which we have no
access whatever except through the Bible.[10] For the same reason it is

impossible merely to try to understand the biblical authors as they understood themselves; every attempt to understand the Bible is of necessity an attempt to understand its authors better than they understood themselves.

There is probably no need for proving that Spinoza considered his own books, and in particular the *Treatise*, intelligible and not hieroglyphic. Hieroglyphic subjects, he indicates, are a matter of curiosity rather than useful, whereas the subjects of the *Treatise* are eminently useful.[11] In order to find out how he wants his own books to be read, we must therefore turn from his biblical hermeneutics to his rules for reading intelligible books.

He does not think that there can be any difficulty that might seriously obstruct the understanding of books devoted to intelligible subjects, and hence he does not see any need for elaborate procedures conducive to their understanding. To understand a book of this kind, one does not need perfect knowledge, but at most "a very common and, as it were, boyish knowledge" of the language of the original; in fact, reading of a translation would suffice perfectly. Nor does one have to know the life of the author, his interests and character, the addressee of his book, its fate, nor the variant readings, etc. Intelligible books are self-explanatory. Contrary to what Spinoza seems to say, not hieroglyphic books, to whose subjects we have no access through our experience or insight, but intelligible books, to whose understanding the reader naturally contributes by drawing on his experience or insight "while he goes," can and must be understood by themselves. For while the meaning of hieroglyphic books must be inferred indirectly from data which are not necessarily supplied by the book itself (the life of the author, the fate of the book, etc.), the meaning of intelligible books can and must be ascertained directly by consideration of its subject matter and of the intention of the author, i.e., of things which become truly known only through the book itself.[12] If we apply this information, as we must, to Spinoza's own books, we realize that according to his view the whole "history" of his works, the whole historical procedure as employed by the modern students of his works, is superfluous; and therefore, we may add, rather a hindrance than a help to the understanding of his books.

We add a few words of explanation. Spinoza says that for the understanding of intelligible books knowledge of the variant readings is superfluous. But he also says that there never was a book without faulty readings. He must have thought that errors which have crept into books or passages dealing with intelligible matters will easily be detected and corrected by the intelligent reader "while he goes."[13] Spinoza says that for the understanding of intelligible books knowledge of the character or mental cast of an author is superfluous. But when discussing the intention of Machiavelli's *Prince*, which he could not have considered a hieroglyphic book, he comes to a decision only by taking into account the author's "wisdom" or "prudence," as well as his love of political liberty.[14] Spinoza would probably answer that he based his decision not on any previous or at any rate extraneous knowledge of Machiavelli's life and character, but on what every intelligent reader of the *Prince* and the *Discourses on Livy* would notice. Spinoza says that even obscure presentations of intelligible matters are intelligible. But he doubtless knew that no negligible number of authors dealing with intelligible matters contradict themselves. He probably would reply that, if an author contradicts himself, the reader does well to suspend his judgment on what the author thought about the subject in question, and to use his powers rather for finding out by himself which of the two contradictory assertions is true. Consideration of whether the usage of the author's language permits the metaphorical interpretation of one of the two contradictory assertions is clearly out of place in the case of intelligible books, since for their understanding it is not even necessary to know in what language they were originally composed.[15]

Our study of Spinoza's rules of reading seems to have led to an impasse. We cannot read his books as he read the Bible because his books are certainly not hieroglyphic. Nor can we read them as he read Euclid and other intelligible books, because his books are not as easily intelligible to us as the nonhieroglyphic books which he knew were to him. If an author of Spinoza's intelligence, who speaks with so much assurance about the most important biblical subjects, simply confesses that he does not understand the Bible, we on our part have to confess that it cannot be easy to understand him. His rules of reading are of little or no use for the understanding of books that are neither hieroglyphic nor as easy of access as a modern manual of Euclidean geometry. One could say of course that by laying down rules for the two extreme cases Spinoza has given us to understand how books of moderate difficulty have to be read: books of this kind are neither absolutely intelligible nor absolutely unintelligible without "history"; "history" is required for the understanding of a book to the extent to which the book is not self-explanatory. But, if one does not want to suppress completely the spirit of Spinoza's statements, one would have to add in the most emphatic manner that according to him the contribution of "history" to the understanding of truly useful books cannot but be trivial.

The modern interpreter of Spinoza on the other hand considers it most useful, and even necessary, to understand Spinoza's books, and is at the same time convinced that "history" makes a most important contribution to their understanding. The interpreter thus contradicts Spinoza in a point which, apparently, is of no small importance: he holds that Spinoza's books cannot be understood on the basis of Spinoza's own hermeneutic principles. Thus the question becomes inevitable, whether it is possible to understand Spinoza on the basis of the rejection of these principles. One's answer will depend on what importance one attaches to the controversial issue. If it is true that the problem of "history," fully understood, is identical with the problem of the nature of philosophy itself, the modern interpreter is separated from Spinoza by a fundamental difference of orientation. The modern interpreter takes it for granted that in order to be adequate to its task, philosophy must be "historical," and that therefore the history of philosophy is a philosophic discipline. He presupposes then from the outset—by the very fact that he is a philosophic historian of philosophy and not a mere antiquarian—that Spinoza's whole position as Spinoza himself presented and understood it, is untenable because it is manifestly not "historical." He lacks then the strongest incentive for attempting to understand Spinoza's teaching as Spinoza himself understood it, that incentive being the suspicion that Spinoza's teaching is *the* true teaching. Without that incentive no reasonable man would devote all his energy to the understanding of Spinoza, and without such devotion Spinoza's books will never disclose their full meaning.

It would seem then that one cannot understand Spinoza if one accepts his hermeneutic principles, nor if one rejects them. To find a way out of this difficulty, we must first understand why Spinoza could rest satisfied with his unsatisfactory remarks about the manner in which serious books must be read. It does not suffice to say that he was exclusively concerned with *the* truth, the truth about the whole, and not with what other people taught about it. For he knew too well how much he was indebted for his grasp of what he considered *the* truth to some books written by other men. The true reason is his contempt for that thought of the past which can become accessible only through the reading of very difficult books. Other things being equal, one needs more of "history" for understanding books of the past than for understanding contemporary books. If a man believes that the most useful or important books are contemporary ones, he will hardly ever experience the need for historical interpretation. This was the case of Spinoza. The only book which he published under his name is devoted to the philosophy of Descartes. The only books (apart from the Bible) on which he ever wrote extensively, were books by Descartes and Boyle, i.e., by contemporaries. The authority of Socrates, Plato, and Aristotle, to say nothing of their followers, did not carry much weight with him. He admired Epicurus, Democritus, Lucretius and their followers much more.[16] Yet there are hardly any unambiguous traces of his having studied their works, or the remnants of their works, with any assiduity; he had easy access to their teaching through the writings of Gassendi, a contemporary. As regards political philosophy in particular, he flatly declares that all political philosophy prior to his own is useless.[17] He confesses to owe much to certain "outstanding men who have written many excellent things about the right way of life, and who have given counsels full of wisdom to mortals";[18] he probably has in mind authors like Seneca and Cicero; but the doctrines to which he refers are by their nature easy for everyone to understand. Regarding a much more difficult and basic teaching, viz. the thesis that God is the immanent cause of all things, he surmises that he says the same thing as "all ancient philosophers, although in a different manner," and as "all ancient Hebrews, as far as one can conjecture from some traditions, which however have been adulterated in many ways." This is not the way in which one would speak of definite literary sources. Besides, he was probably more sincere when he indicated that his doctrine of God deviated radically from all other teachings which he knew.[19] Naturally, he had read a considerable number of old books, especially in his youth; but the question is what importance the mature Spinoza attached to them and to their study. His attitude is not surprising: the conviction that they were achieving a progress beyond all earlier philosophy or science, a progress condemning to deserved oblivion all earlier efforts, was rather common among the men who were responsible for the emergence of modern philosophy or science.

But Spinoza, who wrote for posterity rather than for his contemporaries, must have realized that the day would come when his own books would be old books. Yet, if they contain *the* true, i.e., *the* clear and distinct account of the whole, there seems to be no reason why they should not be directly intelligible at all times, provided they survive at all. This very reply however seems to prove conclusively that Spinoza did not consider a crucial possibility which to us is so obvious: the possibility that the whole orientation of a period may give way to a radically different orientation, and that after such a change has taken place one cannot bridge the gulf between the thought of the later age and that of the earlier age but by means of historical interpretation. From Spinoza's point of view one would have to retort that he denied, not the possibility of such a change occurring after the emergence of his doctrine, but its legitimacy. The abandonment of his approach in favor of a radically different one would have been in his eyes a manifest blunder, and not more than a new example of the frequently experienced relapse of human thought into the servitude of superstition.

Spinoza's rules of reading derive from his belief in the final character of his philosophy as *the* clear and distinct and, therefore, *the* true account of the whole. If we reject Spinoza's belief *a limine*, we will never be able to understand him because we will lack the necessary incentive for attempting to understand him properly. On the other hand, if we open our minds, if we take seriously the possibility that he was right, we can understand him. Apart from the fact that we would have the indispensable incentive, we would be in a position to correct his insufficient rules of reading without having to fear that in doing so we would deviate radically from his fundamental principles. For if these principles are sound, questions of hermeneutics cannot be central questions. More precisely, the need for a correction of Spinoza's hermeneutics follows directly from the assumption that his teaching is *the* true teaching. On the basis of this assumption, *the* true teaching is accessible to us only through certain old books. Reading of old books becomes extremely important to us for the very reason for which it was utterly unimportant to Spinoza. We shall most urgently need an elaborate hermeneutics for the same reason for which Spinoza did not need any hermeneutics. We remain in perfect accord with Spinoza's way of thinking as long as we look at the devising of a more refined historical method as a desperate remedy for a desperate situation, rather than as a symptom of a healthy and thriving "culture."

Our argument implies the suggestion that today *the* truth may be accessible only through certain old books. We still have to show that this suggestion is compatible with Spinoza's principles. Spinoza knew that the power of the natural obstacles to philosophy, which are the same at all times, can be increased by specific mistakes.[20] The natural and sporadic outbursts against philosophy may be replaced by its deliberate and relentless suppression. Superstition, the natural enemy of philosophy, may arm itself with the weapons of philosophy and thus transform itself into pseudophilosophy. Of pseudophilosophies there is an indefinitely large variety, since every later pseudophilosopher can try to improve on the achievements, or to avoid certain blunders, of his predecessors. It is therefore impossible even for the most far-sighted man to foresee which pseudophilosophies will emerge, and gain control of the minds of men in the future. Now, not indeed philosophy, but the way in which the introduction to philosophy must proceed, necessarily changes with the change of the artificial or accidental obstacles to philosophy. The artificial obstacles may be so strong at a given time that a most elaborate "artificial" introduction has to be completed before the "natural" introduction can begin. It is conceivable that a particular pseudophilosophy may emerge whose power cannot be broken but by the most intensive reading of old books. As long as that pseudophilosophy rules, elaborate historical studies may be needed which would have been superfluous and therefore harmful in more fortunate times.

Before we consider whether the dominant thought of the present age would have to be described from Spinoza's point of view as a pseudophilosophy of this kind, we shall venture to express our suggestion in terms of the classic description of the natural obstacles to philosophy. People may become so frightened of the ascent to the light of the sun, and so desirous of making that ascent utterly impossible to any of their descendants, that they dig a deep pit beneath the cave in which they were born, and withdraw into that pit. If one of the descendants desired to ascend to the light of the sun, he would first have to try to reach the level of the natural cave, and he would have to invent new and most artificial tools unknown and unnecessary to those who dwelt in the natural cave. He would be a fool, he would never see the light of the sun, he would lose the last vestige of the memory of the sun, if he perversely thought that by inventing his new tools he had progressed beyond the ancestral cave-dwellers.

According to Spinoza, the natural obstacle to philosophy is man's imaginative and passionate life, which tries to secure itself against its breakdown by producing what Spinoza calls superstition. The alternative that confronts man by nature is then that of a superstitious account of the whole on the one hand, and of the philosophic account on the other. In spite of their radical antagonism, superstition and philosophy have this in common, that both attempt to give a final account of the whole, and both consider such an account indispensable for the guidance of human life. Philosophy finds itself in its natural situation as long as its account of the whole is challenged only by superstitious accounts and not yet by pseudophilosophies. Now, it is obvious that that situation does not exist in our time. The simplicity and directness of the two original antagonists, who fought their secular struggle for the guidance of mankind on the one plane of truth, has given way to a more "sophisticated" or a more "pragmatic" attitude. The very idea of a final account of the whole—of an account which necessarily culminates in, or starts from, knowledge of the first cause or first causes of all things—has been abandoned by an ever-increasing number of people, not only as incapable of realization but as meaningless or absurd. The authorities to which these people defer are the twin-sisters called Science and History. Science, as they understand it, is no longer the quest for the true and final account of the whole. Accordingly, they are used to distinguish between science and philosophy, or between the scientist and the philosopher.[21] Thus they tacitly, and sometimes even openly, admit the possibility of an unphilosophic science and of an unscientific philosophy. Of these two endeavors, science naturally enjoys a much higher prestige: it is customary to contrast the steady progress of science with the failure of philosophy. The philosophy which is still legitimate on this basis would not be more than the hand-maid of science called methodology, but for the following consideration. Science, rejecting the idea of a final account of the whole, essentially conceives of itself as progressive, as being the outcome of a progress of human thought beyond the thought of all earlier periods, and as being capable of still further progress in the future. But there is an appalling discrepancy between the exactness of science itself and the quality of its knowledge of its progressive character as long as science is not accom-panied by the effort, at least aspiring to exactness, truly to prove the fact of progress, to understand the conditions of progress, and therewith to secure the possibility of future progress. Science in the present-day meaning of the term is therefore necessarily accompanied by history of human thought either, as originally, in a most rudimentary form or, as today, in a much more elaborate form. It is the history of human thought which now takes the place formerly occupied by philosophy or, in other words, philosophy transforms itself into history of human thought. The fundamental distinction between philosophy and history, which was implied in the original meaning of philosophy, gives way to a fusion of philosophy and history. If the history of human thought is studied in the spirit of modern science, one reaches the conclusion that all human thought is "historically conditioned," or that the attempt to liberate one's thought from one's "historical situation" is quixotic. Once this has become a settled conviction constantly reinforced by an ever-increasing number of new observations, the idea of a final account of the whole, of an account which as such would not be "historically condi-tioned," appears to be untenable for reasons which can be made mani-fest to every child. Thereafter, there no longer exists a direct access to the original meaning of philosophy, as quest for the true and final account of the whole. Once this state has been reached, the original meaning of philosophy is accessible only through recollection of what philosophy meant in the past, i.e., for all practical purposes, only through the read-ing of old books.

As long as the belief in the possibility and necessity of a final account of the whole prevailed, history in general and especially history of human thought did not form an integral part of the philosophic effort, however much philosophers might have appreciated reports on earlier thought in their absolutely ancillary function. But after that belief has lost its power, or after a complete break with the basic premise of all earlier philosophic thought has been effected, concern with the various phases of earlier thought becomes an integral part of philosophy. The study of earlier thought, if conducted with intelligence and assiduity, leads to a revitalization of earlier ways of thinking. The historian, who started out with the conviction that true understanding of human thought is understanding of every teaching in terms of its particular time or as an expression of its particular time, necessarily familiarizes himself with the view, constantly urged upon him by his subject matter, that his initial conviction is unsound. More than that: he is brought to realize that one cannot understand the thought of the past as long as one is guided by that initial conviction. This self-destruction of historicism is not altogether an unforeseen result. The concern with the thought of the past gained momentum, and increased in seriousness, by virtue of the late eighteenth- and early nineteenth-century critique of the modern approach, of modern natural science and of the moral and political doctrines which went with that science. Historical understanding, the revitalization of earlier ways of thinking, was originally meant as a corrective for the specific shortcomings of the modern mind. This impulse was however vitiated from the outset by the belief which accompanied it that modern thought (as distinguished from modern life and modern feeling) was superior to the thought of the past. Thus, what was primarily intended as a corrective for the modern mind was easily perverted into a confirmation of the dogma of the superiority of modern thought to all earlier thought. Historical understanding lost its liberating force by becoming historicism, which is nothing other than the petrified and self-complacent form of the self-criticism of the modern mind.

We have seen how one has to judge of the predominant thought of the present age in the light of Spinoza's principles, or how one can enlarge, in strict adherence to his principles, his view regarding the obstacles to philosophy and therewith to the understanding of his own books. One thus acquires the right in reading his books to deviate from his own rules of reading. One realizes at the same time that one cannot simply replace his rules of reading by those actually followed by numerous modern historians. It is true that what today is frequently meant by historical understanding of Spinoza's thought, viz. the understanding of his thought in terms of his time, could be described as a more elaborate form of what he himself would have called the "history" of his books. But it is also true that he limited the need for "history" to the understanding of hieroglyphic books. We have no right simply to disregard his view according to which books like his own can and must be understood by themselves. We merely have to add the qualification that this must be done within the limits of the possible. We have to remain faithful to the spirit of his injunction. Contrary to what he implies, we need for the understanding of his books such information as is not supplied by him and as is not easily available to every reasonable reader regardless of time and place. But we must never lose sight of the fact that information of this kind cannot have more than a strictly subordinate function, or that such information has to be integrated into a framework authentically or explicitly supplied by Spinoza himself. This holds of all knowledge which he did not supply directly and which he did not therefore consider relevant for the understanding of his books: information regarding his life, character, and interests, the occasion and time of the composition of his books, their addressees, the fate of his teaching and, last but not least, his sources. Such extraneous knowledge can never be permitted to supply the clue to his teaching except after it has been proved beyond any reasonable doubt that it is impossible to make head and tail of his teaching as he presented it. This principle creates from the outset a healthy suspicion against the attempts, so vastly different among themselves, to understand Spinoza's teaching as a modification of the Kabbala or of Platonism, or as an expression of the spirit of the barocco, or as the culmination of medieval scholasticism. Every deviation from that principle exposes one to the danger that one tries to understand Spinoza better than he understood himself before one has understood him as he understood himself; it exposes one to the danger that one understands, not Spinoza, but a figment of one's imagination.

Historical understanding, as it is frequently practiced, seduces one into seeing the author whom one studies primarily as a contemporary among his contemporaries, or to read his books as if they were primarily addressed to his contemporaries. But the books of men like the mature Spinoza, which are meant as possessions for all times, are primarily addressed to posterity. Hence he wrote them in such a manner as not to require for their understanding the previous knowledge of facts which, to the best of his knowledge, could be really relevant and easily accessible only to his contemporaries. The flight to immortality requires an extreme discretion in the selection of one's luggage. A book that requires for its adequate understanding the use, nay, the preservation of all libraries and archives containing information which was useful to its author hardly deserves being written and being read at all, and it certainly does not deserve surviving its author. In particular, there must have been facts and teachings which were very important to Spinoza during his formative years when he was naturally less capable than later of distinguishing between the merely contemporary—which from Spinoza's point of view probably included much of what he knew of medieval philosophy—and what he considered deserving preservation. Information about his "development" can justly be regarded as irrelevant until it has been shown that Spinoza's final teaching remains mysterious without such information. Since his teaching is primarily addressed to posterity, the interpreter has always to be mindful of the difference in specific weight of the books of the mature Spinoza and his letters. The letters are primarily addressed, not to posterity. but to particular contemporaries. Whereas the works of his maturity may be presumed to be addressed primarily to the best type of readers, the large majority of his letters are obviously addressed to rather mediocre men.

The need for extraneous information derives from the fact that a man's foresight as to what could be intelligible to posterity is necessarily limited. To mention only the most striking and at the same time most important example: Spinoza could not have foreseen, or at any rate he could not have taken effective precaution against the fact, that the traditional terminology of philosophy, which he employed while modifying it, would become obsolete. Thus the present-day reader of Spinoza has to learn the rudiments of a language which was familiar to Spinoza's contemporaries. To generalize from this, the interpreter of Spinoza has to reconstruct that "background" which from Spinoza's point of view was indispensable for the understanding of his books but could not reasonably be supplied through his books, because no one can say everything without being tedious to everyone. This means that in his work of reconstruction the interpreter must follow the signposts erected by Spinoza himself and, secondarily, the indications which Spinoza left accidentally in his writings. He must start from a clear vision, based on Spinoza's explicit statements, of Spinoza's predecessors as seen by Spinoza. He must pay the greatest attention to that branch of "the philosophic tradition" that Spinoza himself considered most important or admired most highly. For instance, he cannot disregard with impunity what Spinoza says about Plato and Aristotle on the one hand, and about Democritus and Epicurus on the other. He must guard against the foolish presumption, nourished by unenlightened learning, that he can know better than Spinoza what was important to Spinoza, or that Spinoza did not know what he was talking about. He must be willing to attach greater weight to mediocre textbooks quoted by Spinoza than to classics which we cannot be sure that Spinoza has even known of. In attempting to interpret Spinoza, he must try his utmost not to go beyond the boundaries drawn by the terminology of Spinoza and of his contemporaries; if he uses modern terminology in rendering Spinoza's thought, or even in describing its character, he is likely to introduce a world alien to Spinoza into what claims to be an exact interpretation of Spinoza's thought. Only after one has completed the interpretation of Spinoza's teaching, when one is confronted with the necessity of passing judgment on it, is one at liberty, and even under the obligation, to disregard Spinoza's own indications. Spinoza claims to have refuted the central philosophic and theologic teaching of the past. To judge of that claim, or of the strength of the arguments in support of it, one must naturally consider the classics of the tradition regardless of whether or not Spinoza has known or studied them. But the understanding of Spinoza's silence about a fact or a teaching with which he must have been familiar, and whose mention or discussion would have been essential to his argument, belongs to the interpretation proper. For the suppression of something is a deliberate action.

II

According to Spinoza, his rules for reading the Bible are not applicable to the study of his own writings for the additional reason that the Bible is addressed to the vulgar, whereas his own writings are addressed to philosophers. In the preface to the *Treatise* he explicitly urges the vulgar to leave that book alone, and he explicitly recommends the book to "the philosophic reader" or "the philosophers."[22] Books addressed to the vulgar must be adequately intelligible if read in the way in which the vulgar is used to read, i.e., their substance must disclose itself to very inattentive and careless reading. In other words, in vulgar books written for instruction the most fundamental teaching must be written large on every page, or it must be the clearest teaching, whereas the same does not hold of philosophic books.

Spinoza held that intelligible books can be fully understood without the readers knowing to whom they are addressed. By stressing the fact that the *Treatise* is addressed to a specific group of men, he supplies us with the first clue to the specific difficulty of the work. He says that the work is meant especially for those "who would philosophize more freely if this one thing did not stand in the way, that they think that reason ought to serve as handmaid to theology." Those who think that reason or philosophy or science ought to be subservient to theology are characterized by Spinoza as skeptics, or as men who deny the certainty of reason, and the true philosopher cannot be a skeptic.[23] Thus, the *Treatise* is addressed, not to actual philosophers, but to potential philosophers. It is addressed to "the more prudent sort" or to those who cannot easily be duped,[24] i.e., to a class of men which is clearly more comprehensive than, and therefore not identical with, the class of the actual philosophers.

The potential philosophers to whom the *Treatise* is addressed believe in the authority of theology, i.e., of the Bible. By the Bible Spinoza understands the Old Testament and the New Testament.[25] The *Treatise* is then addressed to the potential philosophers among Christians. According to Spinoza's explicit declaration, it was the contrast between Christian belief and Christian practice that induced him to write that work.[26] If we could trust numerous explicit statements of Spinoza, his addressing Christian potential philosophers would have to be explained as follows. Christianity, and not Judaism, is based on the most perfect divine revelation. Both its universalist and its spiritual character, as contrasted with the particularist and carnal character of Judaism in particular, explain why the ascent to philosophy is easier or more natural for the Christian than for the Jew, who as such "despises" philosophy. Moreover, Spinoza's aim is to liberate philosophy from the theological domination which culminates in the persecution of philosophers by theologians and their disciples. If Christianity is the religion of love par excellence, whereas the Old Testament commands "thou shalt love thy neighbor, and hate thine enemy," Spinoza's plea for toleration is more naturally addressed to Christians than to Jews.[27]

In spite of this, the subject matter of the *Treatise* is obviously much more Jewish than Christian. Not only does Spinoza speak more fully of the Old than of the New Testament; he also refers in numerous cases, either polemically or approvingly, to Jewish commentators in the widest sense of the term, and hardly, if ever, to Christian ones. Moreover, he is much more indebted for his interpretations to Jewish than to Christian sources. He indicates that he is so well versed in Jewish lore that he can safely rely on his memory when speaking of Jewish subjects, or of what he had ascertained about them "a long time ago." Probably the most striking example of this Jewish background of the *Treatise* is the fact that, in illustrating the two opposed views of the relation between Bible and philosophy, Spinoza refers only to the two men whom he considered the leaders of the two camps within Judaism. He explains his refraining from philologic examination of the New Testament by his insufficient knowledge of the Greek language.[28] Generalizing from this remark, we may explain the preponderance of Jewish subject matter in the *Treatise* by the fact that Spinoza was much more versed in the Jewish than in the Christian tradition. One may go a step further in the same direction and surmise that he incorporated into that work a considerable amount of materials which he had originally used for justifying his defection from Judaism. Certain incongruities which strike the reader of the *Treatise* do not seem to admit of any other explanation. For our purpose it suffices to mention the two most outstanding examples. Spinoza says that the subject of the third chapter (the election of the Jews) is not required by the guiding purpose of the work; and one could consider applying this statement to the fourth and fifth chapters as well, which culminate in the critique of the Jewish ceremonial law. Chapters III-V would thus appear to be relics of a work primarily addressed to Jews. Besides, the *Treatise* stands or falls by the principle that the true meaning of any biblical passage has to be established exclusively out of the Bible, and not at all with regard to the philosophic or scientific truth. But in discussing the question of miracles, Spinoza asserts, in striking contradiction to that principle, that the biblical teaching fully agrees with the philosophic teaching, and that any biblical passage which contradicts the philosophic teaching has to be rejected as a sacrilegious addition to Holy Writ. This method of solving the conflict between philosophy and Bible had been used with particular energy by Spinoza's older Jewish contemporary Uriel da Costa. It would seem that Spinoza's occasional use of that method is another relic of his youthful, as it were intra-Jewish, reflections.

The assertion that Spinoza incorporated into his *Treatise* parts of his youthful apology for his defection from Judaism is at best a plausible hypothesis. Besides, no author who deserves the name will incorporate into a book parts of an earlier writing which do not make sense in the new book. Every concern with the question, of what parts of the *Treatise* might have been taken from Spinoza's early apology, seduces the interpreter into escaping from his plain duty, to understand the book as composed and published by Spinoza, to the questionable pleasures of higher criticism. While it can only be surmised what parts, if any, of the *Treatise* were taken from an earlier writing of Spinoza, it can be known what function these parts fulfill in the *Treatise* itself. Let us discuss from this point of view the two difficulties to which we have referred.

Spinoza says that his principal aim in the *Treatise* is the separation of philosophy from theology, and that this aim requires the discussion of "prophets and prophecy" but does not require the discussion of the questions as to whether the prophetic gift was peculiar to the Jews and as to what the election of the Jews means.[29] This is perfectly correct as far as the surface argument of the *Treatise* is concerned. Yet the deeper argument requires the proof, as distinguished from the assertion, that prophecy is a natural phenomenon. The proof offered in the first two chapters of the *Treatise* remains unsatisfactory as long as it has not been shown that prophecy is a universal phenomenon, i.e., that it is not peculiar to the Jews. This in its turn cannot be demonstrated without previous discussion of what kind of phenomena can possibly be peculiar to a nation, or a discussion of the privileges to which a nation as nation can be chosen. Not only the third chapter, however, but the fourth and fifth chapters as well are indispensable for the fully understood argument of the *Treatise*. The largest part of the work is in fact devoted more directly to an investigation of the Old rather than of the New Testament. In his discussion of the Old Testament, or of Judaism in general, Spinoza quite naturally follows a traditional Jewish arrangement of the subject matter. According to the tradition in question (which ultimately goes back to the Islamic *kalam*), what we may call "theology" is divided into two parts, the doctrine of God's unity and the doctrine of God's justice. The doctrine of divine justice deals especially with prophecy, law, and providence. This order is necessary because providence, or divine reward and punishment, presupposes the existence of a divine law, and the divine law in its turn presupposes divine revelation or prophecy. It is this order which underlies the plan of the first six chapters of the *Treatise* as one sees at once if one considers the connection, clearly indicated by Spinoza, between "miracles" and "providence."[30]

It is equally possible to understand from the context of the *Treatise* why Spinoza disregards in his discussion of miracles the principle of his biblical hermeneutics. For reasons which we shall state later, Spinoza tries to present his views about theological subjects with a great deal of restraint. There is, however, one fundamental point regarding which he consistently refuses to make any unambiguous concessions, and this is precisely the possibility of miracles as supranatural phenomena. Whereas he speaks without hesitation of suprarational teachings, he consistently rejects the possibility of miracles proper. If he had always rejected the possibility of suprarational teachings, he would have had no choice but either simply to identify the biblical teaching with the rational teaching—and this would have been fatal to the separation of philosophy from theology—or else simply to deny all truth to all biblical teachings as revealed teachings. The utmost he could dare was not always to deny the fact of suprarational revelation but always to deny its supranatural or miraculous character, and he could not do this consistently or conveniently without denying the possibility of miracles proper altogether. To avoid the break with the Bible in the crucial point, he had to assert that the possibility of miracles proper is denied by the

Bible itself. To maintain this assertion in the presence especially of the New Testament accounts of the resurrection of Jesus—of accounts which, as Spinoza admitted, are incompatible with his spiritualistic interpretation of Christianity—, he had no choice but to suggest that any biblical accounts of miracles proper cannot be really biblical but must be sacrilegious additions to Holy Writ.[31]

There are no valid reasons for doubting that the *Treatise* and all its parts are addressed to Christians. As a consequence, one does not sufficiently explain the preponderance of Jewish subject matter in the *Treatise* by referring to the fact that Spinoza had greater knowledge of the Jewish than of the Christian tradition. For this very fact would disqualify him from speaking with authority to Christians on the central subject of Christianity. The peculiarly "Jewish" character of the work must be understood in the light of Spinoza's guiding intention. If one assumes that he believed in the superiority of Christianity to Judaism, one cannot help suggesting that he wanted to give to Christians the following counsel: that they should abandon the Jewish carnal relics which have defaced Christianity almost from its beginning, or that they should return to the purely spiritual teaching of original Christianity. If the chief aim of the *Treatise* is the liberation of Christianity from its Jewish heritage, Jewish subjects will quite naturally be in the foreground of the discussion, and the author's qualification as a teacher of things Christian to Christians will be enhanced rather than diminished by the fact that he is more deeply versed in the Jewish than in the Christian tradition.

The modern historian is inclined to interpret the purpose of the *Treatise*, and therewith to answer the question regarding its addressees, in terms of the particular circumstances of Spinoza's life or of his time. There are even some statements of Spinoza which apparently support such an approach. But the statements in question are necessarily misunderstood if they are not grouped around the central fact that the *Treatise* is not addressed to Spinoza's contemporaries in particular. It is addressed to potential philosophers who are Christians. Men of this kind, and hence Spinoza's problem as well as its solution, are coeval with Christianity, and not peculiar to Spinoza's age. This does not do away with the fact that, according to Spinoza's explicit statement, not only philosophy and the subject matter itself, but "the time" as well required of him the investigations presented in the *Treatise*.[32] We have to see how this agrees with what one might call the timeless character of the purpose, and of the thesis, of the work.

Spinoza starts from the contrast between the Christian preaching of universal love and the Christian practice of persecution, especially the persecution of philosophers. This contrast existed at all times except at the very beginning of Christianity. For the decline of Christianity began very early, and its primary cause was not any guilty action. Since the Gospel was unknown to their contemporaries, the apostles were compelled to introduce it by appealing to views that were well-known and accepted at that time. Thus they laid the foundation for that fusion of faith and philosophy that contradicts the original intention of the Gospel and justifies the persecution of philosophy in the name of religion. Since the power of errors increases with the length of the time during which they remain uncontested, things became worse and worse as time went on and, but for certain facts to be mentioned immediately, the situation is worse in Spinoza's time than it had ever been before. Still, there are reasons for hoping that just in "our age" Christian society will return for the first time to the pure teaching of the Gospel. This hope is grounded on facts such as these: there are now in existence Christian republics or democracies, i.e., societies which by their nature require freedom of public discussion; there are no longer any prophets whose authoritative demeanor is incompatible with urbanity; the unitary ecclesiastical system of Christianity has been dissolved.[33] All this does not mean more, however, than that the chances of a general acceptance by Christian society of the true Christian teaching in its purity, or the possibilities of its publication, are greater in Spinoza's time than ever before. It does not mean at all that that teaching was not equally accessible to the free minds of all ages since the beginnings of Christianity.

III

The theological part of the *Treatise* opens and concludes with the implicit assertion that revelation or prophecy as certain knowledge of truths which surpass the capacity of human reason is possible. This assertion is repeated, explicitly or implicitly, in a considerable number of other passages of the work.[34] Yet there are also passages in which the possibility of any suprarational knowledge is simply denied.[35] Spinoza contradicts himself then regarding what one may call the central subject of his book. To suspend one's judgment on what he thought about that subject would be tantamount to throwing away the *Treatise* as a completely unintelligible book. Now, there is no reason why a sincere believer in revealed and suprarational teachings should declare that man has no access whatever to truth except through sense perception and reasoning, or that reason or philosophy alone, as distinguished from revelation or theology, possesses and justly claims for itself the realm of truth, or that belief in invisible things which cannot be demonstrated by reason is simply absurd, or that what are said to be teachings "above reason" are in truth dreams or mere fictions and "by far below reason." This observation by itself solves the difficulty: Spinoza did not admit the possibility of any suprarational teachings. Yet we cannot dispense with a more detailed discussion of Spinoza's self-contradictions. For there occur in the *Treatise* a considerable number of them, some of which cannot be disposed of as easily as the one just mentioned. We are in need of an exact and universal rule that would enable us to decide with certainty in all cases which of two given contradictory statements of Spinoza expresses his serious view.

We shall first enumerate a few additional examples of important contradictions. Spinoza asserts that once philosophy and theology (or reason and faith) are radically separated from each other or restricted to their peculiar realms, there will be no conflict between them. Philosophy, and not theology, aims at truth; theology, and not philosophy, aims at obedience. Now, theology rests on the fundamental dogma that mere obedience, without the knowledge of the truth, suffices for salvation, and this dogma must be either true or untrue. Spinoza asserts that it is a suprarational truth. But he also asserts that suprarational truths are impossible. If the second assertion is accepted, it follows that the very foundation of theology is an untruth.[36] Hence, philosophy and theology, far from being in perfect accord with each other, actually contradict each other. Another form of the same contradiction is presented by the assertions that theology (or the Bible or prophecy) is not authoritative regarding any merely speculative matters, and that theology is authoritative regarding some merely speculative matters.[37] —Spinoza asserts that the biblical teaching regarding providence is identical with the philosophic teaching. On the other hand, he asserts that only philosophy (and hence not the Bible) teaches the truth about providence; for only philosophy can teach that God cares equally for all men, i.e., that one fate meets the just and the unjust;[38] in other words, that there is no providence at all. This agrees with the implicit thesis that there is a fundamental antagonism between reason and faith. —Spinoza uses "prophecy" and "Bible" as virtually synonymous terms, and he asserts that the only source for our knowledge of the phenomenon of prophecy is the Bible. But he also asserts that the augurs of the pagans were true prophets,[39] and thus implies that the first book of Cicero's *De divinatione*, for example, would be as good a source for the study of prophecy as the Bible.

The contradictions regarding Christianity, or the New Testament, require a somewhat more extensive treatment. Spinoza asserts first that no one except Jesus (whom he regularly calls Christ) has reached the superhuman excellence sufficient for receiving, without the aid of the imagination, revelations of suprarational content; or that he alone—in contradistinction to the Old Testament prophets in particular—truly and adequately understood what was revealed to him. He is therefore prepared to say that the wisdom of God has taken on human nature in Christ, and that Christ is the way of salvation.[40] These statements must be understood, i.e., corrected, in the light of Spinoza's denial of supranatural phenomena. Since the laws of nature in general, and of human nature in particular, are always and everywhere the same, or since there is never anything radically "new," the mind of Jesus, who had a human body, cannot have been superhuman.[41] In other words, since man has no higher faculty than reason, or since there cannot be suprarational truths, Jesus cannot possibly have been more than the greatest philosopher who ever lived. The second of the two thematic treatments of Jesus which occur in the *Treatise* fully confirms this conclusion. If Spinoza affirms "with Paul" that all things are and move in God, he can be presumed to have believed that his own doctrine of God as the immanent cause of all things goes back to Jesus himself. He even proves that Jesus' knowledge was of necessity purely rational, because Jesus was sent to teach the whole human race and therefore he had to conform to the opinions common to the whole human race, i.e., to the fundamental principles of reason; whereas the Old Testament prophets had to conform merely to the opinions of the Jews, i.e., to a particular set of prejudices.[42] Or, more precisely, whereas the Old Testament prophets were themselves under the spell of the popular prejudices, Jesus and the apostles only adapted freely the expression of their rational thoughts to the popular prejudices.[43] Not indeed the exoteric teaching of the New Testament but its esoteric teaching is genuinely philosophic. This conclusion is, however, strikingly at variance with the chief purpose of the *Treatise*. The radical separation of philosophy and Bible would be a preposterous demand if the esoteric teaching of the New Testament were the peak of philosophic wisdom. Besides, when Spinoza affirms "with Paul" that all things are and move in God, he adds that the same view was perhaps held by all ancient philosophers and by all ancient Hebrews. He speaks with high regard of Solomon's teaching about God and he calls Solomon simply "the philosopher." Yet philosophy, as Spinoza conceives of it, presupposes the knowledge of mathematics, and Solomon had hardly any mathematical knowledge; moreover, the people accepted Solomon's sayings as religiously as those of the prophets, whereas the people would deride rather than respect philosophers who lay claim to authority in religious matters. Thus it would be more accurate to ascribe to Solomon, not philosophy, but popular wisdom, and accordingly to apply the same description to the teaching of Jesus.[44] This agrees with the facts that, according to Spinoza, the doctrine of "the Scripture," i.e., of both Testaments, contains "no philosophic things but only the most simple things," and that he probably regarded his teaching, i.e., the true philosophic teaching, about God as opposed to all earlier teachings.[45] The rational teaching that Spinoza would seem to have seriously ascribed to Jesus, was hardly more than rational morality. Yet he does not consistently maintain that the true moral teaching was discovered, or preached for the first time, by Jesus. To say nothing of the fact that it is by nature accessible to all human beings at all times, it was certainly known to, and preached by, the prophets and wise men of the Old Testament.[46] The teaching that is characteristic of Jesus or of the New Testament in general is not rational morality itself but its combination with such a "history" as permitted its being preached to the common people of all nations. In other words, the substance of the teaching of the two Testaments is identical. They differ only in this: the Old Testament prophets preached that identical teaching by virtue of the Mosaic Covenant, and therefore addressed it only to the Jews, whereas the apostles preached it by virtue of the passion of Jesus, and therefore addressed it to all men.[47] Now the combination of rational morality with a "historical" basis of either kind implies that the rational morality is presented in the form of a divine command, and hence that God is presented as a lawgiver. Thus the New Testament demands obedience to God as does the Old, and therefore both Testaments are equally in conflict with the philosophic teaching according to which God cannot be conceived as a lawgiver. "To know Christ according to the spirit" means to believe that God is merciful; but philosophy teaches that it does not make sense to ascribe mercy to God.[48] In short, the New Testament is not more rational than the Old. There is then no reason why the apostles, for example, should have been more emancipated from the prejudices of their age than the Old Testament prophets had been. In defending his *Treatise* in one of his letters, if not in the *Treatise* itself, Spinoza admits that all apostles believed in the bodily resurrection of Jesus and hence were under the spell of popular prejudices.[49] There may be more of reasoning in the New Testament than in the Old, and the greatest Old Testament prophet may never have produced a single legitimate argument; but this does not mean of course that there are no illegitimate arguments in the New Testament.[50] Philosophic statements occur especially in Paul's Epistles, but no more than in the writings ascribed to Solomon. Paul's philosophic utterances could be traced to his desire to be a Greek with the Greeks, or to make the Gospel acceptable to a multitude tainted by philosophy; the most philosophic utterances of the New Testament would thus appear to be simply borrowings from Greek philosophy. Furthermore, since these utterances were made in deliberate accommodation to the prejudices of their addressees, they do not necessarily agree with Paul's own views. Above all, Paul's pedagogic use of philosophy seems to have laid the foundation for the fatal fusion of philosophy and theology against which the whole *Treatise* is directed. Certainly Paul's teaching of justification "by faith alone" contradicts what Spinoza considers the central and most useful teaching of the Bible.[51] One could think for a moment that by insisting on the universalistic character of the New Testament, as distinguished from the particularistic character of the Old, Spinoza denies the identity, which he elsewhere asserts, of the moral teaching of the two Testaments. Yet he quotes the statement "love thy neighbor and hate thine enemy" in order to prove, not the difference, but the basic identity of the teaching of the Sermon on the Mount with that of Moses. The difference between the commands "hate thine enemy" (i.e., the foreigner) and "love thine enemy" is exclusively due to the changed political circumstances of the Jewish people: Moses could think of the establishment of a good polity, whereas Jesus (just as Jeremiah before him) addressed a people which had lost its political independence.[52] Spinoza does not consistently grant that what the New Testament teaches in regard to private morality is superior to the Old Testament teaching. But even if he did, this would be outweighed in his opinion by the fact that Christianity, owing to the circumstances of its origin, offers much stronger support for the dualism of spiritual and temporal power, and therewith for perpetual civil discord, than the Old Testament teaching, which was originated by Moses, who was king in fact if not in name. For the safety of the community is the highest law.[53] To sum up: Spinoza's identification of the teaching, or the esoteric teaching, of the New Testament with the true teaching is contradicted in numerous passages of the *Treatise*.

Our last example shall be a contradiction which we have been forced to imitate in our own presentation and which has the advantage that we can resolve it by having recourse to Spinoza's own explanation of a similar difficulty. In one set of passages of the *Treatise* Spinoza suggests that the Bible is hieroglyphic, i.e., unintelligible on account of its subject matter. In accordance with this view, he explicitly says in one of his letters that he simply does not understand the Bible. This view exposes him to the danger of being forced to admit that the Bible is rich in mysteries and requires for its understanding suprarational illumination;[54] it is at any rate incompatible with the whole meaning and purpose of the *Treatise*. There is another set of passages in which Spinoza says with equal definiteness that the Bible is easily intelligible on account of its subject matter, that all difficulties obstructing its understanding are due to our insufficient knowledge of the language, the poor condition of the text and similar causes,[55] and that almost all these difficulties can be overcome by the use of the right method: there is no need whatsoever for suprarational illumination nor for an authoritative tradition. What then does he mean by saying that he does not understand the Bible? When mentioning in the *Treatise* the Christology of "certain Churches," he says that he does not speak at all about these things nor deny them, "for I willingly confess that I do not understand them." In what is the authentic commentary on this passage, he first repeats his statement that he does not understand the Christology of "certain Churches," but then adds that, "to confess the truth," he considers the doctrines in question absurd, or evidently self-contradictory.[56] Accordingly, he says that he does not understand the Bible because he does not want "to confess the truth" that he regards the biblical teaching as self-contradictory. His view concerning the intelligibility of the Bible must then be stated as follows: since one cannot realize that the teaching of a book is absurd if one does not understand that teaching, the Bible is certainly intelligible. But it is easier to understand a book whose teaching is lucid than a book whose teaching is self-contradictory. It is very difficult to ascertain the meaning of a book that consists to a considerable extent of self-contradictory assertions, of remnants of primeval prejudices or superstitions, and of the outpourings of an uncontrolled imagination.[57] It is still more difficult to understand a book of this kind if it is, in addition, poorly compiled and poorly preserved. Yet many of these difficulties can be overcome by the use of the right method.

Spinoza, who regarded the Bible as a book rich in contradictions, has indicated this view in a book that itself abounds in contradictions. We have to see whether his treatment of biblical contradictions does not supply us with some help for the understanding of his own work. We must limit ourselves to what he has to say about contradictions between nonmetaphoric statements of one and the same speaker. His rule is that in such cases one has to suspend one's judgment as to what the speaker thought about the subject in question, unless one can show that the contradiction is due to the difference of the occasion or of the addressees of the two statements.[58] He applies this rule to the (real or alleged) contradiction between certain views of Jesus and Paul: while one of the views is addressed to the common people, the other is addressed to the wise. But Spinoza goes beyond this. The mere fact that Paul says on some occasions that he speaks "after the manner of man," induces Spinoza to dismiss all statements of Paul which agree with what Spinoza considers the vulgar view, as mere accommodations on the part of Paul, and to say of them that they are spoken "after the manner of man."[59] If we reduce this procedure to its principle, we arrive at the following rule: if an author, who admits, however occasionally, that he speaks "after the manner of man," makes contradictory statements on a subject, the statement contradicting the vulgar view has to be considered as his serious view; nay, every statement of such an author which agrees with views vulgarly considered sacred or authoritative must be dismissed as irrelevant, or at least it must be suspected even though it is never contradicted by him.[60]

Spinoza himself is an author of this kind. The first of the three "rules of living" which he sets forth in his *Treatise on the Improvement of the Understanding* reads as follows: "To speak with a view to the capacity of the vulgar and to practice all those things which cannot hinder us from reaching our goal (sc. the highest good). For we are able to obtain no small advantage from the vulgar provided we make as many concessions as possible to their capacity. Add to this that in this way they will lend friendly ears to the truth,"[61] i.e., the vulgar will thus be induced to accept such truths as the philosopher may wish to communicate to them, or they will not resent occasional heresies of the philosopher. At any rate, Spinoza means not merely that the choice of the form of his external worship, or of his religious affiliation, is a matter of mere expediency for the philosopher, but, above all, that he will adapt the expression of his thought to the generally accepted opinions by professing, as far as it is possible or necessary, these very opinions, even though he considers them untrue or absurd. That this is the correct interpretation of the phrase "ad captum vulgi loqui" appears from what Spinoza says on the subject in the *Treatise*. For in the *Treatise* he teaches that God, and Jesus and Paul as well, in speaking to men who held vulgar opinions, accommodated themselves to the capacity of their addressees by professing or at any rate not questioning those opinions. Even in the case of Moses Spinoza suggests that he may have taught things which he did not believe ("Moses believed, or at least he wished to teach . . .").[62] And he calls this kind of communication to speak "ad captum vulgi" or, more frequently, "ad captum alicuius." For to speak with a view to the capacity of the vulgar necessarily means to argue *ad hominem*, or to accommodate oneself to the particular prejudices of the particular vulgar group or individual whom one happens to address.[63] The author or authors of the Bible speak "ad captum vulgi" by communicating a salutary or pious teaching, while not only not questioning but even professing, and thus confirming, the untrue or absurd principles or premises of the addressees.[64]

It is no accident that practically the only authentic information about the precise character of Spinoza's method of communication is supplied by the *Treatise*. A full and direct explanation of this subject was, for obvious reasons, out of the question. But it was possible to assert that in the Bible a superior mind or superior minds condescend to speak in the language of ordinary people, and that there occur in the Bible a number of statements which contradict those biblical statements that are adapted to vulgar prejudices. Spinoza was thus led to assert that at least some of the biblical contradictions are conscious or deliberate, and therewith to suggest that there is an esoteric teaching of the Bible, or that the literal meaning of the Bible hides a deeper, mysterious meaning. By contradicting this ultimate consequence,[65] he leaves no doubt in the reader's mind as to the ironical or exoteric character of his assertion that the statements of the Bible are consciously adapted by its authors to the capacity of the vulgar. But the temporary device has fulfilled its most important function, which is to supply the reader with an urgently needed piece of information. We may say that Spinoza uses the sketch of his exoteric interpretation of the Bible for indicating the character of his own exoteric procedure.

There must be scholars who believe that "to speak with a view to the capacity of the vulgar" merely means to express oneself in not too technical a language, and who argue that the alternative interpretation would be a reflection on Spinoza's character. Those scholars are requested to consider that, if their reason were valid, Spinoza would impute to the author or authors of the Bible a morally questionable practice. Whatever may be the sound moral rule, Spinoza had certainly no compunctions to refrain from "confessing the truth," or to reveal his views while hiding them behind more or less transparent accommodations to the generally accepted opinions. When he says that the wise man will never, not even in the greatest danger, act *dolo malo*, he does not mean that the wise man will never employ any ruses; for he explicitly admits that there are good or legitimate ruses.[66] If the statesman is under an obligation to employ all kinds of ruses in the interest of the material welfare of the ruled,[67] the same duty must be incumbent on those to whom nature has entrusted the spiritual guidance of mankind, i.e., on the philosophers, who are much more exposed to the suspicions of the multitude[68] than statesmen, and therefore in greater need of caution than anyone else. "Caute" was the inscription of Spinoza's signet. By this he did not primarily mean the caution required in philosophic investigations but the caution that the philosopher needs in his intercourse with nonphilosophers. The only reason which he can find for showing that the reading of histories is most useful is that we may learn through their study "to live more cautiously among men and more successfully to accommodate our actions and our life, within the limits of reason, to their way of thinking."[69] For he considered caution, and especially caution in speech, extremely difficult: "not even the most learned or experienced, to say nothing of the common people, know how to be silent. This is a common vice of men, to confide their intentions to others, even though silence is needed." If it is of the essence of the wise man that he is able to live under every form of government, i.e., even in societies in which freedom of speech is strictly denied, it is of his essence that he is able to live without ever expressing those of his thoughts whose expression happens to be forbidden.[70] The philosopher who knows the truth must be prepared to refrain from expressing it, not so much for reasons of convenience as for reasons of duty. Whereas truth requires that one should not accommodate the words of the Bible to one's own opinions, piety requires that everyone should accommodate the words of the Bible to his own opinions,[71] i.e., that one should give one's own opinions a biblical appearance. If true religion or faith, which according to him requires not so much true dogmas as pious ones, were endangered by his biblical criticism, Spinoza would have decided to be absolutely silent about this subject; nay, he would have gladly admitted—in order to escape from all difficulties—that the deepest mysteries are hidden in the Bible.[72] That is to say, he would have suppressed the truths in question and asserted their contraries, if he had felt that these truths could do harm to the mass of readers.

If we disregard, as we must, Spinoza's references to his alleged biblical models, the only man to whom he almost explicitly refers in the *Treatise* as a predecessor regarding his technique of presentation is Abraham ibn Ezra, of whom he speaks with unconcealed respect. Ibn Ezra "did not dare to explain openly" what he thought about the authorship of the Pentateuch, but indicated his view "in rather obscure words." One cryptic statement of ibn Ezra, that is quoted by Spinoza, ends with the words: "He who understands, should be silent." A certain allusion made by Spinoza himself ends with the words that he wished to remain silent on the subject in question for reasons which the ruling superstition or the difficult times do not permit to explain, but that "it suffices to indicate the matter to the wise."[73] Spinoza did not indicate what he owed to Maimonides, to whom he refers more frequently than to ibn Ezra, although in a much less friendly tone. But when saying that Moses "believed or at least wished to teach" that God is zealous or angry, he merely makes explicit what Maimonides had implied when intimating that the belief in God's anger is required, not for man's ultimate perfection, but for the good ordering of civil society.[74] For Moses, whom Maimonides considered the wisest of all men, was necessarily aware of the particular character of the belief in question, to which he gave so forceful an expression. In his *Guide of the Perplexed*, Maimonides presents his teaching by using deliberate contradictions, hidden from the vulgar, between nonmetaphoric statements; it is in this way that he reveals the truth to those who are able to understand by themselves, while hiding the truth from the vulgar. He raises the question as to whether the same kind of contradiction is also used in the Bible, but he does not answer it.[75] If he has answered it in the affirmative—as, in a sense, he necessarily did—the *Guide* would be the model for Spinoza's sketch of an exoteric interpretation of the Bible, an interpretation according to which the Bible consists partly of vulgar statements and partly of philosophic statements which deliberately and secretly contradict the vulgar ones. At any rate, there can be no doubt that, generally speaking, Maimonides' method of presentation is meant to be an imitation of what he declared to be the method of the Bible. Maimonides in his turn was indebted for his method to "the philosophers" of his period. The typical philosopher, as presented in Yehuda Halevi's *Kuzari*, considered it perfectly legitimate for the philosopher to adhere in his speeches as well as in his actions to a religion to which he does not adhere in his thought, and he took it for granted that the philosophic teaching proper is necessarily accompanied by an exoteric teaching. Farabi, whom Maimonides regarded as the greatest philosophic authority of his period, virtually denied all cognitive value to religion, and yet considered conformity with the laws and the beliefs of the religious community in which one is brought up as a necessary qualification for the future philosopher.

But it would be a mistake to think that one has to look for Spinoza's models exclusively in Islamic philosophy. Farabi himself traces the procedure to which we have referred to Plato. Practically the same expression that Spinoza applies to Moses ("he believed, or at least he wished to teach . . .") is applied to Socrates by Lessing, who had studied Spinoza very closely, and who stated that there is no other philosophy than that of Spinoza. According to Lessing, Socrates "believed in eternal punishment in all seriousness, or at least believed in it to the extent that he considered it expedient to teach it in words that are least susceptible of arousing suspicion and most explicit." Lessing held that "all ancient philosophers" had made a distinction between their exoteric and their esoteric teaching, and he ascribed the same distinction to Leibniz.[76] Spinoza's rules of living which open with "ad captum vulgi loqui" are modeled on the rules of Descartes' "morale par provision" which open with the demand for intransigent conformism in everything except in the strictly private examination of one's own opinions.[77] We can barely allude to the question of Descartes' technique of writing, to a question which seems to baffle all his students because of the extreme caution with which that philosopher constantly acted. The traditional distinction between exoteric (or "disclosed") and esoteric (or "enigmatical") presentation was accessible to Spinoza also through Bacon, who insisted especially on the "secret and retired" character of the science of government. The student of Spinoza must pay particular attention to Bacon's principles regarding the use of terms: "it seemeth best to keep way with antiquity *usque ad aras*; and therefore to retain the ancient terms, though I sometimes alter the uses and definitions, according to the moderate proceeding in civil government; where although there be some alteration, yet that holdeth which Tacitus wisely noteth, *Eadem Magistratuum vocabula.*"[78] It is well-known how much Spinoza silently complied with this politic rule. He seems to allude to it when saying that if a man wishes to alter the meaning of a term to which he is accustomed, he will not be able "without difficulty" to do it consistently in speech and in writing.[79] We merely have to remember the fact that "all excellent things are as difficult as they are rare."

Spinoza's caution or thrift in communicating his views is far from being excessive if we judge his procedure by the standards admitted by a number of earlier thinkers. In fact, judged by these standards, he proves to be extraordinarily bold. That very bold man Hobbes admitted after having read the *Treatise* that he himself had not dared to write as boldly. Spinoza was very bold insofar as he went to the extreme to which he could go as a man who was convinced that religion, i.e., positive religion, is indispensable to society, and who took his social duties seriously. He was cautious insofar as he did not state the whole truth clearly and unequivocally but kept his utterances, to the best of his knowledge, within the limits imposed by what he considered the legitimate claims of society. He speaks then in all his writings, and especially in the *Treatise*, "ad captum vulgi." This is not at variance with the fact that the *Treatise* is explicitly addressed, not to the vulgar, but to philosophers. For Spinoza was not in a position effectively to prevent the Latin-reading part of the vulgar from reading the *Treatise* and from thus becoming obnoxious to him. Accordingly, that book serves the purpose, not merely of enlightening the potential philosophers, but also of counteracting the opinion which the vulgar had of Spinoza, i.e., of appeasing the *plebs* itself.[80] Furthermore, the *Treatise* is addressed, not so much to philosophers simply, as to potential philosophers, i.e., to men who, at least in the early stages of their training, are deeply imbued with the vulgar prejudices: what Spinoza considers the basic prejudice of those potential philosophers whom he addresses in the *Treatise* is merely a special form of the basic prejudice of the vulgar mind in general.[81]

In the *Treatise* Spinoza addresses potential philosophers of a certain kind while the vulgar are listening. He speaks therefore in such a way that the vulgar will not understand what he means. It is for this reason that he expresses himself contradictorily: those shocked by his heterodox statements will be appeased by more or less orthodox formulae. Spinoza boldly denies the possibility of miracles proper—in a single chapter. But he speaks of miracles throughout the work without making it clear in the other chapters that he understands by miracles merely such natural phenomena as seemed to be strange to the particular vulgar thinkers who observed or recorded them. To exaggerate for purposes of clarification, we may say that each chapter of the *Treatise* serves the function of refuting one particular orthodox dogma while leaving untouched all other orthodox dogmas.[82] Only a minority of readers will take the trouble of keeping firmly in mind the results of all chapters and of adding them up. Only a minority of readers will admit that if an author makes contradictory statements on a subject, his view may well be expressed by the statements that occur least frequently or only once, while his view is concealed by the contradictory statements that occur most frequently or even in all cases but one; for many readers do not fully grasp what it means that the truth, or the seriousness, of a proposition is not increased by the frequency with which the proposition is repeated. One must also consider "the customary mildness of the common people,"[83] a good-naturedness which fairly soon shrinks from, or is shocked by, the inquisitorial brutality and recklessness that is required for extorting his serious views from an able writer who tries to conceal them from all but a few. It is then not misleading to say that the orthodox statements are more obvious in the *Treatise* than the heterodox ones. It is no accident, for example, that the first sentence of the first chapter is to the effect that prophecy or revelation is such certain knowledge of any subject as is revealed by God to human beings. We may call the more or less orthodox statements the first statements, and the contradictory statements the second statements. Of the two thematic statements about Jesus, the first is definitely nearer to the orthodox Christian view than is the second one.[84] This rule must be taken with a grain of salt: the conclusion of the theological part of the *Treatise* is hardly less orthodox than its opening. The "second statements" are more likely to occur—according to a rule of forensic rhetoric[85]—somewhere in the middle, i.e., in places least exposed to the curiosity of superficial readers. Thus even by presenting his serious view in one set of explicit statements, while contradicting it in another set, Spinoza could reveal it to the more attentive readers while hiding it from the vulgar. But not all of Spinoza's contradictions are explicit. In some cases, not the explicit statements, but the necessary consequences from explicit statements contradict other explicit statements. In other cases, we are confronted with a contradiction between two explicit statements, neither of which is necessarily heterodox or expresses directly Spinoza's view on the subject; but the incongruity presented by the contradiction points to an unexpressed and unambiguously heterodox view, by which the surface contradiction is resolved, and which thus proves to be obliquely presented by the surface contradiction.[86]

The sound rule for reading the *Treatise* is that, in case of a contradiction, the statement most opposed to what Spinoza considered the vulgar view has to be regarded as expressing his serious view; nay, that even a necessary implication of a heterodox character has to take precedence over a contradictory statement that is never explicitly contradicted by Spinoza.[87] In other words, if the final theses of individual chapters of the *Treatise* (as distinguished from the almost constantly repeated accommodations) are not consistent with each other, we are led by the observation of this fact and our ensuing reflection to a consistent view that is no longer explicitly stated, but clearly presupposed, by Spinoza; and we have to recognize this view as his serious view, or as the secret par excellence of the *Treatise*. Only by following this rule of reading can we understand Spinoza's thought exactly as he himself understood it and avoid the danger of becoming or remaining the dupes of his accommodations.

Since Spinoza states the rule "ad captum vulgi loqui" without any qualification, there is a reasonable presumption that he acted on it also when writing his *Ethics*. This presumption cannot be disposed of by reference to the "geometric" character of that work, for "ad captum vulgi loqui" does not mean to present one's thoughts in a popular garb, but to argue *ad hominem* or *ex concessis*, i.e., from a covered position. Spinoza presented the teaching of Descartes' *Principia* also in "geometric" form, although he did not even pretend that that teaching was the true teaching.[88] Nor is the strictly esoteric or scientific character of the *Ethics* guaranteed by the fact that Spinoza did not explicitly address that work to a human type other than actual or mature philosophers, for there are many other ways in which an author can indicate that he is speaking "ad captum alicuius." To mention one of them, there has scarcely ever been a serious reader of the *Ethics* who has not also read the *Treatise*; those for whom indications suffice understood from the *Treatise* what Spinoza seriously thought of all positive religions and of the Bible, and they recognized at once from the pious references to biblical teachings which occur in the *Ethics*[89] that this book is by no means free from accommodations to the accepted views. In other words, one cannot leave it at the impression that while the *Treatise* is, of course, exoteric, the *Ethics* is Spinoza's esoteric work simply, and that therefore the solution to all the riddles of the *Treatise* is presented explicitly and clearly in the *Ethics*. For Spinoza cannot have been ignorant of the obvious truth which, in addition, had been pointed out to him if not by Plato, at any rate by Maimonides,[90] that every book is accessible to all who can read the language in which it is written; and that therefore, if there is any need at all for hiding the truth from the vulgar, no written exposition can be strictly speaking esoteric.

In the absence of statements of Spinoza which refer specifically to the manner of communication employed in the *Ethics*, most students will feel that the question regarding the esoteric or exoteric character of that work can be settled only on the basis of internal evidence. One of the most learned contemporary students of Spinoza speaks of "the baffling allusiveness and ellipticalness of (the) style" of the *Ethics*, and he notes that in that work "statements are not significant for what they actually affirm but for the denials which they imply." He explains Spinoza's procedure by the circumstance that Spinoza, a Jew, lived in a non-Jewish environment in which he "never felt himself quite free to speak his mind; and he who among his own people never hesitated to speak out with boldness became cautious, hesitant, and reserved." In the spirit of this "historical" reason (i.e., of a reason primarily based, not on Spinoza's explicit statements, but on the history of the author's life), he finally asserts: "Little did he understand the real cause of his own behavior," i.e., he admits that he is trying to understand Spinoza better than he understood himself. Apart from this, one can hardly say that Spinoza "never" hesitated to state his views when speaking to Jews; for only while he was very young did he have normal opportunities of conversing with Jews, and caution is not a quality characteristic of youth. On the principle expressed by Spinoza himself, he would have had to be extremely "cautious, hesitant, and reserved" "among his own people" if he had lived in an age when the separation from the Jewish community was impossible for a self-respecting man of Jewish origin, who was not honestly convinced of the truth of another religion. Professor Wolfson also explains the particular style of the *Ethics* by Spinoza's talmudic and rabbinic training, and he accordingly demands that one must approach the study of the *Ethics* in the spirit "in which the old rabbinic scholars approach the study of their standard texts." He admits, however, by implication the very limited value of this approach by saying that "we must constantly ask ourselves, with regard to every statement he makes, what is the reason? What does he intend to let us hear? What is his authority? Does he reproduce his authority correctly or not?"[91] For, clearly, Spinoza did not know of any authorities in philosophic investigation. There is all the difference in the world between an author who considers himself merely a link in the chain of a venerable tradition, and for this very reason uses allusive and elliptical language, i.e., language that is intelligible only on the basis of the tradition in question, and an author who denies all value to tradition and therefore uses various stylistic means, especially allusive and elliptical language, in order to eradicate the traditional views from the minds of his best readers. Wolfson indicates a much more adequate reason for the particular style of the *Ethics* by stating that Spinoza's "'God' is merely an appeasive term for the most comprehensive principle of the universe," or that it was merely a "literary pretension that his entire philosophy was evolved from his conception of God." For it is easily understandable that Spinoza could not neutralize accommodations of this magnitude but by allusions, ellipses, or similar devices. In other words, if, as Wolfson consistently suggests, Spinoza's doctrine of God is fundamentally nothing but an "internal criticism" of traditional theology,[92] one has to admit, on the basis of Spinoza's explicit demand for, and authentic interpretation of, "ad captum vulgi loqui," that Spinoza's doctrine of God—apparently the basis or starting point of his whole doctrine—belongs as such to a mere argument *ad hominem* or *ex concessis*, that rather hides than reveals his real starting point. To express this in technical language, what Spinoza presents in his *Ethics* is the "synthesis," whereas he suppresses the "analysis" which necessarily precedes it.[93] That is, he suppresses the whole reasoning, both philosophic and "politic," leading up to the definitions by which the reader is startled and at the same time appeased when he opens that book. If it is true that Spinoza's "'God' is merely an appeasive term," one would have to rewrite the whole *Ethics* without using that term, i.e., by starting from Spinoza's concealed atheistic principles. If it is true that Spinoza's "'God' is merely an appeasive term," one certainly has no longer any right to assume that, according to Spinoza, the idea of God, to say nothing of God's existence, is "immediately known as an intuition,"[94] and therefore the legitimate starting point for philosophy. However this may be, Spinoza's general principle of accommodation to the generally accepted views imposes on the interpreter the duty to raise the question as to what are the absolute limits to Spinoza's accommodation; or, in more specific terms, as to what are the entirely nontheological considerations that brought Spinoza into conflict with materialism, and to what extent these considerations vouch for the explicit teaching of the *Ethics*. In other words, one has to see whether there are not anywhere in Spinoza's writings indications, however subtle, of a strictly atheistic beginning or approach. This is, incidentally, one reason why the *Treatise* should be read, not merely against the background of the *Ethics*, but also by itself. Precisely the more exoteric work may disclose features of Spinoza's thought which could not with propriety be disclosed in the *Ethics*. While former generations publicly denounced Spinoza as an atheist, today it is almost a heresy to hint that, for all we know prior to a fresh investigation of the whole issue, he may have been an atheist. This change is due not merely, as contemporary self-complacency would have it, to the substitution of historical detachment for fanatical partisanship, but above all to the fact that the phenomenon and the causes of exotericism have almost completely been forgotten.

To return to the *Treatise*, we are now in a position to state the true reasons for certain features of that work which have not yet been sufficiently clarified. The *Treatise* is addressed to Christians, not because Spinoza believed in the truth of Christianity or even in the superiority of Christianity to Judaism, but because "ad captum vulgi loqui" means "ad captum hodierni vulgi loqui" or to accommodate oneself to the ruling opinions of one's time, and Christianity, not Judaism, was literally ruling. Or, in other words, Spinoza desired to convert to philosophy "as many as possible,"[95] and there were many more Christians in the world than there were Jews. To this one may add two "historical" reasons: after his open and irrevocable break with the Jewish community, Spinoza could no longer with propriety address Jews in the way in which, and for the purpose for which, he addresses Christians in the *Treatise*; in addition, there existed in his time a considerable group of Christians, but not of Jews, who were "liberal" in the sense that they reduced religious dogma to a minimum, and at the same time regarded all ceremonies or sacraments as indifferent, if not harmful. At any rate, Spinoza was "a Christian with the Christians" in exactly the same way in which, according to him, Paul was "a Greek with the Greeks and a Jew with the Jews."[96] It is the political and social power of Christianity which also explains why the subject matter of the *Treatise* is Jewish rather than Christian. It was infinitely less dangerous to attack Judaism than to attack Christianity, and it was distinctly less dangerous to attack the Old Testament than the New. One has only to read the summary of the argument of the first part of the *Treatise* at the beginning of the thirteenth chapter in order to see that while the explicit argument of that part is chiefly based upon, or directed against, the Old Testament, the conclusions are meant to apply to "the Scripture," i.e., to both

Testaments alike.[97] When Spinoza criticizes at relatively great length the theological principle accepted by "the greatest part" of the Jews, he clearly has in mind "the greatest part" of the Christians as well, as appears from his reference, in the passage in question, to the doctrine of original sin, and from parallels elsewhere in the *Treatise*.[98] After having indicated the doubtful character of the genealogies of Jeconiah and Zerubbabel in 1 Chronicles 3, Spinoza adds the remark that he would rather have wished to remain silent on this subject, for reasons which the ruling superstition does not permit to explain. Since he had not felt any hesitation to point out the doubtful character of other Old Testament records of a similar nature, his cryptic remark can only refer to the connection between the genealogy in question and the genealogy of Jesus in the first chapter of the Gospel according to Matthew.[99] The preponderance of Jewish subject matter in the *Treatise* is then due to Spinoza's caution rather than to his insufficient knowledge of Christianity or of the Greek language.[100] His relative reticence about specifically Christian subjects could be expected to protect him against persecution by the vulgar, while it was not likely to disqualify him in the eyes of the "more prudent" readers, who could be relied upon to understand the implication of his attack on Judaism, and especially on the Old Testament.

From Spinoza's authentic interpretation of "ad captum vulgi loqui" it follows that he cannot have meant the exoteric teaching of the *Treatise* as a "timeless" teaching. But for the same reason the *Treatise* is linked to its time, not because Spinoza's serious or private thought was determined by his "historical situation" without his being aware of it, but because he consciously and deliberately adapted, not his thought, but the public expression of his thought, to what his time demanded or permitted. His plea for "the freedom of philosophizing," and therefore for "the separation of philosophy from theology," is linked to its time in the first place because the time lacked that freedom and simultaneously offered reasonable prospects for its establishment. In another age, or even in another country, Spinoza would have been compelled by his principle of caution to make entirely different proposals for the protection of philosophy, without changing in the least his philosophic thought. The weakening of ecclesiastical authority in Christian Europe, the great variety of Christian sects in certain Protestant countries, the increasing unpopularity of religious persecution, the practice of toleration in Amsterdam in particular, permitted Spinoza to suggest publicly "the separation of philosophy from theology" in the interest, not merely of philosophy or of the philosophers, but of society in general; and to suggest it, not merely on philosophic grounds, but on biblical grounds as well.[101] Spinoza's argument is linked to his time especially because his plea for "the freedom of philosophizing" is based on arguments taken from the character of the biblical teaching. For, as is shown by his references to classical authors, he believed that the legitimation of that freedom on social grounds alone was also possible in classical antiquity, and hence would be possible in future societies modeled on the classical pattern. More exactly, Spinoza considered this particular kind of legitimation of the freedom of inquiry a classical rather than a biblical heritage.[102] Apart from this, it follows from our previous argument that the exoteric teaching of the *Treatise* is not meant to be "contemporaneous" with Christianity. The *Treatise* is "contemporaneous" not with the specific assumptions which it attacks, but with those to which it appeals. The assumptions to which Spinoza appeals, in the most visible part of the argument of the *Treatise*, are these: the good life simply is the practice of justice and charity, which is impossible without belief in divine justice; and the Bible insists on the practice of justice and charity combined with the belief in divine justice as the necessary and sufficient condition of salvation. At the moment these assumptions cease to be publicly defensible,[103] the exoteric teaching of the *Treatise* would lose its *raison d'être*.

Almost everything we have said in the present essay was necessary in order to make intelligible the particular complexity of the argument of the *Treatise*. A considerable part of that argument is actually an appeal from traditional theology to the Bible, whose authority is questioned by the other part of the argument. The hermeneutic principle that legitimates the whole argument, and thus blurs the fundamental difference between its heterogeneous parts, is expressed by the assertion that, as a matter of principle, the literal meaning of the Bible is its only meaning. The return to the literal sense of the Bible fulfills an entirely different function within the context of the criticism, based on the Bible, of traditional theology on the one hand and within the contrary context of the attack on the authority of the Bible on the other. Arguing from the conceded premise that the Bible is the only document of revelation, Spinoza demands that the pure word of God be not corrupted by any human additions, inventions, or innovations, and that nothing be considered a revealed doctrine that is not borne out by explicit and clear statements of the Bible.[104] The hidden reason for this procedure is twofold. Spinoza considers the teaching of the Bible partly more rational and partly less rational than that of traditional theology. Insofar as it is more rational, he tries to remind traditional theology of a valuable heritage which it has forgotten; insofar as it is less rational, he indicates to the more prudent readers the precarious character of the very basis of all actual theology. He thus leads the reader insensibly toward the criticism of the authority of the Bible itself. This criticism requires the return to the literal meaning of the Bible for the additional reason that the Bible is a popular book: a popular book meant for instruction must present its teaching in the most simple and easily accessible manner.[105] The opposition of the two approaches finds what is probably its most telling expression in the opposite ways in which Spinoza applies the term "ancient" to the Bible: viewed as the standard and corrective for all later religion and theology, the Bible is the document of "the ancient religion"; viewed as the object of philosophic criticism, the Bible is a document transmitting "the prejudices of an ancient nation."[106] In the first case, "ancient" means venerable; in the second case, "ancient" means rude and obsolete. The confusion becomes still greater since Spinoza gives in the *Treatise* the outlines of a purely historical interpretation of the Bible. In fact, his most detailed exposition of hermeneutic rules might seem exclusively to serve the purpose of paving the way for a detached, historical study of the Bible. One is therefore constantly tempted to judge Spinoza's use of the Bible as an authoritative text, as well as his use of the Bible as the target of philosophic criticism, by what he himself declares to be the requirements of a "scientific" study of the Bible; and one is thus frequently tempted to note the utter inadequacy of Spinoza's arguments. Yet one must never lose sight of the fact that the detached or historical study of the Bible was for Spinoza a *cura posterior*. Detached study presupposes detachment, and it is precisely the creation of detachment from the Bible that is Spinoza's primary aim in the *Treatise*. The philosophic criticism of the biblical teaching, and still more the appeal from traditional theology to the authority of the Bible, cannot be judged in terms of the requirements of the historical study of the Bible, because both uses of the Bible essentially precede that historical study. Whereas the historical study of the Bible, as Spinoza conceives of it, demands that the Bible not be taken as a unity, his two primary purposes require just the opposite; for the claims, to which he either defers or which he attacks, are raised on behalf of the Bible as a unitary whole. The first six chapters of the *Treatise*, which lay the foundation for everything that follows, and especially for Spinoza's higher criticism of the Bible, do not in any way presuppose the results of that criticism; in fact, they contradict these results; in these basic chapters, Moses' authorship of the Pentateuch is taken for granted. *Mutatis mutandis* the same applies to Spinoza's attempt to utilize the Bible for political instruction (chapters XVII-XIX).[107] The possible value of Spinoza's philosophic criticism of the biblical teaching is not impaired by this apparent incongruity; for regardless of who were the authors of

the various theological theses asserted in the Bible, or the originators of
the institutions recorded or recommended in the Bible, the proof of the
absurdity or unsoundness of the theses and institutions in question is
the necessary and sufficient condition for the rejection of biblical authority.

The validity of Spinoza's philosophic criticism of the Bible certainly requires that he has grasped the intention of the Bible as a whole.
It is at this point that the distinction between his use of the Bible as
authority and his use of the Bible as the target of philosophic criticism
becomes decisive for the understanding of the *Treatise*. For it is possible
that what Spinoza says about the intention of the Bible as a whole
belongs to the context of his appeal from traditional theology to the
authority of the Bible. It would certainly not be incompatible with
Spinoza's principle "ad captum vulgi loqui" if he had used the Bible in
that exoteric context in the way in which counsel for defense sometimes uses the laws: if one wants to bring about an acquittal—the liberation of philosophy from theological bondage—one is not necessarily
concerned with ascertaining the true intention of the law. We cannot
take it for granted then that Spinoza really identified the fundamental
teaching of the Bible with what the Bible teaches everywhere clearly, or
that he really believed that the moral teaching of the Bible is everywhere clearly expressed and in no way affected by defective readings
and so on.[108] The fact that he teaches these and similar things regarding
the general character of the Bible does not yet prove that he believed
them; for, not to repeat our whole argument, he also asserts that there
cannot be any contradictions between the insight of the understanding
and the teaching of the Bible because "the truth does not contradict the
truth,"[109] and we know that he did not believe in the truth of the biblical
teaching. In addition, there is some specific evidence that supports the
particular doubt we are raising. In his list of those biblical teachings
which allegedly are presented clearly everywhere in the Bible, Spinoza
mentions the dogma that in consequence of God's decree the pious are
rewarded and the wicked are punished; but elsewhere he says that,
according to Solomon, the same fate meets the just and the unjust, the
pure and the impure.[110] He enumerates among the same kind of teachings the dogma that God takes care of all things; it is hard to see how
this can be taught in the Bible everywhere clearly if, as Spinoza maintains, the Bible teaches in a number of important passages that God is
not omniscient, that He is ignorant of future human actions, and that He
takes care only of His chosen people. He also lists among the teachings
in question the dogma that God is omnipotent; again, it is hard to see
how this can be taught in the Bible everywhere clearly if, as Spinoza

suggests, Moses himself believed that the angels or "the other gods," as well as matter, are not created by God.[111] Furthermore, Spinoza says that charity is recommended most highly everywhere in both Testaments, and yet he also says that the Old Testament recommends, or even commends, hatred of the other nations.[112] Above all, Spinoza makes the following assertions: the only intention of the Bible is to teach obedience to God, or the Bible enjoins nothing but obedience; obedience to God is fundamentally different from love of God; the Bible also enjoins love of God.[113] Precisely because Spinoza openly abandoned in the *Treatise* the belief in the cognitive value of the Bible, his maxim to speak "ad captum vulgi" forced him to assign the highest possible value to the practical or moral demands of the Bible. It is for this reason that he asserts that the practical teaching of the Bible agrees with the true practical teaching, i.e., the practical consequences of philosophy. For obvious reasons, he had to supplement this assertion by maintaining that the practical teaching of the Bible is its central teaching, that it is everywhere clearly presented in the Bible, and that it could not possibly be corrupted or mutilated by the compilers and transmitters of the Bible.

The *Treatise* is primarily directed against the view that philosophy ought to be subservient to the Bible, or against "skepticism." But it is also directed against the view that the Bible ought to be subservient, or to be accommodated, to philosophy, i.e., against "dogmatism."[114] Furthermore, while the work is primarily directed against Christianity, it is also directed against Judaism. The *Treatise* is then directed against these four widely different positions: Christian skepticism, Christian dogmatism, Jewish skepticism, and Jewish dogmatism. Now, arguments which might be decisive against one or some of these positions, might be irrelevant if used against the others. For example, arguments taken from the authority of the New Testament might be conclusive against one or the other form of Christian theology, or even against all forms of Christian theology, but they are clearly irrelevant if used against any Jewish position. Hence, one should expect that Spinoza would criticize each of the four positions by itself. But with very few exceptions he directs one and the same criticism against what might appear to be a fantastic hybrid constructed *ad hoc* out of Judaism and Christianity, and of dogmatism and skepticism. His failure to distinguish throughout between the various positions which he attacks, and to pay careful attention to the specific character of each, might seem to deprive his criticism of every claim to serious attention. For example, he prefaces his denial of the possibility of miracles by such an account of the vulgar view on the subject as probably surpasses in crudity everything ever said or suggested by the most stupid or the most obscurant smatterer in

Jewish or Christian theology. Here, Spinoza seems to select as the target of his criticism a possibly nonexistent position that was particularly easy to refute. Or, to take an example of a different character, he prefaces his denial of the cognitive value of revelation by the assertion that "with amazing rashness" "all" writers have maintained that the prophets have known everything within the reach of the human understanding, i.e., he imputes to all theologians a view which is said to have been rejected "by all important Christian theologians of the age."[115] The view in question was held by Maimonides, and Spinoza seems, "with amazing rashness," to take Maimonides as the representative of all theologians. Here, he seems to select as the target of his criticism an actual theological position for the irrelevant reason that he had happened to study it closely during his youth.

The *Treatise* remains largely unintelligible as long as the typical difficulties represented by these two examples are not removed. We intend to show that these difficulties cannot be traced to Spinoza's caution, and thus to express our agreement with the view, which we never contradicted, that Spinoza's exotericism is not the only fact responsible for the difficulties of the *Treatise*. We start from the observation that a certain simplification of the theological issue was inevitable if Spinoza wanted to settle it at all. He effects the necessary simplification in two different ways which are illustrated by our two examples. In the first example, he starts from the implicit premise that all possibly relevant Jewish and Christian theologies necessarily recognize the authority, i.e., the truth, of the thematic teaching of the Old Testament; he assumes moreover that the true meaning of any Old Testament passage is, as a rule, identical with its literal meaning; he assumes finally that the most fundamental teaching of the Old Testament is the account of creation. Now, Moses does not explicitly teach creation *ex nihilo*; Genesis 1:2 seems rather to show that he believed that God has made the visible universe out of preexisting "chaos"; his complete silence about the creation of the angels or "the other gods" strongly suggests that he believed that the power of God is, indeed, superior to, but absolutely different from, the power of other beings. To express Moses' thought in the language of philosophy, the power of nature (which is what he meant by "chaos," and by which he understood a blind "force or impulse") is coeval with the power of God (an intelligent and ordering power), and the power of nature is therefore not dependent on, but merely inferior or subject to, the power of God. Moses taught that uncreated "chaos" precedes in time the ordered universe which is the work of God, and he conceived of God as king. It is therefore reasonable to suppose that he understood the subordination of the power of nature to the power of God as the subjugation of the smaller by the greater power. Accordingly, the power of God will reveal itself clearly and distinctly only in actions in which the power of nature does not cooperate at all. If that only is true which can be clearly and distinctly understood, only the clear and distinct manifestation of God's power will be its true manifestation: natural phenomena do not reveal God's power; when nature acts, God does not act, and vice versa. It does not suffice, therefore, for the manifestation of God's power, that God has subjugated and reduced to order the primeval chaos; He has to subjugate "the visible gods," the most impressive parts of the visible universe, in order to make His power known to man: God's power and hence God's being can be demonstrated only by miracles. This is the core of the crude and vulgar view which Spinoza sketches before attacking the theological doctrine of miracles. The seemingly nonexistent theologian whom Spinoza has in mind when expounding that view is none other than Moses himself, and the view in question is meant to be implied in Genesis 1, in a text of the highest authority for all Jews and all Christians.[116] Spinoza does then not go beyond reminding his opponents of what he considers "the original" of their position. As is shown by the sequel in the *Treatise*, he does not claim at all that that reminder suffices for refuting the traditional doctrine of miracles. To conclude, our example teaches us that Spinoza tries to simplify the discussion by going back from the variety of theologies to the basis common to all: the basic doctrine of the Old Testament.

To turn now to the second example, in which Spinoza identifies the view of all theologians with the view of Maimonides, Spinoza here starts from the implicit premise that not all theological positions are of equal importance. He certainly preferred "dogmatism," which admits the certainty of reason, to "skepticism," which denies it: the former ruins the Bible (i.e., it commits only a historical error), whereas the latter ruins reason (i.e., it makes brutes out of human beings).[117] Furthermore, I take it that Spinoza rejected *a limine* the view according to which the teaching of reason is simply identical with the teaching of revelation; for this view leads to the consequence that, in the first place the philosophers, and indirectly all other men, would not need revelation, revelation would be superfluous, and an all-wise being does not do superfluous things.[118] His critical attention was thus limited to the view that the teaching of revelation is partly or wholly above reason but never against reason, or that natural reason is necessary but not sufficient for man's salvation or perfection. At this point he was confronted with the alternative that the process of revelation is, or is not, above human comprehension. Certain biblical accounts satisfied him that the phenomenon of revelation or prophecy is, in principle, intelligible, i.e., that revelation is effected, not directly by the divine will, but by the intermediacy of secondary causes. Accordingly, he had to seek for a natural explanation of the fact that certain human beings, the prophets, proclaimed a teaching that was partly or wholly above reason but never against reason. The only possible natural explanation was that the prophets were perfect philosophers and more than perfect philosophers. This view of prophecy was explicitly stated in part, and partly suggested, by Maimonides.[119] When Spinoza says that "all" theologians have asserted that the prophets have known everything within the reach of the human understanding, he then simplifies the controversial issue by limiting himself, not to the theological position which was easiest to refute, or which he just happened to know best, but to the one which he regarded as the most reasonable and therefore the strongest.

All the difficulties discussed in the preceding pages concern the reasons with which Spinoza justifies the practical proposals made in the *Treatise*. These proposals themselves are very simple. If they were not, they could not reach many readers, and hence they would not be practical. The practical proposals are supported by both the obvious and the hidden reasoning. The practical proposals together with the obvious reasoning are that part of the teaching of the *Treatise* that is meant for all its readers. That part of the teaching of the *Treatise* must be understood completely by itself before its hidden teaching can be brought to light.

Notes

1. The *Theologico-Political Treatise* will be cited as "the *Treatise*" in the text and as "*Tr.*" in the notes. In the notes, Roman figures after *Tr.* indicate the chapters of the work, Arabic figures following the comma and preceding the brackets indicate the pages in Gebhardt's edition of the *Opera omnia*, and Arabic figures within the brackets indicate the §§ [paragraph numbers] inserted by Bruder in his edition.

2. Consider the following statement of Spinoza (*ep.* 15): ". . . ubi pag. 4. lectorem mones, quâ occasione primam partem composuerim, vellem ut simul ibi, aut ubi placuerit, etiam moneres me eam intra duas hebdomadas composuisse. hoc enim praemonito nemo putabit, haec adeo clare proponi, ut quae clarius explicari non possent, adeoque verbulo uno, aut alteri, quod forte hic illic ofendent [sic], non haerebunt."

3. *Tr.* IX, 135 (§31).

4. *Tr.* VII, 98–101, 104–5, 108–9, 114–15 (§§6, 7, 9–14, 16–19, 22, 35, 37–39, 52, 55, 56, 77ff., 84); XV, 181–82 (§8); XVI, 190–91 (§§10–11); praef., 9–10 (§§20, 25).

5. *Tr.* VII, 98–104, 106–7, 112 (§§7, 13, 15–17, 23–24, 26–29, 36, 44–47, 70); V, 77 (§39).

6. *Tr.* VII, 105 (§40).

7. Compare, e.g., *Tr.* IX, 140 (§58).

8. Compare, e.g., the distinction between histories, revelations, and moral teachings in *Tr.* VII, 98–99 (§§9–11).

9. *Tr.* VII, 100, 102–4, 112 (§§16, 27–29, 36, 70).

10. Compare esp. *Tr.* VII, adnot. 8 (§66n.) with VII, 98–99, 105 (§§9–10, 37), and VII, 109–11 (§§58–68) with ibid., 101 (§23). See also *ep.* 21 (34 §3): "plane et sine ambagibus profiteor me sacram scripturam non intelligere." See *Tr.* VII, 98–99, 114 (§§6–10, 78). The distinction between what we have called the essential unintelligibility of the Bible, which is due to its subject matter (or its origin), and its accidental unintelligibility, which is due to the condition of the text, etc., is underlying also Isaac de la Peyrère's biblical criticism. See his *Systema theologicum, ex Praeadamitarum hypothesi. Pars Prima* (1655), IV, 1.

11. *Tr.* praef., 12 (§33); VII, 111–12 (§69).

12. *Tr.* VII, 98–99, 109–11 (§§9–10, 59–60, 67–68).

13. *Tr.* IX, 135 (§32); X, 149 (§42); XII, 165–66 (§§34–35, 37). Carl Gebhardt (Spinoza, *Opera*, vol. II, 317) says: "Dieses Fehlen der Controlle (des Drucks durch den Autor) macht sich namentlich bei der *Ethica* bemerkbar. Zum Teil gehen die dadurch verschuldeten textkritischen Zweifel so tief, dass selbst die Interpretation spinozanischer Lehren von ihrer Entscheidung abhängt."

14. *Tr. pol.* V, 7. See *Tr.* VII, 102, 111 (§§24, 67, 68); *ep.* 43 (49 §2).

15. *Tr.* VII, 101, 111 (§§21, 66–68). Spinoza implies that in the case of intelligible books one need not know in what manner and on what occasion they were written—*Tr.* VII, 102, 111 (§§23, 67)—; but compare what he says about his own *Renati Des Cartes Principia Philosophiae* (see note 2, above). When Spinoza indicates in *Tr.* XVII adnot. 38 (§55n.) that one has to consider the different "states" in which the Hebrews were at different times in order not to ascribe to Moses, e.g., such institutions as originated at a much later time, he does not formally contradict what he implies in *Tr.* VII adnot. 8 (§65n.), viz. that the understanding of institutions does not require "history." For in the former passage he is speaking only of institutions recorded in the Bible, i.e., in a book which is altogether unintelligible without "history."

16. *Ep.* 56 (60 §13). See *Tr.* praef., 9 (§§18–19); I, 19 (§19).

17. *Tr. pol.* I, 1.

18. *Ethics* III, praef. See *Tr.* VII, 111 (§68).

19. *Ep.* 73 (21 §2). See *Ethics* II, 7 schol. See *ep.* 6 *vers. fin.*: "dico quod multa attributa quae ab iis (*sc.* concinnatoribus) et *ab omnibus mihi saltem notis* deo tribuuntur; ego tanquam creaturas considero, et contra alia, propter praejudicia ab iis tanquam creaturas considerata, ego attributa dei esse . . . contendo. et etiam quod Deum a natura non ita separem ut *omnes, quorum apud me est notitia*, fecerunt." See also Spinoza's polemics against what "all" teach regarding the infinite in *ep.* 12 (29 §2). As for the reference to "all ancient Hebrews," see *Tr.* III, 48 (§18) and XI, 158 (§24).

20. *Tr.* XI end, and praef., 7 (§9). Compare Maimonides, *Guide of the Perplexed* 1.31 (34b Munk).

21. As for Spinoza's synonymous use of "philosophy" and "science," see, e.g., *Tr.* II, 35–36 (§§26–27); IV, 60 (§11); XIII, 167–68, 172 (§§4, 7, 27); XIV, 174 (§§5, 7); XV, 187 (§38); XIX, 237–38 (§§54, 62).

22. *Tr.* praef., 12 (§§33–34); V, 77–79 (§§37–46); XIV, 173–74 (§§1–2, 10); XV, 180 (§§2–3).

23. *Tr.* praef., 12 (§34); XV, 180 (§§1–3); XX, 243 (§26). *Tr. de intellectus emendatione* 18, 29–30 (§§47–48, 78–80). Spinoza frequently uses "philosophy" and "reason" synonymously, implying of course that philosophy is the perfection of man's natural capacity of understanding; see *Tr.* VII, 117 (§94) with XV, 180, 182–84, 187 (§§1–3, 12, 17, 21, 38); XIV, 179 (§38); praef., 10 (§27). See IV, 59 (§10). That Spinoza understands by "philosopher" a man who is not limited in his investigations by any regard whatsoever for theology, is indicated in passages such as these: *Tr.* VI, 88, 95 (§§34, 37, 67–68); XII, 166 (§40); XIII, 167 (§5); XV, 188 (§42); *ep.* 23 (36 §2).

24. *Ep.* 30. See *Tr.* XVII, 205, 219 (§§24, 103); XVIII, 223 (§11); X, adnott. 21, 25 (§§1n., 43n.).

25. *Tr.* XII, 163 (§24); XIV, 174 (§6); XV, 180, 184–85 (§§1–3, 24).

26. *Tr.* praef., 7–8 (§§13–14). See XIX, 234–35 (§§38–39).

27. *Tr.* I, 21 (§§23, 25); compare II, 43 (§§56–57) and XI, 158 (§23) with II, 42–43 (§§52–55); III, 48 and adnot. 5 (§§21, 21n., 22); IV, 64–65 (§§30–34); V, 70, 77 (§§8, 38); XI, 152, 158 (§§4, 24); XII, 158–59, 163 (§§3, 24); XVII, 214–15, 221 (§§77–82, 115); XVIII, 221 (§2); XIX, 233–34 (§§29–30, 38). See *epp.* 73 (21 §§4, 7) and 19 (32 §10).

28. *Tr.* I, 18 (§13); IX, 135–36 (§§30–31, 36); X, 150 (§48); XV, 180–81 (§§1–5).

29. Compare *Tr.* II, 44 (§58) with the heading as well as the plan of III. See XIV, 180 (§40).

30. *Tr.* I–III: prophecy; IV–V: law; VI: miracles. As for the connection between miracles and providence, see *Tr.* VI, 82, 88–89 (§§6, 34, 37, 39). Spinoza could be familiar with the order which he adopted, of the three cardinal subjects, partly from the plans of Maimonides' discussion, and partly from explicit utterances of that authority; see *Guide* 3.17 (34b–35a Munk) and 45 (98b–99a). In the light of the tradition in question, the theological part par excellence of the *Treatise* proves to be devoted to the subject of divine justice as distinguished from the subject of divine unity. That this inference is justified appears from a comparison of *Tr.* I–VI with *Ethics* I, appendix. It would be an exaggeration, but it would not be misleading, if one were to say that the subject of the *Treatise* as a whole is divine justice and human justice; consider *Tr.* XIX, 229–32 (§§5–20).

31. Compare *Tr.* VI, 91 (§51) with *epp.* 75 and 78 (23 §§5–7 and 25 §6). See *Tr.* XV, 185 (§27). The explicit denial of the resurrection of Jesus in the cited letters is confirmed by the implication of *Tr.* XII, 163, 166 (§§24, 39). What we have said in the text throws light on another difficulty presented by Spinoza's discussion of miracles. In his thematic discussion of the biblical teaching, he says that the Bible teaches only indirectly that there are no miracles proper, and yet he adds that any contradictory biblical passage must be rejected as a sacrilegious addition. But in the concluding section of the chapter on miracles he says that the Bible teaches directly that there are no miracles proper, and yet he adds that this explicit biblical teaching is not in any way obligatory. That is to say, the biblical teaching is either merely implicit and at the same time sacred, or it is explicit and at the same time indifferent from a religious point of view: it is certainly not explicit and at the same time obligatory. Compare *Tr.* VI, 89–91 (§§39–51) with ibid., 95–96 (§§66–71).

32. *Tr.* II, 29 (§2).

33. *Tr.* praef., 7–9 (§§12, 14–20); I, 16 (§7); VII, 97–98, 105, 112 (§§1–5, 38–39, 70); VIII, 118 (§§2–3); XI, 153, 157–58 (§§8, 21–24); XII, 159 (§4); XIV, 173, 180 (§§2, 4, 40); XVIII, 225–26 (§§24–25); XIX, 235–37 (§§43, 50, 52–53); XX, 245–46 (§§39–40).

34. *Tr.* I, 15–16, 20–21, 28 (§§1–4, 6–7, 22–23, 45); XV, 184–85, 188 (§§22, 26–27, 44). See, e.g., VI, 95 (§65); VII, 98–99, 114 (§§8–10, 78); XI, 155–56 (§§14–15); XII, 162–63 (§§21–22); XIII, 168, 170 (§§6–8, 20); XVI, 198–200 (§§53–56, 61, 64). See *ep.* 21 (34 §§3, 23).

35. *Tr.* V, 80 (§49); XIII, 170 (§17); XIV, 179 (§38); XV, 184, 188 (§§21, 23, 42). See IV, 62 (§20); VII, 112 (§72); also L. Meyer's preface to *Renati Des Cartes Principiorum etc., vers. fin.*

36. This conclusion is confirmed by the facts that obedience (viz. to God) presupposes that God is a lawgiver or ruler, and that reason refutes this presupposition; see *Tr.* IV, 62–65 (§§22–37) and XVI, adnot. 34 (§53n.). In accordance with the conclusion that we have drawn in the text, Spinoza says that faith requires, not so much true dogmas, as pious ones, "although there may be

among them very many which have not even a shadow of truth"; see XIV, 176 (§20) and XIII, 172 (§29). Compare XV, 182, 187, 188 (§§11–12, 38, 43); XII, 159 (§6); *ep.* 21 (34 §§3, 23) on the one hand, with XV, 185 (§§26–27) and the passages cited in the preceding note on the other.

37. Compare *Tr.* XV, 188 (§42) and II, 35 (§24), with V, 77 (§38), XIII, 168 (§6), and XX, 243 (§22).

38. Compare *Tr.* VI, 82, 95–96 (§§6, 66–71) with VI, 87–88 (§§37, 32–34, 36); XIX, 229, 231–32 (§§8, 20); XIV, 177–78 (§27); *Ethics* I, app.

39. Compare *Tr.* III, 53 (§39) with I, 15, 16 (§§1, 7); VI, 95 (§63); VII, 98 (§6); XII, 163 (§27); XIV, 179 (§38); XV, 188 (§44). See also the contradiction between XVII, 219 (§§105–6) and XI, 152 (§§5–6).

40. *Tr.* I, 20–21 (§§22–25); IV, 64–65 (§§30–32). See *epp.* 73 (21 §4) and 75 (23 §9).

41. *Tr.* I, 16 (§3). Consider the use of the *modus irrealis* in I, 20–21 (§22) and I, adnot. 3 (§40n.). See III, 47 (§12); VI, 95 (§§66–67); XII, 159–60 (§7); *Ethics* III, praef.

42. *Tr.* IV, 64–65 (§§30–36). See XI, 154 (§11). See also the preface to the *Ethics* in the *Opera posthuma*.

43. *Tr.* II, 42–43 (§§52–57); V, 77–78 (§§37–40); XI, 158 (§23). See the argument of XI as a whole.

44. *Tr.* II, 36, 41 (§§29, 48); IV, 66 (§40); VI, 95 (§67); VII, 114 (§79); XI, 156 (§15). *Ep.* 73 (21 §2).

45. *Tr.* XIII, 167 (§4); XIV, 174 (§8); XV, 180 (§2). See page 153 above. [See above in the present essay, section I, the thirteenth paragraph, which begins with the words "It would seem then that one cannot understand Spinoza," toward the end of the paragraph. —Ed.]

46. *Tr.* IV, 66–68 (§§40–46, 48); V, 71–72 (§§10–13); VII, 99 (§11); XII, 162 (§19); XIX, 231 (§16).

47. *Tr.* XII, 163, 165–66 (§§24, 37); XIX, 231 (§16).

48. *Tr.* IV, 64 (§30); XIII, 171–72 (§26); XIV, 174, 178 (§§6–8, 28).

49. *Epp.* 75 (23 §5) and 78 (25 §6).

50. *Tr.* XI, 152–53 (§§5–7); XIV, 175–76 (§§17–18). See *ep.* 75 (23 §7).

51. *Tr.* XI, 156–58 (§§15, 21, 23–24); XII, 166 (§40); XIII, 167 (§3); XIV, 175–76 (§§14–19); III, 54 (§46). See the implicit criticism of Paul in I, 21, 28–29 (§§25, 46).

52. *Tr.* XIX, 233 (§§29–30); XII, 165–66 (§37); VII, 103–4 (§§30–33).

53. *Tr.* XVIII, 225–26 (§25); XIX, 232, 236–38 (§§22–24, 50–59). See V, 70–72 (§§8–9, 13–14).

54. *Tr.* VII, 98, 112 (§§9, 23); XII, 159 (§4); II, 35, 36 (§§25, 29).

55. *Tr.* V, 76–77 (§§35–39); VII, 112 (§§70, 73); XIII, 167 (§§3–4). See XIV, 174 (§§6–8) and II, 34 (§21).

56. *Tr.* I, 21 (§24); *ep.* 73 (21 §5).

57. *Tr.* XV, 180, 184 (§§3, 20); VI, 81–82, 88 (§§1–5, 36). See especially the explicit addition to the teaching of the *Treatise* in *ep.* 73 (21 §3), an addition clarifying the meaning of "superstition."

58. *Tr.* VII, 101, 103–4 (§§21, 29–33).

59. *Tr.* IV, 65 (§§33–36); II, 42 (§51); XVI, adnot. 34 (§53n.).

60. For a somewhat different formulation of the same principle, see E. E. Powell, *Spinoza and Religion* (Boston: Chapman and Grimes, 1941), 65.

61. *Tr. de int. em.* 9 (§17). See *Tr. pol.* III, 10.

62. *Tr.* VII, 101 (§22). This statement is prepared by an allusion in II, 38–39 (§§36, 38). See IV, 45, 53 (§§6, 41).

63. "Ad captum vulgi": VI, 84 (§14); XV, 180 (§2). "Secundum captum vulgi": XIII, 172 (§26); XV, 178–79 (§33). "Ad captum plebis": V, 77 (§§37–38); "Ad captum alicuius": II, 37, 43 (§§31–33, 53, 55, 57); III, 44–45, 54 (§§3, 6, 46). "Ad hominem sive ad captum alicuius": II, 43 (§57). In III, 45 (§6) Spinoza applies the expression "ad captum (Hebraeorum) loqui" to a remark of his own. See also XIV, 173 (§§1–2); VII, 104, 115 (§§35, 81–82); praef., 6 (§§7–8).

64. *Tr.* VI, 88 (§36); XV, 180 (§§2–3). See II, 32–33, 35–43 (§§15, 24, 29, 31–35, 41–45, 47, 50, 52–57); IV, 65 (§§33–37); V, 76–78 (§§35–40); VII, 98–99 (§10); XI, 156, 158 (§§15, 23–24); XIV, 173 (§§1–3).

65. *Tr.* praef., 9 (§18); II, 36–37 (§30); VII, 105 (§37); X, 149 (§41); XII, 163 (§27); XIII, 167–68 (§§4–5). When saying that God spoke with a view to the capacity of the prophets, or of the vulgar, Spinoza himself is speaking "ad captum vulgi" by accommodating himself to the belief, which he rejects, in divine revelation. The fact that he refers with particular emphasis to Paul's speaking "after the manner of man" does not prove that, in his opinion, Paul was emancipated from the vulgar opinions as such, as will have appeared from what we said on page 174 above. [See above in the present essay, section III, the third paragraph, which begins with the words "The contradictions regarding Christianity, or the New Testament," toward the end of the paragraph. —Ed.]

66. *Tr.* XVI, 192 and adnot. 32 (§§16n., 18). *Tr. pol.* III, 17. See *Ethics* IV, 72.

67. See *Tr.* XVI, 197 (§46). *Tr. pol.* I, 2, and III, 14, 17.

68. *Tr.* praef., 12 (§§7–8); II, 29–30 (§2); VII, 114 (§79); XX, 244–45 (§§32–35); *ep.* 30.

69. *Tr.* IV, 61–62 (§19). See *Ethics* IV, 69, 70 and schol. —Regarding Spinoza's caution, see also *epp.* 7 (7 §§4–5), 13 (9 §§1–4), 82 (71 §2). Compare the discussion of this subject by Powell, *Spinoza and Religion*, 51–65.

70. *Tr.* XX, 240 (§§8–9); XVI, adnot. 33 (§34n.).

71. Compare *Tr.* XIV, 173, 178–79 (§§3, 32–33) with VII, 115, 101 (§§85, 22).

72. *Tr.* XII, 159 (§4).

73. *Tr.* VIII, 118–19 (§§4–5, 9); X, adnot. 21 (§1n.). As regards the use of "openly" (*aperte*), compare the parallels in II, 36 (§27); IV, 65 (§35); V, 80 (§49); XV, 180 (§4); *ep.* 13 (9 §1).

74. *Tr.* VII, 101 (§§21–22). *Guide* 3.28 (61a Munk).

75. *Guide* 1, Introduction (11b, 3b, 8b Munk). See *Tr.* VII, 113 (§75).

76. "Leibniz von den ewigen Strafen," *Werke*, eds. Petersen and von Olshausen, XXI, 147 and 160.

77. *Discours de la méthode*, III and VI *in princ.*

78. *Advancement of Learning*, Everyman's Library ed., 92, 141–42, 205–6. See *De augmentis* III, 4 and VI, 2.

79. *Tr.* VII, 106 (§42). v. Dunin-Borkowski, *Spinoza*, II, 217–18: "Nur im Notfall brachte (Spinoza) eine selbstersonnene Terminologie auf. . . . Die altgewohnte Form sollte gleichsam die gefährliche Beunruhigung beschwichtigen. Die Leser konnten zuerst meinen, dass sie sich in einer ihnen wohl bekannten philosophischen Welt bewegten."

80. *Epp.* 30 and 43 (49 §2).

81. Compare *Tr.* praef., 12 (§34) with I, 15 (§2). See V, 69 (§3). See the analyses of superstition in *Tr.* praef., 5 (§4) and in *Ethics* I, app.

82. Fundamentally the same procedure is followed by Hobbes in the third part of his *Leviathan*.

83. Aristotle, *Resp. Ath.* 22. 4.

84. Compare also *Tr.* VII, 98–99 (§§6–10) with ibid., 109–11 (§§58–66)— note the "consulto omisi" on 109 (§59)—; and XIV, 173 (§3: licet) with ibid., 178–79 (§§32–33: tenetur).

85. Cicero, *Orator* 15. 50. See *De oratore* II 77. 313.

86. An example would be the statements "I understand the Bible" and "I do not understand the Bible." Regarding implicit contradictions, see *Tr.* XV, 184 (§20).

87. See page 177 above. [See above in the present essay, section III, the fourth paragraph, toward the end, and the fifth paragraph, toward the beginning; the fourth paragraph begins with the words "Our last example shall be a contradiction which we have been forced to imitate in our own presentation"; the fifth paragraph begins with the words "Spinoza, who regarded the Bible as a book rich in contradictions." —Ed.]

88. *Ep.* 13 (9 §§1–2). See L. Meyer's preface to the *Renati Des Cartes Principiorum etc.*

89. *Ethics* IV, 68 schol.; V, 36 schol. See *Tr. pol.* II, 6, 22; III, 10; VII, 25.

90. Maimonides, *Guide* 1, Introduction (4a Munk). See Plato, *Seventh Letter* 341d4–e3 and 344c3–d5; *Phaedrus* 275c5ff.

91. H. A. Wolfson, *The Philosophy of Spinoza* (Cambridge: Harvard University Press, 1934), I, 22–24.

92. Wolfson, *Philosophy of Spinoza*, I, 20–22, 159, 177; II, 4. See *Tr.* II, 43 (§§56–57); VI, 88 (§36).

93. See the end of Descartes' "Secundae Responsiones" to objections to his *Meditationes*. See also *Regulae* IV.

94. Wolfson, *Philosophy of Spinoza*, I, 375.

95. *Tr. de int. em.* 8–9 (§14); see *Ethics* V, 20. See pages 177f. above. [See above in the present essay, section III, the fourth paragraph, toward the end, and the fifth paragraph, toward the beginning; the fourth paragraph begins with the words "Our last example shall be a contradiction which we have been forced to imitate in our own presentation"; the fifth paragraph begins with the words "Spinoza, who regarded the Bible as a book rich in contradictions." —Ed.] As to the oppressed condition of the Jews, see *Tr.* III, 55, 57 (§§47, 55); VII, 106 (§45).

96. See *Tr.* III, 54 (§46); VI, 88 (§36).

97. To this may be added that the accusation of tampering with the biblical text, or of pious fraud, is directed by Spinoza not only against the Jews in regard to the Old Testament, but also against the Christians in regard to the New Testament; see *Tr.* VI, 91 (§51) with *epp.* 75 (23 §5) and 78 (25 §6).

98. *Tr.* XV, 181–82 (§§4, 10). See the brief reference to fundamentally the same theological principle in V, 80 (§49), a reference characteristically concluding with the words: "Sed de his non est opus apertius loqui." See praef., 8 (§§14–17).

99. *Tr.* X, adnot. 21 (§1n.). For the use of "superstition" in this passage, see *ep.* 76 (74 §§4, 14).

100. At the end of the tenth chapter of the *Treatise*, Spinoza explains his refraining from literary criticism of the New Testament by his insufficient knowledge of the Greek language. But this does not explain why he limits his remarks on the New Testament in the eleventh chapter to the Epistles of the apostles. The reason of this striking fact is his desire to remain silent about the Gospels. See also V, 76 (§34). Hermann Cohen (*Jüdische Schriften* [Berlin: C. A. Schwetschke, 1924], III, 367): "Die Furcht hat (Spinoza) zu zweierlei Mass am Alten und Neuen Testament getrieben."

101. *Tr.* XIV, 173, 179 (§§2, 34); XX, 245–46 (§40). *Ep.* 30.

102. Compare the heading of *Tr.* XX with Tacitus, *Histories* I 1, and *Tr.* XVII, 201 (§9) with Curtius Rufus VIII 5. 17. See also XVII, 206 (§32); XVIII, 225–26 (§25); XIX, 236–37 (§§50–53); XI, 157–58 (§§22–24); II, 43 (§§55–57). See Machiavelli, *Discorsi* I 11: in the age of the good Roman emperors, everyone could hold and defend every opinion he pleased; also Hobbes, *Leviathan* ch. 46 (Everyman's Library ed., 374), and the argument of Milton's *Areopagitica* as a whole.

103. By a publicly defensible view we understand here, not so much a view whose propagation is permitted by law, as a view backed by the sympathy of a powerful section of society.

104. *Tr.* I, 16 (§7); VI, 95 (§65).

105. *Tr.* VII, 116 (§87); XIII, 172 (§§27–28).

106. Compare *Tr.* praef., 8 (§16); XVIII, 222 (§§7–9); XIV, 180 (§40) on the one hand, with XV, 180 (§2); VI, 81 (§4) on the other.

107. Consider also the difference between the correct sequence of questions to be raised by the interpretation of the Bible—*Tr.* VII, 102–4 (§§26–36)—and the sequence of the topics discussed in the *Treatise*.

108. *Tr.* VII, 102–3, 111 (§§27–29, 68–69); IX, 135 (§32); XII, 165–66 (§§34–38).

109. *Ep.* 21 (34 §3). See *Cogitata metaphysica* II 8 §5.

110. Compare *Tr.* XII, 165 (§36) with VI, 87 (§33); XIX, 229, 231–32 (§§8, 20).

111. Compare *Tr.* V, 77 (§38); VII, 102 (§27); XII, 165 (§36) with II, 37–39 (§§32–35, 37–40); III, 44–45 (§3); VI, 81–82 (§§2, 4); XVII, 206, 214–15 (§§30, 77–79).

112. Compare *Tr.* XII, 166 (§37) with XVII, 214 (§77); XIX, 233 (§29).

113. Compare *Tr.* XIII, 168 (§§7–8); XIV, 174 (§§5–9) with XVI, adnot. 34 (§53n.). See IV, 59, 60–61, 65 (§§7–8, 14–15, 34); XII, 162 (§19); XIV, 177 (§§24–25).

114. *Tr.* XV, 180 (§1).

115. v. Dunin-Borkowski, *Spinoza*, IV, 315. See Maimonides, *Guide* 3.32 and 36. See also Abravanel's criticism in his commentary on these chapters, as well as in his commentary on Amos 1:1 and on 1 Kings 3:14; see *Tr.* II, 29 (§1).

116. Compare *Tr.* VI, 81–82 (§§1–4) with II, 38–39 (§§37–40); IV, 64 (§30). See II, 37 (§31); VI, 87–89 (§§34, 39); VII, 115 (§83).

117. Compare *Tr.* XV, 180 (§§1–3) with praef., 8 (§§16–17) and XIII, 170 (§17).

118. Compare *Tr.* XV, 180 (§§1–3) with praef., 8 (§§16–17); XIII, 170 (§17). —XV, 188 (§44).

119. Compare *Tr.* V, 79–80 (§§47–49) with VII, 115 (§83); II, 29 (§2). See XVI, 191 (§11); IV, 58 (§4).

4

Preface to Isaac Husik, *Philosophical Essays: Ancient, Medieval, and Modern*

A decade ago Isaac Husik died. To the many men and women who knew him and came within the influence of a life marked by simplicity, gentleness, and genuine humor, no fitter description could be made than that "self-portrait" of Hume which Husik's death recalled to a friend: ". . . a man of mild dispositions, of command of temper, of an open, social and cheerful humor, capable of attachment, but little susceptible of enmity. . . ." To his colleagues in the academic world and to his peers in the search for "the unity of human learning," his death was that of one of the most distinguished historians of philosophy America had produced. To some, the two aspects of his life appeared to be wholly distinct. A closer study will show them to have been whole and integrated.

The years since Husik's death have served to establish more firmly a reputation founded upon sound scholarship and breadth of interest in the history of ideas and of learning. His papers on Aristotle's philosophy are among the best on that subject. His *A History of Mediaeval Jewish Philosophy*, now in its second edition, was not only justly described by a contemporary reviewer as "the first attempt in the English language to present completely the history . . . of systematic speculation among Jewish thinkers from the ninth to the fifteenth centuries," but was also recognized as a work which for its soundness and penetration "place son auteur au rang des meilleurs historiens de la philosophie,"[1] ". . . un travail de tout premier ordre et dont on peut dire qu'il aura été classique dès le jour même de son apparition."[2] His four-volume edition and translation of Joseph Albo's *Sefer ha-Ikkarim* was the first complete translation on scientific principles into English of an important text first printed in 1485. And to his laurels as historian and philologist Husik had added those of a scholar in jurisprudence who had translated von Ihering's *Law as a Means to an End*, had edited and translated Stammler's *The Theory of Justice*, and had made original contributions to jurispru-

dence. These contributions to scholarship, in the historical and speculative fields, might be regarded, indeed, as sufficient and enduring monuments to Husik's superb linguistic skill and to his devotion to learning.
The gathering together and publication of his essays in ancient,
medieval, and modern philosophy is, however, no act of supereroga-
tion. The essays themselves attest an interest by Husik in rounding out
and deepening his knowledge of systematic philosophy and his speculation upon problems which perhaps—and almost certainly in the
instance of philosophy of law—were preparatory for more extended
studies. The essays are, however, neither tentative nor incomplete. They
are the well-considered writings of a great scholar in fields central to
philosophy, religion, and law. It has been one of the principal reasons for
publishing this book that the essays will serve the useful purpose of
bringing together writings scattered beyond easy access by Husik's
very versatility in learned journals so varied as the *Philosophical Review*,
the *Jewish Quarterly Review*, the *Columbia Law Review*, *Mind*, and the
Archiv für Geschichte der Philosophie. And were they not so widely scattered, the justification for their publication—if justification be needed—
is perhaps sufficiently indicated in a comment Husik once made concerning the fortunes of the study he judged to be his outstanding
contribution to scholarship and philosophy: "*Habent sua fata libelli*," he
wrote. "Thirty-four years ago I published a paper on 'The Categories of
Aristotle' in the *Philosophical Review*. Like the case of the proverbial
Irishman who desired to be buried in a Jewish cemetery because that
was the last place the devil would look for an Irishman, so it seems
that the *Philosophical Review* at the time was the last place that an
Aristotelian scholar would look for a literary-historical article on the
Categories of Aristotle." Perhaps, because of the breadth of Husik's interests, a published essay or unprinted manuscript may be saved from
"sua fata" of incarceration within the covers of rank upon rank of
"learned journals" to find among the readers of this volume those who
will, in its reading, imbue it with new life.

Of their author, it has already been suggested in this prefatory
essay that his life bore the outward semblance of simplicity and gentleness. So marked, indeed, were these characteristics associated with a
retired and retiring life that they evoked in one who knew him as a student and colleague for some forty years a "wonder at the strength of
gentle, the power of quiet, and the fullness of uneventful lives." Husik's
life was in fact not uneventful, however full it was. It was a life of difficult decisions and one which required for its fulfillment the greatest
tenacity of purpose. And however uneventful it may have been in such
superficial circumstances as pertain to physical adventure, it was a life,

on Husik's own testimony, of the most magnificent adventures of the imagination, of the opening and investigation of a world of scholarship rich beyond even the most fantastic dream of a small immigrant boy, and of the meeting of minds, embodied and in books and manuscripts, which enriched an academic life and turned it upon the most diverse paths of interest.

Few men, indeed, have evidenced greater courage and persistence in the pursuit of the object of their heart's desire than did Husik in following the course which eventually led him to a professorship in philosophy at the University of Pennsylvania and to a worldwide reputation among scholars. He was born at Vasseutinez, in the province of Poltava, near Kiev, Russia, on 10 February 1876. His was a pious Jewish family which emigrated to America in 1888. His father's scholarly interests—Wolf Husik was a teacher—and Isaac's early training in Hebrew and in Jewish studies suggested the rabbinate as a career. For the two years before he began his theological training, Isaac studied at Central High School in Philadelphia and earned his livelihood by giving private lessons in Hebrew.

His formal theological studies ended abruptly, and with their termination the suggestion of a career as a rabbi likewise ended. Writing shortly after Husik's death, Louis E. Levinthal[3] recalled the circumstances and in so doing underlined an aspect of Husik's character which is essential for an understanding of his career. Judge Levinthal remarked that Husik "was a scholar who loved not only wisdom. He loved justice and truth even more. His personal integrity and high sense of honor would not permit him to tell a 'white lie' nor to live a lie, white or black. This was strikingly illustrated early in his life. He had planned to become a rabbi, an ambition which greatly pleased his mentor and guide, Rabbi Sabato Morais. He became a student of the Jewish Theological Seminary of America, but when Husik found himself questioning the orthodox beliefs of his ancestral religion, and when the traditional practices of Judaism could no longer command his complete obedience, he unhesitatingly left the seminary, and devoted himself to the study of philosophy instead of theology." In this move, following upon perhaps the most dramatic decision in Husik's scholarly career and certainly the one most far-reaching in its consequences, one discovers the pattern of the man's life. As will be evident, the decision led him from the comparatively restricted interests of the theologian into the wider fields of nonsectarian scholarship. His action, however, signified more than this. With it began a lifelong pursuit of objective truth in fields in which Husik proposed to apply the tools of scholarship rather than accept the dictates of authority. The consequences were decisive not only for his controversy with Neumark[4] but in the calm acceptance of a life for many years bordering on actual poverty, with weary hours devoted year after year to the teaching of languages, hours which Husik must necessarily have thought would be more fruitfully devoted to his historical and speculative studies. For it should be remembered that Husik took a "calculated risk." It was not until 1911 that he became a lecturer at the University of Pennsylvania, and not until five years later that he was made a member of the faculty, with rank of assistant professor. Finally, it is well to note that in this pattern of a man's life, the constant devotion to the "impractical," to the acquisition of knowledge for itself, there is recurrence: he turned from assurance of a distinguished career as rabbi or theologian or both, precisely as he entered later upon the study of the law with no thought of practicing in the courts. His action was ultimately motivated by his profound interest in "pure" scholarship.

Upon leaving the Jewish Theological Seminary, Husik entered by examination the University of Pennsylvania, as a sophomore. In the course of his study at Pennsylvania, he was awarded four degrees, the B.A. in 1897, the M.A. in 1899, the Ph.D. in 1903, and the LL.B. in 1919. His undergraduate career was scholastically outstanding. In but two instances was his recorded mark less than "distinguished" in a course marked by unusual diversification of studies. It is, however, a career particularly notable as a record of linguistic, philological, and literary achievement. In 1895–96, the year in which Husik received a full scholarship, he was also awarded first prize in Hebrew. The following year, he was awarded separate prizes for senior work in French language and literature, and German language and literature, as well as first prize for the Alumni Latin Essay.

In 1897 Husik received his bachelor's degree. It is also the year in which Gratz College was founded and in which Husik was appointed a member of its faculty. He was to remain there as a teacher of Bible, Hebrew grammar, Jewish philosophy, and rabbinics until 1916.[5]

While teaching at Gratz College, Husik entered the graduate school of the University of Pennsylvania. As a candidate for the master of arts degree, his principal interest at this time lay in mathematics, with "minors" in astronomy and Hebrew. He had by this time acquired mastery of Latin, Greek, Hebrew, Aramaic, German, French, and Russian, and now began studies in Arabic, having taught Hebrew since 1894 in one of the Hebrew Education Society schools in the city of Philadelphia.[6] Husik's university scholarship in mathematics and astronomy continued until 1899, when he turned to classics. He continued his studies, principally in Greek and Latin, as a university scholar, until 1902. In 1903, he was appointed fellow for research in philosophy, a status in which he continued until 1911. In classics, he studied with Professors Rolfe and Lamberton; in philosophy, with Professors Fullerton, Newbold, and Singer. And it was the latter two distinguished members of the department of philosophy who principally influenced Husik's philosophical career.

The factual story of academic careers may interest academicians, although the pattern of studies undertaken and degrees awarded tends to pall upon even the most assiduous researcher into dusty archives. The story of academic friendships and the influence of men in university relationships preserves a warmth not ordinarily associated with the routine of seminars and the techniques of research. More than that, it is sometimes, as it was in the instance of the friendship of Newbold and Husik, the occasion for a quickening of imagination and deepening of interests which in themselves cast light upon the motives of men's actions. Husik's relation to Edgar A. Singer, Jr., was one of long-continued friendship, but it was more than that. Husik's speculation upon philosophy of law fell within the framework of Singer's systematic philosophy of "empirical idealism." But it must be remembered that the young Husik was a man principally gifted in languages and that, in Newbold, he discovered a scholar no less gifted in languages, a mature philosopher, and a man so enormously erudite as to have become a figure to conjure with. It is given to few to find, embodied, as Husik did find in Newbold, their ideal of a man. It is given to even fewer to find an ideal which remains such throughout life. It is given to even fewer still to be able to portray that ideal. And, perhaps the most extraordinary fact of all, the portrait of that ideal is not only the portrait of Newbold, but, unconsciously, of Husik himself, of what he hoped to attain, and what in large part he did achieve.

Newbold presented Husik to the graduate faculty of the University of Pennsylvania on 17 June 1903, and characterized his doctoral dissertation, *Judah Messer Leon's Commentary on the Vetus Logica*, as "a substantial contribution to our knowledge of Jewish medieval philosophy." It was Newbold, with Singer, who vigorously supported Husik's appointment as fellow for research from 1903 and as lecturer in 1911, in the face of at least one administrative officer's comment that the appointment would constitute a "luxury" for the department. A "luxury"—at a few hundred dollars a year for twenty years—it was in one sense: Husik's principal interest, ancient philosophy, was the field in which Newbold researched and taught, and Newbold was one of the most brilliant scholars and lecturers in the history of the university. But it was Newbold who fought for the appointment.

It was an act of courage and understanding which Husik never forgot. In a letter prepared for the Newbold memorial meeting, 1 December 1926, he wrote from the heart: "I cannot refrain from recording here, for everyone to read, my great indebtedness to William Newbold. He was more to me than a teacher, a colleague, and a friend; though what more can one want than a true friend? But there are so many different kinds of friends, and William Newbold was to me the one kind that made all the difference. At a time when the slough of disappointed hopes was nigh overwhelming, it was William Newbold who cheered and encouraged me, and not content with kind words he exerted himself to the utmost to help me realize my fond hopes."

Husik saw in his mentor the man to whom was due "whatever I have accomplished." More than this, Newbold stood firmly for what Husik held to be the ground for the philosophical attitude. He regarded Newbold as that rare person "who loves learning for its own sake. I emphasize the word 'learning.' I do not mean science, I do not mean philosophy, nor have I in mind history or literature. Learning is necessary, to be sure, in a serious study of all these subjects, and the majority of persons with an intellectual turn of mind possess, as they must, a certain measure of learning and a certain love thereof, using it as a means to further their specific ends as scientists, philosophers, men of letters, historians. But there is such a thing as learning as an end in itself, the love of books, the love of ideas, and the love of languages, as a means of getting into touch with the books and the ideas and the learning of all the world through the ages.

"There is a grave danger, if a person becomes addicted to learning, that he may lose touch with everything that is not books and become a bookworm. But if one avoids this pitfall and joins with his love of learning a love of his fellowman, he is thrice blessed. The combination is rare in our day because of the many temptations that lead one astray, and the deliberate teachings also of many persons in our midst, that one must above all be practical. Fortunately, there are still a few who believe, or who feel, with Aristotle, that practicality does not necessarily mean being busy with the material affairs of this world, and that a life of study and contemplation is just as worthwhile as one that is concerned with the economics or the politics of the moment. As Aristotle quaintly puts it, if only a life that is devoted to external things is worthwhile and leads to true happiness, then God and nature, who have nothing external to themselves and whose life therefore must needs be one of internal contemplation, would be neither complete nor happy."[7]

In temperament, Newbold and Husik were unlike. Newbold was brisk, fiery, enormously energetic; Husik quiet, contemplative, controlled. Nor were they fundamentally alike as scholars. Both were enormously learned and each had superb control of languages. Yet Newbold's interests lay principally in working at the solution to erudite puzzles and scarcely at all in publishing the results of his research. The one notable exception was his study of Philolaus and the Pythagorean philosophy. Husik had no liking for puzzles, if by puzzles one means philosophy expressed in myth and metaphor. Philosophy to him meant propositions and verification. He preferred Aristotle to all other thinkers. He was painstaking in his effort to set free the meaning of an obscure text by bringing to it philosophical, historical, and philological techniques. He prepared his material for publication, perfecting it as a work of scholarship to be judged by his peers.

Despite these divergences, Newbold's influence upon Husik was enormous. He could, however, only have exerted its full force in a great university. And what the scholar and the University of Pennsylvania did is significant not alone for what they eventually produced in Husik, but also because the event suggests something of the effects which the best in humanism in America produced in the youth of eastern Europe who had come to this country from a closed community and who, in normal circumstances, would have remained isolated in a translated community of the same kind. Husik's natural gift for languages would have gained preeminence for him in any scholarly company. It is true that he had taught Hebrew while yet a student in high school, and was an instructor at Gratz College while his doctoral dissertation was being printed in Leiden. A glance at the introduction to his doctoral dissertation indicates, as well, that he had mastered the art of editing a text. The edition of the *Vetus Logica* clearly anticipates those requirements of perfection which marked all of Husik's later work: "careful collection" of texts, recognition of corrupt readings, knowledge of sources, and an understanding of the philosophies of Aristotle and Averroes. Knowledge and skill are no doubt presupposed in his coming upon a catalogue which informed him that in the Royal Library in Munich there was "a Hebrew manuscript containing a commentary on Averroes's commentary on Aristotle's logic." But there is more in the incident than a man's evident skill in reading languages. For Husik, the memory of the event was green thirty years later and he himself remarks that it was a "revelation" to him. As he wrote in "The Unity of Human Learning": "I did not know that any Jew in the Middle Ages wrote in Hebrew on such a non-Jewish and nonreligious topic as Aristotle's logic, and at once I realized in imagination the joy of studying that manuscript, of seeing how the Jewish rabbi of Mantua in the fifteenth century was grappling with the technical Aristotelian logic in the Hebrew language, *which up to that time I knew of only as a medium used in the prayer book, in the Bible, and in rabbinic law.*"⁸ Newbold and the University of Pennsylvania emancipated Husik from a narrow provincialism. Some instances of such emancipation leave the freed one derelict and without stable foundations. For Husik, in the process of winning his freedom by proper employment of philosophical and philological tools he had sharpened, the process of emancipation led to "insight" into "the unity of human learning."

To one interested in this career, it is difficult to overestimate what had occurred to the man who now was twenty-seven years old. The immediate consequences of this discovery were evident: "in working out that thesis I brought together a Greek philosopher who lived in Athens in the fourth century B.C., an Arab of the Mohammedan faith who lived in Cordova in the eleventh century, a Christian scholastic of the late Middle Ages, and a rabbi of Mantua, who lived in the fifteenth century. And on the way I met many other Greeks, Christians, and Jews, writing in Greek, in Latin, in Arabic, and in Hebrew, all trying to solve the same problem of the nature of logic and of the human ideas and concepts."

The joy he took in the two years of research was undiminished by the reiterated suggestion that the task was "not worthwhile." In a negative sense, he had discovered that "he who has real enthusiasm and interest in ideas will not be content with popularization or sugar-coated pills." Likewise, in a negative sense, he had emancipated himself from "absorption in such a study of the Talmud as among Jews in Russia and Poland" produced "excessive narrowness and provincialism," without understanding "of the relation of talmudic law to other laws, ancient and modern, or perhaps even the true relation of the talmudic law to the law of the Bible." In an affirmative and positive sense, he was brought to realize the truth that "learning is universal, that it is as broad as Humanity and the human spirit." He learned, also, that "all human learning is interrelated, and the truly learned man says, to paraphrase a well-known Latin maxim: 'Nihil humanarum literarum a me alienum puto'."

The vision of a career of learning and scholarship had been granted to Husik, but the practical means which would enable him to pursue that career were not readily available. He had experience of teaching, but in the field of his principal interest there was no opening. Newbold taught undergraduate and graduate course work in classical philosophy, and the brilliance of his teaching was only paralleled by the breadth of the research he pursued and supervised. But Husik, once he had experienced the vision of the unity of human learning and had come to closer grips, not with commentaries upon commentaries, but with Aristotle's text itself, turned not only to the task of perfecting his knowledge in the field of medieval thought and to jurisprudence, but to that of resolving one of the most debated and difficult problems in Aristotelian studies. He set out to examine the problem of the authenticity of the whole of Aristotle's *Categories*. The problem was familiar to Aristotelian scholars of the ancient world and puzzled no less those who had perfected modern scholarly techniques. Husik's findings were published in 1904 in the *Philosophical Review*. "The Categories of Aristotle"[9] remained throughout Husik's life the contribution to philosophy of which he was most proud. He had reason to take pride in it. Sir David Ross, one of the great Aristotelian scholars of our time, remarked of the article thirty-four years later,[10] not only that Husik had "done a service to students of Aristotle by reminding them of his earlier article," but that in building up an "impressive series of resemblances between the *Categories* and the *Topics*," and by refuting the arguments of scholars disinclined to accept the authenticity of the work, he had come to a sound conclusion in his proof of its authenticity.

His paper on Aristotle's *Categories* is the work of a mature scholar who has perfected the instruments of his art. It signalizes Husik's freedom from theology and from the influence of authoritarian pronouncements. The evidence is that his "Aristotle on the Law of Contradiction and the Basis of the Syllogism,"[11] published in *Mind* in 1906, is a no less valuable contribution to philosophy. But while his freedom had been gained, it was not easily maintained and its implications were shortly to be seriously attacked. On 8 May 1908, Husik published in the *Jewish Exponent* a review of Professor David Neumark's *Geschichte der jüdischen Philosophie des Mittelalters;*[12] and he followed this with a review in the *Philosophical Review*.[13] Husik held that Neumark's work was "of great value" written by an author who had "mastered his field." Leaving from present consideration his disagreement with Neumark on the possibility of formulating a Jewish philosophy,[14] Husik expressed fundamental disagreement with Neumark's interpretation of Aristotle's theory of matter and form, and indicated an additional disagreement concerning the author's translations of passages from the *Physics* and the *Metaphysics*.

In 1910, Husik got down to essentials concerning Neumark's book in "A Recent View of Matter and Form in Aristotle."[15] He now regarded the undertaking as "pretentious in its scope and aim." He examined the translations made by Neumark and, in effect, indicated clearly enough his low evaluation of Neumark's Aristotelian scholarship. Neumark replied in *Archiv*.[16] Husik replied with "Matter and Form in

Aristotle: A Rejoinder,"[17] and Neumark again replied in the *Anhang* to *Geschichte der jüdischen Philosophie*.[18] Neumark's attack on Husik was scurrilous to a degree. Scholars, the most renowned of whom was Bäumker, supported Husik's interpretation of Aristotle. The sequel to the controversy come with the publication of Husik's *A History of Mediaeval Jewish Philosophy* in 1916, when Neumark, in the *Hebrew Union College Monthly*, attacked Husik in such wise that his review was described in the following terms: "for unblushing ferocity, for delight in revenge, for bad manners, one will hardly find anything to equal it in the history of American scholarship."[19] The controversy is of little importance now. Husik stood for an objective interpretation, the need for which has long since been recognized. It is significant, however, for the vigor with which Husik was attacked for denying that there is a "Jewish philosophy," and for denying the dictates of authority in scholarship.

Husik's interest in Aristotelian studies continued throughout his lifetime. He conducted seminars in the university in Aristotelian texts until the time of his retirement. Indeed, in 1938, he prepared a brief paper, read at the annual meeting of the American Philosophical Association and published the following year in the *Journal of Philosophy*,[20] bringing up to date his studies in the authenticity of Aristotle's *Categories*. He taught medieval philosophy, having been appointed lecturer in the university in 1911. In 1916, he published *A History of Mediaeval Jewish Philosophy*. A new interest appeared, however, and it was one in the development of which Husik most completely becomes a speculative philosopher. Husik was commissioned by the Committee of the Association of American Law Schools to translate Rudolf von Ihering's *Zweck im Recht* for the Modern Legal Philosophy series. His translation, published under the title *Law as Means to an End*, appeared in 1913. Three years later, an assistant professor in philosophy, he matriculated at the University of Pennsylvania law school. The event did not pass unnoticed. Louis E. Levinthal[21] was at the time a postgraduate student at the law school, working with Professor David W. Amram. Writing on "The Memory of Isaac Husik," in 1940, he recounts his surprise "to learn that Dr. Husik had enrolled as a freshman in law. Mr. Amram told me then that Dr. Husik had become interested in jurisprudence, having translated from the German a learned volume on the philosophy of law. Mr. Amram humorously remarked that, like another Alexander, eager to conquer unknown territories, Husik was starting upon the wide ocean of Anglo-Saxon law." Husik completed the course in law and took his LL.B. in 1919. Again the mystery recurred: "I recall his appearance before the County Board of

Law Examiners," continues Levinthal, "when he informed the rather awe-struck and admiring members of the Board that he would like to be admitted to our bar but had no intention or desire to practice as a lawyer. Some of my colleagues on the Board, never having heard of *Tora lishma*, were somewhat skeptical about such unadulterated study for a profession. I still recall the whispered remark of one of the men, after Dr. Husik had left the meeting room: 'I wonder why he really studied law!'"

Precisely why Husik did study law probably remained to the end a mystery to the members of the legal profession. Not only had he no intention of practicing law or even of passing his examinations for the bar; he had no intention, when he began his studies at the law school, of taking a degree. His analysis of the legal philosophy of Hans Kelsen was judged by editors to be "above the heads" of the readers of law reviews and eventually was published in a philosophical journal.[22] It is evident that Husik was drawn to law ultimately because he was interested in all aspects of human learning. It is also evident that the influence of his friend Edwin R. Keedy, professor of law at the University of Pennsylvania, provided the occasion for his determination to take regular courses in law, precisely as Newbold had earlier influenced his career. Following various discussions upon legal subjects, Keedy practically challenged Husik to answer his own question, "How is the law taught?" Husik entered the law school, as Keedy puts it, with "a chip on his shoulder." His first question, after the first examination of a law case, was "But where's the logic in that?" Keedy explained that there was no logic in it, that the law, "like Topsy, just growed." Husik was to spend many of his mature years attempting to determine the nature of the logic of law. As we shall see, his interest centered upon the problem of justice, its grounds and sanctions, and led him finally to examine the limits of subjectivity and objectivity expressed in egoism and altruism.

Meanwhile, in 1916, Husik had been appointed to an assistant professorship in philosophy at the University of Pennsylvania. In 1922 he advanced to a professorship, and the following year was appointed editor of the Jewish Publication Society of America. By this time, full recognition of his scholarship had occurred, and his life was devoted to teaching and to the presentation in articles and books of the fruits of his learning. He lectured at Yeshiva College in New York and at the Hebrew Union College in Cincinnati, which later invited him to become a member of its faculty. Husik's study of Stammler's *The Theory of Justice* appeared in 1925, and of Kelsen's legal philosophy in 1938. His great edition of Albo's *Ikkarim* in four volumes appeared from the press of the Jewish Publication Society in 1929–30. In 1933 he became editor for the philosophical section of the *Jewish Encyclopaedia*. He was a member of the governing board of Gratz College, and of the Board of License of the Associated Talmud Torahs. He was active in the American Oriental Society and the Pharisees, the American Philosophical Association and the American Academy for Jewish Research.

The latter years of his life were also the richest in terms of happiness and friendships. In 1926 he married Rose Gorfine of Baltimore, Maryland, and shortly after purchased the land in Churchville, Bucks County, on which the Husiks built their home. To it came their many friends. Conversation was equally divided between music—Mrs. Husik being a gifted pianist—and philosophy. The ties of friendship at the University of Pennsylvania remained close, and Husik counted among his intimates Henry Bradford Smith, Edgar A. Singer, Jr., and Louis W. Flaccus, his colleagues in the department of philosophy.

In 1931 Husik was seriously ill, but his recovery was complete. His health failed again in 1938 and the university granted him leave of absence. He returned, in the second semester of that year, both to his teaching and to his editing for the Jewish Publication Society, but a recurrence of the heart ailment ended fatally on 22 March 1939.

The three principal aspects of Husik's contribution to scholarship are classical philosophy, more particularly in the Aristotelian field, medieval Jewish philosophy, and philosophy of law. His interests in these fields are not compartmentalized. They are bound together in his thinking and writing by the "unity of human learning"—"most useful because it is most useless"—and by the ideal of scholarship, and control of the tools of scholarship, which he employed with equal facility in all fields. He wrote once that to "understand Hebrew" the scholar "must know Assyrian and Babylonian and Arabic and Syriac and even Egyptian. To understand the Semitic languages from a philological point of view, he must know the characteristics of the non-Semitic languages, hence he must be familiar with Sanscrit, Greek, Latin, and the Teutonic and Slavonic languages . . . a student in the phenomenon of human speech." He might similarly have laid down these enormous demands for scholarship in classical philosophy and in philosophy of law. Indeed, it is precisely the point of his article, "A Recent View of Matter and Form";[23] or, better, that article is a practical illustration of the application of his enormous resources as a scholar, precisely as "The Law of Nature, Hugo Grotius, and the Bible"[24] manifests it in the field of the law.

There is, however, a deeper interrelation of this triadic field of interest. The Western tradition, in Husik's judgment, is the result of the best of the two diverse streams of culture in which his own interests lay: Hebraism and Hellenism, the "two points of view" which "represent the fundamental elements of human civilization." For Husik, the Greek spirit was the embodiment of "sheer intellectual power," manifesting itself in humanism, in reason, and in science and art. The Hebraic spirit, he believed, was primarily moral and spiritual. His understanding of the Greek spirit produced the finest single study of his career, "The Categories of Aristotle." His understanding of the Hebraic spirit, fructified by his knowledge of that of the Greeks, led to speculation which enabled him to bridge the gaps between the eastern and western thought in Jewish medieval philosophy. But the true mediation of the two spirits for Husik is philosophy of law, where he found that combination of "science" and "justice" best displayed to make "a progressive humanity possible."

Sufficient has been said of Husik's contribution to Aristotelian scholarship. To the other two aspects of his thought we may now turn, mindful at the outset, while we endeavor to ascertain relations, that the center of gravity of his scholarship is to be found in his studies on Jewish medieval philosophy. This fact, obvious in the contents of the present volume, is even more evident upon consideration of those of his writings which appeared in book-form, principally *A History of Mediaeval Jewish Philosophy*, *Judah Messer Leon's Commentary on the Vetus Logica*, and *Ikkarim*. Even the formal study of "Matter and Form in Aristotle" was occasioned by Neumark's history of Jewish philosophy and belongs to the context of Husik's discussion of Neumark's work.[25]

The direction which Husik's interest took might seem to find its sufficient explanation in the fact that he was both a Jew and a philosopher. It would be more accurate, however, to say that, while this fact would account for his interest in Jewish philosophy, it was his realization of the problematic character of Jewish philosophy that explains his interest in the history of Jewish philosophy and, therefore, especially in Jewish medieval philosophy.

No one could insist more strongly than Husik did on the purely historical, nay, antiquarian character of all relevant modern studies on Jewish medieval philosophy. He knew too well, however, that "History for History's sake" is an absurdity. His insistence on the merely antiquarian character of all relevant modern studies on Jewish medieval philosophy was only the consequence, or the reverse side, of his conviction that in the modern world Jewish philosophy is not merely nonexistent but impossible. To establish this conviction, he had to explain why Jewish philosophy was possible in the past. And since he believed "that we cannot speak of a Jewish philosophy until the movement in the Middle Ages which culminated in the philosophy of Maimonides," it was only the study of Jewish medieval philosophy that enabled him to discern the precise reason why in the modern world Jewish philosophy is impossible. It was because of his view that in the modern world Jewish philosophy is impossible that Jewish medieval philosophy could not be of immediate, but only of historical interest to him. But the historical studies which established and elucidated this view served a function that was ultimately philosophic rather than historical.

To the superficial observer, Husik's attitude towards Jewish philosophy might appear to have been little more than an expression of his attitude towards the Jewish problem as a social problem. Husik had his roots in the Jewish tradition or, more specifically, in the closed Jewish community of eastern Europe of the late nineteenth century. The young Husik had to liberate himself from what he then called "the spiritual bondage of the ghetto," "the self-centered spirit" of traditional Judaism, "the narrow bigotry of racial and religious exclusiveness." He broke away from a manner of life which was "a life apart from the rest of the world." Thus he was naturally attracted by Jewish medieval philosophy, which was the greatest monument remembered within the ghetto walls of Jewish participation in the life of "the world." Yet most of the medieval Jewish philosophers appeared to be Jews in the very act of their philosophizing. They addressed their philosophic works to Jews and to Jews only. The emancipation of the Jews in the modern era, however, required that the Jew should contribute to civilization "not as a Jew, but as a man." Desiring to participate without reserve in modern civilization, the modern Jew could not take as his models the medieval Jewish philosophers. Thus Husik had to show that the type of procedure characteristic of Jewish medieval philosophy was no longer viable. Or, to stress another aspect of the same strand in Husik's thought, if self-respecting Jews were to participate in modern civilization, they had frankly to admit to themselves and to others the limitations of the Jewish heritage. Those who are in the habit of calling this whole attitude "assimilationist" are free to follow their bent provided they do not forget that philosophy itself is a kind of assimilation, assimilation to God or the Truth.

In fact, in order to judge fairly Husik's attitude towards Jewish philosophy, one merely has to consider his notion of philosophy. Philosophy, he says, "cannot afford to be either Jewish or Christian. It must aim to be universal and objective." Philosophy is "independent reflection" or "free inquiry." It is incompatible with "any belief in authority as such." It cannot "be bound by the religion in which one is born." "Philosophy qua philosophy [cannot] have a given basis forced upon it. Philosophy will be of value so long, and only so long, as it keeps itself independent of any special religious or other dogmatic doctrines." Furthermore, philosophy strives for knowledge for its own sake and hence cannot as such be enlisted in the service of any other cause, not even in that of ethical monotheism. Finally, philosophy is the attempt to discover the all-important truth on the basis of premises at the disposal of man as man. It is therefore essentially the affair of man as man, not of the Jew as Jew. From this point of view, the idea of a Jewish philosophy is as self-contradictory as the idea of a Christian mathematics or of a German physics.

Husik reached the same conclusion by considering the idea of a Jewish philosophy from the point of view of Judaism. "Judaism is not a philosophy or a science; it is a religion. It is a positive and historic faith." More specifically, Judaism is Law, divine, unchangeable, all-comprehensive law. Judaism means the Torah, and the correct translation of *tora* is law. Accordingly, "the most important monuments of postbiblical Jewish literature are devoted to the legal aspects of the Bible," not in any way to philosophy. The attitude characteristic of Judaism is "naive dogmatism," as distinguished from, and opposed to, the "rationalism" characteristic of philosophy. Philosophy is therefore not "indigenous to Judaism." The belief in an original Jewish philosophy is "unhistorical." "We can scarcely speak of philosophy in connection with the Bible" or with the talmudic literature. "The impulse to philosophizing came from the Greeks." "Philo can scarcely be called a philosopher." "The first Jew, so far as we know, to devote himself to philosophical and scientific discussions" was Isaac Israeli (c. 855–955). "We have no Thomas Aquinas. Maimonides does not occupy that place, and no one dreams of giving him such a place." Considering the basic relation of Judaism and philosophy, it is not surprising to observe that in times of persecution "the philosophic and scientific devotees" among the Jews "were the first to yield, and many of them abandoned Judaism."

From these premises, Husik was led to the conclusion that "the attempt of the medieval Jewish philosophers to establish Judaism on a philosophical basis could not, from the nature of the case, have been a success" or that the task which they set themselves was "hopeless." Husik's detailed argument can be reduced to three main assertions. In the first place, he questioned the genuinely philosophic character of Jewish medieval philosophy. To the extent to which the medieval thinkers admitted the authority of the divine law and conceived of the efforts of reason as necessarily subservient to that authority, they ceased to be philosophers. Naturally, they believed that they were accepting the authority of the divine law on the basis of stringent historical proof and that they were following in their philosophic reflections reason alone. This, however, was a delusion. Their philosophic activity "was the outcome of an intellectual naiveté which we have lost forever." In the second place, Husik denied that the efforts of Jewish medieval philosophy led to a justification of the teaching of the Bible. In attempting to reconcile the Bible with philosophy, they read Greek philosophy "into the Bible by a method which we do not now regard as legitimate." The agreement between the Bible and reason was proved by "the fiction of interpretation," i.e., by the substitution of an allegorical meaning for the genuine meaning of the biblical texts. Finally, insofar as Jewish medieval philosophers did use arguments of a genuinely philosophic character to prove genuinely biblical teachings, Husik denied that they were successful. In particular, he did not believe that the problem of divine knowledge and divine providence could be solved "on the basis of ordinary theism." It is possible that this belief led him to take a sympathetic view of the frankly antitheological philosophy of Spinoza.

Jewish philosophy was, then, possible in the Middle Ages and is impossible in the modern time because the medieval thinkers had "an intellectual naiveté which we have lost forever." Husik traced that naiveté to the absence in medieval thought of historical and literary criticism and, indeed, of an adequate historical knowledge. Medieval rationalism failed because rationalism can "not take the place of a knowledge of history." As regards historical criticism of the biblical text in particular, it was dangerous in the Middle Ages to state in plain terms even the most modest suggestions pointing in that direction. The absence of a historical approach is the crucial negative condition for the employment of the allegorical method, as well as for the development of "a harmonistic attitude in the presence of conflicting authorities." The modern turn to history culminates in "the modern theory of evolution." This doctrine forces us to trace the Bible not to God, but to the genius of the Jewish people. It destroys therewith forever the foundation, not only of the Jewish tradition in general, but of Jewish medieval philosophy in particular. Above all, the study of both Greek philosophic and Jewish literature that is conducted in the spirit of historical objectivity leads to "a truer understanding . . . of the provinces of positive religion and of scientific and philosophical thought." It was with the rise of that truer understanding that "Jewish philosophy has ceased."

To hold the view that the idea of a Jewish philosophy is a delusion is perfectly compatible with the admission that this delusion was under certain conditions inevitable and even salutary. Husik did not stint his praise of the achievement of Maimonides and other Jewish medieval philosophers. In the Middle Ages, only a philosophy that was emphatically Jewish could vindicate within Judaism the authority of reason or take up successfully the fight against superstition and obscurantism. It is true that the authority of reason was recognized by the classical philosophers. It is also true, however, that the classical philosophers were not confronted by the claims of Revelation. To have succeeded in vindicating the authority of reason in the presence of the claims of Revelation "is an achievement of absolute, not of relative value."

This will, perhaps, suffice to clarify the reasons for Husik's conception that his medieval studies were simply historical. They do explain in fact why there is no immediate connection between his philosophic and his historical studies. His chief philosophic interest was in the philosophy of law, and he insisted on the fact that "Judaism always meant law." He thought that "the most important question in law is justice" and, while "the spirit of science is still Greek in its origin," "the passion for justice is still Hebrew." He never attempted, however, to establish a connection between the philosophy of law and the philosophy of Judaism, unless his purely historical effort to show the biblical as well as the classical influences on Grotius be judged an exception. He attached particular importance to the efforts of Stammler and Kelsen. He paid little attention, however, to the work of Hermann Cohen, from which the doctrines of Stammler and Kelsen derive, a fact which can only be explained by Husik's attitude towards Jewish philosophy. He admitted that "the philosophical greatness of Hermann Cohen is beyond question," but he was dissatisfied "with Cohen as a Jewish philosopher." Cohen "made his Judaism tell in his philosophy," with the result that he was forced into "doubtful interpretations" of Judaism and especially of Jewish medieval philosophy. In interpreting the thought of the past, and especially Jewish thought, Cohen employed a method which he called "idealizing" interpretation. This consisted, to use the famous Kantian expression, in understanding the great thinkers of the past better than they understood themselves. Husik rejected this approach as "subjectivistic." He may well have thought that only if "systematic" philosophy and history of philosophy are kept strictly separate can the requirements of historical objectivity be fulfilled.

Husik's achievement bears witness to the fact that most valuable work can be done on the basis of his philosophy. "Objectivity," as Husik understood it, means in the first place the insistence upon the difference between facts and hypotheses. That difference had become somewhat obscured by the temporary success of the "higher criticism" of the nineteenth century. One cannot but admire the courage and the learning with which Husik maintained against all other contemporary students the genuine character of the entire *Categories* of Aristotle. "Objectivity" means, furthermore, impartiality or the refusal to engage in special pleading. Animated by the unobtrusive and unshakeable pride that prevents a man from stooping to make unwarranted claims for the group to which he belongs, Husik never for a moment attached to Jewish philosophies a greater philosophic or historical importance than they in fact possessed. His freedom from any apologetic tendencies has rarely been rivaled by other students in his field. "Objectivity" means also the ability to withstand the temptation to interpret the thought of the past in terms of modern thought, to say nothing of modern fashions. In the case of the study of Jewish medieval philosophy, that ability pre-supposes clarity, based on solid knowledge of the texts, concerning the fundamental difference between modern and medieval philosophy. Historians who try to modernize Jewish medieval philosophy cannot help but lay greater stress on its Platonic than upon its Aristotelian ele-ments, since Plato is, or seems to be, nearer to modern thought than Aristotle. Husik's sober picture of Jewish medieval philosophy brings out very forcefully the almost overwhelming influence of Aristotle. But this by itself would not be enough. History of philosophy is a modern discipline, a product of modern philosophy. And modern philosophy emerged by way of transformation of, if in opposition to, Latin or Christian scholasticism. Modern students are therefore tempted to inter-pret Jewish medieval philosophy on analogy to Christian scholasticism, or to conceive of Maimonides as the Jewish counterpart to Thomas Aquinas. A special effort is needed to realize the fundamental difference between Jewish medieval philosophy and Christian scholasticism. Husik has made this special effort. In this he was doubtless assisted by his familiarity with that tradition of Jewish rationalism the main sup-ports of which were the writings of Maimonides and which, as a tradi-tion, was perhaps never completely interrupted.

The character of a thing sets it off from other things. It is its "limit." One cannot describe the work of a scholar which has a character with-out speaking of that work's limitations. Were we to conceal the diffi-culties with which his position is beset we should certainly not act in the spirit of the Husik who never ceased extolling and practicing the duty of intellectual honesty. These difficulties may be reduced to three heads. They are related to the problems of objectivity, of historical evolution, and of the idea of a Jewish philosophy.

Husik especially opposed the "subjectivism" of Hermann Cohen. Yet, in reviewing a work of one of Cohen's disciples, he granted that "it is better frankly and deliberately to embrace subjectivity than to claim its opposite which cannot be realized, for pure objectivity does not exist." One cannot demand pure objectivity in such matters as are essentially controversial among honest and competent people. If it be true that all philosophic subjects are of this nature, or that all philosophic controversies reveal "our helpless struggle . . . in the face of the unknown," there can be no objective history of philosophy, unless the history of philosophy can be made independent of any specifically philosophic assumptions. Now, the very first thing that the historian of philosophy has to do is to delimit his field of inquiry or to distinguish his subject matter clearly from the subject matter of the other branches of history. History of philosophy presupposes knowledge of what philosophy is. But what philosophy is, is as controversial as any other philosophic subject. History of philosophy will then necessarily be subjective because its very basis is necessarily subjective. To begin with, there is indeed no reason why one should not define philosophy as the attempt to replace opinions about God, world, and man by genuine knowledge of God, world, and man. It is controversial, nevertheless, whether there is direct experience of God—or, more specifically, mystical experience—which supplies genuine knowledge of God as the first cause of all beings, and it is obvious that the manner in which this question is answered determines completely the precise meaning of philosophy. Husik summarily identified Jewish philosophy with Jewish rationalist philosophy and excluded Jewish mysticism and, in particular, the Kabbala from his history of that philosophy. We need not insist on the fact that he dealt in his work with the teaching of Yehuda Halevi, who, according to Husik's own presentation, is a mystic rather than a rationalist. What is decisive is the fact that Husik's definition of the subject matter of the history of Jewish philosophy would appear to be as subjective as that suggested by others whom he blamed for having unduly broadened the term "philosophy" by identifying Jewish philosophy with Jewish thought in general. It is true that all arbitrariness could be avoided if the historian would regard as philosophers only those competent thinkers who regarded themselves as philosophers. In fact, this would appear to be the only legitimate historical procedure or the only procedure compatible with the demands of objectivity, if the task of the historian of philosophy be indeed that of understanding the great thinkers of the past as they understood themselves. But this leads to a new and perhaps still more serious difficulty in regard to Jewish medieval philosophy. It would be easy to show that certainly the greatest of the Jewish medieval thinkers, Maimonides, did not regard himself as a philosopher. The ultimate consequence of a strictly objective procedure would then resemble the evaporation of the subject matter of the history of Jewish medieval philosophy.

The specific philosophic assumption that underlies Husik's historical studies is revealed not so much by the definitions of philosophy which he suggested, as by what he indicated concerning the relation of truth and history. He considered the emergence of a historical approach as the decisive reason for the obsolescence of Jewish medieval philosophy and, with it, of Jewish philosophy as such. "We are all the products of history," and this must be understood not only of our habits and prejudices but of our purest and freest thoughts as well. A man's thought will in the best case still be dependent on "the science of his day." Therefore, there cannot be final certainty. There cannot be certainty, that is, that the science of one's day is not fundamentally false. "It matters not whether the science is true or false. There have been many false sciences, and who knows whether a century later our science will not be upset in turn?" One cannot express the difficulty more tellingly than Husik himself does by speaking of "our helpless struggle in the face of the unknown." In his analysis of Jewish philosophy, Husik assumed that the foundations of Jewish orthodoxy had been destroyed "forever" by historical criticism. The modern Jew cannot help but reject "the old theory" of Judaism, according to which the substance of Judaism is the Torah as the unchangeable divine law, in favor of "the modern theory of evolution," according to which the Torah is the historical product of the genius of the Jewish people. Hence, the modern Jew is entitled and even obliged to "differentiate between the essential and the unessential in the Jewish *Weltanschauung*." "As a result of this process of selection a great part of the material is simply thrown overboard as unessential and the result of historical accident. What remains is kept for the time being as the eternal root of Judaism. But since we are all the products of history, who can warrant that the future may not see things otherwise than we do, and either go back or forward in the process of selection?" It is impossible to accept this too sanguine prospect, which still takes it for granted that in spite of our uncertainty concerning the modes of "selection" which may prevail in the future, we can be certain that the principle of "selection" (as opposed to the principle of obedient acceptance of the whole) is established forever. If human thought is radically historical, if the science of the day, and hence especially the historical science of the nineteenth and twentieth centuries which has destroyed "the old theory" of Judaism, may very well be upset in turn, one must admit, in fact one has already admitted, the possibility of a full restoration of "the old theory," i.e., of Jewish orthodoxy.

Husik's studies on Jewish medieval philosophy are animated by the spirit of historical objectivity. They are not animated by a distinctly Jewish spirit or conceived from a distinctly Jewish point of view. These studies could have been the work of a sufficiently equipped non-Jew or of a sufficiently equipped Jew for whom his being a Jew was merely an accident of birth. But Husik was deeply attached to Judaism. Being a philosopher, he was forced to clarify the meaning of that attachment and to bring it into harmony with his attachment to philosophy. His statements on this subject betray a certain vacillation which is not surprising, since "one scarcely knows what so-called modern Judaism stands for." He was not always sure whether the Judaism to which he was attached was primarily a spiritual force and not rather a racial entity. What keeps Judaism in existence "is the desire of the Jew to retain his identity. The philosophy which puts this desire in articulate terms may vary from age to age, the instinctive desire which prompts it is one and unchangeable. The blood of race is thicker than the water of metaphysics." Still, the view that seems to have prevailed with Husik was that "the genius of the Jewish people . . . created certain ideas and institutions which have proved their value by being accepted by the greater part of civilized humanity," and that these ideas and institutions rather than mere race commanded his allegiance. "The unity of God, and the idea of Ethics and Social Justice, is all that is left of Judaism." This Jewish heritage, he felt, is as essential for civilization as the Greek spirit of science and philosophy. From this conclusion, he was naturally led to demand that the Jewish heritage—"the passion for justice" or "the fear of the Lord"—be brought into some working relation with philosophy and science, or, more precisely, with modern philosophy and science. He was led, in other words, to subscribe to the demand for a modern philosophy of Judaism. "All will not be well in Judaism until the position of the Bible as a Jewish authority is dealt with in an adequate manner by Jewish scholars who are competent to do it . . . the scholar who is going to undertake it . . . must be a philosopher and thinker of eminent abilities. And he must have a love of his people and sympathy with its aspirations." That is to say, what is needed is a modern Jewish philosopher. This whole strand in Husik's thought is in full agreement with the principles of Hermann Cohen. It is therefore hard to see how Husik could with consistency have avoided agreeing with the principle of Cohen's approach to Jewish medieval philosophy. For the fundamental problem for the modern Jewish philosopher—the relation of the spirit of science and of the spirit of the Bible—was also the fundamental problem for the medieval Jewish philosopher. The modern Jewish philosopher will naturally try to learn as much as possible for his own task from his illustrious predecessors. Since he has achieved greater clarity at least about certain aspects of the fundamental issue than the medieval thinkers had, he will not be exclusively concerned with what the medieval thinkers explicitly or actually intended in elaborating their doctrines. He will be much more concerned with what these doctrines mean in the light of the fundamental issue, regardless of whether the medieval thinkers were aware of that meaning or not.

It would be wrong to belittle the strength of these objections. It might be more dangerous, especially in our time, to overestimate their force and to believe that they make doubtful the guiding intention of Husik the scholar. In spite of certain vacillations, he was convinced that a Jewish philosophy is impossible. This conviction was supported by the observation of the difficulties in which the greatest Jewish thinker of his time had become entangled. Owing to the historical character of all modern thought, Cohen was forced to accompany his philosophy of Judaism with interpretations of Jewish medieval philosophy, and these interpretations were extremely objectionable from the point of view of historical exactness. The concern with the "idealizing" interpretation proved to be ruinous to the concern with exact interpretation. A position that forces its holder to attach great importance to historical studies and at the same time prevents him from conducting these studies in an exact manner appears to be untenable. The demand for objectivity, for understanding the thought of the past as it really has been, without distorting it—this demand is not the powerless last gesture of the dying and deadening spirit of the nineteenth century, but the vivifying and invigorating call of that desire in man which prompts him to hate the lie in the soul more than anything else. This was the solid ground on which Husik stood. On this basis, the difficulties with which his position remains beset must be soluble. They cannot be solved without a far-reaching revision of his general views as well as of his interpretation of Jewish medieval thought. But all these changes will have to be inspired by the intention that guided his scholarly work.

That demand for objectivity met its severest speculative test for Husik in his research into the philosophy of law. In this field, he faced fundamental difficulties raised for philosophical analysis by the status of values and evaluation. And he faced them because, as he well realized, since the time of the Greek sophists the grounds for moral and legal sanctions, for obligation and of justice, had presented crucial problems for those who attack and those who defend the theory that the sanctions of law and morality are conventional and subjective.

As we have seen, the translation of von Ihering's *Law as Means to an End* was the occasion for Husik's initiation into jurisprudence. We have seen, as well, evidence of the genuine puzzle which his entrance into the law school of the University of Pennsylvania and which his appearance before the County Board of Law Examiners posed. Professor Amram's suggestion that Husik, like another Alexander, proposed to conquer the world of Anglo-Saxon law is significant in the light of the man's hunger for learning. More significant, certainly, is his remark to Professor Keedy concerning the logic of the law. But the logic or lack of logic of the law was for Husik but another way of expressing his profound interest in the grounds for the evaluation of just and unjust acts, and this interest, in turn, stems from his conviction that in practical action Hellenism and Hebraism, the two great streams of the Western tradition to the understanding of which he devoted his life, are most nearly conjoined.

Husik noted that Greek thought had encroached upon the province of practice which was regarded as "peculiarly the strong point of Judaism." The issue is a crucial one. In general, Husik regarded Hebraism and Hellenism as "two points of view" which, while they "represent the fundamental elements of human civilization," and supply the means to make "a progressive humanity possible," are antithetical. For Hebraism, in his estimation, is primarily a moral and spiritual power manifesting itself in "justice," while Hellenism is the embodiment of "sheer intellectual power," manifesting itself in humanism, in reason, in science, and in art. He sought the mediation of the two opposed traditions. Science by itself tends to be "hard and cruel and destructive as much as constructive"; justice without science is "blind and helpless." In particular, the mediation is difficult. Hellenism and Hebraism meet in the province of practice, but for the students of the Torah "sin and crime and vice and tort and breach of contract become simply violations of the one Law of God," and the problem of law itself is the "meaning of the eternal law." The source of this conception of the law Husik traces to the historical fact that the Jews had no state of their own, interpreted the law as the law of God as revealed in the Bible and in the Talmud, and were strictly limited in a rational approach to jurisprudence by the assumption that the Bible is a direct word of God, "supposed to be complete and perfect, irrespective of time and place."[26] Husik maintained that theoretical speculation among the Jews, resulting from the clash of Hebraism and Hellenism, left Jewish thought unaltered only in the fields of political and legal theory. In jurisprudence, he saw a meeting point in practice between the two spirits. He believed that in the philosophical and scientific techniques of Hellenism could be found the ground for substituting criticism for faith. But he also believed that the formal and rational contribution of Hellenism to the conception of justice needed the passion for justice which "is still Hebrew." He hoped to discover rational grounds for norms of justice. But he would no more embrace such a theory of absolute justice as that propounded by Plato than he would accept the unalterable mandate of "God's law." Paradoxically, he hoped to resolve the problem by substituting the variable for the objective standard.

It is evident that Husik realized early that no historical examination, such as that which he made of Grotius' jurisprudence, would satisfy the conditions of this enormously difficult problem. What is needed is not an examination of the interpretations and contexts of interpretations of a concept such as that of "natural law" but, rather, a methodology expertly employed in the concrete context of law itself. For if, as he maintains, Greek and Jew alike are concerned with conduct which is subject to evaluation, there must be a methodology for the philosopher of law, and the methodology must be applicable to a definable field of endeavor. As regards methodology, Husik's views are perhaps most explicitly stated in his reviews. Despite his high estimate of de Tourtoulou,[27] he disagrees fundamentally with the author of *Philosophy in the Development of Law* upon the meaning of the "conventional." Far from holding that a definition is devoid of interest because it is built upon convention, Husik maintains that it may be of interest if a useful system may be established upon a definition of the law, and furthermore he argues that this outcome may be forthcoming even if one jurist is in agreement with himself. More basically, the law is not merely conventional. It is also experimental, "experimental because the jurist picks out for study those facts which by general consensus are termed juridical and by a study of those facts he establishes a definition." Husik grants that the law is "conventional" simply because the jurist assumes that the definition, however vague and lacking in precision, exists in the general consciousness. But he insists finally that to be conventional does *not* mean to be arbitrary. Indeed, he holds that the law is not unique in this respect, inasmuch as all definitions are similarly conventional and experimental.

Still, the philosophical question remains: what is the law that exists in the general consciousness, "forced upon the human mind by the situation, natural and social," a definition of which is partly experimental and partly conventional? Husik sees clearly the relation of the question to similar questions arising in the field of mechanical and physical law. Moreover, he sees clearly its relation to morality and ethics, to its central problem of justice, and to its general sociological as well as analytical framework of reference. Some clue to Husik's answer to his own question is found in his review[28] of Hohfeld's *Fundamental Legal*

Conceptions. Here Husik maintains that Hohfeld's limitation of the law to the problem of "right" as the sufficient term at the basis of law, to the exclusion of "duty," deprives the author of a generic term basic to the entire science of jurisprudence. But Husik goes farther, insisting, by implication, that law is a science, that in jurisprudence, which is the science of law, it is necessary to have "*necessary* and *sufficient* basic concepts." What is required, he holds, is "insight into the conceptual basis of law."

But if law is a science, it is one which does differ from the sciences of mechanics and physics. And the differences suggest again the conflict between objectivity and subjectivity of judgment. In this regard, it is evident that Husik's approach to the problem is affected not only by the subject matter of the law, but also by the speculative philosophy of his colleague, Professor Edgar A. Singer, Jr. Singer, in his philosophy of "empirical idealism," insists upon a sharp distinction between sciences which are mechanically definable, and those which are definable in terms of teleology. It is fundamental to Singer's position that objective judgments may be made of events which occur "only for the most part," i.e., more than once and less than always. But this substructure of systematic philosophy, which appealed to Husik in part because of its Aristotelian implications, remains bare and abstract outside the structure of jurisprudence. A philosophy of law grounded on a not dissimilar speculative structure he found in Hans Kelsen's jurisprudence. Kelsen makes the significant differentiation between the natural law, which has no exceptions and cannot be violated, and a norm, which can be violated but can have no exception.

It is evident, moreover, in Husik's interest in Kelsen, that he fully realized the difficulty presented by his own question to Keedy in 1916. For the answer to the question, "Where's the logic in that?" could not now be one framed in terms of either abstract logic or even of mechanical laws. This is evident if we compare his attitude toward the systems of jurisprudence which he analyzed with such care in the articles "The Legal Philosophy of Rudolph Stammler"[29] and "The Legal Philosophy of Hans Kelsen."[30] Husik preferred Stammler's jurisprudence to Holland's because of Stammler's interest in reason and justice, rather than in positive law, his search for *a priori* rather than *a posteriori* principles of explanation, and his statement of the problem in terms of a theory of those propositions about law which have universal validity. He grants more than this, indeed, in his evaluation of Stammler. "The choice between two equally plausible definitions may seem arbitrary," he writes, but "preference should be given to that which gives the better results." And, on this pragmatic test, Husik maintains that Stammler "succeeds in deriving a great deal from his definition which does not lie in Holland's programme at all."

Nevertheless, the "very essence" of Stammler's method, in Husik's opinion, constitutes not only his strength but his weakness. Stammler's philosophy of law concerns *a priori* principles and must "deal with pure forms of legal thinking, i.e., with concepts which contain nothing of concrete legal material." It is the "vice of abstract logic," he concludes, which "taints all the reasoning of Stammler."

Husik holds that, while he as a jurist is no less rigorous in method than Stammler, Kelsen's philosophy of law is far the richer in content. Here, indeed, he found speculative philosophy concerned with "the conceptual basis of the law," allied with brilliant suggestions concerning "justice," rights, duties, and the problems of oughtness. Husik describes Kelsen's effort as one intended "to establish the presuppositions of a legal science on the basis of positive law," without taint of abstract logic or intrusion of concern with ethics. He is struck by Kelsen's identification of political theory (*Allgemeine Staatslehre*) and jurisprudence, by his distinctions between natural and normative sciences, between laws and norms, between cause and effect and "ought," between the indefinable and independent primary categories of thought, and between "Being" and "Ought."

It has been noted above that Husik emphasizes Kelsen's differentiation of the natural law, as that which has no exception and cannot be violated, from the norm, which can be violated but can have no exception. But Kelsen uses the differentiation primarily because the methodology of the science of norms will show the interrelations of norms, and will produce a concrete body of data for the solution to the most difficult problems of jurisprudence.

It is interesting, in the light of Husik's earlier investigations into natural law and as an application of the problem of subjective and objective judgments, that Kelsen's treatment of norms enables him to distinguish between the "ought" category and the habit which is its origin, as well as between norm and ground in natural law. This is the concrete application of the principle, implicit in Singer's philosophy, of teleology, that its principles operate for the most part. For the invariability of the norm is unaffected by the fact that the rule of law, "'The State wills to punish' does not mean that punishment invariably takes place, for it does not, but that punishment should take place. This is invariable if the norm is valid." And it is likewise interesting that, in the implications of Kelsen's jurisprudence, Husik finds the systematic denial of Hohfeld's hypothesis that right is the sufficient term at the basis of the law. Rather, duty is the fundamental concept, while right is secondary, and "it exists, where it does, only by grace of the law."

It is not necessary to enter in detail upon either Kelsen's jurisprudence or Husik's interpretation of it. It will suffice to point out that Husik agrees with Kelsen that there can be no *regressus in infinitum* in the establishment of the validity of a legal norm; that the "fundamental norm is merely the necessary presupposition of a positivistic conception of law"; and that "the content of the fundamental norm . . . must be gathered from the actual behavior of the people." And, for our purposes, it is more important to understand Husik's position than to examine his analysis of Kelsen's establishment of the state, in juristic terms, as the law and as "person," the "end point of legal imputation." For it is clear that in Kelsen's masterly interpretation of the law as norm and presupposition of positivistic law Husik found the ground for his own speculation upon jurisprudence, the systematic account which accorded with his own view of the law as definitional (i.e., conventional) and experimental. These are also the grounds for definability, objectivity, and for the enforcement of sanctions. Husik had brought the tools of scholarship and knowledge to the historical and systematic problems of interpretation of Aristotle, and was content with the knowledge those tools wrought. Granted knowledge and increasing knowledge, interpretation remained fundamental. He had reestablished, by his study of philosophy of law, his conviction that in philosophy only propositions are true or false. His courageous denial of the validity of the demand for faith and of the need for acceptance of authority now began to bear fruit. Faced by a seeming breakdown in causal law, if there be one exception, he also faced up to the problem of value judgments and oughtness. And in the "norm theory" and in teleology he discovered sound grounds for speculation.

The results of Husik's own speculation are evident in the unhappily too few manuscripts of his studies in jurisprudence which remain. These papers indicate the line of his thought, although they do not provide the whole system. In two extant manuscripts,[31] "Judge Made Law" and "The Theory of Justice," Husik makes two basic points. The first is his conviction that the law is not merely definitional and abstract but, rather, that it grows from human acts, conventions, and customs, and is legislated by the court. The second is the firm belief, in contrast to his skepticism concerning Jewish philosophy, that the grounds for juristic systems and for justice may be revealed.

As we have seen, the conception of norms is an essential portion of Kelsen's thinking. This phenomenological basis for values becomes fundamental to Husik's analyses. In his essay on "Judge Made Law," the abstract principles of this phenomenology begin to take shape. Husik regards the judge as one who uses inductive and deductive methods, and whose "universe is the accumulation of decisions as the field of the astronomer is the motion of the heavenly bodies and that of the biologist the animal species, past and present." He is doubtful that the first principles of the law ever had a beginning, but if they did so, he hazards the opinion that they were probably determined by "chance and convenience," and that conflict gave rise to rational reflection and "deliberate decisions in case of conflict," with the result that principles resulted. The legal sphere of the common law is, in this view, constantly invaded by extralegal customs until the courts, recognizing social necessity, adopt the customs to "keep the law in touch with life." And he reiterates Kelsen's view that "there is no law without a state."

"The Theory of Justice" gives the most rounded view of Husik's jurisprudence. The paper is notable for its recognition that two forms of "subjectivism," the cynicism of the sophists and the method of "trial by strength" of the courts of the Middle Ages, are both applications of the theory that justice is the rule of the stronger—a theory which, as Husik acutely points out, may sound reasonable until it is applied to the inhumanity the thug exercises in assaulting his innocent victim. Husik's principal concern is with human freedom in the law. He criticizes "justice" as explained in Marxian and Nietzschean terms: for "all talk of justice and injustice becomes idle" in economic determinism, "just as mechanical determinism makes all moral values meaningless." The theory of norms and that of freedom are now allied, and the "caprice" which subjective philosophy attempts to substitute for true freedom is denied the efficacy it is often thought to have.

But before we examine some consequences of this conception of freedom, it is essential to an understanding of Husik's thought to describe his attitude toward the ancient theory which attributes objective existence to abstract universals or ideas such as justice. Husik regards it as a necessary corollary to such a theory that difficulties of application of principles should arise, for "since the conditions of human society are constantly changing, applications of judgment in specific cases are bound to change." He insists, however, that "we must have some idea of justice if we want to do justice." The real issue arises—and this shows how deeply both Singer's philosophy and Kelsen's jurisprudence had affected his thought—when he turns to the formulation of the idea of justice. He sees that there is a difference between definitions, capable of verification, and propositions concerning natural phenomena, which are "true or not" according to their correspondence or lack of correspondence to facts.

Correspondence is, however, but a partial solution to the problem and, in fact, to depend upon it alone is an evasion of the essential issue. For we "do not describe an act" as just; we "put values in it." Husik maintains that what we now have is a real fact in nature and an evaluation. He is content to regard the universal occurrence of the word "justice" among men as sufficient justification for assuming that there is a common concept of it. He is not content, however, to leave unexamined the problem whether divergence and variations of definitions offered concerning the concept of value mean that any philosopher or jurist "intended to express what mankind has actually meant by Justice and no more." He observes acutely, and with the observation goes to the heart of the issue, that man is the carrier of values, and that the various definitions offered at various times were "intended to impose values on human acts, institutions, and relations."

There is no elaboration of this phenomenological theory. But the reader of "The Theory of Justice" approaches Husik's most mature speculation. The law, and with it, justice, are not abstracted from men's actions and institutions. They are not merely conventional or definitional. Their roots lie in morality and custom, yet the law is enforceable and the judge does legislate. Doubts concerning the grounds for these phenomena were settled in Husik's own mind. But no philosophical mind, unless it has converted philosophical principles into tenets of religious faith, hopes for, envisages, or would welcome absolute conviction. Husik still doubted, but his was the doubt a philosopher could welcome. To the problems it raised he could bring philosophical techniques and knowledge. No longer was he confronted by absolutes, either of religion or of Hellenistic rationalism. The problem with which "The Theory of Justice" ends is the conflict between the principles of action for one's own good and for the good of others. Husik urges that "the only answer is that we are as a matter of fact so constituted that we have by nature two opposite tendencies, the selfish and the altruistic, and that we feel by nature that we ought to follow the second while all our desire tends to follow the first."

It may well be that in this and in his concluding remarks may be found the expression of faith of a good man who has discovered in philosophy a haven from doubt: "the ethical imperative is innate and is felt instinctively to have the higher value, while at the same time being the more difficult to carry out. This social or altruistic sense grows in strength and precision as time and history advance. There is no possibility of getting beyond these brute facts of our being—justice and injustice are ultimate values and cannot find their sanction in anything more original." But if, on the other hand, this is an article of faith supplanting a deeply rooted skepticism which itself was the outcome of the blow the conception of the unity of human learning dealt to narrow provincialism, it is well to recall that Husik had achieved that faith by forty years of rigorous effort. Behind the assertion that justice is a primitive concept lay the stores of knowledge in history, theology, languages, and law. But whether his conclusion was the statement of a conviction or a problem, it was intended neither as an easy nor as a simple solution to the grim problems of egoism and altruism, the practical application of the antithesis of subjectivity and objectivity which Husik faced.

The editors of this book have been content to place Husik's essays in the chronological order suggested by their titles rather than by the dates of publication. They have assumed responsibility for selecting from the papers made available to them by the executrix of Husik's estate, Mrs. Rose Husik Forman, those they judged to be of permanent interest and value. They are well aware that other and perhaps equally important essays may have escaped their notice. Husik's publications were widely scattered and, in the task of editing, it became evident that the record of his publications is incomplete. For similar reasons, no definitive bibliography of Husik's writing could now be prepared. Moreover, the editors, rather than delay longer the publication of writings which have increasingly impressed them both by range and value, would regard completeness as less important than the immediate publication of the essays.

The editors acknowledge their indebtedness to Mrs. Forman, who initiated the plan for the publication of Professor Husik's essays and gave of her time and resources to the completion of the edition. They wish also to express appreciation of a generous subvention from the University of Pennsylvania.

Notes

1. *Revue Philosophique*, vol. 91, 291–94.

2. *Revue de Métaphysique et de Morale*, vol. 29 (Supplement), 11–12.

3. Now Judge of Common Pleas, Court No. 6, in Philadelphia. Judge Levinthal's "The Memory of Isaac Husik" appeared in *The Jewish Exponent* of 19 April 1940. It was read at the memorial exercises for Isaac Husik, held on 4 April 1940.

4. See below, chapters 7 and 8. [These chapters in the original book contain: "Review of *Geschichte der jüdischen Philosophie des Mittelalters, nach Problemen dargestellt*, von David Neumark," 68–72; and "Review of Professor Neumark's 'Attributenlehre'," 71–85. —Ed.]

5. After leaving his instructorship at Gratz College, he continued as a member of its governing board.

6. In Henry Samuel Morais' *The Jews of Philadelphia* it is noted (p. 158) that Husik was teacher "at 2856 and 2858 Lark Street, Port Richmond, with about sixty pupils."

7. Compare "The Unity of Human Learning," delivered at the Dropsie College Founder's Day Exercises, 9 May 1925, in which he expresses similar views. See below, 15–16. [Strauss's reference is to the first two pages of Husik's "The Unity of Human Learning," which essay appears in the original book on 15–26. —Ed.]

8. Editor's [i.e., Strauss's] italics.

9. See below, chapter 10. [This is the chapter that in the original book contains Husik's essay "The Categories of Aristotle," 96–112. —Ed.]

10. *Journal of Philosophy*, 3 August 1939, 431–33.

11. See below, chapter 9. [This is the chapter that in the original book contains Husik's essay "Aristotle on the Law of Contradiction and the Basis of the Syllogism," 87–95. —Ed.]

12. The first volume of Neumark's book appeared in 1907.

13. Vol. 17, 1908. See below, chapters 7 and 8. [These chapters in the original book contain: "Review of *Geschichte der jüdischen Philosophie des Mittelalters, nach Problemen dargestellt*, von David Neumark," 68–72; and "Review of Professor Neumark's 'Attributenlehre'," 71–85. —Ed.]

14. See below, xxiiiff., for Husik's opinion on this problem. [See above in the present essay, approximately beginning with the paragraph which commences "To the superficial observer, Husik's attitude towards Jewish philosophy . . . ," and ending with the paragraph which commences "To hold the view that the idea of a Jewish philosophy is a delusion. . . ." —Ed.]

15. *Archiv für Geschichte der Philosophie*, Bd. XXIII, 1910.

16. "Materie und Form bei Aristoteles," *Archiv für Geschichte der Philosophie*, Bd. XXIV, 1911.

17. *Archiv*, Bd. XXV, 1912.

18. *Anhang zum ersten Bande, Kapitel: Materie und Form bei Aristoteles*. Berlin, 1913.

19. See "Professor David Neumark, Ph.D., and 'Mr.' Husik," by S. Baruch, February 1917.

20. See below, chapter 10. [This is the chapter that in the original book contains Husik's essay "The Categories of Aristotle," 96–112. —Ed.]

21. See above, ix and footnote. [See above in the present essay, the fifth paragraph from the beginning, which commences with "His formal theological studies ended abruptly." Also see supra, note 3. —Ed.]

22. See below, chapter 20. [This is the chapter that in the original book contains Husik's essay "The Legal Philosophy of Hans Kelsen," 292–321. —Ed.]

23. *Archiv für Geschichte der Philosophie,* Bd. XXIII, no. 7.

24. *Hebrew Union College Annual,* vol. 2.

25. Its effect upon his "The Categories of Aristotle" has been mentioned. See above, xviff. [See above in the present essay, the paragraph containing notes 9 and 10, which commences with "The vision of a career of learning and scholarship had been granted to Husik." —Ed.]

26. This appears in Husik's analysis of the influence of the Bible upon Hugo Grotius' theory of jurisprudence.

27. Husik's review was published in the *University of Pennsylvania Law Review* 71, no. 4.

28. *University of Pennsylvania Law Review* 72, no. 3.

29. See below, chapter 19. [This is the chapter that in the original book contains Husik's essay "The Legal Philosophy of Rudolph Stammler," 273–91. —Ed.]

30. See below, chapter 20. [This is the chapter that in the original book contains Husik's essay "The Legal Philosophy of Hans Kelsen," 292–321. —Ed.]

31. See below, chapters 21 and 22. [These chapters in the original book contain: "The Theory of Justice," 322–31; and "Judge Made Law," 332–42. —Ed.]

5

Introductory Essay to Hermann Cohen,
Religion of Reason out of the Sources of Judaism

I doubt whether I am the best mediator between Hermann Cohen (1842–1918) and the present-day American reader. I grew up in an environment in which Cohen was the center of attraction for philosophically minded Jews who were devoted to Judaism; he was the master whom they revered. But it is more than forty years since I last studied or even read the *Religion of Reason*, and within the last twenty years I have only from time to time read or looked into some of his other writings. I write this introduction at the request of the publisher and of the translator. I can do no more than to give an account of the thoughts that occurred to me at a renewed reading of *Religion of Reason*. Perhaps they will be helpful to some readers.

Present-day readers can hardly avoid feeling that *Religion of Reason out of the Sources of Judaism* (first published in German in 1919) is a philosophic book and at the same time a Jewish book. It is philosophic since it is devoted to the religion of reason, and it is Jewish since it elucidates, nay, articulates that religion out of the sources of Judaism. This impression, while correct, is not as clear as it appears at first sight.

The Jewish religion might be understood as revealed religion. In that case the philosopher would accept revelation as it was accepted by Jews throughout the ages in an uninterrupted tradition and would bow to it; he would explicate it by the means of philosophy and especially defend it against its deniers or doubters, philosophic and non-philosophic. But this pursuit would not be philosophic since it rests on an assumption that the philosopher as philosopher cannot make or on an act of which the philosopher as philosopher is not capable. Cohen excludes this manner of understanding the relation between philosophy and Judaism by speaking of the religion of reason. "Revelation is [God's] creation of reason." Revelation is not "a historical act." For Cohen there are no revealed truths or revealed laws in the precise or traditional sense of the terms.

267

Let Judaism then be the religion of reason. Yet this can hardly mean that Judaism and the religion of reason are identical. Is the religion of reason found also, hence accidentally, in Judaism? Or is it the core of Judaism and only of Judaism? Cohen rejects both extremes. In particular he refuses to claim that Judaism is "the absolute religion." (This is not to deny that Cohen sometimes calls Judaism, and only Judaism, "the pure monotheism.") His solution of the difficulty is indicated by the word "source." Judaism is the source, the fountainhead of the religion of reason. The Jews "created the religion of reason." Judaism has taught mankind the religion of reason. The other religions either are altogether inadequate or they are derivative from Judaism. It is true that Judaism was not always in every respect the religion of reason. It needed the aid of Platonic, and above all of Kantian, philosophy to free itself completely from mythical and other irrelevancies. But this aid merely enabled Judaism to actualize fully what it meant to be from the beginning and what it fundamentally was at all times.

When one says that Cohen's *Religion of Reason* is a philosophic book, one is likely to assume that the religion of reason belongs to philosophy, that it is perhaps the most exalted part of philosophy. Yet Cohen makes a distinction between philosophy as philosophy, i.e., as scientific philosophy, and religion, and accordingly says that "Judaism has no share in philosophy" or that "Israel has no creative share in science." Nevertheless, there is according to him a kind of philosophic speculation whose matrix is religion and especially Judaism. This does not, however, do away with the fact that Cohen's *Religion of Reason* forms no part of his *System of Philosophy* (*System der Philosophie*).

The relation between religion and philosophy, between the *Religion of Reason* and the *System of Philosophy*, is complicated by the fact that the central part of the *System*, the *Ethics of the Pure Will* (*Ethik des reinen Willens*, first published in 1904), contains, and in a way culminates in, doctrines that at first glance seem to belong to the religion of reason: the doctrines of the unique God and the messianic future. Cohen has made these doctrines integral parts of his *Ethics*; he has transplanted them out of the sources of Judaism into his *Ethics*. He solves this difficulty by distinguishing between the God of ethics and the God peculiar to religion. Yet since it is reason that shows why and how ethics must be transcended by religion, religion "enters into the system of philosophy." Accordingly, the *Religion of Reason* would have to be understood as the crowning part of Cohen's *System of Philosophy*.

However, the last part of the title ("out of the Sources of Judaism") suggests that the *Religion of Reason* transcends the boundaries of the *System of Philosophy*, or of any system of philosophy. It suffices, perhaps, to compare the full title of Cohen's work with that of Kant's *Religion within the Limits of Mere Reason.* The obscurity that remains is ultimately due to the fact that while Cohen had a rare devotion to Judaism, he was hardly less devoted to what he understood by culture (science and secular scholarship, autonomous morality leading to socialist and democratic politics, and art); hence his insistence in particular on the "methodic distinction between ethics and religion." That distinction implies that while religion cannot be reduced to ethics, it remains dependent on "the method of ethics." Man's moral autonomy must not in any way be called in question. Cohen's goal was the same as that of the other Western spokesmen for Judaism who came after Mendelssohn: to establish a harmony between Judaism and culture, between *Tora* and *derekh erez.* But Cohen pursued this goal with unrivaled speculative power and intransigence.

Cohen's *Ethics* and, in fact, his whole *System of Philosophy* precedes his *Religion of Reason* "methodically." Furthermore, he is compelled now and then, especially in Chapters X and XI, to take issue with the Protestant, especially German, biblical criticism of his time and with the philosophy of history on which it is based. Finally, the order of the argument within the chapters does not always have the lucidity of which it is susceptible. These facts are likely to cause considerable difficulties to the reader of the *Religion of Reason.* They can be overcome by repeated readings. In the following remarks I could not help reproducing or imitating difficulties that Cohen has left unresolved.

The *Religion of Reason* presupposes, fundamentally, the *System of Philosophy*, but it does not force the Jewish data into that system as into a Procrustean bed. Cohen follows the intrinsic articulation of that Judaism which was authoritative for him as a liberal Jew who abhorred mysticism. He interprets Jewish thought by "idealizing" or "spiritualizing" it, i.e., by thinking it through and by understanding it in the light of its highest possibilities. In so doing he claims not merely to follow the only sound rule of interpreting any worthwhile text but to continue the process that had been going on in Judaism starting with the Bible itself.

Cohen follows the intrinsic articulation of the Bible by devoting the first chapter to the uniqueness of God. For the account of creation with which the Bible opens presupposes that one knows somehow what is meant by God. The decisive elucidation of what the Bible understands by God is given in the words that "the Eternal is one" and that His name is "I am": He is the one, the only one who or what is; compared to Him, nothing else is. "There is not only no other God but altogether no being except this unique being." Nature, the world, man included, is nothing. Only God's uniqueness thus strictly understood can justify the demand that man should love God with his whole heart, with his whole soul, and with his whole might.

It would not have been in accordance with the Bible or with Cohen's *System of Philosophy* if he had opened his work with a demonstration of the existence of God. God's uniqueness excludes His having existence, existence being essentially related to sense perception. According to Cohen, the idea of God, God as an idea and not a person, is required in the first place in order to establish the indispensable harmony between nature and morality: the ethically required eternity of ethical progress, the ethically required prospect of an infinite future of ethical progress, is not possible without the future eternity of the human race and therefore of nature as a whole; God "secures the ideal." It is incorrect but not altogether misleading to say that, according to Cohen, God is postulated by ethical reason.

The uniqueness of God demands or implies the rejection of the worship of "other gods." Cohen is himself animated by the prophets' "holy zeal against the false gods" when he says in his own name that "the service of other gods or of idols must be altogether exterminated." That holy zeal must overcome all hesitations stemming from the charm exerted by Greek plastics and even from compassion for the worshipers of false gods. At this point more than at any other Cohen reveals how radically he had come to question "culture" as he and his contemporaries understood it. The worship of the other gods is, according to him, necessarily worship of images. In agreement with the Decalogue, but not with Deuteronomy 4:15–19, he denies that there can be worship of sun, moon, and stars as such.

It follows furthermore from God's uniqueness that all things or beings other than God (except human artifacts) are His work. They do not come into being out of God, through emanation, for this would mean that Becoming is part of the true Being, whereas there is only and indeed "an immanent relation" of Being, the unique Being, to Becoming, of God to the world; Becoming is implied in the concept of God, in the definition of God as the unique being. It is in this way that Cohen is able to speak of creation. Creation is "the logical consequence" of the uniqueness of the divine being, nay, it is simply identical with it. Creation is therefore necessary. Cohen does not speak of creation as a free act. Nor is creation according to him a single act in or before time. Creation is continuous creation, continuous renewal. The sources of Judaism that Cohen uses for elucidating creation are almost all postbiblical. He derives his main support from Maimonides. Maimonides' doctrine of creation as set forth in the *Guide of the Perplexed* is, however, not easily recognizable in Cohen's interpretation.

Creation is above all the creation of man. But whereas creation as such is the immanent relation of God as the unique Being to Becoming, and Becoming is coeval with God, surely man, the human race, is not coeval with God. Cohen begins to treat the creation of man in the chapter on revelation. In revelation, he says, God enters into relation with man; he had not said that in creation God enters into relation with the world. Revelation is the continuation of creation since man as the rational and the moral being comes into being, i.e., is constituted, by revelation. Revelation is as little miraculous as creation. That is to say, it is not a unique event or a number of unique events in the remote past. Cohen follows closely the first and classic document of this idealization, Moses' extensive speech in Deuteronomy in which revelation is presented as not in heaven or, as Cohen almost contends, stemming from heaven, but as originating in the heart and reason of man, which are indeed God-given. "Man" here means the children of Israel. Hence, while revelation is not a unique event, it is primarily addressed to a unique people. Monotheism is to have its foundation in a national consciousness, or, more precisely, monotheism is to be the foundation of the consciousness of a nation: Israel, and Israel alone, came into being by virtue of dedication to the only God. Monotheism is not to have its foundation in the consciousness of select individuals. The outstanding individuals, in the first place Moses himself, are only the instruments of the spiritual liberation of the nation, representatives of the Jewish people, teachers of Israel, but by no means mediators between God and Israel.

Cohen had no doubt that in teaching the identity of Reason and Revelation he was in full agreement with "all," or "almost all," Jewish philosophers of the Middle Ages. He mentions in this respect with high praise, apart from Maimonides himself, Ibn Daud, who had assigned a very low status to "the prescriptions of obedience" as distinguished from "the rational principles" and had inferred from the weakness of their rank the weakness of their causes. Cohen abstracts from the fact that Ibn Daud says also—and this he says at the very end of his *Emuna Rama*—that "the prescriptions of obedience" are superior to the rational ones since they call for absolute obedience and submission to the divine will or for faith. The perfect emblem of "the prescriptions of obedience" is God's command to Abraham that he sacrifice his only child Isaac—a command that flagrantly contradicted His previous promise and therefore transcended reason. One need not be concerned here with whether and how Ibn Daud resolved the contradiction between the thought of which Cohen approves and the thought that Cohen dismisses, but one cannot help being impressed by his attempt to find the highest or deepest ground of "the prescriptions of obedience" in Abraham's willingness to sacrifice Isaac. The religion of reason leaves no place for absolute obedience or for what traditional Judaism considered the core of faith. The reader will have no difficulty in grasping the connection between the disappearance of obedience proper and the idealization or spiritualization of creation and revelation.

Owing to its peculiar function, which was to articulate the meaning of revelation especially from Moses' speech in Deuteronomy, the chapter on revelation had left obscure the relation of revelation and hence of God to man as distinguished from Israel. This relation becomes the theme in the next chapter. Cohen takes his bearings by the second account of the creation of man (Genesis 2), which he regards as freer from myth than the first (Genesis 1). The tree of knowledge indicates that it is knowledge that distinguishes man from all other creatures and that it is knowledge, especially the knowledge of good and evil, that characterizes his relation to God. That relation is correlation. Although God is not thinkable except as creator of the world and the world is not thinkable except as God's creature, the relation of God and the world is not yet correlation. God's relation to the world points to, or is absorbed by, His relation to man. In Cohen's deliberately exaggerated expression, God's being becomes actual in and through His correlation with man. "God is conditioned by the correlation with man. And man is conditioned by the correlation with God." God cannot be thought properly as being beyond His relation to man, and it is equally necessary to understand man, the creature constituted by reason or spirit, as essentially related to the unique God Who is spirit. Reason is the link between God and man. Reason is common to God and man. But it would contradict reason if man were only the passive partner in his correlation with God. Correlation means therefore also and especially that God and man are equally, if in different ways, active toward one another. (The reader must keep in mind the question of whether Cohen has always done justice to divine activity in the correlation.) Since these insights concern man as such, the "original universalism of the spirit in Israel" leads to the final universalism of the spirit in all men without any difference of rank whatever.

The full meaning of the correlation between God and man begins to come to sight only when human action is taken into consideration. Human action must be understood in the light of divine action and vice versa. The divine attributes of action (Exodus 34:6–7), as Cohen, following Maimonides, calls them and which he reduces to love and justice, are not meant to reveal the essence of God; yet they are adequate as the norm and model for man's actions. Love and justice together are holiness. "You shall be holy, for I, the Lord your God, am holy."

(Leviticus 19:2) Here the correlation is appropriately expressed, "and with the correlation mythology and polytheism cease. Holiness becomes morality." For with the progress of biblical thought Might recedes into the background and Holiness comes to the fore. As the quoted verse from Leviticus makes clear, holiness is for man a task, a never-ending, infinite task or an ideal, while it characterizes God's being; it is the ground of God's being, of His uniqueness. But God is only in regard to man: God is the Holy One for the sake of the holiness of man, which consists in man's sanctifying himself. Accordingly, the holy spirit is the spirit of man as well as of God, as Cohen tries to show by interpreting Psalm 51, "the classical passage" on the holy spirit, or rather on the spirit of holiness. To understand the holy spirit in isolation, as a person of its own, is tantamount to destroying the correlation: the holy spirit is the correlation between God and man. The competence of the holy spirit is limited to human morality—"the holy spirit is the human spirit"—but human morality is the only morality and therefore includes God's morality: there is no other standard of goodness and justice for God than for man. Cohen's notion of holiness does not seem to have much in common with "the so-called Holiness code" (Leviticus 17ff.), but—and this is of no mean significance—according to him morality, human, rational morality demands the unqualified abstention from incest.

Human action is, to begin with, action directed toward other men whom we know or believe to know from experience. The others, the men who live at our side, become inevitably those against whom we live; they are therefore not yet our fellowmen. Our fellowmen we do not know through experience pure and simple but only by virtue of the command that we love them. Only on the basis of this intrahuman correlation can the correlation of God and man become actual: in man's behavior toward men, not in his behavior toward God, the distinction between good and evil arises. It is in the light of "the social love" of our fellowmen that we must understand the love that proceeds from God and the love that is directed toward Him. Cohen discusses the intrahuman relation first on the political and legal level. He takes his bearings by the talmudic concept of the sons of Noah and the seven commandments given to them. The sons of Noah do not have to adhere to the religion of Israel, i.e., they do not have to acknowledge the only God although they are forbidden to blaspheme and to worship other gods; they are not believers and yet they may be citizens of the Jewish state. In this way Judaism laid the foundation for freedom of conscience and for toleration. Cohen does not claim to have proved that Judaism has laid the foundation for the freedom of conscience of all Jews.

Cohen then goes on to discuss "the discovery of man as the fellow-man" on the plane of "the social question" or, as he also says, of "the economic problem," i.e., of "the social distinction of the poor and the rich." For the prophets and the psalms it is poverty and not death and pain that constitutes the great suffering of man or the true enigma of human life. Our compassion for the poor, our love of the poor makes us understand or divine that God loves the poor and therefore in particular Israel (cf. Isaiah 41:14 and Amos 7:5), but Israel is only the symbol of mankind. God's love of the poor animates the whole social legislation of the Bible and above all the institution of the Sabbath, which prescribes rest also and in particular for servants and maids. Poverty becomes the prime object of compassion, of the affect that is a factor, nay, the factor of the moral law. In his *Ethics* Cohen had characterized the affect in general as a motor of the moral law. In his *Religion of Reason* he goes much beyond this by almost identifying the affect that fulfills that function with compassion. Here more than in the preceding chapters Cohen's heart speaks, and the fear that the Jewish heritage might be eroded vanishes. In his *Ethics* he had denied that love is the affective basis of virtue as such, and he replaced compassion by the virtue of humanity to which he devoted the last and crowning chapter. But the last and crowning chapter of the *Religion of Reason* is devoted to peace in the full Jewish meaning of *shalom*. This does not mean that he abandons the teaching of his *Ethics*; he keeps it intact as the ethical teaching; he merely supplements it by the religious teaching; but in so doing he profoundly transforms it. Humanity is among other things the virtue of art; peace is the virtue of eternity. The chapter on peace, and hence the *Religion of Reason*, concludes with an articulation of the Jewish posture toward death and the grave.

The chapter entitled "The Problem of Religious Love" is the only chapter that carries "problem" in its heading. One cannot say that this is intentional: Cohen does not write like Maimonides. But intentional or not, it is surely remarkable. Cohen speaks of the problem of religious love because he finds that religious love is taken too much for granted. Particularly striking is what he says about man's love of God. The love of God is love of an idea. To the objection that one cannot love an idea but only a person Cohen replies that "one can love only ideas; even in sensual love one loves only the idealized person." Pure love is directed only toward models of action, and no human being can be such a model in the precise sense. Pure love is love of the moral ideal. It is longing, not for union with God, but for nearness to God, that is to say, for never-ceasing, infinite sanctification of man: God alone is holy.

"The discovery of man as the fellowman," while articulated out of the sources of Judaism, belongs in itself, as one can say with some exaggeration, to the competence of ethics; the discovery of "the individual as the I" surely goes beyond that competence and is peculiar to religion. The discovery of man as the fellowman was achieved by "the social prophets"; the discovery of the individual as the I was the great progress due to Ezekiel, who seems to be unduly concerned with sacrifices and the temple and therefore to be regressive. It could seem that the discovery of the fellowman, the Thou, implies the discovery of the individual as the I. According to Cohen this is not the case, if one understands "individual" in the strict sense, "the absolute individual," "the isolated individual," whose concern transcends state and society—which are ultimately "only dark blind masses"—and therefore transcends ethics. The correlation between God and man is above all the correlation between God and the individual; the absolute individual, "the seeing individual," is man standing before God.

Regardless of whether one accepts Cohen's religion of reason, one must ponder carefully his confrontation of the seeing individual with the dark blind masses of state and society. Only in the I can the individual be discovered; only on the basis of this discovery can the fellowman be seen as an individual and thus truly become a fellowman. The reason is this: I have no right to set myself up as a moral judge of other human beings, be they poor or rich; even the judge who condemns the criminal is not meant to pass a moral judgment. But I must pass moral judgment on myself. The individual is discovered by his realization that he is morally guilty and by what that realization leads to. He cannot acquit himself, and yet he needs liberation from his feeling of guilt, i.e., purification from his guilt, his sin. Only God can liberate the individual from his sin and thus transform the individual into an I. The I liberated from sin, the redeemed I, the I redeemed before God, the I reconciled with God is the ultimate goal toward which man must strive.

For the reconciliation with God can only be the consummation of the reconciliation of man with himself. This reconciliation consists in man's "repentance," in his return from his evil ways or, more tellingly, in his making himself a new heart and a new spirit. The first step in this return is man's confession of his sin, his self-punishment, in and before the stateless congregation, i.e., together with all other members of the congregation as his fellow sinners. The return is the return to God Who alone redeems from sin. This redemptive aspect of God is what is meant by His goodness or grace as distinguished from His holiness. "It is the essence of God to forgive man's sin . . . for His essence consists in His correlation with man." When Cohen speaks, deeply moved, of God's help in reconciling man to Him, he is never oblivious of man's autonomy, which is indeed inseparable from his finiteness or frailty; he is not even oblivious of it when he interprets the verses in the prophets and the psalms in which God is compared to the shepherd and men or the souls to His lambs. But it should be noted that in speaking of God's goodness Cohen calls His good action "personlike."

Cohen confirms and deepens his doctrine of reconciliation in his discussion of the Day of Atonement, which in German is called the Day of Reconciliation, and of its primacy over all other festivals in the Jewish year. In this context he makes clear how he understands the relation of sin and punishment: the punishment is the suffering that is inseparable from human life and that leads to man's redemption provided he recognizes it as divine dispensation, as necessary for the development of his self.

The justification of suffering, and hence in particular of Israel's suffering, and not the prospect of the messianic age as the ideal goal of political and social progress, leads Cohen in his *Religion of Reason* to the discussion of "the idea of the Messiah and mankind." According to him, the idea of mankind, of all men without distinctions like those between Greeks and barbarians or between the wise and the vulgar, has at least its historical origin in religion, in monotheism; the unique God is the God of all men, of all nations. "For the Greek, man was only the Greek," despite the fact that the Stoa at any rate was "cosmopolitan," for the Stoa thought only of the individuals, not of the nations. The universalism of the prophets, which comprehends in one thought and hope all nations, is "a thought of the boldest and world-political courage"; the prophets thus became "the originators of the concept of world history," nay, of "the concept of history as the being of the future," for they placed the ideal, which is opposed to all present and past reality, not beyond time but in the future. Mankind as one, because unified in its highest aspiration, never was or is, but will be; its development never comes to an end; that development is progress. By turning toward the future the prophets completed the break with myth that had been achieved by monotheism, the message of the unique God as the God of morality. Israel, the eternal people, is the symbol of mankind. Israel had to survive the destruction of the Jewish state; it has to survive for all times because it is the creator of the Bible, and creation is in this case, too, a never-ending renewal. The Jewish state as one state among many would not point as unmistakably to the unity of mankind as the one stateless people dedicated uniquely to the service of the unique God, the Lord of the whole earth.

This is the meaning of Israel's election: to be an eternal witness to pure monotheism, to be *the* martyr, to be the suffering servant of the Lord. The misery of Jewish history is grounded in messianism, which demands humble submission to suffering and hence the rejection of the state as the protector against suffering. Israel has the vocation not only to preserve the true worship of God but also to propagate it among the nations: through its suffering Israel acquires the right to convert them; the freely accepted suffering makes manifest the historic worthiness of the sufferer. For the prophets and by the prophets Israel became the rest or remainder of Israel, the ideal Israel, the Israel of the future, that is to say, the future of mankind. The patriotism of the prophets is at bottom nothing but universalism.

In this spirit Cohen discusses the messianic passages in the prophetic books. In his idealizing interpretation there is no place for the hope that Israel will return to its own country, to say nothing of the restoration of the temple. He justifies this interpretation in particular by the fact that Jeremiah foretold the return from captivity of Israel's bad neighbors who had also been deported, but this does not do away with the fact that he brought the same good message to Israel. Nor does Ezekiel's prophecy, that after Israel's "merely political restoration" it will extirpate the abominations, do away with the fact that he prophesied also and in the first place Israel's "merely political restoration." It is perhaps more important to note that according to Cohen's interpretation of Isaiah 9:6–7 the day of the Lord can no longer seriously be thought to be imminent, for the new time is meant to be a new eternity: could not eternity, even a new eternity, be imminent? Cohen himself admits that the prophets did not explicitly place the end of the days in a wholly remote future; he traces that fact to the preponderance of their concern with a political future of their own nation and of mankind. He, however, regards as the essence of messianism the "suprasensuousness"—the eternal futurity—of the earthly future of mankind within its natural development, which is a progressive movement.

.   The concern with the earthly and natural (nonmiraculous) future seems to be weakened by the beliefs in the immortality of the soul and in the resurrection of the body. These beliefs are unacceptable to Cohen in their traditional, "dogmatic" form. He is therefore compelled to examine the sources of Judaism on these subjects and to idealize what they say as much as possible. Belief in the survival of the souls is in an early stage connected with the worship of ancestors. In this stage the grave is of utmost importance, as it still is in the biblical stories of Abraham and Joseph. Dying is understood in the Bible as going to one's fathers: the individual soul goes or enters into the soul of the people, and the people does not die. Immortality means, therefore, the historical survival of the fathers, i.e., of the individual in the historical continuity of his people. Cohen uses this apparently redundant expression in order to exclude any thought of the survival of the souls in the literal sense. On the basis of messianism, immortality comes to mean the survival of the soul in the historical process of the human race. Even more than immortality can the "image" of resurrection convey the thought of the eternal sequence of generations of men in the historical unity of the peoples in general, and of the messianic people in particular. This does not mean that the individual is only a link in a chain, for through the discovery of the individual in the light of holiness, i.e., morality, resurrection takes on the purely moral meaning of rebirth, of self-renewal; the link gives life to the chain of the generations.

It is characteristic of monotheism, as distinguished from myth, that it seeks a meaning of death only for the sake of the morally concerned individual. Accordingly, Koheleth says that when man dies the soul returns to God Who has given it—and not to the nether world of myth. Only in this way can one reconcile death with the infinite task of morality or self-purification. This infinite endeavor must be understood in the spirit of messianism: the other life is the historical future, the future in the unending history of the human race. Under "Persian influence" the beliefs in immortality and resurrection combined, became active in the Jewish mind, and were identified with the belief in the messianic age throughout rabbinical antiquity; hence the historical character of the messianic future became endangered: the messianic future, which is to come by virtue of man's actions, was in danger of being understood as the shadowy kingdom of heaven in the Beyond for whose coming one can only wait and pray. This danger was averted in Judaism, however, because of the persistent awareness of the difference between the messianic age, on the one hand, and immortality and resurrection, on the other; that awareness was most clearly expressed by Maimonides in his *Code*.

Cohen especially loathed the notion of hell; concern with eternal punishment, as more obviously the concern with reward, stems from man's natural eudaemonism and is therefore incompatible with ethics proper. It is true that justice, and hence also punitive justice, is thought to be an attribute of God; but, as Cohen says, tacitly but all the more remarkably deviating from Maimonides (*Guide of the Perplexed* 1.54), His justice, as distinguished from His love, cannot be the model of human action; His punitive justice remains entirely His mystery and cannot be the concern of morally concerned men. For an understanding of this assertion one must consider that, according to Cohen, Maimonides asserts for the messianic time "in precise clarity the principle of socialism"; he probably means by this the disappearance of all obstacles to the knowledge of God. He is, of course, silent about the

"Laws concerning Kings and Their Wars" with which Maimonides so impressively concludes his *Code*. It is therefore all the more praiseworthy that Cohen accepts the notion, so deeply rooted in Jewish piety, of "the merit of the fathers": "the patriarchs alone have every merit that their descendants can acquire." Here enthusiasm for the future gives way to gratitude for the past; it would be better to say that enthusiasm for the future reveals its being rooted in a past to which veneration and gratitude are due. These apparently contradictory tendencies are reconciled by an idealizing interpretation or by the fact that the religion of reason is the religion of reason out of the sources of Judaism. Under no circumstances must the merit of the fathers be permitted to cast the slightest doubt or veil on the autonomy of the individual.

The most obvious difficulty to which Judaism is exposed in modern times is caused by its being Law, an all-comprehensive, sacred law. Cohen was assisted in overcoming these difficulties by his failure to take into consideration the extreme questioning of law as such as it was known to him from Plato's *Statesman*. He has the courage to say that Revelation and Law are identical. According to him, the Law is either the moral law or is meant to contribute to man's moral education. More precisely, all particular commandments concern means; their suitability is therefore subject to examination. In the last analysis, the Law is symbol. The only danger entailed in the universal supremacy of the Law, the subservience of everything a man does to the ideal of holiness, is that it leaves no room for man's theoretical and esthetic interests, for "culture" in one sense of the term; but these interests lack the firm center that only the unique God of Jewish monotheism can supply. Besides, this danger can be reduced, and partly has been reduced, by correctives that do not render questionable the Law as a whole.

Cohen admits that, indirectly through Moses Mendelssohn and directly through the Reform movement through which the Jews gained access to the culture of the nations in whose midst they live, the power of the Law has been weakened, but he insists that it has not been destroyed. The survival of Judaism still calls for a certain self-isolation of the Jews within the world of culture and therefore for the Law, however much its scope and its details may have to be modified; it calls for such an isolation "as long as the Jewish religion stands in opposition to other forms of monotheism" or the other forms of monotheism stand in opposition to the Jewish religion, in other words, as long as the messianic age has not yet come.

Yet isolation is not the sole purpose of the Law; its main purpose is the idealization or sanctification of the whole of human life through the living correlation with God. In the chapter on the Law, Cohen engages in a critique of Zionism about which it is not necessary to say anything since it is easily intelligible to every reader. As the reader can hardly fail to notice, in the same context Cohen seems almost to face the possibility actualized not long after his death by national socialism. But his "optimism" was too strong.

The soul and inwardness of the Law is prayer. Prayer gives life to all actions prescribed by the Law, so much so that one may doubt whether prayer is commanded in any of the 613 particular commandments of which the Law is traditionally held to consist. Prayer is the language of the correlation of man with God. As such it must be a dialogue while being a monologue. It is this because it expresses man's love of God as an actual experience of the soul, for the soul is given by God and hence is not exclusively the human soul; therefore it can speak to God and with God. Love of God is the highest form of human love; it is longing for God, for nearness to Him. This must not make one forget that man's longing for God is longing for his redemption, for his moral salvation—a longing that originates in anguish. But man is not merely his soul; all human cares and sorrows become legitimate themes of prayer. Above all, the dangers to intellectual probity are impenetrable for man; if all other purposes of prayer could be questioned, its necessity for veracity, for purity of the soul cannot: God alone can create in man a pure heart. Cohen speaks with emphasis of the danger to veracity that comes from one's fear of being despised by flesh and blood for confessing and professing the religious truth. The Jewish notion of prayer is characterized by the fact that the synagogue is not called a house of prayer but a house of learning or study, for that house is built not for the individual who prays in solitude but for the congregation that lives in anticipation of the messianic kingdom of God; for its coming "in your lives and in your days and in the life of the whole house of Israel" Jews pray in the Kaddish. Yet the congregation cannot be preserved without the Law and therefore without the study of the Law.

The headings of the last five chapters are the only ones that are identical or almost identical with chapter headings in the *Ethics*. The chapter entitled "The Virtues" takes the place of the chapters of the *Ethics* that are entitled, "The Concept of Virtue," "Truthfulness," and "Modesty." The reason for this change is the following. In the *Ethics* Cohen had said that, according to the prophets, God is truth, and they meant by this that "the true God is the ground of morality." But he had continued: "But this is the difference, this is the gulf between religion and ethics, that in ethics no extraneous foundation can be laid; even God must not be for ethics the methodic ground of moral knowledge." Accordingly, in the *Religion of Reason* the true God becomes the ground of morality or more specifically of the virtues; the discussion of the virtues in general and of truth and truthfulness in particular cannot even externally be separated from one another. This is not to deny that even in the *Religion of Reason,* while insisting that "religion must be truth," he still says: "what would truth be without scientific knowledge as its foundation?" It is possible, though, that he means here by "scientific knowledge" rational knowledge and in particular ethical knowledge. Since God is the truth, He cannot in any way be or become a symbol. Truthfulness or intellectual probity animates Judaism in general and Jewish medieval philosophy, which always recognized the authority of reason, in particular. But truthfulness requires knowledge, and our knowledge is imperfect. Therefore truthfulness must be accompanied by modesty, which is the virtue of skepticism. In his *Religion of Reason* Cohen makes no distinction between modesty and humility except to say that he who is humble before God is modest toward men. In his *Ethics* he had said that modesty keeps unimpaired the feeling of one's own worth whereas humility makes the assumption of one's own worthlessness.

In the chapter on fidelity in the *Ethics* Cohen had said that religion must transform itself or be transformed into ethics: religion is a state of nature while the state of maturity is ethics. The transformation must be prepared by the idealization of religion. But this presupposes in the first place fidelity to religion, fidelity to one's religion. In the same chapter he comes to speak of the apparent conflict between fidelity to one's "lost nationality" and fidelity to the state: did he have in mind the Jews in particular? He speaks of gratitude only to the state. In the much shorter chapter on fidelity in the *Religion of Reason* he speaks much more fully of the connection between fidelity and gratitude; he quotes there "If I forget thee, let my right hand forget me." A peculiarly Jewish act of fidelity is the study of the Torah. "Fidelity in the study of the Torah did not permit that the noble character of the folk soul perish amidst the oppression of millennia." He does not speak of the moral obligation not to desert one's people especially when they are in need—and when are Jews not in need?—because for him this went without saying. Almost his whole work, his whole life bears testimony to this fidelity and his gratitude to the Jewish heritage—a fidelity limited only by his intellectual probity, by a virtue that he traced to that very heritage.

Cohen was a faithful warner and comforter to many Jews. At the very least he showed them most effectively how Jews can live with dignity as Jews in a non-Jewish, even hostile, world while participating in that world. In showing this he assumed indeed that the state is liberal or moving toward liberalism. Yet what he said about Jewish martyrdom

III

Lectures on Contemporary Jewish Issues

promised. So I shall limit myself in my exposition tonight to a discussion of Freud's thesis. If anyone is interested in the question regarding Machiavelli, we can perhaps take this up in the discussion.[4]

From the outset I knew that I would not deal with two subjects necessarily connected with the subject of tonight. The first is psychoanalysis, and the second is Freud the Jew. Regarding the second subject, I am so fortunate as to be able to tell you that there appeared an article on this subject—"Sigmund Freud, the Jew"—by Ernst Simon of the Hebrew University in the Yearbook 2 of the Leo Baeck Institute of Jews from Germany (1957).[5] Ernst Simon has read, it seems, everything which Freud wrote, and in addition the numerous writings which deal with Freud's life and character. Freud, it appears, regarded himself as a good Jew. What he meant by this can be stated as follows. The nonreligious Jews of our time may be divided into two classes. There are those who wish that they had not been born Jews, who regard their Jewish origin as a misfortune; and there are those who do not wish not to be born as Jews or are even perhaps glad to be born as Jews. They feel that the best in them is due to their Jewish origin, or at any rate inextricably linked with that. In a strange way they still believe somehow that the Jews are the chosen people. In continental Europe they revealed themselves frequently by the fact that they regarded themselves as Jews and not as Germans, Austrians, and so on. Freud was certainly a good Jew in this sense. I go a step further. I believe that Jews of type number two are both better and happier men than Jews of type number one, and I think that this preference can be defended on rational and not merely Jewish grounds. There is a proverb of old: "Adorn the Sparta which was given to you at birth." One must not run away from one's place, from one's fate, but accept it, and even love it and praise it. Surely people, and in particular Jews, may be so unfortunately born that no one can blame them if they run away from the locus of their birth. But this cannot reasonably be said of Jews as Jews, of a group of men which, humanly speaking, still exists because of the unequalled heroic dedication and decision made by our ancestors three thousand years ago and repeated innumerable times since. Sacrifices of the highest order had to be brought by every generation of Jews, not the least of them being the bearing of indescribable indignities. But we held our heads high since we knew in our bones that only he is contemptible who depends in his self-respect on the respect of others. I am not quite certain whether Freud was a good Jew in this sense. The reason why I am not certain is this—that he was somewhat too concerned with what he called "anti-Semitism." This overconcern arose not only in Freud but in quite a few other Jews of his generation, and perhaps even of younger generations, from the expectation of a truly or unqualifiedly liberal society in which the rights of man as man would be recognized not only legally but by every noncriminal member of society in private life. This expectation presupposed that practically all men can be habitually rational in their conduct. Freud questioned this presupposition, but he did not draw the necessary consequences from this questioning. He remained vulnerable to "anti-Semitism."

I deem it appropriate to read to you a few passages from Ernst Simon's analysis. After having quoted a couple of passages from this work, *Moses and Monotheism*, he says:

> These words are penetrated by deep pathos, the pathos of a Jew who is proud of the life-force of his ancient people. This is the first positive position taken in the book: it is a direct continuation of Freud's Jewish nationalism, which previously had taken on a vague and ambivalent form and now attained clearer and less hesitant expression. The second positive note is struck when Freud speaks of the pathos of Jewish suffering. . . . How strong is the Jewish pride of the aged Freud! On the basis of his opinions we would expect him to add that the entire outlook of the people of Israel, despite its stubborn clinging to its religion, is founded on a fundamental misconception—the holiness of an 'illusion' without any 'future.' Freud would not have denied the truth of his argument during any rational debate, but here it does not influence his choice of words and his style and, indeed, seems to have been forgotten at the time he wrote these and some similar passages. . . . Freud speaks here like a great Jewish *spiritual patriot*, and the positive effect upon him is so great that he uses arguments which cancel one another out. We may presume that he realized these discrepancies, but did not attach decisive importance to them and thought that they could be resolved by a higher stage of synthesis. But there is another contradiction which almost annihilates the main theory of his book. At the beginning of the second essay Freud claims that Jewish monotheism was borrowed from Egypt. But later, in the third essay, he states that the teacher of Moses, King Ikhnaton, 'followed perhaps intimations which through his mother or by other ways had reached him from the Near or the Far East.' Thus 'the idea of monotheism must (!) have returned in the fashion of a boomerang (!) into the country of its origin.' (Note the logical jump from *'perhaps* the Near or the Far East' to a cogent conclusion as to Palestine as the homeland of monotheism!)[6]

Simon tries to give a kind of psychoanalytical interpretation into which I cannot go because I am not competent.

Instead I prefer to suggest another definition of the good Jew, that is, the nonreligious good Jew. He is a man who knows that he is a Jew, that he belongs to the Jewish people, and that the root of his problem is the fact that he cannot believe what his ancestors believed. This leads to a dedicated concern with the truth of the Jewish tradition. I believe one can say that Freud was a good Jew without qualifications in this sense. The question is whether he was a good thinker on this august theme.

After reading the book I found it indispensable not to give a lecture proper but a kind of commentary on various passages. I begin, naturally, at the beginning. The opening words are "To deny." Freud immediately makes clear, I do not know whether with full intention, that what he is doing is something negative, something destructive, something subversive, a reprobation of something. In Jewish literature we have an interesting parallel to that, although Freud was probably unaware of it. In one of the greatest Jewish works of the Middle Ages, Yehuda Halevi's *Kuzari*, a pagan king is converted to Judaism by a conversation with a rabbi, after having had conversations, first, with a philosopher, then with a Christian, and finally with a Muslim. The philosopher is the only individual among these four men who begins his speech with a negation.[7] The use of the term philosopher at this time meant automatically not a Jew.

The first sentence is: "To deny a people the man whom it praises as the greatest of its sons is not a deed to be undertaken lightheartedly—especially by one belonging to that people."[8] The denial of Freud is directed against himself, a self-denial, a moral action, an action requiring self-sacrifice. "No consideration, however, will move me to set aside truth in favor of supposed national interests. Moreover, the elucidation of the mere facts of the problem may be expected to deepen our insight into the situation with which they are concerned." The act of Freud is an act of self-denial, but also an act which looks like an act of treason against the national interest. The justification is that it is done for the sake of truth. The question arises, is truth a part of the national interest? Does the true national interest necessarily lead to truth? Does this apply to the Jewish people in particular or to all peoples? At any rate Freud seems to make a suggestion of the utmost importance—that truth is more important than society. Truth means knowing the truth as distinguished, in the first place, from proclaiming the truth. Freud, however, tacitly identifies knowing the truth and proclaiming the truth. This is justifiable only if the truth is essentially salutary. This would be the case if knowledge of the truth and only knowledge of the truth makes us good men and good citizens. But if truth is essentially edifying, as I believe it is, one should not begin with "To deny." Moreover, if this is so, knowledge of the truth, quest for truth, and communication of the truth, would be *the* key to the understanding of man, to the analysis of man, to the analysis of the soul, to psychoanalysis. Let us see how Freud's argument proceeds.

It is generally held that the name of Moses is Egyptian.

> It might have been expected that one of the many authors who recognized Moses to be an Egyptian name would have drawn the conclusion, or at least considered the possibility, that the bearer of an Egyptian name was himself an Egyptian. [pp. 5–6]

I do not comment on this passage, because I know a bit, as you all do, about Jewish names. Freud suggests the conclusion that Moses was an Egyptian. It is not hard to understand why men have failed to draw this conclusion. Freud explains this failure.

> . . . we have no word of him [Moses—*L.S.*] except from the Holy Books and the written traditions of the Jews. Although the decision lacks final historical certainty, the great majority of historians have expressed the opinion that Moses did live and that the exodus from Egypt, led by him, did in fact take place. It has been maintained with good reason that the later history of Israel could not be understood if this were not admitted. Science today has become much more cautious and deals much more leniently with tradition than it did in the early days of historical investigation. [pp. 3–4]

Freud refers to the early history of biblical criticism; the then prevailing unqualified distrust of tradition is now recognized as unsound. This explains why one does not draw the conclusion that the Egyptian name of Moses bespeaks Egyptian origin. The conclusion that Moses was an Egyptian is reached not from his name but from psychoanalysis as the starting point. Therefore, Freud says: "The consideration thus reached will impress only that minority of readers familiar with analytical reasoning and able to appreciate its conclusions. To them I hope it will appear of significance."[9]

This, of course, raises a great question as to the relationship of psychoanalysis to scientific caution regarding tradition. The story of Moses' miraculous salvation by the daughter of Pharaoh reminds us of similar stories told of Cyrus, Romulus, Hiero of Syracuse, Oedipus, and so on. Of this kind of story, which is regarded here as a typical myth, there exists a psychoanalytical interpretation.

> A hero is a man who stands up manfully against his father and in the end victoriously overcomes him. The myth in question traces this

> struggle back to the very dawn of the hero's life, by having him born
> against his father's will and saved in spite of his father's evil inten-
> tions. [p. 9]

The intention shows itself in the exposure. But the story of Moses differs
in striking respects. He was not exposed by an evil father as Cyrus, for
example, was exposed. In the other stories the hero is of noble descent
and exposed by these noble parents, but saved and brought up by humble parents. Moses, however, stems from humble parents, is hidden out
of fear of a tyrannical and alien ruler, discovered by the ruler's daughter,
and brought up by the royal family. Why this change? Some scholars,
who are partly inclined to go along with Freud in his interpretation of
stories, say that the original version was that Moses was a child of
Pharaoh's daughter; Jews saved him and brought him up as their own.
Freud rejects this on the following ground: the Egyptians had no reason
to make this myth, for to them Moses was not a hero. Nor did the Jews
have any reason to make their hero into an alien. Therefore, this view
must be discussed. "The Moses myth as we know it today lags sadly
behind its secret motives. If Moses is not of royal lineage our legend
cannot make him into a hero; if he remains a Jew it has done nothing to
raise his status."[10] The purpose of the story, then, must be to raise Moses'
status, to make him into a hero, to glorify him. How does Freud know?
In trying to understand a story occurring in a book, be it the story of
Moses' birth or any other story, it is always wise to consider the context,
the immediate context as well as the larger context. That means to consider the book as a whole. What does the Bible say regarding glorification? A man should not glory in being wise and courageous and so on,
but should glory in the fact that he fears God.[11] This is the biblical notion
of glorification. It says of Moses: "the man Moses was very humble."
The great legislator was taught the great science of administration by an
alien, and this is not conducive to his glorification. He has to learn the
art of administration from a foreigner. The Bible does not wish to glorify
Moses, but God. The story of Moses' exposure and salvation shows the
extreme improbability of the survival of the baby Moses, the extreme
improbability of the emergence of the Jewish people, because that was
bound up with the salvation of Moses. This is in perfect accord with *the*
story in Genesis, the story of the binding of Isaac, where all probabilities
are against a son being born to Abraham, and after he was born and
Abraham had been promised a great future for his race through his
only son, he was commanded to slaughter this son. And Abraham, in
spite of the seeming absurdity of that command, is willing to obey it.
The extreme improbability of the survival of a people without arms

and without a land, a people which has no visible means of support—
only God; if that is not one expression of the broad message of the Bible
which every child can see, I do not know what it is. And if this is sufficient for understanding a particular biblical story, it is prudent to leave
it at that. Freud has no understanding of this peculiar quality ascribed to
Moses, which is called in English humility, and at the same time he is
concerned with humiliating man.

Freud explains the peculiarity of the story of Moses by having
recourse to a feature which is common to all similar stories. In all such
stories, to the extent to which they contain a historical core, the family
which brings up the allegedly exposed baby is the real family. The family which is said to have exposed the baby is fictitious. A humble shepherd and his wife bring up a baby and he proves to be an extremely able
man and he becomes the ruler. What will he do as a sensible, that is,
politically sensible, man? He will say that the shepherd and his wife
are not his parents, that they only brought him up. If we accept this
canon for interpreting stories of this kind, it would mean that Moses
was an Egyptian brought up by Jews.

> The divergence of the Moses legend from all others of its kind might
> be traced back to a special feature in the story of Moses' life. Whereas
> in all other cases the hero rises above his humble beginnings as his
> life progresses, the heroic life of the man Moses began by descending
> from his eminence to the level of the children of Israel. [p. 13]

In other words, whereas Cyrus was really the son of poor shepherds
and then became the founder of the Persian empire and claimed to have
been the exposed child of some royal family, the case of Moses is just the
opposite: Moses stemmed from a royal family and was adopted by
humble parents. Freud makes it clear that this is entirely hypothetical. In
fact one could say, to be a bit more exact, that there is no shred of evidence for his contention. Yet he says, "The interpretation of the exposure
myth attaching to Moses *necessitated* the conclusion [i.e., not only 'led to'
but 'necessitated'—*L.S.*] that he was an Egyptian whom a people
needed to make into a Jew."[12]

It is never sufficient to show that a certain theory is entirely baseless, because as a theory it intends to explain a difficulty. Here is the difficulty. Why had Moses to be presented as brought up in all the wisdom
of the Egyptians? As you see, I make now the tentative assumption that
the biblical stories are not necessarily literally true. The man who had to
liberate the Jews from Egyptian rule had to be competent to deal with
the Egyptians and with Pharaoh himself on their own level, in a way

intelligible to the Egyptians. To establish the superiority of Moses' craft or skill to that of the Egyptians, the Bible gives a comparison of Moses' miracles and the Egyptian sorcerers' miracles or marvels. It makes sense to say that humanly speaking, politically speaking, a man who wants to liberate a nation from the imperial nation which oppresses it has to know very well the imperial nation. We have some contemporary examples of people who have studied at Oxford and Cambridge and then affected some changes in a dependency of the British empire.

We have now "established" the fact that Moses was an Egyptian. But if Moses was an Egyptian, two great difficulties arise: (1) if Moses was an Egyptian, his religion was the Egyptian religion, but the Egyptians were polytheists and idolators, and Moses is known to be the founder of the monotheistic religion most strongly opposed to polytheism and idolatry; (2) what could possibly have induced an Egyptian prince to make himself the leader of "culturally inferior immigrants"?[13] As for the first question, Freud has a simple answer. Shortly before Moses' time (there are certain chronological difficulties which Freud did not straighten out and which I cannot straighten out) there was a great change in the Egyptian religion—what Freud calls the great heresy of Ikhnaton. He was an Egyptian king who founded a strictly monotheistic religion: there is only one universal god, the sun god Aton. This god manifests himself in the sun and is not himself the sun. Furthermore, Ikhnaton's heresy was characterized by great intolerance to polytheism and idolatry. Conclusion—there was a monotheistic Egyptian religion which fits the requirements of Moses and his religion. As to the second question, what could have induced an Egyptian prince to step down and mingle with these "culturally inferior immigrants," the following answer is offered. The religion of Ikhnaton was wiped out very shortly after its emergence by reactionary polytheistic priests. Moses was an adherent of the heretical and persecuted Aton worship, and the only hope for his religion consisted in finding a new people which would dedicate itself to the cult of Aton.

The argument is based on a mere assumption—on the assumption that Moses was an Egyptian. Freud gives another confirmation, as he calls it, of this thesis.

> . . . Moses was said to have been "slow of speech"—that is to say, he must have had a speech impediment or inhibition—so that he had to call on Aaron (who is called his brother) for assistance in his supposed discussions with Pharaoh. This again may be historical truth and would serve as a welcome addition to the endeavor to make the picture of this great man live. It may, however, have another and more important significance. The report may, in a slightly distorted way,

recall the fact that Moses spoke another language and was not able to communicate with his Semitic neo-Egyptians [our ancestors—*L.S.*] without the help of an interpreter [this so-called brother Aaron—*L.S.*]—at least not at the beginning of their intercourse. Thus [and this sentence certainly is worthy of being reprinted in a good textbook of logic—*L.S.*] a fresh confirmation of the thesis: Moses was an Egyptian.[14]

I have to read to you another passage. As regards the derivation of the biblical religion from Aton, Freud says:

The most essential difference—apart from the name of its God—is that the Jewish religion entirely relinquishes the worship of the sun, to which the Egyptian one still adhered.[15]

This is an amazing understatement. The Bible is the document of the greatest effort ever made to deprive all heavenly bodies of all possibility of divine worship. But what then happens to the Egyptian origin of Moses' religion?

Considerations of the kind sketched here, which would make quite an impression on some people, do not make any impression on Freud, who knows better. He is disturbed by a difficulty of an entirely different kind. Certain modern scholars deny, explicitly or implicitly, that the founding of a new religion by Moses had anything to do with Egypt. These are other higher critics who have different preoccupations: they say the decisive event took place somewhere in the Sinai desert, for which there is some biblical evidence; they say furthermore that the new god was not the sun god Aton but an "uncanny, blood-thirsty demon who walks by night and shuns the light of day."[16] This is the Old Testament God whom these people called Jahve. The Moses of the desert with whom we are so familiar and who is associated with this god, this volcano god, has nothing in common with the "august Egyptian Moses" "deduced" by Freud. We have, then, two Moses—the Egyptian Moses deduced by Freud, and this other Moses of the desert deduced by some other Old Testament scholars. Here Freud finds another higher critic who helps him greatly.

In 1922 Ernst Sellin made a discovery of decisive importance. He found in the book of the prophet Hosea (second half of the eight century) unmistakable traces of a tradition to the effect that the founder of their religion, Moses, met a violent end in a rebellion of his stubborn and refractory people. The religion he had instituted was at the same time abandoned. . . . Let us adopt from Sellin the surmise that the Egyptian Moses was killed by the Jews, and the religion he instituted abandoned. [pp. 42–43]

The Egyptian Moses was murdered and his religion was abandoned, but he had an Egyptian retinue with him, the original Levites. A fair number of them survived the massacre and the putting down of the Aton worship. The Levites became the elite of the Jewish people. The Jewish people emerged out of the confluence of the Jewish tribe which had come from Egypt under the leadership of Moses and the other tribes which had never been in Egypt. The latter had adopted in the desert the cult of the volcano god and their leader was a Midianite priest, let us say Jethro. The decisive event was a compromise. The Levites adopt the volcano god but insist on circumcision as a price, circumcision being an Egyptian institution. Everything else was abandoned except circumcision. What happens later on can be said in a few words. The story of the exodus from Egypt was rewritten from a volcanistic point of view, just as the sun god became overlaid by the volcano god. And Moses is overlaid by the Midianite priest, the original worshiper of the volcano god. We know nothing, however, about this other Moses. He is entirely obscured by the first, the Egyptian Moses. The only opening might be the clues provided by the contradictions to be found in the Bible's characterization of Moses. "He is often enough described as masterful, hot-tempered, even violent, and yet it is also said of him that he was the most patient and 'meek' of all men." (p. 49) That is a contradiction. I raise this question. We know the Egyptian Moses was masterful and hot-tempered, but why should the savage priest of the savage demon god be meeker than the refined Egyptian? One does not need a profound study of psychoanalysis for realizing that there are people who are both hot-tempered and meek. I have seen such people.

Then comes the big event. The big event is not the introduction of monotheism; the big event is the murder of Moses, of course.

> Among all the events of Jewish prehistory that poets, priests, and historians of a later age undertook to portray, there was an outstanding one the suppression of which was called for by the most obvious and best of human motives. . . . Moses, trained in Ikhnaton's school, employed the same methods as the king; he gave commands and forced his religion on the people. . . . But while the tame Egyptians waited until fate had removed the sacred person of their Pharaoh, the savage Semites took their destiny into their own hands and did away with their tyrant. [pp. 57–58]

Later on the people regretted the murder of Moses and tried to forget it. This was due to the increased influence of the Levites. The spiritual and humane conception of the Egyptian Moses asserted itself gradually against this savage conception which the Midianite Moses had of that volcano god.

Jahve maintains that he had been the god of those patriarchs [Abraham, Isaac, and Jacob—*L.S.*]; it is true—and he has to admit this himself—they did not worship him under this name.[17]

He does not add under what other name he used to be worshiped. [If you look up the passage you see that he appeared under the name God Almighty.—*L.S.*]. . . . There was yet another purpose in bringing the patriarchs into the new Jahve religion. They had lived in Canaan; their memory was connected with certain localities in the country. Possibly they themselves had been Canaanite heroes or local divinities whom the immigrating Israelites had adopted for their early history. By evoking them one gave proof, so to speak, of having been born and bred in the country, and denied the odium that clings to the alien conqueror. It was a clever turn: the god Jahve gave them only what their ancestors had once possessed.[18]

I note here a strange lack of sympathy. From an extremely skeptical point of view one can say that we do not know anything about what happened and, as Freud remarked on another occasion, science (meaning higher criticism) has now become more lenient to tradition; why, then, not regard it as possible that Abraham lived and was a very honest and pious man (as he is described in the Bible)? Why not—if one is not full of hate or ingratitude toward one's origins.

The most interesting remark in this section is this:

None can doubt that it was only the idea of this other god that enabled the people of Israel to surmount all their hardships and to survive until our time. . . . It is honor enough for the Jewish people that it has kept alive such a tradition and produced men who lent it their voice, even if the stimulus had first come from outside, from a great stranger.[19]

In short, the pride of the Jewish people should not be affected by the proof that the founder of the Jewish religion had been an alien.

Considering the flimsiness of the proofs, one is entitled to say that the rationale of the argument cannot consist of the proofs but only of the conclusion. Freud published the conclusion in 1937. Did he wish to make sure that the catastrophe of 1933 did not lead him back to the social neurosis called Judaism? Did he wish to give the Christian Germans a lesson by showing them how a Jew behaves if confronted with the foreign origin of the founder of his religion? One thing is certain: on the basis of Freud's suggestion, the situation of the Jews in regard to Moses is identical with the situation of the Gentile (and hence in particular the German) in regard to Jesus. At the moment of the complete collapse of the assimilation of Jews to Germans, Freud commits a supreme act of assimilation: he assimilates the situation of the Jews in regard to Moses to the situation of the Germans in regard to Jesus.

The third part of Freud's book is by far the largest. It is devoted to psychological discussions. These psychological discussions presuppose the truth of his historical findings, according to which Moses was an Egyptian and there were two Moses. We can safely say that the psychological discussion is an attempt to explain something which is a figment of Freud's imagination. That psychological explanation has the scientific status of an explanation not of the belief in witchcraft but of witchcraft. What precisely is the problem? One could argue that the question of Moses' origin and even of his religion is ultimately of no importance since we have solid information about the lives and the teachings of the great literary prophets. Here we have a unique development of high spirituality regardless of what were its humble and obscure origins. What we can do and must do is to try to understand that accessible teaching or message. If at all possible one must try to find out whether it is true. Freud's approach is different; what we need is a causal explanation: why did monotheism emerge among the Jews?; why did the Jews come to believe that they are the chosen people? Strictly speaking, the question does not concern the emergence of monotheism among Jews, for monotheism, we have learned, emerged in Egypt, and the Egyptian Moses merely transplanted it among the Jews. The question, therefore, is why did it take such a long time until the Jews became entirely and radically monotheistic?

> I thus believe that the idea of an *only* God, as well as the emphasis laid on ethical demands in the name of that God and the rejection of all magic ceremonial, was indeed Mosaic doctrine, which at first found no hearing but came into its own after a long space of time and finally prevailed. How is such a delayed effect to be explained and where do we meet with similar phenomena? [p. 82]

On the basis of Freud's assumptions I would make this suggestion. The Jews in Egypt accepted Moses' leadership not because they were convinced of the truth of his extremely spiritualistic religion (they were simple, underdeveloped immigrants, as we have heard), but because he had promised them freedom. Simpleminded people can easily understand that. They were wholly unprepared for Moses' lofty message, especially so after their union in the desert with their completely savage brethren, those who worshiped the volcano god. There was no possibility of their understanding anything of Moses' message; but on the other hand, they had a sound, practical motive to follow an Egyptian of high rank who offered them leadership with a view to their liberation. Who would not do that if he lives in subjection and slavery, when some member of the ruling empire comes and tells him, "I will liberate you." They would have been insane if they had not followed Moses under these conditions. After the conquest of Canaan they fell naturally victim to the endemic fertility cults and so on. The Levites preserved an inkling of the Mosaic religion, of course in a very corrupted fashion or version. Even this crude version could not have survived if the Egyptian origin of Moses and of his religion, as well as the original character of this religion, had not been successfully suppressed. Otherwise they would always have said, naturally, "We don't want to hear of this foreigner." Still, in some way the tradition of what truly happened at the beginning lingered on. Only with the coming of the supreme crisis did the Jews become receptive to the Mosaic message restored by the prophets. They could no longer trust in any political support—arms or alliances. To this suggestion Freud in effect replies that this explanation does not take proper cognizance of the fact that the repressed memory of the original monotheism became stronger in the course of time, not weaker. Again I would say, the reason that the resistance to the lofty monotheism grew weaker was due to the increasing education of the Jews through the experience they underwent. The lofty monotheism was the only doctrine which was not refuted by events in the way in which the belief in a purely national god, for example, is refuted by the destruction of the people whom he is supposed to protect. We explain the fate of monotheism among the early Jews by the loftiness of monotheism, by an assumption which Freud makes all the time, for he speaks all the time about the high spirituality of this belief.

But apparently I have misunderstood Freud completely. I shall try to "verbalize" his reply to my argument as follows: Spirituality, my foot! "Religious phenomena must of course be regarded as a part of mass psychology." (p. 91) You see that I did not exaggerate by using a crude, vulgar expression, for what can high spirituality mean if it is a part of mass psychology? Let us bow to this announcement of Freud from on high, although what we have heard from Freud about Ikhnaton's revolutionary heresy did not suggest a phenomenon of mass psychology. Let us, then, forget about spirituality and turn to mass psychology, because otherwise we will never make headway with Freud.

The understanding of religion in the context of mass psychology forces us to understand the subject under consideration in the light supplied by our knowledge of neuroses. The fact that Mosaic monotheism disappeared for such a long time must be understood as "latency" of that monotheism. Latency is an essential part of neuroses. Neuroses are delayed effects of a compulsory character which are due to trauma; for example, to certain kinds of early childhood experiences related to sex. There is this formula from Freud: early trauma—defense—latency—outbreak of the neurosis—partial return of the repressed material. The application of this observation to religion is justified by two considerations. First, there is a fundamental correspondence between the experience of the individual, say, the neurotic individual observed by Freud, and the experience of the human race (which Freud could not have observed). Second, religions are neuroses, and this is proven easily by the compulsive character of religious convictions. Religion involves a belief "against which all logical objections remain powerless" (p. 107), and such belief is an obsession.

What, then, is the traumatic experience of the human race which gave rise to the monotheistic neurosis? The primeval horde, ruled with an iron hand by a father who monopolizes all available women—that is the first step. The sons, banding together, kill the father and eat him—that is the second step. The killing is caused by hatred, and the eating is caused by reverence or love. The sons wish to be like the father, to *be* the father, therefore they eat the father. After some time they abandon the desire to be the father and recognize one another as brothers. A kind of social compact is made, with which law and morality begin. An essential part of the compact is that there is to be no community of women, although there are to be limitations of some kind (prohibitions against incest and so on). But the thought of the father lingers on: a father substitute is worshiped. This is the beginning of religion; this is religion. Freud assumes a complicated development from the first and original father substitute to the various forms of polytheism; in these forms, the original form of the father substitute is hardly recognizable. But then there is a sudden reappearance of the single god who is omnipotent, i.e., of the murdered father who was then deified, and therewith of the guilt connected with the awful deed. From here we understand the fact that the Greeks did not have such a deep sense of guilt as Jews or Christians: they were polytheists and thus *the* father was not in the foreground of their thought, nor was their guilt feeling linked to the murder of the father.

We understand from here why monotheism took hold of the Jews, although it did not emerge among them in Egypt; in Egypt, monotheism remained the concern of an inconsequential sect. The psychological motive did not exist in the Egyptians because they had not murdered a fatherlike being. But the Jews had murdered Moses, an eminent father substitute; they had not merely remembered the original crime but had reenacted it; thus, there existed a particularly strong feeling of guilt, fixation, and so on. They became *the* God-killers who had to repress this deed. Freud's theory is worthy of consideration under the following conditions: (a) *if* religion is a kind of neurosis; (b) *if* the original status of man was the horde as described; (c) *if* the original horde was transformed into the fraternal tribe in the manner described; (d) *if* the rationale of religious symbols is remembered as long as the symbols persist, or, if there is such a thing as racial memory proper; (e) *if* there are no reasons inherent in polytheism which make intelligible the transition from polytheism into monotheism; and (f) *if* the Jews murdered Moses.

Freud discusses some difficulties. First, he notes the fact that he knows of only one example of this neurotic development, and scientific theories cannot well be based on a single example. In this context he makes the following observation:

> . . . it is a good rule in analytic work to be satisfied with explaining what exists and not to try to explain what has not happened. [pp. 118–19]

Secondly, in the case of neuroses of individuals there exist memory traces of the past in the unconscious. What is the equivalent of this in the case of neuroses of peoples? Traditions, "active traditions." But are there any "active traditions" of the primeval murder of the father by the brothers? Let us read a few more passages.

> A new complication arises, however, when we become aware that there probably exists in the mental life of the individual not only what he has experienced himself, but also what he brought with him at birth, fragments of phylogenetic origin, an archaic heritage. . . . The first and most certain answer is that it consists in certain dispositions, such as all living beings possess. . . . Analytic research, however, has also brought to light other things, which exceed in significance anything we have so far discussed. In studying reactions to early traumata we often find to our surprise that they do not keep strictly to what the individual himself has experienced, but deviate from this in a way that would accord much better with their being reactions to genetic events and in general can be explained only through such an influence. The behavior of a neurotic child to his parents when under the influence of an Oedipus and castration complex is very rich in such reactions, which seem unreasonable in the individual and can only be understood phylogenetically, in relation to the experiences of earlier generations. . . . On second thought I must admit that I have argued as if there were no question that there exists an inheritance of memory—traces of what our forefathers experienced, quite indepen-

dently of direct communication and of the influence of education by example. When I speak of an old tradition still alive in a people, of the formation of a national character, it is such an inherited tradition, and not one carried on by word of mouth, that I have in mind. Or at least I did not distinguish between the two, and was not quite clear about what a bold step I took by neglecting this difference. This state of affairs is made more difficult, it is true, by the present attitude of biological science, which rejects the idea of acquired qualities being transmitted to descendants. I admit, in all modesty, that in spite of this I cannot picture biological development proceeding without taking this factor into account. [pp. 125–28]

Here is a great difficulty which is in no way disposed of but merely noted. To put it mildly and politely, we do not have knowledge of the possibility of a group memory different from that actualized by tradition.

I turn to a related issue.

If we are quite clear in our minds that a procedure like the present one—to take from the traditional material what seems useful and to reject what is unsuitable, and then to put the individual pieces together according to their psychological probability—does not afford any security for finding the truth, then one is quite right to ask why such an attempt was undertaken. In answer to this I must cite the result. If we substantially reduce the severe demands usually made on a historical and psychological investigation, then it might be possible to clear up problems that have always seemed worthy of attention and that, in consequence of recent events, force themselves again on our observation. [p. 133]

That is to say, quite a few problems may be easily solved if we are not squeamish regarding proof and truth. Freud admits here that what he offers is at best a plausible hypothesis. In fact, it is a wild guess. As far as religion is concerned, Freud's work is based, as Freud always admitted, on the work of Robertson Smith.

I still adhere to this sequence of thought [the Smithian theory—L.S.]. I have often been vehemently reproached for not changing my opinions in later editions of my book [*Totem and Taboo*], since more recent ethnologists have without exception discarded Robertson Smith's theories and have in part replaced them by others which differ extensively. I would reply that these alleged advances in science are well known to me. Yet I have not been convinced either of their correctness or of Robertson Smith's errors. Contradiction is not always refutation; a new theory does not necessarily denote progress. Above all, however, I am not an ethnologist, but a psychoanalyst. [p. 169]

But he uses all the time ethnological theories, although ethnology is a field wholly outside his competence, as he readily admits, and he chooses to reject ethnological theories without even attempting to discuss them. The problem which Freud tries to solve is the amazing power of survival of the Jewish people in spite of, or because of, its being an intensely disliked people. Freud traces this phenomenon in the first place to the Jews' belief in their election, which is very sound; but he immediately interprets the belief in election as extraordinary pride or self-confidence. He traces that extreme self-confidence to the Jews' extraordinary spirituality, and he wonders why such spirituality should raise the self-confidence of the people. This is a question for him, because he believes that spirituality does not belong to man's fundamental constitution. It is a derivation from primary urges.

I cannot go into this comprehensive question, but must limit myself to the question regarding religious spirituality. Religious spirituality implies sacred prohibitions which have a very strong affective note (I try to use his terminology), but not a rational motivation. Freud's example here is the prohibition against incest with daughter or sister. Freud does not consider the fact that without a law of exogamy the enlargement of the family to a political society is not possible, and the order of exogamy must be understood from the end which it brings about. However this may be, the psychological problem of religion arises only if it is certain that God does not exist. The denial of God's existence is only the negative condition of Freud's analysis, a condition which he shares with many men throughout the ages. But his predecessors explained the genesis of religion differently, for example, politically, or by the notion that fear together with ignorance caused religion. Taking for a moment the psychological problem as a necessary and legitimate problem, what strikes us first in religion is the phenomenon of reverence. Reverence is familiar to us first, and from childhood on, as reverence for our parents, our origins. We imply that our origins are greater than we ourselves, and this implies a sense of our defects. Is such a sense of our defects pathological?

> How comprehensive, exhaustive, and final are the doctrines of the believers compared with the labored, poor, and patchy attempts at explanation which are the best we can produce! [p. 157]

It would seem that all serious men are aware of their defects, and have a realization, a nonpathological realization, of their defects. And that always implies some reverence for people or beings possibly greater than us. Every serious man is aware of the defects of his understanding, and of the fact that these defects are partly due to insufficient effort, to guilt. Most men know men who are superior to them, men to whom they look up—reasonably. Surely they do not necessarily believe everything these other men say. They are critical. But there are also cases in which intelligent and otherwise critical men look up without the possibility of criticism, and this seems to be the crucial case. The crucial case is the founder-legislator. We cannot know what went on in the minds of the most intelligent men of early times, but we know a bit about the phenomenon called ancient law, understood as unchangeable. The unchangeable character was traced to its perfection—and to the perfection of the legislator. That is to say, it was traced to something which is no longer admitted. We are then confronted with the phenomenon of uncritical reverence. This phenomenon is well known in Judaism as well as in other legal systems where changes to the law can take place only through legal fictions and so on. What is underlying this seemingly irrational conservatism of ancient societies? Change of laws means change of human beings, and this takes away the sanctity of all laws. Sanctity of the laws cannot be understood except in terms of the divine origin of the laws. Behind this is the notion that law, order, is preceded by a chaos, not only by extreme discord but by a total lack of security in any sense. The order gave meaning; outside the order there is meaninglessness and chaos. Therefore, cling to the law. Freud calls this clinging an obsession. He implies that there is no rational ground for such clinging. But conduct which is not rational for some men may be very rational for others. For a citizen of a modern republic it would be irrational to cling to a law made by Congress last year as something unchangeable, although the clinging to the Constitution would already have a somewhat different status.

Freud's standard of rationality is taken from modern man. He tacitly measures the conduct of early man by a standard of rationality applicable to modern man. We do not call a man obsessed if being shipwrecked he clings with all his might to a plank, or if he frantically runs away from a tiger. Now let us assume that what he was running away from was not a tiger but something which he mistook for a tiger. Mistakes of this kind are not necessarily pathological. Even if the mistake was prompted by a habitual fear of tigers one might easily say that in one's intercourse with tigers even exaggerated caution is indicated. Now let us assume that early man was more ignorant than modern man, and that he had less facility for distinguishing between truly dangerous things and things which only looked dangerous. He would be reasonably afraid of many things of which we reasonably are not afraid. He could not help thinking about the whole. Will the sun always rise? Will the unheard of flood of last year not be followed by one infinitely worse in the coming year? He assumed that what he was depending on was more powerful and greater than he, and that whatever was greater than he must be greater than he in every respect. He was, therefore, inclined to believe that he depended on superhuman powers who think and will, who thus can know his thoughts and actions. Given these premises, was he not reasonably afraid? And if a superior man arose and said, "If you act in this and this way, but only if you act in this and this way, you will not have to be afraid," would he not reasonably cling to that way without having an obsession; as little as a man can be said to have an obsession when he is running away from a tiger. Even people of an entirely different stamp have known this feeling of everything turning around. How often does Plato speak of that into which we come when we cease to take for granted the obvious, when we become aware of the enigmatic character of the obvious? Freud contends that all the assertions made by early legislators have been empirically refuted. Were they? Let us take the most simple example. The man who fears the tiger fears being killed by the tiger. He fears death. Now a part of the founder's promise may have been that if you conduct yourself in the way pointed out by him, and only if you do that, you will have a perfectly blessed life after your death. Is there an empirical refutation of this assertion? Freud does not speak, however, of empirical objections but of logical objections. Religious convictions are mass neuroses since all logical arguments remain powerless against the absurdity of these convictions. Freud presupposes, I think rightly, the validity of the principle of contradiction. But what is the locus of that principle? I find only this answer:

> . . . a standard is created in the Ego which opposes the other faculties by observation, criticism, and prohibition. We call this new standard the *Superego*. [p. 149]

Now the standard of criticism is in all probability characterized by self-contradiction, because "the superego is the successor and representative of the parents . . . who superintended the actions of the individual in his first years of life; it perpetuates their functions almost without a change."[20] Since we cannot assume that all parents are free from self-contradiction, the superego seems to contain contradictions within itself. But above all, what are these logical objections? What are these massive self-contradictions inherent in the religious assertions? I will simplify the discussion by speaking only of liberal religion. It would be absurd to deny that there are men who are religious without being orthodox.

Liberal religion makes a distinction between the core of the religious tradition and its periphery. Freud tacitly refuses to make a distinction between the periphery and the core without justifying this refusal. He does not consider the possibility that the religious doctrines may be inadequate expressions of a fundamental experience, and that there is a great variety of levels of that experience. By proving that certain expressions of the fundamental experience and perhaps even some forms of that experience itself are self-contradictory, one does not disprove all of the experience itself, one does not disprove at all that the experience itself, at its highest level, is not self-contradictory. The reason for Freud's failure is simple: he does not know anything of the experience in question. He has never experienced what some people call the Presence or the Call, because he has built up a wall, a very weak wall to boot, against this experience.

Let us try to see how that basic experience comes to sight in Freud's work in a prereligious or even a religious manner. The psychological problem of the genesis of religion arises only if we are certain that no God exists. If a God exists, the psychological explanation of the experience of God is unimportant. If one is merely an agnostic and not an atheist, one cannot exclude the possibility that the ground of religion is the Presence or the Call of God. The certainty that no God exists would presuppose that there is no possible place for God in the whole; in other words, there is no mystery. For Freud, mysteries are no more than unsolved problems. All problems are in principle solvable. For if there were true mysteries, religion may be a way, perhaps *the* way, of experiencing and expressing these mysteries. I have to correct myself. Freud does recognize mysteries.

> We know that genius is incomprehensible and unaccountable and it should therefore not be called upon as an explanation until every other solution has failed. [p. 81]

The problem how the Jews could survive until today is not one that has proved easy to solve. "One cannot, however, reasonably demand or expect exhaustive answers of such enigmas."[21] That is to say, the mystery fundamentally remains. But Freud does not draw any conclusions from this. He seems to live in the perspective of infinite progress of science, without realizing that the infinite progress of science implies the perpetuity of unsolved problems, for otherwise the progress would not have to be infinite. But the problems which remain always unsolved are hard to distinguish from mysteries. The scientific explanation of the genesis of religion, and therefore of religion itself, cannot be truer than science in general. If the basic premises of science are hypothetical, any scientific explanation of religion, even one which is free from the grave defects of Dr. Freud's, is bound to be hypothetical. Freud takes for granted the validity of the principle of causality. But what is the status of that principle? What can be its status on the basis of Freud's doctrine of man? If the scientific explanation of religion is necessarily hypothetical, the alternative, namely, a religious interpretation of religion, cannot possibly be absurd. We must go a step further. If the basic premises of science are not of such a character that they can be denied as absurd, science as such is radically hypothetical. In addition, science is unable to prove that science is good, for value judgments are impossible for science. Science itself rests, then, ultimately on a nonrational choice. We shall not draw the conclusion that therefore the man wholly dedicated to science, to say nothing of those wholly dedicated to their more or less flimsy theories, are driven by a neurotic compulsion. On the contrary we would say that if their premises are correct, man has no choice but to choose nonrationally between science and nonscience, e.g., between science and religion, unless he wants to be a thoughtless drifter or a moneymaker. This being compelled to choose would be *the* fundamental phenomenon behind which we cannot go and which cannot possibly be explained by science, because any scientific explanation presupposes already the groundless choice of science.

Freud's book completely lacks a philosophic basis. By a philosophic basis I mean also a reflection on philosophy itself, or an understanding of man in the light of philosophy as an outstanding human possibility which is not derivative but which belongs to man as man. I conclude with a remark on a casual remark by Freud. In speaking about the origins of Christianity, Freud says:

> Here we also find the real source of the "tragic guilt" of the hero in drama—a guilt hard to demonstrate otherwise. We can hardly doubt that in Greek tragedy the hero and the chorus represent this same rebel hero and the brother horde . . . [p. 111]

The implication is this—there cannot be tragic conflict. For example, such a conflict as between loyalty to the city and loyalty to one's convictions cannot be a tragic conflict. All men can become well-functioning cogs in a big machine. This view has been supremely presented, unforgettably presented, by a man from whom Freud is said to have learned certain things—Nietzsche. I read to you from *Thus Spoke Zarathustra* about the last man.

"What is love? What is creation? What is longing? What is a star?" thus asks the last man, and he blinks.

The earth has become small, and on it hops the last man, who makes everything small. His race is as ineradicable as the flea-beetle; the last man lives longest.

"We have invented happiness," say the last men, and they blink. They have left the regions where it was hard to live, for one needs warmth. One still loves one's neighbor and rubs against him, for one needs warmth.

Becoming sick and harboring suspicion are sinful to them: one proceeds carefully. A fool, whoever still stumbles over stones or human beings! A little poison now and then: that makes for agreeable dreams. And much poison in the end, for an agreeable death.

One still works, for work is a form of entertainment. But one is careful lest the entertainment be too harrowing. One no longer becomes poor or rich: both require too much exertion. Who still wants to rule? Who obey? Both require too much exertion.

No shepherd and one herd! Everybody wants the same, everybody is the same: whoever feels different goes voluntarily into a madhouse.

"Formerly, all the world was mad," say the most refined, and they blink.

One is clever and knows everything that has ever happened: so there is no end of derision. One still quarrels, but one is soon reconciled—else it might spoil the digestion.

One has one's little pleasure for the day and one's little pleasure for the night: but one has a regard for health.

"We have invented happiness," say the last men, and they blink.[22]

Notes

["Freud on Moses and Monotheism" was a lecture delivered by Leo Strauss at the Hillel House, University of Chicago. It seems to have been delivered in the spring quarter (March–June) of 1958, although the precise date is not known to the editor. Strauss was apparently using notes which had been prepared previously, but these do not survive. A transcription was made by an unknown transcriber from a tape recording of the lecture. This published version is based on that transcription. It must be added that it appears Strauss did not either review or formally approve the above lecture in its transcribed version. The notes below to this lecture are entirely the work of the present editor. —Ed.]

1. This allusion to a plea for "a philosophy which is wholly alien to me, but by which I could not help being impressed," may refer to a "Conversation with Martin Buber," which was introduced by Strauss, and which occurred at the Hillel House of the University of Chicago on 3 December 1951.

2. The English translation, to which Strauss refers by page numbers in the lecture, seems to have been: Sigmund Freud, *Moses and Monotheism*, translated by Katherine Jones (New York: Alfred Knopf, 1949). The original German version is: *Der Mann Moses und die monotheistische Religion: Drei Abhandlungen* (Amsterdam: Allert de Lange, 1939). It also appears in the *Gesammelte Werke* (1950), vol. 16, 101–246. Also useful is the "authorized" English translation by James Strachey (London: The Hogarth Press, 1974).

3. See Leo Strauss, *Thoughts on Machiavelli* (Glencoe, Ill.: Free Press, 1958). This book is an augmented version of the Walgreen Lectures that were delivered at the University of Chicago in 1953. For some of Strauss's reflections on Machiavelli and the Bible in general, see *Thoughts on Machiavelli*, 174–232; for Machiavelli and Moses specifically, see 70–84, 204–5; for whether Machiavelli "heard the Call" or "sensed the Presence," see 203.

4. A tape or a transcript of the discussion period that followed this lecture does not survive. The subject on which Strauss had "quasi-promised" to lecture, but which he could not deal with, is somewhat unclear. It seems to have been: Machiavelli's view of Moses as compared with Freud's. He suggests that he regards their views as essentially similar in the most important respects (a coin "where both sides look exactly alike"). Yet this leads him to imply equally important differences, determined by the different objects of their critiques: to refute anti-Semitic arguments (Freud) versus to deconstruct Western religion (Machiavelli). In line with the preceding clarification, I believe that the contradictions between the spoken verb tenses in the transcription of this paragraph of Strauss's lecture can only be resolved by emending the text. Thus, certain additions and corrections have been made by the editor so that the meaning of what Strauss says in this paragraph can be rendered fully consistent with itself. But to enable the reader to judge for himself, I reproduce the three unemended passages as they appear in the text of the transcription:

> . . . Of course, I have not heard that lecture, . . . but I will present the other side of the coin making the assumption, ... What I heard that evening over the dinner table. . . .

5. Ernst Simon, "Sigmund Freud, the Jew." *Leo Baeck Institute Yearbook* 2 (1957): 270–305.

6. Ibid., 287–89. Strauss quotes the page citations for the passages which are taken from Freud's *Moses and Monotheism* in the sentences from Simon's article which Strauss also quotes, and he does so as they are given in the footnotes of Simon's article. Simon also uses the translation by Katherine Jones. (See note 2, supra.) The passage Simon quotes from the third essay on King Ikhnaton and the origin of "the idea of monotheism" appears in *Moses and Monotheism*, 141. Freud's original discussion of the Egyptian origins of Mosaic monotheism in the second essay, to which Simon refers, starts on 16, and continues through 38. As a further note to these issues, Yosef H. Yerushalmi in his

Freud's Moses: Judaism Terminable and Interminable (New Haven: Yale University Press, 1991) observes that Thomas Mann in his novel *Joseph and His Brothers* takes a bold step beyond Freud and gives to Joseph the responsibility for this teaching of monotheism to Ikhnaton. For the chapter to which Yerushalmi refers, see *Joseph and His Brothers*, translated by H. T. Lowe-Porter (New York: Alfred A. Knopf, 1948) [in Part 4, *Joseph the Provider*], "All Too Blissful," 962–70. (See *Freud's Moses*, 89.)

7. See Yehuda Halevi, *Kuzari* 1.1–4 and 10–14; Leo Strauss, "The Law of Reason in the *Kuzari*," in *Persecution and the Art of Writing* (Glencoe, Ill.: Free Press, 1952), 95–141; Kenneth Hart Green, "Religion, Philosophy, and Morality: How Leo Strauss Read Judah Halevi's *Kuzari*," in *Journal of the American Academy of Religion* 61, no. 2 (Summer 1993): 225–73.

8. Sigmund Freud, *Moses and Monotheism*, translated by Katherine Jones, 3.

9. Ibid., 7.

10. Ibid., 12.

11. Jeremiah 9:22–23 seems to be the core of the biblical text to which Strauss refers:

> Thus saith the Lord:
> Let not the wise man glory in his wisdom,
> Neither let the mighty man glory in his might,
> Let not the rich man glory in his riches;
> But let him that glorieth glory in this,
> That he understandeth, and knoweth Me,
> That I am the Lord who exercise mercy,
> Justice, and righteousness, in the earth;
> For in these things I delight,
>   Saith the Lord.

These verses seem to have been combined with, or completed by, such verses as: "The fear of the Lord is the beginning of knowledge" (Proverbs 1:7); "The fear of the Lord is the beginning of wisdom" (Proverbs 9:10 and Psalm 111:10); and "The reward of humility is the fear of the Lord" (Proverbs 22:4). (I quote the translations of these passages from *The Holy Scriptures* [Philadelphia: The Jewish Publication Society of America, 1955].) For Moses' humility, see Numbers 12:3. For the reference in the next sentences to the "alien" or "foreigner" who taught "the great legislator . . . the great science of administration," he alludes to Moses' Midianite father-in-law Jethro and the events narrated in Exodus 18:13–27. But see also Numbers 11:10–30, and Deuteronomy 1:9–18. And for Maimonides on the passage in Jeremiah to which Strauss refers, see *The Guide of the Perplexed* 3.54, with comments on glory, wisdom, and human perfection.

12. Sigmund Freud, *Moses and Monotheism*, translated by Katherine Jones, 16.

13. Ibid., 18.

14. Ibid., 37–38.

15. Ibid., 28.

16. Ibid., 39.

17. Ibid., 53–54.

18. Ibid., 54–56. For the name God Almighty (*El Shaddai*), see Exodus 6:3.

19. Ibid., 62–63.

20. Ibid., 149. Strauss's quotation omits the words "(and educators)," which in Freud's original follow the phrase "successor and representative of the parents."

21. Ibid., 176. For Strauss on the "mystery" of being, see "Why We Remain Jews," infra, 328–29. For the importance of the search for *the* truth, see "Progress or Return?," supra, 116–17; "Preface to Isaac Husik, *Philosophical Essays*," supra, 254–56; "Why We Remain Jews," infra, 343–45; "Jerusalem and Athens," infra, 378–79; "Perspectives on the Good Society," infra, 444. For a critique of modern "dogmatic atheism," see "An Epilogue," in *An Introduction to Political Philosophy* (Detroit: Wayne State University Press, 1989), 148–49. Strauss would no doubt have been in a qualified sympathy with Oskar Pfister's simple theological response to Freud's playful but proud characterization of himself as a "godless Jew." As Pfister put it: "he who lives for truth lives in God." See *Psychoanalyis and Faith: The Letters of Sigmund Freud and Oskar Pfister*, edited by Heinrich Meng and Ernst L. Freud, and translated by Eric Mosbacher (London: The Hogarth Press, 1963), 64. For an opposite purpose, Nietzsche rejected the supposed atheism of the modern scientist as well as of the modern "free spirit," precisely because they both still "believe" in *the* truth. See *On the Genealogy of Morals*, translated by Walter Kaufmann (New York: Vintage, 1969), Third Essay, Sections 24–25, pp. 148–56.

22. "Zarathustra's Prologue," *Thus Spoke Zarathustra*, translated by Walter Kaufmann, in *The Portable Nietzsche* (New York: Viking Press, 1954), 129–30.

7

Why We Remain Jews:
Can Jewish Faith and History
Still Speak to Us?

Joseph Cropsey, Chairman: It is a strange title, and has the simultaneous characteristics of being apparently somewhat narrow and at the same time apparently bold. It seems to be narrow in being apparently addressed to Jews: "why we remain Jews." Why it is a bold-sounding title, I suppose hardly needs to be spelled out, since it suggests that a question remains as to why people should continue to be Jews. This is something which as Jews, perhaps you would never expect to raise as a question. Now, as it happens, the boldness of this fundamental question is connected with the breadth of it. It is not a narrow question, as it will turn out, because the problem seems to arise in virtue of some very deep and far-ranging developments coming from modern science and modern politics. Some developments in modern political life seem to cause a special difficulty for people when they consider their Jewish character; and indeed, this is what makes the question somewhat more than narrow when they consider the question of their religious affiliation at all. And I think that since the question does so much have to do with developments coming from modern science and modern political life, the question is one that probably occurs not only to Jews but to people of every religious persuasion. I am absolutely uncommissioned to speak for any of the subsequent lecturers, and I do not in any way wish to appear to anticipate what they might say; but it would surprise me very much if it did not turn out to be true that in one way or another the lectures will speak to the question that arises in the mind of everybody, not only of a Jew, and can easily be transformed, with some modifications, into the question why anybody should remain anything that he happens to be to begin with. One other consideration might deserve to be mentioned. Not only is the title of this series of lectures a bit bold in its appearance; you might also have been somewhat taken aback by the extensive affiliation of the political science department with the discussion of this question. As to whether that contributes another element of boldness, I will have to allow you to judge on hearing what is forthcoming.

This is one of those occasions on which it literally is true that the speaker needs no introduction. Everybody, I think, knows the reputation of the gentleman whom we will now have the pleasure to hear. I will only say that it is a source of very great personal pleasure, and it would be an honor to anybody, to be in a position of introducing the Robert Maynard Hutchins Distinguished Service Professor of Political Science, Dr. Leo Strauss.

Leo Strauss: Mr. Chairman, ladies and gentlemen, I have to make two prefatory remarks. One was partly anticipated by Dr. Cropsey regarding the title. When Rabbi Pekarsky first approached me and suggested this title, I was repelled by it, not to say shocked by it. But then, on reflection, I found one could say something about it. At any rate, I must say that to the extent to which I prepared this paper, I prepared it on the assumption that I was going to speak on the subject: "Why do we remain Jews?" I learned of the subtitle only a few days ago when, thanks to some mishap in the printing division of the Hillel Foundation, I saw it for the first time. I could not with propriety speak on the theme of the subtitle because, after all, everyone is a specialist, and my specialty is (to use a very broad and nonspecialist name) social science rather than divinity. Now, social science demands from us, as we all know—and the gentlemen from the social science division I see here, some of whom take a very different view than I, would agree with me on this—or at least the characteristic of the social sciences is, to start from solid if low facts and to remain as much as possible on that ground. No flights of fancy, no science fiction, no metaphysics will enter. That is clear.

The second point which I have to make in my introduction is of a more private nature, which I am sad to have to make: I could not prepare this lecture, for entirely private reasons, as I would have wished to prepare it. But nevertheless I did not cancel the lecture because I thought I am prepared, if not indeed for this lecture, then for this subject. I believe I can say, without any exaggeration, that since a very, very early time the main theme of my reflections has been what is called the "Jewish question." May I only mention this single fact perhaps, going very far back in my childhood. I believe I was about five or six years old in some very small German town, in a village, when I saw in my father's house refugees from Russia, after some pogroms which had happened there, women, children, old men, on their way to Australia.

At that time it could not happen in Germany. We Jews there lived in profound peace with our non-Jewish neighbors. There was a government, perhaps not in every respect admirable, but keeping an admirable order everywhere; and such things as pogroms would have been absolutely impossible. Nevertheless this story which I heard on that occasion about pogroms in Russia made a very deep impression on me, which I have not forgotten until the present day.[1] It was an unforgettable moment. I sensed for a moment that it could happen here. That was overlaid soon by other pleasing experiences, but still it went to my bones, if I may say so. Now this and many other experiences, which it would be absolutely boring and improper to rehearse, are the bases of my lecture. You will not expect, then, a lucid presentation. On the other hand, I will promise to give, as I indicated by the reference to the fact that I am a social scientist, what one would call a hard-boiled presentation. I prefer to call it a frank one. I will not beat around the bush in any respect. At the same time I hope that I can reconcile what not necessarily all social scientists do: the avoiding of beating around the bush with a treatment which we would call *be-kavod*, or to translate it, "honorable." I think such would be possible. Now I turn to my subject.

The main title taken by itself implies that we could cease to be Jews, and that there might be very good reasons for not remaining Jews. It even suggests this possibility. The clearest expression of this view, of this premise, was given by Heinrich Heine, the well-known poet: "Judaism is not a religion but a misfortune."[2] The conclusions from this premise are obvious. Let us get rid of Judaism as fast as we can and as painlessly as we can. If I may now use an almost technical word, complete "assimilation" is the only help. Now, this solution to the problem was always possible, and it was always somehow suggested, because at all times it was very difficult to be a Jew. Think of the Middle Ages, think of the Reformation, to say nothing of other times. In a way, that solution was even easier in the past than it is now. It was sufficient in the Christian countries for a Jew to convert to Christianity and then he would cease to be a Jew; and we cannot count, and no statistician will ever be able to find out, how may Jews took this easy way out of what Heine calls "misfortune." Yet it was not quite easy even then. I will not speak of the obvious things like the separation from one's relatives and friends. There was a big experiment made with this solution in Spain, after 1492, when the Jews were expelled from Spain. What I say about these things, of course, is entirely based on authorities I have read.

Spain was the first country in which Jews felt at home, although they knew they were in exile. Therefore the expulsion from Spain was an infinitely greater misfortune for the Spanish Jews than the expulsion from France in 1340 (if I remember well), or the expulsion from England in 1290 or so. Quite a few Jews simply could not tear themselves away from Spain. This difficulty was enhanced if the individuals in question were wealthy, had large possessions, especially landed possessions; some of them, some leaders of Jewish communities, converted to Christianity. And they stayed in Spain. But this time it was different, especially after the Jews were expelled from Spain in 1492, because there were so many converts at the same time, not one here and another there.[3] As a consequence, there was a reaction to these many new Christians. And the reaction showed itself in distrust of them. Many Christians thought that these converts were not sincere believers in Christianity, but simply had preferred their earthly fortunes to their faith. So the Inquisition entered, and all kinds of things were done which are most horrible to read; and of course, in some cases, even if the Inquisition did its worst, it could not give a legal proof of the fact that some former Jew had engaged in Jewish practices or whatever it may be, and so quite a few survived. But one thing was done which was extralegal but not illegal: the Spaniards made a distinction between the "old" Christians and the "new" Christians; and they began to speak of Spaniards of pure blood, i.e., the old Spaniards, and by implication of Spaniards of impure blood, meaning the *conversos*. The Jews who had converted to Christianity were forced to remain Jews, in a manner.

This is ancient history. Assimilation now does not mean conversion to Christianity, as we know, because assimilation now is assimilation to a secular society, a society which is not legally a Christian society, a society beyond the difference between Judaism and Christianity, and—if every religion is always a particular religion (Judaism, Christianity)—an areligious society, a liberal society. In such a society there are no longer any legal disabilities put on Jews as Jews. But a liberal society stands or falls by the distinction between the political (or the state) and society, or by the distinction between the public and the private. In the liberal society there is necessarily a private sphere with which the state's legislation must not interfere. It is an essential element of this liberal society, with its essential distinction between the public and private, that religion as a particular religion, not as a general religion, is private. Every citizen is free to adhere to any religion he sees fit. Now given this—the necessary existence of such a private sphere—the liberal society necessarily makes possible, permits, and even fosters what is called by many people "discrimination." And here, in this well-known fact, the "Jewish problem" (if I may call it that) reappears. There are restricted areas, and in various ways, . . . I do not have to belabor this point; any glance at journals of sociology or at Jewish journals would convince you of the fact if you have any doubt about its existence.

Therefore, the practical problem for the individual Jew, on the low and solid ground, is this: How can I escape "discrimination"? (This is a term which I beg you to understand as always used by me with quotation marks. I would not use it of my own free will.) The answer is simple: By ceasing to be recognizable as a Jew. There are certain rules of that which everyone can guess, I would say, *a priori*; and I would not be surprised if there were an Ann Landers and other writers of this type, who had written perhaps a long list of these techniques. The most well-known of such techniques are mixed marriages, changes of name, and childless marriages. It would be a worthy subject for a sociological study to enlarge on this theme and to exhaust it, if possible. I do not have to go into it because it is not truly important, for this solution is possible at most only for individuals here or there, not for large groups. I once heard the story of some Jews in Los Angeles who tried to solve the "discrimination" problem by becoming Christian Scientists; there were first four, and then ten, and then more. Then, at a certain moment, the chairman (I don't know whether they call him "chairman") said: "Well, that is really nice, but why don't you make another group, a group of your own, of Christian Scientists"—meaning of former Jews. I would say that this possibility, i.e., of escaping "discrimination" by ceasing to be recognizable as Jews, is refuted by a very simple statistical phenomenon, not known to me statistically but only by observation: the Jewish birthrate.[4]

A broad solution would require the legal prohibition against "discrimination" in every manner, shape, or form. And I have seen people, Jews, who wanted just that. Fraternities must not be permitted to pick their own people, and strictly speaking, no man can pick his own company. The prohibition against every "discrimination" would mean the abolition of the private sphere, the denial of the difference between the state and society, in a word, the destruction of liberal society; and therefore, it is not a sensible objective or policy. But some people would say: "Why not the destruction of liberal society if this is the only way in which we can get the abolition of 'discrimination' (or what they call, the 'abolition of injustice')?" Now, we have empirical data about this fact, the abolition of a liberal society and how it effects the fate of Jews. The experiment has been made on a large scale in a famous country, a very large country, unfortunately a very powerful country, called Russia. We all are familiar with the fact that the policy of communism is the policy of the communist government, and not of private, fraternitylike or other, organizations, and this policy is anti-Jewish. That is undoubtedly the fact. I have checked it by some information I received from certain quarters. I asked a gentleman whom I know very well, a friend of mine, who is very much in favor of a deal with Russia. He is a Jew. I asked him: "What did you observe about Jews in Soviet Russia?" And he said, "Of course, it is true: Jews are 'discriminated' against, as a matter of principle, by the government." And he gave me a striking example. Some of you will say, all right, that is the policy of the present Russian government; it is not essential to communism. In other words, it is possible to abolish liberal society, to abolish the difference between state and society, without having to become anti-Jewish. I would like to discuss this objection, that it is not essential to communism to be anti-Jewish. I would say it is very uncommunistic to seek for the essence of communism outside of what they call the "historic reality of communism," in a mere ideal or aspiration.[5] Trotsky's communism, which was different and which was surely not anti-Jewish in this sense, has been refuted by his highest authority: History. A Trotskyite is a living, a manifest contradiction. There is no longer a Western revolutionary proletariat, to put it on a somewhat broader basis, and that settles this issue perfectly. Only thanks to Stalin could the communist revolution survive. Stalin was a wiser statesman from this point of view than Trotsky—and to some extent, than Lenin—by demanding socialism within a single country. Only thanks to Stalin could the communist revolution survive Hitler.

But in order to survive Hitler, Stalin had to learn from Hitler. That is always so: in order to defeat an enemy you have to take a leaf from his book. Stalin learned two grave lessons from Hitler. The first, which has nothing to do directly with our issue but should be mentioned, is that bloody purges of fellow revolutionaries are not only possible, but eminently helpful. The old communist theory, as you surely know, was: no repetition of the bad experiences of the French Revolution, where the revolution ate its own children. And then Hitler showed by his classic act against Röhm that this can be done,[6] and that it makes governing much easier. Hence, the big Stalin purges.

Second (and here I come back to our immediate subject), in pre–World War I socialism, where the distinction between Bolshevism and Menshevism was not so visible, at least not in the western European countries, it was an axiom: "Anti-Semitism is the socialism of the fools"; and therefore, it is incompatible with intelligent socialism.[7] But again, one can state the lesson which Hitler gave Stalin in very simple words, as follows. The fact that anti-Semitism is the socialism of fools is an argument not against, but for, anti-Semitism; given the fact that there is such an abundance of fools, why should one not steal that very profitable thunder. Of course, one must not become a prisoner of this like that great fool Hitler, who believed in his racial theories; that is absurd. But judicially used, politically used, anti-Jewish policies make governing Russians, and Ukrainians, and so on, much easier than if one would be strictly fair to Jews. I do not have to point out the obvious fact that we must think not only of the Russians and the Ukrainians, but also of the Arabs; and everyone can easily see that there are many more Arabs in the world than there are Jews. I mean, a sober statesman for whom "the end sanctifies every means" has no choice. Khrushchev (I think one can say)[8] abandoned lesson number one regarding the desirability and usefulness of bloody purges of party members—let me add, for the time being—but he surely kept lesson number two, and it has come to stay.

I draw a conclusion. It is impossible not to remain a Jew. It is impossible to run away from one's origins. It is impossible to get rid of one's past by wishing it away. There is nothing better than the uneasy solution offered by liberal society, which means legal equality plus private "discrimination." We must simply recognize the fact, which we all know, that the Jewish minority is not universally popular, and we must recognize the consequences which follow from that. We all know that there is in this country an entirely extralegal, but not illegal, what we can call "racial hierarchy" coming down from the Anglo-Saxons, down to the Negroes; and we are just above the Negroes. We must face that. And we must see that there is a similarity between the Jewish question and the Negro question; there are quite a few Jewish organizations which are very well aware of this. But also, in order to keep the record straight, we must not forget the difference. When we Jews fight for something which we may fairly call justice, we appeal to principles ultimately which (if I may say so) were originally our own. When the Negroes fight for justice, they have to appeal to principles which were not their own, their ancestors' in Africa, but which they learned from their oppressors. This is not an altogether negligible difference, which should be stated by someone who does not want to beat around the bush.

I begin again. There is no solution to the Jewish problem. The expectation of such a solution is due to the premise that every problem can be solved. There was a famous writer, a great mathematician in the sixteenth century (as I read somewhere), Vieta, who literally said that there is no problem which cannot be solved.[9] This is, in application to social matters, a premise of many well-meaning men in the West in the nineteenth and twentieth centuries. I disagree with them entirely. It is not self-evident that every problem can be solved, and therefore we should not be altogether surprised if the Jewish problem cannot be solved.

Let us briefly survey the solutions which have been suggested. The first is the assimilation of individuals, of which I disposed before. The second would be assimilation in a different form: Judaism would be understood as a sect like any other sect; I say advisedly, understood as a "sect," and not as a "religion." A sect is a society that is based on an entirely voluntary membership, so that today you belong to sect A, and if you change your mind you leave sect A and enter sect B; and the same applies, of course, to all members of your family. The fact that the man stems from Jewish parents would be entirely irrelevant from this point of view. I do not believe that this opinion can be reconciled with anything ever understood as Jewish, regardless of whether it is orthodox, conservative, or reform.

There is a third solution—the only one, as opposed to the hitherto mentioned solutions, which deserves our serious attention—and that is assimilation as a nation. Here the fact that the Jews are an ethnic group is honestly faced. But it is also implied that Judaism is a misfortune, and hence that we must do something about the problem. But the problem cannot be solved except on a national scale. We Jews are a nation like any other nation; and just as any other nation, we have the right to demand self-determination. It leads necessarily to the demand for a Jewish state. This was the view taken by the strictly political Zionists. I emphasize the word "strictly," because in fact there are all kinds of combinations which are by no means due to accident but to one of the deepest principles of human nature, which is, that man is the animal who wishes to have the cake and to eat it. To make clear what I mean, I remind you of the motto of the most impressive statement of political Zionism: Pinsker's *Autoemancipation,*[10] written in the eighties of the last century. Pinsker's motto is this: "If I am not for myself, who will I be for? And if not now, when?" That is: do not expect help from others; and do not postpone your decision. This is a quotation from a well-known Jewish book, *The Sayings of the Fathers;* but in the original, something else is said which Pinsker omitted: "But if I am only for myself, what am I?"[11] The omission of these words constitutes the definition of pureblooded political Zionism. There was, long before Pinsker, a man who sketched the principles of political Zionism—a great man, but not a good Jew—and that man was Spinoza. Towards the end of the third chapter of his *Theologico-Political Treatise,* he said (I am speaking from memory): "If the principles of their religion did not effeminate the Jews, I would regard it as perfectly possible that one day, if the political constellation is favorable, they might succeed in restoring their state."[12] I do not believe he said "in Palestine" because, from his point of view, Uganda would have been as good as Palestine. I did not explain what he meant by the effeminating character of the Jewish religion. He meant by that: trust in God instead of trust in one's own power and "hardware." But in spite of the undeniable fact that political Zionism, pure and simple, is based on a radical break with the principles of the Jewish tradition, I cannot leave the subject without paying homage to it. Political Zionism was more passionately and more soberly concerned with the human dignity of the Jews than any other movement. What it had in mind ultimately was that the Jews should return to their land with their heads up, but not by virtue of a divine act but rather of political and military action—fighting.

Yet it is impossible to settle all Jews in that very small land. Political Zionism was a very honorable suggestion, but one must add that it was also merely formal or poor. I would like to illustrate this. I was myself (as you might have guessed) a political Zionist in my youth, and was a member of a Zionist student organization. In this capacity, I occasionally met Jabotinsky, the leader of the Revisionists.[13] He asked me, "What are you doing?" I said, "Well, we read the Bible, we study Jewish history, Zionist theory, and, of course, we keep abreast of developments, and so on." He replied, "And rifle practice?" And I had to say, "No."

In this student group, when I talked to my friends—some of whom are now very high officials in Israel—I made this observation. They were truly passionate Zionists, and worked very much, and were filled with enthusiasm. But, after all, you cannot always make speeches, and have political discussions, or do other administrative work: you also have to have, so to say, a life of your own. I was struck by the fact that the substance of the intellectual life of some of these estimable young men—to the extent that it was not merely academic, and therefore of no particular interest outside of academic halls—consisted of their concern with people like Balzac.

But the main point is that this Zionism was strictly limited to political action. The mind was in no way employed, or even the heart was in no way employed, in matters Jewish. Now this led very early to a reaction and opposition to political Zionism by cultural Zionism. Cultural Zionism means simply that it is not enough to have a Jewish state; the state must also have a "Jewish culture." In other words, it must have a life of its own. Jewish culture means, the product of the Jewish mind in contradistinction to other national minds. If we look, however, at what this means in specific terms, we see that the rock bottom of any Jewish culture is the Bible, the Talmud, and the Midrash. And if you take these things with a minimum of respect or seriousness, you must say that they were not meant to be products of the Jewish mind. They were meant to be ultimately "from Heaven," and this is the crux of the matter: Judaism cannot be understood as a culture. There are folk dances, and pottery, and all that—but you cannot live on that. The substance is not culture, but divine revelation. Therefore, the only consistent solution, the only clear solution, is that which abandons, or which goes beyond, cultural Zionism and becomes clearly religious Zionism. And this means: return to the Jewish faith, return to the faith of our ancestors.[14]

But here we are up against a difficulty which underlies the very title of the lecture and everything I said before. What shall those Jews do who cannot believe as our ancestors believed? So while religious Zionism is the only clear solution, it is not feasible, humanly speaking, for all Jews. I repeat: it is impossible to get rid of one's past. It is necessary to accept one's past. That means that out of this undeniable necessity one must make a virtue. The virtue in question is fidelity, loyalty, piety in the old Latin sense of the word *pietas*. The necessity of taking this step appears from the disgraceful character of the only alternative, of denying one's origin, past, or heritage. A solution of a man's problem which can be achieved only through a disgraceful act is a disgraceful solution. But let us be detached; let us be objective or scientific. Is this universally true? We must bust the case wide open in order to understand the difficulty. I am not interested in preaching up any solution; I try to help myself and, if I can, some of you in understanding our difficulty. Let us take a man by nature very gifted for all excellences of man, of the mind and of the soul, who stems from the gutter. Is he not entitled to run away from the gutter? Surely one could even say that by being silent about his gutter origins he acts more decently than by displaying them, and thus annoying others with a bad smell. Yet, however this may be, this interesting case—which deserves all our compassion, I think—is surely not our case. Our worst enemies admit this in one way or another. Our worst enemies are called (since I do not know how many years) "anti-Semites," a word which I shall never use, and which I regard as almost obscene. I think that if we are sensible we abolish it from our usage. I said in a former speech here that it was coined by some German or French pedant: I smelled them. But then I learned, a few weeks ago, that it was coined by a German pedant, a fellow called Marr.[15] The reason he coined it was very simple. "Anti-Semitism" means hatred of Jews. Why not call it as we Jews call it? It is *rish'us*, "viciousness."[16] "Hatred of Jews" is perfectly intelligible. "Anti-Semitism" was coined in a situation in which people could no longer justify their hatred of Jews by the fact that Jews are not Christians. They had to find another reason; and since the nineteenth century was almost as proud of science as the twentieth century, the reason had to be scientific. Science proves that the Western world consists of two races, the Aryan race and the Semitic race; and therefore, by speaking of anti-Semitism, our enemies could claim that they acted on a spiritual principle, not from mere hatred. The difficulty is that the Arabs are also Semites. One of my Arab friends was occasionally asked in the Chicago suburbs, "You are, of course, an anti-Semite." And he would say, "I cannot be that."

So I speak of our enemies, and I want to show that they recognize that we are not from the gutter. Let us take the latest and crudest and simplest example: the Nazis. The Nazis' system was based on the notion of the Aryan. I mean, it was no longer a Christian Germany, it was to be an Aryan Germany. But what does "Aryan" mean? The Nazis were compelled, for example, to give the Japanese the status of Aryans, and quite a few others. In a word, "Aryan" had no meaning but "non-Jewish." The Nazi regime was the only regime of which I know which was based on no principle other than the negation of Jews. It could not define its highest objective except by putting the Jews into the center; that is a great compliment to us, if not intended as such. I take more serious cases; first, the anti-Judaism of late classical antiquity, when we (and incidentally also the Christians) were accused by the pagan Romans of standing convicted of hatred of the human race. I contend that it was a very high compliment. And I will try to prove it.

This accusation reflects an undeniable fact. For the human race consists of many nations or tribes or, in Hebrew, *goyim*. A nation is a nation by virtue of what it looks up to. In antiquity, a nation was a nation by virtue of its looking up to its gods. They did not have ideologies at that time; they did not have even ideas at that time. At the top, there were the gods. And now, our ancestors asserted *a priori*—that is to say, without looking at any of these gods—that these gods were nothings and abominations, that the highest things of any nation were nothings and abominations. (I cannot develop this now; then we would have to go into broader considerations—into that metaphysical, science-fiction thing which I have tried to avoid—but I must make one remark.)[17] In the light of the purity which Isaiah understood when he said of himself, "I am a man of unclean lips in the midst of a nation of unclean lips,"[18] the very Parthenon is impure. This is still alive in Judaism today; perhaps not among all Jews, but among some. I heard the story that, when Ben-Gurion went to Thailand for negotiations or something, he went to a Buddhist temple, and there was quite an uproar in Israel about that on the old, old grounds.[19] And I suggested to the man who told me, that he should wire to Ben-Gurion, and that Ben-Gurion should say that what he was meditating upon in that Buddhist temple was the foreign policy of Israel, which might be pleaded as an extenuating circumstance.

Now, the fight of our ancestors against Rome was unique. We have the two greatest cases: the Jewish fight against Rome, and the German fight against Rome. The Germans were more successful than us from the military point of view: they defeated the Romans; we were defeated. Yet still, victory as opposed to defeat is not the highest criterion. And if we compare these two actions, we see that the fight of our ancestors was not merely a fight against foreign oppression, but it was a fight in the name of what one should very provisionally call an "idea"—the only fight in the name of an idea made against the Roman empire.

The next great anti-Jewish body was the Christian republic. The hatred of Jews persisted, but changed; in some respects, it was even intensified. For the Jewish people's posture toward the God-man was the same as that against the manlike gods of the Greeks and Romans. And since there are many Christians today who are no longer trinitarians, one difference surely remains between Judaism and Christianity which was never, never taken back. The Christian assertion that the redeemer has come was always countered by our ancestors with the assertion that the redeemer has not come. One can perhaps say—and I say this without any animus—that *the* justification of Judaism in its fight with Christianity was supplied by the Crusades. One only has to read that history as a Jew to be satisfied with the fact that one is a Jew. The Crusades consisted partly of a simple orgy of murder of Jews. Wherever the Crusaders went (above all, in Jerusalem itself), how did our ancestors act? Permit me to read a few lines from the writings of the greatest living Jewish historian, Yitzḥak F. Baer's *Galut:*

> The best descriptions left us of the persecutions that took place at the time of the First Crusade are to be found in Hebrew records. These were constructed from shorter reports describing the happenings in individual places and provinces, and encountered similar pamphlets with opposite tendencies that were circulated by the Christians. In this age, religious-national martyrdom reaches its highest expression. These martyrs are no seekers after death like the early Christians, no heroes challenging destiny. Violence and death come unsought. And the whole community suffers—old and young, women and children, willing or not. At first they fight for the preservation of the community, and they hold off their enemies before the walls of the episcopal palace or the fortress just as long as defense is possible. [*Strauss:* One must add here

the remark, which Baer of course does not deny, that the higher clergy behaved on the whole much better than the lower clergy. You know the peasants' sons who became priests were much more fanatical and savage than. . . . Recall among the higher clergy the famous case of Bernard of Clairvaux, who tried to prevent that. But they did not prevail.][20] But then, when all hope for safety is gone, they are ready for martyrdom. No scene is more stirring than the Sabbath meal of the pious Jews in Xanten (1096). Hardly had the grace before the meal been recited when the news came of the enemy's approach; immediately they fulfilled the ceremony of the closing grace, recited the formula expressing faith in the oneness of God, and carried out the terrible act of sacrifice that was renewed again and again, generation after generation, from the time of Masada [in the Roman rule—L.S.]. The martyrologies have described in frightful clarity the ritual of voluntary mutual slaughter (not the sacrifice of enemies, falsely ascribed to the Jews), and have glorified it in poetry modeled after the sacrifice of Isaac (*Akeidat Yitzḥak*).[21]

The Reformation abolished bloody persecution. But the unbloody persecution which remained was in some respects worse than the bloody persecution of the Middle Ages, because it did not call forth the fighting qualities which were still so powerfully visible in that glorious time for us of the Crusades. I summarize. Our past, our heritage, our origin is then not misfortune, as Heine said, and still less, baseness. But suffering indeed, heroic suffering, suffering stemming from the heroic act of self-dedication of a whole nation to something which it regarded as infinitely higher than itself—in fact, which it regarded as the infinitely highest. No Jew can do anything better for himself today than to live in remembering this past.

But someone might say: "Is this sufficient if the old faith has gone? Must the Jew who cannot believe what his ancestors believed not admit to himself that his ancestors dedicated themselves to a delusion—if to the noblest of all delusions? Must he not dedicate himself to a life in a world which is no longer Jewish, and by the same token no longer Christian, but, as one could say, post–Judaeo-Christian? However repulsive the thought of assimilation must be to any proud man, must he not accept assimilation as a moral necessity, and not as a convenience? Is not the noblest in man his capacity to assimilate himself to the truth?" Very well, let us then reconsider assimilation.

We will be helped in that reconsideration by this statement of a non-Jew, of a German. Of a German, in addition, who has a very bad reputation in many quarters, and that man is Friedrich Nietzsche. I would like to read to you an aphorism, which will not please every one of you, from Nietzsche's *Dawn of Day*, aphorism 205:[22]

Of the people of Israel. To the spectacles to which the next century invites us belongs the decision of the destiny of the European Jews. That they have cast their die, crossed their Rubicon, is now quite obvious: it only remains for them either to become the lords of Europe or to lose Europe, as once in olden times they lost Egypt, where they confronted a similar either/or. In Europe, however, they have gone through a schooling of eighteen centuries such as no other people here can show, and in such a way that the experiences of this terrible time of training have benefited not merely the community but even more the individual. As a consequence of this, the psychic and spiritual resources of today's Jews are extraordinary; they, least of all those who inhabit Europe, reach, when in distress, for the cup or for suicide in order to escape a deep dilemma—as the less gifted are so prone to do. [*Strauss:* Every sociologist knows that, regarding suicide, the situation is terribly changeable. That was still the old sturdy Jews of Europe he means.] Every Jew has in the history of his fathers and ancestors a treasure of examples of coldest self-possession and steadfastness in dreadful situations, of bravery under the cloak of wretched submission, their heroism in *spernere se sperni* (despising that one is despised) surpasses the virtues of all the saints. One has wanted to make them contemptible by treating them contemptibly for two millennia, and by barring them access to all honors, to everything honorable, and by all the more deeply pushing them down into the more sordid trades—and indeed, under this procedure they have not become cleaner. But contemptible? They themselves have never ceased to believe themselves called to the highest things,[23] nor have the virtues of all sufferers ever ceased to adorn them. The way in which they honor their fathers and children, the reason in their marriages and marriage customs, distinguish them among all Europeans. In addition they have understood how to create a feeling of power and eternal vengeance out of the very trades that were left to them (or to which one left them); one must say in the excuse even of their usury that without this occasionally pleasant and useful torture of those who hold them in contempt, they could hardly have endured holding fast to their self-respect for so long. For our self-respect is tied to our ability to retaliate in good and evil. In all this their vengeance does not easily carry them too far, for they have all that liberality, also of the soul, to which frequent changes of place, climate, customs of neighbors and oppressors, educates man; they possess by far the greatest experience in all human intercourse, and[24] even in their passions they practice the caution taught by this experience. They are so sure in the exercise of their spiritual versatility and shrewdness that they never, not even in the most bitter circumstances, find it necessary to earn their bread by physical force as manual laborers, porters, or farmhands. [*Strauss:* Well, he knew only Germany.] Their manners still show that one has never put noble chivalric feelings into their soul and beautiful weapons about their body: something obtrusive alternates with an often tender and almost always painful submissiveness. But now that they unavoidably intermarry more and more, from year to year, with the noblest blood of Europe, they will soon have a good heritage of the manners of soul and body so that in a hundred years already they will appear noble enough so that as lords they will not awaken the *shame* of those subdued by them. And that is what matters! Therefore a settlement of their case is still premature! They themselves best know that there can be no thought of a conquest of Europe or of any violence whatsoever; but also that at some time Europe may fall like a perfectly ripe fruit into their hand, which only casually reaches out. In the meantime it is necessary for them to distinguish themselves in all the areas of European distinction and to stand among the first, until they will be far enough along to determine themselves that which distinguishes. Then they will be called the inventors and guides of the Europeans and no longer offend their shame. And[25] how shall it issue forth, this wealth of accumulated great impressions which Jewish history constitutes for every Jewish family, this wealth of passions, virtues, resolutions, renunciations, struggles, victories of every kind, how shall it issue forth if not at last in great spiritual men and works! Then, when the Jews will be able to exhibit as their work such precious stones and golden vessels as the European peoples of shorter and less profound experience neither can nor could bring forth, when Israel shall have changed its eternal vengeance into an eternal blessing of Europe, then that seventh day will once again be here when the old Jewish God will be able to *rejoice* in Himself, His creation, and His chosen people—and we all, all will rejoice with Him!

This is the most profound and most radical statement on assimilation which I have read. It does not lose any of its significance by the fact that Nietzsche has not written without irony. In other words, he had no hopes in this respect; he only thought something through. Assimilation cannot mean abandoning the inheritance, but only giving it another direction, transforming it. And assimilation cannot be an end, it could only be a way toward that. Assimilation is an intermediate stage in which it means distinguishing oneself in pursuits which are not as such Jewish but, as Nietzsche would say, European, or as we would say, Western. After having received a notion of what assimilation in the highest sense could mean (and only in this way can we understand any assimilation), we must look at the actual assimilation. After one has heard such a passage, one trembles to look at the actual assimilation. There exists a kind of Jewish glorification of every clever or brilliant Jewish mediocrity, which is as pitiable as it is laughable. It reminds one of villagers who have produced their first physicist, and hail him for this reason as the greatest physicist that ever was. I refuse to quote chapter and verse, but when I read statements in Jewish periodicals about Jewish celebrities I am always reminded of that. I became so distrustful of it at one time, that I did not believe that Einstein was of any significance. I am not a theoretical physicist and, therefore, I was as entitled to my opinion as any other ignoramus. Then I asked a trustworthy friend of mine about it, who was a physicist and a Jew. I told him my opinion: I had the feeling that this is really a propaganda machine organized by Einstein's wife. (I believe that was, by the way, true; I heard that we have had one.) But then he told me, "You are mistaken." He was present at a seminar in Berlin in which Einstein participated, and that was tops in physics, Max Planck and other such men were present. And it was simply so: Einstein had the defect that he did not know elementary mathematics—I mean, that was his genuine defect—but his conceits, his inventions, were surpassing that of all the others there. And so my physicist friend said to me, "You must believe it. Einstein is really a first-rate physicist, and surely the greatest physicist of this epoch. It is an empirical fact." So I accepted that. But I must say, I am still proud of my resistance, because this inclination to self-glorification, in things in which there is no reason for self-glorification, is a disgrace. That we have today so many outstanding Jews is due (let us not deceive ourselves about that) to the general decline, to a general victory of mediocrity. It is today very easy to be a great man. "Among the blind, the one-eyed is king," goes the proverb.

Nietzsche's analysis has some defects, although his statement (which is almost dithyrambic) is based on a very deep analysis—perhaps on the deepest analysis ever made—of what assimilation could possibly mean.[26] Now, the most patent defect of Nietzsche's analysis seems to be this: the regeneration or cleansing which he had in mind as part of the process proved to be insufficient as a work of individuals, however numerous, dedicated, or gifted. It required and requires an act of national cleansing or purification; and this, in my mind, was the establishment of the state of Israel. Everyone who has seen Israel, nay, everyone who has witnessed the response to that act in New York, will understand what I mean. But this fact refutes Nietzsche's dream. For what the establishment of the state of Israel means, while it may be an act or a progress, in a way, of Jewish assimilation—as it surely is—is also a reassertion of the difference between Jews and non-Jews. Since I said "an act of assimilation," may I tell another story from my youth? I had a friend who was not a Zionist, and his father was an old-fashioned liberal Jew. They called themselves in Germany "German citizens of Jewish faith." And what he said was: when he goes to fetch his father

from the synagogue and sees him together with his other assimilationist friends, and then he sees this young generation of Zionist boys, then
he must admit that this older generation, which is so un-Jewish by
refusing any national character of Judaism, is much more Jewish than
this young generation is, which was accepting of the national character
of the Jews. It is undeniable.[27]

Judaism is not a misfortune (I am back to my beginning) but, let us
say, a "heroic delusion." In what does this delusion consist? The one
thing needful is righteousness or charity; in Judaism these are the same.
This notion of the one thing needful is not defensible if the world is not
the creation of the just and loving God, the holy God. The root of injustice and uncharitableness, which abounds, is not in God, but in the free
acts of His creatures—in sin. The Jewish people and their fate are the living witness for the absence of redemption. This, one could say, is the
meaning of the chosen people; the Jews are chosen to prove the absence
of redemption. The greatest expression of this, surpassing everything
that any present-day man could write, is that great Jewish prayer, which
will be known to some of you and which is a stumbling block to many,
Aleinu leshabeiaḥ. It would be absolutely improper for me to read it now.

[The following is a translation of the *Aleinu* prayer, which Leo Strauss did
not actually read during the lecture. A similar, but not identical, translation was added to the transcription by the original transcribers. —Ed.]

It is our duty to praise the Lord of all things, to ascribe greatness to
Him who formed the world in the beginning, since He has not made
us like the nations of other lands, and He has not placed us like other
families of the earth, since He has not assigned to us a portion as to
them, nor a lot as to all their multitude. (For they worship vain things
and emptiness, and pray to a god which cannot save.[28]) But we bend
the knee and bow in worship and acknowledge thanks before the
supreme King of kings, the Holy One, blessed be He, Who stretched
out the heavens and laid the foundation of the earth, the seat of Whose
honor is in the heavens above, and the abode of Whose might is in
the loftiest heights. He is our God; there is none else. In truth He is our
King; there is none besides Him. As it is written in His Torah: "And
you shall know this day, and lay it to your heart, that the Lord He is
God in the heavens above and on the earth below: there is none else."[29]

We therefore put our hope in You, O Lord our God, that we may
speedily behold the splendor of Your might, when You will remove the
idols from the earth, and the false gods will be utterly cut off, when the
world will be perfected under the kingdom of the Almighty, and all
human beings will call on Your name, and when all the wicked of the
earth will be turned toward You. Let all who dwell in the world rec-

ognize and know that to You every knee must bend, and every tongue must swear allegiance. Before You, O Lord our God, let them bend the knee and prostrate themselves, and to Your glorious name let them render honor. Let them all accept the yoke of Your kingdom, so that You may reign over them speedily, and for ever and ever. For the kingdom is Yours, and You will reign in glory for all eternity. As it is written in Your Torah: "The Lord shall reign for ever and ever."[30] And it is said: "And the Lord shall be King over all the earth: on that day the Lord shall be One, and His name One."[31]

Now let us reflect for a few moments more—be patient—about delusion. What is a delusion? We also say a "dream." No nobler dream was ever dreamt. It is surely nobler to be a victim of the most noble dream than to profit from a sordid reality and to wallow in it. Dream is akin to aspiration. And aspiration is a kind of divination of an enigmatic vision. And an enigmatic vision in the emphatic sense is the perception of the ultimate mystery, of the truth of the ultimate mystery. The truth of the ultimate mystery—the truth that there is an ultimate mystery, that being is radically mysterious—cannot be denied even by the unbelieving Jew of our age. That unbelieving Jew of our age, if he has any education, is ordinarily a positivist, a believer in Science, if not a positivist without any education. As scientist he must be concerned with the Jewish problem among innumerable other problems. He reduces the Jewish problem to something unrecognizable: religious minorities, ethnic minorities. In other words, you can put together the characteristics of the Jewish problem by finding one element of it there, another element of it here, and so on. I am speaking from experience. I once had a discussion with some social scientists in the presence of Rabbi Pekarsky, where I saw how this was done. The unity, of course, was completely missed. The social scientist cannot see the phenomenon, which he tries to diagnose or analyze, as it is. His notion, his analysis, is based on a superficial and thoughtless psychology or sociology. This sociology or psychology is superficial and thoughtless because it does not reflect on itself, on science itself. At the most it raises the question: "What is science?" Nevertheless—whatever may follow from that—I must, by God, come to a conclusion.

Science, as the positivist understands it, is susceptible of infinite progress. That you learn in every elementary school today, I believe. Every result of science is provisional and subject to future revision, and this will never change. In other words, fifty thousand years from now there will still be results entirely different from those now, but still subject to revision. Science is susceptible of infinite progress. But how can science be susceptible of infinite progress if its object does not have an inner infinity? In other words, the object of science is everything that is—being. The belief admitted by all believers in science today—that science is by its nature essentially progressive, and eternally progressive—implies, without saying it, that being is mysterious. And here is the point where the two lines I have tried to trace do not meet exactly, but where they come within hailing distance. And, I believe, to expect more in a general way, of people in general, would be unreasonable.

[End of Lecture]

Joseph Cropsey, Chairman: For various reasons I will not go beyond a short remark. Dr. Strauss is known to have spoken other times on the theme of "Jerusalem and Athens." My only observation tonight is, I believe he has done it again. It seems to me that what Dr. Strauss has said—with respect to the solution of the Jewish problem or the character of the Jewish problem, in a way in which a respectable man can hope to understand the solution of it—is a sort of affirmation of the human unity of the excellences known to the old tradition of the Jews, and also those timeless things that the Greeks, maybe in their own way, first articulated with respect to the moral and intellectual virtues.

Question and Answer Period

Questioner: The title of the lecture, "Why Do We Remain Jews?"—am I correct that your answer is that we have no choice?

Strauss: As honorable men, surely not.

Questioner: Well, even one step back from that, even if we wish to be dishonorable, do we have a choice?

Strauss: Yes. But I tried to show that even then it would not work, because you have to have a very, very special . . . like a murderer, you know, who thinks that the easiest thing is to get the money he wants by murder, and then he lives his whole life with that murder. I mean, that is not a practical thing. And this fellow, who tries to do that, will live for the rest of his life with his solution. In other words, his solution will prove to be a problem. I made this reservation only for this reason: one cannot look into human beings, and of human beings one only knows a limited number. There may be somewhere, perhaps in Alaska, a man of Jewish origin who no one knows as a Jew and who lives happily ever after. That I cannot exclude. But you get my point.

Questioner: I tend to be not quite as pessimistic temperamentally as you, and perhaps younger and more foolish, but it seems to me that one of the things that could contribute to a better outlook for the problem of "discrimination" is just the best of sciences. If we as Jews can better come to understand the Christians and non-Jews sociologically, culturally, as well as just in terms of theological doctrine, and they can come to understand us better sociologically, culturally, and historically—and so also with the Negroes—we can yet remain Jews, non-Jews, and Negroes, and yet win some mutual respect.

Strauss: Well, sure! I would say I deplore the word "pessimism," because that means the belief that this world is the worst of all possible worlds; and that, I think, very few people believe. It is impossible to maintain. But you think I am more apprehensive than you are?

Questioner: Can we not hope, at least? Let us not hope for winning an end to "discrimination." I mean, everyone has his friends, everyone has his likes and his dislikes, and we do not wish to take that away from anyone, although we can certainly hope for increasing the mutual respect of peoples of different religions and different races.

Strauss: Sure! Sure! I mean, everyone should try to educate himself and, if he can, educate others to behave as decent human beings. But whether the so-called prejudices, meaning the erroneous opinions, are so important—in some cases, they may be important—but whether they are universally so important, can be doubted. You see, knowledge of another group—a nation or whatever it might be—is not necessarily conducive to good relations. The cultural exchange between Germany and France shortly before World War I surpassed everything which the most sanguine man could expect now to take place from cultural exchange with Soviet Russia. And there was no security officer at the elbow of every German in Paris or of every Frenchman in Berlin. And yet, when the thing came to the test, all these cultural relations (which were much more intimate than the cultural relations between the United States' scientists and Soviet scientists) meant absolutely nothing for the fate of their political relations.[32] In other words, in political matters the stronger and lower is more powerful than the higher and weaker; that is well known. But, by all means, go on! There is no question that if there are misconceptions, that if a person thinks (to pick a somewhat neutral example) that every Negro is given to violence, of course it is good to tell him that it is a misconception, to tell him: "You are absolutely mistaken; that is a false generalization." Surely! I am all in favor of that. But I do not

longer speak of progress. So why do you not stick to your guns? That would then mean that the theology written in our century—Jewish theology—is in fact superior (if you assert progress) to, say, the theology of Yehuda Halevi, Maimonides, or someone else. I mean, prior to investigation that is surely possible; but let me only draw your attention to one thing, one point. The enormous progresses which have been achieved in every respect—in the standard of living, and even politically—have very much to do with modern technology, which itself is based on modern science. This same science and technology has also made possible for the first time, or is about to make possible, the destruction of the human race. The most wicked and vicious human beings who ever were—Nero himself—could not, even if they wished, think of such devices as the atomic bomb. In other words, his killing capacity did not reach the state of what some people call "overkill." That is exactly the other side. I mean, when we speak of progress, positive progress, we must also say that this progress is essentially, not accidentally, accompanied by a progress in destructiveness. If we look at Jewish history, and if we look at that history as Jews, then we must say that such a thing—we have gone through terrible things—but such a thing as the Nazis has never happened before, I mean, before the twentieth century. If you look at the terrible persecution of the Middle Ages, you have to admit that this was not the *government* which demanded it. The government, represented by the higher clergy, was opposed to it. I mean, one can prove this by a simple picture. In some medieval churches, especially in the Münster in Strassburg, there is a presentation of the Church and the Synagogue. The Church: eyes open; the Synagogue: blindfolded. "Blindness," as the Christians call it. But there is nothing whatever mean and degrading in that, nothing whatever. It is a dogmatic assertion to which the Christians from their point of view are entitled, but it has nothing in itself, it has nothing whatever, to do with a debasement, degradation, and so on, as a *government* policy as it was pursued in Nazi Germany. Even the czarist regime, although it was surely abominable, did not reach that degree of abomination which the Nazis reached. And that is in the twentieth century. So I believe that is why there are many people who have become doubtful whether it is wise to speak of "progress." Progress in certain respects; regress in other, perhaps more important, respects. And therefore, that we are different, that there was a change from our ancestors to us, is undeniable. And it is also prudent to assume that there will be further changes from us to Jews a hundred years from now. But that this should be a progress is an unwarranted assumption. There could be possibly, if everything goes well, a reduction in what is now called "discrimination." That, I believe, is for the time being very possible. And in this respect, I think this lady, if I may use this elegant term, my blessings. But not more.

Questioner: I am afraid I did not make my question very clear. I think you pointed out some things which are not exactly to our taste: not only the Nazis and the Russians, but also the possibility (but not the definite direction) of nuclear destruction. The point of my question was not the discussion of progress or not progress, but rather that there has been an undeniable change, from Judaism as it was defined many centuries ago to what it is today. And it seems to me that this change is continuing, and therefore will continue in the future, and I think it is reasonable.

Strauss: Aha! That is the key point. I mean, change is undeniable. But for better or for worse, that is the question.

Questioner: Well, I bring the question back to the basic discussion: why do we remain Jews? In view of this continuing change going on, we have to define "what is a Jew," and "what are we remaining," "what have we changed from," and "what are we changing to." And is there not a possibility that the various beliefs might eventually come a little closer to something that is not what we call today "Jewish"?

Strauss: Well, that was exactly the dream of the eighteenth century. Lessing put it this way, in a letter to Moses Mendelssohn, if I remember well. Lessing was absolutely sick and tired of religious controversy, you know. He was not an orthodox Lutheran, and he got into all kinds of troubles. And he said: "I wish I could go to a country where there were neither Jews nor Christians."[33] That was his simple epistolary formulation of what a very broad political movement intended. There are people who say that this notion underlies the American Constitution. You know that that is controversial, because it raises the question: what does the First Amendment mean? But it is surely, at first glance, a possible view: a secular society. But this is no longer an aspiration. Now we have some experiences with a secular society. And if we are sensible, we must consider that experience. We have also the experience in an alternative secular society, namely, the communist society. I mean, a religious man who is sure on the basis of divine revelation that this will be the future, namely, that the messianic age will come, then he is consistent if he believes in the face of all evidence to the contrary. But someone who bases his hopes not on divine revelation must show some human grounds for it. And I think you cannot show any. Because, you see, even granting what some people suspect—that a hundred years from now there will no longer be religious people in practical terms, that the members of religious communities, churches, synagogues, and so on, will become a tiny minority—even that would, of course, not mean that the distinction between Jews and Christians, between Jews and non-Jews rather, would disappear. Because a Jewish community is of this peculiar character, that it is indeed what we now call a "religious community"—"religion" not being a Jewish word—but at the same time, it is the people, the seed of Abraham; that goes together. How this goes together in the thought of the Jewish tradition, that is a very deep and very old question—but the fact is undeniable. You see, all practical questions must be settled here and now. The way in which your great-grandchildren might settle it cannot determine the way in which you settle it now, because you cannot possibly know under what circumstances your great-grandchildren will live. If social science claims to predict, it does not mean that it can predict the circumstances in which Jews will live a hundred years from now. The predictions of social scientists are much more circumscribed and, if I may say so, irrelevant. I mean that from a practical point of view. They are theoretically very interesting.

Questioner: I have both uneasiness to express, and a question to ask you. The uneasiness that I want to express first, has to do with the fact that in the contemporary world—and I am directing my comment to the rather easy way in which you talked about the Christians on the one hand, and then the non-Jews on the other—in the contemporary world the outstanding anti-Jews, or Jew haters, have not been Christians, but have been Nazis (on the one hand), who have not been Christians, and communists (on the other), who have also not been Christians. (*Strauss:* That is correct.) The question that I ask is: what implications do you see, if any, in the growth in the kind of friendliness—at least theologically, and in other areas, too—which prevails, say, between people like Tillich on the one hand, and Martin Buber on the other?[34] Where, if you will, the leading theologians, both Jewish and Christian, have referred to each other, with a considerable amount of friendliness, and read and quote each other. Do you see any Judaizing in the contemporary world of Christianity, or Christianizing of Judaism?

Strauss: No. Surely not. I mean, I do not know whether the examples you chose were the ones I would have chosen—I mean, the individuals you mentioned—but that is truly irrelevant. You are right. There are

such figures; Parkes in England is a good example.[35] There are quite a
few Christians now who deplore the decision originally made by
Augustine in favor of forcible persecution. I know that. And I would
assume that there were at all times deep Christians who in their heart of
hearts saw the same thing: that this is incompatible with Christianity.
Glad as I am about these developments, I must not give up a certain
(how shall I say?) sobriety to which I am obliged by virtue of the fact
that I belong to a political science department. In other words, I must
also speak of the seamy side of the matter. By this I do not wish for one
moment to impugn the motives of any individual concerned with these
matters. For example, I know Professor Finkelstein of the Jewish
Theological Seminary, and he is on (as you know) excellent terms with
Reinhold Niebuhr of the Union Theological Seminary,[36] and I know
other such examples. No question. But you cannot be blind to the fact
that, for a hundred years, gradually building up and now coming to the
fore in our century, there is a very powerful movement which is both
anti-Christian and anti-Jewish. And this, of course, leads . . . and here it
is not entirely legitimate to adduce examples from straight politics. You
know, when a new party arises, and it is very powerful, then the older
parties, who were in a dogfight up to this point, might be compelled to
make peace among themselves. That this reconciliation could be, in the
case of Judaism and Christianity, in the spirit of the noblest aspirations
of the noblest Jews and Christians is shown by the fact, you know, that
we Jews find all kinds of statements to this effect in Halevi,
Maimonides, and so on. I do not wish to question the theological legitimacy of this reconciliation,[37] but I would like to say that we must also
look at the other side, and here I come to my point. This was exactly
what I tried to show. I could show it sensibly only in the case of communism: that this new power or powers, which are both anti-Jewish
and anti-Christian, still make the distinction between Jews and
Christians. The Greek church and Islam are treated by the Soviet government very differently from the way in which (to use a Christian
expression) the Synagogue is treated. You see the point? Only someone completely ignorant would say that anti-Jewish things are a matter
of Christianity. Of course not. The Romans and Greeks in Alexandria
and other places were as much anti-Jewish as the most wicked monks in
Germany or in Italy or wherever it was. In other words, this fact, that
quite a few Christians were friendly toward Jews, is significant—and I
mentioned Nietzsche advisedly, from this point of view, although
Nietzsche was surely not a Christian, as you all know; but Nietzsche
surely was very German, and he is held partly responsible for the
Nazis.[38] And there is a certain animosity against Germany among

Jews—which I shared, I believe, as much as anyone could have shared it—but which is also in need of rethinking, I believe. And we find other cases: for example, Max Weber, a man very well known in the social sciences; the philosopher Schelling, much less known; and there were some other famous cases—*precisely* in Germany—who were not only friendly to Jews, but showed a very profound understanding of what one would call the "substance" of Judaism, which a man who is friendly to Jews does not as such possess, as you all know. Surely that exists. But we must not forget the background of this reconciliation. A new power has arisen, Marxist communism, which promised—by a break, by a radical break, with the whole past—to destroy the very possibility of anti-Jewish feelings and thoughts. Marx's well-known anti-Jewish utterances were, of course, not inspired by anti-Jewish feelings in the common sense of the word. Yet Marx's present-day successors, like Khrushchev, have restored anti-Jewish policies on a communist basis. However this may be, communism in principle threatens Judaism and Christianity equally. As a consequence, the Jewish-Christian antagonism—just as the intra-Christian antagonisms—tend to disappear. I would say, in proportion as Jewish-Christian antagonism disappears, other antagonisms come to sight; and these antagonisms cannot be presumed to be indifferent to the difference between Jews and non-Jews, and are likely to exploit this difference for their purposes. But it is most important to realize, as I tried to show by the comparison of the Greek Orthodox church with the Synagogue, that the actual policies of that common enemy are much more anti-Jewish than anti-Christian. I know the facts you mention. My reference to the terrible times in the Middle Ages was due only in order to dispel Heine's crude and simplistic view: misfortune. That was not mere misfortune; that was something much greater than misfortune.

Questioner: Do you agree that there is a basic difference between "discrimination" against Jews and "discrimination" against Negroes, in that those who "discriminate" against Negroes are glad to have some people that they can look down on or around, whereas those who are against Jews would rather have no Jews at all, and therefore have their property belong to Christians or belong to some other sect of which they happen to be members?

Strauss: I never have considered it. I do not know. I mean, in the first place I would say that the desire to have someone to look down on is not limited to anti-Jewish people. I have known Jews who have had the same desire. I mean, every man who has "ambition," in the vulgar sense of the word, has this desire. So let us not be self-righteous at this point. But, you know, every chaser after badges does not have to be vicious, but the element of viciousness is in that. But as for this point which you have made, I am not so familiar with the details of anti-Jewish and anti-Negro propaganda. The facts as you stated them—if they are facts—would simply prove that there is more Jewish property to distribute easily than the Negroes have.

Questioner: As a non-Jew I find that one of my greatest problems is, as you mentioned at the very end of your lecture, the fact of being and the infinity which underlies and holds up the idea of progress. And I find myself standing before this idea of being, and looking at a Jew as if the difference between him and me was irrelevant. The one thing that seems to distinguish us in our attitudes (and I suppose you could call me a "humanist") is that before the fact of being I acknowledge that all our symbols are relevant, and that we all stand under the same dispensation. But the Jew will not admit that. He will never merely say, "You are a man as I." And I find this a real difficulty. (*Strauss:* Oh, that is not true; I mean, that is simply not true.) No, I find that he insists, you see, on saying that he is a Jew. And this question of self-definition creates real difficulties in communication. (*Strauss:* Oh God! That is, I think, really unfair. That is as if you would blame a Christian for saying that he is a Christian. Would you say that a Christian as Christian denies to non-Christians the qualities of men? Or a Muslim or Buddhist? Or if a man says, "I am an American," does he deny that the people who are not Americans are not human beings?) No. But the Christians make certain assertions about dogma. I find that there are certain people, such as you dealt with to some extent in raising the problem of the Jew who cannot believe as his fathers believed. Now, I am inclined to think also that the question of race as a Nazi problem is merely a residual one. That is: there may continue, out of choice, to be people who choose to stay in the tradition and race, and who may continue, for so long as there is a human race, a seed which is what we would call a "distinctive race."

Strauss: Well, race not in any particular biological sense. That is, I suppose, sheer nonsense. But people who—to put it very cynically—people who *believe* themselves to be descended from Abraham, Isaac, and Jacob? Yes, sure. That could be. But I would say, I do not see where there is anything wrong with that.

Questioner: Yes. But the whole point is that given this fact that race as such . . . I mean, one has only to go to New York and watch, for instance, the Maccabee soccer team, which has come from Israel to play soccer on the fields of Yonkers, to realize that the whole business of race is irrelevant. All these peoples call themselves Jews, and the idea of physical race. . . .

Strauss: "Race" as it is used in any human context is not a subject about which biologists can say anything. This is clear.

Questioner: Right. Granted. So this then is my point. We have the Jew who cannot identify himself with any dogmatic fixation of his fathers. And yet withal he insists on calling himself a Jew. Now, he may be a Jew, but his Jewishness consists in a myth. Which can be a reality, I grant you, in the human consciousness, but I cannot lay my hands on it.

Strauss: Well, that is very, very nice of you to say that it might exist, although you cannot lay your hands on it . . . But I would say I have tried to explain that. I took the extreme case of a Jew who feels—I did not take your particular "humanist," but I could also have taken him—who thinks that this was all, well, perhaps a noble belief, but it is not a true belief, and so he cannot share it. And then he sees no reason whatever for perpetuation of this old community. All right. But what is he going to do? How does it look in practice? You see, in all practical matters it is not sufficient to state merely the ends; you must also show the *way* to the end. And the simplest thing you can show is the first step. Now, suppose you tell this man, "All right, you don't wear a beard." (Today beards have changed their meanings, I have been told; there was a time when the beard was a sign by which you could recognize a Jew.) So, in other words, all other things which he can possibly change in his external appearance he will change. He may even change his name. He may even marry a non-Jewish woman; and the children will not be brought up as either Jews or Christians; they will not be circumcised or baptized. I mean, let us go into this; if we want to commit the act of treason, we must go into that. Good, now how do we go from here? I would say you will discover—except in extremely rare cases—somewhere flies in the ointment. For example, this very liberal Jew and this very liberal non-Jewess are not descended from rocks or oaks (to quote an old poet), but from human beings. By which I mean, they belong to families. And the families do not necessarily see eye to eye with their most liberal members. The Jew may be willing to say, "All right, I will never see my father, mother, brother, and sister again." But the non-Jewish wife, owing to an amiable weakness of the female sex, may perhaps say, "Well, it is too hard, I will see my mother." And then they (the family) will always say, "Why did you do it? Why did you marry that Jew?" Then the children must also see the grandmother, and the same difficulty arises again. I mean, you cannot wish away these things. Then you would have to form colonies, in which only people who have broken with their Jewish heritage or past origins, and with their Christian past origins, would live together. People have made such small communities for other purposes; for example, for trying out socialism and communism. But they are mentioned in the histories of social movements as amiable, but wholly ineffective. It does not work. If you take it on the lowest ground of practice—I mean, just Machiavellian recipes for getting rid of their misfortune—it does not work. It can work in individual cases. I do not know whether one could say, if one may speak of a living man in this connection, that perhaps Bernard Baruch is an example where it worked.[39] I had heard this at one time, but I do not know the gentleman, and I do not know how it works in practice. But this is a very old man now, in addition, living in the American South. That I have heard; I do not know that. There may be other cases of this kind. But if it is a problem of a social kind, i.e., not a problem peculiar to him as an individual but to other people of his kind, he would have to think of the other people of his kind. And he would say that a solution which is even *perfect* for him, is imperfect because of these bonds; and the fundamental point seems to me to be this. Again speaking detachedly, hard-boiledly, and disregarding all of the deeper issues—why do you want perfect solutions?

Questioner: But that is the whole point. I am not looking for a solution. You see, I do not want Jews to cease to exist. (*Strauss:* Oh!) That is why a man who is a religious Jew, with a position before the mystery of being, this is a position for which I have respect; rather more, let me say in passing, than many others with which I am acquainted. But I meet people who do not have this orientation. I recognize that the race question is irrelevant; and yet withal, this individual creates a special orientation for himself which seems to me to have just the quality of a myth.

Strauss: No. That is, I believe, empirically wrong. I mean, if you mean by myth something fabricated, merely figured out, . . . [A break in the tape occurred.] . . . and that was the word *galut,* "exile." In other words, this is the recollection, the notion, that there is something—a deep defect—in our situation as Jews, and this deep defect in our situation as Jews is connected with the deep defect with the situation of man. That was an implication of the traditional Jewish faith. This implication—disregarding the theological premises, and so on, and its consequences—is, I think, an empirically tenable assertion. And that the Jews know—most of them. I mean, it is perfectly clear, this difficult position in which modern Jews are; I have not brought it out fully because I thought everyone knows it. Every Jew surely knows it, and every thoughtful non-Jew who knows any Jews also does not have to be told. These are things which are partly very painful to bring out, if no useful purpose is served—in other words, merely for the sake of the record. That is, I would not do that. But, on the other hand, one cannot deny it, and deny, as you call it, its "reality." It is not a myth. The theories of this or that Zionist ideology, these can be said to be myths. When I was still studying these things with intensity many decades ago, I always made a distinction between Pinsker as the clearest case on the one hand, and Nordau on the other.[40] Pinsker really started from the Jewish question as it was hitting him directly; and Nordau had a general theory of nationalism of which the Jewish case was only a special case. And I always went more for the more direct people, you know, who started from what everyone could know. And there are all kinds of other things as well, but I do not wish to go into intra-Jewish polemics. You are aware of the fact that there are Jews, a minority in this country, who regard the state of Israel as (to use a mild expression) a pain in the neck. I know these people, but one can simply say that they are the delusionists. One can also say it as follows, also on the lowest denominator: the Jewish problem, as it is called, is the most simple and available exemplification of the human problem. That is one way of stating that the Jews are the chosen people. If that is properly developed, the whole of the other things would come out. The clean solutions of which people dream and dreamt have led either to nothing, or to a much greater bestiality than the uneasy solutions with which sensible people will always be satisfied.

Questioner: Well, if I were to try to draw a general principle from what you have said—I do not know if this is right—but I would say something like this: a man is being dishonorable if he chooses to disagree with, or break away from, his origins, what his family believes.

Strauss: I qualified that. I said that I could visualize a man, stemming from absolute degradation and simply having a nobler thing in himself, tending away, as it were, in this way. And I could only say, he acts wisely. If he had the singular qualities ascribed to him, he would not go around and peddle them and say, "Look what I achieved." But what I said is that this is not the case of the Jews. However degraded we had to live for centuries in all the various countries, we were not degraded. Surely we were maltreated; all kinds of things were inflicted upon us.

But for the *average* Jew it was perfectly clear that we did not deserve it at the hands of these people. Perhaps we deserved it at the hand of God—that is another matter—but not at the hands of the people as such. I could give you some childhood stories which are illustrative, and older people (or people of my age here) could also give examples, of what the traditional posture was. I remind you of only one essay which is still worthy of being read by everyone who is interested in this. That is an essay by Aḥad Ha'am. (You know who he was? Asher Ginsberg.) I mean an essay by Aḥad Ha'am which he called "In External Freedom and Internal Slavery,"[41] and in which he compared the situation of the Jews in the Russian ghetto to the chief rabbi of France, who was also the head of the Sanhedrin—you know, an institution founded by Napoleon himself. This chief rabbi was highly respectable, with badges and all—you know, like this. And then Aḥad Ha'am showed him, on the basis of what this man said—this chief rabbi—that he was a slave, not a free man. Externally, he was free: he could vote, and do many other things, acquire property, whatever kind he liked. But in his heart he was a slave. Whereas the poorest Polish Jew (if he did not happen to be an individual with a particularly lousy character, which can happen in any community) was externally a man without rights and in this sense a slave, but he was not a slave in his heart. And that is of crucial importance in this matter.

Questioner: My point of view is this. Suppose a person who is an average Jew comes to me and says, "On the basis of my latest thinking, I had a real struggle, but I have decided that I can no longer in conscience remain a Jew. I have decided I will become a positivist, I will suspend judgment, etc." I would say that, even though I realize this is going to cause trouble with his family, and it is going to be dysfunctional for him (*Strauss:* Do you mean "inconvenient"?) yes, inconvenient for him, I would say that if this man remains a Jew he would be dishonorable.

Strauss: Oh! That is another question. You mean to say: is it not morally necessary for certain Jews not to go to synagogue, not to pray, and not to participate in other communal activities?

Questioner: I mean even more than that; I mean, take over, say, the trappings of another religion completely if he so decides that this is the correct thing to do.

Strauss: Yes, prior to any deeper argumentation, one would have to say yes. I was still brought up in the belief, in a very old-fashioned country, that no Jew who ever converted to Christianity was sincere. That was what I learned and what I believed until I met, as a student, a professor who told me of his conversion to Christianity. (He was a son of a rabbi.) I must say I was not impressed by his story, and if I could speak of living people here among more or less strangers I could tell the story, which was more pitiable than an object of any indignation. But I would have to admit that he was subjectively sincere, and no calculation entered into it. I cannot say anything more about that. I know there is a real disproportion between my primitive feelings (which I learned from my wet nurse, as a much greater man put it) and my rational judgment. But I said at the beginning that conversion was always possible. And the question was not simply whether to be a member of a Jewish congregation, with all its implications. Quite a few Jews do not do that—you know what the statistics say about that. But, nevertheless, the interesting point is this: the Jewish question remains. I gave you the example of those people who became Christian Scientists. I assume—because everyone must be regarded as innocent until proven guilty—that they did it out of conviction. In other words, they did not want just to get rid of a "misfortune," but they were convinced of the truth of Christian Science. All right, but what happened to them without any doings on their side? After all, the other Jews who were becoming Christian Scientists had also gotten this conviction—all pure convictions—yet the chairman of this group came to them and said, "Why don't you form a group of Christian Scientists of your own?" You can say: "Well, for people who are *only* concerned with the religious truth— in this case, Christian Science—it does not make any difference whether they or their fellow workers are former Jews or not." Surely. But that is, however, very unfair and, I would say, almost cruel, because these people suffered from that. While they did not become Christian Scientists in order to get rid of the Jewish disability, they felt a "discrimination" was committed. They are right from their point of view; only it is of no use to get indignant about individual occurrences or symptoms, but one must view the whole situation.

Questioner: In a sense, and I guess with some pain, I really think that I— as a Jew who is very concerned with finding some meaningful answer as to why I remain a Jew, and how to do so—must really repeat the question that was asked by the non-Jew. I think that you give us really little reason to want positively to remain Jewish. At best, you tell us that an empirical, hard-boiled analysis of the situation—which is your position tonight (*Strauss:* Absolutely and always.)—would constrain one in this direction. At second best, you tell us there are various flies in the ointment which we might idealize. (*Strauss:* No! I did not say that. No, no.) Well, I guess really I'm reacting, and I think I'm permitted to react. (*Strauss:* Yes, sure, get it out of your system.) But basically, I think that what you are really suggesting—if you talk to the young people here, of whom I number myself (*Strauss:* Rightly.)—is that you are really challenging us, you are really forcing us to say that this is just another one of the things that "we shall overcome." Because, even if we fail, it is worthwhile, from the way you paint the picture. And I think, and I would hope (although this is not my evening to lecture), that I have different reasons for positively wanting to remain a Jew, and for having an answer to in what ways one might be meaningfully different from a Christian. But partly my difference from you stems from my inability to accept your basic premise. I think at least that now—maybe we are deluded, but Americans in my situation, I think, pretty well feel that— it is a voluntary thing; that your anecdotes are out of date, so to speak; that the Christian Science story has no compelling meaning to people of our generation. And I think much of your interpretation of the American scene is based on such anecdotal material which I feel is not compelling, although it may be true that it has happened somewhere else and quite recently. But basically, accepting your premise, I would say that all you offer me positively is to be a religious Zionist. But failing that, you give me the quite comfortable solution—but which I find inadequate because not challenging enough, and not different enough—to be a scientist who somehow can reconcile his scientific positivism with the eternal mystique which, after all, derives from Judaism.

Strauss: Thank you very much for your statement. You misunderstood certain points; but since I know you, I can only say that that must be due to certain defects of my presentation. When you say that my knowledge of American Jewry (and there is a question there) is defective, I simply have to grant that. I came to this country only about twenty-three years ago. (I have not figured that out at the moment, but roughly.) But I do also have some training in seeing, by which I do not necessarily mean the social science training.

You see, what I tried to show is this: I think clarity or honesty about the most important matters is a most important thing. That was my premise. Therefore, I rejected—partly explicitly and partly implicitly, because I could not develop the whole thing—all attempts to interpret the Jewish past in terms of a culture. Therefore the emptiness of which you complain. In other words, for me the question is: truly either the Torah as understood by our tradition, or, say, unbelief. And I think that is infinitely more important than every cultural interpretation, which is based on a tacit unbelief and cannot be a substitute for the belief it has given up. That is, I believe, the basis of our disagreement, as far as I can see it. Let me add one point. When I say "the Jewish faith as our ancestors held it," I do not mean that every particular belief (even if entertained by the majority of Jews, or by the large majority of Jews, for centuries) must necessarily be binding. I happen to know a bit of the Jewish medieval thinkers, and I know that quite a few very powerful and important changes were made even by them. I believe—and I say this without any disrespect to any orthodox Jew—that it is hard for people, for most Jews today, to believe in verbal inspiration (I mean, in verbal inspiration of the Torah), and in the miracles—or most of the miracles—and other things. I know that. My friend Rabbi Harris is not here, but I am in deep sympathy with what he means by a "postcritical Judaism." I think that it offers a perfectly legitimate and sensible goal, namely, to restate the essence of Jewish faith in a way which is by no means literally identical with, say, Rambam's "Creator of the world,"[42] or with something of this kind—I mean, with any traditional statement of principles. That is not the point. But a Judaism which is not belief in the "Creator of the world," that has problems running through it.

Now I will tell you another story, and this story has a somewhat greater dignity. One of the most outstanding Jews in Germany was Hermann Cohen, the founder of the neo-Kantian school.[43] And he was concerned very much with how he could be both a philosopher and a Jew, in the sense of a believing Jew. That was a lifelong struggle, and what he said is by no means irrelevant, and is, I think, worthy of the study of everyone who is concerned with that. At a certain point in his life he read to an orthodox and educated Jew a brief statement of what he thought to be the essence of Judaism. And then the old-fashioned, simple man (of birth and education) said: "And where remains the Creator of the world?" I have heard that in this very building at some time someone said, "I believe in God as a symbol."[44] Then I would say that a man who says, "I do not believe in God," is, other things being equal, a better man. Now I do not deny that a man can believe in God without believing in creation, and particularly without believing in creation out of nothing. After all, the Bible itself does not explicitly teach creation out of nothing, as one might see. But still, Judaism contains the whole notion of man's responsibility and of a final redemption. I mean, you can say: "All right, abolish the personal Messiah, and have only the messianic age"—which is done by most liberal Jews, as you know; and you could add many more of these things. But the very notion of the certainty of final redemption is untenable without belief in a God concerned with justice—and this is such a most important issue. And I would say that it seems to me that the proper posture of a man who does not believe in that is to enter into this mystery, into this mysterious belief. And I think he will come out of it—even if he will not come out of it with belief in this—with some understanding he did not have before.

One of the deepest Jewish thinkers now, in my private opinion (which does not count much in these matters), perhaps the deepest Jewish thinker, is Gershom Scholem of the Hebrew University. Now in his most recent book, which is in German only (I suppose it came out in Hebrew, but I do not even remember the German title),[45] he shows to what amazing lengths some of our mystics went by thinking through these beliefs; and then they came out with views to which many of the objections, which many of us would have to such traditional beliefs, would no longer be tenable. That would be the kind of thing which I would regard as satisfactory. But, I believe, by simply replacing God by the creative genius of the Jewish people, one gives away, one deprives oneself—even if one does not believe—of a source of *human* understanding.[46] Let us also not forget to ask: what does it mean, that one does not believe? How much of the unbelief now existing is as much a matter of hearsay, or even of what someone of your profession would call "social pressure"? Belief and unbelief are not such simple states: here is a camp of the believers, and here is a camp of non-believers. Politically, it may very well appear this way on many occasions; but for most of the more *thoughtful* people in both camps, things would be different. Now I do not wish to minimize folk dances, Hebrew speaking, and many other things—I do not want to minimize them. But I believe that they cannot possibly take the place of what is most profound in our tradition.

But however this may be, I have had my day in court. I have said what I thought about it, and I must say that I am surprised that you are still here.

Notes

["Why We Remain Jews" was a lecture delivered by Leo Strauss at the Hillel House, University of Chicago, on 4 February 1962. It seems as if Strauss was using notes which had been prepared previously, but these do not survive. A transcription was made by Werner Dannhauser and James Lane from a tape recording of the lecture. The lecture preserved in the tape, as the transcribers put it, consisted of "essentially oral material, much of which was developed spontaneously, and none of which was prepared with publication in mind." The transcribers state that Strauss did not either review or formally approve the above lecture in its transcribed version. The transcription was dedicated to the memory of Rabbi Maurice Pekarsky (1905–62), the director of the B'nai B'rith Hillel House at the University of Chicago who arranged the above lecture, among others, delivered by Strauss. This published version is based almost entirely on that transcription, with some slight grammatical changes made by the editor for the sake of clarity. Changes made by the editor which may be regarded as significant have been duly noted. The notes below to this lecture are entirely the work of the present editor. —Ed.]

1. The phrase which occurs in this sentence, "on that occasion about pogroms in Russia," has been added by the editor in order to make clear which story it was that made such a deep impression on Strauss.

2. Heinrich Heine (1797–1856), one of the great modern German poets and essayists, was a Jew who in 1825 resorted to baptism as what he called "the admission ticket to European civilization." His attitude toward Judaism was deeply ambivalent. Strauss seems to refer to the famous lines from Heine's poem, "The New Israelite Hospital in Hamburg" (1844), in which the poet speaks about Judaism not as a religion, but as "that dark misfortune" [das dunkle Weh], and as "that thousand-year-old family affliction" [das tausandjährige Familienübel]. See "Das neue Israelitische Hospital zu Hamburg," in *Heinrich Heine: Historisch-kritische Gesamtausgabe der Werke*, gen. ed. Manfred Windfuhr. Vol. 2, *Neue Gedichte*, ed. Elisabeth Genton (Hamburg: Hoffmann und Campe, 1983), 117–18.

3. The phrase which occurs in this sentence, "especially after the Jews were expelled from Spain in 1492," has been added by the editor in order to make clear what "this time" was, to which Strauss refers, which was so "different." It is constructed from a phrase used by Strauss himself toward the end of the previous paragraph. Strauss refers to what was, until the modern era, an unprecedented historical fact: the great numbers of forced and voluntary conversions of Jews to Christianity which occurred in the face of the anti-Jewish riots and massacres of 1391 in Spain, as well as in their wake. Of course, these great numbers were further hugely augmented by the voluntary and forced conversions of Jews to Christianity which occurred in the face of the 1492 order of expulsion of the Jews from Spain. Also, it should be noted that while Strauss referred above from memory to "the expulsion from France in 1340 (if I remember well), or the expulsion from England in 1290 or so," his memory only served him well on England; regarding France, this event actually occurred in 1306. (To be sure, it was repeated again twice by France during the same century, in 1322 and 1394.) However, Strauss may have been thinking of the massacres of the Jews in France in 1348–49, which resulted from their being blamed for the Black Death.

4. The phrase, "i.e., of escaping 'discrimination' by ceasing to be recognizable as Jews," has been added by the editor in order to make clear what the "possibility" is to which Strauss had just referred. It is constructed from two phrases used by Strauss himself previously in this paragraph to define, or elaborate on, that possibility.

5. See Strauss's further elaboration of these points in the "Preface to *Spinoza's Critique of Religion*," supra.

6. For Ernst Röhm, I quote the passage from Lucy S. Dawidowicz, *The War Against the Jews* (New York: Bantam, 1976), p. 81:

> The only dissatisfaction, it seemed, came from the SA, which had by the end of 1933 become a behemoth of four million, but whose leader, Ernst Röhm, felt unrewarded in the national socialist state. Hitler began to regard the SA as a threat to his authority. Even though Röhm had been one of his old comrades from the Reichswehr days in Munich of 1919, Hitler did not hesitate to move against him. Over a period of months the SS and the army were readied, at Hitler's orders, to attack the SA. It was then that the SS emerged as the "elite" party military organization that would eventually dominate all Europe; it was then that the army smelled its great opportunity. On June 30, 1934, about two hundred SA men, including Röhm himself, were murdered with unspeakable brutality. The SA was finished as a major force in the German dictatorship and would henceforth exist under the shadow of the SS.

7. "Anti-Semitism is the socialism of fools." The phrase was first coined by, or attributed to, August Bebel (1840–1913), a German social democratic (or what the Russians would call "Menshevik") party leader. Subsequently, it was often repeated by Vladimir Ilyich Lenin (1870–1924), the leader of both the majority faction in the Russian Social Democratic Workers party (i.e., the "Bolsheviks"), and eventually also of communist or Soviet Russia as of their coup d'état in October, 1917.

8. Nikita Khrushchev (1894–1971) was the premier of the Soviet Union from 1958 to 1964. Prior to his accession to full power, he was also the member of the communist party leadership who was perhaps most identified with the exposure of some of the monstrous crimes of Stalin. He served as First Secretary of the communist party, and at its 20th congress held in 1956 he delivered a "secret" report on "The Personality Cult [i.e., of Stalin] and Its Consequences." In this report he "informed" the Russian people about some of Stalin's most heinous crimes, and he denounced the worst excesses. Hence he seemed interested in correcting, or at least diminishing, the "methods" of absolute tyrannical rule that had been employed for most of thirty years by Stalin.

9. For Franciscus Vieta (François Viète), see Jacob Klein, *Greek Mathematical Thought and the Origin of Algebra*, translated by Eva Brann (Cambridge: M.I.T. Press, 1968), 150–85. Klein quotes Vieta from the end of his *Isagoge* (*Introduction to the Analytical Art*, translated by J. Winfree Smith in the Appendix to the same book, 315–53): "Analytical art appropriates to itself by right the proud *problem of problems*, which is: TO LEAVE NO PROBLEM UNSOLVED." (See Jacob Klein, *Greek Mathematical Thought and the Origin of Algebra*, 185, 353.)

10. Leon Pinsker (1821–91), *Autoemancipation—ein Mahnruf an seine Stammesgenossen, von einem russischen Juden* (*Autoemancipation—an appeal to his people by a Russian Jew*). Berlin: 1882. Pinsker was an assimilated Jew and a physician in czarist Russia who, in the aforementioned pamphlet, preceded Herzl by fourteen years in presenting a purely political analysis of the "Jewish problem" in nineteenth-century Europe, and also in suggesting a purely political solution.

11. *Pirkei Avot* (*Sayings of the Fathers*) 1:14. The saying is attributed to Hillel the Elder (c. 60 B.C.E.–c. 10 C.E.), a religious sage and scholar in Judea approximately during the reign of Herod the Great. The complete saying may be translated as follows, with the order of the sentences as they are arranged in the original: "If I am not for myself, who will be for me? And if I am only for myself, what am I? And if not now, when?"

12. Benedict (né Baruch) Spinoza, *Theologico-Political Treatise*, chapter 3 ("On the Vocation of the Hebrews"), toward the end. It may be translated literally as follows: ". . . unless the foundations of their religion were to effeminate their spirits, I would absolutely believe, as human things are mutable, that someday, given the occasion, they will erect their imperium again and God will choose them anew." [. . . nisi fundamenta suae religionis eorum animos effoeminarent, absolute crederem eos aliquando, data occasione—ut sunt res humanae mutabiles—suum imperium iterum erecturos, Deumque eos de novo electuram.] (My thanks to Martin D. Yaffe for allowing me to use his translation of the quoted passage, which is offered in note 65 (page 75) to his essay, "'The Histories and Successes of the Hebrews': The Demise of the Biblical Polity in Spinoza's *Theologico-Political Treatise*," vol. 7, nos. 1–2 [Spring 5755/1995]: 57–75 in *Jewish Political Studies Review*.)

13. The Revisionist Zionist movement was formally established in 1925 by Vladimir Ze'ev Jabotinsky (1880–1940). But the movement to which Strauss adhered from his youth (about 1916), and which he calls simply "political Zionism," he identifies with Jabotinsky, who had eloquently espoused what would more or less be the Revisionists' fundamental principles and policies for years prior to 1925 as the leader of a faction in the general Zionist movement. As Jabotinsky presented them, his ideas were merely rooted in the original political theory and practice of Theodor Herzl (1869–1904), the father of the modern Zionist movement. Herzl's teaching, however, had undoubtedly been radicalized somewhat by Jabotinsky. Strauss was originally attracted to Jabotinsky for his honest Herzlianism. It was with this Herzlianism that Strauss identified himself affirmatively for the rest of his life. See "Letter to the Editor: The State of Israel," infra.

14. Again, see Strauss's further elaboration of these points in the "Preface to *Spinoza's Critique of Religion*," supra.

15. Wilhelm Marr apparently coined the term in 1879. On the modern history of "anti-Semitism," or hatred of Jews, see: Jacob Katz, *From Prejudice to*

Destruction—Anti-Semitism, 1700–1933 (Cambridge: Harvard University Press, 1980); Bernard Lewis, *Semites and Anti-Semites* (New York: W. W. Norton, 1987).

16. *Rish'us* (in modern Hebrew, *rish'ut*) may be translated literally as viciousness, wickedness, or cruelty. It was used as a term for the hatred of Jews, or for "anti-Semitism," predominantly by German Jews. The sentence structure as rendered by the transcribers has been altered slightly in order to make Strauss's meaning clearer. Instead of "Why not call it as we Jews call it: *rish'us*, 'viciousness'?" as offered by the transcribers, the two clauses have been rendered as two separate sentences, with the first sentence made Strauss's definite question, and the second sentence made his definite answer; thus, it is offered in the text as: "Why not call it as we Jews call it? It is *rish'us*, 'viciousness'."

17. The word "considerations" has been added to this sentence by the editor, since Strauss apparently did not finish the phrase in speaking, so that the adjective "broader" lacked any noun. (As is also possible, perhaps the tape recording or the transcribers missed the noun, which may have been spoken quietly by Strauss.) In any case, the word "considerations" was chosen because it is one often favored by Strauss in other, similar contexts. In the last clause of the previous sentence, the word "things" has been added, and the verb has been made plural (i.e., changed from "was" to "were"), in order to make the subject of this clause accord with its object. Thus, the unedited clause read: "that the highest of any nation was nothings and abominations."

18. Isaiah 6:5.

19. David Ben-Gurion (1886–1973) was the first prime minister of the modern state of Israel. He served as the leader of the government from 1948 to 1953, and again from 1955 to 1963. It seems likely Strauss was thinking of the state visit which Ben-Gurion made to Burma, and not to Thailand, in December, 1961. During this trip, Ben-Gurion spent eight days meditating, fasting, and reading in a Buddhist temple at the Rangoon residence of his friend U Nu, the prime minister of Burma. It should be noted that while Ben-Gurion did study Buddhist literature during his prolonged stay at the temple, at his request the daily Hebrew newspapers were also brought to him promptly each day.

20. In this side remark made by Strauss, the phrase "Recall among the higher clergy" has been added by the editor, in light of what Strauss had just said in his own words, so that a complete and meaningful sentence might be formed with regard to Strauss's allusion to Bernard of Clairvaux (1090–1153). He was a distinguished churchman and a passionate preacher for the need of the Second Crusade in 1146. But he unconditionally defended the Jews against physical attack, and attempted to prevent further brutality. He also denied any Christian legitimacy to such violence, and he maintained an absolute religious difference for Christians between Jews and Muslims. In an epistle on these matters, he stressed the demise by divine retribution of those knights in the First Crusade who had been persecutors of the Jews.

21. Yitzhak F. Baer, *Galut*, translated by Robert Warshow (New York: Schocken, 1947), 24–25. Xanten is a town in western Germany, on the northern reaches of the Rhine River.

22. As far as I can detect from the English translations then available to Strauss, he translated by himself aphorism 205 from Nietzsche's *Dawn of Day* (*Morganröte*). In fact, there was only available to him a single version of any value: aphorism 205 as it was rendered in *The Portable Nietzsche*, translated and edited by Walter Kaufmann (New York: Viking, 1954), 88–89. However, Kaufmann offered only selections from *The Dawn*, and aphorism 205 only in an abridged form. Strauss (or the transcribers) quoted almost the entire passage; for the omissions, see infra, notes 23, 24, and 25. Strauss's own translation has also been compared with the translation made recently by R.J. Hollingdale, *Daybreak: Thoughts on the Prejudices of Morality* (Cambridge: Cambridge University Press, 1982), 124–25. For the original German, see *Morganröte*, in *Nietzsche Werke: Kritische Gesamtausgabe*, ed. Giorgio Colli and Mazzino Montinari. Sect. 5, vol. 1 (Berlin: Walter de Gruyter, 1971), 180–83.

23. The transcribers record Strauss as rendering the first half of the sentence in the following condensed form: "They themselves chosen for the highest things." What seems closer to a literal translation—"They themselves have never ceased to believe themselves called to the highest things"—has been substituted for the transcribed version, and derives from the Hollingdale translation, *Daybreak*, 124. But see also Walter Kaufmann, *The Portable Nietzsche*, 88, for a slightly different version, which is not closer to Strauss's: "They themselves have never ceased to believe in their calling to the highest things." The German original is as follows: "Sie haben selber nie aufgehört, sich zu den höchsten Dingen berufen zu glauben, ..." See *Morganröte*, 181.

24. A clause from the middle of this sentence had been omitted by Strauss, whether deliberately or not. (Or perhaps the omission must be attributed to the transcribers?) In any case, that clause has been added to the present version of the aphorism quoted from Nietzsche. Thus, what has been added is the following clause: "even in their passions they practice the caution taught by this experience. They are so sure in the . . ." I employ the translation made by Hollingdale, *Daybreak*, 125. (Kaufmann does not translate this phrase, or the one which precedes it, i.e., "they possess by far . . . ," or the entire next section that follows it immediately, but resumes with "And how shall it issue forth," as it is rendered in Strauss's version.) See the German original, *Morganröte*, 182.

25. A clause from the beginning of this sentence had been omitted by Strauss, whether deliberately or not. (Or perhaps the omission must be attributed to the transcribers?) In any case, that clause has been added to the present version of the aphorism quoted from Nietzsche. Thus, what has been added is the following clause: "And how shall it issue forth, this wealth of accumulated great impressions which Jewish history constitutes for every Jewish family, this wealth of passions, virtues, resolutions, renunciations, struggles, victories of every kind." I render it with the aid of the translations both by Kaufmann, *The*

Portable Nietzsche, 89, and by Hollingdale, *Daybreak*, 125. The German original is as follows: "Und wohin soll auch diese Fülle angesammelter grosser Eindrücke, welche die jüdische Geschichte für jede jüdische Familie ausmacht, diese Fülle von Leidenschaften, Tugenden, Entschlüssen, Entsagungen, Kämpfen, Siegen aller Art—wohin soll sie sich ausströmen, . . ." See the German original, *Morganröte*, 182–83.

26. This sentence has been altered slightly by the editor in order to make the first sentence of the paragraph express Strauss's meaning as a separate and intelligible thought, which in the spontaneity of speech was slightly jumbled with the thought of the second sentence. (For one thing, among others, the phrase that Strauss used to begin the next complete sentence—which does form a complete thought—was also uttered but not completed by him in the beginning of the present sentence as well.) Thus, the transcribers recorded Strauss's speech as follows: "The most patent defect, however, of Nietzsche's analysis (and it has some defects) is that his statement, which is almost dithyrambic, is based on a very deep analysis, perhaps on the deepest analysis ever made, of what assimilation could possibly mean. Now the most patent defect of Nietzsche's analysis seems to be this. . . ." As the first sentence stood, it suggested that the defect of Nietzsche's statement was to be based on a very deep analysis, if not the deepest analysis ever made, of what assimilation could possibly mean. I doubt whether this sentence, as originally spoken, was meant by Strauss to criticize Nietzsche for the depth of his analysis. A brief note on the historical facts to which Strauss alludes in the last half of the previous paragraph of the lecture (p. 326 supra) may be helpful to some readers. Albert Einstein (1879–1955), one of the great twentieth-century physicists, is best known for discovering the principle of the relativity of motion; he also received the Nobel Prize in Physics in 1921 for his conception of the "photoelectric effect." Max Planck (1858–1947), another great twentieth-century physicist, first suggested in 1900 the hypothesis of "quanta" of energy and subsequently explored the idea speculatively, which earned him the Nobel Prize in Physics in 1918, and which initiated the beginnings of the "quantum" revolution in modern physics. In 1914 Planck helped to secure for his friend Einstein a professorship at the Prussian Academy of Science in Berlin. Einstein remained with Planck at the Prussian Academy for the next nineteen years; while there he made several further discoveries of high importance to modern physics. It is, then, to this research academy that Strauss alludes. (He calls it a "seminar," perhaps referring to its "physics seminar"?) The accession of Hitler to power in Germany in January of 1933 caused Einstein to resign almost immediately from the Prussian Academy as well as to renounce his German citizenship, and to accept an offer to pursue his research at the Institute for Advanced Studies in Princeton, New Jersey.

27. The transcribers were apparently unable to hear the words that Strauss spoke in the middle of the final clause of this sentence. As a result, the final clause is transcribed as ending with: "which was . . . Jews." The editor has

taken the liberty of giving the phrase "accepting of the national character of the" to the final clause, in light of the contrast between the older and the younger generations of German Jews which Strauss had been discussing in the previous clauses and sentences. The attempt has been made to use, as much as possible, words or their opposites which Strauss himself used to convey his meaning, and especially to do so by a reversal of Strauss's phrase "refusing any national character of," employed by him in the previous clause.

28. According to Joseph H. Hertz, ed., *The Authorized Daily Prayer Book* (New York: Bloch Publishing Co., 1948), 551, this bracketed passage is a conflation of two biblical verses: Isaiah 30:7 and 45:20. It is also the sentence that was falsely accused of slurring Christianity, and was even used as a pretext for persecution of the Jews. (Even Manasse ben Israel believed himself called on to dedicate an entire chapter in his *Vindiciae Judaeorum* [1656] to a defense of the disputed line.) By the eighteenth and nineteenth centuries, through fear of church and state censors, it had been removed from most Ashkenazic prayerbooks. The disputed line is retained by Sephardic prayerbooks; and it has been restored in at least one recent American edition of the orthodox prayerbook of which I am aware—*The Complete Artscroll Siddur*, ed. Nosson Scherman (Brooklyn: Mesorah, 1984), 158. The prayer first appeared in the arrangement by Rav (Abba bar Aivu, or Abba "Arikha") of the New Year's Day liturgy, produced during the third century C.E. in the Babylonia of the Zoroastrians, i.e., a thoroughly non-Christian context. By the twelfth century C.E., it had been adopted as the prayer used to conclude all three daily prayer services during the entire year, and for all holydays as well. Tradition ascribed its composition to Joshua, following the crossing of the Jordan River by Israel in its conquest of Canaan. Two modern opinions about its origin are still upheld: Rav may have been the prayer's author, or it may have been of even greater antiquity, possibly passed down from the Persian period of Jewish history, following the return from the Babylonian exile and prior to Alexander's conquest of Judea. It is certainly a prayer of high and noble spirituality, stressing God's pure and absolute sovereignty, but its popular "authority" derives not only from this nor even from its antiquity. Rather, it seems to issue from its relation to medieval Christian persecution of the Jews, and especially from those events which occurred during and since the Crusades: "It was the death-song of Jewish martyrs in the Middle Ages." (See Philip Birnbaum, ed., *Daily Prayer Book/Ha-Siddur Ha-Shalem* [New York: Hebrew Publishing Co., 1949], 136.) Since Strauss emphasizes so strikingly in this lecture the religious nobility of Jewish martyrdom during the Crusades, it was deemed appropriate that the full text of the prayer which those martyrs recited be conveyed. It also seemed fitting to record the full prayer, with the few additional words of the controversial sentence, because for Strauss the prayer as he refers to it may possibly encompass this much-disputed line in it, which I would suggest for two reasons. First, he alludes enigmatically to the prayer as "a stumbling block to many." (To be sure, he may just mean its crystalization of a high Jewish theology, in which some of his hearers may not believe.) Second, during his dis-

cussion of the anti-Judaism of classical antiquity, he makes a statement which, if not a literal quote of the controversial line in the prayer, is certainly a virtual paraphrase: "And now, our ancestors asserted *a priori*—that is to say, without looking at any of these gods—that these gods were nothings and abominations, that the highest things of any nation were nothings and abominations." Strauss speaks of the *Aleinu* in glowing terms, as "the greatest expression of this, surpassing everything that any present-day man could write." In the context of the lecture, Strauss spoke so eloquently about the *Aleinu* prayer presumably because of the invocation of God against idolatry and against its attendant evils, and because of the call for everlasting fidelity to the special Jewish historical task in helping to bring closer the future redemption of humanity from idolatry in its multifarious forms.

29. Deuteronomy 4:39.

30. Exodus 15:18.

31. Zechariah 14:9.

32. The phrase which occurs in this sentence, "of their political relations," has been added by the editor to the end of the sentence in order to make Strauss's meaning clearer, i.e., to make clear what fate it is that was of concern to Strauss. For my choice of these words, I make use of a construction which combines his earlier "cultural relations" used in the same sentence with his later "political matters" used in the next sentence, and since the sentence clearly seems to intend to express a contrast between cultural and political relations.

33. The last letter Lessing wrote to Mendelssohn, of 19 December 1780:

This emigrant's proper name is Alexander Daveson, and I can testify that our people, incited by yours, behaved abominably toward him. All he wants of you, dear Moses, is that you show him the shortest and surest way to a European country where there are neither Christians nor Jews. I hate losing him; but as soon as he safely arrives there, I shall be the first to follow him.

Translated by Alexander Altmann, in his *Moses Mendelssohn: A Biographical Study* (Philadelphia: Jewish Publication Society, 1973), 581.

34. Martin Buber (1878–1965) was a major twentieth-century philosopher and Jewish thinker, who taught in Germany and Israel, and who was the author of such works as: *I and Thou* (1923); *Moses* (1946); and *Eclipse of God* (1953). Paul Tillich (1886–1965) was the religious thinker who exercised perhaps the greatest influence on Protestant theology since 1945. He taught in Germany and the United States, and among his major works are: *The Courage to Be* (1952); *Dynamics of Faith* (1957); *Systematic Theology* (1963). See also note 44, infra.

35. James Parkes (1896–1981) was an Anglican priest in Great Britain, a scholar of Judaism and especially of its historical and theological relations with Christianity, and an advocate of a fundamental correction in Christian attitudes to Jews, Judaism, and Israel. Among his major works are: *The Conflict of the Church and the Synagogue* (1934); *End of an Exile: Israel, the Jews, and the Gentile World* (1954); and *Whose Land? A History of the Peoples of Palestine* (1970).

36. Louis Finkelstein (1895–1991) was a scholar of rabbinic and medieval Judaism, and a leader of the Conservative religious movement in Judaism in the United States. He was president as well as chancellor of the Jewish Theological Seminary in New York from 1940 to 1971. Among his major scholarly works are: *Jewish Self-Government in the Middle Ages* (1924); *Akiba: Scholar, Saint, and Martyr* (1936); *The Pharisees* (1962); and *New Light from the Prophets* (1970). Reinhold Niebuhr (1892–1971) was one of the leading Protestant theologians of the twentieth century in North America, who taught at the Union Theological Seminary in New York for several decades. He focused on the relation of religion to politics, and he was through his long career a stalwart friend of Jews, Judaism, and Israel in Christian circles as well as in the civic domain. Among his main works are: *Moral Man and Immoral Society* (1932); *The Nature and Destiny of Man* (1943); *Faith and History* (1949); *Christian Realism and Political Problems* (1953).

37. The words "of this reconciliation," as well as the word "reconciliation" at the beginning of the previous sentence, have been added by the editor in order to make the subject of Strauss's discussion clearer. It was chosen because Strauss himself uses the word "reconciliation" in a similar context, and for a directly related point, further along in the paragraph. (See: "But we must not forget the background of this reconciliation.")

38. The words, "were friendly toward Jews, is significant," have been added by the editor in order to make the object of Strauss's sentence clearer, which Strauss himself neglected to provide in the spontaneity of the speech. It is based on similar language used by Strauss further along in the paragraph. (See: "who were not only friendly to Jews," as used with reference to Weber and Schelling.) In the last half of Strauss's response to a questioner (pp. 335–36 supra), he refers in passing to Weber and Schelling as two German thinkers who "showed a very profound understanding of what one would call the 'substance' of Judaism." Perhaps it might be helpful to some readers if their ideas on the substance of Judaism were presented briefly, since Strauss regarded these two thinkers as significant enough to mention only them by name. F. W. J. Schelling (1775–1854) defended a position, in the final stage of his philosophic development, which maintained the irreducible divine revelation to Israel. It has been responsible for conveying the Hebrew Bible, for bringing to light the profundity of the inexpressible divine name, and for bearing divine chosenness as the ground for God's special relation to man. Also, through his *The Ages of the World* (1811), Schelling exercised a deep influence on Franz Rosenzweig's Jewish thought. Max Weber (1864–1920), in his *Ancient Judaism* (1917–19) and in his *The Sociology of Religion* (1921–22), studied carefully the question of the social

sources and subsequent historical unfolding of Judaism as the original ethical rationalism. In his view, through the notion of God in Judaism and through how it was elaborated socially and morally, the Jews contributed decisively to the enduring character and virtue, as well as to the unique and continuing problematics, of Western civilization.

39. Bernard M. Baruch (1870–1965) was an eighth generation American Jew, whose family was long settled in South Carolina. He was a financier as well as an eminent statesman, who served his country with distinction from 1912 to 1951 in the administrations of several presidents.

40. For Leon Pinsker, see note 10 supra. Max Nordau (1849–1923) was a celebrated European Jewish essayist, critic, and journalist. He was one of the first converts made by Theodor Herzl himself to the cause of Zionism. As a spellbinding speaker, he delivered the keynote programmatic address to the delegates of the first World Zionist Congress in 1897 at Basel, Switzerland. Strauss wrote a youthful article on the theme of "Nordau's Zionism" (1923), which was published in *Der Jude* 7 (1923): 657–60, edited by Martin Buber.

41. Aḥad Ha'am, pen name of Asher Ginsberg (1856–1927), was an important modern Jewish thinker, a lucid Hebrew writer and stylist, and the father of "cultural Zionism," the opposite pole to the political Zionism of Theodor Herzl. The well-known essay to which Strauss refers, "*Avdut betokh Ḥerut*" ("Slavery in Freedom"), was first published in 1891. See *Kol Kitvei Aḥad Ha'am* (Tel Aviv: Dvir, 1964), 64–69; *Selected Essays of Ahad Ha'am*, translated and edited by Leon Simon (Philadelphia: Jewish Publication Society, 1962), 171–94.

42. Rambam—the acronym of Rabbi Moses ben Maimon (1135–1204), also known as Moses Maimonides—is the familiar name used by traditional Jews. Rambam in his *The Guide of the Perplexed*, to whose careful study Strauss devoted enormous attention, makes the belief in God as the Creator absolutely crucial to Jewish theology; and he elaborates a theologically sophisticated notion of what such belief in God's creation of the world means, especially in contrast to the doctrine of the eternity of the world enunciated by ancient and medieval Aristotelian philosophy and science. For creation, see *Guide* 2.13-31.

43. Hermann Cohen (1842–1918) was a leader of the neo-Kantian school of philosophy in the nineteenth century, and he was associated for several decades with the University of Marburg in Germany. He developed his own system of philosophy in the neo-Kantian mode, and he composed a major three-volume work to articulate it. In his final years, he returned to Judaism and wrote what is regarded as one of the truly great works of modern Jewish philosophy, *Religion of Reason out of the Sources of Judaism*. For the complex views of Strauss on Cohen, see essay five supra in the present volume; and see also the Editor's Introduction.

44. See *Philosophie und Gesetz* (Berlin: Schocken, 1935), 33, 38–39; *Philosophy and Law*, translated by Eve Adler (Albany: State University of New York Press, 1995) , 44–45, 48–51, 139 note 6; K. H. Green, *Jew and Philosopher* (Albany: State

University of New York Press, 1993), 46–47. Franz Rosenzweig, at the end of his commentary on Yehuda Halevi's poem "The Name," tells the story about Hermann Cohen and the *Borei 'olam* which was first communicated to Rosenzweig by Strauss, and which was supposed by Rosenzweig to convey the fatal flaw in the heart of the rationalist theology of Cohen. For a "rebuttal," see Steven S. Schwarzschild, "Franz Rosenzweig's Anecdotes about Hermann Cohen," in *Gegenwart im Rückblick*, edited by H. A. Strauss and K. R. Grossman (Heidelberg: Lothar Stiehm Verlag, 1970), 209–18. For a translation of the original commentary by Rosenzweig on the Halevi poem, see *Franz Rosenzweig and Jehuda Halevi*, by Barbara E. Galli (Montreal and Kingston: McGill-Queens University Press, 1995), 206–7. The belief in "God as a symbol" may refer to the theology of Paul Tillich, who taught at the Union Theological Seminary in New York, as well as at Harvard University, and who lectured on numerous occasions at the University of Chicago, and then taught there from 1962 to 1965. See his *Dynamics of Faith* (New York: Harper and Row, 1957), 41–54, 89–98. A remark similar to what occurs in the text was made by Strauss in "An Epilogue," in *An Introduction to Political Philosophy*, edited by Hilail Gildin (Detroit: Wayne State University Press, 1989), 148–49. In this remark Strauss makes it clear that, in his opinion, "a frank atheist is a better man than an alleged theist who conceives of God as a symbol." See also note 34, supra.

45. Gershom Scholem (1897–1982) was the great scholar of Jewish mysticism, and of most aspects in the spiritual history of Judaism. Scholem, who was a friend of Strauss from their youth in Germany, and who taught at the Hebrew University in Jerusalem since his emigration to Palestine in 1923, was also an important modern Jewish thinker in his own right. In his remarks on the radical thinking of the Jewish mystics, Strauss probably refers to Gershom Scholem, *Zur Kabbala und ihrer Symbolik* (Zurich: Rhein-Verlag, 1960); idem, *On the Kabbala and Its Symbolism*, translated by Ralph Manheim (New York: Schocken, 1965).

46. In this context, it is perhaps worth considering the remarks that Scholem, to whom Strauss just paid such high tribute, made in his essay "Reflections on Jewish Theology" (1974) on substituting for the belief in God, the belief in "the creative genius of the Jewish people." In these remarks, Scholem also links the doctrine of revelation taught by Jewish religious existentialism, which to him actually implies a humanism, to the humanist positivism of secular cultural Zionism. The remarks are fully quoted in the Editor's Introduction, supra, note 99. See also *On Jews and Judaism in Crisis*, edited by Werner Dannhauser (New York: Schocken, 1976), 274–75.

IV

Studies on the Hebrew Bible

8

On the Interpretation of Genesis

I want to begin with the remark that I am not a biblical scholar; I am a political scientist specializing in political theory. Political theory is frequently said to be concerned with the values of the Western world. These values, as is well known, are partly of biblical and partly of Greek origin. The political theorist must, therefore, have an inkling of the agreement as well as the disagreement between the biblical and the Greek heritage. Everyone working in my field has to rely most of the time on what biblical scholars or classical scholars tell him about the Bible on the one hand, and Greek thought on the other. Still, I thought it would be defensible if I were to try to see whether I could not understand something of the Bible without relying entirely on what the authorities both contemporary and traditional tell me. I began with the beginning because this choice seems to me to be least arbitrary. I have been asked to speak here about Genesis—or rather about the beginning of Genesis. The context of a series of lectures on the "Works of the Mind" raises immediately a very grave question. Works of the mind are works of the human mind. Is the Bible a work of the human mind? Is it not the work of God? The work of God, of the divine mind? The latter view was generally accepted in former ages. We have to reflect on this alternative approach to the Bible, because this alternative is decisive as to the way in which we will read the Bible. If the Bible is a work of the human mind, it has to be read like any other book—like Homer, like Plato, like Shakespeare—with respect but also with willingness to argue with the author, to disagree with him, to criticize him. If the Bible is the work of God, it has to be read in an entirely different spirit than the way in which we must read the human books. The Bible has to be read in a spirit of pious submission, of reverent hearing. According to this view, only a believing and pious man can understand the Bible—the substance of the Bible. According to the view which prevails today, the unbeliever, provided he is a man of the necessary experience or sensitivity, can understand the Bible as well as the believer. This difference between the two approaches can be described as follows. In the past, the Bible was universally read as the document of revelation. Today it is frequently read as one great document of the human mind among many such documents. Revelation is a miracle. This means, therefore, that before we even open the Bible we must have made up our minds as to whether we believe in the possibility of miracles. Obviously we read the account of the burning bush or the Red Sea deliverance in an entirely different way in correspondence with the way in which we have decided previously regarding the possibility of miracles. Either we regard miracles as impossible, or we regard them as possible, or else we do not know whether miracles are possible or not. The last view at first glance recommends itself as the one most agreeable to our ignorance or, which is the same thing, as most open-minded.

I must explain this briefly. The question as to whether miracles are possible or not depends on the previous question as to whether God as an omnipotent being exists. Many of our contemporaries assume tacitly or even explicitly that we know that God as an omnipotent being does not exist. I believe that they are wrong; for how could we know that God as an omnipotent being does not exist? Not from experience. Experience cannot show more than that the conclusion from the world, from its manifest order and from its manifest rhythm, to an omnipotent Creator is not valid. Experience can show at most that the contention of biblical faith is improbable; but the improbable character of biblical belief is admitted and even proclaimed by the biblical faith itself. The faith could not be meritorious if it were not faith against heavy odds. The next step of a criticism of the biblical faith would be guided by the principle of contradiction alone. For example, people would say that divine omniscience—and there is no omnipotence without omniscience—is incompatible with human freedom. They contradict each other. But all criticism of this kind presupposes that it is at all possible to speak about God without making contradictory statements. If God is incomprehensible and yet not unknown, and this is implied in the idea of God's omnipotence, it is impossible to speak about God without making contradictory statements about Him. The comprehensible God, the God about whom we can speak without making contradictions, we can say is the god of Aristotle and not the God of Abraham, Isaac, and Jacob. There is then only one way in which the belief in an omnipotent God can be refuted: by showing that there is no mystery whatever, that we have clear and distinct knowledge, or scientific knowledge, in principle of everything, that we can give an adequate and clear account of everything, that all fundamental questions have been answered in a perfectly satisfactory way; in other words, that there exists what we may call the absolute and final philosophic system. According to that system (there was such a system; its author was Hegel), the previously hidden God, the previously incomprehensible God, has now become perfectly revealed, perfectly comprehensible. I regard the existence of such a system as at least as improbable as the truth of the Bible. But, obviously, the improbability of the truth of the Bible is a contention of the Bible, whereas the improbability of the truth of the perfect philosophic system creates a serious difficulty for that system. If it is true then that human reason cannot prove the nonexistence of God as an omnipotent being, it is, I believe, equally true that human reason cannot establish the existence of God as an omnipotent being. From this it follows that in our capacity as scholars or scientists we are reduced to a state of doubt in regard to the most important question. We have no choice but to approach the Bible in this state of doubt as long as we claim to be scholars or men of science. Yet that is possible only against a background of knowledge.

What then do we know? I disregard the innumerable facts which we know, for knowledge of mere facts is not knowledge, not true knowledge. I also disregard our knowledge of scientific laws, for these laws are admittedly open to future revision. We might say, what we truly know are not any answers to comprehensive questions but only these questions, questions imposed upon us as human beings by our situation as human beings. This presupposes that there is a fundamental situation of man as man which is not affected by any change, any so-called historical change in particular. It is man's fundamental situation within the whole—within a whole that is so little subject to historical change that it is a condition of every possible historical change. But how do we know that there is this whole? If we know this, we can know it only by starting from what we may call the phenomenal world, the given whole, the whole which is permanently given, as permanently as are human beings, the whole which is held together and constituted by the vault of heaven, and comprising heaven and earth and everything that is within heaven and on earth and between heaven and earth. All human thought, even all thought human or divine, which is meant to be understood by human beings, willy-nilly begins with this whole, the permanently given whole which we all know and which men always know. The Bible begins with an articulation of the permanently given whole; this is one articulation of the permanently given whole among many such articulations. Let us see whether we can understand that biblical articulation of the given whole.

The Bible begins at the beginning. It says something about the beginning. Who says that in the beginning God created heaven and earth? Who says it, we are not told; hence we do not know. Is this silence about the speaker at the beginning of the Bible due to the fact that it does not make a difference who says it? This would be a philosopher's reason. Is it also the biblical reason? We are not told; hence we do not know. The traditional view is that God said it. Yet the Bible introduces God's speeches by "And God said," and this is not said at the beginning. We may, therefore, believe the first chapter of Genesis is said by a nameless man. Yet he cannot have been an eyewitness of what he tells. No man can have been an eyewitness of the creation; the only eyewitness was God. Must not, therefore, the account be ascribed to God, as was traditionally done? But we have no right to assert this as definite. The beginning of the Bible is not readily intelligible. It is strange. But the same applies to the content of the account. "In the beginning God created heaven and earth; and the earth was without form and void; and darkness was upon the face of the deep; and the spirit of God moved upon the face of the waters."[1] It would appear, if we take this literally, that the earth in its primeval form, without form and void, was not created, the creation was formation rather than creation out of nothing. And what does it mean that the spirit was moving upon the face of the waters? And what does "the deep," which is perhaps a residue of certain Babylonian stories, mean? Furthermore, if in the beginning God created heaven and earth and all the other things in six days, the days cannot be days in the ordinary sense, for days in the ordinary sense are determined by the movements of the sun. Yet the sun was created only on the fourth creation day. In brief, all these difficulties, and we could add to them, create the impression, which is shared by many people today, that this is a so-called mythical account. This means in fact, as most people understand it, that we abandon the attempt to understand.

I believe we must take a somewhat different approach. Fortunately, not everything is strange in this account. Some of the things mentioned in it are known to us. Perhaps we may begin with that part of the first chapter of Genesis which we can understand. The Hebrew word for creation used there is applied in the Bible only to God. Yet this term, *bara*, is used synonymously, at least apparently, with the Hebrew word for doing or making, *'asa*. In one case, and twice in this special case, doing or making is used of something other than God: the fruit tree making the fruit, to translate literally. So here we have another case of creation. The word *bara* is applied only to God. What this means is not explained in the Bible. But there is a synonymous term (*'asa*) for creating—making—which is applied also to other beings, to trees for example, to say nothing of human beings.[2] Let us therefore see what this word *making* means in the cases in which it occurs within the first chapter of Genesis. The fruit tree making fruit, what kind of making is this? The fruit is originated almost entirely by the tree and, as it were, within the tree. Secondly, the fruit does not have the looks of a tree. Thirdly, the fruit is a complete and finished product. And last, the fruit can be separated from the tree. Perhaps creation has a certain kinship with this kind of making as distinguished from the following kinds of making: first, the making of something which does not originate almost entirely in the maker, artifacts, which require clay and so on in addition to the maker; secondly, the making of something which looks like the maker, the generation of animals; third, the making of something which is not complete but needs additional making or doing, the eggs; and finally, the making of something which cannot be separated from the maker: for example, deeds, human deeds, cannot be separated from the man who does them (deeds and makings would be the same word in Hebrew, *ma'asim*). We keep only one thing in mind: creation seems to be the making of separable things, just as fruits are separable from trees; creation seems to have something to do with separation. The first chapter of the Bible mentions separation quite often. I mean the term; five times it is explicitly mentioned and ten times implicitly in expressions like "after its kind" which means, of course, the distinction or separation of one kind from the other.[3] Creation is the making of separated things, of species of plants, animals, and so on; and creation means even the making of separating things—heaven separates water from water, the heavenly bodies separate day from night.

Let us consider now the most glaring difficulty, namely, the difficulty created by the fact that the Bible speaks of days prior to the creation of the sun. The sun was created only on the fourth creation day. We have no difficulty in admitting that the sun came into being so late; every natural scientist would say this today; but the Bible tells us that the sun was created after the plants and trees, the vegetative world, was created. The vegetative world was created on the third day and the sun on the fourth day.[4] That is the most massive difficulty of the account given in the first chapter of the Bible. From what point of view is it intelligible that the vegetative world should precede the sun? How are the vegetative world, on the one hand, and the sun, on the other, understood so that it makes sense to say the vegetative world precedes the sun? The creation of the vegetative world takes place on the third day, on the same day on which the earth and the sea were created first.[5] The vegetative world is explicitly said to have been brought forth by the earth. The vegetative world belongs to the earth. Hence the Bible does not mention any divine making in the creation of the vegetative world. The earth is told by God to bring forth the plants, and the earth brings them forth, whereas God made the world of heaven and sun and moon and stars, and above all, God commands the earth to bring forth the animals and God made the animals.[6] The earth does not bring them forth. The vegetative world belongs to the earth. It is, we may say, the covering of the earth, as it were, the skin of the earth, if it could produce skin. It is not separable from the earth. The vegetative world is created on the same day on which the earth and the seas are created; the third day is the day of the double creation. In most of the six cases, one thing or a set of things is created. Only on the third day and the sixth day are there double creations.[7] On the sixth day the terrestrial brutes and man are created. There seems to be here a kind of parallelism in the biblical account. There are two series of creation, each of three days. The first begins with the creation of light, the second with that of the sun.[8] Both series end with a double creation. The first half ends with the vegetative world, the second half ends with man. The vegetative world is characterized by the fact that it is not separable from the earth. Could the distinction between the nonseparable and the separable be the principle underlying the division? This is not sufficient. The kinds of plants are separable from each other, although they are not separable from the earth; and creation altogether is a kind of separation. Creation is the making of separated things, of things or groups of things which are separated from each other, which are distinguished from each other, which are distinguishable, which are discernible. But that which makes possible distinguishing and discerning is light. The first thing created is, therefore, light. Light is the beginning, the principle of distinction or separation.[9] Light is the work of the first day. We know light primarily as the light of the sun. The sun is the most important source of light for us. The sun belongs to the work of the fourth day. There is a particularly close kinship between light and the sun. This kinship is expressed by the fact that the light is the beginning of the first half of the creation, and the sun is the beginning of the second half of creation.[10]

If this is so, we are compelled to raise this question: could the second half of creation have a principle of its own, a principle different from light or separation or distinction? This must be rightly understood. Separations or distinctions are obviously preserved in the second half. Men are distinguished from brutes, for example. Hence, a principle different from light or separation or distinction would have to be one which is based on, or which presupposes, separation or distinction but which is not reducible to separation or distinction. The sun presupposes light, but is not light. Now let us look at the creations of the fourth to sixth days—on the fourth day, sun, moon, and stars; on the fifth day, the water animals and birds; on the sixth day, land animals and man.

Now, what is common to all creations of the second half? I would say local motion. I shall therefore suggest that the principle of the first half is separation or distinction simply. The principle of the second half, the fourth to sixth day, is local motion. It is for this reason, and for this very important reason, that the vegetative world precedes the sun; the vegetative world lacks local motion. The sun is what it is by rising and setting, by coming and going, by local motion. The difficulty from which I started is solved or almost solved once one realizes that the account of creation consists of two main parts which are parallel. The first part begins with light, the second part begins with the sun. Similarly there is a parallelism of the end of the two parts. Only on the third and sixth days were there two acts of creation. To repeat, on the third day, earth and seas, and the vegetative world; on the sixth day, the land animals and man. I have said that the principle of the first half of creation is separation or distinction, and that of the second half of the creation is local motion, but in such a way that separation or distinction is preserved in the idea underlying the second part, namely, local motion. Local motion must be understood, in other words, as a higher form of separation. Local motion is separation of a higher order, because local motion means not merely for a thing to be separated from other things; an oak tree is separated or distinguished from an apple tree. Local motion is separation of a higher order because it means not merely for a thing to be separated from other things, but to be able to separate itself from its place, to be able to be set off against a background which appears as a background by virtue of the thing's moving. The creation of the heavenly bodies on the fourth day is immediately followed by the creation of the water animals and the birds. These animals are the first creatures which are blessed by God, and He blesses them by addressing them: "Be fruitful and multiply."[11] They are the first creatures which are addressed, addressed in the second person, not like the earth: "the earth should bring forth"; whereas the earth and water are addressed, they are not addressed in the second person.[12] Water animals and birds belong to the class, or the genus, of living beings. (I try to translate the Hebrew term, *nefesh haya*.)[13] What does it mean that on the fourth day we have the first beings capable of local motion, the heavenly bodies, and that on the fifth day we have animals? Local motion is followed by life. Life too must be understood as a form of separation. In the first place, life is here characterized by the capacity of being addressed, of hearing, of sense perception. It is of the greatest importance that the Bible singles out hearing, and not seeing or touch, as characteristic of the living being.[14] But for our present purpose it is more important to note that animal life appears in the context of the whole chapter as representing a still higher degree of separation than do the heavenly bodies. Animals can change not only their place, but also their courses. The sun and moon and stars cannot change their courses, except miraculously; but as you see from every dog, for example, when he is running along, he can change his course; as a matter of fact, he does not have such a course. Animals are not limited to changing their places. From this it follows that the being created last, namely, man, is characterized by the fact that he is a creature which is separated in the highest degree; man is the only being created in the image of God. If we consider the parallelism of man and plants, and that plants are the only creatures to which the term *making* is explicitly ascribed, we may also recognize that man is capable of doing, making deeds, to the highest degree of all creatures.[15]

It seems then that the sequence of creation in the first chapter of the Bible can be stated as follows: from the principle of separation, light; via something which separates, heaven; to something which is separated, earth and sea; to things which are productive of separated things, trees, for example; then things which can separate themselves from their courses, brutes; and finally a being which can separate itself from its way, the right way. I repeat, the clue to the first chapter seems to be the fact that the account of creation consists of two main parts. This implies that the created world is conceived to be characterized by a fundamental dualism: things which are different from each other without having the capacity of local motion, and things which in addition to being different from each other do have the capacity of local motion. This means the first chapter seems to be based on the assumption that the fundamental dualism is that of distinctness, otherness, as Plato would say, and of local motion. To understand the character of this dualism, otherness and local motion, let us confront it with the only other fundamental dualism referred to in the chapter. I quote the twenty-sixth verse: "And God created man in His image, in His image, in the image of God, did God create him, male and female did He create them."[16] That is a very difficult sentence. The dualism of the male and female could well be used for the fundamental articulation of the world, and it was used in this way in many cosmogonies—the male and female gender of nouns seems to correspond to the male and female gender of all things, and this could lead to the assumption of two principles, a male and a female, a highest god and a highest goddess. The Bible disposes of this possibility by ascribing the dualism of male and female, as it were, to God Himself by locating, as it were, the root of their dualism within God. God created man in His image and, therefore, He created him male and female. And also, the Bible mentions the distinction of male and female only in the case of man, hence saying, as it were, that male and female are not universal characters. There are many things that are neither male nor female, but all things are what they are by being distinguished from each other; and all things are either fixed to a place or capable of local motion. Therefore, the fundamental dualism, male and female, is replaced by the fundamental dualism, distinctness or otherness, and local motion. This latter dualism, distinctness–local motion, does not lend itself to the assumption of two gods, a distinguishing god and a moving god, as it were. Furthermore, it excludes the possibility of conceiving of the coming into being of the world as an act of generation, the parents being two gods, a male and a female god; or, it disposes of the possibility of conceiving of the coming into being of the world itself as a progeny of a male and of a female god. The dualism chosen by the Bible, the dualism as distinguished from the dualism of male and female, is not sensual but intellectual, noetic, and this may help to explain the paradox that plants precede the sun. Another point which I mentioned of which I will have to make use: all created beings mentioned in the Bible are nonmythical beings in the vulgar sense of the word; I mean, they are all beings which we know from daily sense perception. Having reached this point, we reconsider the order of creation: the first thing created is light, something which does not have a place. All later creatures have a place. The things which have a place either do not consist of heterogeneous parts—heaven, earth, seas; or they do consist of heterogeneous parts, namely, of species or individuals. Or as we might prefer to say, the things which have a place either do not have a definite place but rather fill a whole region, or something to be filled— heaven, earth, seas; or else they do consist of heterogeneous parts, of species and individuals, or they do not fill a whole region but a place within a region, within the sea, within heaven, on earth. The things which fill a place within a region either lack local motion—the plants; or they possess local motion. Those which possess local motion either lack life, the heavenly bodies; or they possess life. The living beings are either nonterrestrial, water animals and birds; or they are terrestrial. The terrestrial living beings are either not created in the image of God, brutes; or in the image of God—man. In brief, the first chapter of Genesis is based on a division by two, or what Plato calls *diairesis* (division by two).[17]

These considerations show, it seems to me, how unreasonable it is to speak of the mythical or prelogical character of biblical thought as such. The account of the world given in the first chapter of the Bible is not fundamentally different from philosophic accounts; that account is based on evident distinctions which are as accessible to us as they were to the biblical author. Hence we can understand that account; these distinctions are accessible to man as man. We can readily understand why we should find something of this kind in the Bible. An account of the creation of the world, or more generally stated, a cosmogony, necessarily presupposes an articulation of the world, of the completed world, of the cosmos, that is to say, a cosmology. The biblical account of creation is based on a cosmology. All the created things mentioned in the Bible are accessible to man as man regardless of differences of climate, origin, religion, or anything else. Someone might say, that is very well, we all know what sun, moon, and stars, fruits and plants are, but what about the light as distinguished from the sun? Who knows it? But do we not all know a light which is not derivative from the sun, empirically, ordinarily? I say yes: lightning. And perhaps there is a connection between what the Bible says about the light and the biblical understanding of lightning. The Bible starts then from the world as we know it and as men always knew it and will know it, prior to any explanation, mythical or scientific. I make only this remark about the word "world". The word "world" does not occur in the Bible. The Hebrew Bible says "heaven and earth" where we would ordinarily say "world." The Hebrew word which is mostly translated by "world," *'olam*, means something different; it means, in the first place, the remote past, "once" in the sense of "then," the early time or since early time. It means, secondly, "once" or "then" in the future. And it means finally, "once and for all," for all times, never ceasing, permanent. It means, therefore, that which is permanent. The Hebrew word for world, in other words, means therefore primarily something connected with time, a character of time rather than something which we see. If there are other beings mentioned in other cosmogonies where all kinds of so-called mythical beings are mentioned, for example, in Babylonian stories, we must go back behind these dragons or whatnot, at least by wondering whether these beings exist. And we must go back to those things mentioned in the first chapter of the Bible, and familiar to all of us now, and familiar to all men at all times. The Bible really begins, in this sense also, with the beginning.

But you will say, and quite rightly, that what I have discussed is the least important part or aspect of the first chapter. The cosmology used by the biblical author is not the theme of the biblical author. That cosmology, that articulation of the visible universe, is the unthematic presupposition of the biblical author. His theme is that the world has been created by God in these and these stages. We prepare our reflection on this theme by considering another feature of the account which we have disregarded hitherto. The Bible in this first chapter makes a distinction between things which are named by God and things which are not named by God, and a distinction between things which are called good by God and things which are not called good by God. The things named by God are day, as the name of light, and night, as the name of darkness, and furthermore, heaven, earth, and seas.[18] All other things are not named by God; only these general things, only the things which lack particularization, which do not have a place, properly speaking, are named by God. The rest is left to be named by man. Almost all things are called good by God; the only ones excepted are heaven and man. But one can say that it was not necessary to call man good, explicitly, because man is the only being created in the image of God and because man is blessed by God. However this may be, certainly the only thing which is not called good without being redeemed, as it were, by being blessed by God or by being said to be created in the image of God, is heaven.[19] We may say that the concern of the author of this chapter is a depreciation or a demotion of heaven; in accordance with this, creation appears to be preceded by a kind of rudimentary earth, "in the beginning God created heaven and earth, and the earth. . . ." There is no kind of rudimentary heaven, and the heavenly bodies—sun, moon, and stars—are, according to the first chapter, nothing but tools, instruments, for giving light to the earth; and, most important, these heavenly bodies are lifeless; they are not gods. Heaven is depreciated in favor of the earth, life on earth, man. What does this mean? For cosmology, strictly understood, Greek cosmology, heaven is a more important theme than earth, than life on earth. Heaven means for the Greek thinkers the same as the world, the cosmos. Heaven means a whole, the vault which comprises everything else. Life on earth needs heaven, rain, and not vice versa. And if the more sophisticated Greek cosmologists realized that one cannot leave it at the primacy of heaven, they went beyond heaven, as Plato says, to a superheavenly place. The human thing is a word of depreciation in Greek philosophy.

There is then a deep opposition between the Bible and cosmology proper, and, since all philosophy is cosmology ultimately, between the Bible and philosophy. The Bible proclaims cosmology is a non-thematic implication of the story of creation. It is necessary to articulate the visible universe and understand its character only for the sake of saying that the visible universe, the world, was created by God. The Bible is distinguished from all philosophy because it simply asserts that the world is created by God. There is not a trace of an argument in support of this assertion. How do we know that the world was created? The Bible declared it so. We know it by virtue of declaration, pure and simple, by divine utterance ultimately. Therefore, all knowledge of the createdness of the world has an entirely different character than our knowledge of the structure or articulation of the world. The articulation of the world, the essential distinction between the plants, brutes, and so on, is accessible to man as man; but our knowledge of the createdness of the world is not evident knowledge. I will read you a few verses from Deuteronomy, chapter 4, verses 15 to 19: "Take ye, therefore, good heed unto yourselves, for ye saw no manner of similitude on the day that the Lord spake unto you in Horeb out of the midst of the fire, lest ye corrupt yourselves and make you a graven image, the similitude of any figure, the likeness of male or female, the likeness of any beast that is on the earth, the likeness of any winged fowl that flieth in the air, the likeness of any thing that creepeth on the ground, the likeness of any fish that is in the waters beneath the earth; and lest thou lift up thine eyes unto heaven, and when thou seest the sun, and the moon, and the stars, even all the host of heaven, shouldest be driven to worship them, and serve them, which the Lord thy God hath divided unto all nations under the whole heaven," which means, which the Lord thy God has assigned, attributed, to all nations under the whole heaven. All nations, all men as men, cannot help but be led to this cosmic religion, if they do not go beyond the created things. "But the Lord has taken you and brought you forth out of the iron furnace, out of Egypt, to be under Him a people of inheritance as you are this day." In other words, the fact that the world has a certain structure is known to man as man. That the world is created is known by the fact that God speaks to Israel on the Horeb; that is the reason why Israel knows that sun and moon and stars do not deserve worship, that heaven must be depreciated in favor of human life on earth, and ultimately, that the origin of the world is divine creation. There is no argument in favor of creation except God speaking to Israel. He who has not heard that speech either directly or by tradition will worship the heavenly bodies, will remain, in other words, within the horizon of cosmology.

I would like to say a very few words about the second chapter, because one great difficulty of the beginning of the Bible is that there is a twofold account of creation, one in chapter one and another in chapters two to three. The first chapter of the Bible contains a cosmology which is overarched by an account of the creation of the world, a cosmology which is integrated into an account of the creation of the world. This integration of cosmology into an account of creation implies the depreciation of heaven. Heaven is not divine; heaven is subordinate in rank to earth, to life on earth. But this cosmology used by the Bible, as distinguished from the assertion regarding creation, I mean the articulation of the visible world, this cosmology is based on evidence accessible to man as man, whereas the assertion of the createdness of the world is not based on such evidence. Hence the question arises: with what right is the horizon of cosmology—of the things we see, describe, and understand—transcended? Or, in other words, what is wrong with cosmology? What is wrong with man's effort to find his bearing in the light of what is evident to man as man? What is the true character of human life? What is the right life of man? This question is the starting point of the second account of creation, in the second chapter. The first account ends with man; the second account begins with man. It seems that an account which ends with man is not sufficient. Why? In the first account, man is created on the same day as the terrestrial animals, he is seen as part of the whole—if as its most exalted part. In this perspective, the absolute difference between man and all other creatures is not adequately seen. It appears from the first account that man is separated to the highest degree, that he can move or change his place, in a very metaphorical sense even, to the highest degree. But this privilege, this liberty—freedom—is also a great danger. Man is the most ambiguous creature; hence man is not called good, just as heaven is not called good. There is a connection between the ambiguity of man, the danger to which man is essentially exposed, and heaven, with what heaven stands for, the attempt to find one's bearing in the light of what is evident to man as man, the attempt to possess knowledge of good and evil like the gods. Now, if man is the most ambiguous creature, in fact the only ambiguous creature, we need a supplement to that account in which man appears also as part of the whole. We need an account which focuses on man alone; more precisely, since ambiguity means ambiguity in regard to good and evil, we need an additional account in which man's place is defined, not only as it was in the first account by a command, "Be fruitful and multiply" in general, but by a negative command, a prohibition. For a prohibition sets forth explicitly the limitations of man—up to this point, and not beyond!—the limit separating the good from the evil. The second chapter of the Bible answers the question not about how the world has come into being, but how human life, human life as we know it, has come into being. Just as the answer to the question regarding the world as a whole requires an articulation of the world, the answer to the question regarding human life requires an articulation of human life. Human life, the life of most men, is the life of tillers of the soil, or is at least based on that life. If you do not believe the Bible, you may believe Aristotle's *Politics*.[20] Human life is, therefore, characterized most obviously by need for rain and need for hard work. Now, this cannot have been the character of human life at the beginning; for if man was needy from the very beginning and essentially, he is compelled or at least seriously tempted to be harsh, uncharitable, unjust; he is not fully responsible for his lack of charity or justice because of his neediness. But somehow we know that man is responsible for his lack of charity and justice; therefore, his original state must have been one in which he was not forced or seriously tempted to be uncharitable or unjust. Man's original condition was, therefore, a garden, surrounded by rivers; originally man did not need rain nor hard work; there was a state of affluence and of ease. The present state of man is due to man's fault, to his transgression of a prohibition with which he could easily have complied. But man was created in the image of God, in a way like God. Was he not, therefore, congenitally tempted to transgress any prohibitions, any limitations? Was this likeness to God not a constant temptation to be literally like Him? To dispose of this difficulty, the second account of creation distributes accents differently than the first account had done. Man is now said to be, not created in the image of God, but dust from the earth. Furthermore, in the first account, man is created as the ruler of the beasts. In the second account, the beasts come to sight rather as helpers or companions of man. Man is created in lowliness; he was not tempted therefore to disobey either by need or by his high estate. Furthermore, in the first account, man and woman were created in one act. In the second account, man is created first, thereafter the brutes, and finally only the woman out of the rib of man. Woman, that is the presupposition, is lower than man. And this low creature, I apologize, woman, lower still than man, begins the transgression. Disobedience is shockingly ill-founded. Note, furthermore, that in spite of these differences, the second account fundamentally continues the tendency of the first account in two points. First, there was no need for rain at the beginning, which again means a depreciation of heaven, the source of rain. And secondly, the derivative character of woman implies a further depreciation of the dualism male–female, which plays such a role in the first part. Only one more word about this second chapter. Man's original sin, his original transgression, consisted in eating of the fruit of the tree of knowledge of good and evil. We have no reason to suppose on the basis of the biblical account, as distinguished from later explanations, that man was guided by desire for knowledge of good and evil, for he would have had to have some knowledge of good and evil in order to have such desire. It is even hard to say that man desired to transgress the divine command. It comes out rather accidentally. Man's transgression is a mystery, but he did transgress and he knew that he did. Man certainly chose to disobey. He chose therewith the principle of disobedience. This principle is called knowledge of good and evil. We may say that disobedience means autonomous knowledge of good and evil, a knowledge which man possesses by himself, the implication being that the true knowledge is not autonomous; and, in the light of later theological developments, one could say the true knowledge of good and evil is supplied only by revelation.

What I am suggesting then is this: the crucial thesis of the first chapter, if we approach it from the point of view of Western thought in general, is the depreciation of heaven. Heaven is a primary theme of cosmology and of philosophy. The second chapter contains this explicit depreciation of the knowledge of good and evil, which is only another aspect of the thought expressed in the first chapter. For what does forbidden knowledge of good and evil mean? It means ultimately such knowledge of good and evil as is based on the understanding of the nature of things, as philosophers would say; but that means, somewhat more simply expressed, knowledge of good and evil which is based on the contemplation of heaven. The first chapter, in other words, questions the primary theme of philosophy; and the second chapter questions the intention of philosophy. The biblical authors, as far as we know, did not know anything of philosophy, strictly so-called. But we must not forget that they were probably familiar with things, and certainly familiar with certain things—in Babylon, for example—which are primitive forms of philosophy, contemplation of heaven and becoming wise in human conduct through contemplation of heaven. The fundamental idea is the same as that of philosophy in the original sense. Chapters two and three of Genesis are animated by the same spirit as the first chapter; what the Bible presents is the alternative to the temptation, and this temptation we can call, in the light of certain things we happen to know, philosophy. The Bible, therefore, confronts us more clearly than any other book with this fundamental alternative: life in obedience to revelation, life in obedience, or life in human freedom, the latter being represented by the Greek philosophers. This alternative has never been disposed of, although there are many people who believe that there can be a happy synthesis which is superior to the isolated elements: Bible on the one hand, and philosophy on the other. This is impossible. Syntheses always sacrifice the decisive claim of one of the two elements. And I shall be glad if we can take up this point in the discussion.[21]

I would like to make only one concluding remark, because I understand that in this group you are particularly interested in books. And therefore I would like to say something about the problem of books insofar as it affects the Bible on the one hand, and philosophy on the other. The Greek philosophic view has as its primary basis the simple notion that contemplation of heaven, an understanding of heaven, is the ground by which we are led to the right conduct. True knowledge, the Greek philosophers said, is knowledge of what is always. Knowledge of things which are not always, and especially knowledge of what happened in the past, is knowledge of an entirely inferior character. As regards knowledge of the remote past, in particular, it comes to be regarded as particularly uncertain. When Herodotus speaks of the first inventor of the various arts, he does not say, as the Bible does, that X was the first inventor of this or that art. Herodotus says he was the first inventor as far as we know.[22] Now this kind of thought, which underlies all Greek thought, creates as its vehicle the book, in the strict sense of the term, the book as a work of art. The book in this sense is a conscious imitation of living beings. There is no part of it, however small and seemingly insignificant, which is not necessary so that the whole can fulfill well its function. When the artisan or artist is absent or even dead, the book is living in a sense. Its function is to arouse to thinking, to independent thinking, those who are capable of it; the author of the book, in this highest sense, is sovereign. He determines what ought to be the beginning and the end and the center. He refuses admission to every thought, to every image, to every feeling, which is not evidently necessary for the purpose or the function of the book. Aptness and graces are nothing except handmaids of wisdom. The perfect book is an image or an imitation of that all-comprehensiveness and perfect evidence of knowledge which is aspired to but not reached. The perfect book acts, therefore, as a countercharm to the charm of despair which the never satisfied quest for perfect knowledge necessarily engenders. It is for this reason that Greek philosophy is inseparable from Greek poetry. Now let us look, on the other hand, at the Bible. The Bible rejects the principle of autonomous knowledge and everything that goes with it. The mysterious God is the last theme and highest theme of the Bible. Given the biblical premise, there cannot be a book in the Greek sense, for there cannot be human authors who decide in the sovereign fashion what is to be the beginning and the end, and who refuse admission to everything that is not evidently necessary for the purpose of the book. In other words, the purpose of the Bible, as a book, partakes of the mysterious character of the divine purpose. Man is not master of how to begin; before he begins to write he is already confronted with writings, with the holy writings, which impose their law on him. He may modify these holy writings, compile these holy writings, so as to make out of them a single writing, as the compilers of the Old Testament probably did, but he can do this only in a spirit of humility and reverence. His very piety may compel him to alter the texts of the holy writings which came down to him. He may do this for reasons of piety because certain passages in an older source may lend themselves to misunderstanding which is grave. He may change, therefore, but his principle will always be to change as little as possible. He will exclude not everything that is not evidently necesssary for an evident purpose, but only what is evidently incompatible with a purpose whose ground is hidden. The sacred book, the Bible, may then abound in contradictions and in repetitions which are not intended, whereas a Greek book, the greatest example being the Platonic dialogue, reflects the perfect evidence to which the philosopher aspires; there is nothing which does not have a knowable ground because Plato had a ground. The Bible reflects in its literary form the inscrutable mystery of the ways of God, which it would be impious even to attempt to comprehend.[23]

Notes

["On the Interpretation of Genesis" was originally a lecture delivered by Leo Strauss on 25 January 1957, in the "Works of the Mind" series, at University College, University of Chicago. The text of the lecture prepared by Strauss was first published posthumously in *L'Homme* 21, no. 1 (January–March, 1981): 5–20, followed by a French translation. The present version reproduces the previously published text, with two difficulties flagged: see note 16, infra. The notes below to this lecture are entirely the work of the present editor. —Ed.]

1. See Genesis 1:1–2.

2. For divine "creating" (*bara*), see 1:1, 21, 27 (as well as 2:3, 4); for "making" (*'asa*), both by the Creator and by the creatures, see 1:7, 11, 12, 16, 25, 26, 31 (as well as 2:2, 3, 4); for specifically the trees "making" fruit, see 1:11–12.

3. For separation or division, see: 1:4, 6, 7, 14, and 18; for "after its kind" (*l-mino, l-mineihu, l-mineihem,* and *l-mina*), see: 1:11, 12 (twice), 21 (twice), 24 (twice), and 25 (thrice).

4. Compare 1:14–19 (what was created on the fourth day) with 1:11–13 (what was created on the third day).

5. See 1:9–10.

6. Compare 1:11–12 with 1:7, 16, and 24–25.

7. Compare 1:9–13 with 1:24–30.

8. Compare 1:3–5 with 1:14–19.

9. See 1:4.

10. See 1:3–5 and 1:14–19. For a remark about the biblical notion of the subordination of the sun and all of the planets to God in order to avoid the worship of false gods, and how this fundamental point suggests that Moses could not have been a mere student or imitator of Ikhnaton, see "Freud on Moses and Monotheism," supra, and esp. p. 293: "The Bible is the document of the greatest effort ever made to deprive all heavenly bodies of all possibility of

divine worship." For the meaning of the priority, in the order of creation, of light (first day) to the sun (fourth day) in Genesis 1, see further on in this lecture for an elaboration of that and related points. See also "Jerusalem and Athens," infra, 382–84, for a related discussion.

11. See 1:22.

12. See 1:11, 20.

13. For *nefesh ḥaya* ("living being"), see 1:20, 21, 24, 28, 30. But see also 1:28 for just *ḥaya* (pl., *ḥayot*), traditionally translated as just "living thing."

14. See 1:22, 28–30.

15. Compare 1:12 with 1:27, 28.

16. In the version of the text of Strauss's lecture published in *L'Homme* (p. 12), Genesis 1:26 (actually the verse should have been cited as 1:27) has been misquoted: following "And God created man in His image," i.e., in the first half of the biblical verse quoted by Strauss, the phrase "in His image" is repeated in the printed text of the lecture, but it is not so repeated in the Bible. These two errors were apparently not made accidentally by the printer, but rather may have been made deliberately by Strauss, as a check of the original typed manuscript of the lecture proves. The repetition of "in His image," as well as the miscited verse number, have both not been removed from the present version.

17. For a further comment by Strauss on *diairesis* and theology in Plato, see *On Tyranny*, edited by Victor Gourevitch and Michael S. Roth (New York: Free Press, 1991), 278–79.

18. See 1:5, 8, 10.

19. Compare the creation of heaven on the second day, 1:6–8, with the creation of man on the sixth day, 1:26–31. But see also two paragraphs, infra, for a further discussion and elaboration of these points by Strauss.

20. See, e.g., Aristotle, *Politics* 1264a12–15, 1290b40–41, 1318b7–14, 1319a20.

21. No record, tape, or transcript of the discussion that followed this lecture is known to the present editor. However, for Strauss's most succinct criticisms of the idea of philosophic synthesis, see "Progress or Return?," supra, 104–5, 116–17; as well as *Natural Right and History* (Chicago: University of Chicago Press, 1971), 70–76; and *On Tyranny*, edited by Victor Gourevitch and Michael S. Roth (New York: Free Press, 1991), 191–92.

22. For inventors in Genesis, see, e.g., 4:17, 20–22; 10:8–9. For Herodotus, see, e.g., *The History* 1.68, 94, 171; 2.4, 82, 167.

23. For important additional remarks by Strauss on the Bible as a book, see: "Jerusalem and Athens," infra, 380–82, 394; "Progress or Return?," supra, 120.

the scientist of culture do or did not know that they are or were cultures. This causes no difficulty for him: electrons also do not know that they are electrons; even dogs do not know that they are dogs. By the mere fact that he speaks of his objects as cultures, the scientific student takes it for granted that he understands the people whom he studies better than they understood or understand themselves.

This whole approach has been questioned for some time but this questioning does not seem to have had any effect on the scientists. The man who started the questioning was Nietzsche. We have said that according to the prevailing view there were or are *n* cultures. Let us say there were or are 1,001 cultures, thus reminding ourselves of the Arabian Nights, the 1,001 Nights; the account of the cultures, if it is well done, will be a series of exciting stories, perhaps of tragedies. Accordingly Nietzsche speaks of our subject in a speech of his Zarathustra that is entitled "Of 1,000 Goals and One." The Hebrews and the Greeks appear in this speech as two among a number of nations, not superior to the two others that are mentioned or to the 996 that are not mentioned. The peculiarity of the Greeks is the full dedication of the individual to the contest for excellence, distinction, supremacy. The peculiarity of the Hebrews is the utmost honoring of father and mother. (Up to this day the Jews read on their highest holiday the section of the Torah that deals with the first presupposition of honoring father and mother: the unqualified prohibition against incest between children and parents.) Nietzsche has a deeper reverence than any other beholder for the sacred tables of the Hebrews as well as of the other nations in question. Yet since he is only a beholder of these tables, since what one table commends or commands is incompatible with what the others command, he is not subject to the commandments of any. This is true also and especially of the tables, or "values," of modern Western culture. But according to him, all scientific concepts, and hence in particular the concept of culture, are culture-bound; the concept of culture is an outgrowth of nineteenth-century Western culture; its application to "cultures" of other ages and climates is an act stemming from the spiritual imperialism of that particular culture. There is then a glaring contradiction between the claimed objectivity of the science of cultures and the radical subjectivity of that science. Differently stated, one cannot behold, i.e., truly understand, any culture unless one is firmly rooted in one's own culture, or unless one belongs in one's capacity as a beholder to some culture. But if the universality of the beholding of all cultures is to be preserved, the culture to which the beholder of all cultures belongs must be the universal culture, the culture of mankind, the world culture; the universality of beholding presupposes, if only by anticipating it, the universal culture which is no longer one culture among many. The variety of cultures that have hitherto emerged contradicts the oneness of truth. Truth is not a woman so that each man can have his own truth as he can have his own wife. Nietzsche sought therefore for a culture that would no longer be particular and hence in the last analysis arbitrary. The single goal of mankind is conceived by him as in a sense superhuman: he speaks of the superman of the future. The superman is meant to unite in himself Jerusalem and Athens on the highest level.

However much the science of all cultures may protest its innocence of all preferences or evaluations, it fosters a specific moral posture. Since it requires openness to all cultures, it fosters universal tolerance and the exhilaration deriving from the beholding of the diversity; it necessarily affects all cultures that it can still affect by contributing to their transformation in one and the same direction; it willy-nilly brings about a shift of emphasis from the particular to the universal: by asserting, if only implicitly, the rightness of pluralism, it asserts that pluralism is *the* right way; it asserts the monism of universal tolerance and respect for diversity; for by virtue of being an ism, pluralism is a monism.

One remains somewhat closer to the science of culture as commonly practiced if one limits oneself to saying that every attempt to understand the phenomena in question remains dependent on a conceptual framework that is alien to most of these phenomena and therefore necessarily distorts them. "Objectivity" can be expected only if one attempts to understand the various cultures or peoples exactly as they understand or understood themselves. Men of ages and climates other than our own did not understand themselves in terms of cultures because they were not concerned with culture in the present-day meaning of the term. What we now call culture is the accidental result of concerns that were not concerns with culture but with other things and above all with the Truth.

Yet our intention to speak of Jerusalem and Athens seems to compel us to go beyond the self-understanding of either. Or is there a notion, a word that points to the highest that the Bible on the one hand and the greatest works of the Greeks claim to convey? There is such a word: wisdom. Not only the Greek philosophers but the Greek poets as well were considered to be wise men, and the Torah is said in the Torah to be "your wisdom in the eyes of the nations." We must then try to understand the difference between biblical wisdom and Greek wisdom. We see at once that each of the two claims to be true wisdom, thus denying to the other its claim to be wisdom in the strict and highest sense. According to the Bible, the beginning of wisdom is fear of the

Lord; according to the Greek philosophers, the beginning of wisdom is wonder. We are thus compelled from the very beginning to make a choice, to take a stand. Where then do we stand? We are confronted with the incompatible claims of Jerusalem and Athens to our allegiance. We are open to both and willing to listen to each. We ourselves are not wise but we wish to become wise. We are seekers for wisdom, *philo-sophoi*. By saying that we wish to hear first and then to act to decide, we have already decided in favor of Athens against Jerusalem.

This seems to be necessary for all of us who cannot be orthodox and therefore must accept the principle of the historical-critical study of the Bible. The Bible was traditionally understood as the true and authentic account of the deeds of God and men from the beginning till the restoration after the Babylonian exile. The deeds of God include His legislation as well as His inspirations of the prophets, and the deeds of men include their praises of God and their prayers to Him as well as their God-inspired admonitions. Biblical criticism starts from the observation that the biblical account is in important respects not authentic but derivative, or consists not of "histories" but of "memories of ancient histories," to borrow a Machiavellian expression.[1] Biblical criticism reached its first climax in Spinoza's *Theologico-Political Treatise*, which is frankly antitheological; Spinoza read the Bible as he read the Talmud and the Koran. The result of his criticism can be summarized as follows: the Bible consists to a considerable extent of self-contradictory assertions, of remnants of ancient prejudices or superstitions, and of the outpourings of an uncontrolled imagination; in addition it is poorly compiled and poorly preserved. He arrived at this result by presupposing the impossibility of miracles. The considerable differences between nineteenth- and twentieth-century biblical criticism and that of Spinoza can be traced to their difference in regard to the evaluation of imagination: whereas for Spinoza imagination is simply subrational, it was assigned a much higher rank in later times; it was understood as the vehicle of religious or spiritual experience, which necessarily expresses itself in symbols and the like. The historical-critical study of the Bible is the attempt to understand the various layers of the Bible as they were understood by their immediate addressees, i.e., the contemporaries of the authors of the various layers. The Bible speaks of many things that for the biblical authors themselves belong to the remote past; it suffices to mention the creation of the world. But there is undoubtedly much of history in the Bible, i.e., accounts of events written by contemporaries or near-contemporaries. One is thus led to say that the Bible contains both "myth" and "history." Yet this distinction is alien to the Bible; it is a special form of the distinction between *mythos* and *logos*; *mythos* and *historie* are of Greek origin. From the point of view of the Bible the "myths" are as true as the "histories": what Israel "in fact" did or suffered cannot be understood except in the light of the "facts" of Creation and Election. What is now called "historical" is those deeds and speeches that are equally accessible to the believer and to the unbeliever. But from the point of view of the Bible, the unbeliever is the fool who has said in his heart "there is no God"; the Bible narrates everything as it is credible to the wise in the biblical sense of wisdom. Let us never forget that there is no biblical word for doubt. The biblical signs and wonders convince men who have little faith or who believe in other gods; they are not addressed to "the fools who say in their hearts 'there is no God'."[2]

It is true that we cannot ascribe to the Bible the theological concept of miracles, for that concept presupposes that of nature and the concept of nature is foreign to the Bible. One is tempted to ascribe to the Bible what one may call the poetic concept of miracles as illustrated by Psalm 114: "When Israel went out of Egypt, the house of Jacob from a people of a strange tongue, Judah became his sanctuary and Israel his dominion. The sea saw and it fled; the Jordan turned back. The mountains skipped like rams, the hills like lambs. What ails thee, sea, that thou fleest, thou Jordan that thou turnst back? Ye mountains that ye skip like rams, ye hills like lambs? From the presence of the Lord tremble thou earth, from the presence of the God of Jacob who turns the rock into a pond of water, the flint into a fountain of waters." The Presence of God or His Call elicits a conduct of His creatures that differs strikingly from their ordinary conduct; it enlivens the lifeless; it makes fluid the fixed. It is not easy to say whether the author of the psalm did not mean his utterance to be simply or literally true. It is easy to say that the concept of poetry—as distinguished from that of song—is foreign to the Bible. It is perhaps more simple to say that, owing to the victory of science over natural theology, the impossibility of miracles can no longer be said to be simply true but has degenerated to the status of an indemonstrable hypothesis. One may trace to the hypothetical character of this fundamental premise the hypothetical character of many, not to say all, results of biblical criticism. Certain it is that biblical criticism in all its forms makes use of terms having no biblical equivalents and is to this extent unhistorical.

How then must we proceed? We shall not take issue with the findings and even the premises of biblical criticism. Let us grant that the Bible and in particular the Torah consists to a considerable extent of "memories of ancient histories," even of memories of memories; but memories of memories are not necessarily distorting or pale reflections of the original; they may be re-collections of re-collections, deepenings through meditation of the primary experiences. We shall therefore take the latest and uppermost layer as seriously as the earlier ones. We shall start from the uppermost layer—from what is first for us, even though it may not be the first simply. We shall start, that is, where both the traditional and the historical study of the Bible necessarily start. In thus proceeding we avoid the compulsion to make an advance decision in favor of Athens against Jerusalem. For the Bible does not require us to believe in the miraculous character of events that the Bible does not present as miraculous. God's speaking to men may be described as miraculous, but the Bible does not claim that the putting together of those speeches was done miraculously. We begin at the beginning, at the beginning of the beginning. The beginning of the beginning happens to deal with *the* beginning: the creation of heaven and earth. The Bible begins reasonably.

"In the beginning God created heaven and earth." Who says this? We are not told; hence we do not know. Does it make no difference who says it? This would be a philosopher's reason; is it also the biblical reason? We are not told; hence we do not know. We have no right to assume that God said it, for the Bible introduces God's sayings by expressions like "God said." We shall then assume that the words were spoken by a nameless man. Yet no man can have been an eyewitness of God's creating heaven and earth;[3] the only eyewitness was God. Since "there did not arise in Israel a prophet like Moses whom the Lord saw face to face," it is understandable that tradition ascribed to Moses the sentence quoted and its whole sequel. But what is understandable or plausible is not as such certain. The narrator does not claim to have heard the account from God; perhaps he heard it from some man or men; perhaps he retells a tale. The Bible continues: "And the earth was unformed and void. . . ." It is not clear whether the earth thus described was created by God or antedated His creation. But it is quite clear that while speaking about how the earth looked at first, the Bible is silent about how heaven looked at first. The earth, i.e., that which is not heaven, seems to be more important than heaven. This impression is confirmed by the sequel.

God created everything in six days. On the first day He created light; on the second, heaven; on the third, the earth, the seas, and vegetation; on the fourth, sun, moon, and the stars; on the fifth, the water animals and the birds; and on the sixth, the land animals and man. The most striking difficulties are these: light and hence days (and nights) are presented as preceding the sun, and vegetation is presented as preceding the sun. The first difficulty is disposed of by the observation that creation-days are not sun-days. One must add, however, at once that there is a connection between the two kinds of days, for there is a connection, a correspondence, between light and sun. The account of creation manifestly consists of two parts, the first part dealing with the first three creation-days and the second part dealing with the last three. The first part begins with the creation of light, and the second with the creation of heavenly light-givers. Correspondingly the first part ends with the creation of vegetation, and the second with the creation of man. All creatures dealt with in the first part lack local motion; all creatures dealt with in the second part possess local motion.[4] Vegetation precedes the sun because vegetation lacks local motion and the sun possesses it. Vegetation belongs to the earth;[5] it is rooted in the earth; it the fixed covering of the fixed earth. Vegetation was brought forth by the earth at God's command; the Bible does not speak of God's "making" vegetation; but as regards the living beings in question, God commanded the earth to bring them forth and yet God "made" them. Vegetation was created at the end of the first half of the creation-days; at the end of the last half the living beings that spend their whole lives on the firm earth were created. The living beings—beings that possess life in addition to local motion—were created on the fifth and sixth days, on the days following the day on which the heavenly light-givers were created. The Bible presents the creatures in an ascending order. Heaven is lower than earth. The heavenly light-givers lack life; they are lower than the lowliest living beast; they serve the living creatures, which are to be found only beneath heaven; they have been created in order to rule over day and night: they have not been made in order to rule over the earth, let alone over man. The most striking characteristic of the biblical account of creation is its demoting or degrading of heaven and the heavenly lights. Sun, moon, and stars precede the living things because they are lifeless: they are not gods. What the heavenly lights lose, man gains; man is the peak of creation. The creatures of the first three days cannot changes their places; the heavenly bodies change their places but not their courses; the living beings change their courses but not their "ways"; men alone can change their "ways." Man is the only being created in God's image. Only in the case of man's creation does the biblical account of creation reportedly speak of God's "creating" him; in the case of the creation of heaven and the heavenly bodies, that account speaks of God's "making" them. Only in the case of man's creation does the Bible intimate that there is a multiplicity in God: "Let us make man in our image, after our likeness. . . . So God created man in His image, in the image of God He created him; male and female He created them." Bisexuality is not a preserve of man; but only man's bisexuality could give rise to the view that there are gods and goddesses: there is no biblical word for "goddess." Hence creation is not begetting. The biblical account of creation teaches silently what the Bible teaches elsewhere explicitly but not therefore more emphatically: there is only one God, the God Whose name is written as the Tetragrammaton, the living God Who lives from ever to ever, Who alone has created heaven and earth and all their hosts; He has not created any gods and hence there are no gods beside Him. The many gods whom men worship are either nothings that owe such being as they possess to man's making them, or if they are something (like sun, moon, and stars), they surely are not gods.[6] All nonpolemical references to "other gods" occurring in the Bible are fossils whose preservation indeed poses a question, but only a rather unimportant one. Not only did the biblical God not create any gods; on the basis of the biblical account of creation one could doubt whether He created any beings one would be compelled to call "mythical": heaven and earth and all their hosts are always accessible to man as man. One would have to start from this fact in order to understand why the Bible contains so many sections that, on the basis of the distinction between mythical (or legendary) and historical, would have to be described as historical.

According to the Bible, creation was completed by the creation of man; creation culminated in the creation of man. Only after the creation of man did God "see all that He had made, and behold, it was very good." What then is the origin of the evil or the bad? The biblical answer seems to be that since everything of divine origin is good, evil is of human origin. Yet if God's creation as a whole is very good, it does not follow that all its parts are good or that creation as a whole contains no evil whatever: God did not find all parts of His creation to be good. Perhaps creation as a whole cannot be "very good" if it does not contain some evils. There cannot be light if there is not darkness, and the darkness is as much created as is light: God creates evil as well as He makes peace.[7] However this may be, the evils whose origin the Bible lays bare after it has spoken of creation are a particular kind of evils: the evils that beset man. Those evils are not due to creation or implicit in it, as the Bible shows by setting forth man's original condition. In order to set forth that condition, the Bible must retell man's creation by making man's creation as much as possible the sole theme. This second account answers the question, not of how heaven and earth and all their hosts have come into being, but of how human life as we know it—beset with evils with which it was not beset originally—has come into being. This second account may only supplement the first account, but it may also correct it and thus contradict it. After all, the Bible never teaches that one can speak about creation without contradicting oneself. In postbiblical parlance, the mysteries of the Torah (*sitrei Tora*) are the contradictions of the Torah; the mysteries of God are the contradictions regarding God.

The first account of creation ended with man; the second account begins with man. According to the first account, God created man and only man in His image; according to the second account, God formed man from the dust of the earth and He blew into his nostrils the breath of life; the second account makes clear that man consists of two profoundly different ingredients, a high one and a low one. According to the first account, it would seem that man and woman were created simultaneously; according to the second account, man was created first. The life of man as we know it, the life of most men, is that of tillers of the soil; their life is needy and harsh; they need rain, which is not always forthcoming when they need it, and they must work hard. If human life had been needy and harsh from the very beginning, man would have been compelled or at least irresistibly tempted to be harsh, uncharitable, unjust; he would not have been fully responsible for his lack of charity or justice. But man is to be fully responsible. Hence the harshness of human life must be due to man's fault. His original condition must have been one of ease: he was not in need of rain nor of hard work; he was put by God into a well-watered garden that was rich in trees good for food. While man was created for a life of ease, he was not created for a life of luxury: there was no gold or precious stones in the garden of Eden.[8] Man was created for a simple life. Accordingly, God permitted him to eat of every tree[9] of the garden except of the tree of knowledge of good and evil (bad), "for in the day that you eat of it, you shall surely die." Man was not denied knowledge; without knowledge he could not have known the tree of knowledge nor the woman nor the brutes; nor could he have understood the prohibition. Man was denied knowledge of good and evil, i.e., the knowledge sufficient for guiding himself, his life. While not being a child, he was to live in childlike simplicity and obedience to God. We are free to surmise that there is a connection between the demotion of heaven in the first account and the prohibition against eating of the tree of knowledge in the second. While man was forbidden to eat of the tree of knowledge, he was not forbidden to eat of the tree of life.

Man, lacking knowledge of good and evil, was content with his condition and in particular with his loneliness. But God, possessing knowledge of good and evil, found that "it is not good for man to be alone, so I will make him a helper as his counterpart." So God formed the brutes and brought them to man, but they proved not to be the desired helpers. Thereupon God formed the woman out of a rib of the man. The man welcomed her as bone of his bones and flesh of his flesh but, lacking knowledge of good and evil, he did not call her good. The narrator adds that "therefore [namely, because the woman is bone of man's bone and flesh of his flesh] a man leaves his father and his mother, and cleaves to his wife, and they become one flesh." Both were naked but, lacking knowledge of good and evil, they were not ashamed.

Thus the stage was set for the fall of our first parents. The first move came from the serpent, the most cunning of all the beasts of the field; it seduced the woman into disobedience and then the woman seduced the man. The seduction moves from the lowest to the highest. The Bible does not tell what induced the serpent to seduce the woman into disobeying the divine prohibition against eating of the tree of knowledge of good and evil. It is reasonable to assume that the serpent acted as it did because it was cunning, i.e., possessed a low kind of wisdom, a congenital malice; everything that God has created would not be very good if it did not include something congenitally bent on mischief. The serpent begins its seduction by suggesting that God might have forbidden man and woman to eat of any tree in the garden, i.e., that God's prohibition might be malicious or impossible to comply with. The woman corrects the serpent and in so doing makes the prohibition more stringent than it was: "we may eat of the fruit of the other trees of the garden; it is only about the tree in the middle of the garden that God said: you shall not eat of it or touch it, lest you die." God did not forbid the man to touch the fruit of the tree of knowledge of good and evil. Besides, the woman does not explicitly speak of the tree of knowledge; she may have had in mind the tree of life. Moreover, God had said to the man: "thou mayest eat . . . thou wilt die"; the woman claims that God had spoken to both her and the man. She surely knew the divine prohibition only through human tradition. The serpent assures her that they will not die, "for God knows that when you eat of it, your eyes will be opened and you will be like God, knowing good and evil." The serpent tacitly questions God's veracity. At the same time, it glosses over the fact that eating of the tree involves disobedience to God. In this it is followed by the woman. According to the serpent's assertion, knowledge of good and evil makes man immune to death, but we cannot know whether the serpent believes this. But could immunity to death be a great good for beings that did not know good and evil, to men who were like children? But the woman, having forgotten the divine prohibition, having therefore in a manner tasted of the tree of knowledge, is no longer wholly unaware of good and evil: she "saw that the tree was good for eating and a delight to the eyes and that the tree was to be desired to make one wise"; therefore she took of its fruit and ate. She thus made the fall of the man almost inevitable, for he was cleaving to her: she gave some of the fruit of the tree to the man, and he ate. The man drifts into disobedience by following the woman. After they had eaten of the tree, their eyes were opened and they knew that they were naked, and they sewed fig leaves together and made themselves aprons: through the fall they became ashamed of their nakedness; eating of the tree of knowledge of good and evil made them realize that nakedness is evil (bad).

The Bible says nothing to the effect that our first parents fell because they were prompted by the desire to be like God; they did not rebel highhandedly against God; they rather forgot to obey God; they drifted into disobedience. Nevertheless God punished them severely. He also punished the serpent. But the punishment did not do away with the fact that, as God Himself said, as a consequence of his disobedience "man has become like one of us, knowing good and evil." As a consequence, there was now the danger that man might eat of the tree of life and live forever. Therefore God expelled him from the garden and made it impossible for him to return to it. One may wonder why man, while he was still in the garden of Eden, had not eaten of the tree of life of which he had not been forbidden to eat. Perhaps he did not think of it because, lacking knowledge of good and evil, he did not fear to die and, besides, the divine prohibition drew his attention away from the tree of life to the tree of knowledge.

The Bible intends to teach that man was meant to live in simplicity, without knowledge of good and evil. But the narrator seems to be aware of the fact that a being that can be forbidden to strive for knowledge of good and evil, i.e., that can understand to some degree that knowledge of good and evil is evil for it, necessarily possesses such knowledge. Human suffering from evil presupposes human knowledge of good and evil and vice versa. Man wishes to live without evil. The Bible tells us that he was given the opportunity to live without evil, and that he cannot blame God for the evils from which he suffers. By giving man that opportunity God convinces him that his deepest wish cannot be fulfilled. The story of the fall is the first part of the story of God's education of man. This story partakes of the unfathomable character of God.

Man has to live with knowledge of good and evil and with the sufferings inflicted on him because of that knowledge or its acquisition. Human goodness or badness presupposes that knowledge and its concomitants. The Bible gives us the first inkling of human goodness and badness in the story of the first brothers. The oldest brother, Cain, was a tiller of the soil; the youngest brother, Abel, a keeper of sheep. God preferred the offering of the keeper of sheep, who brought the choicest of the firstlings of his flock, to that of the tiller of the soil. This preference has more than one reason, but one reason seems to be that the pastoral life is closer to original simplicity than the life of the tillers of the soil. Cain was vexed and, despite his having been warned by God against sinning in general, killed his brother. After a futile attempt to deny his guilt—an attempt that increased his guilt ("Am I my brother's keeper?")—he was cursed by God as the serpent and the soil had been after the Fall, in contradistinction to Adam and Eve who were not cursed; he was punished by God, but not with death: anyone slaying Cain would be punished much more severely than Cain himself. The relatively mild punishment of Cain cannot be explained by the fact that murder had not been expressly forbidden, for Cain possessed some knowledge of good and evil, and he knew that Abel was his brother, even assuming that he did not know that man was created in the image of God. It is better to explain Cain's punishment by assuming that punishments were milder in the beginning than later on. Cain—like his fellow fratricide Romulus—founded a city, and some of his descendants were the ancestors of men practicing various arts: the city and the arts, so alien to man's original simplicity, owe their origin to Cain and his race rather than to Seth, the substitute for Abel, and his race. It goes without saying that this is not the last word of the Bible on the city and the arts, but it is its first word, just as the prohibition against eating of the tree of knowledge is, as one may say, its first word simply, and the revelation of the Torah, i.e., the highest kind of knowledge of good and evil that is vouchsafed to men, is its last word. One is also tempted to think of the difference between the first word of the first book of Samuel on human kingship and its last word. The account of the race of Cain culminates in the song of Lamech who boasted to his wives of his slaying of men, of his being superior to God as an avenger. The (antediluvian) race of Seth cannot boast of a single inventor; its only distinguished members were Enoch, who walked with God, and Noah, who was a righteous man and walked with God: civilization and piety are two very different things.

By the time of Noah the wickedness of man had become so great that God repented of His creation of man and all other earthly creatures, Noah alone excepted; so He brought on the Flood. Generally speaking, prior to the Flood man's life span was much longer than after it. Man's antediluvian longevity was a relic of his original condition. Man originally lived in the garden of Eden, where he could have eaten of the tree of life and thus have become immortal. The longevity of antediluvian man reflects this lost chance. To this extent the transition from antediluvian to postdiluvian man is a decline. This impression is confirmed by the fact that before the Flood rather than after it the sons of God consorted with the daughters of man and thus generated the mighty men of old, the men of renown. On the other hand, the fall of our first parents made possible or necessary in due time God's revelation of His Torah, and this was decisively prepared, as we shall see, by the Flood. In this respect the transition from antediluvian to postdiluvian mankind is a progress. The ambiguity regarding the Fall—the fact that it was a sin and hence evitable, and that it was inevitable—is reflected in the ambiguity regarding the status of antediluvian mankind.

The link between antediluvian mankind and the revelation of the Torah is supplied by the first Covenant between God and men, the Covenant following the Flood. The Flood was the proper punishment for the extreme and well-nigh universal wickedness of antediluvian men. Prior to the Flood mankind lived, so to speak, without restraint, without law. While our first parents were still in the garden of Eden, they were not forbidden anything except to eat of the tree of knowledge. The vegetarianism of antediluvian men was not due to an explicit prohibition (see 1:29); their abstention from meat belongs together with their abstention from wine (see 9:20); both were relics of man's original simplicity. After the expulsion from the garden of Eden, God did not punish men, apart from the relatively mild punishment which He inflicted on Cain. Nor did He establish human judges. God as it were experimented, for the instruction of mankind, with mankind living in freedom from law. This experiment, just as the experiment with men remaining like innocent children, ended in failure. Fallen or awake, man needs restraint, must live under law. But this law must not be simply imposed. It must form part of a Covenant in which God and man are equally, though not equal, partners. Such a partnership was established only after the Flood; it did not exist in antediluvian times either before or after the Fall. The inequality regarding the Covenant is shown especially by the fact that God's undertaking never again to destroy almost all life on earth as long as the earth lasts is not conditioned on all men or almost all men obeying the laws promulgated by God after the Flood: God's promise is made despite, or because of, His knowing that the devisings of man's heart are evil from his youth. Noah is the ancestor of all later men just as Adam was; the purgation of the earth through the Flood is to some extent a restoration of mankind to its original state; it is a kind of second creation. Within the limits indicated, the condition of postdiluvian men is superior to that of antediluvian men. One point requires special emphasis: in the legislation following the Flood, murder is expressly forbidden and made punishable with death on the ground that man was created in the image of God (9:6). The first Covenant brought an increase in hope and at the same time an increase in punishment. Man's rule over the beasts, ordained or established from the beginning, was only after the Flood to be accompanied by the beasts' fear and dread of man (compare 9:2 with 1:26–30 and 2:15).

The Covenant following the Flood prepares the Covenant with Abraham. The Bible singles out three events that took place between the Covenant after the Flood and God's calling Abraham: Noah's curse of Canaan, a son of Ham; the excellence of Nimrod, a grandson of Ham; and men's attempt to prevent their being scattered over the earth through building a city and a tower with its top in the heavens. Canaan, whose land came to be the promised land, was cursed because of Ham's seeing the nakedness of his father Noah, because of Ham's transgressing a most sacred, if unpromulgated, law; the curse of Canaan was accompanied by the blessing of Shem and Japheth, who turned their eyes away from the nakedness of their father; here we have the first and the most fundamental division of mankind, at any rate of postdiluvian mankind, the division into a cursed and a blessed part. Nimrod was the first to be a mighty man on earth—a mighty hunter before the Lord; his kingdom included Babel; big kingdoms are attempts to overcome by force the division of mankind; conquest and hunting are akin to one another. The city that men built in order to remain together and thus to make a name for themselves was Babel; God scattered them by confounding their speech, by bringing about the division of mankind into groups speaking different languages, groups that cannot understand one another: into nations, i.e., groups united not only by descent but by language as well. The division of mankind into nations may be described as a milder alternative to the Flood.

The three events that took place between God's Covenant with mankind after the Flood and His calling Abraham point to God's way of dealing with men knowing good and evil and devising evil from their youth; well-nigh universal wickedness will no longer be punished with well-nigh universal destruction; well-nigh universal wickedness will be prevented by the division of mankind into nations in the sense indicated; mankind will be divided, not into the cursed and the blessed (the curses and blessings were Noah's, not God's), but into a chosen nation and the nations that are not chosen. The emergence of nations made it possible that Noah's Ark floating alone on the waters covering the whole earth be replaced by a whole, numerous nation living in the midst of the nations covering the whole earth. The election of the holy nation begins with the election of Abraham. Noah was distinguished from his contemporaries by his righteousness; Abraham separates himself from his contemporaries and in particular from his country and kindred at God's command—a command accompanied by God's promise to make him a great nation. The Bible does not say that this primary election of Abraham was preceded by Abraham's righteousness. However this may be, Abraham shows his righteousness by at once obeying God's command, by trusting in God's promise the fulfillment of which he could not possibly live to see, given the short life spans of postdiluvian men: only after Abraham's offspring will have become a great nation will the land of Canaan be given to them forever. The fulfillment of the promise required that Abraham not remain childless, and he was already quite old. Accordingly, God promised him that he would have issue. It was Abraham's trust in God's promise that, above everything else, made him righteous in the eyes of the Lord. It was God's intention that His promise be fulfilled through the offspring of Abraham and his wife Sarah. But this promise seemed to be laughable to Abraham, to say nothing of Sarah: Abraham was one hundred years old and Sarah ninety. Yet nothing is too wondrous for the Lord. The laughable announcement became a joyous announcement. The joyous announcement was followed immediately by God's announcement to Abraham of His concern with the wickedness of the people of Sodom and Gomorra. God did not yet know whether those people were as wicked as they were said to be. But they might be; they might deserve total destruction as much as the generation of the Flood. Noah had accepted the destruction of his generation without any questioning. Abraham, however, who had a deeper trust in God, in God's righteousness, and a deeper awareness of his being only dust and ashes, than Noah, presumed in fear and trembling to appeal to God's righteousness lest He, the judge of the whole earth, destroy the righteous along with the wicked. In response to Abraham's insistent pleading, God as it were promised to Abraham that He would not destroy Sodom if ten righteous men were found in the city: He would save the city for the sake of the ten righteous men within it. Abraham acted as the mortal partner in God's righteousness; he acted as if he had some share in the responsibility for God's acting righteously. No wonder that God's Covenant with Abraham was incomparably more incisive than His Covenant immediately following the Flood.

Abraham's trust in God thus appears to be the trust that God in His righteousness will not do anything incompatible with His righteousness, and that while or because nothing is too wondrous for the Lord there are firm boundaries set to Him by His righteousness, by Him. This awareness is deepened and therewith modified by the last and severest test of Abraham's trust: God's command to him to sacrifice Isaac, his only son from Sarah. Before speaking of Isaac's conception and birth, the Bible speaks of the attempt made by Abimelech, the king of Gerar, to lie with Sarah; given Sarah's old age Abimelech's action might have forestalled the last opportunity that Sarah bear a child to Abraham; therefore God intervened to prevent Abimelech from approaching Sarah. A similar danger had threatened Sarah many years earlier at the hands of the Pharaoh; at that time she was very beautiful. At the time of the Abimelech incident she was apparently no longer very beautiful, but despite her being almost ninety years old she must have been still quite attractive;[10] this could seem to detract from the wonder of Isaac's birth. On the other hand, God's special intervention against Abimelech enhances that wonder. Abraham's supreme test presupposes the wondrous character of Isaac's birth: the very son who was to be the sole link between Abraham and the chosen people, and who was born against all reasonable expectations, was to be sacrificed by his father. This command contradicted not only the divine promise, but also the divine prohibition against the shedding of innocent blood. Yet Abraham did not argue with God as he had done in the case of Sodom's destruction. In the case of Sodom, Abraham was not confronted with a divine command to do something, and in particular, not with a command to surrender to God, to render to God, what was dearest to him: Abraham did not argue with God for the preservation of Isaac because he loved God, and not himself or his most cherished hope, with all his heart, with all his soul, and with all his might. The same concern with God's righteousness, that had induced him to plead with God for the preservation of Sodom if ten just men should be found in that city, induced him not to plead for the preservation of Isaac, for God rightfully demands that He alone be loved unqualifiedly: God does not command that we love His chosen people with all our heart, with all our soul, and with all our might. The fact that the command to sacrifice Isaac contradicted the prohibition against the shedding of innocent blood must be understood in the light of the difference between human justice and divine justice: God alone is unqualifiedly, if unfathomably, just. God promised to Abraham that He would spare Sodom if ten righteous men should be found in it, and Abraham was satisfied with this promise; He did not promise that He would spare it if nine righteous men were found in it; would those nine be destroyed together with the wicked? And even if all Sodomites were wicked and hence justly destroyed, did their infants who were destroyed with them deserve their destruction? The apparent contradiction between the command to sacrifice Isaac and the divine promise to the descendants of Isaac is disposed of by the consideration that nothing is too wondrous for the Lord. Abraham's supreme trust in God, his simple, single-minded, childlike faith was rewarded, although or because it presupposed his entire unconcern with any reward, for Abraham was willing to forgo, to destroy, to kill the only reward with which he was concerned; God prevented the sacrifice of Isaac. Abraham's intended action needed a reward although he was not concerned with a reward because his intended action cannot be said to have been intrinsically rewarding. The preservation of Isaac is as wondrous as his birth. These two wonders illustrate more clearly than anything else the origin of the holy nation.

The God Who created heaven and earth, Who is the only God, Whose only image is man, Who forbade man to eat of the tree of knowledge of good and evil, Who made a Covenant with mankind after the Flood and thereafter a Covenant with Abraham which became His Covenant with Abraham, Isaac, and Jacob—what kind of God is He? Or, to speak more reverently and more adequately, what is His name? This question was addressed to God Himself by Moses when he was sent by Him to the sons of Israel. God replied: "*Ehyeh-Asher-Ehyeh.*" This is mostly translated: "I am That (Who) I am." One has called that reply "the metaphysics of Exodus" in order to indicate its fundamental character. It is indeed the fundamental biblical statement about the biblical God, but we hesitate to call it metaphysical, since the notion of *physis* is alien to the Bible. I believe that we ought to render this statement by "I shall be What I shall be," thus preserving the connection between God's name and the fact that He makes covenants with men, i.e., that He reveals Himself to men above all by His commandments and by His promises and His fulfillment of the promises. "I shall be What I shall be" is as it were explained in the verse (Exod. 33:19), "I shall be gracious to whom I shall be gracious and I shall show mercy to whom I shall show mercy." God's actions cannot be predicted, unless He Himself predicted them, i.e., promised them. But as is shown precisely by the account of Abraham's binding of Isaac, the way in which He fulfills His promises cannot be known in advance. The biblical God is a mysterious God: He comes in a thick cloud (Exod. 19:9); He cannot be seen; His presence can be sensed but not always and everywhere; what is known of Him is only what He chose to communicate by His word through His chosen servants. The rest of the chosen people knows His word—apart from the Ten Commandments (Deut. 4:12 and 5:4–5)—only mediately, and does not wish to know it immediately (Exod. 20:19 and 21, 24:1–2, Deut. 18:15–18, Amos 3:7). For almost all purposes the word of God as revealed to His prophets and especially to Moses became *the* source of knowledge of good and evil, the true tree of knowledge which is at the same time the tree of life.

This much about the beginning of the Bible and what it entails. Let us now cast a glance at some Greek counterparts to the beginning of the Bible, and in the first place at Hesiod's *Theogony* as well as the remains of Parmenides' and Empedocles' works. They all are the works of known authors. This does not mean that they are, or present themselves as, merely human. Hesiod sings of what the Muses, the daughters of Zeus, who is the father of gods and men, taught him or commanded him to sing. One could say that the Muses vouch for the truth of Hesiod's song, were it not for the fact that they sometimes say lies resembling what is true. Parmenides transmits the teachings of a goddess, and so does Empedocles. Yet these men composed their books; their songs or speeches are books. The Bible on the other hand is not a book. The utmost one could say is that it is a collection of books. But are all parts of that collection books? Is in particular the Torah a book? Is it not rather the work of an unknown compiler or of unknown compilers who wove together writings and oral traditions of unknown origin? Is this not the reason why the Bible can contain fossils that are at variance even with its fundamental teaching regarding God? The author of a book in the strict sense excludes everything that is not necessary, that does not fulfill a function necessary for the purpose that his book is meant to fulfill. The compilers of the Bible as a whole and of the Torah in particular seem to have followed an entirely different rule. Confronted with a variety of preexisting holy speeches, which as such had to be treated with the utmost respect, they excluded only what could not by any stretch of the imagination be rendered compatible with the fundamental and authoritative teaching; their very piety, aroused and fostered by the preexisting holy speeches, led them to make such changes in those holy speeches as they did make. Their work may then abound in contradictions and repetitions that no one ever intended as such, whereas in a book in the strict sense there is nothing that is not intended by the author. Yet by excluding what could not by any stretch of the imagination be rendered compatible with the fundamental and authoritative teaching, they prepared the traditional way of reading the Bible, i.e., the reading of the Bible as if it were a book in the strict sense. The tendency to read the Bible and in particular the Torah as a book in the strict sense was infinitely strengthened by the belief that it is the only holy writing or the holy writing par excellence.

Hesiod's *Theogony* sings of the generation or begetting of the gods; the gods were not "made" by anybody. So far from being created by a god, earth and heaven are the ancestors of the immortal gods. More precisely, according to Hesiod everything that is has come to be. First there arose Chaos, Gaia (Earth), and Eros. Gaia gave birth first to

Ouranos (Heaven) and then, mating with Ouranos, she brought forth
Kronos and his brothers and sisters. Ouranos hated his children and
did not wish them to come to light. At the wish and advice of Gaia,
Kronos deprived his father of his generative power and thus uninten-
tionally brought about the emergence of Aphrodite; Kronos became the
king of the gods. Kronos' evil deed was avenged by his son Zeus, whom
he had generated by mating with Rheia and whom he had planned to
destroy; Zeus dethroned his father and thus became the king of the
gods, the father of gods and men, the mightiest of all the gods. Given his
ancestors it is not surprising that while being the father of men and
belonging to the gods who are the givers of good things, he is far from
being kind to men. Mating with Mnemosyne, the daughter of Gaia and
Ouranos, Zeus generated the nine Muses. The Muses give sweet and
gentle eloquence and understanding to the kings whom they wish to
honor. Through the Muses there are singers on earth, just as through
Zeus there are kings. While kingship and song may go together, there is
a profound difference between the two—a difference that, guided by
Hesiod, one may compare to that between the hawk and the nightin-
gale. Surely Metis (Wisdom), while being Zeus's first spouse and having
become inseparable from him, is not identical with him; the relation of
Zeus and Metis may remind one of the relation of God and Wisdom in
the Bible.[11] Hesiod speaks of the creation or making of men not in the
Theogony but in his *Works and Days*, i.e., in the context of his teaching
regarding how man should live, regarding man's right life, which
includes the teaching regarding the right seasons (the "days"): the question of the right life does not arise regarding the gods. The right life for
man is the just life, the life devoted to working, especially to tilling the
soil. Work thus understood is a blessing ordained by Zeus who blesses
the just and crushes the proud: often even a whole city is destroyed for
the deeds of a single bad man. Yet Zeus takes cognizance of men's justice and injustice only if he so wills (35–36, 225–85). Accordingly, work
appears to be not a blessing but a curse: men must work because the
gods keep hidden from them the means of life and they do this in order
to punish them for Prometheus' theft, inspired by philanthropy, of fire.
But was not Prometheus' action itself prompted by the fact that men
were not properly provided for by the gods and in particular by Zeus?
Be this as it may, Zeus did not deprive men of the fire that Prometheus
had stolen for them; he punished them by sending Pandora to them
with her box that was filled with countless evils such as hard toils (42,
105). The evils with which human life is beset cannot be traced to
human sin. Hesiod conveys the same message by his story of the five
races of men, which came into being successively. The first race, the

golden race, was made by the gods while Kronos was still ruling in heaven; these men lived without toil and grief; they had all good things in abundance because the earth by itself gave them abundant fruit. Yet the men made by father Zeus lack this bliss; Hesiod does not make clear whether this is due to Zeus's ill will or to his lack of power; he gives us no reason to think that it is due to man's sin. He creates the impression that human life became ever more miserable as one race of men succeeds the other: there is no divine promise, supported by the fulfillment of earlier divine promises, that permits one to trust and to hope.

The most striking difference between the poet Hesiod and the philosophers Parmenides and Empedocles is that according to the philosophers not everything has come into being: that which truly is has not come into being and does not perish. This does not necessarily mean that what is always is a god or gods. For if Empedocles, e.g., calls one of the eternal four elements Zeus, this Zeus has hardly anything in common with what Hesiod, or the people generally, understood by Zeus. At any rate, according to both philosophers the gods as ordinarily understood have come into being, just as heaven and earth, and therefore will perish again.

At the time when the opposition between Jerusalem and Athens reached the level of what one may call its classical struggle, in the twelfth and thirteenth centuries, philosophy was represented by Aristotle. The Aristotelian god like the biblical God is a thinking being, but in opposition to the biblical God he is only a thinking being, pure thought: pure thought that thinks itself and only itself. Only by thinking himself and nothing but himself does he rule the world. He surely does not rule by giving orders and laws. Hence he is not a creator-god: the world is as eternal as god. Man is not his image: man is much lower in rank than other parts of the world. For Aristotle it is almost a blasphemy to ascribe justice to his god; he is above justice as well as injustice.[12]

It has often been said that the philosopher who comes closest to the Bible is Plato. This was said not the least during the classical struggle between Jerusalem and Athens in the Middle Ages. Both Platonic philosophy and biblical piety are animated by the concern with purity and purification: the "pure reason" in Plato's sense is closer to the Bible than the "pure reason" in Kant's sense or, for that matter, in Anaxagoras' and Aristotle's sense. Plato teaches, just as the Bible, that heaven and earth were created or made by an invisible God whom he calls the Father, who is always, who is good, and hence whose creation is good. The coming-into-being and the preservation of the world that he has created depends on the will of its maker. What Plato himself calls the theology consists of two teachings: 1) God is good and hence is no way the cause of evil; 2) God is simple and hence unchangeable. On the divine concern with men's justice and injustice, the Platonic teaching is in fundamental agreement with the biblical teaching; it even culminates in a statement that agrees almost literally with biblical statements.[13] Yet the differences between the Platonic and the biblical teaching are no less striking than the agreements. The Platonic teaching on creation does not claim to be more than a likely tale. The Platonic God is a creator also of gods, of visible living beings, i.e., of the stars; the created gods rather than the creator God create the mortal living beings and in particular man; heaven is a blessed god. The Platonic God does not create the world by his word; he creates it after having looked to the eternal ideas which therefore are higher than he. In accordance with this, Plato's explicit theology is presented within the context of the first discussion of education in the *Republic*, within the context of what one may call the discussion of elementary education; in the second and final discussion—the discussion of the education of the philosophers—theology is replaced by the doctrine of ideas. As for the thematic discussion of providence in the *Laws*, it may suffice here to say that it occurs within the context of the discussion of penal law.

In his likely tale of how God created the visible whole, Plato makes a distinction between two kinds of gods, the visible cosmic gods and the traditional gods—between the gods who revolve manifestly, i.e., who manifest themselves regularly, and the gods who manifest themselves so far as they will. The least one would have to say is that according to Plato the cosmic gods are of much higher rank than the traditional gods, the Greek gods. Inasmuch as the cosmic gods are accessible to man as man—to his observations and calculations—whereas the Greek gods are accessible only to the Greeks through Greek traditions, one may ascribe in comic exaggeration the worship of the cosmic gods to the barbarians. This ascription is made in an altogether non-comic manner and intent in the Bible: Israel is forbidden to worship the sun and the moon and the stars, which the Lord has allotted to the other peoples everywhere under heaven.[14] This implies that the other peoples', the barbarians', worship of the cosmic gods is not due to a natural or rational cause, to the fact that those gods are accessible to man as man, but to an act of God's will. It goes without saying that according to the Bible the God Who manifests Himself as far as He wills, Who is not universally worshiped as such, is the only true god. The Platonic statement taken in conjunction with the biblical statement brings out the fundamental opposition of Athens at its peak to

Jerusalem: the opposition of the God or gods of the philosophers to the God of Abraham, Isaac, and Jacob, the opposition of Reason and Revelation.

II. On Socrates and the Prophets

Fifty years ago, in the middle of World War I, Hermann Cohen, the greatest representative of German Jewry and spokesman for it, the most powerful figure among the German professors of philosophy of his time, stated his view on Jerusalem and Athens in a lecture entitled "The Social Ideal in Plato and the Prophets."[15] He repeated that lecture shortly before his death. We may then regard it as stating his final view on Jerusalem and Athens, and therewith on *the* truth. For, as Cohen says right at the beginning, "Plato and the prophets are the two most important sources of modern culture." Being concerned with "the social ideal," he does not say a single word on Christianity in the whole lecture. Crudely but not misleadingly one may restate Cohen's view as follows. *The* truth is the synthesis of the teaching of Plato and that of the prophets. What we owe to Plato is the insight that the truth is in the first place the truth of science, but that science must be supplemented, overarched, by the idea of the good, which to Cohen means, not God, but rational, scientific ethics. The ethical truth must not only be compatible with the scientific truth, the ethical truth even needs the scientific truth. The prophets are very much concerned with knowledge: with the knowledge of God; but this knowledge as the prophets understood it has no connection whatever with scientific knowledge; it is knowledge only in a metaphorical sense. It is perhaps with a view to this fact that Cohen speaks once of the divine Plato but never of the divine prophets. Why then can he not leave matters at Platonic philosophy? What is the fundamental defect of Platonic philosophy that is remedied by the prophets and only by the prophets? According to Plato, the cessation of evils requires the rule of the philosophers, of the men who possess the highest kind of human knowledge, i.e., of science in the broadest sense of the term. But this kind of knowledge, as to some extent all scientific knowledge, is according to Plato the preserve of a small minority: of the men who possess certain gifts that most men lack—of the few men who possess a certain nature. Plato presupposes that there is an unchangeable human nature. As a consequence, he presupposes that there is such a fundamental structure of the good human society as is unchangeable. This leads him to assert or to assume that there will be wars as long as there will be human beings, that there ought to be a class of warriors, and that that class ought to be higher in rank and honor than the class of producers and exchangers. These defects are remedied by the prophets precisely because they lack the idea of science and hence the idea of nature, and hence they can believe that men's conduct toward one another can undergo a change much more radical than any change ever dreamt of by Plato.

Cohen has brought out very well the antagonism between Plato and the prophets. Nevertheless we cannot leave matters at his view of that antagonism. Cohen's thought belongs to the world preceding World War I. Accordingly he had a greater faith in the power of modern Western culture to mold the fate of mankind than seems to be warranted now. The worst things that he experienced were the Dreyfus scandal and the pogroms instigated by czarist Russia: he did not experience communist Russia and Hitler Germany. More disillusioned regarding modern culture than Cohen was, we wonder whether the two ingredients of modern culture, of the modern synthesis, are not more solid than that synthesis. Catastrophes and horrors of a magnitude hitherto unknown, which we have seen and through which we have lived, were better provided for, or made intelligible, by both Plato and the prophets than by the modern belief in progress. Since we are less certain than Cohen was that the modern synthesis is superior to its premodern ingredients, and since the two ingredients are in fundamental opposition to each other, we are ultimately confronted by a problem rather than by a solution.

More particularly, Cohen understood Plato in the light of the opposition between Plato and Aristotle—an opposition that he understood in the light of the opposition between Kant and Hegel. We, however, are more impressed than Cohen was by the kinship between Plato and Aristotle on the one hand, and the kinship between Kant and Hegel on the other. In other words, the quarrel between the ancients and the moderns seems to us to be more fundamental than either the quarrel between Plato and Aristotle or that between Kant and Hegel.

We prefer to speak of Socrates and the prophets rather than of Plato and the prophets, for the following reasons. We are no longer as sure as Cohen was that we can draw a clear line between Socrates and Plato. There is traditional support for drawing such a clear line, above all in Aristotle; but Aristotle's statements on this kind of subject no longer possess for us the authority that they formerly possessed, and this is due partly to Cohen himself. The clear distinction between Socrates and Plato is based, not only on tradition, but on the results of modern historical criticism; yet these results are in the decisive respect hypothetical. The decisive fact for us is that Plato as it were points away from himself to Socrates. If we wish to understand Plato, we must take him seriously; we must take seriously in particular his deference to Socrates. Plato points not only to Socrates' speeches but to his whole life, to his fate as well. Hence Plato's life and fate do not have the symbolic character of Socrates' life and fate. Socrates, as presented by Plato, had a mission; Plato did not claim to have a mission. It is in the first place this fact—the fact that Socrates had a mission—that induces us to consider, not Plato and the prophets, but Socrates and the prophets.

I cannot speak in my own words of the mission of the prophets. Surely here and now I cannot do more than remind you of three prophetic utterances of singular force and grandeur. Isaiah 6: "In the year that King Uzziah died I saw also the Lord sitting upon a throne, high and lifted up, and His train filled the temple. Above it stood the seraphim: each one had six wings; with twain he covered his face, and with twain he covered his feet, and with twain he did fly. And one cried unto another, and said, Holy, holy, holy is the Lord of hosts: the whole world is full of His glory. And the posts of the door moved at the voice of him that cried, and the house was filled with smoke. Then I said, Woe is me! for I am undone; because I am a man of unclean lips, and I dwell in the midst of a people of unclean lips: for mine eyes have seen the King, the Lord of hosts. Then flew one of the seraphim unto me, having a live coal in his hand, which he had taken with the tongs from off the altar: And he laid it upon my mouth, and said, Lo, this hath touched thy lips; and thine iniquity is taken away, and thy sin purged. Also I heard the voice of the Lord, saying, Whom shall I send, and who will go for us? Then said I, Here am I; send me." Isaiah, it seems, volunteered for his mission. Could he not have remained silent? Could he refuse to volunteer? When the word of the Lord came unto Jonah, "Arise, go to Nineveh, that great city, and cry against it; for their wickedness is come up before me," "Jonah rose up to flee unto Tarshish from the presence of the Lord"; Jonah ran away from his mission; but God did not allow him to run away; He compelled him to fulfill it. Of this compulsion we hear in different ways from Amos and Jeremiah. Amos 3:7–8: "Surely the Lord God will do nothing but He revealeth His secret unto His servants the prophets. The lion hath roared, who will not fear? the Lord God hath spoken; who will not prophesy?" The prophets, overpowered by the majesty of the Lord, by His wrath and His mercy, bring the message of His wrath and His mercy. Jeremiah 1:4–10: "Then the word of the Lord came unto me, saying, Before I formed thee in the belly I knew thee and before thou camest out of the womb I sanctified thee, and I ordained thee a prophet unto the nations. Then said I, Ah, Lord God! behold, I cannot speak; for I am a child. But the Lord said unto me, Say not, I am a child; for thou shalt go to all that I shall send thee, and what-soever I command thee thou shalt speak. Be not afraid of their faces; for I am with thee to deliver thee, saith the Lord. Then the Lord put forth his hand, and touched my mouth. And the Lord said unto me, Behold, I have put my words in thy mouth. See, I have this day set thee over the nations and over the kingdoms, to root out, and to pull down, and to destroy, and to throw down, to build, and to plant."

The claim to have been sent by God was raised also by men who were not truly prophets but prophets of falsehood, false prophets. Many or most hearers were therefore uncertain as to which kinds of claimants to prophecy were to be trusted or believed. According to the Bible, the false prophets simply lied in saying that they were sent by God: "they speak a vision of their own heart, and not out of the mouth of the Lord. They say . . . the Lord hath said, Ye shall have peace." (Jer. 23:16–17) The false prophets tell the people what the people like to hear; hence they are much more popular than the true prophets. The false prophets are "prophets of the deceit of their own heart" (ibid., 26); they tell the peo-ple what they themselves imagined (consciously or unconsciously) because they wished it or their hearers wished it. But: "Is not My word like as a fire? saith the Lord, and like a hammer that breaketh the rock in pieces?" (ibid., 29) Or, as Jeremiah put it when opposing the false prophet Hananiah: "The prophets that have been before me and before thee of old prophesied both against many countries, and against great kingdoms, of war, and of evil, and of pestilence." (28:8) This does not mean that a prophet is true only if he is a prophet of doom; the true prophets are also prophets of ultimate salvation. We understand the difference between the true and the false prophets if we listen to and meditate on these words of Jeremiah: "Thus saith the Lord: Cursed is the man that trusteth in man, and makes flesh his arm, and whose heart departeth from the Lord. . . . Blessed is the man that trusteth in the Lord, and whose hope the Lord is." [17:5, 7] The false prophets trust in flesh, even if that flesh is the temple in Jerusalem, the promised land, nay, the chosen people itself, nay, God's promise to the chosen people if that promise is taken to be an unconditional promise and not as a part of a Covenant. The true prophets, regardless of whether they predict doom or salvation, predict the unexpected, the humanly unforeseeable—what would not occur to men, left to themselves, to fear or to hope. The true prophets speak and act by the spirit, and in the spirit, of *Ehyeh-Asher-Ehyeh*. For the false prophets on the other hand there cannot be the wholly unexpected, whether bad or good.

Of Socrates' mission we know only through Plato's *Apology of Socrates*, which presents itself as the speech delivered by Socrates when he defended himself against the charge that he did not believe in the existence of the gods worshiped by the city of Athens and that he corrupted the young. In that speech he denies possessing any more than human wisdom. This denial was understood by Yehuda Halevi among others as follows: "Socrates said to the people: 'I do not deny your divine wisdom, but I say that I do not understand it; I am wise only in human wisdom'."[16] While this interpretation points in the right direction, it goes somewhat too far. At least Socrates refers, immediately after having denied possessing any more than human wisdom, to the speech that originated his mission, and of this speech he says that it is not his, but he seems to ascribe to it divine origin. He does trace what he says to a speaker who is worthy of credence to the Athenians. But it is probable that he means by that speaker his companion Chairephon, who is worthy of credence to the Athenians, more worthy of credence to the Athenians than Socrates, because he was attached to the democratic regime. This Chairephon, having once come to Delphi, asked Apollo's oracle whether there was anyone wiser than Socrates. The Pythia replied that no one was wiser. This reply originated Socrates' mission. We see at once that Socrates' mission originated in human initiative, in the initiative of one of Socrates' companions. Socrates takes it for granted that the reply given by the Pythia was given by the god Apollo himself. Yet this does not induce him to take it for granted that the god's reply is true. He does take it for granted that it is not meet for the god to lie. Yet this does not make the god's reply convincing to him. In fact he tries to refute that reply by discovering men who are wiser than he. Engaging in this quest he finds out that the god said the truth: Socrates is wiser than other men because he knows that he knows nothing, i.e., nothing about the most important things, whereas the others believe that they know the truth about the most important things. Thus his attempt to refute the oracle turns into a vindication of the oracle. Without intending it, he comes to the assistance of the god; he serves the god; he obeys the god's command. Although no god had ever spoken to him, he is satisfied that the god had commanded him to examine himself and the others, i.e., to philosophize, or to exhort everyone he meets to the practice of virtue: he has been given by the god to the city of Athens as a gadfly.

While Socrates does not claim to have heard the speech of a god, he claims that a voice—something divine and demonic—occurs to him from time to time, his *daimonion*. This *daimonion*, however, has no connection with Socrates' mission, for it never urges him forward but only keeps him back. While the Delphic oracle urged him forward toward philosophizing, toward examining his fellow men, and thus made him generally hated and thus brought him into mortal danger, his *daimonion* kept him back from political activity and thus saved him from mortal danger.

The fact that both Socrates and the prophets have a divine mission means, or at any rate implies, that both Socrates and the prophets are concerned with justice or righteousness, with the perfectly just society which as such would be free from all evils. To this extent Socrates' figuring out of the best social order and the prophets' vision of the messianic age are in agreement. Yet whereas the prophets predict the coming of the messianic age, Socrates merely holds that the perfect society is possible: whether it will ever be actual depends on an unlikely, although not impossible, coincidence, the coincidence of philosophy and political power. For, according to Socrates, the coming-into-being of the best political order is not due to divine intervention; human nature will remain as it always has been; the decisive difference between the best political order and all other societies is that in the former the philosophers will be kings or that the natural potentiality of the philosophers will reach its utmost perfection. In the most perfect social order as Socrates sees it, knowledge of the most important things will remain, as it always was, the preserve of the philosophers, i.e., of a very small part of the population. According to the prophets, however, in the messianic age "the earth shall be full of knowledge of the Lord, as the waters cover the earth" (Isaiah 11:9), and this will be brought about by God Himself. As a consequence, the messianic age will be the age of universal peace: all nations shall come to the mountain of the Lord, to the house of the God of Jacob, "and they shall beat their swords into plowshares, and their spears into pruning hooks: nation shall not lift up sword against nation, neither shall they learn war any more." (Isaiah 2:2–4) The best regime, however, as Socrates envisages it, will animate a single city which as a matter of course will become embroiled in wars with other cities. The cessation of evils that Socrates expects from the establishment of the best regime will not include the cessation of war.

The perfectly just man, the man who is as just as is humanly possible, is according to Socrates the philosopher and according to the prophets the faithful servant of the Lord. The philosopher is the man who dedicates his life to the quest for knowledge of the good, of the idea of the good; what we would call moral virtue is only the condition or by-product of that quest. According to the prophets, however, there is no need for the quest for knowledge of the good: God "hath shewed thee, o man, what is good; and what doth the Lord require of thee, but to do justly, and to love mercy, and to walk humbly with thy God." (Micah 6:8) In accordance with this the prophets as a rule address the people and sometimes even all the peoples, whereas Socrates as a rule addresses only one man. In the language of Socrates the prophets are orators, while Socrates engages in conversations with one man, which means he is addressing questions to him.

There is one striking example of a prophet talking in private to a single man, in a way addressing a question to him. 2 Sam. 12:1–7: "And the Lord sent Nathan unto David. And he came unto him, and said unto him, There were two men in one city; the one rich, and the other poor. The rich man had exceeding many flocks and herds: But the poor man had nothing, save one little ewe lamb, which he had brought and nourished up: and it grew up together with him, and with his children; it did eat of his own meat, and drank of his own cup, and lay in his bosom, and was unto him as a daughter. And there came a traveler unto the rich man and he spared to take of his own flock and of his own herd, to dress for the wayfaring man that was come unto him; but took the poor man's lamb, and dressed it for the man that was come unto him. And David's anger was greatly kindled against the man; and he said to Nathan, As the Lord liveth, the man that hath done this thing shall surely die; And he shall restore the lamb fourfold, because he did this thing, and because he had no pity. And Nathan said to David, Thou art the man." The nearest parallel to this event that occurs in the Socratic writings is Socrates' reproof of his former companion, the tyrant Critias. "When the thirty were putting to death many citizens and by no means the worst ones, and were encouraging many in crime, Socrates said *somewhere*, that it seemed strange that a herdsman who lets his cattle decrease and go to the bad should not admit that he is a poor cowherd; but stranger still that a statesman when he causes the citizens to decrease and go to the bad should feel no shame nor think himself a poor statesman. This remark was *reported* to Critias. . . ." (Xenophon, *Memorabilia* 1.2.32–33)

Notes

1. *Discorsi* I.16.

2. Bacon, "Of Atheism," *Essays.*

3. Job 38:4.

4. See U. Cassuto, *A Commentary on the Book of Genesis* (Jerusalem: Magnes Press, 1961), part I, 42.

5. See the characterization of the plants as *engeia* ("in or of the earth") in Plato's *Republic* 491d1. See Empedocles A70.

6. See the distinction between the two kinds of "other gods" in Deut. 4:15–19, between the idols on the one hand, and sun, moon, and stars on the other.

7. Isaiah 45:7.

8. Cassuto, *Commentary*, 77–79.

9. One does not have to stoop in order to pluck the fruits of trees.

10. The Bible records an apparently similar incident involving Abimelech and Rebekah (26:6–11). That incident took place after the birth of Jacob; this alone would explain why there was no divine intervention in this case.

11. *Theogony* 53–97 and 886–900; see Proverbs 8.

12. *Metaphysics* 1072b14–30, 1074b15–1075a11; *De Anima* 429a19–20; *Eth. Nic.* 1141a33–b2, 1178b1–12; *Eth. Eud.* 1249a14–15.

13. Compare *Laws* 905a4–b2 with Amos 9:1–3 and Psalm 139:7–10.

14. *Timaeus* 40d6–41a5; Aristophanes, *Peace* 404–13; Deut. 4:19.

15. *Hermann Cohens Jüdische Schriften* (Berlin: C. A. Schwetschke und Sohn Verlag, 1924), I, 306–30; see the editor's note, on p. 341.

16. *Kuzari* 4.13 and 5.14. See Leo Strauss, *Persecution and the Art of Writing* (Glencoe, Ill.: Free Press, 1952), 105–6.

V

Comments on Jewish History

10

What Is Political Philosophy?
[The First Paragraph]

The Problem of Political Philosophy

It is a great honor, and at the same time a challenge, to accept a task of particular difficulty, to be asked to speak about political philosophy in Jerusalem. In this city, and in this land, the theme of political philosophy—"the city of righteousness, the faithful city"—has been taken more seriously than anywhere else on earth. Nowhere else has the longing for justice and the just city filled the purest hearts and the loftiest souls with such zeal as on this sacred soil. I know all too well that I am utterly unable to convey to you what in the best possible case, in the case of any man, would be no more than a faint reproduction or a weak imitation of our prophets' vision. I shall even be compelled to lead you into a region where the dimmest recollection of that vision is on the point of vanishing altogether—where the Kingdom of God is derisively called an imagined principality—to say here nothing of the region which was never illumined by it. But while being compelled, or compelling myself, to wander far away from our sacred heritage, or to be silent about it, I shall not for a moment forget what Jerusalem stands for.

11

Review of J. L. Talmon,
The Nature of Jewish History—
Its Universal Significance

This is an earnest statement by a man who is both a Jew and a historian rather than a Jewish historian. According to him, the historian who studies the fate of the Jewish people cannot and need not go back behind the fact that the Jewish people was constituted by its belief in its being the chosen people; this belief made possible and in effect caused its exiles and its precarious existence throughout the ages up to the present day; for the establishment of the state of Israel has not removed "the problematic ambiguity attached to Jewish existence everywhere and at all times" (p. 9 n.). Both economic and "psychological" accounts are radically inadequate. Nor, on the other hand, is the historian as historian compelled or able to accept the theological understanding of "election." The author lays bare the parochialism informing the common notion according to which the belief in election stems from ethnic pride. The idea of "the chosen people" as of a "holy nation" or "a people of priests" expresses "what Matthew Arnold called the Jewish passion for right acting as distinct from the Greek passion for right seeing and thinking" (p. 18). It is therefore one of the two basic elements of Western civilization. It is at the root of "the fundamentally and peculiarly Western relationship between Church and State" which prevented the emergence in the West of "Oriental despotism" (p. 19). It is to be hoped that the author will develop this theme further by showing more precisely than he has hitherto done why "the passion for right acting," as distinguished from "the passion for right seeing and thinking," requires primarily a peculiar nation as its bearer.

12

Letter to the Editor:
The State of Israel

For some time I have been receiving *National Review*, and I agree with many articles appearing in the journal. There is, however, one feature of the journal which I completely fail to comprehend. It is incomprehensible to me that the authors who touch on that subject are so unqualifiedly opposed to the state of Israel.

No reasons why that stand is taken are given; mere antipathies are voiced. For I cannot call reasons such arguments as are based on gross factual error, or on complete noncomprehension of the things which matter. I am, therefore, tempted to believe that the authors in question are driven by an anti-Jewish animus; but I have learned to resist temptations. I taught at the Hebrew University in Jerusalem for the whole academic year of 1954–55, and what I am going to say is based exclusively on what I have seen with my own eyes.

The first thing which strikes one in Israel is that the country is a Western country, which educates its many immigrants from the East in the ways of the West: Israel is the only country which as a country is an outpost of the West in the East. Furthermore, Israel is a country which is surrounded by mortal enemies of overwhelming numerical superiority, and in which a single book absolutely predominates in the instruction given in elementary schools and in high schools: the Hebrew Bible. Whatever the failings of individuals may be, the spirit of the country as a whole can justly be described in these terms: heroic austerity supported by the nearness of biblical antiquity. A conservative, I take it, is a man who believes that "everything good is heritage." I know of no country today in which this belief is stronger and less lethargic than in Israel.

But the country is poor, lacks oil and many other things which fetch much money; the venture on which the country rests may well appear to be quixotic; the university and the government buildings are within easy range of Jordanian guns; the possibility of disastrous defeat or failure is obvious and always close. A conservative, I take it, is a man who despises vulgarity; but the argument which is concerned exclusively with calculations of success, and is based on blindness to the nobility of the effort, is vulgar.

I hear the argument that the country is run by labor unions. I believe that it is a gross exaggeration to say that the country is run by the labor unions. But even if it were true, a conservative, I take it, is a man who knows that the same arrangement may have very different meanings in different circumstances.

The men who are governing Israel at present came from Russia at the beginning of the century. They are much more properly described as pioneers than as labor unionists. They were the men who laid the foundations under hopelessly difficult conditions. They are justly looked up to by all nondoctrinaires as the natural aristocracy of the country, for the same reasons for which Americans look up to the Pilgrim fathers. They came from Russia, the country of Nicolai II and Rasputin; hence they could not have had any experience of constitutional life and of the true liberalism which is only the reverse side of constitutional democracy adorned by an exemplary judiciary.

On page 16 of the November 17 issue of the *Review*, Israel is called a racist state. The author does not say what he understands by a "racist state," nor does he offer any proof for the assertion that Israel is a racist state. Would he by any chance have in mind the fact that in the state of Israel there is no civil marriage, but only Jewish, Christian, and Muslim marriages, and therefore that mixed marriages in the nonracist sense of the term are impossible in Israel? I am not so certain that civil marriage is under all circumstances an unmitigated blessing, as to disapprove of this particular feature of the state of Israel.

Finally, I wish to say that the founder of Zionism, Herzl, was fundamentally a conservative man, guided in his Zionism by conservative considerations. The moral spine of the Jews was in danger of being broken by the so-called emancipation, which in many cases had alienated them from their heritage, and yet not given them anything more than merely formal equality; it had brought about a condition which has been called "external freedom and inner servitude"; political Zionism was the attempt to restore that inner freedom, that simple dignity, of which only people who remember their heritage and are loyal to their fate are capable.

Political Zionism is problematic for obvious reasons. But I can never forget what it achieved as a moral force in an era of complete dissolution. It helped to stem the tide of "progressive" leveling of venerable, ancestral differences; it fulfilled a conservative function.

Leo Strauss, Chicago

VI

Miscellaneous Writings
on Jews and Judaism

13

Introduction to
Persecution and the Art of Writing

The subject matter of the following essays may be said to fall within the province of the sociology of knowledge. Sociology of knowledge does not limit itself to the study of knowledge proper. Being critical in regard to its own basis, it studies impartially everything that pretends to be knowledge as well as genuine knowledge. Accordingly, one should expect that it would devote some attention also to the pursuit of genuine knowledge of the whole, or to philosophy. Sociology of philosophy would thus appear to be a legitimate subdivision of sociology of knowledge. The following essays may be said to supply material useful for a future sociology of philosophy.

One cannot help wondering why there does not exist today a sociology of philosophy. It would be rude to suggest that the founders of the sociology of knowledge were unaware of philosophy or did not believe in its possibility. What one can safely say is that the philosopher appeared to them, eventually or from the beginning, as a member of a motley crowd which they called the intellectuals or the Sages. Sociology of knowledge emerged in a society which took for granted the essential harmony between thought and society, or between intellectual progress and social progress. It was more concerned with the relation of the different types of thought to different types of society than with the fundamental relation of thought as such to society as such. It did not see a grave practical problem in that fundamental relation. It tended to see in the different philosophies exponents of different societies or classes or ethnic spirits. It failed to consider the possibility that all philosophers form a class by themselves, or that what unites all genuine philosophers is more important than what unites a given philosopher with a particular group of nonphilosophers. This failure can be traced directly to the inadequacy of the historical information on which the edifice of sociology of knowledge was erected. The firsthand knowledge at the disposal of the early sociologists of knowledge was limited, for all practical purposes, to what they knew of nineteenth- and early twentieth-century Western thought.

To realize the necessity of a sociology of philosophy, one must turn to other ages, if not to other climates. The present writer happened to come across phenomena whose understanding calls for a sociology of philosophy while he was studying the Jewish and Islamic philosophy of the Middle Ages.

There is a striking contrast between the level of present-day understanding of Christian scholasticism and that of present-day understanding of Islamic and Jewish medieval philosophy. This contrast is ultimately due to the fact that the foremost students of Christian scholasticism believe in the immediate philosophic relevance of their theme, whereas the foremost students of Islamic and Jewish medieval philosophy tend to regard their subject as only of historical interest. The rebirth of Christian scholasticism has given rise to a philosophic interest in Islamic and Jewish medieval philosophy: Averroes and Maimonides appeared to be the Islamic and Jewish counterparts of Thomas Aquinas. But from the point of view of Christian scholasticism, and indeed from the point of view of any position which accepts the very principle of faith, Islamic and Jewish medieval philosophy are likely to appear inferior to Christian scholasticism, and at best only trail blazers for the approach characteristic of the latter.[1] If Islamic and Jewish medieval philosophy must be understood properly, they must be of philosophic and not merely of antiquarian interest, and this in turn requires that one ceases to regard them as counterparts of Christian scholasticism.

To recognize the fundamental difference between Christian scholasticism on the one hand, and Islamic and Jewish medieval philosophy on the other, one does well to start from the most obvious difference, the difference in regard to the literary sources. This difference is particularly striking in the case of practical or political philosophy. The place that is occupied in Christian scholasticism by Aristotle's *Politics*, Cicero, and the Roman law, is occupied in Islamic and Jewish philosophy by Plato's *Republic* and his *Laws*. Whereas Plato's *Republic* and *Laws* were recovered by the West only in the fifteenth century, they had been translated into Arabic in the ninth century. Two of the most famous Islamic philosophers wrote commentaries on them: Farabi on the *Laws*, and Averroes on the *Republic*. The difference mentioned implied a difference not only in regard to the content of political philosophy, but, above all, in regard to its importance for the whole of philosophy. Farabi, whom Maimonides, the greatest Jewish thinker of the Middle Ages, regarded as the greatest among the Islamic philosophers, and indeed as the greatest philosophic authority after Aristotle, was so much inspired by Plato's *Republic* that he presented the whole of philosophy proper within a political framework. That of Farabi's works which Maimonides recommended especially consists of two parts, the first discussing God and the universe, and the second discussing the city; the author entitled it *The Political Governments.* A parallel work composed by him bears the title *The Principles of the Opinions of the People of the Virtuous City;* it is called in the manuscripts that I have seen "a political book." It is significant that Farabi was definitely less known to Christian scholasticism than were Avicenna and Averroes.[2]

To understand these obvious differences, one must take into consideration the essential difference between Judaism and Islam on the one hand, and Christianity on the other. Revelation as understood by Jews and Muslims has the character of Law (*Tora, Shari'a*) rather than of Faith.[3] Accordingly, what first came to the sight of the Islamic and Jewish philosophers in their reflections on Revelation was not a creed or a set of dogmas, but a social order, if an all-comprehensive order, which regulates not merely actions but thoughts or opinions as well. Revelation thus understood lent itself to being interpreted by loyal philosophers as the perfect law, the perfect political order. Being philosophers, the *falasifa*,[4] as they were called, attempted to arrive at a perfect understanding of the phenomenon of Revelation. Yet Revelation is intelligible to man only to the extent to which it takes place through the intermediacy of secondary causes, or to the extent to which it is a natural phenomenon. The medium through which God reveals Himself to man is a prophet, i.e., a human being. The *falasifa* attempted therefore to understand the process of Revelation as essentially related to, or as identical with, a peculiar "connatural" perfection, and in fact, the supreme perfection, of man. Being loyal philosophers, the *falasifa* were compelled to justify their pursuit of philosophy before the tribunal of the divine law. Considering the importance which they attached to philosophy, they were thus driven to interpret Revelation as the perfect political order which is perfect precisely because it lays upon all sufficiently equipped men the duty to devote their lives to philosophy. For this purpose they had to assume that the founder of the perfect order, the prophetic lawgiver, was not merely a statesman of the highest order but at the same time a philosopher of the highest order. They had to conceive of the prophetic lawgiver as a philosopher-king, or as the supreme perfection of the philosopher-king. Philosopher-kings, and communities governed by philosopher-kings, were however the theme not of Aristotelian but of Platonic politics. And divine laws, which prescribe not merely actions but opinions about the divine things as well, were the theme of Plato's *Laws* in particular. It is therefore not surprising that, according to Avicenna, the philosophic discipline which deals with prophecy is political philosophy or political science, and the standard work on prophecy is Plato's *Laws*. For the specific function of the prophet, as Averroes says, or of the greatest of all prophets, as Maimonides suggests, is legislation of the highest type.

Plato's *Laws* were known in the period under consideration as "Plato's rational laws (*nomoi*)." The *falasifa* accepted then the notion that there are "rational laws." Yet they rejected the notion of "rational commandments." The latter notion had been employed by a school of what one may call Islamic theology (*kalam*), and had been adopted by certain Jewish thinkers. It corresponded to the Christian notion of "the natural law," which may be identified with "the law of reason" and "the moral law." By rejecting the notion of "rational commandments," the *falasifa* implied that the principles of morality are not rational, but "probable" or "generally accepted." "The rational laws (*nomoi*)" which they admitted are distinguished from "the rational commandments," or the natural law, by the fact that they do not have obligatory character. The Stoic natural law teaching, which was transmitted to the Western world chiefly through Cicero and some Roman lawyers, did not influence the practical or political philosophy of the *falasifa*.

The philosophic intransigence of the *falasifa* is not sufficiently appreciated in the accepted interpretations of their teachings.[5] This is partly due to the reticence of the *falasifa* themselves. The best clues to their intentions are found in the writings of men like Yehuda Halevi and Maimonides. The value of the testimony of these great men may be thought to be impaired by the fact that they opposed the *falasifa*. Yet at least some writings of Farabi confirm the interpretation which Halevi and Maimonides suggest. In the present state of our knowledge it is impossible to say to what extent Farabi's successors accepted his views in regard to the crucial point. But there can be no doubt that those views acted as a leaven as long as philosophy exercised an influence on Islamic and Jewish thought.

Farabi expressed his thought most clearly in his short treatise on the philosophy of Plato.[6] The *Plato* forms the second and shortest part of a tripartite work which apparently was entitled *On the Purposes of Plato and of Aristotle*, and which is quoted by Averroes as *The Two Philosophies*.[7] The third part, which has not yet been edited, deals with the philosophy of Aristotle. In the first part (*On the Attainment of Happiness*), Farabi discusses the human things which are required for bringing about the complete happiness of nations and of cities. The chief requirement proves to be philosophy, or rather the rule of philosophers, for "the meaning of *Philosopher, First Leader, King, Legislator,* and *Imam* is one and the same." The Platonic origin of the guiding thesis is obvious and, in addition, pointed out by the author. He concludes the first part with the remark that philosophy as previously described stems from Plato and Aristotle, who both "have given us philosophy" together with "the ways toward it and the way toward its introduction after it has been blurred or destroyed," and that, as will become clear from the presentation of the philosophies of Plato and Aristotle in the two subsequent parts, the purpose of Plato and of Aristotle was one and the same. Two points in Farabi's *On the Purposes of Plato and of Aristotle* strike one most. The work owes its origin to the concern with the restoration of philosophy "after it has been blurred or destroyed"; and it is more concerned with the purpose common to Plato and Aristotle than with the agreement or disagreement of the results of their investigations. What Farabi regarded as the purpose of the two philosophers, and hence what he regarded as the sound purpose simply, appears with all the clarity which one can reasonably desire from his summary of Plato's philosophy, and from no other source. This purpose is likely to prove the latent purpose of all *falasifa* proper. Farabi's *Plato* would thus prove to be the clue par excellence to the *falsafa*[8] as such.

According to Farabi, Plato started his inquiry with the question regarding the essence of man's perfection or of his happiness, and he realized that man's happiness consists in a certain science and in a certain way of life. The science in question proves to be the science of the essence of every being, and the art which supplies that science proves to be philosophy. As for the way of life in question, the art which supplies it proves to be the royal or political art. Yet the philosopher and the king prove to be identical. Accordingly, philosophy by itself is not only necessary but sufficient for producing happiness: philosophy does not need to be supplemented by something else, or by something that is thought to be higher in rank than philosophy, in order to produce happiness. The purpose of Plato, or of Aristotle, as Farabi conceived of it, is sufficiently revealed in this seemingly conventional praise of philosophy.

The praise of philosophy is meant to rule out any claims of cognitive value which may be raised on behalf of religion in general and of revealed religion in particular. For the philosophy on which Farabi bestows his unqualified praise is the philosophy of the pagans Plato and Aristotle. In his *Enumeration of the Sciences*, he presents the "Islamic sciences" (*fiqh* and *kalam*) as corollaries to political science. By this very fact, the pursuits in question cease to be Islamic; they become the arts of interpreting and of defending any divine law or any positive religion.

Whatever obscurity there might seem to be in the *Enumeration*, every ambiguity is avoided in the *Plato*. Through the mouth of Plato, Farabi declares that religious speculation, and religious investigation of the beings, and the religious syllogistic art, do not supply the science of the beings in which man's highest perfection consists, whereas philosophy does supply it. He goes so far as to present religious knowledge as the lowest step on the ladder of cognitive pursuits, as inferior even to grammar and to poetry. The purpose of the *Plato* as a whole makes it clear that this verdict is not affected if one substitutes the religious knowledge available in Farabi's time for the religious knowledge available in Plato's time.

At the beginning of the treatise *On the Attainment of Happiness*, with which he prefaces his summaries of the philosophies of Plato and of Aristotle, Farabi employs the distinction between "the happiness of this world in this life" and "the ultimate happiness in the other life" as a matter of course. In the *Plato*, which is the second and therefore the least exposed part of a tripartite work, the distinction of the two kinds of happiness is completely dropped. What this silence means becomes clear from the fact that in the whole *Plato* (which contains summaries of the *Gorgias*, the *Phaedrus*, the *Phaedo*, and the *Republic*), there is no mention of the immortality of the soul: Farabi's Plato silently rejects Plato's doctrine of a life after death.

Farabi could go so far in the *Plato*, not merely because that treatise is the least exposed and the shortest part of a larger work, but also because it sets forth explicitly the views of another man. As has been mentioned, he treats differently the two kinds of happiness in *On the Attainment of Happiness* and in the *Plato*; and he treats religious knowledge somewhat differently in the *Enumeration of the Sciences* and in the *Plato*. Proceeding in accordance with the same rule, he pronounces more or less orthodox views concerning the life after death in *The Virtuous Religious Community* and *The Political Governments*, i.e., in works in which he speaks in his own name. More precisely, in *The Virtuous Religious Community* he pronounces simply orthodox views, and in *The Political Governments* he pronounces views which, if heretical, could nonetheless still be considered tolerable. But in his commentary on the *Nicomachean Ethics* he declares that there is only the happiness of this life, and that all divergent statements are based on "ravings and old women's tales."[9]

Farabi avails himself then of the specific immunity of the commentator or of the historian in order to speak his mind concerning grave matters in his "historical" works, rather than in the works in which he speaks in his own name. Yet could not Farabi, as a commentator, have expounded, without a muttering of dissent, such views as he rejected as a man? Could he not have been attracted, as a student of philosophy, by what he abhorred as a believer? Could his mind not have been of the type that is attributed to the Latin Averroists? It almost suffices to state this suspicion in order to see that it is unfounded. The Latin Averroists gave a most literal interpretation of extremely heretical teachings. But Farabi did just the reverse: he gave an extremely unliteral interpretation of a relatively tolerable teaching. Precisely as a mere commentator of Plato, Farabi was compelled to embrace the doctrine of a life after death. His flagrant deviation from the letter of Plato's teaching, or his refusal to succumb to Plato's charms, proves sufficiently that he rejected the belief in a happiness different from the happiness of this life, or the belief in another life. His silence about the immortality of the soul in a treatise designed to present the philosophy of Plato "from its beginning to its end" places beyond any reasonable doubt the inference that the statements asserting the immortality of the soul, which occur in some of his other writings, must be regarded as accommodations to the accepted views.

Farabi's Plato identifies the philosopher with the king. He remains silent, however, about the precise relationship between the philosopher and the king on the one hand, and the legislator on the other; to say the least, he does not explicitly identify the legislator with the philosopher-king. Whatever this may mean,[10] Farabi suggests in the *Plato* that philosophy is not simply identical with the royal art: philosophy is the highest theoretical art, and the royal art is the highest practical art; and the fundamental difference between theory and practice remains a major theme throughout the *Plato*. Since he contends that philosophy and the royal art together are required for producing happiness, he agrees in a way with the orthodox view according to which philosophy is insufficient for leading man to happiness. Yet the supplement to philosophy which, according to him, is required for the attainment of happiness is not religion or Revelation but politics, if Platonic politics. He substitutes politics for religion. He thus may be said to lay the foundation for the secular alliance between philosophers and princes friendly to philosophy, and to initiate the tradition whose most famous representatives in the West are Marsilius of Padua and Machiavelli.[11] He speaks of the need for the virtuous city which he calls "another city." He means to replace the other world or the other life by the other city. The other city stands midway between this world and the other world, since it is an earthly city indeed, yet a city existing not "in deed" but "in speech."

In fact, it is by no means certain that the purpose of Plato or of Aristotle, as Farabi understood it, required the actualization of the best political order or of the virtuous city. Farabi adumbrates the problem by making a distinction between Socrates' investigations and Plato's investigations, as well as between "the way of Socrates" and the way adopted eventually by Plato. "The science and the art of Socrates," which is to be found in Plato's *Laws*, is only a part of Plato's, the other part being "the science and the art of Timaeus," which is to be found in the *Timaeus*. "The way of Socrates" is characterized by the emphasis on "the scientific investigation of justice and the virtues," whereas the art of Plato is meant to supply "the science of the essence of every being," and hence especially the science of the divine and of the natural things. The difference between the way of Socrates and the way of Plato points back to the difference between the attitude of the two men toward the actual cities. The crucial difficulty was created by the political or social status of philosophy: in the nations and cities of Plato's time, there was no freedom of teaching and of investigation. Socrates was therefore confronted with the alternative whether he should choose security and life, and thus conform with the false opinions and the wrong way of life of his fellow-citizens, or else nonconformity and death. Socrates chose nonconformity and death. Plato found a solution to the problem posed by the fate of Socrates in founding the virtuous city in speech: only in that "other city" can man reach his perfection. Yet, according to Farabi, Plato "repeated" his account of the way of Socrates, and he "repeated" the mention of the vulgar of the cities and nations which existed in his time.[12] The repetition amounts to a considerable modification of the first statement, or to a correction of the Socratic way. The Platonic way, as distinguished from the Socratic way, is a combination of the way of Socrates with the way of Thrasymachus; for the intransigent way of Socrates is appropriate only for the philosopher's dealing with the elite, whereas the way of Thrasymachus, which is both more and less exacting than the former, is appropriate for his dealings with the vulgar. What Farabi suggests is that, by combining the way of Socrates with the way of Thrasymachus, Plato avoided the conflict with the vulgar and thus the fate of Socrates. Accordingly, the revolutionary quest for the other city ceased to be necessary: Plato substituted for it a more conservative way of action, namely, the gradual replacement of the accepted opinions by the truth or an approximation to the truth. The replacement of the accepted opinions could not be gradual if it were not accompanied by a provisional acceptance of the accepted opinions: as Farabi elsewhere declares, conformity with the opinions of the religious community in which one is brought up is a necessary qualification for the future philosopher.[13] The replacement of the accepted opinions could not be gradual if it were not accompanied by the suggestion of opinions which, while pointing toward the truth, do not too flagrantly contradict the accepted opinions. We may say that Farabi's Plato eventually replaces the philosopher-king who rules openly in the virtuous city by the secret kingship of the philosopher who, being "a perfect man" precisely because he is an "investigator," lives privately as a member of an imperfect society which he tries to humanize within the limits of the possible. Farabi's remarks on Plato's policy define the general character of the activity of the *falasifa*.

In the light of these considerations, it would appear to be rash to identify the teaching of the *falasifa* with what they taught most frequently or most conspicuously. The attempt to establish their serious teaching is rendered still more difficult by the fact that some opponents of the *falasifa* seem to have thought it necessary to help the *falasifa* in concealing their teaching, because they feared the harm which its publication would cause to those of their fellow-believers whose faith was weak.

What Farabi indicates in regard to the procedure of the true philosophers is confirmed by a number of remarks about the philosophic distinction between the exoteric and the esoteric teaching which occur in the writings of his successors. Farabi's *Plato* informs us about the most obvious and the crudest reason why this antiquated or forgotten distinction was needed. Philosophy and the philosophers were "in grave danger." Society did not recognize philosophy or the right of philosophizing. There was no harmony between philosophy and society. The philosophers were very far from being exponents of society or of parties. They defended the interests of philosophy and of nothing else. In doing this, they believed indeed that they were defending the highest interests of mankind.[14] The exoteric teaching was needed for protecting philosophy. It was the armor in which philosophy had to appear. It was needed for political reasons. It was the form in which philosophy became visible to the political community. It was the political aspect of philosophy. It was "political" philosophy. From here we shall perhaps understand sometime why Farabi presented the whole of philosophy within a political framework, or why his most comprehensive writings are "political books." It is not impossible that the title "the two philosophies," by which his treatise *On the Purposes of Plato and of Aristotle* was known, intimated the difference between "the two philosophies" or "the two doctrines": the exterior and the interior. This possibility cannot be neglected in any serious evaluation of the Platonism or rather neo-Platonism of the *falasifa*, and in particular of the use which they sometimes made of the neo-Platonic *Theology of Aristotle*. It suffices here to remark that Farabi's *Plato* shows no trace whatever of neo-Platonic influence.

In most of the current reflections on the relation between philosophy and society, it is somehow taken for granted that philosophy always possessed political or social status. According to Farabi, philosophy was not recognized in the cities and nations of Plato's time. He shows by his whole procedure that there was even less freedom of philosophizing in the cities and nations of his own time, i.e., "after philosophy had been blurred or destroyed." The fact that "philosophy" and "the philosophers" came to mean in the Islamic world a suspect pursuit and a suspect group of men, not to say simply unbelief and unbelievers, shows sufficiently how precarious the status of philosophy was: the legitimacy of philosophy was not recognized.[15] Here, we are touching on what, from the point of view of the sociology of philosophy, is the most important difference between Christianity on the one hand, and Islam as well as Judaism on the other. For the Christian, the sacred doctrine is revealed theology; for the Jew and the Muslim, the sacred doctrine is, at least primarily, the legal interpretation of the divine law (*talmud* or *fiqh*). The sacred doctrine in the latter sense has, to say the least, much less in common with philosophy than the sacred doctrine in the former sense. It is ultimately for this reason that the status of philosophy was, as a matter of principle, much more precarious in Judaism and in Islam than in Christianity: in Christianity philosophy became an integral part of the officially recognized and even required training of the student of the sacred doctrine. This difference explains partly the eventual collapse of philosophic inquiry in the Islamic and in the Jewish world, a collapse which has no parallel in the Western Christian world.

Owing to the position which "the science of *kalam*" acquired in Islam, the status of philosophy in Islam was intermediate between its status in Christianity and in Judaism. To turn therefore to the status of philosophy within Judaism, it is obvious that while no one can be learned in the sacred doctrine of Christianity without having had considerable philosophic training, one can be a perfectly competent talmudist without having had any philosophic training. Jews of the philosophic competence of Halevi and Maimonides took it for granted that being a Jew and being a philosopher are mutually exclusive. At first glance, Maimonides' *Guide of the Perplexed* is the Jewish counterpart of Thomas Aquinas' *Summa Theologica*; but the *Guide* never acquired within Judaism even a part of the authority which the *Summa* enjoyed within Christianity; not Maimonides' *Guide*, but his *Mishneh Torah*, i.e., his codification of the Jewish law, could be described as the Jewish counterpart to the *Summa*. Nothing is more revealing than the difference between the beginnings of the *Guide* and of the *Summa*. The first article of the *Summa* deals with the question as to whether the sacred doctrine is required besides the philosophic disciplines: Thomas as it were justifies the sacred doctrine before the tribunal of philosophy. One cannot even imagine Maimonides opening the *Guide*, or any other work, with a discussion of the question as to whether the *halakha* (the sacred Law) is required besides the philosophic disciplines. The first chapters of the *Guide* look like a somewhat diffuse commentary on a biblical verse (Genesis 1:27) rather than like the opening of a philosophic or theological work. Maimonides, just as Averroes, needed much more urgently a legal justification of philosophy, i.e., a discussion in legal terms of the question whether the divine law permits or forbids or commands the study of philosophy, than a philosophic justification of the divine law or of its study. The reasons which Maimonides adduces in order to prove that certain rational truths about divine things must be kept secret were used by Thomas in order to prove that the rational truth about the divine things was in need of being divinely revealed.[16] In accordance with his occasional remark that the Jewish tradition emphasized God's justice rather than God's wisdom, Maimonides discerned the Jewish equivalent to philosophy or theology in certain elements of the *aggada* (or Legend), i.e., of that part of the Jewish lore which was generally regarded as much less authoritative than the *halakha*.[17] Spinoza bluntly said that the Jews despise philosophy.[18] As late as 1765, Moses Mendelssohn felt it necessary to apologize for recommending the study of logic, and to show why the prohibition against the reading of extraneous or profane books does not apply to works on logic.[19] The issue of traditional Judaism versus philosophy is identical with the issue of Jerusalem versus Athens. It is difficult not to see the connection between the depreciation of the primary object of philosophy—the heavens and the heavenly bodies—in the first chapter of Genesis, the prohibition against eating of the tree of knowledge of good and evil in the second chapter, the divine name "I shall be What I shall be," the admonition that the Law is not in heaven nor beyond the sea, the saying of the prophet Micah about what the Lord requires of man, and such talmudic utterances as these: "for him who reflects about four things—about what is above, what is below, what is before, what is behind—it would be better not to have come into the world," and "God owns nothing in His world except the four cubits of the *halakha*."[20]

The precarious status of philosophy in Judaism as well as in Islam was not in every respect a misfortune for philosophy. The official recognition of philosophy in the Christian world made philosophy subject to ecclesiastical supervision. The precarious position of philosophy in the Islamic-Jewish world guaranteed its private character, and therewith its inner freedom from supervision. The status of philosophy in the

Islamic-Jewish world resembled in this respect its status in classical Greece. It is often said that the Greek city was a totalitarian society. It embraced and regulated morals, divine worship, tragedy and comedy. There was however one activity which was essentially private and transpolitical: philosophy. Even the philosophic schools were founded by men without authority, by private men. The Islamic and Jewish philosophers recognized the similarity between this state of things and the one prevailing in their own time. Elaborating on some remarks of Aristotle, they compared the philosophic life to the life of the hermit.

Farabi ascribed to Plato the view that in the Greek city the philosopher was in grave danger. In making this statement, he merely repeated what Plato himself had said. To a considerable extent, the danger was averted by the art of Plato, as Farabi likewise noted. But the success of Plato must not blind us to the existence of a danger which, however much its forms may vary, is coeval with philosophy. The understanding of this danger and of the various forms which it has taken, and which it may take, is the foremost task, and indeed the sole task, of the sociology of philosophy.

Notes

1. Compare Isaac Abravanel, Commentary on Joshua X, 12 (ed. Frankfurt, 1736, fol. 21–22).

2. See *Church History* 15 (1946): 62. Louis Gardet and M.-M. Anawati, *Introduction à la théologie musulmane* (Paris: J. Vrin, 1948), 245: ". . . les Farabi, les Avicenne, les Averroès. Deux noms émergèrent (en chrétienté): Avicenne . . . et plus tard Averroès. . . ."

3. Compare, e.g., Gardet and Anawati, *Introduction*, 332, 335, and 407.

4. The Arabic transcription of the Greek word for "philosophers."

5. See Gardet and Anawati, *Introduction*, 268–72, and 320–24.

6. The full title is "The philosophy of Plato, its parts, and the grades of dignity of its parts, from its beginning to its end." The original has been edited, annotated, and translated into Latin by F. Rosenthal and R. Walzer, *Alfarabius De Platonis Philosophia* (London: Warburg Institute, 1943). [See now *Alfarabi's Philosophy of Plato and Aristotle*, translated with an introduction by Muhsin Mahdi (Ithaca: Cornell University Press, 1969). —Ed.]

7. The latter title is used also by a contemporary of Averroes, Joseph ibn Aknin. See A. S. Halkin, "Ibn Aknin's Commentary on the Song of Songs," in *Alexander Marx Jubilee Volume*, ed. Saul Lieberman (New York: Jewish Theological Seminary, 1950), 423.

8. The Arabic transcription of the Greek word for "philosophy."

9. Ibn Tufail, *Hajj ibn Yaqdhan*, ed. L. Gauthier (Beirut: Imprimerie Catholique, 1936), 14. Compare the remarks of Averroes which are quoted by Steinschneider, *Al-Farabi*, 94 and 106 ("In libro enim de Nicomachia videtur [Alfarabius] negare continuationem esse cum intelligentiis abstractis: et dicit hanc esse opinionem Alexandri, et quod non est opinionandum quod finis humanus sit aliud quam perfectio speculativa"). Compare Thomas Aquinas, Commentary on *Eth. Nic.* X, lect. 13 *vers. fin.*, and *S. c. G.* III cap. 48 *vers. fin.*

10. The meaning is indicated by the fact that in the three last paragraphs of the *Plato*, "philosopher," "king," "perfect man" and "investigator" on the one hand, and "legislator" and "virtuous men" on the other, are treated as interchangeable.

11. See below, p. 91, note 156. [See the page and note referred to in: Leo Strauss, *Persecution and the Art of Writing*. —Ed.]

12. As regards the precise meaning of "repetition," see below, pp. 62–64. [See the pages referred to in: Leo Strauss, *Persecution and the Art of Writing*. —Ed.]

13. *On the Attainment of Happiness, k. tahsil as-sa'ada* (Hyderabad, 1345), 45. Compare the first two maxims of Descartes' "morale par provision" (*Discours de la méthode*, III).

14. Farabi, *Plato*, para. §17.

15. Compare Gardet and Anawati, *Introduction*, 78, 225, and 236.

16. Compare *Guide* 1.34 with Thomas, *S. c. G.* I 4 and *Quaest. disput. De Veritate* q. 14 a. 10.

17. Compare the passages indicated below, p. 39 n. 5 [see the page and note referred to in: Leo Strauss, *Persecution and the Art of Writing*. —Ed.] with *Guide* 3.17 (35a Munk).

18. *Tr. Theol.-pol.* XI *vers. fin.* See ibid., I (§41 Bruder). See also Georges Vajda, *Introduction à la pensée juive du moyen age* (Paris: J. Vrin, 1947), 43.

19. *Gesammelte Schriften: Jubiläums-Ausgabe* II, 202–7.

20. Compare Maimonides, *Guide* 1.32 (36b Munk), and his Introduction to his *Commentary on the Mishna* (*Porta Mosis*, ed. E. Pococke [Oxford, 1655], 90).

14

Perspectives on the Good Society

At the request of Professor Rylaarsdam I attended a Jewish-Protestant colloquium sponsored by the Divinity School of the University of Chicago and the Anti-Defamation League of B'nai B'rith. I attended the colloquium as an observer with the understanding that I would write a report about it. I am a Jew, but I was not meant to write the report as a Jew, but as an observer, an impartial and friendly observer, or as a social scientist, for the social scientist is supposed to be particularly concerned with every effort directed toward the good society. This concern was the common ground of the participants and the observer, for the colloquium was based on the premise that in spite of their profound disagreements Jews and Protestants can be united in their concern for the good society and in their effort to bring it about or to secure it.

The colloquium consisted of two parts: of three discussion sessions and two meal sessions. The discussion sessions dealt with (1) "Common Ground and Difference," (2) "Faith and Action," and (3) "Needs and Justice"; they descended from the question regarding the highest principles to the question regarding the most important social action here and now; at each of these sessions a Protestant and a Jew spoke. The speaker at the luncheon session was a Protestant, and the speaker at the dinner session was a Jew; the meal sessions may be said to have been devoted to the situation which has rendered possible a Jewish-Protestant colloquium about the perspectives on the good society. Since not indeed the highest principles by themselves, but the manner in which they are approached or come to light, depends decisively on the given situation, it will be best to speak first of the meal sessions.

At the luncheon session Professor Nathan A. Scott, Jr. (Professor of Theology in Literature, Divinity School, University of Chicago), spoke of "Society and the Self in Recent American Literature." He concentrated on the American novel of the time following World War II, since the novel enjoys a particularly high prestige in present-day America. Above all, the contemporary American novel—especially if contrasted with the contemporary British novel—shows how much Judaism and Christianity are embattled in present-day America. According to Mr. Scott, this kind of literature preaches up the radical divorce of the self from contemporary society or the existence without roots. By confining itself "to the narrow enclave of the self," recent American fiction has compelled itself to produce—apart from very few exceptions—nothing but "pale and bloodless ghosts." Since it does not see human beings in the light of the biblical faith in creation, it does not see them with humility and charity: the individual without history and hence authenticity creates beings without history and hence authenticity. Of this literature it has been claimed that it corresponds to the "post-Christian" character of our world. Mr. Scott rejected this claim with contempt. If I understood him correctly, in his view it is not the non-Christian character of our world, but the non-Christian or non-Jewish character of the writers concerned, which is responsible for their sterility. I cannot comment on the literature in question since I do not know it. Yet living in this country at this time in constant contact with young Americans who are compelled to face and to resist that literature, I cannot help having some familiarity with the moral phenomenon of which the contemporary American novel as characterized by Mr. Scott seems to be an expression if not a cause.

Not a few people who have come to despair of the possibility of a decent secularist society, without having been induced by their despair to question secularism as such, escape into the self and into art. The "self" is obviously a descendant of the soul; that is, it is not the soul. The soul may be responsible for its being good or bad, but it is not responsible for its being a soul; of the self, on the other hand, it is not certain whether it is not a self by virtue of its own effort. The soul is a part of an order which does not originate in the soul; of the self it is not certain whether it is a part of an order which does not originate in the self. Surely the self as understood by the people in question is sovereign or does not defer to anything higher than itself; yet it is no longer exhilarated by the sense of its sovereignty, but rather oppressed by it, not to say in a state of despair. One may say that the self putting its trust in itself and therefore in man is cursed.[1] It is an unwilling witness to the biblical faith. Mr. Scott was right in rejecting the view that our world is "irredeemably post-Christian" on the ground that "the Holy Spirit bloweth where it listeth," but I believe that one should admit the fact that the unbelief in question is in no sense pagan, but shows at every point that it is the unbelief of men who or whose parents were Christians or Jews. They are haunted men. Deferring to nothing higher than their selves, they lack guidance. They lack thought and discipline. Instead they have what they call sincerity. Whether sincerity as they understand it is necessary must be left open until one knows whether sincerity is inseparable from shamelessness; sincerity is surely not sufficient; it fulfills itself completely in shrill and ugly screams, and such screams are not works of art. "Life is a tale told by an idiot" is a part of a work of art, for life is such a tale only for him who has violated the law of life, the law to which life is subject. It is true that the message of the writers in question is not that of Macbeth. They scream that life is gutter. But one cannot sense that life is gutter if one has not sensed purity in the first place, and of this which is by nature sensed first, they say nothing, they convey nothing. The self which is not deferential is an absurdity. Their screams are accusations hurled against "society"; they are not appeals to human beings uttered in a spirit of fraternal correction; these accusers believe themselves to be beyond the reach of accusation; their selves constitute themselves by the accusation; the self as they understand it is nothing but the accusation or the scream. Every accusation presupposes a law; accusations of the kind voiced by them would require a holy law; but of this they appear to be wholly unconscious. Their screams remind one of the utterances of the damned in hell; they themselves belong to hell. But hell is for them not society as such, but "life in the United States in 1963." Their despair is due to their having believed in the first place that life in the United States in 1963 is heaven or could be heaven or ought to be heaven. They condemn contemporary American society; their selves constitute themselves by this condemnation; they are nothing but this condemnation or rejection—a condemnation not based on any law; they belong to this society as completely as their twin, the organization man; their only difference from the latter is, or seems to be, that they are miserable and obsessed.

The speaker at the dinner session, Mr. Dore Schary (Anti-Defamation League of B'nai B'rith), agreed with Mr. Scott in implicitly suggesting that contemporary America is fundamentally healthy, that is, possesses within itself the remedies for the ills from which it suffers, and that this fundamental health is connected with its being not purely secularist and its not meaning to be it. The society attacked by the literary avant-gardists is held together, or is what it is, by the dedication to freedom in the sense that the freedom and dignity of anyone is supposed to require the freedom and dignity of everyone. According to Mr. Schary, democracy is not primarily the rule of the majority, but recognition of the dignity of the individual, that is, of every individual in his individuality. Only a society in which everyone can be what he is or can develop his unique potentialities is truly free and truly great or excellent. What is true of the individual is true also of the groups of which society consists and in particular of the religious groups; the freedom and excellence of this country require, above all, that its citizenry belong to a variety of faiths. Why this is so appears from a consideration of the ills from which American society suffers. Those ills can be reduced to one head: the tendency toward homogeneity or conformism, that is, toward the suppression by nonpolitical means of individuality and diversity; all Americans are to be remolded in the likeness of "the typical American." American society is in danger of becoming ever more a mass society which is "informed" in the common and in the metaphysical meaning of the term by mass communication, by the mass communication industry, the most visible and audible part of which is the advertising industry. Everyone can see that the youngest girl and the oldest great-grandmother tend ever more to look alike; the natural differences of age and beauty are overlaid by the conventional identity of the ideal, formed not without the support of the cosmetics industry. It is not merely amusing to observe that whereas there is a single model of womanhood—say, the attractive young woman of twenty-one—there is a dual model of manhood which one may describe as that of the good-looking and successful junior executive on the one hand, and that of the good-looking and successful senior executive on the other; in this sphere cosmetics cannot help respecting the most important natural difference: "the body is at its peak from thirty to thirty-five years of age, the soul at about forty-nine."[2] On the whole, however, mass society succeeds amazingly well in rendering irrelevant all natural differences and therefore in particular also the racial differences: one can easily visualize a society consisting of racially different men and women each of whom dresses, has "fun," mourns, talks, feels, thinks, and is buried exactly like everyone else. It is for this reason, I suppose, that Mr. Schary found religious diversity most annoying to the lovers of homogeneity. The difference in religious faith—in dedication to what simply transcends humanity —is the obstacle par excellence to conformism.

One may well find it paradoxical that a society dedicated to the free development of each individual in his individuality should be threatened by a particularly petty kind of conformism, but the paradox disappears on reflection. It is merely a shallow hope to expect that the uninhibited "growth" of each individual to its greatest height will not lead to serious and bloody conflict. The growth must be kept within certain limits: everyone may grow to any height and in any direction provided his growth does not prevent the growth of anybody else to any height and in any direction. The limits, the right limits, are to be set by the law. But in order to fulfill this function, the lawmakers and ultimately the sovereign must possess both knowledge and good will. The sovereign must be enlightened, free from prejudice; such freedom can be expected to come from exposure to science (both natural and social) and its consequences (technology, facility of traveling, and so on). "People and ideas all over the world are increasingly accessible, and the sense of what is 'alien' grows dimmer"; the "more remarkable differences [among the races of men] tend to dissipate." Mr. Schary was, to say the least, not quite certain whether this is a pure gain. One must be grateful to science and its concomitants for the liberation from prejudice which it achieves; but, as was indicated, the same power also endangers diversity or fosters homogeneity. As for good will, democracy was originally said to be the form of government the principle of which is virtue. But it is obviously impossible to restrict the suffrage to virtuous men, men of good will, conscientious men, responsible men, or whichever expression one prefers. While in a democracy the government is made responsible to the governed in the highest degree possible—ideally the government will not have any secrets from the governed—the governed cannot be held responsible in a comparable manner: the place par excellence of sacred secrecy or privacy is not the home, which may be entered with a search warrant, but the voting booth. In the voting booth the prejudices can assert themselves without any hindrance whatever. Voting is meant to determine the character of the legal majority. The legal majority is not simply the majority, but it is not irrelevant to the legal majority how the simple majority feels. There may be a stable or permanent majority; in the United States the stable majority is "white Protestant." As a consequence, there is a social hierarchy at the bottom of which are the Negroes (or colored people in general), and barely above them are the Jews. There is then a prejudice which is both constitutional and unconstitutional against Negroes and Jews. If I understood Mr. Schary correctly, the conformism against which he directed his attack has the unavowed intention either to transform all Americans into white Protestants, or else to deny those Americans who are not white Protestants full equality of opportunity. Yet would not one have to say that this pressure toward conformism is not the same as that which is exerted by the communications and cosmetics industries?

Recognition of religious diversity, as Mr. Schary understood it, is not merely toleration of religions other than one's own, but respect for them. The question arises as to how far that respect can be extended. "We who are religiously oriented state that there *is* God; clearer identification than that is denied us." Who are the "we"? If the "we" are Jews or Christians, Mr. Schary admits too little; if they are religious human beings as such, he admits too much. The singular "God" would seem to exclude the possibility of respect for Greek polytheism, and still more of the polytheism of the Egyptians who had "a bizarre pantheon of their own . . . they invented monsters to worship." Can one respect a religion which worships monsters or, to use the biblical expression, abominations? Mr. Schary concluded the paragraph from which these quotations are taken with the remark that "all men of decency, self-respect, and good will are joined in a common brotherhood." I take it that he does not deny that men who are not "religiously oriented" may be "men of decency, self-respect, and good will" and that men who lack decency, self-respect, and good will and therefore refuse to join the common brotherhood do not for this reason cease to be our brothers. But under no circumstances can we be obliged to respect abominations, although it may be necessary to tolerate them.

Mr. Schary, I thought, in contradistinction to Mr. Scott, was less concerned with the truth common to Judaism and Christianity than with the virtues of diversity. But this very concern made him a defender of the religious point of view since religion rather than science is the bulwark of genuine diversity. As is shown in our age especially by the U.S.S.R., the secularist state is inclined to enforce irreligious conformism, just as in the past the religious state was inclined to enforce religious conformism. It seems that only a qualifiedly secularist, that is, a qualifiedly religious, state which respects equally religious and nonreligious people can be counted upon to contain within itself the remedy against the ill of conformism. However this may be, it is the danger caused by radical secularism in its communist or noncommunist form which provides the incentive for such undertakings as a Protestant-Jewish colloquium.

This is perfectly compatible with the fact that the condition of the colloquium is the secular state. This fact was pointed out by the chairman of the session devoted to "Common Ground and Difference," Professor J. T. Petuchowski (Hebrew Union College), in his comment on the papers read by Professor J. Coert Rylaarsdam (Professor of Old Testament, Divinity School, University of Chicago) and Mr. Arthur A. Cohen (Director of Religious Publishing for Holt, Rinehart and Winston, Inc.). The secular state may be said to derive from the view that the basis of the civil order must be reason alone, and not revelation, for if revelation, that is, a particular revelation, were made that basis, one would use compulsion open or disguised in the service of faith to the detriment of the purity of faith. In other words, a Protestant-Jewish colloquium as an *amica collatio* presupposes friendship, and friendship presupposes equality, at least civic equality, of Jews and Christians; without civic equality not even the necessary civility is likely to be forthcoming. On the other hand, as Mr. Petuchowski indicated, if the secular state were self-sufficient, there would be no secure place within it for transsecular Judaism and Christianity: Judaism and Christianity must have something to say to the secular state which secularism is unable to say, and in order to be effective the message of Judaism and the message of Christianity must be to some extent identical. It was taken for granted by all participants in the colloquium that that message could not be the natural religion or the religion of reason which was in the past sometimes regarded as the basis of the secular state, for the religion of reason (assuming that it is possible) would tempt one to believe in the self-sufficiency of reason, or to regard the specifically Jewish or Christian message as an unnecessary and peace-disturbing addition to the one thing needful, and it tends to lead toward the euthanasia of religious belief, or toward "ethical culture." The common ground on which Jews and Christians can make friendly *collatio* to the secular state cannot be the belief in the God of the philosophers, but only the belief in the God of Abraham, Isaac, and Jacob—the God who revealed the Ten Commandments, or at any rate such commandments as are valid under all circumstances regardless of the circumstances. That common ground was indeed not articulated in the meeting devoted to the common ground. The reason was not that that ground is trivial—in an age in which both Judaism and Christianity have been affected by existentialist ethics, it is surely not trivial—but because, as is shown by the whole history of Christian-Jewish relations, recognition of that common ground is not in any way sufficient for mutual recognition of the two faiths.

What can such recognition mean? This much: that Church and Synagogue recognize each the noble features of its antagonist. Such recognition was possible even during the Christian Middle Ages: while the Synagogue was presented as lowering its head in shame, its features were presented as noble. However far the mutual recognition may go in our age, it cannot but be accompanied by the certainty on the part of each of the two antagonists that in the end the other will lower its head. Recognition of the other must remain subordinate to recognition of the truth. Even the pagan philosophers Plato and Aristotle remained friends, although each held the truth to be his greatest friend, or rather because each held the truth to be his greatest friend. The Jew may recognize that the Christian error is a blessing, a divine blessing, and the Christian may recognize that the Jewish error is a blessing, a divine blessing. Beyond this they cannot go without ceasing to be Jew or Christian.

To say the least, it was always easier for Christians to recognize the divine origin of Judaism than for Jews to recognize the divine origin of

Christianity. On the other hand, it was easier for Jews to recognize that Christians may have a "share in the world to come" than it was for Christians to recognize that Jews may be "saved." This is due to the Jewish union of the "carnal" and the "spiritual," of the "secular" and the "eternal," of the "tribal" and the "universal": the Torah which contains the promise of the eventual redemption of all children of Adam[3] was given to, or accepted by, Israel alone. As a consequence, it was easier for Jews to admit the divine mission of Christianity[4] than it was for Christians to admit the abiding divine mission of Judaism. It is therefore not surprising that, as Mr. Rylaarsdam pointed out, the first genuine meeting of Jews and Christians should have been initiated by a Jew, Franz Rosenzweig, and that a comparable Christian response to this Jewish call should not yet have been forthcoming. Such a response, including above all the recognition of the abiding mission of Judaism, is urgently demanded in the opinion of Mr. Rylaarsdam because of what happened to the Jewish people in our lifetime: the butchery of six million Jews by Hitler-led Germany and the establishment of the state of Israel; Jewish agony and Jewish rebirth are not adequately understandable on the basis of the traditional Christian view of Judaism. In addition, the traditional Christian judgment on the Jew is at least partly responsible for the persecution of the Jews in the Christian world and therefore, if indirectly, for Hitler Germany's action. The Christian must begin to ask himself whether he can "acknowledge that the mission of Israel did not end when his own mission began." One cannot leave matters at asserting the undeniable fact that the Jew denies and the Christian maintains that the Messiah, that Redemption, has come. Judaism says that "there is no redemption yet God has redeemed His people"; Christianity says that there is no redemption yet God has redeemed mankind in the death and resurrection of Jesus Christ. Judaism, in contradistinction to Christianity, "is concerned with the redemption of history," with redemption on this side of death, with redemption on earth: according to Judaism, the Elect One is Israel which never dies; according to Christianity, the Elect One is Jesus the Christ who died on the cross. Yet "the Christian must agree with the Jew that the world [*this* world] is unredeemed," and that "this world matters to God." The agony of the Jew and the agony of the Cross belong together; "they are aspects of the same agony." Judaism and Christianity need each other.

One may say that Mr. Rylaarsdam stated what Christianity has to learn from Judaism; he did not presume to tell the Jews what they have to learn from Christianity; he left the performance of that task to his Jewish partner. But Mr. Cohen did not perform this task. I do not think that he can be blamed for this. He did not, of course, mistake learning from Christianity for assimilation to Christianity. For instance, to move the day of rest from the seventh day of the week to the first day is an act of assimilation to Christianity which does not involve learning from Christianity. Nor did he deny, he even asserted, that Judaism and Christianity need each other; in fact, in this respect he agreed entirely with Mr. Rylaarsdam. But in the main he limited himself to reasserting vigorously the traditional Jewish position toward Christianity: there is an irreconcilable disagreement beween Judaism and Christianity; Christianity depends on Judaism, and not vice versa; Christianity has to learn from Judaism; there is no Judaeo-Christian tradition; at least from Paul on, Christianity has never understood Judaism. And yet he stressed the fact that the contemporary Jew and Christian are not, and can never become again, the Jew and the Christian of old: they confront each other "no longer as dogmatic enemies, but as common seekers of the truth." He admitted, in other words, that the misunderstanding has been mutual. But he did not explain what the Jewish misunderstanding of Christianity was. He did not go beyond alluding to certain defects of Jewish messianism at the time of Jesus and to the deplorable if excusable alliance of Judaism with secularist, anti-Christian movements. Why did he fail to make clear what Judaism may have to learn from Christianity? Are Jews still in greater danger to abandon Judaism in favor of Christianity than Christians are to abandon Christianity in favor of Judaism? Is there still a greater worldly premium on being a Christian than on being a Jew? Or is it obvious to everyone what the Jews have learned from modernity and it is obvious that modernity is secularized Christianity? But is modernity in fact secularized Christianity? Mr. Cohen seemed to doubt this. However this may be, he surely referred to the Jew's "pain of his historical encounter with Christendom."

Which Jew can indeed forget that pain? But confronted by the fact that the most noble Christians of our age have shown sincere repentance and sincerely offer us peace, we Jews must not regard Christendom as if it were Amalek; we must even cease to regard it as Edom. Above all, *noblesse oblige*. Mr. Cohen rightly rejected the common Christian notion of Jewish "pharisaism": no Jew who ever took the Torah seriously could be self-righteous, or believe that he could redeem himself from sin by the fulfillment of the Law, or underestimate the power of sin over him. The true "Pharisee" in the Christian sense is not the Pharisee proper, but Aristotle's perfect gentleman who is not ashamed of anything or does not regret or repent anything he has done because he always does what is right or proper. Mr. Cohen went beyond this. He demanded that the Christian view of the power and the depth of sin be mitigated in the light of "a realistic humanism," and he asserted that that humanism is found in the Jewish Bible. Isaiah's words in 6:5–7 and David's prayer in Psalm 51:12 sound "realistic" enough; they are, however, hardly "humanistic." Similar considerations apply to Mr. Cohen's remark about Pauline theology as "a theology for disappointment." I had thought that the days of historicist "debunking" had gone. Yet I cannot but agree with his concluding sentence: "What more has Israel to offer the world than eternal patience?" This sentence calls indeed for a long commentary. One sentence must here suffice: what is called "eternal patience" is that fortitude in suffering, now despised as "ghetto mentality" by shallow people who have surrendered wholeheartedly to the modern world, or who lack the intelligence to consider that a secession from this world might again become necessary for Jews and even for Christians.

If I understood him correctly, Mr. John Wild (Professor of Philosophy, Northwestern University) introduced the meeting devoted to "Faith and Action" with the observation that while Judaism and Christianity agree in believing that faith must issue in action, Christianity has sometimes succumbed to the Greek, intellectualist understanding of faith and accordingly severed or almost severed the connection between faith and action. M. Paul Ricoeur (Professor of Philosophy, Sorbonne), presenting "a Christian view" of faith and action, started from the facts that the opposition between the contemplative life and the active life stems from Greek philosophy and is wholly alien to Judaism, and that in this respect Christianity is simply the heir to Judaism. One may agree with M. Ricoeur while admitting that there is some evidence supporting the view that Greek philosophy did not as such assert that opposition. It suffices to mention the name of the citizen-philosopher Socrates. But perhaps one will be compelled eventually to say that his being a citizen culminated in his transcending the city, not only the city of Athens but even the best city, in speech, as well as that the only comprehensive and effective reply to the claim of contemplation to supremacy is supplied by the Bible. Be this as it may, M. Ricoeur was chiefly concerned with the question as to whether the doctrines distinguishing Christianity from Judaism do not lead again to the depreciation of action. His answer was in the negative. He conveyed to me the impression that the doctrine of original sin, for instance, is "the speculative expression" alien to Judaism of an experience which is not alien to Judaism. Differently stated, the Christian doctrine of justification by faith was perhaps "present from the beginning in the Bible"; the Jewish saying that everything is in the hands of God except fear of God would contradict the doctrine of justification by faith only if it were meant, as it surely is not meant, to arouse or confirm "any desire to draw glory" over against God from one's fearing God. M. Ricoeur asserted that Christianity sometimes succumbed to "Hellenistic" ways of understanding the relation of faith and action by divorcing faith from action, especially from social action, or by denying that there is any connection between the salvation of the individual and "historical redemption," or by being unconcerned with the evil embodied in "impersonal institutions" (the state, property, and culture) as distinguished from sin proper; yet in his view this is simply a "reactionary conception," incompatible with original Christianity. At any rate, there is no serious difference in this respect between Christianity and Judaism: "it is always its Jewish memory that guards (Christianity) against its own deviations."

Mr. Nahum N. Glatzer (Professor of Jewish History, Brandeis University) presented "a Jewish view of faith and action." He gave a comprehensive survey of Jewish thought on this subject from the days of the Bible down to the present. According to what one may call the classic Jewish view, "knowledge of God," study, faith, learning, or wisdom both presupposes and issues in righteous action or active piety or "fear of Heaven," but in such a way that what counts is action. The basis of this view appeared to be the talmudic theologoumenon that by his right or pious action man becomes "a participant with God in the work of creation": whereas regarding revelation and redemption, man is merely a recipient; regarding creation, or rather regarding the continuity of creation, "man is an active partner" of God. The Jewish view of faith and action was obscured in different ways and for different reasons in the Middle Ages on the one hand, and in modern times on the other. Owing to their subjugation many medieval Jews came to believe that "the world matters little; the rectification of its ills and, finally, its redemption, would come in God's good time." As a consequence of the emancipation of the Jews in the nineteenth century, an important part of Jewish opinion came to identify social and other progress with the process of redemption; that which transcends progress and action, that with which faith is concerned, tended to be forgotten. Modern secularism believed that it would put an end to the Jewish-Christian antagonism by depriving Judaism and Christianity of their *raisons d'être*; its manifest failure, which affects equally Jews, Christians, and nonbelievers, calls for a community of seeking and acting of both Jews and Christians—a community which has originally been rendered possible by secularism. The failure of secularism shows itself, for instance, in the ever increasing cleavage between science and humanism. In Mr.

Glatzer's view that gulf cannot be bridged by a "synthesis" of science and humanism because science is "neutralist" and humanism is "traditionalist": the required "redefinition of the image of man" is beyond the competence of either or both, not in spite but because of the fact that it must be a redefinition of man as created in the image of God. "The *hybris* of scientism" cannot be overcome with the help of a humanism which is inspired by the belief in man as a creator. Over against scientism and humanism Judaism and Christianity are at one.

The greatest divisive power in the past was revealed religion. Even today, as we have been led to see by reflecting on one of the papers read at the colloquium, religious diversity is the obstacle par excellence to conformism in this country. The differences at any rate between Judaism and Christianity do not preclude the availability of a common ground. What divides the human race today in the most effective manner is, however, the antagonism between the liberal West and the communist East. Even in this case there exists, as Mr. Gibson Winter (Divinity School, University of Chicago) pointed out in his paper on "National Identity and National Purpose," a "common ground": "their common ground is the limit set upon their opposition by [their] nuclear power." Thermonuclear war being manifestly an act of madness, the common ground must become the basis of dialogue—a dialogue to be conducted, not in ideological terms, but with a view to the duties of this country faced by the worldwide "struggle against hunger and the aspiration for human dignity"; this country must cease to "endorse a status quo position in a hungry world." The dialogue required is then in the first place a dialogue, not with Soviet Russia, but with the "have-nots" within the U.S.A. and without. As for the dialogue with the U.S.S.R., it requires that the "purpose and interest" of "our enemies" be respected and, above all, that the "apocalyptic framework" for the dialogue be recognized: in the spirit of Deuteronomy 30:19, we must choose life—"a future in justice and community"—in the certainty that the alternative choice leads to thermonuclear annihilation as God's judgment. What will enable us to continue the dialogue with the U.S.S.R. in spite of all its hazards is faith, not, of course, in the good will of the Soviet rulers, but in God. It goes without saying that no such faith can be expected from the Soviet rulers: unilateral disarmament is out of the question. Faith equally forbids preventive war. On the other hand one cannot simply assert that this country must not under any circumstances initiate the use of nuclear weapons. "The most difficult problem in the use of nuclear power," however, concerns retaliation. "Retaliation after a destructive attack becomes simply vengeance" and seems therefore to be incompatible with Christian ethics: "to choose

the life of others over our own—this is the message of the Cross." Yet
"the possibility of retaliation is the power which restrains aggression."
    Two comments on this proposal seem to be appropriate. First, the
possibility of retaliation would lose much of its restraining power if the
enemy knew that a second strike force which survived his successful
attack would never be used against him; hence a decision allegedly
demanded by faith must remain the most closely guarded secret; in
other words, the tongue must pronounce the opposite of what the heart
thinks. Second, by saving the lives of the Soviet people in the contin-
gency under consideration, one would surrender all the have-not
nations to Soviet rule and thus deprive them for all the foreseeable
future of the possibility to be nonatheistic nations or, more generally
stated, to have a future of their own, neither Russian nor American; in
other words, Mr. Winter's proposal is based on a tacit claim to know
what God alone can know. Considerations like these may explain the
fact deplored by him that "the institutional weight of our religious traditions [viz. Christian and Jewish] falls . . . on the conservative side in
the struggle which separates the world." At any rate there seems to be a
tension between his plea for universal prosperity and freedom, and his
remark that "the grave danger for Judaism at this moment is the prosperity which distracts her from [her] vocation. . . . External oppression
can fortify the [chosen] people."
    The Jewish partner of Mr. Winter, Mr. Nathan Glazer (Housing
and Financing Agency, Washington, D.C.), spoke on "The Shape of the
Good Society." He did not speak from a distinctly Jewish point of view.
He dealt with the most successful revolution of our age, "the organiza-
tional revolution, or the scientific revolution," and its implications.
Through this revolution the gap between "the intellectuals," "the radical and liberal critics," on the one hand, and the organizations "representing the status quo" on the other, has been closed or at least very
much narrowed. The reason was that the intellectuals proved to possess
"new techniques for making organizations more efficient." One might
say that in proportion as the scientists drew all conclusions from their
basic premise, which is the assertion that science is limited to "factual"
assertions as distinguished from "value" assertions, they lost the right to
be radical critics of institutions and became willing servants of any
institutions. Yet, strangely, the cooperation of scientists and men of
affairs has affected the "values" of the latter: could there be a pre-
established harmony between the allegedly value-free science and the
liberal values? Be this as it may, the question which troubled Mr. Glazer
was whether the society rendered possible by the cooperation of the
scientists and the managers—the society guaranteeing to everyone

"simple justice and simple freedom"—can be regarded as the good society: "both conservatives or reactionaries on the one hand, and intellectuals and radicals and anarchists on the other, often come together in opposition to what we might call establishment Liberalism." Both the reactionary and the intellectual question the claim of the welfare state— "the whole organization, the machine for doing good"—to be the good society. Mr. Glazer sees only one way out: "to improve the organizations" by setting up "the great organization" or "the big organization" or "the determining center of allocation," which is enabled to direct all other organizations because it "will have far more information and will make much better diagnoses" than anyone else can. Hence it will be "the good big society." Alongside it, Mr. Glazer predicted "there will be developing . . . good small societies," composed "of reactionaries and anarchists and radical intellectuals." But he was not sure whether "the organization will be tolerant enough to let them be" nor whether "they will be clever enough to evade it." Faced with the grim prospect of universal philistinism, we are forced to wonder whether, according to Mr. Glazer, Judaism and Christianity belong on the side of the big organization or on that of the anarchists. I believe that Jews and Christians would have to choose anarchism or secession—a kind of secession radically different from that castigated by Mr. Scott. The reason why I believe this is Exodus 13:17: "And it came to pass, when Pharaoh had let the people go, that God led them not through the way of the land of the Philistines, although that was near." The land of the Philistines is perhaps nearer today than it ever was. The meaning which we ascribe to the scriptural verse may not be its literal meaning; it may nevertheless be its true meaning. For, as Jews and Christians agree, the literal meaning isolated from everything else "killeth." Pharisaic rabbinical Judaism always held that the written Torah must be understood in the light of the oral or unwritten Torah, and the most profound reason for this is that the most profound truth cannot be written and not even said: what Israel heard at Sinai from God Himself "was nothing but that [inaudible] *aleph* with which in the Hebrew text of the Bible the First Commandment begins."[5]

Notes

1. Jeremiah 17:5–8.

2. Aristotle, *Rhetoric* 2.14.1390a29–b10.

3. See Maimonides, *Mishneh Torah, Hilkhot Melakhim* 11–12.

4. See Yehuda Halevi, *Kuzari* 4.23.

5. Gershom Scholem, *Zur Kabbala und ihrer Symbolik* (Zurich: Rhein-Verlag, 1960), 47; *On the Kabbala and Its Symbolism*, translated by Ralph Manheim (New York: Schocken, 1965), 30.

VII

Autobiographical Reflections

15

An Unspoken Prologue
to a Public Lecture at St. John's College
in Honor of Jacob Klein[1]

The common sense of mankind has granted old men certain privileges in order to compensate them for the infirmities of old age or to
make it easier for them to indulge those infirmities. Not the least of
these privileges is the permission granted to old men to speak about
themselves in public more freely than young men can in propriety do.
I have always regarded it as both an honor and a pleasure to come to
St. John's to lecture and to meet faculty members and students. But I
also had a private reason for enjoying my journeys to St. John's. St.
John's harbors—it is a perfect harbor for—my oldest friend, Jacob
Klein. Permit me to pay homage to Mr. Klein on the present occasion,
the first occasion after his sixtieth birthday. What I intend to do I regard
as an act of duty although of a pleasant duty. Yet however innocent our
actions may be as regards their intentions, the circumstances in which
they are performed may cloak these actions with an appearance of
malice. In such a situation one must not be squeamish and still do
one's duty. In addition—such is the complexity of the things of the
heart—even if we are virtuous men, we may derive some pleasure
from the appearance of malice, provided we keep within certain
bounds. In the present case the appearance of malice arises from Mr.
Klein's idiosyncratic abhorrence of publicity—of anything which even
remotely reminds of the limelight. I always found that Mr. Klein went
somewhat too far in this but all too justified abhorrence. When we
were in our twenties we worked every day during a longish period
for some hours in the Prussian State Library in Berlin, and we relaxed
from our work in a coffee house close by the library. There we sat
together for many hours with a number of other young men and talked
about everything which came to our mind—mixing gravity and levity
in the proportion in which youth is likely to mix them. As far as Mr.

Klein was concerned, there was, I am tempted to say, only one limit: we must not appear to the public as young men cultivating their minds; let us avoid at all costs—this was his silent maxim—the appearance that we are anything other than idle and inefficient young men of business or of the lucrative professions or any other kind of drones. On such occasions I derived enjoyment from suddenly exclaiming as loudly as I could, say, "Nietzsche!" and from watching the anticipated wincing of Mr. Klein.

Nothing affected us as profoundly in the years in which our minds took their lasting directions as the thought of Heidegger. This is not the place for speaking of that thought and its effects in general. Only this much must be said: Heidegger, who surpasses in speculative intelligence all his contemporaries and is at the same time intellectually the counterpart to what Hitler was politically, attempts to go a way not yet trodden by anyone or rather to think in a way in which philosophers at any rate have never thought before. Certain it is that no one has questioned the premise of philosophy as radically as Heidegger. While everyone else in the young generation who had ears to hear was either completely overwhelmed by Heidegger, or else, having been almost completely overwhelmed by him, engaged in well-intentioned but ineffective rearguard actions against him, Klein alone saw why Heidegger is truly important: by uprooting and not simply rejecting the tradition of philosophy, he made it possible for the first time after many centuries— one hesitates to say how many—to see the roots of the tradition as they are and thus perhaps to know, what so many merely believe, that those roots are the only natural and healthy roots. Superficially or sociologically speaking, Heidegger was the first great German philosopher who was a Catholic by origin and by training; he thus had from the outset a premodern familiarity with Aristotle; he thus was protected against the danger of trying to modernize Aristotle. But as a philosopher Heidegger was not a Christian: he thus was not tempted to understand Aristotle in the light of Thomas Aquinas. Above all, his intention was to uproot Aristotle: he thus was compelled to disinter the roots, to bring them to light, to look at them with wonder. Klein was the first to understand the possibility which Heidegger had opened without intending it: the possibility of a genuine return to classical philosophy, to the philosophy of Aristotle and of Plato, a return with open eyes and in full clarity about the infinite difficulties which it entails. He turned to the study of classical philosophy with a devotion and a love of toil, a penetration and an intelligence, an intellectual probity and a sobriety in which no contemporary equals him. Out of that study grew his work which bears the title "Greek Logistics and the Genesis of Algebra."[2] No title could be less expressive of a man's individuality and even of a man's intention; and yet if one knows Klein, the title expresses perfectly his individuality, his idiosyncrasy mentioned before. The work is much more than a historical study. But even if we take it as a purely historical work, there is not, in my opinion, a contemporary work in the history of philosophy or science or in "the history of ideas" generally speaking which in intrinsic worth comes within hailing distance of it. Not indeed a proof but a sign of this is the fact that less than half a dozen people seem to have read it, if the inference from the number of references to it is valid. Any other man would justly be blamed for misanthropy, if he did not take care that such a contribution does not remain inaccessible to everyone who does not happen to come across volume 3 of section B of *Quellen und Studien zur Geschichte der Mathematik, Astronomie, und Physik* and in addition does not read German with some fluency. One cannot blame Klein because he is excused by his idiosyncrasy. I hope that you, faculty and students of St. John's, do not accuse me of trespassing if I say: some man or body of men among you should have compelled Klein, if need be by starving him into submission, to close his eyes while you arrange for a decent English translation and its publication.[3] The necessity for this is in no way diminished by the fact that Mr. Klein is said to prepare now a new book which may contain a very long footnote giving the first intelligent account of the Platonic dialogue, and which will probably be entitled *Mathematics in the Curriculum of the School of Gorgias*.[4] But it was not in order to make to you the foregoing suggestion that I made these prefatory remarks: I ask you to rise and join me in giving Mr. Klein an ovation.

Notes

[The notes below to the Prologue were not provided by Leo Strauss, but are based on those added to its original publication by the editors of *Interpretation*. However, they have been modified slightly as well as supplemented by the present editor, and hence they are entirely his responsibility.—Ed.]

1. In 1959, on the occasion of the sixtieth birthday of Jacob Klein (1899–1978), Leo Strauss delivered a lecture at St. John's College in honor of his oldest and best friend. He wrote this tribute as a prologue to the lecture which, however, was apparently not spoken on that occasion or subsequently. From the first paragraph, it is possible to suggest that this prologue was not spoken by Strauss due to the specific and urgent request of Klein, who suffered from an "idiosyncratic [i.e., extreme] abhorrence of publicity." See also "A Giving of Accounts," infra.

2. Jacob Klein, "Die griechische Logistik und die Entstehung der Algebra," in *Quellen und Studien zur Geschichte der Mathematik, Astronomie, und Physik* (Berlin). Abteilung B: *Studien*, vol. 3, no. 1 (1934), 18–105; vol. 3, no. 2 (1936), 122–235.

3. Jacob Klein, *Greek Mathematical Thought and the Origin of Algebra*, translated by Eva Brann (Cambridge: M.I.T. Press, 1968) [with an Appendix containing: Franciscus Vieta, *Introduction to the Analytical Art*, translated by J. Winnfree Smith, 315–53].

4. Jacob Klein, *A Commentary on Plato's Meno* (Chapel Hill: University of North Carolina Press, 1965). See also: *Plato's Trilogy—Theaetetus, The Sophist, and The Statesman* (Chicago: University of Chicago Press, 1977).

16

Preface to
Hobbes Politische Wissenschaft[1]

The present study of Hobbes, which now appears for the first time in the German original, was composed in 1934–35 in England, and published in 1936 in English translation. Ernest Barker wrote a preface for the English edition and I added an introductory note, which may now be replaced by the following comments:

The leading thought of my Hobbes book arose from positive and negative stimuli received while I still lived in Germany. The first time I heard about Hobbes in a way that caused me to take notice was in the lectures of Julius Ebbinghaus on the social teaching of the Reformation and the Enlightenment, given in Freiburg im Breisgau in the summer semester of 1922. Ebbinghaus appreciated in an unconventional way the originality of Hobbes; in his lively presentation, Hobbes's teaching became not merely plastic but vital. He was anything but a Hobbesian; if my memory does not deceive me, he already believed at that time that the significant part of Hobbes's teaching had been "sublated" [*aufgehoben*] in the Kantian philosophy. Carl Schmitt, in quite unconscious opposition to Ebbinghaus, asserted in his essay, "The Concept of the Political" ("Der Begriff des Politischen," *Archiv für Sozialwissenschaft und Sozialpolitik*, 1927),[2] that Hobbes is "by far the greatest and perhaps the only truly systematic political thinker." Schmitt's judgment about the greatness and the significance of Hobbes, a judgment which corresponded to my feelings or taste at that time, strengthened, understandably, my interest in Hobbes.

My study of Hobbes began in the context of an investigation of the origins of biblical criticism in the seventeenth century, namely, of Spinoza's *Theologico-Political Treatise*. The reawakening of theology, which for me is marked by the names of Karl Barth and Franz Rosenzweig, appeared to make it necessary to investigate how far the critique of orthodox theology—Jewish and Christian—deserved to be victorious. Since then the theological-political problem has remained *the* theme of my investigations. As far as the political, especially, is concerned, the contrast between Hobbes and Spinoza seemed to me at that time to be more important, more illuminating, than their agreement. In any case, I believed that I had learned, through my first study of Hobbes, that the prior accounts and aperçus had not done justice to what is decisive in him.

When a fate that was in a certain way kind drove me to England and I gained in this way access to sources which cannot be studied elsewhere, I saw the opportunity not to limit my work to an analysis of the teaching of the mature Hobbes but to investigate at the same time how and from what source this teaching had been formed in Hobbes's mind. This double intention gave the present study its character.

Philosophic interest in theology linked me with Gerhard Krüger; his review of my Spinoza book expressed my intention and result more clearly than I myself had done.[3] The final sentence of his Kant book,[4] which corresponded completely to my view at that time and with which I would still today, with certain reservations, agree, explains why I directed myself wholly to the "true politics,"[5] and why I did not write about Hobbes as a Hobbesian. Insight into the necessity of understanding the dispute of the ancients and the moderns more thoroughly and more exactly than had previously been done, before one decided for the modern or the ultramodern, linked me with Jacob Klein; his "Die griechische Logistik und die Entstehung der Algebra" (*Quellen und Studien zur Geschichte der Mathematik, Astronomie, und Physik*, Band 3, Heft 1–2),[6] a masterly and exemplary investigation led by this insight, received the distinction of being passed over in near total silence in our everything-but-silent era.

As far as the defects of the present book are concerned, I have tacitly corrected them, so far as they have become known, in *Natural Right and History* (chapter V, section A), and in my critique of Polin's Hobbes book (*What Is Political Philosophy?*, 170–96). Only in the latter publication (176, note)[7] did I succeed in laying bare the simple leading thought of Hobbes's teaching about man. For obscure reasons Hobbes himself never did this; his famous clarity is limited to his conclusions, while his presuppositions are shrouded in obscurity. His obscurity is, of course, not in every respect involuntary.

What I stated thirteen years ago in the preface to the American edition of the present book I will still allow to stand. I said then. . . .[8]

Notes

[The notes below to the Preface were not provided by Leo Strauss, but are based on those contributed by the English translator, Donald J. Maletz. Those which appear in square brackets have been added by the present editor.—Ed.]

1. Leo Strauss, *Hobbes Politische Wissenschaft* (Neuwied am Rhein und Berlin: Hermann Luchterhand Verlag, 1965). [The Preface was added by Strauss to the first publication in 1965 of the German original of his book, *The Political Philosophy of Hobbes*, translated by Elsa M. Sinclair (Oxford: The Clarendon Press, 1936), which had only been available in its English translation. The Preface first appeared in English translation in *Interpretation* 8 (1979–80): 1–3, translated by Donald J. Maletz. It is this translation that is reproduced in the present book. —Ed.]

2. [See Carl Schmitt, *The Concept of the Political*, with the "Comments" on it by Leo Strauss, edited by George Schwab (New Brunswick, N.J.: Rutgers University Press, 1976). See now also Heinrich Meier, *Carl Schmitt and Leo Strauss: The Hidden Dialogue* (Chicago: University of Chicago Press, 1995). —Ed.]

3. Krüger's review of Strauss's *Die Religionskritik Spinozas als Grundlage seiner Bibelwissenschaft: Untersuchungen zu Spinozas Theologisch-politischen Traktat* (Berlin: Akademie Verlag, 1930), appeared in the *Deutsche Literarzeitung*, vol. 51 (20 December 1931): 2407–12. [It is also available in English translation as: Gerhard Krüger, "Review of Leo Strauss, *Die Religionskritik Spinozas als Grundlage seiner Bibelwissenschaft: Untersuchungen zu Spinozas Theologisch-politischen Traktat*," translated by Donald J. Maletz, in *The Independent Journal of Philosophy* 5/6 (1988): 173–75. —Ed.]

4. The last several paragraphs of Krüger's *Philosophie und Moral in der Kantischen Kritik* (Tübingen: Verlag J.C.B. Mohr, 1931), attempt to state the basis for a "philosophical, that is, unlimited questioning," in the light of the fact that, since Kant, "the *aporias* of the Enlightenment have become greater." Krüger argues that "Kant's problem is thoroughly contemporary," in that "the unpenetrated opposition of 'dogmatism' and 'skepticism' has become prominent in thought as in life itself with new sharpness, while the living and unifying *tradition*, upon which the Enlightenment fed, has disappeared and been replaced by the *historicism of knowledge*." The concluding sentences of Krüger's book may be translated as follows: "The question will only be in reality unlimited if it *inquires into the good in the knowledge of the historical passion*. Let the *answer* to this question—and thus also the Christian answer of Augustine—be left undecided. That the decisive question remains *true*, even if it finds *no* answer, can be taught him who questions thus by the example of Socrates."

5. This term occurs in Kant's "Zum Ewigen Frieden," Anhang, I, end, in: Immanuel Kant, *Kleinere Schriften zur Geschichtsphilosophie, Ethik, und Politik*, ed. Karl Vorländer (Hamburg: Felix Meiner Verlag, 1964), 162. See the translation of "Perpetual Peace" in: Immanuel Kant, *On History*, ed. Lewis White Beck (Indianapolis: Bobbs-Merrill, 1963), 128.

6. Jacob Klein, *Greek Mathematical Thought and the Origin of Algebra*, translated by Eva Brann (Cambridge: M.I.T. Press, 1968).

7. [What is likely the key section of the note in *What Is Political Philosophy?* (p. 176, note 2), to which Strauss refers above, is reproduced in the paragraph below. —Ed.:]

According to Hobbes, the only peculiarity of man's mind which precedes the invention of speech, i.e., the only natural peculiarity of man's mind, is the faculty of considering phenomena as causes of possible effects, as distinguished from the faculty of seeking the causes or means that produce "an imagined effect," the latter faculty being "common to man and beast": not "teleological" but "causal" thinking is peculiar to man. The reason why Hobbes transformed the traditional definition of man as the rational animal into the definition of man as the animal which can "inquire consequences" and hence which is capable of science, i.e., "knowledge of consequences," is that the traditional definition implies that man is by nature a social animal, and Hobbes must reject this implication (*De Cive* I, 2). As a consequence, the relation between man's natural peculiarity and speech becomes obscure. On the other hand, Hobbes is able to deduce from his definition of man his characteristic doctrine of man: man alone can consider himself as a cause of possible effects, i.e., man can be aware of his power; he can be concerned with power; he can desire to possess power; he can seek confirmation for his wish to be powerful by having his power recognized by others, i.e., he can be vain or proud; he can be hungry with future hunger, he can anticipate future dangers, he can be haunted by long-range fear. See *Leviathan*, chs. 3 (15), 5 (27, 29), 6 (33–36), 11 (64), and *De homine* X, 3.

8. The remaining three paragraphs of the Preface to *Hobbes Politische Wissenschaft* are a German translation of the "Preface to the American Edition," *The Political Philosophy of Hobbes* (Chicago: University of Chicago Press, 1952), xv–xvi.

17

A Giving of Accounts:
Jacob Klein and Leo Strauss

The following giving of accounts took place at St. John's College, Annapolis, Maryland, on 30 January 1970. Jacob Klein and Leo Strauss were introduced by Dean Robert A. Goldwin.

Dean Goldwin: Mr. Klein and Mr. Strauss are going to present us tonight with two "accounts."

The origin of this event is, I think, quite simple. Many of us have known them both, as our teachers, for many, many years. In a sense we can say that we know much about their teachings.

But, in fact, most of us know very little of the genesis of their thought. And it occurred to us that it would be, very simply, enlightening, to hear from them their own accounts of the origin and development of their thoughts in those matters of greatest interest to us, their students.

It is arranged that Mr. Klein will speak and then Mr. Strauss will speak. Then we will have questions, in our accustomed style.

Jacob Klein: This meeting has two reasons, one is accidental, the other is important. The first is the fact (and any fact is some kind of accident) that Mr. Strauss and I happen to have known each other closely, and have been friends, for fifty years, and happen both to be now in Annapolis at St. John's College. The other reason, the important one, is that Mr. Strauss is not too well known in this community, and that we as a real community of learners should begin to understand better why he is now a member of this community. We thought it might be not too bad an idea, although a somewhat embarrassing one, to tell you what we have learned in our lives, what preoccupied us and what still preoccupies us. Dead Week might perhaps indeed provide the right opportunity, the *kairos*, to do that. I shall begin.

Up to my twenty-fifth year I had one great difficulty. I was a student, and so was Mr. Strauss—we studied at the same university—and I studied all kinds of things, something called philosophy, and mathematics, and physics, and I did that quite superficially. But what preoccupied me mostly during those years was this: whatever thought I might have, and whatever interest I might have in anything, seemed to me to be located completely within me, so that I always felt that I could not really understand anything outside me, could not understand anything uttered or written by another person. I felt that I was in a kind of vicious circle out of which I could find no escape. I wrote a dissertation, which is not worth the paper on which it was written, obtained my Ph.D. degree, and then after a short while, returned to studies.

Now, while Mr. Strauss and I were studying we had many, I should say, endless conversations about many things. His primary interests were two questions: one, the question of God; and two, the question of politics. These questions were not mine. I studied, as I said, quite superficially, Hegel, mathematics, and physics. When I resumed my studying, a certain man happened to be at the university in the little town in which I was living. This man was Martin Heidegger. Many of you have heard his name, and some of you might have read some of his works in impossible English translations. I will not talk too much about Martin Heidegger, except that I would like to say that he is the very great thinker of our time, although his moral qualities do not match his intellectual ones. When I heard him lecture, I was struck by one thing: that he was the first man who made me understand something written by another man, namely, Aristotle. It broke my vicious circle. I felt that I could understand. Then I began studying seriously, for myself, seriously, not superficially.

It became clear to me that one had to distinguish the classical mode of thinking from the modern mode of thinking. Our world and our understanding, as it is today, is based on a certain change that occurred about five hundred years ago, and this change pervades not only our thinking but the whole world around us. It made possible one of the greatest achievements of man, mathematical physics, and all the auxiliary disciplines connected with it. It made possible what we call with a strange Latin word, science. This science is derived from the classical mode of thinking, but this derivation is also a dilution which blinds our sight. My studies led me to conclude: we have to relearn what the ancients knew; we should still be able to persist in scientific investigations, where real progress is possible, although the science with which we are familiar is also capable of regress and of bringing about a fundamental forgetfulness of most important things. As a consequence of these studies and of this understanding, a question arose: how should people be educated?

At that time a certain political upheaval made it necessary for me to come to these United States, and to land on the St. John's campus. This great question, how to educate people, became suddenly a "practical" question. I found here a man, an extraordinary man, whose name you all know, Scott Buchanan. He was also struggling with this question, as he had been struggling all his life. Since then, as the Dean told you, I have stayed here on this campus.

Mr. Strauss, meanwhile, worked on his own, tenaciously, indefatigably, and in an exemplary way. His erudition, his zeal, his tenacity brought fruit—resplendent fruit. As so many others, I learned from him. There are indeed, I think, differences between us, although it is not quite clear to me in what they consist. And I do think that at this point it is not too important to find out what they are. Mr. Strauss might allude to them.

Leo Strauss: I must begin with an introduction to my introduction. Some faculty members, I was told, had misgivings about this meeting. The only ones which are justified concern this question: is it proper for people to talk about themselves in public? The general answer is: no. But there are exceptions. First, what is true of men in general is not equally true of old men. Second, and above all, people may talk about their thoughts concerning matters of public concern, and virtue is a matter of public concern. Those thoughts, it is true, are connected with our lives, and I for one will have to say something about my life. But this is of interest even to me only as a starting point of considerations, of studies, which I hope are intelligible to those who do not know my starting point. Why then speak of one's life at all? Because the considerations at which I arrived are not necessarily true or correct; my life may explain my pitfalls.

The subject is the relations between Klein and me, i.e., our agreements and our differences. In my opinion we are closer to one another than to anyone else in our generation. Yet there are differences. I wish to learn from Klein how he sees these differences. It is possible that our disagreements have something to do with the differences of our temperaments or humors. It is more helpful and worthy, however, if I tell the tellable story of my life with special regard to how Klein affected it. I must warn you: I may commit errors of memory. Apart from this I shall not always keep to the chronological order.

I was brought up in a conservative, even orthodox Jewish home somewhere in a rural district of Germany. The "ceremonial" laws were rather strictly observed but there was very little Jewish knowledge. In the *Gymnasium* I became exposed to the message of German humanism. Furtively I read Schopenhauer and Nietzsche. When I was sixteen and we read the *Laches* in school, I formed the plan, or the wish, to spend my life reading Plato and breeding rabbits while earning my livelihood as a rural postmaster. Without being aware of it, I had moved rather far away from my Jewish home, without any rebellion. When I was seventeen, I was converted to Zionism—to simple, straightforward political Zionism.

When I went to the university I tended towards the study of philosophy. For reasons of local proximity I went to the University of Marburg, which had been the seat and center of the neo-Kantian school of Marburg, founded by Hermann Cohen. Cohen attracted me because he was a passionate philosopher and a Jew passionately devoted to Judaism. Cohen was at that time no longer alive, and his school was in a state of disintegration. The disintegration was chiefly due to the emergence and ever increasing power of phenomenology—an approach opened up by Edmund Husserl. Husserl told me a few years later: the Marburg school begins with the roof, while he begins with the foundation. But also, Cohen belonged definitely to the pre–World War I world. This is true also of Husserl. Most characteristic of the post–World War I world was the resurgence of theology: Karl Barth. (The preface to the first edition of his commentary on the Epistle to the Romans is of great importance also to nontheologians: it sets forth the principles of an interpretation that is concerned exclusively with the subject matter as distinguished from historical interpretation.) Wholly independently of Barth, Jewish theology was resurrected from a deep slumber by Franz Rosenzweig, a highly gifted man whom I greatly admired to the extent to which I understood him.

It was in Marburg in 1920 that I met Klein for the first time. He stood out among the philosophy students not only by his intelligence but also by his whole appearance: he was wholly nonprovincial in a wholly provincial environment. I was deeply impressed by him and attracted to him. I do not know whether I acted merely in obedience to my duty or whether this was only a pretense: I approached him in order to win him over to Zionism. I failed utterly. Nevertheless, from that time on we remained in contact up to the present day.

Academic freedom meant in Germany that one could change one's university every semester, and that there were no attendance requirements nor examinations in lecture courses. After having received my Ph.D. degree (a disgraceful performance) in Hamburg I went to the University of Freiburg in 1922 in order to see and hear Husserl. I did not derive great benefit from Husserl; I was probably not mature enough. My predominant interest was in theology: when I once asked Husserl about the subject, he replied, "If there is a datum 'God' we shall describe it." In his seminar on Lotze's *Logic* I read a paper in the first sentence of which the expression "sense perception" occurred. Husserl stopped me immediately, developed his analysis of sense perception, and this took up the rest of the meeting: at the end Husserl graciously apologized. I attended regularly the lecture courses on the social doctrines of the Reformation and the Enlightenment by Julius Ebbinghaus: I still remember gratefully Ebbinghaus's lively presentation of Hobbes's doctrine; Ebbinghaus shared with Hobbes a certain boyish quality. One of the unknown young men in Husserl's entourage was Heidegger. I attended his lecture course from time to time without understanding a word, but sensed that he dealt with something of the utmost importance to man as man. I understood something on one occasion: when he interpreted the beginning of the *Metaphysics*. I had never heard nor seen such a thing—such a thorough and intensive interpretation of a philosophic text. On my way home I visited Rosenzweig and said to him that compared to Heidegger, Max Weber, till then regarded by me as the incarnation of the spirit of science and scholarship, was an orphan child.

I disregard again the chronological order and explain in the most simple terms why in my opinion Heidegger won out over Husserl; he radicalized Husserl's critique of the school of Marburg and turned it against Husserl: what is primary is not the object of sense perception but the things which we handle and with which we are concerned, *pragmata*. What I could not stomach was his moral teaching, for despite his disclaimer he had such a teaching. The key term is "resoluteness," without any indication as to what are the proper objects of resoluteness. There is a straight line which leads from Heidegger's resoluteness to his siding with the so-called Nazis in 1933. After that I ceased to take any interest in him for about two decades.

To return to 1922, the resurgence of theology, of what sometimes was even called orthodoxy, was in fact a profound innovation. This innovation had become necessary because the attack of the Enlightenment on the old orthodoxy had not been in every respect a failure. I wished to understand to what extent it was a failure and to what extent it was not. The classical statement on this subject in Hegel's *Phenomenology of the Mind* had become questionable because Hegel's whole position had been called into question by the new theology. One had to descend to a level which is, in the good and the bad sense, less sophisticated than Hegel's. The classic document of the attack on orthodoxy within Judaism, but not only within Judaism, is Spinoza's

Theologico-Political Treatise. Spinoza's *Treatise* had been subjected to a fierce criticism by Cohen—a criticism which was impressive because Cohen was entirely free from the idolatry of Spinoza as the God-intoxicated thinker—but it was nevertheless inadequate. In order to form an independent judgment I began, therefore, a fresh study of the *Theologico-Political Treatise*. In this study I was greatly assisted by Lessing, especially his theological writings, some of them with forbidding titles. Incidentally, Lessing is also the author of the only improvised live dialogue on a philosophic subject known to me. Lessing was always at my elbow. This meant that I learned more from him than I knew at that time. As I came to see later, Lessing had said everything I had found out about the distinction between exoteric and esoteric speech and its grounds.

In 1925 Heidegger came to Marburg. Klein attended his classes regularly, and he was, naturally, deeply impressed by him. But he did not become a Heideggerian. Heidegger's work required and included what he called *Destruktion* of the tradition. (*Destruktion* is not quite so bad as destruction. It means taking down, the opposite of construction.) He intended to uproot Greek philosophy, especially Aristotle, but this presupposed the laying bare of its roots, the laying bare of it as it was in itself and not as it had come to appear in the light of the tradition and of modern philosophy. Klein was more attracted by the Aristotle brought to light and life by Heidegger than by Heidegger's own philosophy. Later Klein turned to the study of Plato, in which he got hardly any help from Heidegger. Klein convinced me of two things. First, the one thing needed philosophically is in the first place a return to, a recovery of, classical philosophy; second, the way in which Plato is read, especially by professors of philosophy and by men who do philosophy, is wholly inadequate because it does not take into account the dramatic character of the dialogues, also and especially of those of their parts which look almost like philosophic treatises. The classical scholar Paul Friedländer had seen this to some extent, but Friedländer had no inkling of what Plato meant by philosophy. Klein and I differ somewhat in our ways of reading Plato, but I have never been able to find out precisely what that difference is. Perhaps the following remarks are helpful.

The first offshoot of Klein's Platonic studies is his work on Greek logistics and the genesis of modern algebra—a work which I regard as unrivaled in the whole field of intellectual history, at least in our generation.

While Klein was engaged in this work, I continued my study of Spinoza's *Treatise*, from which I had been led to Hobbes on the one hand, and to Maimonides on the other. Maimonides was, to begin with, wholly unintelligible to me. I got the first glimmer of light when I concentrated on his prophetology and, therefore, the prophetology of the Islamic philosophers who preceded him. One day, when reading in a Latin translation Avicenna's treatise *On the Division of the Sciences*, I came across this sentence (I quote from memory): the standard work on prophecy and revelation is Plato's *Laws*. Then I began to begin to understand Maimonides's prophetology and eventually, as I believe, the whole *Guide of the Perplexed*. Maimonides never calls himself a philosopher; he presents himself as an opponent of the philosophers. He used a kind of writing which is, in the precise sense of the term, exoteric. When Klein had read the manuscript of my essay on the literary character of the *Guide of the Perplexed*, he said: "We have rediscovered exotericism." To this extent we completely agreed. But there was from the beginning this difference between us: that I attached much greater importance than Klein did and does to the tension between philosophy and the city, even the best city.

I arrived at a conclusion that I can state in the form of a syllogism: Philosophy is the attempt to replace opinion by knowledge; but opinion is the element of the city, hence philosophy is subversive, hence the philosopher must write in such a way that he will improve rather than subvert the city. In other words, the virtue of the philosopher's thought is a certain kind of *mania*, while the virtue of the philosopher's public speech is *sophrosyne*. Philosophy is as such transpolitical, transreligious, and transmoral, but the city is and ought to be moral and religious. In the words of Thomas Aquinas, only reason informed by faith knows that God must be worshiped, and the intellectual virtues with the exception of prudence do not presuppose moral virtue. To illustrate this point, moral man, merely moral man, the *kaloskagathos* in the common meaning of the term, is not simply closer to the philosopher than a man of the dubious morality of Alcibiades.

This view of philosophy was derived from my study of premodern philosophy. It implies that modern philosophy has a radically different character. In modern times the gulf between philosophy and the city was bridged, or believed to have been bridged, by two innovations: (1) the ends of the philosopher and the nonphilosopher are identical, because philosophy is in the service of the relief of man's estate, or "science for the sake of power"; (2) philosophy can fulfill its salutary function only if its results are diffused among the nonphilosophers, if popular enlightenment is possible. The high point was reached in Kant's teaching on the primacy of practical, i.e., moral reason, a teaching prepared to some extent by Rousseau: the one thing needful is a good will, and of a good will all men are equally capable. If we call moralism the view that morality or moral virtue is the highest, I am doubtful if it occurs in antiquity at all.

I was confirmed in my concentration on the tension between philosophy and the *polis*, i.e., on the highest theme of *political* philosophy, by this consideration. What distinguishes present-day philosophy in its highest form, in its Heideggerian form, from classical philosophy is its historical character; it presupposes the so-called historical consciousness. It is therefore necessary to understand the partly hidden roots of that consciousness. Up to the present day when we call a man a historian without qualification (like economic historian, cultural historian, etc.), we mean a political historian. Politics and political philosophy is the matrix of the historical consciousness.

Selection from the Question Period

Questioner: Concerning the differences between Mr. Klein and Mr. Strauss.

Klein: I do suppose that his emphasis on the political aspect of our lives, which can never be disregarded, of course, is something I do not quite agree with. On the other hand, we do agree that if there is philosophizing, it is a completely immoderate undertaking that cannot find, ultimately, its goal, although one has to persist in it. Now where the difference here is, is really not quite clear.

Strauss: I believe that there is another way of stating the difference. Mr. Klein and I differ regarding the status of morality.

Klein: (Laughter) I am not entirely certain of that. That is all I can say. Well, I will add something to that. And that is again a question of a difference of emphasis. I think I would not emphasize it so much, the morality of man, but I do think that man ought to be moral.

Strauss: Yes—sure. I did not mean that when I spoke of our difference. I think that in your scheme of things morality has a higher place than in my scheme.

Klein: I really do not think so. Why do you say that?

Strauss: Because we have frequently had quite a few conversations . . . now and then, and one general formula which suggested itself to me was that you attach a higher importance to morality, as morality, than I do. Now, let me explain this. That the philosophic life, especially as Plato and Aristotle understood it, is not possible without self-control and a few other virtues almost goes without saying. If a man is habitually drunk, and so on, how can he think? But the question is, if these virtues are understood only as subservient to philosophy and for its sake, then that is no longer a moral understanding of the virtues.

Klein: That may be. [A break in the tape occurred.]

Strauss: . . . a statement by a modern extremist, but who had a marvelous sense for Greek thought, Nietzsche—in his *Genealogy of Morals,* third treatise, "What is the Significance of Ascetic Ideals," he explains: why is a philosopher ascetic? And he makes this clear, that he is ascetic. And, he says, that is not different from the asceticism of a jockey, who in order to win a race must live very restrainedly, but that is wholly unimportant to the jockey, what is important is to win the race. If one may compare low to high things, one may say similarly of the philosopher, what counts is thinking and investigating and not morality. Of course the word morality is a "bad word" because it has so many connotations which are wholly alien to the ancients, but I think, for provisional purposes, we can accept it.

Klein: If there is something that I learned from Plato, or that I think that I learned from Plato, it is to understand that nothing can be—*nothing* can be—that is not in some way—and that is very difficult—good. That is why I do understand why Mr. Strauss says that the philosopher is in a certain way superior to the concern about morality; but I cannot agree that the ultimate consideration of things, as far as one is capable of doing that, ever, *ever,* frees men of the compulsion to act rightly.

Strauss: Yes, I think that you believe that. Yes, that is what I meant.

Questioner: Of what use is the city to the philosopher?

Strauss: Without cities, no philosophers. They are the conditions.

Klein: You would not deny that, would you?

Questioner: But it seems to me that the city provides for the needs of the body.

Strauss: Yes, sure.

Questioner: But does it provide for the needs of the soul?

Strauss: To some extent, sure.

Questioner: Is it necessary for its existence?

Strauss: To some extent, obviously. In one way or another, even if there is no compulsory education, the city educates its citizens.

Questioner: Would not the philosopher get his education from nature?

Strauss: His first education, surely not. His first education he would usually get from his father and mother, and other relatives, that is to say, from the city.

Questioner: How does it follow from the saying that everything that is, is somehow or other good, that a man should act rightly?

Klein: I would answer that very simply: he must try to *be* what he is. And, by the way, to be a man, a human being, is not a simple matter. The trouble with us human beings is that we are not quite complete, neither when we are born nor when we die.

Appendix 1:
Plan of a Book Tentatively Entitled
Philosophy and the Law: Historical Essays[1]

Although certain parts of the book will necessarily be of a more technical nature, the book as a whole is meant as an introduction to the understanding of Jewish medieval philosophy. Its purpose is to remind, not merely the scholar, but the intelligent and educated layman as well, of certain crucial problems whose bearing can be grasped immediately on the basis of modern life and of modern experiences. This does not mean that I plan to give a popularized version of the current scholarly interpretation of Jewish medieval philosophy. On the contrary, by starting in the way which I have mentioned, I shall be compelled to discuss important aspects of Jewish medieval philosophy which have not been sufficiently treated, or have not been treated at all, in the scholarly literature.

Each of the twelve essays outlined below is meant to be intelligible by itself, while forming a link in a broader argument.

The expected size of the book is about 350 pages. It is expected to be ready for publication at some time in 1948.

I. Modern Jewish Philosophy and Its Limitations

The essay will start with a description of the spiritual-intellectual situation of the modern Jew. The attempt will be made to trace that situation to its basic philosophic premises. Those premises find their least ambiguous expression in the modern rejection of the belief in miracles on the one hand, and in modern biblical criticism on the other. A discussion of the most significant attempts to restore the fundamental principles of the Jewish tradition on the basis of modern science and criticism leads to the result that those attempts have not been altogether successful, and that important lessons for our most vital and most personal problem might have to be learned from our medieval philosophy.

The suggestion of a partial return to medieval philosophy is open to the objection that medieval philosophy made the impossible attempt to reconcile two utterly irreconcilable traditions, viz. the biblical tradition and that of Greek philosophy. This problem will be discussed in:

II. Jerusalem and Athens

An elementary discussion of the most important points of agreement and divergence between Judaism and classical Greek philosophy. In spite of the ultimate and fundamental conflict between these two spiritual powers, a reconciliation between them became possible because classical Greek philosophy permitted, nay, demanded an exoteric teaching (as a supplement to its esoteric teaching) which, while not claiming to be strictly speaking true, was considered indispensable for the right ordering of human society.

While Aristotle was generally considered *the* philosopher, the representative of the philosophic attitude, or of philosophy as a human possibility, was not so much Aristotle as Socrates. According to a medieval view, "Socrates" represented precisely the synthesis of the two forms in which philosophy appears, the esoteric and the exoteric form. That this view is not merely a medieval myth, but has a solid basis in the classical Socratic literature, will be shown in:

III. The Two Faces of Socrates

After these preliminary discussions, I turn to Jewish medieval philosophy.

IV. How to Study Jewish Medieval Philosophy

A number of observations regarding the most obvious obstacles to a genuine understanding of Jewish medieval philosophy. Much will be made of the fact that modern study of Jewish medieval philosophy is constantly exposed to the danger of approaching Jewish medieval philosophy from the point of view of Christian medieval philosophy. Stress will be laid on the fundamentally different social situation, and social function, of philosophy in our time, in the Christian Middle Ages, and in the Jewish Middle Ages.

Hitherto, the study of Jewish medieval philosophy has chiefly been concerned with its theoretical, and especially its metaphysical, part. Such important aspects of Jewish medieval philosophy as its social philosophy, and its manner of understanding the relation of philosophy to society at large, have barely been touched upon. It can be shown that, for instance, Maimonides' doctrine of prophecy, and this means his doctrine of revelation and of the divine law, cannot be adequately understood if one starts from his theoretical philosophy, but becomes truly transparent if one starts from his political philosophy. Maimonides' political philosophy in its turn can be shown to be a modified form of the teaching of Plato's *Republic* and of his *Laws*. What I consider the most important aspects of the more neglected part of Maimonidean thought will be treated in the three following essays:

V. Maimonides' Political Science

VI. Maimonides' Ethics

VII. The Literary Character of the *Guide of the Perplexed*
(Already published in: *Essays on Maimonides:*
An Octocentennial Volume, edited by Salo Wittmayer Baron
[New York: Columbia University Press, 1941].)

From these three essays it will become clear that Plato's philosophy in general and his political philosophy in particular are, in the form which was given to them by Farabi, of crucial importance for the understanding of Maimonides' thought. This fact requires the insertion of:

VIII. Farabi's Treatise on Plato's Philosophy
(Already published in: *Louis Ginzberg Jubilee Volume*
[New York: American Academy for Jewish Research, 1945].)

The objection might be made that the interpretation suggested in the preceding essays is relevant only for the understanding of Maimonides (or of his Islamic predecessors). I shall therefore try to show that that interpretation is fruitful also for the understanding of the other classic of Jewish medieval philosophy, of Yehuda Halevi's *Kuzari*:

IX. The Law of Reason in the *Kuzari*
(Already published in: *Proceedings of the American*
Academy for Jewish Research vol. 13 [1943].)

What we can observe in the totalitarian societies of our time, i.e., in societies which as a matter of avowed policy suppress freedom of speech, supplies us with important clues to the understanding of the conditions under which many free minds of former centuries thought, spoke, and wrote. This subject will be dealt with in:

X. Persecution and the Art of Writing
(Already published in: *Social Research* vol. 8 [1941].)

I shall incorporate into that essay some observations about the controversy regarding Maimonides' writings in the early thirteenth century.

In essay X, I shall have to mention the question of how the emergence of modern liberal society, which is characterized by the recognition of the right of everyone to freedom of speech, radically changed the conditions of literary production by heterodox or not wholly orthodox thinkers. It would seem to be desirable that I discuss an example taken from the period of transition, from the period in which the two views of freedom of speech, the older view and the modern or liberal view, were still fighting each other. The most interesting example within the context of the present subject would be the controversy between Moses Mendelssohn and F. H. Jacobi on Lessing's Spinozism. While preparing the edition of Mendelssohn's metaphysical writings for the *Jubilee Edition* of Mendelssohn's works, I discovered some unknown material which throws new light on that controversy. A discussion of that controversy would enable me to treat of Spinoza's philosophy in its relation to Jewish medieval philosophy.

XI. A Controversy on Spinoza

The recollection of the man Maimonides was probably one of the motives underlying Lessing's *Nathan the Wise*, the outstanding poetic monument erected in honor of Jewish medieval philosophy. A discussion of this "gospel of tolerance" and of the message which it offers to modern Jewry appears to be a proper conclusion to the suggested book.

XII. Nathan the Wise

Note

[The note below to the Plan is entirely the work of the present editor. —Ed.]

1. The Plan of a Book is a previously unpublished proposal for a book of essays in Jewish philosophy which Strauss sketched in 1946. It was discovered by the editor in the Leo Strauss Archive in the Library of the University of Chicago (box 11, folder 11). Although it may never have been submitted to a publisher by Strauss, it does reflect his mature view of Jewish philosophy in its current condition.

Appendix 2:
Restatement on Xenophon's *Hiero*
[The Last Paragraph][1]

The utmost I can hope to have shown in taking issue with Kojève's thesis regarding the relation of tyranny and wisdom is that Xenophon's thesis regarding that grave subject is not only compatible with the idea of philosophy but required by it. This is very little. For the question arises immediately whether the idea of philosophy is not itself in need of legitimation. Philosophy in the strict and classical sense is quest for the eternal order or for the eternal cause or causes of all things. It presupposes then that there is an eternal and unchangeable order within which History takes place and which is not in any way affected by History. It presupposes, in other words, that any "realm of freedom" is not more than a dependent province within the "realm of necessity." It presupposes, in the words of Kojève, that "Being is essentially immutable in itself and eternally identical with itself." This presupposition is not self-evident. Kojève rejects it in favor of the view that "Being creates itself in the course of History," or that the highest being is Society and History, or that eternity is nothing but the totality of historical, i.e., finite time. On the basis of the classical presupposition, a radical distinction must be made between the conditions of understanding and the sources of understanding, between the conditions of the existence and perpetuation of philosophy (societies of a certain kind, and so on) and the sources of philosophic insight . On the basis of Kojève's presupposition, that distinction loses its crucial significance: social change or fate affects being, if it is not identical with Being, and hence affects truth. On the basis of Kojève's presuppositions, unqualified attachment to human concerns becomes the source of philosophic understanding: man must be absolutely at home on earth, he must be absolutely a citizen of the earth, if not a citizen of a part of the inhabitable earth. On the basis of the classical presupposition, philosophy requires a radical detachment from human concerns: man must not be absolutely at home on earth, he must be a citizen of the whole. In our discussion, the conflict between the two opposed basic presuppositions has barely been mentioned. But we have always been mindful of it. For we both apparently turned away from Being to Tyranny because we have seen that those who lacked the courage to face the issue of Tyranny, who therefore *et humiliter serviebant et superbe dominabantur*,[2] were forced to evade the issue of Being as well, precisely because they did nothing but talk of Being.

Notes

[The notes below to the last paragraph of the Restatement are entirely the work of the present editor. —Ed.]

1. This is the last paragraph of Strauss's "Restatement on Xenophon's *Hiero*." The "Restatement" served as Strauss's response to the essay by Alexandre Kojève, "Tyranny and Wisdom," which was an explication in counterpoint to Strauss's own interpretation of the text of Xenophon's dialogue, *Hiero*. Hence, the "Restatement" concluded the high philosophic debate contained in *On Tyranny*. However, the famous last paragraph, which was present in the French version, *De la tyrannie* (Paris: Gallimard, 1954), was missing from the first complete English version of *On Tyranny* (Glencoe, Illinois: Free Press, 1963). Fortunately, it has been added to the revised and augmented version of *On Tyranny*, edited by Victor Gourevitch and Michael S. Roth (New York: Free Press, 1991). Unfortunately, Gourevitch and Roth were forced to rely on their own English translation from the French version, which was itself a translation from Strauss's original English version! Thanks to Laurence Berns, who received a copy of the typescript of the original English version from Strauss, this is the first appearance in print of that famous last paragraph as it was actually written. I would suggest that this is the closest thing we possess to a metaphysical confession of faith by Strauss, and I would also further suggest that it points us to some important theological implications which would seem to follow directly from it. See, e.g., "On the Interpretation of Genesis," supra, 361.

2. Gourevitch and Roth, 212, translate the Latin phrase of Livy, *History of Rome* 24.25.8, in the following words: "themselves obsequiously subservient while arrogantly lording it over others." I believe that Strauss, in this use of the words of Livy, means to allude unambiguously to Martin Heidegger. For how Strauss viewed Heidegger, one must add (as supplementary to what he says explicitly in some of the essays of this book, in other immediately relevant essays, as well as in passing remarks of seemingly unrelated essays and books) the implicit critique that is contained in a brief reference: Strauss refers the reader to C. F. Meyer, *Die Versuchung des Pescara* (1887). (See note 23, p. 174

supra, which is a note to a passage on p. 150 supra, in the text of "Preface to *Spinoza's Critique of Religion*.") The novella by Meyer might be characterized as a literary treatment of the following theme: how a truly noble man deals with the temptation of the promise of immortal glory, with immortal glory to be achieved through committing a base act, and with the promise itself couched in the language of a religious Call. See Conrad Ferdinand Meyer, "Die Versuchung des Pescara," in *Sämtliche Werke*, ed. Hans Zeller and Alfred Zäch, vol. 13, pp. 151–275 (Bern: Benteli, 1962). See also, for an English translation, "The Temptation of Pescara," in *The Complete Narrative Prose of Conrad Ferdinand Meyer*, ed. and trans. George F. Folkers, David B. Dickens, and Marion W. Sonnenfeld, vol. 2, pp. 225–306 (Lewisburg: Bucknell University Press, 1976).

Appendix 3:
Memorial Remarks for Jason Aronson[1]

We are struck by the awesome, unfathomable experience of death, of the death of one near and dear to us. We are grieved particularly because our friend died so young—when he was about to come into his own, to enter on a career which would have made him esteemed beyond the circle of his friends here and elsewhere and his pupils in the Liberal Arts Program. It is not given to me to say words of comfort of my own. I can only try to say what, I believe, Jason Aronson had come to know. I saw him for the last time about three weeks ago in my office. He knew where he stood. He jokingly reminded me of an old joke: all men are mortal but some more than others. He decided bravely and wisely to continue his study of Shaftesbury. At his suggestion we agreed that we would read the Bible together, starting from the beginning

Death is terrible, terrifying, but we cannot live as human beings if this terror grips us to the point of corroding our core. Jason Aronson had two experiences which protected him against this corrosive as well as its kin. The one is to come to grips with the corrosives, to face them, to think them through, to understand the ineluctable necessities, and to understand that without them no life, no human life, no good life, is possible. Slowly, step by step, but with ever greater sureness and awakeness did he begin to become a philosopher. I do not know whether he knew the word of a man of old: may my soul die the death of the philosophers, but young as he was he died that death.

The other experience which gave him strength and depth was his realizing ever more clearly and profoundly what it means to be a son of the Jewish people—of the 'am 'olam—to have one's roots deep in the oldest past and to be committed to a future beyond all futures.

He did not permit his mind to stifle the voice of his heart nor his heart to give commands to his mind.

I apply to his life the daring, gay, and noble motto: *courte et bonne*—his life was short and good. We shall never forget him and for what he stood.

I address to his wife, his mother, and brother, and his sister the traditional Jewish formula: "May God comfort you among the others who mourn for Zion and Jerusalem."

Note

[The note below to the Memorial Remarks is entirely the work of the present editor. —Ed.]

1. These memorial remarks were made by Leo Strauss in honor of Jason Aronson at his funeral in Chicago on 6 December 1961. Jason Aronson was a thirty-two year old graduate student who had been studying with Strauss at the University of Chicago. A pamphlet entitled "Jason Marvin Aronson: Three Funeral Addresses" (20 pages) was published by his friends at the University of Chicago. It contains words spoken in remembrance of his life by George Anastaplo, Leo Strauss, and Thomas McDonald, as well as his "Proposal for a Dissertation" on Shaftesbury. The memorial remarks by Strauss were subsequently published by George Anastaplo in a provocative article, "On Leo Strauss : A Yahrzeit Remembrance," *University of Chicago Magazine* 67 (Winter 1974): 30–38. (It is reprinted with notes and corrections as an epilogue to his book, *The Artist as Thinker: From Shakespeare to Joyce* [Athens, Ohio: Ohio University Press, 1983], 249–72, 473–85.) As a non-Jew and a careful observer, Anastaplo in his article keenly appreciates what he regards as the twofold beneficial influence which Judaism exercised on Strauss, and through him on his students both Jewish and non-Jewish. First, it somehow helped make Strauss, as both a thinker and a careful reader, receptive to the premodern idea of philosophy and resistant to certain modern ideas. Second, it overflowed through him as a Jewish thinker and scholar so as to leave a deep and vivifying impression on those who encountered him, through his intellectual seriousness about Judaism, and through his human example of devotion to Judaism. In the words of Anastaplo: "One can see in these remarks [of Strauss] . . . the solace which Judaism can provide mankind in the face of death, especially an untimely death." The Hebrew phrase from Strauss's remarks, *'am 'olam*, may be translated as "the eternal people."

Sources

"Progress or Return?" was first delivered as a series of lectures at the Hillel House, University of Chicago in November 1952. It was originally published in two parts. The first part appeared as "Progress or Return? The Contemporary Crisis in Western Civilization" in *Modern Judaism* 1 (1981): 17–45. The second part appeared as "The Mutual Influence of Theology and Philosophy" in *The Independent Journal of Philosophy* 3 (1979): 111–18.

"Preface to *Spinoza's Critique of Religion*" first appeared in Leo Strauss, *Spinoza's Critique of Religion* (New York: Schocken, 1965), 1–31. It was republished with slight changes in Leo Strauss, *Liberalism Ancient and Modern* (New York: Basic Books, 1968), 224–59.

"How to Study Spinoza's *Theologico-Political Treatise*" first appeared in *Proceedings of the American Academy for Jewish Research* 17 (1948): 69–131.

"Preface to Isaac Husik, *Philosophical Essays: Ancient, Medieval, and Modern*" first appeared in Isaac Husik, *Philosophical Essays: Ancient, Medieval, and Modern*, edited by Milton Nahm and Leo Strauss (Oxford: Basil Blackwell, 1952), vii–xli.

"Introductory Essay to Hermann Cohen, *Religion of Reason out of the Sources of Judaism*" first appeared in Hermann Cohen, *Religion of Reason out of the Sources of Judaism* (New York: Frederick Ungar, 1972), xxiii–xxxviii.

"On the Interpretation of Genesis" first appeared in *L'Homme* 21 (1981): 5–36.

"Jerusalem and Athens" first appeared as *Jerusalem and Athens: Some Preliminary Reflections*. The First Frank Cohen Public Lecture in Judaic Affairs, The City College Papers, Number 6 (New York: City College, 1967). 28 pp. pamphlet.

The first paragraph of "What Is Political Philosophy?" (1954) first appeared in Leo Strauss, *What Is Political Philosophy?* (New York: Free Press, 1959), 9–10.

"Review of J.L. Talmon, *The Nature of Jewish History*" first appeared in *The Journal of Modern History* 29 (1957): 306.

"Letter to the Editor: The State of Israel" first appeared in *National Review* 3, no. 1 (5 January 1957): 23.

"Introduction to *Persecution and the Art of Writing*" first appeared in Leo Strauss, *Persecution and the Art of Writing* (Glencoe, Ill.: Free Press, 1952), 7–21.

"Perspectives on the Good Society" first appeared in *Criterion* 2, no. 3 (Summer 1963): 2–9.

"An Unspoken Prologue to a Public Lecture at St. John's College" first appeared in *Interpretation* 7, no. 3 (1978): 1–3.

"Preface to *Hobbes Politische Wissenschaft*" first appeared in *Interpretation* 8, no. 1 (1979–80): 1–3. Translated by Donald J. Maletz.

"A Giving of Accounts" first appeared in *The College* 22, no. 1 (April 1970): 1–5.

Bibliography:
Selected Works on Leo Strauss
as a Modern Jewish Thinker

Adler, Eve. "Leo Strauss's *Philosophie und Gesetz.*" In *Leo Strauss's Thought: Toward a Critical Engagement*, ed. Alan Udoff, 183–226. Boulder, Colorado: Lynne Rienner, 1991.

———. "Translator's Introduction." In *Philosophy and Law: Contributions to the Understanding of Maimonides and His Predecessors*, by Leo Strauss, 1–19. Albany: State University of New York Press, 1995.

Almaleh, Gérard, Albert Baraquin, and Mireille Depadt-Ejchenbaum. "Présentation." In *Le Testament de Spinoza*, by Leo Strauss, 9–39. Paris: Les Editions du Cerf, 1991.

Altizer, Thomas J. J. "The Theological Conflict Between Strauss and Voegelin." In *Faith and Political Philosophy: The Correspondence Between Leo Strauss and Eric Voegelin*, eds. Peter Emberley and Barry Cooper, 267–77. University Park, Pennsylvania: Pennsylvania State University Press, 1993.

Altmann, Alexander. "Leo Strauss: 1899–1973." *Proceedings of the American Academy for Jewish Research* 41–42 (1975): xxxiii–xxxvi.

———. Review of *The Guide of the Perplexed*, by Moses Maimonides, translated with an introduction and notes by Shlomo Pines, and with an introductory essay by Leo Strauss. *Journal of Religion* 44 (1964): 260–61.

Altwicker, Norbert. "Vorwort." In *Die Religionskritik Spinozas als Grundlage seiner Bibelwissenschaft*, by Leo Strauss, IX–XII. Hildesheim: Georg Olms, 1981.

Anastaplo, George. "On Leo Strauss: A Yahrzeit Remembrance." *University of Chicago Magazine* 67 (Winter 1974): 30–38. Also in *The Artist as Thinker: From Shakespeare to Joyce*, by George Anastaplo, 249–72, 473–85. Athens, Ohio: Ohio University Press, 1983.

Arkes, Hadley. "Athens and Jerusalem: The Legacy of Leo Strauss." In *Leo Strauss and Judaism: Jerusalem and Athens Revisited*, ed. David Novak, 1–24. Lanham, Maryland: Rowman and Littlefield, 1996.

Arkush, Allan. "Leo Strauss and Jewish Modernity." In *Leo Strauss and Judaism: Jerusalem and Athens Revisited*, ed. David Novak, 111–30. Lanham, Maryland: Rowman and Littlefield, 1996.

Auerbach, Maurice. "The Philosophical Politics of Leo Strauss." *Teaching Political Science* 12, no. 2 (Winter 1985): 52–60.

Ben-Asher, Mordechai. "Religion and Reason in Maimonides. Contribution to an Explanation of the Views of Julius Guttmann and Leo Strauss" (in Hebrew). *Bash-Sha'ar* 4 (1961): 78–87.

Berns, Laurence. "Leo Strauss: 1899–1973." *The Independent Journal of Philosophy* 2 (1978): 1–3.

———. "The Relation Between Religion and Philosophy: Reflections on Leo Strauss's Suggestion Concerning the Source and Sources of Modern Philosophy." *Interpretation* 19, no. 1 (Fall 1991): 43–60.

Biale, David. "Leo Strauss: The Philosopher as Weimar Jew." In *Leo Strauss's Thought: Toward a Critical Engagement*, ed. Alan Udoff, 31–40. Boulder, Colorado: Lynne Rienner, 1991.

Blanchard, Kenneth C. "Philosophy in the Age of Auschwitz: Emil Fackenheim and Leo Strauss." In vol. 2 of *Remembering for the Future*, ed. Yehuda Bauer, et al., 1815–29. Oxford, England: Pergamon, 1989.

Bloom, Allan. "Leo Strauss: September 20, 1899–October 18, 1973." In *Giants and Dwarfs: Essays 1960–1990*, 235–55. New York: Simon and Schuster, 1990. Also in: *Political Theory* 5 (1977): 315–30.

Bouganim, Ami. "Un judaïsme politique: Léo Strauss." In *Le juif égaré*, 65–105. Paris: Desclée de Brouwer, 1990.

———. "Une désillusion héroïque: Une étude de la pensée de Léo Strauss." *Pardès* 4 (1986): 54–72.

Brague, Rémi. "Leo Strauss and Maimonides." In *Leo Strauss's Thought: Toward a Critical Engagement*, ed. Alan Udoff, 93–114. Boulder, Colorado: Lynne Rienner, 1991. For a French version, see: "Leo Strauss et Maïmonide." In *Maimonides and Philosophy*, eds. Shlomo Pines and Yirmiyahu Yovel, 246–68. Dordrecht, The Netherlands: Martinus Nijhoff, 1986.

Buijs, Joseph A. "The Philosophical Character of Maimonides' *Guide*—A Critique of Strauss's Interpretation." *Judaism* 27 (1978): 448–57. Also in *Maimonides: A Collection of Critical Essays*, ed. Joseph A. Buijs, 59–70. Notre Dame, Indiana: University of Notre Dame Press, 1988.

Caton, Hiram. "Explaining the Nazis: Leo Strauss Today." *Quadrant* 30, no. 10 (October 1986): 61–65.

Clay, Jenny Strauss. "Afterword." In *Leo Strauss and Judaism: Jerusalem and Athens Revisited*, ed. David Novak, 193–94. Lanham, Maryland: Rowman and Littlefield, 1996.

Cohen, Jonathan. "Strauss, Soloveitchik, and the Genesis Narrative: Conceptions of the Ideal Jew as Derived from Philosophical and Theological Readings of the Bible." *Journal of Jewish Thought and Philosophy* 5, no. 1 (1995): 99–143.

———. "Jew and Philosopher: The Return to Maimonides in Leo Strauss: A Review Essay." *Modern Judaism* 16, no. 1 (February 1996): 81–91.

Colmo, Christopher A. "Reason and Revelation in the Thought of Leo Strauss." *Interpretation* 18, no. 1 (Fall 1990): 145–60.

Coser, Lewis A. "Leo Strauss (1899–1973): Political Philosopher and Guide to the Modern Perplexed." In *Refugee Scholars in America: Their Impact and Their Experiences*, 202–7. New Haven: Yale University Press, 1984.

Dannhauser, Werner J. "Leo Strauss: Becoming Naive Again." *American Scholar* 44 (1974–75): 636–42. Also in *Masters: Portraits of Great Teachers*, ed. Joseph Epstein, 253–65. New York: Basic Books, 1981.

———. "Leo Strauss as Citizen and Jew." *Interpretation* 17, no. 3 (Spring 1991): 433–47.

———. "Athens and Jerusalem or Jerusalem and Athens?" In *Leo Strauss and Judaism: Jerusalem and Athens Revisited*, ed. David Novak, 155–72. Lanham, Maryland: Rowman and Littlefield, 1996.

Deutsch, Kenneth L., and Walter Nicgorski. "Introduction." In *Leo Strauss: Political Philosopher and Jewish Thinker*, eds. Kenneth L. Deutsch and Walter Nicgorski, 1–37. Lanham, Maryland: Rowman and Littlefield, 1994.

Eidelberg, Paul. *Jerusalem versus Athens*. Lanham, Maryland: University Press of America, 1983.

Emberley, Peter, and Barry Cooper, "Introduction." In *Faith and Political Philosophy: The Correspondence Between Leo Strauss and Eric Voegelin*, eds. Peter Emberley and Barry Cooper, ix–xxvi. University Park, Pennsylvania: Pennsylvania State University Press, 1993.

Fackenheim, Emil L. "Leo Strauss and Modern Judaism." *Claremont Review of Books* 4, no. 4 (Winter 1985): 21–23.

———. "Jewish Philosophy and the Academy." In *Jewish Philosophy and the Academy*, eds. Emil L. Fackenheim and Raphael Jospe, 23–47. London: Associated University Presses, 1996.

Fortin, Ernest L. "Rational Theologians and Irrational Philosophers: A Straussian Perspective." *Interpretation* 12 (1984): 349–56.

——— . "Between the Lines: Was Leo Strauss a Secret Enemy of Truth?" *Crisis* 7, no. 12 (December 1989): 19–26.

Fox, Marvin. Review of *The Guide of the Perplexed*, by Moses Maimonides, translated with an introduction and notes by Shlomo Pines, and with an introductory essay by Leo Strauss. *Journal of the History of Philosophy* 3 (1965): 265–74.

——— . *Interpreting Maimonides: Studies in Methodology, Metaphysics, and Moral Philosophy.* Chicago: University of Chicago Press, 1990.

Fradkin, Hillel. "Leo Strauss." In *Interpreters of Judaism in the Late Twentieth Century*, ed. Steven T. Katz, 343–67. Washington, D.C.: B'nai B'rith, 1993.

——— . "Philosophy and Law: Leo Strauss as a Student of Medieval Jewish Thought." In *Leo Strauss: Political Philosopher and Jewish Thinker*, eds. Kenneth L. Deutsch and Walter Nicgorski, 129–41. Lanham, Maryland: Rowman and Littlefield, 1994.

——— . "A Word Fitly Spoken: The Interpretation of Maimonides and the Legacy of Leo Strauss." In *Leo Strauss and Judaism: Jerusalem and Athens Revisited*, ed. David Novak, 55–86. Lanham, Maryland: Rowman and Littlefield, 1996.

Fuller, Timothy. "Philosophy, Faith, and the Question of Progress." In *Faith and Political Philosophy: The Correspondence Between Leo Strauss and Eric Voegelin*, eds. Peter Emberley and Barry Cooper, 279–95. University Park, Pennsylvania: Pennsylvania State University Press, 1993.

Gadamer, Hans-Georg. "Philosophizing in Opposition: Strauss and Voegelin on Communication and Science." In *Faith and Political Philosophy: The Correspondence Between Leo Strauss and Eric Voegelin*, eds. Peter Emberley and Barry Cooper, 249–59. University Park, Pennsylvania: Pennsylvania State University Press, 1993.

Gebhardt, Jürgen. "Leo Strauss: The Quest for Truth in Times of Perplexity." In *Hannah Arendt and Leo Strauss: German Émigrés and American Political Thought After World War II*, eds. Peter Graf Kielmansegg, Horst Mewes, Elisabeth Glaser-Schmidt, 81–104. New York: Cambridge University Press, 1995.

Germino, Dante. "Leo Strauss versus Eric Voegelin on Faith and Political Philosophy." *Political Science Reviewer* 24 (1995): 251–75.

Grant, George P. "Tyranny and Wisdom: The Controversy Between Leo Strauss and Alexandre Kojève." *Social Research* 31 (1964): 45–72. Also in *Technology and Empire*, by George P. Grant, 81–109. Toronto: Anansi, 1969.

Green, Kenneth Hart. "'In the Grip of the Theological-Political Predicament': The Turn to Maimonides in the Jewish Thought of Leo Strauss." In *Leo Strauss's Thought: Toward a Critical Engagement*, ed. Alan Udoff, 41–74. Boulder, Colorado: Lynne Rienner, 1991.

——. *Jew and Philosopher: The Return to Maimonides in the Jewish Thought of Leo Strauss*. Albany: State University of New York Press, 1993.

——. "Religion, Philosophy, and Morality: How Leo Strauss Read Judah Halevi's *Kuzari*." *Journal of the American Academy of Religion* 61, no. 2 (Summer 1993): 225–73.

——. "Leo Strauss." In *The Routledge History of Jewish Philosophy*, eds. Daniel H. Frank and Oliver Leaman, 820–53. London: Routledge, 1997.

Gunnell, John G. "Strauss Before Straussianism: Reason, Revelation, and Nature." In *Leo Strauss: Political Philosopher and Jewish Thinker*, eds. Kenneth L. Deutsch and Walter Nicgorski, 107–28. Lanham, Maryland: Rowman and Littlefield, 1994.

Guttmann, Julius. "Philosophie der Religion oder Philosophie des Gesetzes?" *Proceedings of the Israel Academy of Sciences and Humanities* 5 (1976): 146–73 (in Hebrew translation, pp. 188–207).

Harvey, Warren Zev. "The Return of Maimonideanism." *Jewish Social Studies* 42 (1980): 249–68.

Herberg, Will. "Athens and Jerusalem: Confrontation and Dialogue." *The Drew Gateway* 28, no. 3 (Spring 1958): 178–200.

Himmelfarb, Milton. "On Leo Strauss." *Commentary* 58, no. 8 (August 1974): 60–66. For responses to the article in letters to the editor, and a reply by the author, see *Commentary* 59, no. 1 (January 1975): 14, 16.

Hyman, Arthur. "Interpreting Maimonides." *Gesher* 5 (1976): 46–59.

Ivry, Alfred L. "Leo Strauss on Maimonides." In *Leo Strauss's Thought: Toward a Critical Engagement*, ed. Alan Udoff, 75–91. Boulder, Colorado: Lynne Rienner, 1991.

Jaffa, Harry V. "Leo Strauss, the Bible, and Political Philosophy." In *Leo Strauss: Political Philosopher and Jewish Thinker*, eds. Kenneth L. Deutsch and Walter Nicgorski, 195–210. Lanham, Maryland: Rowman and Littlefield, 1994.

Lachterman, David R. "Laying Down the Law: The Theological-Political Matrix of Spinoza's Physics." In *Leo Strauss's Thought: Toward a Critical Engagement*, ed. Alan Udoff, 123–53. Boulder, Colorado: Lynne Rienner, 1991.

Lawrence, Frederick G. "Leo Strauss and the Fourth Wave of Modernity." In *Leo Strauss and Judaism: Jerusalem and Athens Revisited*, ed. David Novak, 131–54. Lanham, Maryland: Rowman and Littlefield, 1996.

Lerner, Ralph. "Leo Strauss." Vol. 15 in the *Encyclopedia Judaica*, ed. Cecil Roth, et al., 434. Jerusalem: Keter, 1971.

———. "Leo Strauss: 1899–1973." *American Jewish Year Book* 76 (1976): 91–97.

———. "Foreword. " In *Philosophy and Law*, by Leo Strauss, ix–xiii. Philadelphia: Jewish Publication Society, 1987.

Luz, Ehud. "The Judaism of Leo Strauss" (in Hebrew). *Daat* 27 (Summer 1991): 35–60.

Mendes-Flohr, Paul R. "The Theological-Political Predicament of Modern Judaism: Leo Strauss's Neo-Maimonidean Political Ethic." Unpublished manuscript, 40 pp.

Momigliano, Arnaldo. "Hermeneutics and Classical Political Thought in Leo Strauss." In *Essays on Ancient and Modern Judaism*, 178–89. Chicago: University of Chicago Press, 1994.

Morgan, Michael L. "The Curse of Historicity: The Role of History in Leo Strauss's Jewish Thought." *Journal of Religion* 61 (1981): 345–63. Also in *Dilemmas in Modern Jewish Thought*, by Michael L. Morgan, 40–54. Bloomington, Indiana: Indiana University Press, 1992.

———. "Leo Strauss and the Possibility of Jewish Philosophy." *Dilemmas in Modern Jewish Thought*, by Michael L. Morgan, 55–67. Bloomington, Indiana: Indiana University Press, 1992.

———. "Teaching Leo Strauss as a Jewish and General Philosopher. In *Jewish Philosophy and the Academy*, eds. Emil L. Fackenheim and Raphael Jospe, 174–88. London: Associated University Presses, 1996.

Novak, David. "Philosophy and the Possibility of Revelation: A Theological Response to the Challenge of Leo Strauss." In *Leo Strauss and Judaism: Jerusalem and Athens Revisited*, ed. David Novak, 173–92. Lanham, Maryland: Rowman and Littlefield, 1996.

Orr, Susan, *Jerusalem and Athens: Reason and Revelation in the Works of Leo Strauss*. Lanham, Maryland: Rowman and Littlefield, 1995.

———. "Strauss, Reason, and Revelation: Unraveling the Essential Question." In *Leo Strauss and Judaism: Jerusalem and Athens Revisited*, ed. David Novak, 25–54. Lanham, Maryland: Rowman and Littlefield, 1996.

———. Review Essay on *Jew and Philosopher: The Return to Maimonides in the Jewish Thought of Leo Strauss*, by Kenneth Hart Green. *Interpretation* 23, no. 2 (Winter 1996): 307–16.

Pangle, Thomas L. "On the Epistolary Dialogue Between Leo Strauss and Eric Voegelin." In *Leo Strauss: Political Philosopher and Jewish Thinker*, eds. Kenneth L. Deutsch and Walter Nicgorski, 231–56. Lanham, Maryland: Rowman and Littlefield, 1994.

Pines, Shlomo. "On Leo Strauss," translated by Aryeh Leo Motzkin. *The Independent Journal of Philosophy* 5/6 (1988): 169–71. For the Hebrew original, see: "On Leo Strauss." *Molad* 30, nos. 247–48 / n.s. 7, nos. 37–38 (1976): 455–57.

Polak, Joseph A. "Progress as a Category in the Writings of Classical Judaism and of Leo Strauss." Unpublished manuscript, 20 pp.

Rhodes, James M. "Philosophy, Revelation, and Political Theory: Leo Strauss and Eric Voegelin." *Journal of Politics* 49, no. 4 (November 1987): 1036–60.

Rosen, Stanley. "Hermeneutics as Politics." In *Hermeneutics as Politics*, 87–140. New York: Oxford University Press, 1987.

——— . "Leo Strauss and the Quarrel Between the Ancients and the Moderns." In *Leo Strauss's Thought: Toward a Critical Engagement*, ed. Alan Udoff, 155–68. Boulder, Colorado: Lynne Rienner, 1991.

——— . "Politics or Transcendence? Responding to Historicism." In *Faith and Political Philosophy: The Correspondence Between Leo Strauss and Eric Voegelin*, eds. Peter Emberley and Barry Cooper, 261–66. University Park, Pennsylvania: Pennsylvania State University Press, 1993.

Rotenstreich, Nathan. "Between Athens and Jerusalem" (in Hebrew). *Studies in Contemporary Jewish Thought*, 139–43. Tel Aviv: Am Oved, 1978.

Sandoz, Ellis. "Medieval Rationalism or Mystic Philosophy? Reflections on the Strauss-Voegelin Correspondence." In *Faith and Political Philosophy: The Correspondence Between Leo Strauss and Eric Voegelin*, eds. Peter Emberley and Barry Cooper, 297–319. University Park, Pennsylvania: Pennsylvania State University Press, 1993.

Schall, James V. "Revelation, Reason and Politics: Catholic Reflexions on Strauss." *Gregorianum* 62 (1981): 349–65, 467–97.

——— . "A Latitude for Statesmanship? Strauss on St. Thomas." In *Leo Strauss: Political Philosopher and Jewish Thinker*, eds. Kenneth L. Deutsch and Walter Nicgorski, 211–30. Lanham, Maryland: Rowman and Littlefield, 1994.

Schwarcz, Moshe. "The Enlightenment and Its Implications for Jewish Philosophy in the Modern Period, in Light of the Controversy between L. Strauss and J. Guttmann" (in Hebrew). *Daat* 1, no. 1 (Winter 1978): 7–16.

Schweid, Eliezer. "Religion and Philosophy: The Scholarly-Theological Debate Between Julius Guttmann and Leo Strauss." *Maimonidean Studies* 1 (1990): 163–95.

Seeskin, Kenneth. "Maimonides' Conception of Philosophy." In *Leo Strauss and Judaism: Jerusalem and Athens Revisited*, ed. David Novak, 87–110. Lanham, Maryland: Rowman and Littlefield, 1996.

Shell, Susan. "Taking Evil Seriously: Schmitt's 'Concept of the Political' and Strauss's 'True Politics.'" In *Leo Strauss: Political Philosopher and Jewish Thinker*, eds. Kenneth L. Deutsch and Walter Nicgorski, 175–93. Lanham, Maryland: Rowman and Littlefield, 1994.

Smith, Steven B. "Leo Strauss: Between Jerusalem and Athens." In *Leo Strauss: Political Philosopher and Jewish Thinker*, eds. Kenneth L. Deutsch and Walter Nicgorski, 81–105. Lanham, Maryland: Rowman and Littlefield, 1994.

——— . "Gershom Scholem and Leo Strauss: Notes Toward a German-Jewish Dialogue." *Modern Judaism* 13 (1993): 209–29.

Soffer, Walter. "Modern Rationalism, Miracles, and Revelation: Strauss's Critique of Spinoza." In *Leo Strauss: Political Philosopher and Jewish Thinker*, eds. Kenneth L. Deutsch and Walter Nicgorski, 143–73. Lanham, Maryland: Rowman and Littlefield, 1994.

Söllner, Alfons. "Leo Strauss: German Origin and American Impact." In *Hannah Arendt and Leo Strauss: German Émigrés and American Political Thought After World War II*, eds. Peter Graf Kielmansegg, Horst Mewes, Elisabeth Glaser-Schmidt, 121–37. New York: Cambridge University Press, 1995.

Udoff, Alan. "On Leo Strauss: An Introductory Account." In *Leo Strauss's Thought: Toward a Critical Engagement*, ed. Alan Udoff, 1–29. Boulder, Colorado: Lynne Rienner, 1991.

Vajda, Georges. Review of *The Guide of the Perplexed*, by Moses Maimonides, translated with an introduction and notes by Shlomo Pines, and with an introductory essay by Leo Strauss. *Revue des Études Juives* 123 (1964): 209–16.

Walsh, David. "The Reason-Revelation Tension in Strauss and Voegelin." In *Faith and Political Philosophy: The Correspondence Between Leo Strauss and Eric Voegelin*, eds. Peter Emberley and Barry Cooper, 349–68. University Park, Pennsylvania: Pennsylvania State University Press, 1993.

Wiser, James L. "Reason and Revelation as Search and Response: A Comparison of Leo Strauss and Eric Voegelin." In *Faith and Political Philosophy: The Correspondence Between Leo Strauss and Eric Voegelin*, eds. Peter Emberley and Barry Cooper, 237–59. University Park, Pennsylvania: Pennsylvania State University Press, 1993.

Yaffe, Martin D. "On Leo Strauss's *Philosophy and Law*: A Review Essay." *Modern Judaism* 9 (1989): 213–25.

―――. "Leo Strauss as Judaic Thinker: Some First Notions." *Religious Studies Review* 17, no. 1 (January 1991): 33–41.

―――. "Autonomy, Community, Authority: Hermann Cohen, Carl Schmitt, Leo Strauss." In *Autonomy and Judaism*, ed. Daniel H. Frank, 143–60. Albany: State University of New York Press, 1992.

Zank, Michael. "Translator's Introduction." In *The Early German Jewish Writings*, by Leo Strauss. Albany: State University of New York Press, 1998. (forthcoming)

Index

Abel, 109, 387–88
Abimelech, 392, 405n10
Abraham, 110, 121, 271–72, 277, 290, 295, 360, 390–93
Academy for the Science of Judaism (Berlin), 4
Action and faith, 440–42
Adam, 105, 372, 385–86, 387
Aggada (midrash), 319–20, 427
Aḥad Ha'am (Asher Ginsberg), 80(nn84,85), 81n93, 82n99, 144–45, 174n10, 341, 354n41. *See also* Cultural Zionism; "In External Freedom and Internal Slavery" (Aḥad Ha'am)
Akeida (binding of Isaac), 110, 271–72, 290, 323, 391, 392–93
Albo, Joseph, 235, 245
Alcibiades, 463
Aleichem, Sholem, 54n10
Aleinu prayer, 327–28, 351n28
Alfarabi, 210, 418–19, 420–26, 428, 469
Altmann, Alexander, 2, 51n6, 59n20, 71n51
American Academy for Jewish Research, 5
American Constitution, 302, 333
Amos, 106, 274, 400
Anastaplo, George, 55n12, 59n23, 476n1
Ancestral as good, 87–88, 89, 112–13, 118, 120
Ancient philosophy, *see* Greek philosophy
Anthropocentrism, in modern thought, 102
Anti-Semitism, 321, 334, 336–37, 348n15, 349n16; Freud's concern with, 286–87; in Germany, 139–41, 320–21, 335–36; in liberal democracies, 29–30, 31,

143–44, 314–15; in Soviet Union, 54n10, 144, 282, 315–17, 335, 336; Strauss avoids term, 79n83, 92, 320–21. *See also* "Discrimination" (prejudice); Persecution of Jews; *Rish'us*
Apollo, 110, 402
Apologetic thinkers, 16, 17, 252
Apology of Socrates (Plato), 401–4
Aquinas, Thomas, 252, 426–27, 429n9, 463
Arabs, 317, 321, 419–21, 425, 426
Aristotle, 37, 121, 133n13, 152, 173, 437, 439, 450, 468; god of, 113–14, 121, 360, 396; on human life, 240, 371; Husik's studies on, 235, 236, 241–44, 247, 252, 259, 261; Maimonides and, 8; *Metaphysics*, 243, 461; on morality, 105–110 passim, 114, 115, 152, 155, 465; on Plato and Socrates, 399; *Politics*, 371, 418; on progress, 95
Arkush, Allan, 68n47
Arnold, Matthew, 411
Aronson, Jason, 475–76
Arts and crafts, 102, 115–16, 119, 388
"Aryan," 139, 321
Assimilation, 30, 31, 32, 91–92, 248, 323–27, 439; Freud and, 295–96; of individuals, 142, 313, 314, 315, 318; of nation, 142, 295–96, 318; Nietzsche on, 323–25, 326; Spinoza on, 14, 91, 156, 161
Atheism, 99, 171–72, 344–45; Freud and, 301, 304; and miracles, 128; in Nietzsche and "new thinking," 150; of Spinoza, 172, 215–16; and Strauss, 55n12; Zionism and, 33–34
Athens, *see* Greek philosophy; Jerusalem and Athens

489

Aton, 292–93
Autoemancipation (Pinsker), 141, 318, 348n10
Averroes, 241, 418, 419, 420, 427, 429n9
Avicenna, 419, 420, 463
Awareness (*noesis*), 118–19, 120, 124, 367

Baal, 126–27
Babel, tower of, 390
Bacon, Francis, 9, 10, 14, 16, 127–28, 154, 211
Baer, Yitzhak F., 322–23, 349n21
Balaam, 153
Barbarism: in twentieth century, 26, 100–1, 131–32, 332; in the past, *see* Persecution of Jews. *See also* Evil; Holocaust; Nuclear warfare
Baron, Salo Wittmayer, 57n19
Barth, Karl, 22, 73n52, 453, 460
Baruch, Bernard M., 339, 354n39
Bebel, August, 347n7
Benardete, Seth, xivn4, 134n24
Ben-Gurion, David, 321–22, 349n19
Benjamin, Walter, 56n12
Berdyczewski, M.J., 63n30
Berlin, Isaiah, 79n80
Bernard of Clairvaux, 323, 349n20
Berns, Laurence, xvin8, 134n35, 472n1
Bezalel, 115
Bible (Scripture), 73n52, 76n61, 146, 168, 170, 293, 319–20, 375n10); as a book, 120, 380–82, 373–75, 394; conception of God in, 89, 114–15, 119–20, 148–49, 157; contradictions in, 120, 125, 128, 206, 360–61, 375, 380, 382–83, 384–85; creation in, 83n96, 110, 115, 128, 344, 361–72, 380, 381, 382–86; faith (belief) in, 99, 119, 127, 151–52, 160, 360, 377, 381, 393, 432; as hieroglyphic book, 185–86, 205–8, 210; as history, 117–18, 380–82, 384; humanism in, 440; morality and, 28, 44, 99, 105–110, 118, 150–51, 204–5, 389; mystery of, 374–75, 393; myths in, 367, 380–81, 384; philosophy and, 104–123, 152, 250, 369, 373–74; poetry in, 59n23, 381; and progress, 96–97; rules for reading, 182–86, 187, 190, 196; Spinoza on, 10–11, 12, 15, 196–207, 216–23, 225(nn10,15); Strauss's "postcritical"

approach to, xii, xivn4, 48; and Western civilization, 98–99, 104, 116, 117, 120–21; on wisdom, 379–80; work of human or divine mind?, 359–60, 362. *See also* Deuteronomy; Exodus; Genesis; Leviticus; Prophets; Psalms; Torah (*Tora*)
Biblical criticism, 45, 128, 145, 250, 269, 360, 380–81, 453–54, 467; Freud on, 289; originated by Spinoza, 9, 10, 15, 93, 168, 209, 218–19, 380. *See also* Spinoza, Baruch; Wellhausen, Julius
Bismarck, Otto von, 137
Blessing: biblical notion of, 365, 390; Cohen's life and writings as, 282; divine, Jewish and Christian, 437; Greek notion of, 395; state of Israel as, 34–35, 142; modern victory of orthodoxy not unmitigated, 47–48, 172; Nietzsche on Jewish assimilation as, 325; Strauss "thinks" his, 333; Strauss's life and teachings as, xvin7, 1.
Bloom, Allan, 1, 49n2, 50n6, 52n7, 59n20
Bloom, Harold, xivn4
Bodin, Jean, 9, 166
Books, Bible contrasted with Greek philosophy as, 120, 373–75, 380–82, 394
Buber, Martin, 4, 5, 148, 149, 150, 306n1, 334, 353n34
Buchanan, Scott, 459
Burke, Edmund, 112, 135n45

Cain, 109, 115, 387, 388
Canaan, 295, 297, 352n28, 390–91
Caro, Joseph, 164
Cassirer, Ernst, 4, 60n26
Cassuto, Umberto, xivn4
Categories (Aristotle), Husik on, 236, 243, 244, 247, 252
Causality, 110, 114, 119, 126, 155–56, 191, 259, 305. *See also* Teleology
Chosen people (divine election): Bible in light of, 370, 381, 393; and Covenant with Abraham, 390–93; Freud on, 296, 301; Israel symbolizes mankind as, 79n82, 141, 143, 276–77, 327–28, 340, 352n28, 411, 438, 443; and Jewish survival, 286, 301; Nietzsche on, 324–25; persecution as proof of, 91, 443; in prophets, 401; in Rosenzweig's

thought, 152; Spinoza on, 160, 198–99, 220. *See also* Faith (belief), Jewish; Jewish people (nation); Judaism

Christianity: difference from Islam and Judaism, 419, 426; Freud on, 305; Jewish and Christian faith, 124, 141, 163, 197–205, 220–24, 314, 333–36, 437; and Judaism, 156, 334–36, 426, 436–42; persecution of Jews, *see* Persecution of Jews; Spinoza on, 13–14, 158, 159–60, 197, 200–1, 202–5, 216–17, 221–23; Strauss on, 335. *See also* Bible (Scripture); Church; Faith (belief), Jewish and Christian; Jesus; New Testament; Scholasticism

Church: Catholic, 125–26, 139, 450; Orthodox, 335–36; Protestant, 125–26, 217–18, 431; of Spinoza, 91, 156, 160; and Synagogue, 332, 437

Churchill, Winston, 65n43

City, 116, 388, 463, 465–66. *See also* *Republic* (Plato)

Claremont College (Berkeley, California), 6

Cohen, Arthur A., 436, 439–40

Cohen, Hermann, xvin7, 24, 49n1, 72n51, 73n52, 344, 354n43, 355n44, 460; belief in progress, 19, 23, 24–25, 399; and faith, 19–21, 23, 25, 154, 161–62, 399; Husik on, 251, 252–53, 255, 256; "idealization," 18–19, 21, 24, 165–66, 251, 256, 269, 277, 279; on immortality, 277–78; and modern Judaism, 17–22, 27, 54n10, 256, 267–82; on morality, 20, 161–62, 273, 280–81; on Plato and the prophets, 398–99; *Religion of Reason* (Strauss's introductory essay), xi, 6, 54n10, 267–82; on revelation, 19, 22, 25, 279; on Spinoza, 12, 154, 158–69, 462; Strauss and, 17–25, 54n10, 61n28, 65n42, 68n48, 70n50, 71n51, 76(nn62,63,66), 267–82; *System of Philosophy*, 268, 269, 270

Commentary on the Mishna (Maimonides), 164, 429n20

Communism: anti-Jewish policy of, 144, 282, 315–17, 335, 336; opposition to religion, 436; in Russia, 7, 23, 61(nn27–28), 123, 138, 144, 347n8, 442–43

Compassion: Cohen on, 274; Nietzsche on, 150; Spinoza and, 158–59

Conformism: religious, 210–11, 436; social, 434–35, 442

Conservatism, 166, 169, 443–44; Zionism and, 32, 413–14

Contemplation, 109, 113–14, 115–16, 118, 154–56, 373–74, 440

Contradictions: in Bible, 120, 125, 128, 206, 360–61, 375, 380, 382–83, 384–85, 392–93; in Maimonides, 210; principle of, 167, 285; in Spinoza, 198–99, 201–24 passim, 231n86; in state of Israel, 34; in the Torah (*sitrei Tora*), 167, 385; in Zionism, 33

Conversion, 342, 346n3. *See also* Assimilation

Copernicus, Nicolaus, 102

Cosmocentrism, in ancient thought, 102

Cosmology, 368–71, 471–72

Costa, Uriel da, 198

Covenant, 114–15, 119, 128, 133n14, 149, 344, 393; with Abraham, 390, 391; with Noah, 96, 389–90

Creation: in the Bible, 82n96, 106, 110, 115, 128, 361–73, 382–85; Cohen on, 270–71, 272, 276; defining belief for Judaism, 344–45; Hebrew word, 362–63; Maimonides on, 40, 46, 78n76, 83n96, 96, 110, 270, 354n42; Plato on, 106, 397; Spinoza on, 155, 222–23; twofold account in Genesis of, 115, 370–73, 383, 384–85; vs. eternity, 40, 78n76, 95, 110, 354n42

Cropsey, Joseph, xi, 311–12, 329

Crusades, 13, 139, 322–23, 352n28

Cultural Zionism, 35, 92, 143, 144–45, 319–20, 354n41. *See also* Ahad Ha'am (Asher Ginsberg)

Culture, 166, 269–70, 279, 344, 377–79

"Custom" or "way," 111–12, 261–62, 383. *See also* Good, ancestral as; Tradition

Czarist regime, 53n10, 312–13, 332, 399

Daimonion, of Socrates, 402–3

Damnation, 122, 278. *See also* Divine punishment

Dannhauser, Werner, xiiin2, xvn5, 58n20, 345

Darwin, Charles, 144–45

David, 107, 109, 125, 134n32, 404, 440
Dawidowicz, Lucy, 347n6
Dawn of Day (Nietzsche), 323–25, 349n22, 350(nn23–25), 351n26
Day of Atonement, Cohen on, 276
Death: Cohen's view of, 277–78; Strauss on, 475–76
Delphic oracle, 402–3
Delusion, 124, 171–72, 250, 323; heroic: 327–28
Democracy, *see* Liberal democracy
Descartes, René, 9, 10, 14, 154, 188, 210–11, 213
Deuteronomy, 27, 172, 270, 271, 272, 370, 405n6, 442
Dharma, 112
Diairesis, 367, 376n17
Dialogues (Plato), 462
"Discrimination" (prejudice): against Jews and Negroes in U.S., 143–44, 317, 330–31, 336–37, 435; lessening of?, 330–37; in liberal state, 29–31, 77n73, 91–93, 143–44, 314–15, 435. *See also* Anti-Semitism; Persecution of Jews; *Rish'us*
Diversity, religious, 434, 435–36, 442
Divine law, 119, 199, 257–58, 278, 279, 302, 344, 389, 419–20, 426–27, 433; Aquinas on, 426–27; in Bible and in Greek philosophy, 106–7, 112–13, 114; Cohen on, 272, 278–79; disobedience of, 87, 89, 106, 115, 372, 386–87; Farabi on, 420–26 passim; Husik on, 249–50, 254, 257–58; individual selection from, 153; Maimonides' defense of, 37–40, 41, 46, 81n94, 426–27; and philosophy, 37–38, 113–14, 118, 249, 426; Spinoza on, 91, 167–68, 199, 218, 227n30. *See also* Covenant; God; Ten Commandments (Decalogue); Torah (*Tora*)
Divine mission: of Israel, 141, 439–40; of Israel, in Cohen, 276–77; of the prophets, 400–1, 403; of Socrates, 400, 402–3
Divine omnipotence, 40, 41, 81n94, 110, 114, 119, 129, 153, 220–21, 360, 361
Divine punishment, 106, 122, 141, 276, 387, 388, 389
Dostoyevsky, Fyodor, 123–24, 135n52

Doubt: historical, 48; Maimonides on, 41–42; no biblical word for, 381; Strauss on, 44–45
Dream, noble, 328
Dualism, fundamental, 120, 366–67, 372

Ebbinghaus, Julius, 453, 461
Eden, garden of, 87, 385, 387, 389
Education, 459, 466; of ancient Jews in history, 297; divine: 387; Plato on theology and, 397
"Effeminizing" effect of Judaism, Spinoza on, 80n89, 90, 142, 161, 318, 319
Ehyeh-Asher-Ehyeh, *see* "I shall be What I shall be"
Einstein, Albert, 326, 351n26
Elijah, 126–27
Elite: doubt confined to, 41–42, 44–45; and philosophic search, 41–45, 196–97, 208–9, 424; Zionism and, 142
Empedocles, 394, 396
Empiricism, 147, 152
Emuna Rama (Ibn Daud), 271
Engels, Friedrich, 97, 133n17
Enlightenment, 7–8, 13, 24, 27, 62n29, 64n39, 71n51; and Jewish orthodoxy, 15–17, 27, 171–72, 461; Mendelssohn and, 15–17; Spinoza and, 9
Enoch, 388
Epicureanism, 95, 171
Esoteric and exoteric: of Bible, 185–86, 205–8; distinction between, 211, 214, 216, 218, 222–23, 224, 425, 462–63, 468; of Kabbala, 83n99; Lessing and, 462; of Maimonides, 7, 41–43, 44, 84n99, 209–10, 462–63; in philosophy, 7, 44–45, 210, 425, 468; of Spinoza, 207–24; Strauss on, 45, 462–64
Eternal, vs. historical, 98, 257–58, 274, 471–72
Eternity, of the universe, 133n13, 471; vs. creation, 40, 78n76, 95, 110, 354n42
Ethics, *see* Divine law; Good; Justice; Morality; Natural law
Ethics, Nicomachean (Aristotle), 105, 106, 107, 108, 155
Ethics of the Pure Will (Cohen), 268, 269, 274, 280, 281
Ethics (Spinoza), 11, 12, 64n37, 130, 155, 169, 170, 213–16

Euthyphro (Plato), 78n76
Eve, 105, 372, 385–87
Evil, 24, 98, 109, 115, 153, 157, 161–62, 272–73, 324, 371–73, 384–89, 393, 397, 398, 403, 441. *See also* Sin
Exile (*galut*), 32, 34, 90–91, 143, 313, 339, 380
Existentialism, 82n99, 117, 355n46, 437
Exodus, 114, 272, 393, 444; "metaphysics" of, 393
Explanation: distinct from interpretation, 181–82, 184–85, 187–88; for reading Spinoza's books, 193–94
Ezekiel, 88, 275, 277

Fackenheim, Emil L., xvin7, 1, 2, 48n1, 50n6, 63n30, 66n43
Faith (belief): and action, 440–42, 443; in America, 93; biblical, 99, 119, 127, 151–52, 160, 360, 377, 381, 393, 432; Cohen and, 19–21, 23, 25, 154, 161–62, 399; critique of, 11, 13, 15, 197, 257, 302–4, 425; diversity of, 434, 435–36, 442; Jewish and Christian, 124, 125, 141, 163, 197–205, 220–24, 314, 333–36, 437; Jewish and Muslim, 124, 165, 418–20, 425–28; Jewish (*see other subentries also*), 11–12, 17, 27–28, 34–35, 37, 39–41, 46–48, 55n12, 66n43, 77n72, 82n99, 87, 89–90, 143–46, 249, 271–72, 281, 301, 320, 323, 326–29, 342–45, 403, 409; and miracles, 126, 128, 360, 381; neurotic, Freud on, 297–98; and philosophy, 10, 23, 27, 127–28, 131, 170–73, 181, 201–2, 209–10, 257, 261, 263–64, 327–29, 338–40, 425–28; principle of, 418–19; and religious community, 42–44, 109, 425; Rosenzweig and, 27, 146–53; Spinoza's "universal," 160, 220–21
Falasifa, 419, 420, 421, 425
Fall, biblical account of, 87, 89, 105, 115, 372, 386–87, 389
Farabi, Abu Nasr al-, *see* Alfarabi
Father substitute, Freud on God as, 298–99
Fellowman, love of, 273–75
Fidelity, 54n11, 89, 159, 165, 281, 286, 320
Finkelstein, Louis, 57n19, 335, 353n36
First principles, search for, 111, 118–19

Flood, biblical account of, 388, 389, 390, 391, 393
Fox, Marvin, 2, 58n19
Fradkin, Hillel, xivn4
Frank Cohen Memorial Lectureship, 5, 377
Frankl, Viktor, 1
Freedom: in Genesis, 371, 373, 389; Husik's conception, 262; in modern thought, 103–4, 433, 444; of philosopher, 37, 38–39, 43–44, 45, 161, 217–18, 248–49, 424, 426, 469–70
Free Jewish House of Learning (Frankfurt), 4
"Freud on Moses and Monotheism" (Strauss), xii, 2, 55n12, 285–309
Freud, Sigmund: as a Jew, 286, 287; on monotheism, 287, 292, 293, 296, 297, 298–99; on religion as neurosis, 298–99, 303
Friedländer, Paul, 462

Gadamer, Hans-Georg, 52n7, 54n11, 58n20, 59n22
Galut (exile), 32, 34, 90–91, 143, 313, 339, 380; writings of Baer, 322–23, 349n21
Garden of Eden, *see* Eden, garden of
Gassendi, Pierre, 189
Genesis, xii, 87, 110, 115, 222–23, 272, 290, 359–76, 427; cosmology of, 368–71. *See also* Abraham; Creation; Moses
"Genius," of the Jewish people, 46–47, 82n99, 92, 143, 152–53, 156–57, 250, 254, 255, 319–20, 345, 355n46
Gentiles, 34, 55n12, 81n90, 163–64, 176n58, 295–96
Gentleman, Bible vs. philosophy on, 107–8
Germany: Cohen's hope for, 19, 25; Nazism in, 7, 60n26, 61n27, 65n43, 139, 321, 332, 438; Weimar Republic, 73n54, 137–38, 139
Gersonides, Levi, 4
Ginsberg, Asher, *see* Ahad Ha'am
"Giving of Accounts" (Klein and Strauss), 53n8, 457–66
Glatzer, Nahum N., 441–42
Glazer, Nathan, 443–44
God, 120–32 passim, 148, 157, 229n65, 327, 344–45, 354, 380; Aristotle's concept of, 396; Bible as word of, 125; biblical con-

God *(continued)*
ception of, 89, 114–16, 119–20, 148–49, 157, 361–75 passim, 380–94 passim; Cohen on, 161–62, 270–81 passim, 344, 398; common belief for Jews and Christians, 437, 440–42; concern with man, 108, 109, 110–11; as creator, 222–23, 327, 361–72, 382–85; existence of, 113–14, 145–46, 170, 270, 360–61; as first cause, 110–11, 114, 119, 155, 191–92, 253, 270, 360–61, 471–72; Freud's denial of, 301, 304; human understanding of, 12, 14, 119, 124, 129, 130, 131, 146, 147, 149–50, 253, 269–70; Maimonides on, 43, 344, 354n42; mystery of, 304–5, 328–29, 343–45, 374–75, 387, 393; name of, 114, 119, 295, 384, 393, 427, 444; and omnipotence, 40–41, 81n94, 110, 114, 119, 129, 153, 220–21, 360, 361; perfection of, 129, 130, 155; Plato's concept of, 396–97; prophets on, 89, 148–49, 400–1; punishment by, 122, 278, 388; Rosenzweig on, 19–20, 25–26, 145–53 passim; Spinoza on, 10–12, 130, 155, 156, 157–58, 166, 189, 207, 215, 220–24, 226n19, 229n65; Strauss on, 47, 83n99, 453–54, 458, 460–62; will of, 396–98. *See also* Creation; Divine law; Divine mission; Divine omnipotence; Divine punishment; Faith (belief); "I shall be What I shall be"; Revelation

Goethe, Johann Wolfgang von, 137, 140, 153

Goldwin, Robert A., 457

Good: ancestral as, 112–13, 118–20; ancients vs. moderns on, 94–95, 99; biblical vs. philosophic notions of the, 109, 115–16, 369–73, 384–87, 396–97; Cohen vs. Spinoza on highest, 162, 167–68, 207; soul vs. self on, 432

Good life, 103, 122–23, 218, 466, 475–76; biblical and philosophic notions of, 104, 116

Good society, 423–25, 431–45

Greek Mathematical Thought and the Origin of Algebra (Klein), 347n9, 450–51, 454, 462

Greek philosophy, 115, 124, 373–74; and Bible, 104–123; Hesiod, 394–96; idea of progress, 94–96; Klein's study of,

450–51, 454; Maimonides and, 8; morality in, 105–10, 118; Spinoza and, 189, 195; and Western civilization, 99, 104, 120–21, 247, 257, 458; on wisdom, 121, 122, 379, 380. *See also* Aristotle; Jerusalem and Athens; Plato; Socrates

Group memory, Freud on, 299–300

Guide of the Perplexed (Maimonides), 5, 58n19, 72n51, 78(nn76,77), 81n93, 110, 151, 270, 278, 354n42, 426–27, 463; esotericism of, 40–44, 209–10

Guilt, 108, 109; Cohen's notion of, 275–76; in Judaism, Freud on, 298–99

Guttmann, Julius, 4, 5, 75n59

Halakha, 427

Halevi, Yehuda, 109, 121, 210, 253, 288, 332, 355n44, 402, 420, 426, 469–70. *See also* Jewish thought (philosophy); *Kuzari* (Halevi)

Halkin, Hillel, 67n43

Hallel, 59n23

Ham (son of Noah), 390

Harvey, Warren Zev, xvin8

Hatred of Jews, *see* Anti-Semitism; Persecution of Jews; *Rish'us*

Heaven: in Genesis, 271, 293, 320, 369, 370, 373, 383, 427, 433, 441; in Greek philosophy, 373–74

Hebraism and Hellenism, *see* Jerusalem and Athens

Hebrew Bible, *see* Bible (Scripture)

Hebrew Union College (Cincinnati), 6, 245

Hebrew University of Jerusalem, 5, 6, 413

Hegel, Georg W.F., 26, 27, 121, 138, 139, 147, 167, 361, 399, 461

Heidegger, Martin, 19, 24, 27, 28, 149, 151; compared with Rosenzweig, 27, 28, 78n78; moral failure of, 140–41, 450, 458, 461, 472n2; "new thinking" in, 8, 26, 147–49, 151; radical historicism of, 6, 8, 22, 35–36, 60n26; Strauss and, 8, 60n26, 63n30, 68n48, 70n48, 79n79, 461; studies of Aristotle, 450, 458, 462

Heine, Heinrich, 139, 313, 323, 336, 346n2

Hell, Cohen on, 278

Heptaplomeres (Bodin), 166

Hermeneutics, Spinoza on, 184–85, 188, 190, 218, 219

Herodotus, 113, 135n45, 374
Herzl, Theodor, 29–31, 79n81, 80n84, 141, 142, 348n13, 414. *See also The Jews'*
State (Herzl); Political Zionism
Hesiod, 394–96
Hidden meaning, *see* Esoteric and exoteric
Hieroglyphic books, 193–94; Bible as, 185–86, 205–8; Maimonides, 7, 41–43, 44, 84n99; and Spinoza's works, 207–224
Hiero (Xenophon), 471–72
Hillel the Elder, 142, 348n11
Hillel House, 5, 58n20, 132, 285, 312, 345–46
Hindenburg, Paul von, 137
Hindu religion, 112
Historical criticism, 26–27, 125, 126, 130–31, 150, 168, 219–21, 250–51, 254, 293, 295, 380–82
Historical experience, 19, 23–24, 26–27, 62n29, 76n64
Historical religion, as revealed religion, 117–18, 249
Historicism, 6, 61n27, 73n52, 74n58, 193; radical, 6, 8, 22, 35–36, 60n26, 153, 450
History: Bible as, 117–18, 380–82, 384; contribution to understanding books, 187, 188, 189, 193–94, 200, 214; discovery of, 93, 98, 104, 117, 276; faith not refuted by, 128–31, 145; of human thought, 192–93, 254, 256; philosophy and, 152, 184–89, 192, 214, 247–48, 250–52, 471–72
History of Mediaeval Jewish Philosophy (Husik), 235, 244, 247
Hitler, Adolf, 61n27, 138, 139, 144, 282, 316, 317, 347n6, 438, 450
Hobbes, Thomas, 4, 9, 10, 14, 16, 102, 130, 154, 211, 462; preface to Strauss's book on, 453–56
Holocaust, 26, 47, 61n29, 66n43, 100–1, 282, 332, 438
Holy Roman Empire, 139
Holy spirit, Cohen on, 272–73
Homer, 110, 120, 359
Honor, Jewish, 29, 33–34, 141–42, 319
Horeb, Mount, 370
"How to Study Spinoza's *Theologico-Political Treatise*" (Strauss), 63n32, 181–233

Hubris, 36, 442
Humanism: in Bible, 440; and science, 441–42
Humility, biblical notion of, 106, 107, 108, 109, 281, 290–91, 308n11, 374, 432
Husik, Isaac: on the Bible, 76n61; character, 235, 236, 237, 240–41; and classical philosophy, 235, 236, 241–44, 246, 247, 251–52; criticisms of Cohen, 22, 252–53, 255, 256; youthful studies, 237–39; friendships, 58n19, 239–41, 245, 246; medieval Jewish philosophy, 22–23, 239, 241–42, 247–56; philosophy of law in, 235–36, 244–45, 247, 256–64; Strauss on, 22–23, 75(nn59,61), 235–66
Husserl, Edmund, 18, 22, 68n48, 460–61; Strauss on, 70n48
Hutchins, Robert Maynard, 5

Ibn Daud, Abraham, 271–72
Ibn Ezra, Abraham, 209
"Idealizing," by Hermann Cohen, 18–19, 21, 24, 165–66, 168, 251, 256, 271–72, 279, 281
Idolatry, 127–28, 164, 176n58, 270, 292, 321–22, 327, 352n28
Ikhnaton, 292, 297
Immortality: Cohen on, 277–78; Farabi on, 422, 423
Inquisition, 166, 314
"In External Freedom and Internal Slavery" (Aḥad Ha'am), 144–45, 174n10, 341, 354n41
Intellectual probity, 144, 151–52, 154, 159, 172, 280–81
Interpretation, distinguished from explanation, 181–82, 184–85, 187–88
"Introduction to Heideggerian Existentialism" (Strauss), xvn6, 60n26
"Introductory Essay to Hermann Cohen, *Religion of Reason*" (Strauss), 267–82
Irrationalism, 8, 24, 27, 62n30, 77n75, 78n76, 100, 163
Isaac, 110, 271–72, 290, 323, 391–93
Isaiah, 87, 106, 126, 145, 274, 277, 321, 400, 403, 440
"I shall be What I shall be" (*Ehyeh-Asher-Ehyeh*), 114, 119, 157, 170, 393, 401, 427. *See also* God, name of

Islam: and Judaism, contrasted with Christianity, 418–20, 425–28; philosophy in, 210, 426. *See also* Faith (belief), Jewish and Muslim; Koran; Mohammed

Israel, 77n72; as modern state, xii, 29, 32, 33–34, 35, 79n80, 142–43, 326, 340, 411, 413–14, 438; state as blessing and cleansing for all Jews, 34–35, 142, 326, 414; people as symbol of mankind, 79n82, 141, 143, 274, 276–77, 327–28, 340, 352n28, 411, 438. *See also* Chosen people (divine election); Jewish people (nation); Zionism

Israeli, Isaac, 249

Jabotinsky, Vladimir Ze'ev, 3, 319, 348n13. *See also* Revisionist Zionist movement

Jacobi, F.H., 4, 156, 470

Jaffa, Harry V., 50n6

James, William, 54n11

Japheth (son of Noah), 390

Jeremiah, 88, 205, 277, 308n11, 400–1

Jerusalem and Athens: attempts to harmonize, 104–7, 468; roots of Western civilization in, 98–99, 104, 116, 117, 120–21, 246–47, 255, 257, 329, 377–79, 397–98, 427. *See also* Bible (Scripture); Greek philosophy

"Jerusalem and Athens" (Strauss), xii, xvn4, 5, 50n6, 51n7, 55n12, 61n29, 377–405

Jerusalem, Strauss on meaning of, 409

Jesus, 41, 160, 438; Spinoza on, 159, 203–7 passim, 212, 217

Jewish culture, 35, 92–93, 143, 319–20, 343–44

Jewish faith, *see* Faith (belief), Jewish; Judaism

Jewish orthodoxy, *see* Orthodoxy, Jewish

Jewish people (nation), 142, 152, 156–57, 281, 321–22; assimilation *see* Assimilation; as chosen people, *see* Chosen people (divine election); creative genius of, 47, 82n99, 250, 254, 255, 345, 355n46; Freud on, 301, 304–5; as nation, 142, 152, 156–57, 281, 321–22; persecution of, *see* Persecution of Jews; self-respect, 91–92, 324. *See also* Israel; Judaism

"Jewish problem (question)," 92–93, 141–44, 161, 314–15, 342; as a human problem, 79n82, 141, 143, 276–77, 327–28, 340, 352n28, 438; solution to?, 14, 29, 30, 31–32, 33, 66n43, 143–44, 317–18

Jewish-Protestant colloquium, 431–45

Jewish Theological Seminary, 5, 58n19, 237–38, 335, 353n36

Jewish thought (philosophy), xiii, xvn8, 1–8 passim, 23, 61n29; Alfarabi and, 210, 418–19, 420–26, 428; *falasifa* and, 419, 420, 421, 425; Husik's studies on, 22–23, 239, 241–42, 247–56; medieval, 4, 6, 8, 468–69; medievals vs. moderns, 23, 37; modern, 6, 8, 22–23, 61n29, 144–73 passim, 247–48, 181–224 passim, 250, 255–56, 267–82 passim; mystics and, 46–47, 83n99, 345, 355n46; Strauss's plan for a book on, 467–70; of Strauss, xiii, 2, 6–8, 52n7, 55n12, 467–70. *See also* Aḥad Ha'am; Cohen, Hermann; Halevi, Yehuda; Herzl, Theodor; Maimonides, Moses (Rambam); Mendelssohn, Moses; Rosenzweig, Franz; Spinoza, Baruch; Strauss, Leo; "Theological-political crisis"; Zionism

Jewish tradition (heritage), 89, 92, 93, 120, 139–40, 143, 163, 200, 218, 248, 250, 255, 274, 281, 288, 319–20, 323, 334, 339, 409, 413–14, 427, 467

Jew and Philosopher (Green), 51n7, 56n12, 60(nn25,26)

Jews' State, The (Herzl), 141

Job, 106

Jonah, 400

Jonathan, 107, 134n32

Judah L. Magnes Lectures, 5, 59n21, 409

Judaism: and Christianity, 156, 334–36, 426, 436–42; in Cohen's modern synthesis, 18, 20–22, 25, 54n10, 267–82; Husik on, 249–50, 251, 254, 255; Maimonides on, 40–41, 81(nn90,92), 82(nn93,94); martyrdom and heroic suffering in, 90–91, 141, 168, 276–77, 280–81, 286, 322–23, 336 439–40; Mendelssohn and, 15–17; modern crisis of, xiii, 7–8, 15, 17, 23, 47, 61n29, 87–136, 145; not refuted by science,

10–11, 128–31, 145, 170–71; orthodox, *see* Orthodoxy, Jewish; and philosophy, 15–28, 427–28, 468; and rationalism, 27, 47, 78(nn73,75–77), 157; return to (*teshuva*), 25–26, 28, 34–35, 45, 63n31, 87, 88–89, 90, 93–94, 144–47, 154, 468; Rosenzweig on, 151–53; Spinoza and, 12–15, 67n44, 90–91, 154–61, 163–71, 197, 198, 199, 221–24; in state of Israel, 34, 35; Strauss on, xiii, 2, 6–9, 50n6, 51n7, 55n12, 66n43, 312–29; truth and, 27, 52, 73, 90, 248, 280–81, 288, 320, 323, 343, 444; universalism of, 163–65. *See also* Chosen people (divine election); Jerusalem and Athens; Jewish thought (philosophy); Faith (belief), Jewish; Jewish people; Jewish tradition (heritage); Jewish culture; Torah (*Tora*)
"Judge Made Law" (Husik), 261, 262
Jurisprudence, Husik's work in, 235–36, 244–45, 256–64
Justice, 99, 106–7, 109, 118, 137, 141, 147–48, 157, 160, 162, 199, 203, 257–58, 272–73, 278, 314, 317, 327, 344, 371–72, 403–4, 424, 427, 443–44; divine, 392, 395, 396–99, 403–4, 409; Husik's views on, 262–64. *See also* Divine law; Morality
Justification by faith, 205, 440–41

Kabbala, 59n20, 83n99, 88, 194, 253
Kalam, 199, 420, 421, 426
Kant, Immanuel, 20, 102, 155, 156, 162, 163, 399, 463
Kass, Leon, xivn4
Keedy, Edwin R., 245, 257, 259
Kelsen, Hans, 245, 251, 259, 260–61, 262
Khrushchev, Nikita, 317, 336, 347n8
Kierkegaard, Sören, 26
Klein, Jacob, 347n9, 454; account of his experiences, with Strauss, 457–66; unspoken prologue honoring, 449–52
Knowledge: dedication to God, 116; function of books in, 373–75; of good and evil, 115, 272, 372–73, 385–87, 427; for the prophets, 398; for Socrates, 122, 124, 402, 403
Kojève, Alexandre, 52n7, 79n80, 471, 472n1
Koran, 380

Kraus, Paul, 57n17
Krüger, Gerhard, 454, 455(nn3,4)
Kuzari (Halevi), 121, 210, 288, 402, 469–70. *See also* Halevi, Yehuda

Lachterman, David R., 52n7
Lane, James, xiii
Law, 278–80; divine, *see* Divine law; natural, *see* Natural law; philosophy of, in Husik's research, 235–36, 244–45, 256–64
Laws (Plato), 105, 106, 109, 111, 114, 397, 418, 420, 463, 469
Leibniz, Gottfried Wilhelm von, 16, 102, 146, 166, 210
Lenin, Vladimir Ilyich, 61n27, 316, 347n7
Leo Baeck Institute, 5, 286
Leo Strauss: Political Philosopher and Jewish Thinker (Deutsch and Nicgorski, eds.), 53n7
Leo Strauss and Judaism (Novak, ed.), x, 53n7
Lessing, Gotthold Ephraim, 16, 133n20, 156, 210, 333, 353n33, 462, 470
Letter on Astrology (Maimonides), 67n44
"Letter to the Editor: The State of Israel" (Strauss), 32, 79n80, 413–14
Levinas, Emmanuel, 63n30
Levinthal, Louis E., 237, 244
Levites, 294, 297
Leviticus, 272–73
Liberal democracy, 433–35; best available solution to Jewish problem, 66n43, 79n82; betrayal of principles, 29–31; conformism in, 434, 435; of Spinoza, 13, 14, 15, 31, 91, 155–61 passim; view of religion in, 139, 143; Weimar Republic as, 137–38, 139
Liberalism, 7, 15, 281, 287, 443–44, 470; and Jews, 30, 92–93, 141–44 passim, 317, 435; limitations of, 29–31, 33, 60n26, 61n29, 66n43, 77n73, 143–44, 314–15; religious, 152, 153, 169; and Zionism, 32, 33
Light, creation of, 364, 365, 366, 367, 368, 382–83
Literature, contemporary, 431–33
Locke, John, 16
Love: Christian, 200–1; Cohen on, 272, 273–75; Scripture on, 104

Löwith, Karl, 63n30, 78n78
Lucretius, 95
Luria, Isaac, 88

Machiavelli, Niccolò, 9, 14, 154, 157, 162,
    285, 307(nn3,4), 380, 423; and origins
    of modernity, 13, 24, 62n30, 64n39; *The
    Prince*, 187
Magnanimity, 134n32; in Greek philoso-
    phy, 107, 108
Maimonideanism, Strauss's, 7, 29, 36–48,
    58n19, 60n25, 64n34, 67n44, 72n51
Maimonides, Moses (Rambam), 27, 93,
    125, 152, 163–65, 176n58, 253, 332, 470;
    on Alfarabi, 418, 419; on creation, 40,
    83n96, 96, 270; on divine law, 37–40, 41;
    esotericism of, 7, 41–44, 83n99, 209–10,
    214; on four elements, 112; *Guide of the
    Perplexed, see Guide of the Perplexed*
    (Maimonides); Husik on, 249, 250–51,
    252; on the Jewish people, 68n44; on
    Judaism, xiii, 16, 37–40, 80n90,
    81(nn92,93,94); on miracles, 153;
    *Mishneh Torah/Code, see Mishneh
    Torah/Code* (Maimonides); on morality,
    40–41, 44, 81n94, 82(nn95,96); political
    views, 38–39, 80(nn89,90), 469; pre-
    modern rational thought, 8, 24, 39–40;
    on prophets, 38, 39, 40, 41, 42, 420;
    Spinoza on, 209, 222, 223, 224; Strauss's
    work on, 4, 5, 6–7, 8, 24, 29, 58n19,
    68n44, 72n51, 462–63; vs. Spinoza, 9,
    11, 38; and Zionism, 80(nn89,90), 81n91
Male and female dualism, in Genesis,
    105–6, 157, 366–67, 372, 383–84, 385–86
Mann, Thomas, 308n6
Mansfield, Harvey C., Jr., 50n5
Marr, Wilhelm, 320, 348n15
Marx, Karl, 97, 262, 336
Mass psychology, and religion, Freud on,
    298
Medieval Jewish philosophy, *see* Jewish
    thought (philosophy)
"Memorial Remarks for Jason Aronson"
    (Strauss), xiii, 475–76
Memory, 120, 380–82
Mendelssohn, Moses, 28, 78n75, 151, 269,
    279, 427, 470; attempted synthesis of
    Judaism and reason, 15–17; Strauss
    edits works of, 4

Messiah, 88, 132n4, 344, 438; Cohen on,
    276, 277
Messianism, 88, 148–49, 159, 403, 439; of
    Cohen, 161, 276–77, 280; in modern
    philosophy, 72n51; and Zionism,
    32–33, 81n86
Metaphysics (Aristotle), 243, 461
Micah, 403, 427
Michal, 107, 134n32
Middle Ages, 99, 121–22, 129, 139, 151–52,
    241–42, 248, 250–51, 262, 271, 288, 313,
    323, 332, 336, 396, 418, 437, 441, 468
Midrash (*aggada*), 319–20, 427
Miracles, 129–30, 131, 145, 227, 344, 467;
    in the Bible, 128, 381, 382; Cohen on,
    168–69; and faith (belief), 126, 128,
    360, 381; Jewish orthodoxy on, 153–54;
    Rosenzweig on, 77n72, 153; Spinoza
    on, 126, 130, 135n54, 169, 198, 199–200,
    212, 221–22, 223, 227n31, 380–81
Mishneh Torah/Code (Maimonides),
    111–12, 132n4, 163–64, 278–79, 426
Modernity, 21, 24, 97–98, 101, 439; charac-
    teristics of, 102–4; countermovement
    to, 101–2; as project, 13, 15, 21, 64n39,
    154–55; waves of, 63n30
Mohammed, 41
Momigliano, Arnaldo, 60n25
Monotheism, 44, 106, 119; Cohen on, 271,
    276, 278–79; ethical, 20, 21, 22; Freud
    on, 287, 292, 293, 296, 297, 298–99
Moral bankruptcy of contemporary phi-
    losophy, in Strauss's view, 6, 24, 36,
    60n26. *See also* Philosophy;
    Rationalism, modern; "Theological-
    political crisis"
Morality (ethics): biblical, 28, 44, 99,
    105–10, 118, 150–51, 204–5, 389; Cohen
    on, 20, 161–62, 273; in Greek philoso-
    phy, 105–10, 118; Klein and Strauss
    discuss, 464–66; Maimonides on,
    40–41, 44, 82(nn94–96); neo-Kantian,
    20, 21; Spinoza on, 204–5
Mosaic law, *see* Divine law; Torah (*Tora*);
    Pentateuch, Mosaic authorship of
Moses, 41, 45, 88, 105, 106, 125, 127, 170,
    219, 263, 271–72, 375n10, 382, 393;
    Freud on, 285, 288–309; Maimonides
    on, 209–10; Spinoza on, 158–60, 170,
    205, 207, 209, 219, 221, 222–23

Muses, 120, 394, 395
Mystery, 304–5, 328–29, 345, 374–75, 393, 444
Mystics, medieval Jewish, 47, 83n99, 253, 345, 355n45. *See also* Kabbala
Myth: in the Bible, 125, 276, 278, 338–40, 367, 380–81, 384; vs. philosophy, 111
Mythology, 119, 273

Name of God, 114, 119, 295, 384, 393, 427. *See also* "I shall be What I shall be"
Nathan, 109, 404
Nathan the Wise (Lessing), 470
National socialism, 7, 60n26, 61n27, 65n43, 138, 139, 141, 144, 280, 321, 332, 334, 347n6, 438
Nation, Jewish, *see* Jewish people (nation)
Natural law, 114, 162–63, 258, 259, 260, 420
Natural rights, 14, 30, 155
Natural theology, 117, 129, 131
Nature, 110–14, 119, 126, 154–56, 158–59, 171–72, 240, 263, 269–70, 281, 318, 381, 398–99, 403, 433, 466; in Bible, 111, 222–23; in Greek philosophy, 111
Nazism, *see* National socialism
Negroes and Jews, discrimination against in U.S., 317, 336–37, 435
Neo-Kantianism, 18, 19, 20, 22, 68n48, 154, 344, 354n43
Neo-orthodox theology, 22, 453, 460
Neo-Platonism, 155, 425
Neumark, David, 243–44
Neuroses, religions as, Freud on, 295, 297–300, 303
Newbold, William, 239–41, 242
New School for Social Research (New York), 5
New Testament, Spinoza on, 197, 200–1, 202–5, 232n100
"New thinking," 8, 26, 27, 28, 146–51, 152; of Heidegger, 8, 26, 147–49, 151; of Rosenzweig, 25–28, 151–54
Newton, Isaac, 75n58, 99
Niebuhr, Reinhold, 335, 353n36
Nietzsche, Friedrich, 26, 139, 140, 166–67, 262, 335, 378–79, 465; on assimilation of the Jews, 323–25, 326; *Dawn of Day*, 323–25, 349n22, 350(nn23–25), 351n26;

influence of his thought, 8, 62n30; and morality, 19, 21, 24, 99, 100, 150–51, 172–73; on Spinoza, 166–67
Nimrod, 390
Noah, 388, 389, 390; covenant with, 96, 163–65, 273, 389–90
Noahidic commandments, 164, 165, 273
Nordau, Max, 340, 354n40
Norms, 259, 260–62
Novak, David, x, 53n7, 62n29
Novels, contemporary American, 431–32
Nuclear warfare, 332, 333, 442–43

"Objectivity": of Husik, 244, 251–53, 254–56, 259, 264; Rosenzweig and Cohen on, 163–68; Strauss and, 379
Odyssey (Homer), 110
On the Attainment of Happiness (Farabi), 420–21, 422
On the Division of the Sciences (Avicenna), 463
"On the Interpretation of Genesis" (Strauss), xii, 359–76
On Tyranny (Strauss), 52n7, 55n12, 471–72
Original sin, 372, 386–87, 440
Orthodoxy, Jewish, 15, 27, 55n12, 125, 169–70, 172, 254, 303, 344, 380, 427, 453, 459, 461; on miracles, 153–54; resistance to Enlightenment, 17, 171–72; return to, 25–28, 45, 64n31, 88–89, 90, 93–94, 144–47, 154; Strauss and, 3, 45–46, 47, 55n12
Overman (superman), Nietzsche on the, 150–51, 379

Palestine, 319
Pangle, Thomas L., 51n6, 72n51
Parkes, James, 335, 353n35
Parmenides, 394, 396
Pascal, Blaise, 131
Passover Haggada, 285
Patriarchal family, 105
Paul, 439, 440; Spinoza on, 203, 204–5, 206–7, 216, 229n65
Pekarsky, Maurice, 312, 328, 346
Pentateuch, Mosaic authorship of, 125–27, 145, 159, 170, 209–10, 219, 382
Perfection of the origin, 87–88, 89, 372, 385

Persecution and the Art of Writing (Strauss), xii, 5; introduction to, 417–29

Persecution of Jews: Crusades, 13, 139, 322–23, 352n28; expulsion from Spain (1492), 313–14, 346n3; Inquisition, 166, 314; in twentieth century, 26, 47, 61n29, 66n43, 100–1, 282, 315–17, 332, 438. *See also* Anti-Semitism; Holocaust

Persian empire, 170, 291

Petuchowski, J.T., 436, 437

Pfister, Oskar, 309n21

Phaedrus (Plato), 103

Pharisees, 439–40, 444

Phenomenology, 18, 22, 69n48, 261, 460–61

Phenomenology of the Mind (Hegel), 461

Philistines, 92, 444

Philosopher: and cities, 463–64, 465–66; freedom of, 37, 38–39, 43–44, 45, 161, 217–18, 248–49, 424, 426, 469–70; Socrates on, 38, 403; students of philosophy, 41–45, 196–97; and theologian, 117, 121

Philosophic system, absolute and final, 121, 129–31, 170–71, 191–92, 360–61

Philosophie und Gesetz/Philosophy and Law (Strauss), xi, 4, 37, 49n4, 55n12

Philosophy: basic premise unprovable, 131–32; Christian *see* Aquinas, Thomas; Neo-orthodox theology; Scholasticism; in classical Greece, *see* Greek philosophy; as distinguished from myth, 111; doubt, *see* Doubt; and faith, *see under* Faith (belief); history and, *see under* History; Husik's view of, 248–49; insufficiency of, 122–23; Islamic *see* Alfarabi; Averroes; Avicenna; Islam; Jewish, *see* Jewish thought (philosophy); Judaism and, 15–28, 427–28, 468; modern, 6, 24, 35–36, 47, 87–136 passim, 252, 463; obstacles to, 190–93; and religion, 36, 37–38, 42, 44–45, 83n96, 268, 369, 373–75; and science, 99–100, 102, 123, 191–92, 458; sociology of, 417, 418, 428. *See also* Jerusalem and Athens; "Theological-political crisis"

Philosophy and the Law, Strauss's proposal for a book, xii, 467–70

Philosophy of law, in Husik's studies, 235–36, 244–45, 256–64

Philosophy of Right (Hegel), 138–39

Philosophy, vs. theology, 107–117, 119, 181; Spinoza, 196–97, 198–99, 202, 203–4, 205, 217–18, 226n23

Piety, 51n6, 118, 209, 279, 320, 388

Pines, Shlomo, 2, 5, 72n51

Pinsker, Leon, 30, 31, 141, 142, 340, 348n10

Pirkei Avot (*Sayings of the Fathers*), 168, 318, 348n11

Plato, 37, 95, 133n21, 149, 257–58, 303, 366, 367, 428, 437, 462, 465, 469; *Apology of Socrates*, 401–3; *Banquet*, 105; *Charmides*, 105; concept of God, 113–14, 396–97; concept of knowledge, 398; contrasted with the prophets, 398–99; on creation, 397; estericism of, 210, 214; *Euthyphro*, 78n76; Farabi on, 420–26, 428, 429n10, 469; *Laches*, 460; *Laws*, 105, 106, 109, 111, 114, 418, 420; Maimonides and, 8, 469; and medieval Jewish philosophy, 252; *Phaedrus*, 103; *Republic*, 106, 108, 397, 418, 419; and religion, 111, 113–14, 367, 396–97, 419–20, 423–23; and Socrates, 399–400; *Statesman*, 279; *Timaeus*, 96, 106, 133n13, 424

Platonism, 20, 21–22, 173, 194, 398–99

Pluralism, 379

Poetry: Greek, 100, 109, 374, 379; vs. song in the Bible, 59n23, 381

Pogroms, 312–13

Political philosophy (theory), 62n29, 260, 359, 409, 456n7, 464, 469. *See also* City; Philosopher; *Politics* (Aristotle); *Republic* (Plato); State; Zionism

Political Zionism, 3, 5, 19, 20, 29–35, 45, 66n43, 90, 92, 141–43, 318–19, 348, 414. *See also* Herzl, Theodor; Pinsker, Leon; Zionism

Politics (Aristotle), 371, 418

Positivism, 22, 328–29

Possessed, The (Dostoyevsky), 123–24, 135n52

Postcritical Judaism, xii, xivn4, 48, 94, 344

Prayer: *Aleinu*, 327–28, 351n28; Cohen on, 280; philosophy and, 117; and Psalm 114, 6, 59n23, 381

Predestination, 157
"Preface to Isaac Husik, *Philosophical Essays*" (Strauss), 235–66
"Preface to *Spinoza's Critique of Religion*" (Strauss), xii, 65n42, 66n43, 67n44, 68n45, 137–77
Prejudice, *see* "Discrimination" (prejudice)
Presence or Call of God, 124, 149, 304, 307n3, 381
Prince, The (Machiavelli), 187
Private sphere, for religion, 30–31, 139, 143–44, 314, 470
Progress: twentieth-century barbarism raises doubts about, 26, 100–1, 131–32, 332; biblical notions, 96–97; classical conception, 94–96; Cohen's optimism, 19, 23, 25, 161–62, 280, 399; Enlightenment and, 7; Hebrew terms, 88, 132n6; modern doubts about, 97–98, 100; questions of Strauss about, 26–27, 77n73, 87, 191–93; reduction in "discrimination"?, 330–37; and science, 98, 132, 192, 304, 328–29, 331, 332; social, 95–96, 97, 417, 441; strives for future perfection, 89–90. *See also* History; Messianism; Modernity
"Progress or Return?" (Strauss), xvn4, 64n37, 87–136
Prohibition to first human beings, 115, 371, 385, 386, 387, 389, 427
Prophets, 21, 126, 277, 296, 400, 419; Cohen on, 274, 275, 276, 277; concept of knowledge, 398, 403; divine mission, 400–1, 403; experience and interpretation, 124; false, 401; Maimonides on, 38, 39, 40, 41, 42, 46, 469; Spinoza on, 158, 159, 163, 198–99, 203–5, 224; view of God, 89, 148–49. *See also* Amos; Ezekiel; Isaiah; Jeremiah; Micah; Moses; Nathan; Samuel
Psalms, 6, 59n23, 106, 273, 274, 276, 381, 440
Pseudophilosophy, 190–91
Purges: abandoned by Khrushchev, 317; started by Hitler, 316, 347n6; under Stalin, 316

Radical historicism, *see* Historicism
Rambam, *see* Maimonides, Moses (Rambam)

Rathenau, Walter, 73n54, 137
Rationalism, modern, 93, 99, 157, 181; challenged by Nietzsche and Heidegger, 7–8, 60n26; decline through modern history, 7–8, 77(nn73,75), 147, 172–73; in Freud, 302–3; and view of Judaism, 27, 47; contrasted with Maimonides' notions, 8, 24, 39–40, 252. *See also* Reason
Reading, Spinoza's rules for, 182–86, 187, 190, 196
Realism, 101, 440
Reason, 6, 8, 21, 61n29, 272, 463; Cohen's view of, 22, 267–82; and Greek philosophers, 251; "historicality" of, 74n58; limitations of, 47, 81n94, 147; Maimonides on, 40–41, 81(nn90,92), 82(nn93,94); Mendelssohn and, 15–17; Rosenzweig's critique of, 26–27; modern "self-destruction" of, 172–73; vs. revelation, 24, 36–37, 123–32, 145–47, 223–24, 267–68, 271–72, 397–98, 426–28. *See also* Rationalism, modern
Redemption (salvation), 88, 96, 109, 118, 148–49, 156, 203, 275, 276, 280, 322, 327, 344, 401, 438, 441
Reformation, 313, 323, 461
Religion: on cognitive value of, 209–11, 293, 296–97, 322, 367, 421–22; critique of, 127–32, 169–71, 181, 218–24, 302–5, 421–22; essential to a healthy society and soul, 44, 211; historical, 117–18; liberal, 152–53, 169, 216–18, 269, 303–4, 326–27, 344; as mass psychology, in Freud, 297–300, 303; modern project and, 13, 15, 21, 64n39, 154–55; origin of, 108, 301, 304–5; philosophy and, 36, 37–38, 42, 44–45, 83n96, 268, 373; and science, 128–29, 145, 255, 305. *See also* Christianity; Faith (belief); Islam; Judaism; Revelation
Religion of Reason (Cohen), 68n48, 71n51, 354n43; Strauss's introductory essay, xi, 6, 54n10, 267–82
Religious experience, Bible vs. philosophy on, 111, 119, 123–24, 146–50, 253, 304, 380, 382
Religious Zionism, 35, 143, 320, 343. *See also* Judaism; Zionism

Repentance (return), 87, 88–89, 90, 93–94,
107–9, 144–47, 320, 439; Cohen on,
275–76. *See also* Return to Judaism;
Teshuva
Republic (Plato), 106, 108, 418, 419, 469;
theology in, 367, 397
"Restatement on Xenophon's *Hiero*"
(Strauss), xiii, 471–72
Resurrection: Cohen on, 278; Farabi on,
422–23; Spinoza on, 200, 204, 227n31
Return to Judaism, 25–26, 28, 34–35, 45,
63n31, 87, 88–89, 90, 93–94, 104,
144–47, 154, 320, 468. *See also*
Repentance (return); *Teshuva*
Revealed religion, 117–18, 170–71, 181,
257, 267–68, 393, 427
Revelation, 15, 78n79, 97, 121–22, 171,
181, 320, 360, 419, 469; Buber on
Heidegger's statement, 148; Cohen's
notion of, 19, 22, 25, 267, 271, 272, 279;
historical criticism of, 117–18, 128–29;
impossibility of proof, 125–26; and
knowledge of God, 119; lacking in the
secular state, 436; Maimonides on, 6,
37, 43, 469; not refuted, 10–11, 128–31,
145, 170–71; Rosenzweig on, 19, 25–26,
28; Spinoza's attack on, 10–12, 181,
201–2, 212, 218, 222, 223–24, 227n36,
229n65; vs. reason, 24, 37, 123–32,
145–47, 223–24, 267–68, 271–72,
397–98, 426–28
Reverence, 298, 301–2, 378, 393
Revisionist Zionist movement, 319,
348n13. *See also* Jabotinsky, Vladimir
Ze'ev
Revolutions, Cohen on, 162–63
Ricoeur, Paul, 440–41
Rish'us, 320, 349n16. *See also* Anti-
Semitism; "Discrimination" (preju-
dice); Persecution of Jews
Röhm, Ernst, 347n6
Roman empire, 322
Romanticism, 139, 169, 172
Romulus, 388
Roosevelt, Franklin Delano, 65n43
Rosen, Stanley, 50n6, 52n7
Rosenzweig, Franz, 65n42, 438; on Cohen,
163, 165, 355n44; compared with
Heidegger, 28, 78n78, 147–48; irra-
tionalism of, 27, 62n30; return to bibli-

cal faith, 25–26, 27, 146–53; Strauss
and, 4, 19, 22, 25–29, 73n52, 76n70,
77n72, 453, 460, 461
Ross, Sir David, 243
Rousseau, Jean-Jacques, 16, 62n30, 138,
139, 155, 463
Routledge History of Jewish Philosophy
(Frank and Leaman, eds.), 52n7
Russian Jews, 54n10, 315–17. *See also*
Soviet Union
Rylaarsdam, J. Coert, 436, 438

SA, 347n6
Sabbath, 274, 323
Sacks, Robert, xivn4
St. John's College (Annapolis), 6, 449,
451n1, 457
Saint-Pierre, Abbé de, 133n14
Salvation, *see* Redemption (salvation)
Samuel, 107, 116, 134n32, 142, 388, 404
Sarah, 391, 392
Saul, 107, 134n32
Sayings of the Fathers (*Pirkei Avot*), 168,
318, 348n11
Schary, Dore, 433–36
Schelling, F.W.J., 336, 354n38
Schmitt, Carl, 4, 453
Scholasticism, 252, 418
Scholem, Gershom, 2, 5, 46–47,
55(nn11,12), 63n30, 82n99, 88, 345,
355(nn45,46)
Schwarzschild, Steven, 2, 74n58, 355n44
Science: Cohen and Husserl on, 20,
69n48; and humanism, 441–42; makes
value of progress questionable, 98,
131–32, 192, 328–29, 331, 332; and phi-
losophy, 99–100, 102, 123; and
"pseudophilosophy," 191–92; and reli-
gion, 23, 255, 305; revelation not refut-
ed by, 10–11, 128–31, 145–47, 170–71
"Science of Judaism," 139–40
Scientific revolution in seventeenth century, 99, 458
Scott, Nathan A. Jr., 431–32
Sect, 318
Secularism, 127, 333, 436, 441–42; of
Zionism, 29, 34–35
Self-definition of Jewishness, 337–42
Self-determination for the Jewish people,
318

Self-respect for Jews, 91–92, 286–87
Self vs. soul, 432–33
Sellin, Ernst, 293
Seneca, 95, 189
Sense perception, 114, 118, 119, 120, 126, 201, 270, 367
Serpent, in Genesis, 386, 387
Seth, 388
Shabbetai Zevi, 14
Shakespeare, William, 359
Shalom, 274
Shem (son of Noah), 390
Simon, Ernst, 286, 287, 307n6
Sin, 87, 89, 96, 107–8, 141, 217, 257, 275–76, 306, 327, 372–73, 386–89, 440
Sinai, Mount, 97, 125, 293, 444
Singer, Edgar A., Jr., 239, 246, 259, 262
Sitrei Tora, 167, 385
Smith, Robertson, 300
Social action, 441
Social structure, 435
Sociology of philosophy, 417, 418, 428
Socrates: conformity or nonconformity, 38, 424, 440; divine mission, 110, 400, 401–3; esotericism and exotericism, 210, 468; and morality, 44, 107–8, 134n33, 403, 404; and Plato, 399–400; on wisdom, 121, 122, 124, 402
Sodom, 391, 392
Solomon, Spinoza on, 203–4, 220
Sophists, 158, 256, 262
Sorel, Georges, 100
Soul, 31, 39, 111, 123, 288–89; Cohen on, 277–80; vs. self, 432–33
Soviet Union, 442, 443; anti-Semitism in, 54n10, 144, 282, 315–17, 335, 336; opposition to religion, 436
Spain: achievements of Spanish Jewry, 140; expulsion of Jews from (in 1492), 313–14, 346; Inquisition, 166, 314
Spengler, Oswald, 100
Spinoza, Baruch, 9–15, 16, 28, 125, 154, 172, 470; accommodation to thought of the time, 207, 215–16, 217–18, 229n65; addresses posterity, 189, 194, 195; atheism, 172, 215–16; on Bible, 182–86, 187, 190, 193–94, 196, 197–98, 199, 205–8, 218–23, 225n15; biblical criticism, 9, 10, 15, 93, 168, 380; caution and boldness, 208–13; on

Christianity, 13–14, 158–60, 197, 200–1, 202–5, 216–17, 221–23; Cohen's criticism of, 12, 154, 158–69, 462; conception of God, 130, 155, 156, 157–58, 166, 189, 207, 215, 220–21, 226n19, 227n30; critique of religion in, 9–12, 36, 64n39, 202–7, 227n36; and Enlightenment, 9; and esoteric writing, 207, 212–13, 215–17; excommunication of, 159; fails to disprove reality of God, 10–12; on freedom of philosopher, 38; historical interpretation of, 189–90, 193–96, 200, 214; Hobbes and, 453–54; on the Jewish people, 14, 90, 142, 318, 319; and Judaism, 12–15, 67n44, 90–91, 154–61, 163–71, 201–2, 203–4, 221–24, 318–19, 348n12, 427; Machiavellianism, 13–14, 65(nn39,42), 157, 161; on miracles, 126, 135n54, 169, 198, 199–200, 212, 221–22, 223, 227n31, 380; new church of, 156, 160; Strauss on, 2, 14, 36, 63–64(nn31–37), 65(nn42,43), 67n44, 68n45, 137–77 passim, 181–233 passim; favors liberal democracy, 13, 14, 15, 31, 91, 153, 155–56, 158, 160–61; terminology, 195–96, 211; vs. Maimonides, 9, 11, 38; Zionism of, 14, 15, 30, 90, 161, 318–19, 348n12. See also Ethics (Spinoza); Theologico-Political Treatise (Spinoza)
Spinoza's Critique of Religion (Strauss), 64n34; preface to, xii, 4, 65n42, 66n43, 67n44, 68n45, 137–77
SS, 347n6
Stalin, Joseph, 144, 316
Stammler, Rudolph, 251, 259–60
Star of Redemption (Rosenzweig), 151
State: Husik's ideas on, 261, 262; of Israel, xii, 29, 32, 33–34, 79n80, 142–43, 326, 340, 411, 413–14, 438; Spinoza's view of, 90, 142, 158, 318–19. See also Political philosophy (theory); Zionism
Statesman (Plato), 279
Stoics (Stoa), 95, 276, 420
Strauss, Bettina (Strauss's sister), 57n17
Strauss, Leo: and Cohen, 17–25, 68n48; experiences affect thought, 26, 53n8, 61n29, 459; as a Jewish thinker, 1–3, 6–9, 17, 50n6, 51n7, 55n12, 66n43; life and work, 3–6, 54n11;

Strauss, Leo *(continued)*
　Maimonideanism of, 7, 29, 36–45, 46,
　　47–48, 58n19, 60n25, 64n34, 67n44,
　　72n51; and Mendelssohn, 4, 15–17, 28,
　　78n75; on "Nietzsche-Heidegger
　　school," 8, 60n26, 62n30; political
　　thought, 52n7, 62n29; "postcritical"
　　approach to Bible, xii, xivn4, 48; and
　　Rosenzweig, 25–28, 77n72; on
　　Spinoza, 9–15, 63–64(nn31–38), 65n43,
　　67n44, 68n45; teacher and thinker, xii,
　　5, 6, 49n1, 58n20; Zionism and, 3, 5,
　　19, 20, 28–35, 46, 54n11, 59n21, 79n80,
　　80n84
"Subjectivistic" approach, 108, 168, 251,
　　252–53, 255, 259, 262, 264
Summa Theologica (Aquinas), 426–27
Sun, in creation account, 363, 364, 365,
　　382–83
Sun god, Egyptian, 292–94
SUNY series of Strauss's Jewish writings,
　　xi, 49n4, 51n7, 65n42
Superego, Freud on, 303–4
Superman (overman), Nietzsche on the,
　　150–51, 379
Superstition, Spinoza on, 190, 191
Swift, Jonathan, 102, 133n20
Synagogue, 280, 332, 335–36, 341–42, 437
System of Philosophy (Cohen), 268, 269, 270

Tacitus, 155, 211, 232n102
Talmon, J.L., 411
Talmud (rabbinic), 58n19, 59n20, 125, 143,
　　168, 214–15, 242, 249, 257, 273, 319–20,
　　380, 426, 427, 441
Technology, *see* Science
Teleology, 145, 156, 259, 260, 261, 276. *See
　　also* Causality
Telluric catastrophes, 96, 133n13
Temple, 31, 81n86, 88, 116, 141, 148, 275,
　　277, 401
Ten Commandments (Decalogue), 81n94,
　　105, 149, 270, 393, 437, 444
Teshuva (repentance), 25–26, 34–35, 87,
　　88–89, 90, 93–94, 109, 144–47, 154. *See
　　also* Repentance (return); Return to
　　Judaism
Theocentrism, in biblical and medieval
　　thought, 102
Theogony (Hesiod), 394–95

"Theological-political crisis," 7, 8, 15, 29,
　　47–48, 61n29, 97–98, 100–1, 137, 453
Theologico-Political Treatise (Spinoza),
　　67n44, 90–91, 318–19, 348n12, 453, 454,
　　461–62; addressed to Christians, 197,
　　200–1, 216–17; biblical criticism in,
　　380; Cohen on, 158–59, 160, 161–69;
　　critique of orthodoxy, 9–12, 380; eso-
　　teric nature, 207, 212–13, 216–24;
　　Jewish context of, 197–98, 200; for
　　potential philosophers, 169–70,
　　196–97, 200, 211–12; Strauss on, xii, 12,
　　50n5, 63n32, 155–56, 169–70, 173,
　　181–233 passim
Theology: and philosophy, 107–117, 119,
　　121, 181; "progress" in?, 331–32,
　　334–35
"Theory of Justice" (Husik), 261, 262, 263
Thrasymachus, 424
"Three Waves of Modernity" (Strauss),
　　62n30
Thus Spoke Zarathustra (Nietzsche), 305–6
Tillich, Paul, 334, 353n34, 355n44
Timaeus (Plato), 96, 106, 133n13, 424
Torah (*Tora*), 88, 92, 269, 378, 379, 385,
　　438; as divine law, 106, 152, 249, 254,
　　257; and Jewish nation, 152, 156–57,
　　281; *lishma*, 245; literal truth of, 23,
　　444; Maimonides on, 41, 42, 163,
　　164–65; revelation of, 388, 389, 419;
　　sitrei, 167, 385; Spinoza's view of, 158,
　　167; study of, 242, 245, 257, 281; as tra-
　　dition, 125, 153, 343, 381–82, 394. *See
　　also* Divine law; Faith (belief), Jewish;
　　Jewish tradition (heritage); Judaism
Tradition, 88–90, 93–94, 125, 144–47, 340,
　　345; Freud's interpretation, 299–300;
　　living nature of, 165, 169
Tragedy, Greek, 108, 305
*Treatise on the Improvement of the
　　Understanding* (Spinoza), 207
Treaty of Versailles, 138
Trotsky, Leon, 316
Truth: Bible vs. philosophy on, 73n52,
　　123, 323, 338, 361; Cohen's concept of,
　　158, 165, 280–81, 398; and culture, 379;
　　Farabi on, 424–25; Freud on, 288–89;
　　Judaism and, 27, 52, 73, 90, 248,
　　280–81, 288, 320, 323, 343, 345, 444;
　　Maimonides on, 39, 40, 42; possible

origin in human thought, 102; Spinoza on, 10, 90, 166, 188–93, 202–6, 222; Strauss vs. Berlin on, 79n80; Strauss vs. Kojève on, 471–72; suprarational, 27, 78n76, 127, 199–200, 202

Udoff, Alan, xvn6, xvin7, 52n7, 71n51
Unbelief, 171–72, 181, 303–4, 344–45, 432–33. *See also* Atheism
Universalism of Judaism, 160, 163–65, 276–77
Universal significance of Jewish history, 79n82, 141, 143, 276–77, 327–28, 340, 352n28, 411, 438, 443
University of Chicago, 5, 6, 58n20
University of Hamburg, 5

Value judgments, question of objective support for, 98, 101, 261, 262–63, 305, 378–79, 443
"Value problem," 131–32
Vieta, Franciscus, 317, 347n9
Voegelin, Eric, 52n7
Volcano god, 294, 297

Walter, Benjamin, 56n12
"Way" or "custom," 111–12, 262–62, 383. *See also* Good, ancestral as; Tradition
Weber, Max, 57n13, 74n54, 336, 351n26, 461
Weimar Republic, 73n54, 137–38, 139
Welfare state, 444
Wellhausen, Julius, 145, 148
Weltanschauungen, 69n48, 254
Western civilization: modern crisis in, 8, 29, 47, 48, 61n29, 97–98, 100–1; two roots of, 98–99, 104, 116, 117, 120–21, 247, 255, 257. *See also* Jerusalem and Athens

"Why We Remain Jews" (Strauss), xii, 53(nn8,10), 311–55
Wild, John, 440
Will, Nietzsche on, 8, 99, 151, 172
Winter, Gibson, 442–43
Wisdom: Bible on, 379–80; conflict about, 109, 120–21, 129, 379–80; Greek philosophers on, 95, 109, 379, 380; Socrates on, 121, 122, 124, 402
Wolfson, Harry Austryn, 58n19, 214–15
Works and Days (Hesiod), 395
"World," in Bible, 368

Xenophon, 471–72

Yaffe, Martin D., 55n12, 68n46, 348n12
Yerushalmi, Yosef H., 307n6
Yeshiva University, 245
Yovel, Yirmiyahu, 68n46

Zeus, 395, 396
Zionism, 29–36, 123, 141–43, 280; atheism and, 33–34; cultural, 35, 92, 143, 144–45, 319–20, 354n41; difficulties, 29, 32–35, 92–93; Maimonides and, 80(nn89,90), 81n91; and messianism, 32–33, 81n86; political, 3, 5, 19, 20, 29–35, 45, 66n43, 90, 92, 141–43, 318–19, 348, 414; religious, 35, 143, 243, 320; revisionist, 348n13; of Spinoza, 14, 15, 30, 90, 161, 318–19; Strauss and, 3, 5, 19, 20, 29–35, 45, 54n11, 59n21, 79n80, 80n84, 460. *See also* Aḥad Ha'am; Ben-Gurion, David; Herzl, Theodor; Israel, as modern state; Israel, state as blessing and cleansing; Jabotinsky, Vladimir Ze'ev; Pinsker, Leon; State, of Israel